ARSENAL WHO'S WHO

By Jeff Harris
Edited by Tony Hogg

Published by
INDEPENDENT UK SPORTS PUBLICATIONS

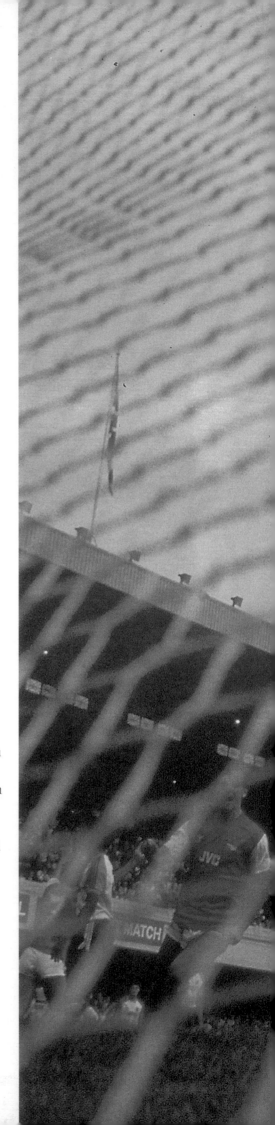

First published in Great Britain by:
Independent UK Sports Publications,
7-9 Rathbone Street, London, W1P 1AF, England.
Telephone: 0171-636 5599 Fax: 0171 636 1617

Text Copyright: Independent UK Sports Publications

Design Copyright: Polar Print Group

ISBN 1-899429-02-6

Designed and printed by:
Polar Print Group,
2 Uxbridge Road, Leicester, LE4 7ST.

Photographs courtesy of:
Les Gold (Les Gold Promotions), Bill Smith, Richard Austin, Allsport, Empics,
Colorsport.

Front Cover photographs:
(Top left)   LIAM BRADY
(Top centre)   ALEX JAMES
(Top right)   IAN WRIGHT
(Bottom left)   DENNIS BERGKAMP
(Bottom right)   THE 1991 FIRST DIVISION CHAMPIONS

ACKNOWLEDGMENTS FROM THE AUTHOR
To Duncan McKay for all his work; Sally, Dawn Harris, Rob Pearce and Marilyn
Harris for their typesetting; John Claypole and Doug Judd for proof reading;
Stephen George Henry Russell; Fred Ollier (Arsenal Complete Record); Stephen
Studd (Herbert Chapman); Ivan Ponting (Arsenal Player By Player); Bob Wall
(Arsenal From The Heart); Tom Whittaker Story; Bernard Joy (Forward
Arsenal); Geoffrey Mowbray (Gunners On The Target); Eddie Hapgood Football
Ambassador; John Harding (Alex James).

DEDICATED TO
The Harris and Judd families – lifetime Gunners followers – and the next
generation, Thomas, Robbie and Callum.

Introduction

ARSENAL! A name synonymous with success since the halcyon days of the 1930s, when, under the leadership of that football visionary, Herbert Chapman, they swept all before them in the British game and became a byword for excellence all over the world.

A name invariably associated with affluence and accomplishment, underlined as two huge new Highbury stands rose phoenix like over the drab N.5. skyline, unchallengeable testaments to their superior status – providing a rare glimpse of grandeur in the heart of the depression.

But the marble halls of Avenell Road were light years away from the meeting place where the forebears of Arsenal FC were born, The Prince of Wales public house at Plumstead, South London in October, 1886.

Gathered there were a group of football enthusiasts from the north. Fred Beardsley, who had kept goal for Nottingham Forest (the club whose red strip Arsenal adopted), David Danskin, a Scotsman from Kirkcaldy, Richard Pearce, from Bolton and Elijah Watkins, who would become the infant club's first secretary.

All had travelled south to gain employment in the munitions factory and they called the club Dial Square, after the workshop in which they plied their trade in Woolwich Arsenal.

Fred Beardsley kept goal in the club's first ever match against Eastern Wanderers at Millwall in December 1886, which Dial won 6-0.

Fred's entry duly appears within these pages along with those of more than 800 others who have been associated with this great club and can have rightly claimed: "I played for Arsenal."

The club changed its name to Royal Arsenal in December 1886, and again in 1893 to Woolwich Arsenal, finally dropping the 'Woolwich' prefix shortly after the move to Highbury in 1913.

But this book is not intended to chronicle the history of the club (although many a fascinating fact can be gleaned within its 300 plus pages), this is the players' story.

From Roy Goulden, son of the famous Len Goulden of West Ham and England, who played just one match versus Leeds United in November 1959 and drifted out of the 'big time' when he joined Southend in 1961, to David O'Leary, who made a record 719 League and Cup appearances between 1973 and 1993 and a few more for Leeds when he left Highbury – they're all here.

As indeed is every player to sign professional forms for Arsenal since the war, irrespective of whether they played in the first team or not.

After all, they all played for Arsenal!

DUCAT, Andy　1905-1912

Birth Place:　Brixton, Surrey
Date of Birth:　16th February 1886

Andy Ducat

☛ Andy Ducat was a sporting legend at the turn of the twentieth century, playing league football 1905-1924 and county cricket for Surrey 1906-1931, becoming one of the privileged few who have played both football (six caps) and cricket (one test) for England. Andy began his footballing career in junior football with Westcliffe Athletic before joining local league side Southend United in 1903, he moved on to Woolwich Arsenal in January 1905, making his Arsenal League debut at centre forward versus Blackburn Rovers 11th February 1905. In 1905-06 he played in only fifteen league games and in 1906-07 only four. However, in 1907-08 Andy switched to right half with great success. He became automatic first team choice in 1908 - 09 when playing in thirty three league games and in the following term his classy performances were rewarded when winning the first of his six England Caps. He played with distinction for two more seasons before a £1,000 offer by Aston Villa was accepted by the club in June 1912. His Villa career got off to a disastrous start when breaking a leg at Maine Road versus Manchester City in September 1912. This being bad enough, it meant him missing the 1913 F A Cup Final. Andy spent one more season at Villa Park before the outbreak of World War One. He played for two more seasons 1919-20 and 1920-21 in which time he captained the club when winning the 1920 F A Cup Final versus Huddersfield Town. He later played for Fulham 1921-24 becoming their Manager in May 1924-26. In his sporting career Andy was beset by injury, in 1924 a broken arm kept him out for the whole of that season. On the cricket front, in his only match versus Australia at Leeds in 1921 he was out in the most unfortunate circumstances when a delivery from McDonald chipped a chunk of wood off the shoulder of Ducat's bat on to his stumps removing a bail. During his twenty five year cricketing career he scored nearly twenty five thousand first class runs. Andy later coached cricket at Eton. He died playing cricket, collapsing, whilst batting for Surrey Home Guard at Lords in July 1942 aged 56.

	Games	Goals
League	175	19
F A Cup	13	2
Other Senior Matches	5	1
Friendly Matches	22	14
London League Reserves	22	11
South Eastern League	30	26
London FA Challenge Cup	6	1
War Time	47	3
Total	**320**	**77**

Honours:
With Aston Villa: 3 England caps
FACup Winners Medal 1919-20
With Arsenal: 3 England Caps
Southern Charity Cup Winners Medal 1905-06
South Eastern League Championship Medal 1906-07
London League Championship Medal 1906-07

DUFF, Hugh　1895-98 & 1899-1900

☛ Hugh Duff was an outside left who was transferred to Woolwich Arsenal as an amateur from Millwall in August 1895, turning professional the following month. He spent all of seasons 1895-96 and 1896-97 playing for the club's reserve sides before making his league 'bow' and scoring at Leicester Fosse 4th December 1897. He returned to Millwall for season 1898-99 before rejoining the club for 1899-1900. He was unable to win a first team place owing to the other contestants for the left wing position (Tennant and Shaw).

	Games	Goals
League	1	1
FA Cup	1	1
Other Senior Matches	1	1
United League	1	0
Kent League	42	22
Friendly Matches	69	35
Southern Combination	1	0
Total	**116**	**60**

Honours:
Kent League Championship
　Medal　1896-97

DUNCAN, David　1912-13

Birth Place:　County Antrim, Ireland
Date of Birth:　1891

☛ David Duncan was a centre forward who has appeared in Scottish Junior Football for Glasgow St Anthony and Bellshill Athletic before joining Albion Rovers. He moved South to join Fulham in the Summer of 1911. He could not command a regular place at Craven Cottage and was transferred to Woolwich Arsenal in December 1912. He made his league debut within forty eight hours of joining the club in the last North London Derby played at the Manor Field versus Tottenham 14th December 1912. However, his stay was short lived leaving soon after. He later returned to Albion Rovers (1916-1921).

	Games	Goals
League	3	1
F A Cup	2	1
Friendly Matches	4	0
South Eastern League	5	1
Total	**14**	**3**

DUNSBEE, Charles　1899-1900

☛ Charles Dunsbee was transferred from Kidderminster to Woolwich Arsenal in June 1899. He played either right or left half in eight league games 1899-1900 in which his debut was at home at the Manor Field 11th November 1899 versus Sheffield Wednesday. He could not oust other wing halfs (Murphy, Moir and Anderson) this resulting him in departing during the summer of 1900.

	Games	Goals
League	8	0
FA Cup	3	0
Kent League	13	0
Friendly Matches	6	0
Southern Combination	6	0
Total	**36**	**0**

DWIGHT, Frederick　1903-05

☛ Frederick Dwight was a left back who joined Woolwich Arsenal from Southern League, Fulham in June 1903. In his initial season with the club 1903-04 he was permanent understudy to the ever reliable James Jackson. In 1904-05 the name of the game was the same. However, he managed to play in one league game at Deepdale versus Preston 7th January 1905. He left the club during that summer when he linked up with Nelson.

ALEX. JAMES
ARSENAL (1ST DIVISION)

DAVID JACK
ARSENAL (1ST DIVISION)

J. HULME
ARSENAL (1ST DIVISION)

Contents

J. CRAYSTON

E. HAPGOOD (ARSENAL)

B. JONES (ARSENAL)

C. BASTIN

C. M. BUCHAN
ARSENAL

E. J. DRAKE

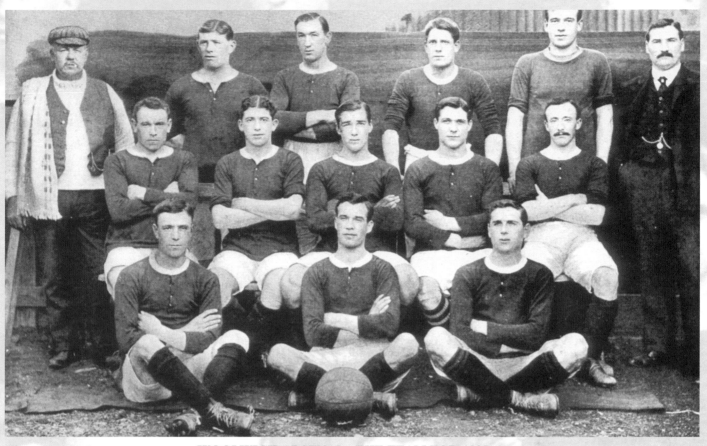

WOOLWICH ARSENAL. THE TEAM FOR 1905-6.

Back Row: P. R. Denmore J. Sharp. J. Ashcroft, Goalkeeper. P. R. Sands. A. Cross. Phil Kelso, Manager.

Middle Row: A. Gray. A. Templeton. A. Duccat. T. T. Fitchie. P. J. McEachrane

Front Row: J. T. Bellamy. J. Dick, Captain. J. Blair.

1886-1915

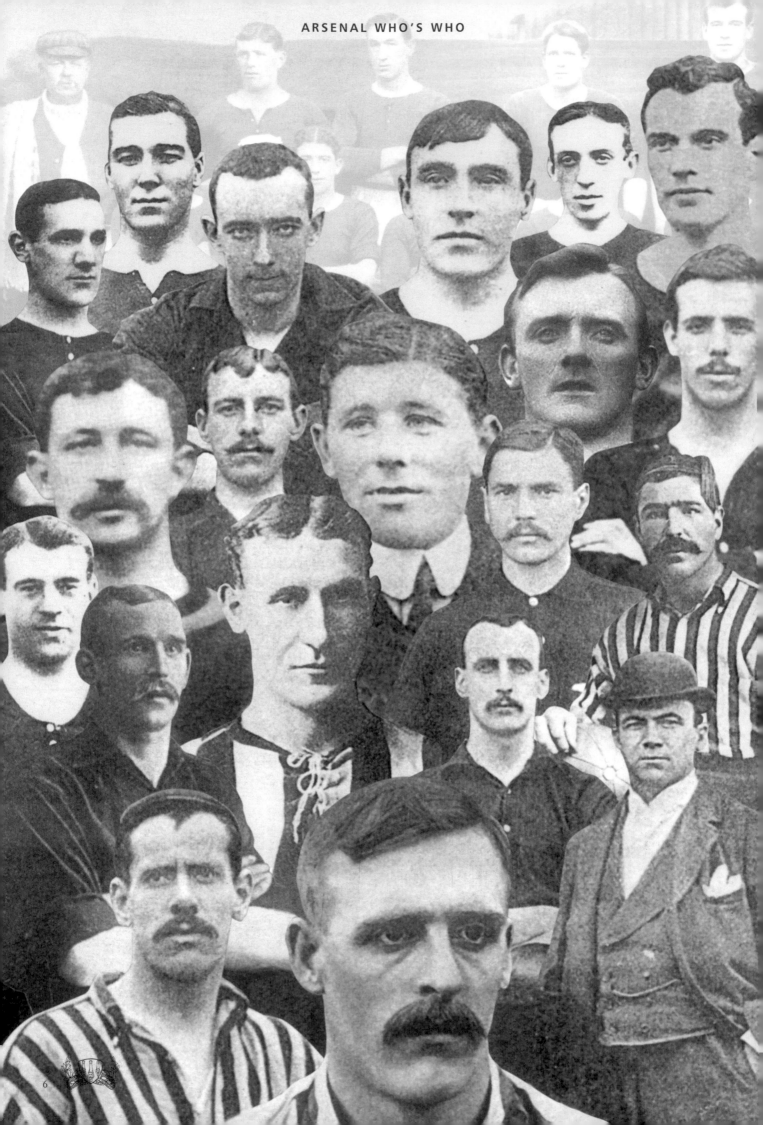

AMBLER, Charles   1891-94 & 1895-96

Birth Place: Hampshire
Date of Birth: 1869

Charles Ambler was recruited by Royal Arsenal from the junior side Bostal Rovers in 1891, not turning professional until nearly two years later. A goalkeeper, during his three seasons at the club in pre-league days his appearances were restricted to just friendly senior games. Was transferred to Tottenham Hotspurs in the summer of 1894 where he stayed six seasons playing in over one hundred and thirty first team appearances. Whilst as an amateur at the club he also appeared for Clapton, Dartford, Luton Town, Gravesend and New Brompton (now Gillingham). He rejoined Woolwich Arsenal in November 1895 when he played in his solitary league game versus Newton Heath (now Manchester United) 30th November 1895. He was released the following summer. He later played for West Ham United 1901-02, and Millwall. Died 1952 aged 83.

	Games	Goals
League	1	0
FA Cup	1	0
Other Senior Matches	5	0
Friendly Matches	22	0
Other Reserve Matches	36	0
Total	**65**	**0**

ANDERSON, Edward   1903-04

Birth Place: Scotland

Edward Anderson was transferred to Woolwich Arsenal from St Mirren in November 1903. In his brief spell at the club Anderson played in two league games in 1903-04 of which his debut was away to Stockport County on new years day 1904. He left the club within eight weeks of joining, when he linked up with southern league side Fulham. He finished his career playing for Queens Park Rangers 1906-08.

	Games	Goals
League	2	0
Friendly Matches	1	0
London League	1	0
London League Reserves	1	2
South Eastern League	3	3
Total	**8**	**5**

ANDERSON, John   1896-1903

Date of Birth: 1878

John Anderson was transferred to Woolwich Arsenal from non league Crook Town in December 1896, making his league debut on New Years Day 1897 in a 1-4 defeat at Darwen. For the remainder of that season he was a first team regular, inter changing between all three half back positions. In 1897-98 he again was a first team choice when playing in twenty one league games, over the next two seasons he played in the majority of the club's first team fixtures without ever becoming an automatic selection in any one position. In 1900-01 John enjoyed his finest season at the club when missing only two league games. However, in 1902-03, after the signing of Roddy McEachrane, his first team duties were limited and he played in only eight league games that season. He later played for Portsmouth in the Southern League.

	Games	Goals
League	144	10
FA Cup	9	1
Other Senior Matches	6	1
United League	32	1
Kent League	23	2
Friendly Matches	59	3
London League	8	0
London League Reserves	9	3
Southern Combination	12	1
Total	**302**	**22**

ANDERSON, Walter   1901-1903

Date of Birth: 1878

Walter Anderson was a reserve forward on the books of Sheffield United when signing for Woolwich Arsenal in December 1901. In the 1901-02 season he established himself in the league side when playing in thirteen of the clubs last fifteen games (scoring five times). His debut being a home encounter versus Preston 11th January 1902. In the 1902-03 season he had many opportunities to hold down a first team place but unfortunately his consistency was not of the required standard. He finished the season having played fifteen league games, scoring five times, he was transferred to Plymouth Argyle in the close season of 1903. Died March 1904 aged 25.

	Games	Goals
League	28	10
FA Cup	2	1
Other Senior Matches	3	1
Kent League	4	6
Friendly Matches	6	1
London League	9	4
London League Reserves	3	1
Total	**55**	**24**

ARNOLD, Thomas   1905-1906

Birth Place: Coventry
Date of Birth: 1879

Thomas Arnold was a right winger who joined Woolwich Arsenal from Coventry City in May 1905. He was brought to the club to understudy for James Bellamy, making his league debut at the Victoria Ground versus Stoke City 23rd September 1905. He played in the following league game versus Everton before the injured Bellamy returned to league action and subsequently, Arnold found himself back in reserve team duties. When the club signed William Garbutt in December 1905 his first team chances were numbered. He returned to Coventry City during the summer of 1906 serving them well for five seasons before becoming trainer at the club and in later years, a director.

	Games	Goals
League	2	0
Friendly Matches	11	1
London League Reserves	12	2
South Eastern League	16	3
Total	**41**	**6**

Honours:
South Eastern League Championship Medal
1905-06

ASHCROFT, James   1900-1908

Birth Place: Liverpool, Lancashire
Date of Birth: September 1878

James Ashcroft can be described as the first of the club's long line of 'great' goalkeepers. James began his career with several Liverpool youth sides. For a short period he was on the books (as an amateur) with Everton before joining Southern League club side Gravesend United in 1899. He was transferred to Woolwich Arsenal in June 1900 when he immediately gained a first team position, replacing Thomas Spicer in the third league game of the season versus Burton 15th September 1900 and he remained ever present for the rest of that season. In 1901-1902 he played in every league game when helping the club, to their then highest ever league position (fourth in division two) conceding only twenty six goals in thirty four games of which he kept seventeen clean sheets which included a run of six games without conceding a goal (which still remains a club record). In 1902-03, he again was ever present when helping the club to third place in division two.

In 1903-04 his amazing consistency was continued when yet again, he was ever present, conceding only twenty two goals in thirty four games of which, unbelievably, he kept twenty clean sheets (in the club's promotion winning team of that season). In 1904-05 his consecutive run of matches ended (154) when he missed one league game early season but he continued ever present for the remainder of the season. In 1905-06 his form was rewarded when he won three England full caps plus football league honours as well as helping the club to the FA Cup Semi Final. In 1906-07 James missed only three league games and again reached the F A Cup semi final with the club. In his final season with Woolwich Arsenal he played in thirty six of the club's thirty eight league games before being transferred to Blackburn Rovers in May 1908. In five seasons with them he played in over one hundred and twenty first team games in which time he was a semi final loser in the FA cup for the third time in 1910-11. Later played for Tranmere Rovers, (1913). Died April 1943 aged 64.

James Ashcroft

	Games	Goals
League	273	0
FA Cup	30	0
Other Senior Matches	12	0
Kent League	1	0
Friendly Matches	48	0
London League	25	0
London League Reserves	3	0
South Eastern League	1	0
Total	**393**	**0**

Honours:
3 England Caps.
2 Football League Caps.
Southern Professional Charity Cup
  Winners Medal   1905-06
Southern Professional Charity Cup
  Finalists Medal   1903-04

ASTON, James   1899-1900

Birth Place: Walsall
Date of Birth: 1st July, 1877

James Aston was a goalscoring inside forward with Walsall Town 1896-99 playing in nearly one hundred first team games scoring nearly forty goals. He was the club's leading goalscorer in 1888-89. He was transferred to Woolwich Arsenal in May 1899. In 1899-1900, he began as the club's regular inside right when he played in eleven of the sides first twelve league games (scoring three times). His debut was on the opening day of the season at home to Leicester Fosse 2nd September 1899. However, he lost his place to Paddy Logan in December 1899. He was transferred to Small Heath (now Birmingham City) during the summer of 1900, where he was a regular for two seasons helping the club to promotion to division one in 1900-01. Moved on to Doncaster in 1902. Died August 1934, aged 57.

	Games	Goals
League	11	3
FA Cup	4	2
Kent League	4	0
Friendly Matches	3	1
Southern Combination	3	0
Total	**25**	**6**

BANNISTER, William   1902-1904

Birth Place: Burnley, Lancashire
Date of Birth: 1879

William Bannister was on the books of junior side Earley, when joining Burnley in 1899. A centre half, he made a rapid rise to fame in his first full season at Turf Moor in 1900 -01 being a mainstay in their defence, gained International Honours when playing for England versus Wales in March 1901. William was transferred to Bolton in November 1901 and whilst at Burnden Park he won another cap versus Ireland. He joined Woolwich Arsenal in December 1902 making his Arsenal league debut on New Years Day 1903 at Stockport County. He eventually finished up playing in sixteen of the club's last seventeen league games. However, in Arsenal's promotion winning season of 1903-04 he played in only two league games, fighting illness and injury during that season. Bannister was transferred to Leicester Fosse in May 1904 where he spent six seasons (being ever present in 1905-06) and helping the club to promotion to division one in 1907-08, he finished his career back at Burnley 1910-11, died March 1942, aged 62.

	Games	Goals
League	18	0
FA Cup	4	0
Other Senior Matches	3	0
Friendly Matches	2	0
London League	8	0
London League Reserves	3	1
South Eastern League	4	0
Total	**42**	**1**

Honours:
(WITH BURNLEY AND BOLTON)
2 England Caps.
(WITH ARSENAL)
Southern Professional Charity Cup
  Finalists Medal   1903-04

BARBOUR, Humphrey   1888-1893

Birth Place: Glasgow

Humphrey Barbour was a prolific goalscoring centre forward who had played for Third Lanark before joining Royal Arsenal from Airdrie in November 1888. Humphrey was a regular for five seasons, in the club's pre league days, for the senior side. When leaving Royal Arsenal he joined Clapton.

	Games	Goals
FA Cup	5	4
Other Senior Matches	66	55
Other Reserve Matches	18	8
Total	**89**	**67**

Honours:
London Senior Cup Winners Medal 1890-91
London Senior Cup Finalists Medal 1889-90
London Challenge Cup Winners
  Medal   1889-90
Kent Senior Cup Winners Medal   1889-90

BASSETT, Spencer   1906-1910

Birth Place: Blackheath, Kent

Spencer Bassett joined Woolwich Arsenal in 1906 turning professional in May 1907 from local side Maidstone, he spent four seasons at the club mainly playing as half back in the South Eastern League team. He played in only one league match versus Notts County 7th October 1909. He later played for Exeter City and Swansea Town. Died in action in France during World War One in April 1917.

	Games	Goals
League	1	0
Other Senior Matches	1	0
Friendly Matches	24	1
London League Reserves	27	2
South Eastern League	95	6
Other Youth Matches	2	1
Total	**150**	**10**

Honours:
South East League Championship
  Medal   1907-08

BATES, Joseph   1888-1891

Date of Birth: 1864

☛ Joseph Bates was a regular half back in the Royal Arsenal side at the beginning of the club's foundation. He joined the club from Nottingham Forest in September 1888. He made three appearances in FA Cup Qualifying games of which the first was against Lyndhurst 5th October 1889. Died 6th September 1905 aged 41. He was a member of the Nottingham side which donated the first red shirt to the Dial Square Club.

	Games	Goals
FA Cup	3	0
Other Senior Matches	70	6
Other Reserve Matches	6	0
Total	**79**	**6**

Honours:
London Challenge Cup Winners
  Medal   1889-90
Kent Senior Cup Winners Medal   1889-90
London Senior Cup Finalists Medal 1889-90

BATEUP, Edward   1905-08 & 1910-11

Birth Place: Croydon, London
Date of Birth: 1886

☛ Edward Bateup was playing Junior football for Faversham (Kent league) when joining Woolwich Arsenal in 1905 as an amateur, turning professional the following month. A former soldier in the seventh Dragoon Guards, Edward was a goalkeeper, who in 1905-06 was one of the many custodians who were to be deputies to Jimmy Ashcroft. His solitary league appearance that season was at Maine Road versus Manchester City 7th April 1906. In 1906-07 he played in three league games, unfortunately his last appearance was when the club were on the wrong end of a 3-5 defeat at Middlesbrough. Much was the same in 1907-08 when again as deputy for Ashcroft he managed to play in only two league games. Disillusioned with reserve team football he joined New Brompton (now Gillingham) during the summer of 1908. After two seasons with them he rejoined Woolwich Arsenal in July 1910. Finally, after years of trying, he became the club's first choice keeper that season playing in all of the club's first twenty seven league games losing his place to George Burdett, in March 1911. He later joined Burslem Port Vale.

	Games	Goals
League	34	0
FA Cup	2	0
Other Senior Matches	2	0
Friendly Matches	20	1
London League Reserves	39	0
South Eastern League	72	0

London FA Challenge Cup	2	0
Total	**171**	**1**

Honours:
3 South Eastern League Championship
  Medals   1905-06, 1906-07, 1907-08
London League Reserve Championship
  Medals   1906-07

BEARDSLEY, Fred   1886-1891

Birth Place: Nottingham

☛ Fred Beardsley was previously with Nottingham Forest when joining, (as one of the originators of the Club) Royal Arsenal in 1886. He was the first choice goalkeeper for five seasons in the pre league days. His first class debut was in an 11-0 victory versus Lyndhurst, 5th October 1889. On retirement he became a businessman and was a director of Woolwich Arsenal, 1906-1910.

	Games	Goals
FA Cup	2	0
Other Senior Matches	67	0
Other Reserve Matches	19	0
Total	**88**	**0**

Honours:
London Challenge Cup Winners
  Medal   1889-90
Kent Senior Cup Winners Medal   1889-90
London Senior Cup Finalists Medal 1889-90

BEE, Edward   1890-1893

Birth Place: Nottingham
Date of Birth: 1868

☛ Edward Bee was the regular goalkeeper for Royal Arsenal between 1890 and 1893, which included his first class debut in the FA Cup versus Derby County, 17th January 1891. Later played for Luton Town and when his playing days had finished he became trainer at Nottingham Forest.

	Games	Goals
FA Cup	4	0
Other Senior Matches	105	0
Other Reserve Matches	11	0
Total	**120**	**0**

Honours:
London Senior Cup Winners Medal 1890-91

BELL, Charles   1913-14

Birth Place: Dumfries, Scotland
Date of Birth: 1894

☛ Charles Bell was a centre forward who had played for various Scottish junior sides when he joined Woolwich Arsenal in September 1913. During his only season with

the club he played regularly in the South Eastern League side. He played his one and only league game (scoring twice) versus Leicester Fosse 27th December 1913. Was transferred to Chesterfield in July 1914. Charles later managed Wigan, Mansfield and Bournemouth.

	Games	Goals
League	1	2
Friendly Matches	3	5
London League Reserves	11	4
South Eastern League	22	17
Other Youth Matches	1	0
Total	**38**	**28**

BELLAMY, James   1903-07

Birth Place: Bethnal Green, London
Date of Birth: 11th September, 1881

James Bellamy

☛ James Bellamy was playing southern league football for Reading when Woolwich Arsenal signed him in May 1903. James spent his first two seasons at Plumstead playing for the club's reserve sides of that period. After a two year wait he eventually made his league debut in a home match versus Everton 22nd April 1905. In 1905-06 he began the season as the club's first choice right winger but when William Garbutt was signed by the club in December 1905 Bellamy was demoted back into reserve team football, in 1906-07 with the position being the same James wanted away after he had played in only eleven league games that season. He joined Portsmouth during the summer of 1907. He then had a short spell at Norwich 1908 before linking up with Dundee 1908-11 where he helped them to the Scottish League Championship Runners up position in 1908-09 and in the following season to a Scottish F A Cup Final Victory versus Clyde. Bellamy then moved to Motherwell 1911-12, before Burnley paid £1,000 for his services and in that 1912-13 season he helped the club to promotion to division one when playing in seventeen league games. He was transferred to Fulham in 1914 where he spent one season prior to the outbreak of World War One. He finished his long career playing for Southend in their first season in the football league in 1919-20. Died March 1969, aged 87.

	Games	Goals
League	29	4
Other Senior Matches	2	0
Friendly Matches	24	7
London League	4	1
London League Reserves	30	7
South Eastern League	48	12
Other Youth Matches	1	1
Total	**138**	**32**

Honours:
(WITH DUNDEE)
Scottish F A Cup Winners Medal   1909-10
(WITH ARSENAL)
South Eastern Counties League
   Championship Medal   1903-04
London League Reserve Championship
   Medal   1903-04
Southern Charity Cup Winners
   Medal   1905-06

BENEY, Albert   1909-10

Birth Place: Hastings, Sussex
Date of Birth: 1887

☛ Albert Beney joined Woolwich Arsenal in February 1909 from Hastings for £200. In his one year at the club he played in sixteen league games (scoring six goals) which included his league debut versus Manchester City 13th February 1909. He was transferred to Carlisle in 1910.

	Games	Goals
League	16	6
FA Cup	1	0
Friendly Matches	11	13
London League Reserves	1	0
South Eastern League	19	18
London FA Challenge Cup	3	0
Total	**51**	**37**

BENSON, Robert   1913-16

Birth Place: Whitehaven
Date of Birth: 9th February, 1883

☛ Robert Benson's story is not dissimilar to the tragic case of Joseph Powell. Robert began his career playing for several North Eastern Junior sides before joining Newcastle United in 1902. However, with the club having many fine full backs on their books he was restricted to playing only one league game in two seasons. He then linked up with Southampton in the Southern League in 1904. At the start of the 1905-06 season he was transferred to Sheffield United and over the course of the following eight seasons he developed into one of the countries finest left backs. The club penalty taker, he won a full England cap versus Ireland in February 1913 as well as football league honours whilst at Bramall Lane. He joined Arsenal (in the Club's first season at Highbury) in November 1913, making his Arsenal League debut at Bristol City, 29th November 1913, playing in all of the club's last twenty five league fixtures of that 1913-14 season, in 1914-15 he again was the club's regular left back except for the last game of the season when manager George Murrell experimented and played Benson at centre forward, Bob took up the challenge and scored twice in a 7-0 home victory versus Nottingham Forest. However, little did the footballing world know of the tragic circumstances of Bob's next game, for on 19th February 1916, he decided to play for the club (after he had not played for nearly a year) when with Arsenal a player short in a wartime game versus Reading. During the match he had to retire from the field feeling unwell, and later died in the dressing room with a burst blood vessel, aged 33.

	Games	Goals
League	52	7
FA Cup	2	0
Other Senior Matches	3	0
Friendly Matches	2	0
London League Reserves	5	0
South Eastern League	10	5
London FA Challenge Cup	4	0
Wartime	1	0
Total	**79**	**12**

Honours:
(WITH SHEFFIELD UNITED)
1 England Cap.
1 Football League Cap.
(WITH ARSENAL)
London F A Challenge Cup Finalists
   Medal   1914-15

BIGDEN, James   1904-1908

Birth Place: London
Date of Birth: 1880

☛ James Bigden had played junior football for Gravesend before joining West Ham United in 1901 where he played in nearly 100 games, he was transferred to Woolwich Arsenal in June 1904. In his four seasons at the Manor Field he played in every position, for the club, in the half back line. In his first season, 1904-05 he had to be content in deputising for either John Dick or Roddy McEachrane (another former West Ham Player). He played in only seven league games that term in which his debut was in an away fixture at Newcastle United on the opening day of the season, 3rd September 1904. At the beginning of the 1905-06 season James was still the understudy to the aforementioned. However, his fortunes changed in November 1905 when after a 0-2 home defeat versus Sheffield Wednesday he was selected for the following game (taking the place of Percy Sands) versus Nottingham Forest, he remained ever present for the rest of the season. In 1906-07 he enjoyed his finest season at the club when playing in thirty seven of the thirty eight league matches and helped Arsenal to their highest ever league position (seventh in division one) and reached the FA Cup Semi Final. In 1907-08 he suffered loss of form, which resulted in John Dick and Andy Ducat being the main rivals for the right half position at the club. He was transferred to Bury in June 1908 and later played for Southend in 1909.

	Games	Goals
League	75	1
FA Cup	12	0
Other Senior Matches	4	0
Friendly Matches	17	1
London League Reserves	10	0
South Eastern League	28	2
Total	**146**	**4**

Honours:
South Eastern Counties League
   Championship Medal   1905-06
Southern Charity Cup
   Winners Medal   1905-06

BLACKWOOD, John   1900-1901

Birth Place: Maine, U.S.A.
Date of Birth: 1877

☛ John Blackwood was one of many scotsman who played for Woolwich Arsenal at the turn of the century. He had begun his career with Patrick Thistle before joining Woolwich Arsenal in May 1900 from Glasgow Celtic. In his one and only season at the club he shared the centre forward position with

Ralph Gaudie and Alex Main. His league debut was versus Gainsborough Trinity 1st September 1900. Transferred to Reading 1901. Later played for West Ham United.

	Games	Goals
League	17	6
FA Cup	1	1
Kent League	2	1
Friendly Matches	11	11
London League Reserves	3	4
Total	**34**	**23**

BLAIR, James   1905-06

Birth Place: Dumfries, Scotland
Date of Birth: 1885

☛ James Blair joined Woolwich Arsenal from Kilmarnock in May 1905, making his league debut versus Liverpool 2nd September 1905. Blair was an inside forward who was later transferred to Manchester City in November 1906. Spent four seasons at Maine Road, 1906-1910 playing in seventy six league games. He joined Bradford City in May 1910 for two seasons. He finished his career with Stockport 1912-13. Took his own life in 1913 aged 28.

James Blair

	Games	Goals
League	13	3
Other Senior Matches	1	0
Friendly Matches	8	1
London League Reserves	8	2
South Eastern League	5	2
Total	**35**	**8**

BOOTH, Charles   1892-1894

Birth Place: Gainsborough, Lincolnshire
Date of Birth: 1869

☛ Charles Booth was an outside left who had served his home club town, Gainsborough Trinity before joining Wolverhampton Wanderers in 1889. He spent three seasons at the newly built Molineux, before joining Royal Arsenal during the summer of 1892. Charles was a permanent fixture in the club's last pre league side of 1892-93. In 1893-94 he made his league debut for the club in Royal Arsenal's first ever league match versus Newcastle United 2nd September 1893. He was a consistent member of the side until a heavy 0-3 defeat at Lincoln City in February 1894 (losing his place to Thomas Bryan). He was transferred to Loughborough Town in 1894. Died in September 1898 aged 29.

	Games	Goals
League	16	2
FA Cup	10	8
Other Senior Matches	42	11
Friendly Matches	14	4
Total	**82**	**25**

BOYD, Henry   1894-1897

Birth Place: Pollokshaws, Scotland
Date of Birth: 1868

☛ Henry Boyd can be described as the club's first prolific marksman. He joined Woolwich Arsenal in May 1894 having served West Bromwich Albion. In his first season at the club it became apparent that they had signed a mercurial talent. After scoring on his debut versus Grimsby Town, 10th September 1894, he went on a goal spree netting eight times in the next five games, which included a hat trick versus Manchester City. However, disaster struck when in a game versus Newton Heath (now Manchester United), 13th October 1894, he suffered a broken leg which put him out of action for over a year. On return to league action he started where he left off by scoring in a 5-0 victory over Burton. Although missing the first seven league games of that 1895-96 season he still managed to finish as the club's leading marksman with thirteen goals in twenty two games. In 1896-97 he had scored ten goals in twelve games when in January 1897, Woolwich Arsenal could not refuse a £45 transfer bid from Newton Heath for Henry's services. He spent three seasons at Bank Street keeping up his scoring ratio (thirty two goals in fifty two games).

	Games	Goals
League	40	31
FA Cup	1	0
United League	4	1
Kent League	2	1
Friendly Matches	32	47
Total	**79**	**80**

BOYLAN, P A   1896-1897

Birth Place: Greenock, Scotland
Date of Birth: 1876

☛ P A Boylan joined Woolwich Arsenal from Scottish junior football in June 1896. In his only season at the club he played in eleven league games as a half back which included his league debut versus Manchester City 5th September 1896. Later played for Greenock Morton.

	Games	Goals
League	11	0
United League	7	0
Kent League	10	4
Friendly Matches	12	1
Total	**40**	**5**

Honours:
Kent League Championship Medal 1896-97.

BOYLE, James   1893-1897

Birth Place: Springburn, Scotland.
Date of Birth: 11th July, 1866

☛ James Boyle was a versatile half back who joined Woolwich Arsenal from Celtic in November 1893, (he had been on their books when they won the Scottish Cup in 1892 and the Scottish Championship in 1892-93. In 1893-94 (the club's first season in the league) he eventually gained a regular place in the side at centre half in February 1894 (taking over from Robert Buist). He had previously made his league debut at centre forward away at Northwich Victoria 9th December 1893. In 1894-95 he was a stalwart in the defence, missing only two league games. However, in 1895-96 James lost his place to Caesar Jenkyns. He regained his first team spot after the suspension of Allen Ward. Showing his true flexibility when the club hit a goalkeeping crisis in December, Boyle filled in and played in four league games between the posts. In 1896-97 he played in his fair share of league encounters without ever gaining a regular position. He was released from his contract during the summer of 1897 when he joined non league Dartford.

	Games	Goals
League	61	7
FA Cup	5	2
United League	4	0
Kent League	26	3
Friendly Matches	81	15
Total	**177**	**27**

Honours:
Kent League Championship Medal 1896-97

BRADSHAW, William — 1900-1904

Birth Place: Burnley, Lancashire.
Date of Birth: 1882

☛ William Bradshaw was the son of the then Woolwich Arsenal manager, when signing for the club as an amateur in March 1900, turning professional four months later. In his four seasons at the club he was a permanent member of the reserve teams of the time. He eventually gained his first team chance on the 8th November 1902 when scoring Arsenal's first goal in a 2-1 victory versus Blackpool. He managed to play in the final three league games of the club's promotion winning season of 1903-04. When his father, Harry, was appointed manager of Fulham William followed him to Craven Cottage during the summer of 1904. He later played for Burton United and Ton Pentre before emigrating to Canada in 1910. His brother, Joseph, was also at one stage on Woolwich Arsenal's books.

	Games	Goals
League	4	2
Other Senior Matches	1	0
Kent League	36	19
Friendly Matches	23	13
London League	7	2
London League Reserves	66	39
South Eastern League	16	12
Other Youth Matches	3	2
Total	**156**	**89**

Honours:
3 Kent League Championship
Medals   1900-01, 1901-02, 1902-03
2 London League Reserve Championship
Medals   1901-02, 1903-04
South Eastern League Championship
Medal   1903-04

BRIERCLIFFE, Thomas — 1901-05

☛ Thomas Briercliffe had played Northern Junior Football for Bacup and Clitheroe before joining Blackburn Rovers in 1897. An outside right, Thomas was a steady member of the Rovers side for three seasons before moving on to Stalybridge for the 1900-01 season. He was transferred to Woolwich Arsenal in May 1901 - in the 1901-02 season Briercliffe enjoyed a very successful campaign, not only was he ever present but he finished as the club's leading goalscorer with eleven, this after making his Arsenal league debut versus Barnsley, 2nd September 1901. In 1902-03 he made the right wing position his own (when missing only one game). In Arsenal's promotion winning season he was an integral part of the forward line which virtually every week

read Briercliffe, Coleman, Gooing, Shanks and Linward. This forward line scored eighty three times between them that season of which Thomas helped himself to a hat trick in an 8-0 demolition of Burton United. In his last season at the club, 1904-05, he was still a mainstay on the club's wing before surprisingly returning to Blackburn Rovers in April 1905. He later played in the Southern League for Plymouth Argyle and for Darwen.

	Games	Goals
League	122	33
FA Cup	11	1
Other Senior Matches	2	0
Friendly Matches	11	5
London League	25	5
London League Reserves	1	0
Total	**172**	**44**

BRIGGS, Stanley — 1893

Birth Place: Stamford Hill, London.
Date of Birth: 7th February, 1872

☛ Stanley Briggs joined Royal Arsenal as an amateur centre half in October 1893. During his three months at the club he played in two league games of which his league debut was versus Rotherham Town 13th November 1893. Later had spells with Tottenham and Millwall. He died in Canada in September, 1935.

	Games	Goals
League	2	0
Friendly Matches	2	0
Total	**4**	**0**

BROCK, James — 1896-1898

Birth Place: Scotland
Date of Birth:

☛ James Brock was Woolwich Arsenal's regular outside right for two seasons 1896-1898, during which time he missed only six of the club's sixty league matches. He made his league debut on the opening day of the season versus Manchester City 5th September 1896. He was transferred to to Cowes, Isle of Wight for £30 in November 1898. He later returned to play in his native Scotland, for Clyde and Paisley Abertorn.

	Games	Goals
League	57	19
FA Cup	6	3
United League	31	10
Kent League	4	2
Friendly Matches	28	11
Total	**126**	**45**

BRYAN, Thomas — 1892-1894

☛ Thomas Bryan spent most of his time at the club as a reserve outside left, although he did manage to play nine league games. His league debut was versus Rotherham Town 6th February 1894. Tom later played junior football for several Kent teams.

	Games	Goals
League	9	1
Friendly Matches	8	3
Other Reserve Matches	5	3
Total	**22**	**7**

BUCHAN, James — 1904-1905

Birth Place: Perth, Scotland
Date of Birth: 1881

☛ James Buchan joined Woolwich Arsenal in April 1904 from Hibernian after helping them to the Scottish League Championship of 1902-1903, and to the Scottish FA Cup of 1902. A half back, he only spent one year at the club and played in only eight league matches which included his league debut versus Newcastle 3rd September 1904. (This was Arsenal's first ever league game in Division One). Transferred to Manchester City in March 1905. He served City well for six seasons playing in over one hundred and fifty league games winning a second division championship medal in 1909-1910. Returned to Scotland in 1911 when he joined Motherwell.

	Games	Goals
League	8	0
Other Senior Matches	1	0
Friendly Matches	5	2
London League Reserves	2	0
South Eastern League	3	0
Other Youth Matches	1	0
Total	**20**	**2**

Honours:
(WITH MANCHESTER CITY)
Second Division Championship
Medal   1909-10

BUCHANAN, Robert — 1894-1896

Birth Place: Paisley, Scotland
Date of Birth: 1868

☛ Robert Buchanan was a skillful inside forward who began his career for Scottish Junior club Johnstone. He then joined Abercorn spending four seasons there, winning a Scottish full cap versus Wales in 1891. He moved South to join Burnley (in their pre league days) in 1892, spending two seasons there before being transferred to Woolwich Arsenal in September 1894. In the 1894-95 season he enjoyed a long spell in the league side, scoring nine goals in twenty five games, which included his league debut in a 4-2 home victory versus Manchester City, 29th September 1894. In 1895-96 he changed from the centre forward role back to his orthodox inside left position playing in seventeen league games, scoring seven goals. He moved on to Southampton St Mary during the summer of 1896. Died December 1907 aged 39.

	Games	Goals
League	42	16
FA Cup	2	0
Kent League	9	8
Friendly Matches	33	21
Total	**86**	**45**

Honours:
(WITH ABERCORN)
1 Scottish Cap.

BUCHANAN, William   1909-1910

Birth Place: Woolwich, London
Date of Birth: 1887

☞ William Buchanan was in the army stationed at Aldershot when he signed for Woolwich Arsenal as an amateur in November 1909. He was the club's regular centre forward that season, 1909-1910, after he made his league debut versus Bristol City, 20th November 1909. Was transferred to Southampton in July 1910. Died June 1954, aged 67.

	Games	Goals
League	21	5
Friendly Matches	1	0
South Eastern League	1	1
Other Youth Matches	1	4
Total	**24**	**10**

BUIST, George   1896-1897

Birth Place: Scotland

☞ George Buist followed his elder brother Robert down to London to play for Woolwich Arsenal from Greenock Morton in September 1896. Made his league debut versus Manchester City 28th April 1897. A full back, he played in only six league games during his seven months with the club.

	Games	Goals
League	6	0
United League	4	0
Kent League	4	0
Friendly Matches	11	0
Total	**25**	**0**

BUIST, Robert   1891-1894

Birth Place: Glasgow
Date of Birth: 1870

☞ Robert Buist played in Royal Arsenal's first ever league game versus Newcastle, 1st September 1893 as centre half in a two all draw. For the first three seasons he was a main stay in the club's defence before the club's introduction to league football.

	Games	Goals
League	17	0
FA Cup	10	0
Other Senior Matches	93	3
Friendly Matches	24	1
Total	**144**	**4**

BURDETT, George   1910-1912

Birth Place: Tottenham

☞ George Burdett was another army man who joined the club as an amateur in August 1910. He was the reserve goalkeeper to Edward Bateup in 1910-11, playing in ten league games. His debut was against Everton, 11th March 1911, keeping a clean sheet. Gained the first team spot in 1911-12 playing in the club's first fifteen league games. However, he lost his place after a three goals to one defeat at Bury.

	Games	Goals
League	28	0
Other Senior Matches	2	0
Friendly Matches	5	0
South Eastern League	32	0
London FA Challenge Cup	2	0
Total	**69**	**0**

BURRELL, George   1912-14

Birth Place: Newcastle Upon Tyne
Date of Birth: 1892

☞ George Burrell was an outside left who joined Arsenal in June 1912 from Leyton FC, having previously played in the North East of England for local sides, Shildon Athletic and South Shields. He made his league debut versus Newcastle, 28th September 1912. He gained a regular place (in an Arsenal side which narrowly missed relegation) at the back end of the season, taking over the left wing position from "Tiny" Winship and made seventeen league appearances. In 1913-14 he could not hold down a regular position playing in only 6 league games and was handed a free transfer during the close season of 1914 when he rejoined South Shields.

	Games	Goals
League	23	3
FA Cup	1	0
Other Senior Matches	1	0
Friendly Matches	4	1
London League Reserves	8	2
South Eastern League	37	11
London FA Challenge Cup	4	0
Total	**78**	**17**

BURROWS, Lycurgus   1892-1895

Birth Place: Ashton-under-Lyme, Lancashire.
Date of Birth: 26th June, 1875

☞ Lycurgus Burrows joined Royal Arsenal as an amateur full back in January 1892, the year before the club entered the Football League. In the club's first season in the league he managed to play in six consecutive league games in February 1894, which included his league debut versus Rotherham Town, 6th February 1894. In 1894-95 season he played in the first three league games at right back before losing his place to Joseph Powell. In 1895-96 season he played his last league game in a 4-3 victory at Notts County in November 1895. Died August 1952, aged77.

	Games	Goals
League	10	0
Other Senior Matches	1	0
Friendly Matches	29	0
Other Reserve Matches	21	0
Total	**61**	**0**

BUSBY, Walter   1903-1905

Birth Place: Wellingborough.
Date of Birth: 1882

☞ Walter Busby was an outside left who joined Woolwich Arsenal in May 1903 from Queens Park Rangers having previously played for Wellingborough. He played in five league games during the 1903-04 season which included his debut versus Manchester United when he scored in a 4-0 victory at home. He also scored in his second game at the Manor Field ground in an 8-0 victory win versus Leicester Fosse, in 1904-05 season the left wing position was "fiercely" contested with the likes of Satterthwaite, Templeton and Linward, this resulting in Busby spending the whole season playing in the South Eastern League reserves. Was transferred to Leyton F C during the summer of 1905.

	Games	Goals
League	5	2
F A Cup	1	0
Other Senior Matches	2	0
Friendly Matches	6	7

London League	3	1
London League Reserves	25	16
South Eastern League	27	21
Other Youth Matches	1	3
Totals	**70**	**50**

Honours:
South Eastern League Championship
  Medal   1903-04
London League Reserves Championship
  Medal   1903-04

CAIE, Alexander   1897

Birth Place: Aberdeen, Scotland
Date of Birth: 1878

Alex Caie was a young centre forward playing Scottish Junior Football for Victoria United (now Aberdeen) before joining Woolwich Arsenal in February 1897. "Big Sandy" affectionately known (because at only five foot nine inches he weighed over thirteen stones) made his league debut versus Burton Swifts 20th February 1897, when scoring the club's third goal in a 3-0 victory. After playing in only eight league games during his five months at the club, he was transferred to Bristol South End (now Bristol City). He later linked up with Southern League side Millwall (at which juncture in his career he had changed to the right half position). His form in this position resulted in Alex Caie returning to league action with Newcastle United 1901-03. He later played for Brentford before finishing his career back in Scotland with Motherwell. He emigrated to Canada and was tragically killed in a rail accident in Massachusetts, USA December 1914 aged 36.

	Games	*Goals*
League	8	4
United League	4	2
Friendly Matches	9	5
Total	**21**	**11**

CALDER, Leslie   1911-1913

Birth Place: Southampton

Leslie Calder was a utility forward, who during his two seasons at the Manor Field played regularly for the club's South Eastern League side. He made his one and only league appearance versus Middlesbrough, 15th April 1911.

	Games	*Goals*
League	1	0
Friendly Matches	13	13
South Eastern League	48	30
Totals	**62**	**43**

CALDWELL, John   1894-98

Birth Place: Ayr, Scotland
Date of Birth: 1873

John Caldwell had played junior football in Scotland for Newmills (Ayr) before joining Hibernian. Transferred to Woolwich Arsenal in August 1894. In the club's second season in the league John Caldwell made Arsenal history becoming their first player to remain ever present in a season, as the club's left back, after making his debut away at Lincoln City, 1st September 1894. In 1895-86 he was again very consistent, missing just one game versus Loughborough Town. In 1896-97 he seemed to lose his way when losing his place to the newly signed Finlay Sinclair. This resulted in John returning to Scotland for a short period with Third Lanark. He came back to the Manor Field and played in fifteen of the last seventeen league encounters of that season. In 1897-98 he shared the left back berth with Alex McConnell when he played in nineteen league games. He was transferred to Brighton United in the summer of 1898.

	Games	*Goals*
League	93	2
F A Cup	4	0
Other Senior Matches	1	0
United League	18	0
Kent League	3	0
Friendly Matches	72	5
Total	**191**	**7**

CALDWELL, James   1913-1914

Birth Place: Carronshore, Scotland
Date of Birth: 1886

James Caldwell had played junior football for Carron Thistle and Dunipace in Scotland before turning professional with East Stirling, he then tried his luck in the Southern League with Tottenham and Reading. Transferred to Everton in 1912 and was their regular goalkeeper in the 1912-13 season. He joined Arsenal in June 1913. Unfortunately in his one season at the club he had to be content as deputy to Joe Lievesley, playing in only three league games. His debut being a home encounter at Highbury versus Hull City, 20th September 1913. It came as no surprise when he was transfer listed and transferred back to Reading in the summer of 1914.

	Games	*Goals*
League	3	0
Friendly Matches	4	0
London League Reserves	11	0
South Eastern League	32	0
London FA Challenge Cup	2	0
Total	**52**	**0**

CALVERT, Frederick   1911-1912

Birth Place: Southend, Essex

Frederick Calvert was a soldier stationed at the garrison at Woolwich, when joining Woolwich Arsenal as an amateur in April 1911. Made his league debut versus Liverpool at Anfield 17th April 1911. He only played in one other league game, scoring the club's only goal in a 1 - 3 defeat at Notts County in December 1912.

	Games	*Goals*
League	2	1
Friendly Matches	1	0
South Eastern League	13	6
Totals	**16**	**7**

CARVER, George   1896-1900

George Carver was a full back who served Woolwich Arsenal well for four seasons. During this time he predominantly played in the Kent League side or friendly matches. He played in only one league game versus Loughborough, 12th December 1896. This game was Arsenal's record league defeat 0 - 8.

	Games	*Goals*
League	1	0
United League	1	0
Kent League	23	0
Friendly Matches	56	0
Other Youth Matches	2	0
Totals	**83**	**0**

CASSIDY, Hugh   1897

Hugh Cassidy was a full back who joined Woolwich Arsenal in February 1897 from the army. His duration at the club was less than three months in which time he played in his one and only league game versus Newcastle at the Manor Field in a 5 - 1 victory.

	Games	*Goals*
League	1	0
Friendly Matches	1	0
Totals	**2**	**0**

CHALMERS, John   1910-1912

Birth Place: Glasgow
Date of Birth: 1885

John Chalmers was a centre forward who started his career with Scottish Junior sides Rutherglen and Glencairn (Glasgow), before turning professional with Glasgow Rangers.
He was transferred to Stoke City in January 1906 and was their leading scorer 1906-07. He then moved to Bristol Rovers before returning

to Scotland to join Clyde in November 1908, where he helped them reach the Scottish F A Cup Final 1910. John joined Woolwich Arsenal in October 1910 (after the club had scored only two league goals in the opening six games). He made his debut at Bradford City October 8th 1910. He finished the season as the club's leading scorer with fifteen goals in twenty nine games. In 1911-12 he began the season as the club's regular centre forward before losing his place to Alf Common. (who had switched from inside forward) Not content with reserve team football, he was transferred to Greenock Morton for £500 in March 1912.

	Games	Goals
League	48	21
F A Cup	3	1
Other Senior Matches	1	1
South Eastern League	4	2
London FA Challenge Cup	3	0
Total	59	25

CHARTERIS, J M   1888-1890

Birth Place: Kirkcaldy, Scotland

☛ J M Charteris was an inside forward who during his three seasons with Royal Arsenal in the Pre league days played regularly in senior and reserve team matches. Was a prolific scorer, twice scoring seven goals in a match for the reserves in 1889-90 season. His career ended after breaking a leg in November 1890.

	Games	Goals
F A Cup	1	0
Other Senior Matches	27	24
Other Reserve Matches	25	35
Totals	53	59

COLEMAN, John   1902-1908

Birth Place: Kettering, Northamptonshire
Date of Birth: 26th October 1881

☛ "Tim" Coleman will be regarded as the club's first ever great goal scorer, for in a total of only twelve seasons, he scored over two hundred first class goals in less than four hundred and fifty games. His career began with his home town club Kettering (the club Arsenal signed in latter years, Eddie Hapgood) before joining Northampton Town in 1901, where he was transferred from, to Woolwich Arsenal along with Everard Lawrence, in May 1902. In his first season at the club he broke the Arsenal league goal scoring record in a season when scoring seventeen times in thirty games, this included, surprisingly, his only hat trick for the club versus Burnley 27th December 1902. His league debut being on the opening day of the season versus Preston, 6th September 1902. In 1903-04, in the club's promotion winning season, he broke his own

Honours:
Kent County Junior Cup Winners
Medal   1889-90

CHISHOLM, Norman   1907-1910

Birth Place: Arbroath, Scotland

☛ Norman Chisholm was a full back, joining the club as an amateur in September 1907 turning professional the following September. In his three seasons at Woolwich Arsenal he played a total of three league games, all in the 1908-09 season, including his debut at Middlesbrough, 3rd October 1908. His appearances being restricted due to the consistency of Archie Gray and Joe Shaw.

	Games	Goals
League	3	0
Friendlies	7	0
London League Reserves	7	0
South Eastern League	31	0
London F A Challenge Cup	1	0
Total	49	0

CHRISTMAS, Arthur   1890-1891

Birth Place: Wolverhampton

☛ Arthur Christmas was a utility forward who joined Royal Arsenal in Pre- League days from Kidderminster in January 1890. In his 2 seasons at the club he played mainly in the senior side. He played in only one first class match, an F A Cup Tie at the Invicta ground versus Derby County 17th January 1891, he later moved on to Gray Wanderers.

individual record by scoring twenty three times in twenty eight games, (Although Tommy Shanks, broke his club record when scoring twenty four times). In a disappointing 1904-05 season John managed to score only five times in twenty six games. In 1905 -06 he maintained his record of scoring in nearly every other game when finding the net fifteen times in thirty four first team games, helping the club to the first of consecutive F.A. Cup Semi Final appearances. In 1906-07 his consistency was rewarded when winning a full England cap versus Ireland in February 1907, after scoring fourteen times in thirty four league games. With the club suffering financially, Everton's transfer bid of £700 in February 1908 was accepted. In three seasons at Goodison Park he played in seventy one league games scoring thirty goals, helping the club to the First Division runners up position in 1908-09 as well as winning three football league caps. He later played for Sunderland 1910-11 (thirty two games and twenty goals), Fulham 1911-14 (ninety four games and forty five goals) and Nottingham Forest

	Games	Goals
F A Cup	1	0
Other Senior Matches	37	18
Other Reserve Matches	5	2
Total	43	20

Honours:
London Charity Cup Winners Medal 1889-90
London Senior Cup Winners Medal 1890-91
Kent Senior Cup Winners Medal   1889-90
Kent Junior Cup Winners Medal   1889-90

CLARK, James   1897-1900

☛ James Clark was Woolwich Arsenal's reserve centre half during his three seasons at the club. He played in only three league games in 1897-98, in which his debut was at Darwen, 12th March 1898. In 1898-99 he played one league match versus Leicester Fosse during 1899-1900, because of the form of John Dick, he was not able to gain a league place. He, subsequently, left the club.

	Games	Goals
League	4	0
United League	1	0
Kent League	23	5
Friendly Matches	36	0
Other Youth Matches	2	0
Totals	66	5

1914-15 (thirty seven games and fourteen goals). He retired during the first world war, but later played non league football for Tunbridge Wells in 1920. He finished his footballing career coaching in Holland. Died November 1940, aged 59.

	Games	Goals
League	172	79
FA Cup	24	5
Other Senior Matches	9	5
Friendly Matches	21	16
London League	11	5
South Eastern League	3	3
Total	240	113

Honours:
(WITH ARSENAL)
1 England Cap
Southern Professional Charity Cup
   Winners Medals   1905-06
Southern Professional Charity Cup Finalists
   Medal   1903-04
(WITH ARSENAL AND EVERTON)
   3 Football League Caps

COLES, Frederick   1900-1904

Birth Place: Nottingham
Date of Birth: 1875

☛Frederick Coles had been a reserve wing half with both Notts County and Nottingham Forest before joining Woolwich Arsenal in June 1900. In 1900-01 he gained a regular position in the side. After making his league debut at home to Chesterfield 29th September 1900, going on to play in twenty seven league games that season. In 1901-02 he missed only two league games (playing in thirty two out of thirty four). However, with the emergence of Percy Sands and with John Dick moving from centre half to right half, Frederick had to be content virtually all that season with reserve team football. This resulted in him being transferred to Grimsby Town in June 1904. He spent three seasons there and later became a football and cricket coach in Sweden and trainer of the Hague Club, in Holland 1910-11. Died April 1947 aged 71.

	Games	Goals
League	78	2
FA Cup	8	0
Other Senior Matches	3	0
Kent League	5	0
Friendly Matches	27	2
London League	22	0
London League Reserves	25	1
South Eastern League	21	2
Other Youth Matches	3	0
Total	**192**	**7**

Honours:
South Eastern League Championship
  Medal   1903-04
London League Reserve Championship
  Medal   1903-04

COMMON, Alf   1910-1912

Birth Place: Sunderland
Date of Birth: 25th May 1880

☛Alf Common started his footballing career playing junior football with South Hylton and Jarrow in the North East of England before joining his home town club Sunderland in 1900. He won a regular place in the Sunderland side of 1901 when helping them to the runners up position in division one. With the club having an overload of classy inside forwards, Alf was allowed to join Sheffield United in the latter part of 1901 and in his first season he became a folk hero when scoring the winning goal in the 1902 FA Cup Final versus Southampton. He stayed at Bramall Lane for a further two seasons in which time he won the first of his three England caps versus Ireland in February 1904. He moved back to Sunderland for the 1904-05 season before making football

history when becoming the first ever player to be transferred for a four figure sum - £1,000 to Middlesbrough in 1905. He spent five seasons at Ayresome Park, playing in one hundred and sixty eight league games, scoring fifty six league goals, Common was transferred to Woolwich Arsenal for £250 in August 1910, making his Arsenal league debut versus Manchester United, 1st September 1910. In that 1910-11 season he was a regular in either inside forward positions when playing in twenty nine league games, scoring six goals. In the 1911-12 season he enjoyed being the club's leading league goal scorer (with seventeen goals) when missing only two league fixtures. In Arsenal's disastrous 1912-13 relegation campaign, Common played in twelve of the club's first fifteen league games (without scoring) before being transferred to Preston North End in December 1912, for £250. In his two seasons at Deepdale he was a member of both the club's Second Division Championship winning side of 1912-13 and their division one relegation season, 1913-14. Retired 1914, died April 1946 aged 65.

	Games	Goals
League	77	23
FA Cup	3	0
Other Senior Matches	3	1
Friendly Matches	4	1
South Eastern League	3	2
London FA Challenge Cup	5	4
Total	**95**	**31**

Honours:
(WITH SHEFFIELD UNITED)
3 England Caps
1 Football League Cap
F A Cup Winners Medal   1901-02
(WITH PRESTON)
Second Division Championship
  Medal   1912-13

CONNOLLY, Peter   1888-1893

Birth Place: Kirkcaldy, Fife, Scotland
Date of Birth: 1867

☛Peter Connolly was an unusual player in the sense that he played either as a full back or centre forward. Peter joined Royal Arsenal in 1888 from the Scottish junior side Kirkcaldy Wanderers. In his five seasons with Royal Arsenal in pre League days, he was a key fixture in the senior side. He made his first class debut in an F A Cup qualifying game versus Lyndhurst, 5th October 1889. Like so many other players of the time he later played for the Royal Ordnance. Died September 1895 aged 28.

	Games	Goals
F A Cup	6	2
Other Senior Matches	127	49
Other Reserve Matches	25	25
Total	**158**	**76**

Honours:
London Charity Cup Winners
  Medal   1889-90
Kent Senior Cup Winners Medal   1889-90
London Senior Cup Winners Medal   1890-91
London Senior Cup Finalists Medal   1889-90

CONNOR, Maurice   1902

Birth Place: Lochee, Scotland
Date of Birth: July 1877

☛Maurice Connor was a footballing nomad who started his career with Scottish junior clubs Dundee Fereday and Queen's Gordon Highlanders. He then linked up with Glentoran in Ireland before trying his luck in English football with West Bromwich Albion in 1897. Transferred to Walsall in 1899. He joined Bristol City in 1901 before leaving for Woolwich Arsenal in 1902. His period at Manor Field was one of less than nine months, making his Woolwich league debut on the opening day of the season (when scoring) at Deepdale versus Preston 6th September 1902. He played in fourteen league games at the beginning of the season but lost his place to Walter Anderson and was subsequently transferred to Brentford in December 1902, where he won the first of his three Irish caps versus Scotland. He later played for New Brompton (now Gillingham) and Fulham before finishing his career with Glentoran. He died August 1934 aged 57.

	Games	Goals
League	14	2
FA Cup	2	1
Friendly Matches	1	2
London League	6	3
Total	**23**	**8**

Honours:
Three Irish Caps.

COOPER, Joseph   1893-1894

Birth Place: Wolverhampton
Date of Birth: 1865

☛Joseph Cooper was a centre forward who had played junior football for Milton FC before signing league forms to play for Wolverhampton Wanderers in the first football league season of 1888-89. He spent five seasons at Molineux (four of these as a permanent reserve) transferred to Woolwich Arsenal in October 1893, making his Arsenal league debut at the Manor Field versus Ardwick (now Manchester City) 11th November 1893. He managed to play in only six league games for the club during that season.

	Games	Goals
League	6	0
FA Cup	2	2
Friendly Matches	19	19
Total	**27**	**21**

COTTRELL, Ernest 1898-1901

Birth Place: Grantham, Limcs.
Date of Birth: 31st January 1877

☞ Ernest Cottrell joined Arsenal in May 1898. A right winger or inside right, he made his Woolwich Arsenal debut versus Small Heath, 5th November 1898 and was a regular in the side that season, scoring nine goals in eighteen league games, which included a hat trick versus Blackpool 18th March 1899. In 1899-1900 he lost his place and only made one league appearance. In 1900-01 he played in just five league games before leaving to join Watford during the summer of 1901. He collapsed and died whilst watching a Watford versus Preston encounter in January 1929, aged 51 years.

	Games	Goals
League	24	12
Other Senior Matches	1	1
United League	7	3
Kent League	32	22
Friendly matches	27	20
London League Reserves	14	7
Southern Combination	1	0
Totals	**106**	**65**

Honours:
Kent League Championships Medal 1900-01

CRAWFORD, Gavin 1891-1898

Birth Place: Kilmarnock, Scotland
Date of Birth: 1867

☞ Gavin had played junior football in Scotland for Glasgow sides Ash Lea FC and Fairfield Rangers when joining Sheffield United in their pre league days of 1890. He was transferred from them to Royal Arsenal during the summer of 1891. In his first two seasons at the club he was a regular in the senior side. In 1893-94, the club's first season in the football league, he played in twenty one league games (which were either at wing half or on the club's right wing) of which his debut was a scoring one versus Walsall Town Swifts, 11th September 1893. In 1894-95 he missed only one league game whilst playing on the right wing, scoring seven goals. However, in 1895-96 he reverted back to the right half position. In the following campaign his consistency earned him the captaincy after the tragic death of Joseph Powell, Gavin playing in twenty six of the clubs thirty league games. His fortune changed in 1897-98, when combined with lack of form and injuries, he played in just nineteen league fixtures which were spread over six spells during that season. This resulted in him moving on to Millwall in the summer of 1898. He later played for Queens Park Rangers and was head groundsman at Charlton Athletic up until the late 1940's. Died March 1955 aged 87.

	Games	Goals
League	122	14
FA Cup	16	4
Other Senior Matches	83	49
United League	21	0
Kent League	3	1
Friendly Matches	94	19
Other Reserve Matches	7	4
Total	**346**	**91**

CRAWFORD, Harold 1911-1913

Birth Place: Dundee, Scotland

☞ Harold Crawford joined Woolwich Arsenal from Hebburn Argyle (Newcastle junior football) in June 1911. A goalkeeper in his first season with the club he was understudy to both George Burdett and Leigh Roose. He played in seven league games that season making his debut at Tottenham in a 5-0 defeat, Christmas Day 1911. Not a good Christmas present for the Arsenal supporters in the 47,000 crowd ! He became automatic choice at the start of the 1912-13 season, playing in the first seventeen league games, but was dropped after a 3 - 0 home defeat versus Tottenham in December 1912. He played in a further 2 league games in March 1913 after losing his position to Hugh McDonald, these being a 4 - 1 defeat at Villa Park and a 5 -2 home defeat against Sheffield Wednesday. The club were subsequently relegated for the only time in the 20th Century. Was granted a free transfer in May 1913 when he joined Reading.

	Games	Goals
League	26	0
F A Cup	1	0
Other Senior Matches	1	0
Friendly matches		14
	0	
South Eastern League	38	0
Other Youth Matches	1	0
Total	**81**	**0**

CROSS, Archie 1900-1910

Birth Place: Kent
Date of Birth: 1881

☞ Arthur "Archie" Cross was a loyal serving full back for ten years at the turn of the century, having joined the club from Dartford in April 1900. In his first season, 1900-01, he had to be content in being right back deputy to David McNichol, playing in just three league games which included his debut at Blackpool, 6th October 1900. In 1901-02 he played in fifteen of the club's first nineteen league games before losing his place to McNichol. After playing in fourteen league games in 1902-03, he finally won a regular position in the side during Woolwich Arsenal's promotion winning season of 1903-04. However, during the next three seasons he played in only forty three of the club's one hundred and ten league games in which time he was understudy to Archie Gray. In his final two seasons at Plumstead, Archie had switched to left back, but could not wrestle the first team birth from the consistent Joe Shaw. His loyalty was rewarded by the many reserve team honours he won. In his ten seasons at the club, he played in one hundred and thirty two league games and in 1905-06 and 06-07 he was good enough to be selected for England International Trials.

Archie Cross

	Games	Goals
League	132	0
FA Cup	17	0
Other Senior Matches	7	0
Kent League	18	1
Friendly Matches	58	0
London League	9	0
London League Reserves	52	1
South Eastern League	66	0
London FA Challenge Cup	3	0
Other Youth Matches	1	0
Total	**363**	**2**

Honours:
Southern Charity Cup Winners Medal	1905-06
Southern Charity Cup Finalist Medal	1903-04
London League Championship Medal	1901-02
Two Kent Championship Medals	1900-01, 1901-02
South Eastern League Championship Medal	1907-08

CROWE, Alfred　　　　1903-1906

☛Alf "Happy" Crowe was a centre forward who joined Woolwich Arsenal as an amateur from North Woolwich Invicta in August 1903. In his three seasons at manor field he was a prolific scorer in all the club's reserve sides scoring well over 100 goals. He played in only six league games during his time with the club, scoring four goals, including two goals on his league debut at Sheffield Wednesday 29th October 1904. He was unfortunate to be at the club when they had such consistent performers as Coleman, Gooing, Shanks, Satterthwaite, Freeman and Fitchie.

	Games	Goals
League	6	4
Friendlies	22	17
London League	4	2
London League Reserves	39	32
South Eastern League	52	56
Other Youth Matches	1	5
Total	124	116

Honours:

South Eastern League Championship
　Medal　　　　　　　　　　1903-04
London League Reserves Championship
　Medal　　　　　　　　　　1903-04

CROZIER, James　　　　1894-1895

☛James Crozier was a goalkeeper who joined Woolwich Arsenal from Partick Thistle in May 1894. He played in only one league game for the club at home versus Grimsby (1 -3) 10th September 1894.

	Games	Goals
League	1	0
Friendlies	14	0
Totals	15	0

CURLE, William　　　　1908-1910

Birth Place:　Glasgow
Date of Birth:　1886

☛William Curle joined Woolwich Arsenal from Scottish junior side Rutherglen Glencairn in May 1908. In his two seasons at Manor Field, he like Alf Crowe, could not command a regular place in the side due to the form of the forwards on the books at this time. However, he appeared regularly in the South Eastern League side. He played in three league games for the club, including his debut at Meadow Lane versus Notts County, 5th September 1908.

	Games	Goals
League	3	0
Other Senior Matches	1	0
Friendly Matches	16	1
London League Reserves	12	0
South Eastern League	52	12

London FA Challenge Cup	1	0
Other Youth Matches	2	1
Totals	87	14

DAILLY, Hugh　　　　1898-1899

Birth Place:　Scotland
Date of Birth:　1879

☛Hugh Dailly was transferred to Woolwich Arsenal in May 1898 from Scottish junior side Dundee North End. An outside left , his spell at the Manor Field was one of only eight months, he played in eight league games during 1898-99, scoring on his debut at Darwen, 17th September 1898. He followed this by scoring twice in the club's next home game versus Gainsborough Trinity in a 5 - 1 win. He lost his place on the left flank to Herbert Shaw and left the club in February 1899 when he joined Dundee.

	Games	Goals
League	8	4
Other Senior Matches	1	0
United League	8	4
Kent League	4	3
Friendly Matches	6	3
Totals	27	14

DAVIDSON, Alexander　　　1904-1905

Birth Place:　Strathclyde, Scotland

☛Alexander Davidson was a Scottish Junior International goal keeper, when joining Woolwich Arsenal in June 1904. He spent one season at the club playing mainly in the South Eastern league team.Because of the brilliance and consistency of Jimmy Ashcroft, managed to play in only one league game at Blackburn Rovers 15th October 1904.

	Games	Goals
League	1	0
Friendly Matches	1	0
London League Reserves	14	0
South Eastern League	19	0
Other Youth Matches	1	0
Totals	36	0

DAVIE, George　　　　1891-1892

Birth Place:　Scotland
Date of Birth:　1865

☛George Davie was a centre forward who had been on the books of Everton and Sunderland before returning home to play for Renton. He joined Royal Arsenal in October 1891. In his period with the club he was a regular goal scorer for the senior side. He made his first class debut in an F A Cup qualifying round versus Millwall Athletic 19th November 1892. He was sacked by the club in December 1892 which resulted in a

court case, in which Davie tried to sue for wrongful dismissal and loss of earnings. The club won the case.

	Games	Goals
F A Cup	4	3
Other Senior Matches	58	39
Total	62	42

DAVIS, Frederick　　　　1893-1899

Birth Place:　Smethwick, Warwick
Date of Birth:　1871

☛Frederick Davis was a wing half who played junior football in the Birmingham area for Soho Villa and Birmingham St Georges before joining Woolwich Arsenal at the beginning of the clubs first ever season in the Football League (September 1893). He made his league debut in the second league game of the season at Notts County, Frederick missing only one league game during the rest of that season. In the following three seasons he remained a consistent member of the side playing at either right or left half. In 1897-98, after missing the first six games of the season he remained virtually ever present when helping the club to their then highest ever league position (fifth in division two). In Davis' last season at Manor Field he played in eighteen league games before leaving the club for Nottingham Forest during the summer of 1909.

	Games	Goals
League	137	8
F A Cup	13	2
Untied League	25	1
Kent League	6	0
Friendly Matches	110	5
Other Youth Matches	2	0
Total	293	16

DEVINE, Archibald　　　　1913-1914

Birth Place:　Lochgelly, Fifeshire, Scotland
Date of Birth:　1886

☛Archibald Devine began his footballing career in Junior football with his home town club Lochgelly United, he joined Hearts in 1904-05, staying with them for two seasons playing only three league games for the club before moving on to Raith Rovers for the 1907 - 08 season. Archibald was transferred to Falkirk in 1908, where he spent two successful seasons, which included in 1909-10, scoring thirteen goals in twenty five league outings from the inside left position, this form catching the eye of the Scottish selectors and he was capped versus Wales, also winning Scottish League Honours. Moved South to join Bradford City in April 1910 and in his first season at the club helped City in winning the 1911 F A Cup Final versus Newcastle. Devine signed for Woolwich Arsenal in February 1913 for £1,000 making his Arsenal league debut at

Stamford Bridge against Chelsea, 15th February 1913. In1913-14 he could not command a regular position in the side when vying with H.T.W Hardinge for the inside left slot. Not happy about this, Archibald rejoined Bradford City during the summer of 1914. Died September 1964 aged 78.

	Games	Goals
League	24	5
Friendly Matches	1	1
London League Reserves	3	0
South Eastern League	10	3
London FA Challenge Cup	3	2
Total	**41**	**11**

Honours:
(WITH FALKIRK)
1 Scottish Cap.
1 Scottish League Cap.
(WITH BRADFORD CITY)
F A Cup Winner Medal   1910-11

DEVINE, Daniel   1892-1893

Birth Place: Dumbarton, Scotland
Date of Birth: 1870

☛Daniel Devine had played junior football for Dumbarton Athletic and Renton before joining Royal Arsenal in November 1892. He is honoured as having played in Arsenal's first ever football league match versus Newcastle United 2nd September 1893, in front of a 10,000 crowd at the Manor Field. Was a reserve wing half to Fred Davis for virtually all of season 1892-93 and played in only two league games at the start of the 1893-94 season. Later joined Partick Thistle.

	Games	Goals
League	2	0
F A Cup	2	0
Other Senior Matches	35	2
Friendly Matches	10	1
Other Reserve Matches	3	2
Totals	**52**	**5**

DEVLIN, James   1897-1898

☛James Devlin was a reserve centre forward, who was languishing in Sunderland's reserve side when snapped up for £80 by Woolwich Arsenal in December 1897. He had previously played in his native Scotland with Dundee and in the Southern League with Tottenham Hotspur. His duration at the Manor Field was one of nine months this largely due to contracting pleurisy soon after joining the club. He played in just one league game (when scoring the first goal) in a 3-3 away fixture at the Athletics ground versus Blackpool on New Years Day 1898. He was transferred (in exchange for John Dick) to Airdrie in August 1898.

DICK, John   1898-1912

John Dick

Birth Place: Eaglesham, Renfrewshire
Date of Birth: 1876

☛John Dick gave Woolwich Arsenal fourteen years magnificent service in which time he captained the side in many of those seasons, also becoming one of the first players in the club's history to play in over two hundred league fixtures. John was transferred to the club, in August 1898 (in an exchange deal with John Devlin from Airdrie). In his first season at Manor Field he was a mainstay in the side when missing only four league games whilst occupying the centre half position. His Arsenal league debut being on the opening day of the season at Luton Town, 3rd September 1898. In 1899-1900, his consistency was shown again, when missing only one league game. He managed to score twice in Arsenal's record league victory (12-0 versus Loughborough Town) March 1900. In 1900-01 he again only missed one league game this being followed by John, playing in twenty eight league games in 1901-02 and twenty six in 1902-03. In the club's promotion winning season of 1903-04 he moved to the right half position (after the signing of Percy Sands) and played in all but one of the club's thirty four league fixtures. He played in Arsenal's first ever game in the first division versus Newcastle 3rd September 1904. In 1904-05 John again only missed one game.In 1905-06, Dick started the season as the club's first choice right half before

losing it to James Bigden. Although he remained at the Club for another six seasons John could never regain a regular first team place being quite content in guiding the youth players in the various reserve teams. In 1911 he became the first player in the club's history to play six hundred competitive matches for Arsenal (a record which stood for many years). When leaving, in June 1912, he moved to Czechoslovakia to coach in Prague.

	Games	Goals
League	262	12
F A Cup	22	1
Other Senior Matches	8	0
United League	19	1
Kent League	3	3
Friendly Matches	88	6
London League	17	0
London League Reserves	39	2
South Eastern League	134	17
London F A Challenge Cup	3	0
Southern Combination	15	0
Other Youth Matches	5	1
Total	**615**	**43**

Honours:
Southern Charity Cup Finalists
   Medal   1903-04
South Eastern League Championship
   Medal   1906-07
London League Reserve Championship
   Medal   1906-07

	Games	Goals
League	1	1
Untied League	1	0
Friendly Matches	1	0
Total	**3**	**1**

DRAIN, Thomas   1909-1910

Birth Place: Pollockshaws, Glasgow
Date of Birth: 1880

☛Thomas Drain was an experienced centre forward, who before joining Woolwich Arsenal in May 1909 had played for Celtic, Ayr United, Bradford City 1903-05, Leeds City 1905-07, Kilmarnock 1907, Exeter City 1908-09. Played in only two league games for the club in 1909-10 which included his debut which was a 5-1 defeat at Villa Park versus Aston Villa in the opening game of the season, 1st September

1909. His only other game was another 5-1 defeat for the club against Notts County at Meadow Lane.

	Games	Goals
League	2	0
Friendly Matches	6	1
South Eastern League	10	0
London FA Challenge Cup	1	0
Total	**19**	**1**

	Games	Goals
League	1	0
Friendly Matches	11	2
London League	5	0
London League Reserves	33	1
South Eastern League	41	2
Other Youth Matches	1	0
Total	**92**	**5**

Honours:
South Eastern League Championship
Medal   1903-04
London League Reserve Championship
Medal   1903-04

DYER, Frank   1892-93

Birth Place: Bishopbriggs, Glasgow
Date of Birth: 1870

☛ Frank Dyer was a utility player, playing at either wing half or in the full back position. He began his career playing junior football for Warwick County before joining West Bromwich Albion in 1890. He spent two successful seasons with the Baggies, helping them win the F A Cup in 1891-92. He joined Royal Arsenal in the summer of 1892, (in the clubs last pre league season). He made his first class Arsenal debut in a 0-6 defeat F A Cup tie at Newcastle Road versus Sunderland 21st January 1893. He was transferred to Ardwick (in Manchester City's first ever season in the football league) in August 1893. He spent five seasons with them before retiring in 1898.

	Games	Goals
F A Cup	5	0
Other Senior Matches	36	2
Other Reserve Matches	7	0
Total	**48**	**2**

Honours:
(WITH WEST BROMWICH)
F A Cup Winners Medal   1891-92

EDGAR, John   1901-02

Birth Place: Scotland
Date of Birth:

☛ John Edgar, an inside forward, played ten times for Woolwich Arsenal's league side in 1901-02 after joining them from junior Scottish side Parkhead FC in October 1901. He made his league debut in a 2-2 draw at Gainsborough Trinity 12th October 1901. He left the club during the close season of 1902, moving back to Scotland where he later played for Aberdeen 1904-1912 helping them to the Scottish Division one runners up position in 1910-11 season.

	Games	Goals
League	10	1
FA Cup	1	0

	Games	Goals
Other Senior Matches	2	0
Kent League	5	6
Friendly Matches	9	3
London League	4	0
London League Reserves	4	6
Total	**35**	**16**

ELLIOTT, Arthur   1892-94

Birth Place: Nottingham
Date of Birth: 1870

☛ Arthur Elliott was an inside forward who started his career with Gainsborough Trinity before joining Accrington Stanley in 1891. He was the club's leading scorer in the 1891 92 season. He joined Royal Arsenal in the summer of 1892. In his first season with the club he was a regular for the senior side (in the last pre league season). He made his league debut (scoring) playing in the club's first ever league match versus Newcastle United 2nd September 1893. During that season he played in twenty nine first team games scoring fifteen goals, which included a hat trick in an F A Cup qualifying match versus Ashford United which the club won 12-0. He wanted to return to amateur status and so he joined Tottenham Hotspur in the summer of 1894.

	Games	Goals
League	24	11
F A Cup	10	9
Other Senior Matches	52	29
Friendly Matches	20	16
Other Reserve Matches	1	1
Total	**107**	**66**

EVANS, Robert   1912-13

Birth Place: London

☛ Robert Evans was an amateur full back when joining Woolwich Arsenal in September 1912. Played in only two first class games during his period at the club, his league debut versus Newcastle at St James's Park resulted in a 1-3 defeat on the 25th January 1913. His other match being in the club's last ever FA Cup appearance at the Manor Field versus Liverpool 2nd February 1913. (1-4 defeat). He moved on to Clapton Orient in August 1913.

	Games	Goals
League	1	0
FA Cup	1	0
South Eastern League	9	0
Total	**11**	**0**

FAIRCLOUGH, William   1895-97

☛ William Fairclough was a soldier in the First Scots Guards and was allowed to join Woolwich Arsenal in December 1895. He made his league debut shortly after on the 25th January 1896, at Leicester Fosse. A goalkeeper, he played in the last 9 league games of that season. At the start of 1896-97 season he was the club's regular keeper until conceding 17 goals in only three matches, (versus Walsall 3-5, Small Heath 2-5 and, in an almost unbelievable match at Meadow Lane versus Notts County, 4-7). However, he regained his place from John Leather after a 3-6 defeat at Leicester Fosse. Was not retained and joined New Brompton (now Gillingham).

	Games	Goals
League	26	0
FA Cup	1	0
United League	9	0
Kent League	3	0
Friendly Matches	28	0
Total	**67**	**0**

FARMER, George   1896

Birth Place: Derbyshire
Date of Birth: 25th November 1874

☛ George Farmer was an outside right who had played junior football for Derby Swifts, Bedford Rangers and Belper Town before joining Woolwich Arsenal in May 1896. He made his one and only league appearance in the opening home game of the season versus Walsall 12th September 1896.

	Games	Goals
League	1	0
FA Cup	1	1
United League	1	1
Kent League	4	6
Friendly Matches	4	1
Total	**11**	**9**

FARRELL, Patrick   1897-98

Birth Place: Belfast
Date of Birth: 3rd April 1872

☛ Patrick Farrell was a half back with Celtic when joining Woolwich Arsenal in May 1897 (having helped Celtic to two league championships in 1893-94 and 1895-96). He spent only one season at Manor Field playing in nineteen league games, which included his debut in 4-1 home defeat of Grimsby (scoring), 1st September

1897. Could not settle at the club and moved into the Southern League to play for Brighton in the summer of 1898. Later played for Distillery 1900-02 where he won two Irish caps in 1900-01 versus Scotland and Wales. Returned to Brighton in 1902.

	Games	Goals
League	19	2
FA Cup	3	0
United League	9	2
Friendly Matches	9	0
Total	**40**	**4**

Honours:
2 Irish Caps.

FERGUSON, James   1906-07

Birth Place: Scotland

An outside left, James Ferguson spent just one season at Woolwich Arsenal, when joining them from the Scottish junior club side Cambuslang Hibs in June 1906. Was a regular in the reserves in 1906-07. He played in only one league game versus Liverpool at Anfield 25th February 1907.

	Games	Goals
League	1	0
Friendly Matches	9	1
London League Reserves	13	0
South Eastern League	21	5
Total	**44**	**6**

Honours:
South Eastern League Championship
 Medal   1906-07
London League Reserve Championship
 Medal   1906-07

FIDLER, Joseph   1913-14

Birth Place: Sheffield, Yorkshire
Date of Birth: 1884

Joseph Fidler was a full back playing Southern League Football for Queens Park Rangers when joining Woolwich Arsenal in February 1913. He immediately gained the first team left back position (taking over from injured J C Peart). He made his league debut in a home fixture versus Oldham Athletic and played in the Club's last thirteen league games of the season. He started the 1913-14 season as the club's regular left back, but lost the position to the newly signed England International Bob Benson. Not happy with reserve team football he joined Port Vale.

	Games	Goals
League	25	0
Other Senior Matches	1	0
Friendly Matches	2	0
London League Reserves	9	0
South Eastern League	12	0
London F A Challenge Cup	4	0
Total	**53**	**0**

FISHER, George   1909

George Fisher spent a month on trial with Woolwich Arsenal in October 1909. A goalkeeper, he played in two league games for the club (deputising for the injured Hugh McDonald). His debut being in 1-5 defeat at Notts County. He was not retained and later joined Manchester United.

	Games	Goals
League	2	0
South Eastern League	1	0
Total	**3**	**0**

FLANAGAN, John   1910-1917

Birth Place: Preston, Lancashire
Date of Birth: 1891

John (little Jack) Flanagan had played junior football for Stourbridge before joining Norwich City in 1908. John was transferred to Fulham during the summer of 1909, his eighteen month stay at Craven Cottage brought this diminutive inside forward little joy, which resulted in him being transferred to Woolwich Arsenal in December 1910, making his Arsenal league debut versus Bradford City 11th February 1911. In 1911-12, Flanagan played in every forward position when scoring seven times in thirty three games. He was in and out of the first team during the club's disastrous 1912-13 relegation campaign, "Little Jack" finishing the season as the club's joint third highest league scorer with two goals! With the club back in Division two in 1913-14 he had a more successful season when scoring twelve times in twenty four games. In his last

FITCHIE, Thomas   1901-06 & 1908-09

Birth Place: Edinburgh, Scotland
Date of Birth: 11th December 1881

Thomas Tindal Fitchie was one of the most talented inside forwards of the early part of the twentieth century. An amateur throughout his career (this due to business commitments). He was, on many occasions, on more than one club's books at a given time his club's, other than Woolwich Arsenal, included West Norwood, as a junior, Tottenham, Queens Park Rangers, two stints at Fulham, Glossop, Brighton and a spell in Scotland at Queens Park (1906-

Thomas Fitchie

08). His career with Woolwich Arsenal began in November 1901, when joining them as a nineteen year old. Thomas showed his prodigious talent when scoring twice in his Arsenal League debut versus Gainsborough Trinity 8th February 1902. In 1902-03 his outside commitments resulted in him playing in only one league game. In 1903-04 his talents were lost to the club for the whole of that promotion winning campaign. With the club back in Division one Thomas managed to find time to play in nine league games (scoring six goals) which included a hat trick at Notts County 17th December 1904. Although playing in so little first team football (the Prince of Dribblers), amazingly won the first of his four

Scottish caps versus Wales during this season. In 1905-06 he spent more time on his footballing career playing in twenty two league games, scoring nine goals as well as helping the club to their first ever F A Cup semi final. Thomas returned to the club for the 1908-09 season, when he finished as the club's leading league goal scorer with nine goals in twenty one games, this wasted footballing talent finished his career scoring thirty goals in sixty three first team games, a ratio bettered by few for the club. Died October 1947 aged 65.

	Games	Goals
League	56	27
F A Cup	7	3
Other Senior Matches	2	1
Friendly Matches	4	2
London League	2	0
Total	**71**	**33**

Honours:

Four Scottish Caps

full season at Highbury, before the outbreak of World War One, he was a regular inside right when figuring in twenty six league games, his last appearance was at his home town club Preston on 17th April 1915. (A match which Preston had to win to gain promotion to Division one). Preston won 3-0, Flanagan being dropped for the last game of the season, he spent another two seasons on the club's books during wartime before retiring through injury in 1917.

	Games	Goals
League	114	28
F A Cup	7	0
Other Senior Matches	7	5
Friendly Matches	7	4
London League Reserves	4	5
South Eastern League	16	12
London F A Challenge Cup	4	0
Other Youth Matches	1	0
Wartime	5	3
Total	165	57

FLETCHER, Alfred   1914-15

Birth Place: Ripley, Derbyshire

☛ Alf Fletcher had played three league games for Glossop as a wing half in 1913-14, before joining Arsenal in June 1914. He was a consistent member of the club's South Eastern league side of that season. He played in three of Woolwich Arsenal's last five league games of that season which included his debut at Bristol City 3rd April 1915.

	Games	Goals
League	3	0
Friendly Matches	2	0
London League Reserves	15	1
South Eastern League	32	3
London FA Challenge Cup	1	1
Total	53	5

FORD, George   1912-15

Birth Place: Woolwich, London
Date of Birth: 1891

☛ George Ford was a full back, who had played for Gravesend and Dartford, before joining Woolwich Arsenal as an amateur in September 1912 (turning professional in November 1912). During his three seasons at the club he was left back understudy to JC Peart, Bob Benson and Joe Fidler. In 1912-13 he played in only three league games (including his debut versus Liverpool 28th December 1912). He spent all of season 1913-14 playing reserve football. In January 1915 returned to league action playing in six consecutive games, before losing his place to Bob Benson.

	Games	Goals
League	9	0

FA Cup	1	0
Friendly Matches	11	0
London League Reserves	24	0
South Eastern League	91	1
London FA Challenge Cup	1	0
Other Youth Matches	1	0
Total	**138**	**1**

FOSTER, R   1889

☛ R Foster was a goalkeeper who played in two FA Cup qualifying games versus Crusaders and Swifts in 1889, four years before the club entered the football league.

	Games	Goals
FA Cup	2	0
Other Senior Matches	3	0
Other Reserve Matches	2	0
Total	7	0

FOXALL, Abraham   1901-02

Birth Place: Sheffield
Date of Birth: 1874

☛ "Abe" Foxall was a left winger who began his football league career with Sheffield youth sides before joining Gainsborough Trinity in 1897. He spent two seasons with them before signing for Liverpool in the summer of 1899. Moved into the Southern League, during the close season of 1900, with Queens Park Rangers before being transferred to Woolwich Arsenal in May 1901. In his solitary season at the club he was a consistant member of the side playing in thirty one league games of which his debut was on the opening day of the season versus Barnsley (Foxall scoring the first goal) 2nd September 1901. When leaving the club he linked up again with Gainsborough Trinity.

	Games	Goals
League	31	3
Other Senior Matches	3	1
Friendly Matches	4	0
London League	5	0
Total	43	4

FREEMAN, Bert   1905-08

Birth Place: Birmingham
Date of Birth: October 1885

☛ Bert Freeman was a footballing legend at the turn of the twentieth century. He started his career with Birmingham youth sides, Gower Old Boys and Aston Manor before joining Aston Villa in April 1904. He spent eighteen months at Villa Park without once getting a first team chance and was transferred to Woolwich Arsenal in November 1905, making his league debut

when scoring (at Nottingham Forest, 25th November 1905). In his first season at the club he showed his goal scoring prowess netting twelve times in twenty one appearances, helping the side to their first ever F A Cup Semi Final. In 1906-07 he lost his place to the newly signed Peter Kyle, Bert still managing to score eight times in twelve games. In 1907-08 the situation remained unchanged, the club deciding to allow him to leave for Everton in April 1908. This can only be described as one of the great transfer blunders of those early years, Freeman later becoming the first and still only player to be the league's leading scorer in three seasons with Everton;1908-09, thirty eight goals and with Burnley in 1911-12 thirty two goals and 1912-13 thirty one goals. With Everton 1908-1911 he scored seventy three times in eighty six league appearances as well as winning five England Caps and four Football League Caps. Transferred to Burnley in 1911, in his six seasons at Turf Moor he scored one hundred and three league goals in only one hundred and sixty three league games. (These figures would have been greater if not for the loss of four seasons at the peak of his career due to the First World War.) His finest hour was when netting the only goal of the 1914 F A Cup Final versus Liverpool. After the resumption of league football he later played for Wigan Borough and Kettering Town. In total, Bert Freeman scored the staggering total of one hundred and ninety seven league goals in only two hundred and ninety three games. His brother Walter, played for Aston Villa, Birmingham and Fulham. Died August 1955 aged 69.

	Games	Goals
League	44	21
F A Cup	5	3
Other Senior Matches	1	0
Friendly Matches	16	27
London League Reserves	24	43
South Eastern League	24	34
Total	**114**	**128**

Honours:
(WITH EVERTON)
5 England Caps.
4 Football League Caps.
(WITH BURNLEY)
F A Cup Winners Medal   1913-14
(WITH ARSENAL)
London League Reserve Championship
Medal   1906-07
South Eastern League Championship
Medal   1907-08

FYFE, JAMES — 1898

Birth Place: Scotland

☛ Born Scotland, James Fyfe was a right back who joined Woolwich Arsenal from Alloa Athletic in May 1898. He played in the first seven league games of 1898-99, his debut being versus Luton Town, 3rd September 1898, but after two heavy defeats against Manchester City and Walsall he lost his place to first John McPhee and then to John McAvoy. He left the club at the back end of 1898 when he returned to Scotland.

	Games	Goals
League	7	0
United League	5	0
Friendly Matches	3	0
Total	**15**	**0**

GARBUTT, William — 1905-08

Birth Place: Stockport, Cheshire.
Date of Birth: 9th January, 1855.

☛ William Garbutt was an outside right who joined Woolwich Arsenal from Southern League side Reading in December 1905, making his league debut within a week of joining, at Deepdale, Preston 23rd December 1905 and for the remainder of that season he was the mainstay on the club's right wing and helped the club to their first F A Cup Semi Final. In 1906-07, although he had long spells out of the side he still managed to play in twenty five league games as well as helping Arsenal to their second successive F A Cup Semi Final. However, in 1907-08 William was replaced by Jackie Mordue and subsequently spent the rest of the season in the reserve team. Garbutt was transferred to Blackburn Rovers in May 1908. In four seasons at Ewood Park he played in nearly one hundred first team games for them which included another F A Cup Semi Final in 1911, William having the unenviable record of being in three losing F A Cup Semi Final sides (in seven seasons). Whilst at Blackburn he won a football league cap versus Ireland, after retiring from the game he enjoyed a long and successful coaching career which included Genoa 1914, Rome 1927, Naples 1929 and Athletica Bilbao 1935 returning to Genoa in 1946.

	Games	Goals
League	52	8
F A Cup	13	6
Other Senior Matches	3	0
Friendlies	4	2
London League Reserves	2	1
South Eastern League	6	2
Total	**80**	**19**

Honours:
(WITH BLACKBURN)
1 Football League Cap.

GARTON, John — 1899

Birth Place: Leicestershire

☛ John Garton spent just two months with Woolwich Arsenal as an amateur (March April 1899) and incredibly played in fourteen games (have times changed?). He played in five consecutive league matches at right back (none were lost) in March 1899 including his debut versus Loughborough Town, when taking over from the injured Alex McConnell.

	Games	Goals
League	5	0
United League	2	0
Friendly Matches	7	0
Total	**14**	**0**

GAUDIE, Ralph — 1899-1901

Birth Place: Guisborough, Yorkshire
Date of Birth: 1876

☛ Ralph Gaudie was a centre forward who made his league debut for Sheffield United in their Championship winning side of 1897-98. He could not command a regular place at Bramall Lane and was transferred to Aston Villa in 1898 when he played in five league games during Villa's Championship winning side of 1898-99. He had a short spell at non league Dudley Town before joining Woolwich Arsenal in October 1899, in season 1899-1900 he was the club's league leading scorer when netting fifteen times in twenty five games. This included a hat trick in the club's record league victory, (12-0 versus Loughborough Town 12th March 1900), after making his Arsenal debut versus Gainsborough Trinity 14th October 1899. In 1900-01, although, missing twelve league games through injury he was still the leading scorer with eight goals in twenty two games. He retired from football due to ill health at the end of that season but made a return to league action in 1903 with Manchester United.

	Games	Goals
League	47	24
F A Cup	3	0
Friendly Matches	13	3
Southern Combination	10	2
Total	**73**	**29**

GEMMELL, Duncan — 1892-94

Birth Place: Glasgow
Date of Birth: 1870

☛ Duncan Gemmell was an inside forward who played Scottish junior football for Elderslee before joining Sheffield Wednesday in their pre-league days in 1890. Transferred to Royal Arsenal in June 1892. In the club's last pre-league season he was a consistent performer in the senior side. He signed full league terms in June 1893, and played in the first five games the club ever played in the league, however, was dropped and never regained his place from Gavin Crawford, after a 6-0 defeat at Newcastle United in September 1893.

	Games	Goals
League	5	0
FA Cup	3	0
Other Senior Matches	46	16
Friendly Matches	16	2
Other Reserve Matches	3	2
Total	**73**	**20**

GILMER, William — 1895-96

☛ William Gilmer, was a goalkeeper and like many other players of the time joined Woolwich Arsenal from the Royal Ordnance factory, this being in December 1895. During his four months duration at the club he played in three consecutive league games his debut being versus Loughborough Town (a 5-0 victory) 4th January 1896. However, after two heavy defeats against Liverpool and Newcastle, he lost his place to William Fairclough.

	Games	Goals
League	3	0
Kent League	9	0
Friendlies	10	0
Total	**22**	**0**

GLOAK, Davis — 1889-91

☛ Davis Gloak played for Royal Arsenal for two pre league seasons 1889-91, being a regular at centre forward or outside left in the senior side. He played in an FA Cup Match versus Derby County at the Invicta ground 17th January 1891. Left the club during the summer of 1891 when he joined Millwall.

	Games	Goals
FA Cup	1	0
Other Senior Matches	33	13
Other Reserve Matches	11	5
Total	**45**	**18**

Honours:
London Senior Cup Winners Medal 1890-91
Kent Junior Cup Winners Medal 1889-90

GOOING, William   1901-05

Birth Place: Penistone, Yorkshire
Date of Birth: 1874

William Gooing started his career in junior football with his home town club Penistone Wath before joining Sheffield Wednesday as a bustling centre forward in their pre league days of 1895. He was never given a real first team chance at Wednesday (playing only three league games in four years). He moved to Chesterfield in 1899 spending two seasons there playing in sixty three league games, scoring twenty five goals. This form caught the eye of the Arsenal management and William signed for the club in November 1901. He made his Arsenal league debut shortly after in a home fixture versus Newton Heath (now Manchester United) 16th November 1901. In his initial season at the club he scored nine goals in twenty four league outings. In 1902 -03 Gooing and John Coleman spearheaded the Arsenal attack with them scoring over half of the club's goals included in his sixteen goals was a hat trick versus Gainsborough Town. In Arsenal's 1903 - 04 promotion winning side he was again amongst the goals (with Coleman and Shanks) the three of them scoring sixty six of the clubs ninety one league goals although appearing in Arsenal's first ever First Division league match versus Newcastle he spent much of that 1904 -05 season as reserve to Charlie Satterthwaite. Subsequently he left the club in early 1905 when he joined Northampton Town.

	Games	Goals
League	94	45
F A Cup	12	3
Other Senior Matches	5	2
Friendly Matches	6	6
London League	12	3
Total	**129**	**59**

GORDON, Robert   1895-96

Birth Place: Leith, Scotland
Date of Birth: 1873

Robert began his career with Scottish Junior side Leigh Rangers in 1889, moving to Hearts in 1990. He played for Middlesbrough Ironopolis 1891-92, before rejoining Hearts for the 1892-93 season. He returned to England, when joining Aston Villa at the beginning of the 1894-95 season. His stay at Villa Park was short lived before being transferred to Leicester Fosse in October 1894, for whom he scored fifteen league goals in twenty one games during the rest of that season. Robert moved to Woolwich Arsenal during the summer of 1895. A centre forward, he scored on his Arsenal league debut versus Grimsby Town on the opening day of the 1895-96 season, 2nd September 1895. He played steadily during his only season at the club before linking up with Reading who were playing in the Southern league.

	Games	Goals
League	20	6
Kent League	4	2
Friendly Matches	20	1
Total	**44**	**9**

GRAHAM, John   1899-1900

Birth Place: Derby
Date of Birth: 12th April, 1873

John Graham began his footballing career with non league Gray Wanderers before joining Millwall Athletic in the Southern League. He signed for Woolwich Arsenal in September 1899 (as a right back cover for David McNichol) he played in only one league game for the club in a home encounter versus Gainsborough Trinity, 14th October 1899. With his first team chances limited he moved on to Fulham during the close season of 1900. He died April 1925 aged 51.

	Games	Goals
League	1	0
Kent League	11	0
Friendlies	6	0
Southern Combination	1	0
Total	**19**	**0**

GRAHAM, Thomas   1891-92

Birth Place: Balloch, Scotland
Date of Birth: 1868

Thomas Graham was an inside forward, who joined Royal Arsenal from the Scottish side Vale of Leven during the summer of 1891, having being a member of the Leven side which lost to Queens Park in the 1890 Scottish FA Cup Final. Graham was a regular at centre forward in the senior side of 1891-92 and played in the FA Cup tie versus Small Heath 16th January 1892.

	Games	Goals
FA Cup	1	0
Other Senior Matches	55	47
Other Reserve Matches	2	3
Total	**58**	**50**

GRANT, George   19010-19

Birth Place: Plumstead, London
Date of Birth: 1871

George Grant played for several Kent sides before joining Woolwich Arsenal from Dartford (as amateur) in March 1910, turning professional in 1911. His first season, 1910-11, was spent entirely playing in reserve and junior football. In 1911-12 he made his only league appearance that season (when deputising for injured Percy Sands at centre half) in a 4-1 defeat at Villa Park 9th Sept. 1911. During the 1912-13 season played in twelve of the club's last thirteen games. Unfortunately he could not help the club from suffering their only relegation in history. In 1913-14 George took part in the first ever league game played at Highbury v Leicester Fosse 6th September 1913. In those two seasons 1913-15 leading up to the outbreak of world war one, Grant was the club's regular right half playing in a further forty league games. He remained on the club's books during those war years later playing for Millwall and QPR.

	Games	Goals
League	54	4
FA Cup	3	0
Other Senior Matches	5	0
Friendly Matches	22	4
London League Reserves	5	1
South Eastern League	110	5
London FA Challenge Cup	4	0
Other Youth Matches	1	0
War Time	43	0
Total	**247**	**14**

Honours:
London FA Challenge Cup Finalist 1914-15

GRANT, John   1912

The son of James Grant who was a director of Woolwich Arsenal 1904-07 John Grant was a centre forward who joined Arsenal as an amateur from Southport Central in February 1912, when the club needed cover at centre forward for either Jackie Chalmers or Alf Common. Made his league debut v Preston at home 8th April 1912, then scored a hat trick v Blackburn at the Manor Ground 22nd April 1912.

	Games	Goals
League	4	3
South Eastern League	1	0
Total	**5**	**3**

GRAY, Archie — 1904-12

Birth Place: Govan, Glasgow, Scotland
Date of Birth: 1883

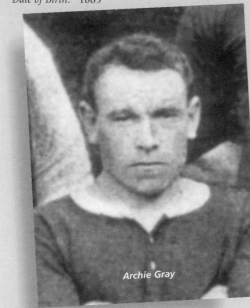

Archie Gray

☞ "Baldie" Gray was an uncompromising, no nonsense, no questions asked full back who began his football career with Scottish junior sides Govan Columbia and Glasgow Ashfield before joining Hibernian in 1899. In his five seasons at the club he enjoyed winning a Scottish league championship medal in 1902-03, a season after him winning a Scottish FA cup winners medal in 1901-02. Whilst at Hibs he won a full Scottish cap versus Ireland as well a Scottish league cap. Archie was transferred to Arsenal in 1904 (ready for the club's first ever first division league campaign) making his league debut on the opening day of the season at Newcastle. In his first five seasons at the Manor Field he was without doubt the club's first choice right back. In 1909-10, however, he lost his first team mantle to Duncan McDonald. In 1910-11 he played in twenty six league games filling in at both full back positions. In his final season at the club 1911-12 he could not reclaim his place to the up and coming J C Peart. "Baldie" playing his two hundredth (and last) first team appearance for the club at Notts County 23rd December 1911. He moved on to Fulham for £250.

	Games	Goals
League	184	0
FA Cup	16	0
Other Senior Matches	5	0
Friendly Matches	32	1
London League Reserves	1	0
South Eastern League	30	0
London FA Challenge Cup	5	0
Other Youth Matches	2	0
Total	**275**	**1**

Honours:
(WITH HIBERNIAN)
1 Scottish Cap
1 Scottish League Cap
Scottish League Championship
Medal 1902-03
Scottish FA Cup Winners
Medal 1901-02

GRICE, Neville — 1906

☞ Neville Grice was an amateur outside right who joined Woolwich Arsenal in March 1906, playing in only one game for the club, in the league, away to Middlesbrough in a 2-0 defeat 21st April 1906.

	Games	Goals
League	1	0
Total	**1**	**0**

GRIEVE, Thomas — 1900-01

☞ Thomas Grieve was an outside right who joined Woolwich Arsenal from Gravesend in May 1900. He became a consistent performer in the reserve side of that season (1900-01), and played in six league games of which his debut was against Barnsley at the Manor Ground 22nd September 1890. He later played in the southern league for Watford and Brighton.

	Games	Goals
League	6	0
Kent League	4	0
Friendly Matches	4	4
London League Reserves	13	3
Total	**27**	**7**

Honours:
Kent League Championship Medal 1900-01

HAMILTON, Thomas — 1898-1900

☞ Thomas Hamilton was a goalkeeper with Stockton when signing for Woolwich Arsenal as an amateur in April 1898, turning professional the following month. In season 1898-99 he was understudy to Roger Ord, playing in just one league game versus New Brighton 10th December 1898. In 1899-00 he played in six of the club's last eight league games taking over from the injured Ord. However, was not retained and was transferred to Gravesend during the summer of 1900.

	Games	Goals
League	7	0
United League	2	0
Kent League	37	0
Friendly Matches	30	0
Southern Combination	9	0
Total	**85**	**0**

HANKS, Ernest — 1912-13

☞ Ernest Hanks was yet another Woolwich Arsenal player who joined them from the army, this as an amateur in April 1912, turning professional in November 1912. He scored on his debut at Bradford City 26th October 1912 and played in a further three league games that season, before being transferred to Southend United in July 1913.

	Games	Goals
League	4	1
Friendly Matches	4	1
South Eastern League	22	13
Total	**30**	**15**

HANNAH, David — 1897-99

Birth Place: County Down, Ireland
Date of Birth: 28th April 1867

☞ David Hannah was an inside forward who was on the books of the Scottish side Renton, when they won the Scottish cup in 1888, before joining Sunderland in their first ever league season of 1890-91. In his four seasons at the club he enjoyed great success when helping the "Rokerites" to the league championship in 1891-92, and 1892-93 the runners up spot in 1893-94 and to an FA Cup semi final in 1891-92. David was transferred to Liverpool in 1894 where he spent three seasons during which time he helped the club gain promotion to the first division for the first time when winning the second division championship in 1895-96. He moved on to Dundee (for a short five month period) before joining Woolwich Arsenal in October 1897, making his Arsenal league debut at Walsall 6th November 1897. He finished the season playing in the club's last twenty league games finishing as joint top league goalscorer with twelve goals (which included a hat trick versus Small Heath (now Birmingham City) 5th March 1898. In the following season he reverted from inside

forward to wing half when playing in twenty six league games. David retired during the close season of 1899.

	Games	Goals
League	46	17
FA Cup	4	0
Other Senior Matches	2	0
United League	27	17
Kent League	3	1
Friendly Matches	19	6
Total	**101**	**41**

Honours:
(WITH SUNDERLAND)
Division One Championship
Medal   1891-92, 1892-93
(WITH LIVERPOOL)
Division Two Championship
Medal   1895-96

HANNIGAN, Richard   1899

☛ Richard Hannigan was an outside right who joined Woolwich Arsenal from Notts County in May 1899. He made his one and only league appearance for the club on the opening day of season 1899-1900 versus Leicester Fosse. He suffered an injury which resulted in him losing his place to Fergus Hunt and then Frank Lloyd. He was transferred to Burnley in December 1899.

	Games	Goals
League	1	0
FA Cup	1	0
Kent League	3	0
Friendly Matches	1	0
Southern Combination	1	0
Total	**7**	**0**

HARDING, Edwin   1896

☛ Edwin Harding spent two months at Woolwich Arsenal at the back end of 1896. A full back, he played in only one first team game for the club in an FA Cup Qualifying match versus Leyton 12th December 1896.

	Games	Goals
FA Cup	1	0
Kent League	3	0
Total	**4**	**0**

HARE, Charles   1895-96

Birth Place: Yardley, Birmingham
Date of Birth: June 1871

☛ Charles began his career with junior side Birmingham United before joining Aston Villa in 1891. He spent four seasons at Villa Park, without ever gaining a regular place-

although he did win a first division championship medal in 1893-94. He was transferred to Woolwich Arsenal in February 1895. He made his Arsenal league debut versus Leicester Fosse 9th March 1895. A match in which the referee was attacked and the ground at Plumstead was later closed for five weeks. In the 1895-96 season, Hare was in and out of the league side at inside right, although at the end of that term he filled in at right back for the injured Joe Powell. Moved on to Small Heath (now Birmingham City) in November 1896. Later played in the Southern league for Watford and Plymouth Argyle. Died February 1934 aged 63.

	Games	Goals
League	19	7
FA Cup	1	0
Kent League	8	6
Friendly Matches	38	12
Total	**66**	**25**

Honours:
(WITH ASTON VILLA)
Division One Championship Medal   1893-94

HARTLEY, Abraham   1899

Birth Place: Dumbarton, Scotland
Date of Birth: 8th February 1872

☛ Abraham began his footballing career with Dumbarton youth side, Artizan Thistle before joining Dumbarton in Scotland's first ever league campaign of 1890-91, being on their books when they won the first two Scottish titles of 1890-91 and 1891-92 as well as the Scottish cup final of 1891. Hartley was transferred to Everton in 1892, spending five seasons at the club in which time he helped them to the league runners up position in 1894-95 and to the 1896-97 FA Cup final versus Aston Villa. He moved on to fellow neighbours Liverpool in December 1897, having a short stay there before leaving for Southern league side Southampton in May 1898. In his one season with the Saints 1898-99, he helped them to the Southern League Championship before being transferred to Woolwich Arsenal in July 1899. In his five months at Manor Field, Hartley played in only five league games at centre forward which included his club league debut at Walsall 23rd September 1899. However, after the signing of Ralph Gaudie in October 1899 from Sheffield United his first team chances were limited, this resulting in him being transferred to Burnley in December 1899. Abe, who was one of three brothers who assisted Dumbarton in their early years. Died suddenly at Southampton Docks in October 1909 aged 37.

	Games	Goals
League	5	1
FA Cup	4	0
Kent League	2	2
Friendly Matches	1	0
Southern Combination	4	2
Total	**16**	**5**

Honours:
(WITH EVERTON)
FA Cup Finalist Medal   1896-97
(WITH SOUTHAMPTON)
Southern League Championship
Medal   1898-99

HATFIELD, Thomas   1895-96

Birth Place: London
Date of Birth: 1874

☛ Thomas Hatfield was a goalkeeper who joined Woolwich Arsenal as an amateur in January 1895, turning professional three months later. He made his league debut on the final day of the 1894-95 season versus Burton, 20th April 1895. He played in just one other league game the following season before being transferred to Tottenham during the close season of 1896, where he played 10 games. Later with Royal Engineers.

	Games	Goals
League	2	0
Kent League	11	0
Friendly Matches	16	0
Other Youth Matches	2	0
Total	**31**	**0**

HAYWOOD, Adam   1896-99

Birth Place: Nr Burton-on-Trent, Derby
Date of Birth: 23rd March 1875

☛ Adam was a diminutive inside forward, who had played for many junior clubs in the Derbyshire leagues, before joining Woolwich Arsenal in January 1896, making his league debut versus Leicester Fosse, 25th January 1896. He was ever present in the side for the rest of that campaign. In 1896-87, Adam was a mainstay for the club playing in twenty six league games scoring eleven goals. The goals dried up for him in the following term when scoring only four times in twenty six games, although in 1898-99 his goalscoring ability returned when finding the net on twelve occasions in twenty three games, which included a hat trick in a home game versus Luton Town. The club needing a financial injection, accepted a £50 transfer bid for Haywood from Glossop during the summer of 1899. He later played in the Southern league for QPR and New Brompton (now Gillingham) before enjoying a four year stint with Wolverhampton Wanderers. He was transferred to West Bromwich in 1905 being the clubs leading scorer in 1905-06 and helping them to the FA Cup semi final of 1906-07. Moved on again to Blackpool before finishing his career with Crystal Palace. Died May 1932 aged 57.

	Games	Goals
League	84	31
FA Cup	7	5
United League	41	16
Kent League	3	0
Friendly Matches	48	33
Other Youth Matches	2	0
Total	**185**	**85**

HEATH, Joseph   1893-95 & 1896-99

Birth Place: Bristol
Date of Birth: 1869

Joseph Heath's career saw him play in many positions which included right and left half as well as all forward births. This after starting out in life in junior football in pre league days with Walsall Town Swifts and Wednesbury Old Athletic before joining Wolverhampton Wanderers (in their pre league days). Joseph could never command a regular place at Molineux and was transferred to Woolwich Arsenal in June 1893, making his Arsenal league debut in the second game of Arsenal's first ever season in the football league at Notts County 9th September 1893. He created history by becoming the first ever Arsenal player to score a league hat trick, versus Walsall Town Swifts 11th September 1893. In that first season in the league, although scoring four times in eight games he remained a reserve to Walter Shaw. In 1894-95 although being a consistent member of the reserve side he could not oust Robert Buchanan from the centre forward position. This resulted in Joseph being transferred to Southern League side Gravesend United in September 1895. Rejoined the club during the summer of 1896 when he spent three seasons assisting the reserve and junior sides at which time he was the club's reserve team coach.

	Games	Goals
League	10	5
FA Cup	2	2
Kent League	22	13
Friendly Matches	89	47
Other Reserve Matches	2	0
Other Youth Matches	5	2
Total	**130**	**69**

Honours:
Kent League Championship
  Medal   1896-87

HENDERSON, James   1892-95

Birth Place: Dumfries, Scotland
Date of Birth: 1867

An inside forward who joined Woolwich Arsenal from Glasgow Rangers during the summer of 1892 (being on their books when they won their first league championship in 1890-91). In his first season at the Invicta Ground (Arsenal's last pre league season) he was a consistent goalscoring member of the senior side. He made his league debut in the club's first ever league game versus Newcastle, 2nd September 1893. In that first season he finished as the club's leading goalscorer in major competitions (with eighteen in only twenty seven games) which included hat tricks versus Crewe in the league and Ashford United in the FA Cup. In 1894-95 ,James could not find the form of the previous season, his fifteen league appearances being inter spread over three periods - this resulting in the club releasing him during the summer of 1895 when he returned to Scotland.

	Games	Goals
League	38	18
FA Cup	9	12
Other Senior Matches	49	30
Friendly Matches	38	25
Other Reserve Matches	2	0
Other Youth Matches	1	1
Total	**137**	**86**

HEPPINSTALL, Frank   1909-11

Birth Place: South Hiendley, Yorks
Date of Birth: **1885**

Frank Heppinstall was an outside left who played junior football for Denaby United, league football for Barnsley and Southern League football for Swindon, before joining Woolwich Arsenal in May 1909. He made his league debut in a 1-5 defeat at Villa Park at the opening game of season 1909-10, 1st September 1909. He appeared in the first three games of that season before losing his place to David Neave, regained it in February 1910 and played in the last thirteen league games of that season. He played in the opening four league games of the 1910-11 season but lost out again to David Neave, and later to "Tiny" Winship and Charlie Lewis. He left the club at the end of that season and later played for Hamilton.

	Games	Goals
League	23	0
Friendly Matches	10	1
South Eastern League	30	4
London FA Challenge Cup	1	1
Other Youth Matches	1	0
Total	**65**	**6**

HOARE, Gordon   1907-09 & 1910-12

Birth Place: Blackheath, Kent
Date of Birth: 18th April 1884

Was a utility forward who throughout his thirteen year career remained as an amateur. Gordon began it in junior football with West Norwood, Woolwich Polytechnic and Bromley before joining Woolwich Arsenal in May 1907, making his league debut in the last game of the 1907-08 season versus Sheffield Wednesday, 20th April 1908. In 1908-09 he performed well in the limited amount of matches he played (scoring five times in eleven games). However, with a lack of first team opportunities he was transferred to Glossop in December 1909. He was limited to occasional appearances for them before rejoining Woolwich a year later in December 1910. On his return he played in fourteen league games and scored six goals in 1910-11. At the start of the 1911-12 season he had to be content to be understudy forward to Randall and Chalmers. Not satisfied with this position he rejoined Glossop. In February 1912 and whilst on their books he won a gold medal in the 1912 olympic games (scoring twice in England's 4-2 victory over Denmark). He later played for Queens Park Rangers and Fulham. Died October 1973 aged 89.

	Games	Goals
League	30	12
FA Cup	4	1
Other Senior Matches	1	0
Friendly Matches	5	2
London League Reserves	3	1
South Eastern League	16	7
London FA Challenge Cup	1	1
Total	**60**	**24**

Honours:
England Amateur International 1912
Olympic Games Football Gold Medal 1912.

HORSINGTON, Richard   1889-90

Richard Horsington was an outside right who joined Royal Arsenal from Swindon Town in 1889. He was a regular for the club in senior football at the back end of season 1888-89 and in season 1889-90. He played in two first class games for the club of which his senior debut was versus Lyndhurst in an FA Cup Qualifying game, 5th October 1889.

	Games	Goals
FA Cup	2	1
Other Senior Matches	31	9
Other Youth Matches	2	0
Total	**35**	**10**

Honours:
London Senior Cup Finalist Medal   1889-90

28

HOWAT, David — 1889-1896

Birth Place: Preston, Lancashire
Date of Birth: 1st October 1870

☛David Howat joined his home town club Preston North End in 1887, spending two seasons at Deepdale as a reserve half back. Transferred to Royal Arsenal as an amateur in the early part of 1889. Turning professional soon after. In his first five seasons (pre league days) he was a consistent member of the club's senior side. He became one of the few players to make the breakthrough from the pre league days in to league football. David made his league debut in the clubs first ever game in the football league versus Newcastle United, 2nd September 1893. During that initial season, Howat missed only one league game whilst making the left half position his own. In 1895-96 with Gavin Crawford moving from the right wing position to right half and Fred Davis switching from right half to left half his opportunities were now limited. (Playing in only one league game that season), he later played for Third Lanark. After becoming the first Arsenal player to play in three hundred games for the club.

	Games	Goals
League	56	2
FA Cup	16	1
Other Senior Matches	143	10
Kent League	17	0
Friendly Matches	71	4
Other Reserve Matches	8	3
Total	**311**	**20**

Honours:
London Senior Cup Winners Medal 1890-91
London Senior Cup Finalist Medal 1889-90
London Charity Cup Winners Medal 1889-90
Kent Senior Cup Winners Medal 1889-90

HUNT, Fergus — 1897-1900 & 1902-03

Date of Birth: 1876

☛A prolific goal scorer of his time, Fergus Hunt began his footballing career in junior football with Mexborough before joining Middlesborough Ironopolis, in their pre league days. He was transferred to Darwen in 1895 and was that club's leading scorer in both 1895-96 and 1896-97. Fergus joined Woolwich Arsenal in May 1897, making his Arsenal league debut on the opening day of the season versus Grimsby Town, 1st September 1897. He finished his first season at the club as the first team's leading marksman with fifteen goals in twenty four games (which included a hat trick in a 9-0 victory versus St Albans in an FA Cup tie). In 1898-99 he again was the leading scorer with fifteen goals in thirty one games, scoring another hat trick versus Luton Town on New Years Eve, 1898. However, in 1899-1900 he had to be content in sharing his first team position after the signing of Frank Lloyd. Not happy with this he moved on to West Ham United in the summer of 1900. He spent two seasons playing Southern League football for them before rejoining Woolwich Arsenal in October 1902. In his second spell at the club, which spanned less than eight months, he played in only three league games. Hunt moved on to Fulham in the Southern League, 1903-05 before returning to league action, and finishing his career with Burton Albion 1905-06.

	Games	Goals
League	72	30
FA Cup	9	5
Other Senior Matches	1	0
United League	28	12
Kent League	13	8
Friendly Matches	29	10
London League Reserves	10	3
Southern Combination	7	1
Other Youth Matches	6	2
Total	**175**	**71**

Honours:
Kent League Championship Medal 1902-03

HUNTER, John "Sailor" — 1904-05

Birth Place: Johnstone, Renfrewshire, Scotland
Date of Birth: 6th April 1878

☛John Hunter began his career with Scottish Junior side Westmarch (Paisley) before joining Abercorn in 1897. An inside forward, his next move was to Liverpool in 1899, and he spent three seasons at Anfield without ever gaining a regular first team place. Transferred to Heart of Midlothian in May 1902 for £300, plus a player exchange. During his two seasons with Hearts he helped the club to the Scottish F A Cup Final of 1903 which they lost to Rangers 2-0 (after two drawn games). He moved on to Woolwich Arsenal in May 1904. In his only season at the Manor ground 1904 - 05 he was a regular in the league side when playing in twenty two league matches which included his Arsenal league debut in the club's first ever first division fixture at Newcastle United, 3rd September 1904. In the summer of 1905 he decided to try his luck in the Southern League with Portsmouth, spending two seasons with Pompey before returning to Scotland with Dundee. In 1907, "Sailor" enjoyed three seasons at Dens Park helping the club to a Scottish F A Cup Final victory versus Clyde in 1910 also winning his solitary Scottish Cap versus Wales during the 1908-09 season. He finished his playing career with Clyde in 1910-11 before embarking on one of the longest managerial careers in the history of British football. He became, at the age of thirty two, manager of Motherwell in May 1911, a position he held for thirty five years until May 1946. During that period he managed the club to a Scottish League Championship in 1931-2, to three losing Scottish Cup finals in 1931, 1933 and 1939, also guiding the club in four promotion seasons from Division two to Division one, 1927, 1930, 1933 and 1935. He was later secretary of the club 1946-1959 finally retiring after forty eight years with them, when in his eighty first year. Died Jan. 1966 aged 87.

	Games	Goals
League	22	4
Other Senior Matches	1	0
Friendly Matches	7	7
Total	**30**	**11**

Honours:
With Dundee, One Scottish Cap. Scottish
  F A Cup Winners Medal 1909-10
With Hearts, Scottish F A Cup
  Finalists Medal 1902-03

HYNDS, Thomas — 1906-07

Birth Place: Hurlford, Scotland
Date of Birth: 1880

☛Thomas Hynds was a young centre half on the books of Glasgow Celtic when joining Manchester City in September 1901. He served City for five seasons, in which time he played in over one hundred and seventy first team games, helping them win the Second Division championship in 1902-03 and the F A Cup in 1903-04. In the 1905-06 season he was regarded as the best centre half the club ever had, this being shown in the fact that his weekly wage of six pounds and ten shillings was more than the club was paying the legendary Billy Meredith. However, his career turned sour when he was one of seventeen City players found guilty in a sensational illegal payments scandal, which saw Hynds banned for four months and fined £75. In context this is the equivalent of a player today on £5,000 per week being fined £60,000, he was transferred to Woolwich Arsenal (whilst still under suspension in December 1906) spending just five months at the club taking over the centre half position, from Percy Sands in thirteen of the club's last eighteen league encounters. His Arsenal league debut being at Hillsborough versus Sheffield Wednesday on New Years Day 1907, and he helped the club in reaching the F A Cup Semi-Final of that season also versus Sheffield Wednesday. He later played for Leeds City whom he joined in May 1907 finishing his career with Hearts 1908-10.

Later coached in British Columbia and Italy.

	Games	Goals
League	13	0
F A Cup	4	1
Total	**17**	**1**

Honours:
(With Manchester City)
F A Cup Winners Medal   1903-04
Second Division Championship
     Medal   1902-03

JACKSON, James   1899-1905

Birth Place: Cambuslang, Scotland
Date of Birth: 15th September 1875

☞ James Jackson's family emigrated to Australia in 1877 where the young James began his footballing career with Rosebud. He returned to Scotland in 1893 linking up with Newton Thistle's youth side. In 1894 he was transferred to Glasgow Rangers and was on their books when they won the Scottish F A Cup in 1897 versus Dunbarton. Jackson was transferred to Newcastle United in August 1897 and during his two seasons at the club he helped United to promotion to division one in 1897-98. Woolwich Arsenal was his next port of call when joining them in May 1899. For six seasons James was not only a mainstay for the club playing either full back or wing half he also Captained the side on many occasions. He made his Arsenal league debut versus Leicester Fosse on the 2nd September 1899 and went on to play in twenty eight league games that season which included the club's highest ever league victory, 12-0 versus Loughborough, 12th March. In 1900-01 he missed only two league games when again showing his consistency at left back. The same applied in 1901-02 when he missed just one game. However, in 1902-03 (at the begining of the season) he lost his place to Archie Cross although he still managed to play in twenty eight league games. In Woolwich Arsenal's promotion winning side 1903-04, he was virtually ever present when captaining the club, to division one for the first time. In his last season at Manor Field, 1904-05, an offer from Southern League side Leyton, during the summer of 1905, to become their new player manager, at the age of twenty nine, was too great a challenge for Jackson to resist. But his stay at Leyton was short lived and later he went on to play for West Ham 1905, Glasgow Rangers, 1906, before retiring to become a blacksmith. He came out of retirement to play for Morton 1911. His two sons Archie (Tranmere) and the Reverend James Jackson (Liverpool) also played league football, whilst his nephew was the legendary Australian test cricketer Archie Jackson.

	Games	Goals
League	183	0
F A Cup	21	1
Other Senior Matches	4	0
Friendly Matches	32	0
London League	16	0
Southern Combination	12	0
Total	**268**	**1**

Honours:
Southern Professional Charity Cup
     Finalists   1903-04
For picture of James Jackson see page 52.

JACQUES, G H   1894

☞ G H Jacques was an outside left who spent two months with Woolwich Arsenal at the end of the club's first ever season in the football league, joining them from Rushden in March 1894. He played in just two league games which included his debut, when he scored twice versus Northwich Victoria at the Manor Field 23rd March 1894.

	Games	Goals
League	2	2
Friendly Matches	3	1
Total	**5**	**3**

JEFFREY, William   1892-1894

Birth Place: Dalderby, Lincolnshire
Date of Birth: 1868

☞ William Jeffrey was unusual in the sense that whilst playing for Royal Arsenal he played for the club in both full back positions and as a goalkeeper. William began his career playing junior football for West Manchester before playing for three teams who had yet to join the football league, Lincoln City, Grimsby Town and Gainsborough Trinity. He played one season in the league with Burnley in 1891-92 before joining Royal Arsenal at the back end of that season. He played regularly for the senior side in the club's last pre league season of 1892-93. In 1893-94 he made his Arsenal league debut (at left back) in the club's opening league encounter in the football league versus Newcastle United, 2nd September 1893. When the club's first choice goalkeeper, Charles Williams was injured for two periods during that season, William deputised in nine league games between the sticks. Transferred to Southampton St Mary's where he played in their first season in the newly formed Southern league.

	Games	Goals
League	22	0
F A Cup	9	0
Other Senior Matches	61	2
Friendly Matches	24	1
Other Reserve Matches	2	0
Total	**118**	**3**

JENKYNS, Caesar   1895-96

Birth Place: Builth Wells, Wales
Date of Birth: 24th August 1866

☞ Caesar Jenkyn's name will remain in the Arsenal record books for all time, this is because in the 1895-96 season he became the club's first ever current International, winning a cap for Wales versus Scotland (he in total won eight caps over a six year period). Jenkyns began his career playing for several Birmingham Youth sides before joining Small Heath (now Birmingham City) in their pre league days of 1888. Caesar spent seven seasons at Small Heath helping them to the Second Division title in 1892-93. Was transferred to Woolwich Arsenal in April 1895, when he was immediately made Captain for his one and only season at the club. Caesar scored six times (from the centre half position) in twenty seven league games. However, Arsenal could not hold on to their prized asset and he was lured away by Newton Heath (now Manchester United) in May 1896. He spent two seasons with them in which time he helped the club to promotion to division one in 1897-98. He finished his career back in the Midlands with Walsall, died July 1941 aged 74.

	Games	Goals
League	27	6
Kent League	1	0
Friendly Matches	27	3
Total	**55**	**9**

Honours:
(WITH ARSENAL AND BIRMINGHAM)
8 Welsh Caps
(WITH BIRMINGHAM)
Division Two Championship Medal   1892-93

JOBEY, George   1913-14

Birth Place: Tyneside
Date of Birth: 1886

☞ George Jobey was playing junior football for Morpeth Harriers when joining Newcastle United in May 1906. He spent seven seasons with the Geordies playing in fifty three league games and helping the club to the football League Championship in 1908-09 and to the 1911 F A Cup Final versus Bradford City. George was transferred to the newly named Arsenal in May 1913. Jobey holds two Arsenal records neither of which can ever be taken, firstly he was the first player ever to score a goal at Highbury, against Leicester Fosse and secondly he was the first player to be carried off at Highbury. Apparently George was transferred to nearby lodgings on a cart borrowed from a local milkman! In his one season at the club he played in twenty eight league games scoring three goals when mainly playing at right or centre half. Transferred to Bradford in June 1914. He later played for Hamilton Academicals and Leicester City before becoming player manager of Northampton Town, 1920-22, this being the beginning of his thirty year managerial career. He managed Wolves 1922-25, guiding them to the Third Division North Championship in 1923-24. George then managed Derby County for sixteen years, 1925-41 leading the club to two First Division Championship runners up positions in 1929-30 and 1935-36 and to promotion to Division One in his first season 1925-26. In 1941, an F A League joint commission investigated all of Derby County's transfer dealings between 1925 and 1938. The question being asked was how was a small town club like Derby County attracting the likes of Hughie Gallagher etc,etc, Derby were found to have paid out illegal bonuses and inducements. Jobey was suspended from all football but the ban was lifted in 1945. He managed Mansfield Town 1952-53. Died May 1962 aged 76.

	Games	Goals
League	28	3
Other Senior Matches	1	0
London F A Challenge Cup	3	1
War Time	6	0
Total	**38**	**4**

Honours:
(WITH NEWCASTLE)

Football League Championship	1908-09
F A Cup Finalists Medal	1910-11

JULIAN, John   1889-92

Birth Place: Boston, Lincolnshire
Date of Birth: 10th July, 1867

John Julian was a wing half who was a regular for three seasons in the club's pre league days. He joined Royal Arsenal from Boston Town during the summer of 1889. He captained the club on many occasions which included four FA Cup ties of which his senior debut was versus Lyndhurst, 5th October 1889. He later played in the Southern League for Luton Town 1892-94, Tottenham Hotspur 1894-1896 and Dartford. He died March 1957 aged 89.

	Games	Goals
FA Cup	4	0
Other Senior Matches	71	3
Other Reserve Matches	31	15
Total	**106**	**18**

Honours:

London Charity Cup Winners Medal	1889-90
London Senior Cup Winners Medal	1890-91
London Senior Cup Finalist Medal	1889-90
Kent Senior Cup Winners Medal	1889-90

KANE, Edward   1896-97

Edward Kane spent just one season with Woolwich Arsenal as a reserve centre half. He signed for the club from the army in October 1896. He played in just one league game versus Darwen 19th April 1897.

	Games	Goals
League	1	0
Total	**1**	**0**

KEMP, Frederick   1905-06

Birth Place: Tottenham, London
Date of Birth: 1887

Frederick Kemp was playing junior football for Barking when joining Woolwich Arsenal, in August 1905, An outside left, he spent just one season at the Manor Field when he was a regular member of the club's South Eastern league side. His first team chances were limited due to the consistency of Bobby Templeton and David Neave. He played in only two league games of which his debut was at St Andrews versus Birmingham City, 28th October 1905. He was transferred to West Ham United in the summer of 1906 spending a season playing for them in the Southern League.

	Games	Goals
League	2	0
Friendly Matches	6	3
London League Reserves	10	6
South Eastern League	20	5
Total	**38**	**14**

Honours:

South Eastern League Championship Medal	1905-06

KING, Edward   1912-14

Birth Place: Blyth, Northumberland
Date of Birth: 1890

Edward King joined Woolwich Arsenal from Leyton FC in August 1912. In the 1912-13 season, he took over the right half position from Matthew Thomson, making his League debut versus West Bromwich, at the Hawthorns on the 9th November 1912. He eventually played in eleven league games that season (of which the team did not win on any occasion and were later relegated) in 1913-14 his appearances were restricted due to the presence of Grant, Jobey and Thomson. He was transferred to Clapton Orient in June 1914.

	Games	Goals
League	11	0
FA Cup	2	0
Other Senior Matches	1	0

Friendlies	1	0
London League Reserves	9	0
South Eastern League	40	2
London FA Challenge Cup	1	0
Other Youth Matches	1	0
Total	**66**	**2**

KINGTON, Edward   1895-1898

Edward Kington joined Woolwich Arsenal from junior club Charlton United as an amateur in 1895, turning professional in September 1896. A left half who served the club well for three seasons during which time he played in only one senior game versus Leyton in the FA Cup 12th December 1896.

	Games	Goals
FA Cup	1	0
United League	1	0
Kent League	28	2
Friendly Matches	30	1
Other Youth Matches	1	0
Total	**61**	**3**

Honour:

Kent League Championship Medal	1896-97

KIRK, Frank   1892-94

Frank Kirk was an outside left who joined Woolwich Arsenal from local league football in 1892. In his two seasons with the club he played in the majority of games for the reserve side, appearing in just one league game on New Years Day 1894 versus Liverpool.

	Games	Goals
League	1	0
Other Senior Matches	6	0
Friendly Matches	9	2
Other Reserve Matches	21	7
Total	**37**	**9**

KYLE, Peter   1906-08

Birth Place: Rutherglen, Glasgow
Date of Birth: September 1880

A Centre forward who had played junior football for Larkhill and Royal Albert before joining Partick Thistle in 1888. Peter was transferred to Liverpool during the summer of 1899, in his season at the club he was centre forward understudy to Charles Satterthwaite. (A player with whom he would link up again at Woolwich Arsenal). Not happy with reserve team football he left for Leicester Fosse for the 1900-01 season. He then went on a five season period in the Southern League playing for West Ham United, 1901 -02, Kettering Town, 1902-05 and Tottenham Hotspur 1905-06 whom he joined from Woolwich Arsenal in April 1906. He made his Arsenal league debut on the opening day of the season (scoring twice) in a 4-1 victory at Manchester City, 1st September 1906. In that season he played in twenty nine league games scoring thirteen goals as well as helping the club to the FA Cup Semi-Final versus Sheffield Wednesday. In 1907-08 he was joint top league goal scorer with Coleman and Lewis when scoring eight times in twenty three games.Kyle was transferred to Aston Villa in March 1908. He spent less than one year at Villa Park. Peter moved to Sheffield United 1908 -09 before returning to the southern league to play for Watford. Died 1961 aged 81.

	Games	Goals
League	52	21
FA Cup	8	2
Other Senior Matches	2	0
Friendly Matches	10	2
South Eastern League	1	0
Total	73	25

LAIDLAW, James   1901

Birth Place: Scotland
Date of Birth: 1877

James Laidlaw was an inside forward with Burnley when in August 1900, Newcastle United approached Laidlaw who was on a loan period with Leith. The signing of James caused a massive controversy at the time with Burnley claiming that Laidlaw was still on their books. This resulted in Newcastle being fined and censored by the football league. He spent only one season on Tyneside before joining Woolwich Arsenal in August 1901. His stay at the club was of under three months in which time he played in only three league games which included his debut (when scoring) ironically versus Burnley at the Manor Field 21st September 1901. He returned to Scotland in November 1901.

	Games	Goals
League	3	2
London League	2	0
London League Reserves	2	1
Total	7	3

LAWRENCE, Everard   1902-03

Date of Birth: 1880

Everard was an outside left who had previously played for Kettering and Northampton Town before joining Woolwich Arsenal (with John Coleman) in May 1902. During season 1902-03 he shared the left wing spot with William Linward, playing in twenty league games which included his debut on the opening day of the season at Preston, 6th September 1902. He lost his place to Linward and was subsequently transferred to Fulham during the summer of 1903, stayed one season before joining Glossop in 1904.

	Games	Goals
League	20	3
FA Cup	3	0
Kent League	6	4
Friendly Matches	4	4
London League	6	0
London League Reserves	1	0
Total	40	11

Honour:
Kent League Championship Medal   1902-03

LAWRENCE, Walter   1909-10

Walter Lawrence joined Woolwich Arsenal from Crystal Palace as an amateur in May 1909, turning professional the same month. An inside forward, he was a regular member of the league side during his only season at the club, playing in twenty five league games scoring five goals (which made him, with Greenaway and Buckenham joint top scorer that season). His debut was made in a 0 - 0 home, draw versus Sheffield United on the 4th September 1909. Transferred back to Crystal Palace in the summer of 1910 and later played for Merthyr.

	Games	Goals
League	25	5
FA Cup	1	0
Other Senior Matches	1	0
Friendly Matches	4	3
South Eastern League	2	0
Total	33	8

LEATHER, John   1896-98

Date of Birth: 1875

Joined Woolwich Arsenal in August 1896 from Macclesfield. John Leather was a goalkeeper who in 1896-97 played in eight league games which included his debut at the Manor Field versus Notts County 26th September 1896. He vied for the regular goalkeeping position which was held by

William Fairclough with Arthur Talbot. He enjoyed a four game run in the side in January 1897. But his joy was short lived as two of the games he played in resulted in heavy defeats 3-6 at Leicester Fosse and 1-4 at Darwen. He spent all of season 1897-98 as permanent understudy to the club's new keeper Roger Ord. Was transferred to Queens Park Rangers in the summer of 1898.

	Games	Goals
League	8	0
FA Cup	2	0
United League	4	0
Kent League	8	0
Friendly Matches	44	0
Other Youth Matches	2	0
Total	68	0

Honours:
Kent League Championship Medal   1896-97

LEE, Harold   1905-09

Birth Place: Erith, Kent
Date of Birth: 1886

Harold Lee was a utility forward who had played junior football for Erith, Gray Wanderers and Sittingbourne before joining Woolwich Arsenal in September 1905. In his first two seasons at the club he was a permanent fixture in the southern league side. He had to wait over two years before making his league debut in a home match versus Bristol City 7th September 1907. During that season, 1907-08, he mainly played on the right wing after the departure of William Garbutt in December 1907, Harold playing in eighteen league games scoring five times. In 1908-09 he played all along the front line when scoring eight goals in seventeen league games (of which five were scored in the last four games of the season). At the beginning of the 1909-10 season he made a further six league appearances, until he was transferred to Bury in October 1909. Lee spent three seasons at Gigg Lane 1909-1912. He fininshed his career with Dartford.

	Games	Goals
League	41	15
Other Senior Matches	1	0
Friendly Matches	18	12
London League Reserves	34	16
South Eastern League	78	55
London FA Challenge Cup	2	0
Total	174	98

Honours:
Three South Eastern League Championship
  Medals   1905-06, 1906-07, 1907-08
London League Reserve Championship
  Medal   1906-07

LIEVESLEY, Joe — 1913-15

Birth Place: Staveley, Derbyshire
Date of Birth: 1883

☛ Joe Lievesley had a long and successful career with Sheffield United, being their regular custodian keeper for eight seasons and playing in over three hundred first team games, as well as winning a football league cap in 1910. However, in 1912-13 (whilst playing in a united side which contained future Arsenal players Benson and Hardinge) he lost his place to J T Mitchell. This, subsequently resulted in Joe joining Arsenal in June 1913. He made his Arsenal league debut in the first ever game at Highbury versus Leicester Fosse 6th September 1913. During that 1913-14 season he kept twelve clean sheets whilst conceding only thirty six goals in thirty five league games. His consistency being shown in the fact that eleven of these goals were conceded in just two games. In 1914-15 he became only the fourth goalkeeper in the club's history (after Ord, McDonald and Ashcroft) to remain everpresent in a season whilst conceding only forty one goals in thirty eight games. He retired at the outset of World War one. Died October 1941, aged 58.

	Games	Goals
League	73	0
FA Cup	2	0
Other Senior Matches	4	0
Friendly Matches	2	0
South Eastern League	3	0
London FA Challenge Cup	6	0
Total	**90**	**0**

Honours:
(WITH SHEFFIELD UNITED)
1 Football League Cap.
(WITH ARSENAL)
London FA Challenge Cup Finalist
Medal   1914-15

LINWARD, William — 1902-05

Birth Place: Hull, Yorkshire
Date of Birth: 1877

☛ William Linward had been on the books of Grimsby Town and Doncaster Rovers before moving south to play for southern league side West Ham United. Spending one season there, as an everpresent, before being transferred to Woolwich Arsenal in December 1902. Within a week of joining the club he had made his league debut in a 5-1 home victory versus Burnley 27th December 1902. For the remainder of that 1902-03 season he established himself as the club's first choice on the left wing. In 1903-04 he kept his position (in the best Arsenal side up to this point in time) William playing in twenty seven league games in the club's promotion season. However, with Arsenal in the first division for the first time in

their history, Linward found it difficult to adjust to the higher grade and was replaced by the newly signed, Scottish international, Bobby Templeton. He later played for Norwich City 1905-06, Kilmarnock 1906-07, finishing his career with Maidstone 1907-08.

	Games	Goals
League	47	10
FA Cup	3	0
Friendly Matches	12	8
London League	9	2
London League Reserves	15	1
South Eastern League	18	3
Other Youth Matches	1	0
Total	**105**	**24**

Honours:
Kent Charity Cup Winners Medal   1904-05

LLOYD, Frank — 1899-1900

Date of Birth: 1881

☛ Frank Lloyd was an outside right who joined Woolwich Arsenal from Wednesbury in May 1899. Lloyd took over the right wing spot from Fergus Hunt and made his league debut at New Brighton 2nd December 1899. He retained his place for virtually the rest of the season and finished on a bright note when scoring twice in the club's last game at home to Barnsley. Was transferred to Aston Villa during the summer of 1900 and spent his first season at Villa Park as right wing understudy to the legendary Charlie Athersmith. Transferred to Dundee 1902.

	Games	Goals
League	18	3
FA Cup	1	0
Kent League	5	2
Friendly Matches	8	1
Southern Combination	8	4
Total	**40**	**10**

LOGAN, Harry — 19010-11

Birth Place: Glasgow
Date of Birth: 1888

☛ Harry Logan was a reserve forward at Sunderland when signing for Woolwich Arsenal in July 1910, in his one and only season at the club Logan played in eleven league games at either inside right or inside left. However, he did not prove to be a lucky mascot, the club only winning one of the eleven games in which he played. His debut being at Bury 3rd September 1910.

	Games	Goals
League	11	0
Other Senior Matches	1	0
Friendly Matches	1	0
South Eastern League	10	4
London FA Challenge Cup	1	0
Total	**24**	**4**

LOGAN, Peter — 1899-1900 & 1901

Birth Place: Glasgow, Scotland

☛ "Paddy" Logan began his career with Motherwell before coming to England to try his luck with Notts County in 1898-99, spending only one season at the Trent Bridge ground before being transferred to Woolwich Arsenal in May 1899. In his first spell at the club, 1899-1900, he was a consistent member of the side at inside right when playing in twenty six league games. His Arsenal league debut was on the opening day of the season versus Leicester Fosse (He being one of nine Arsenal players making their league debuts). In the summer of 1900 he left to play Southern league football for Reading. Re-joining the club a year later. Paddy's second spell (which lasted less than six months), 1901-02, he began as regular centre forward playing in five of the first eight league games before losing his place to the newly signed William Gooing. He moved on to Brentford in November 1901.

	Games	Goals
League	28	7
FA Cup	1	0
Kent League	6	5
Friendly Matches	6	4
Southern Combination	12	5
Total	**53**	**21**

LOW, Archibald — 1906-1908

Birth Place: Scotland

☛ Archibald Low was a left half playing in Scottish junior football with Ashfield of Glasgow when joining Woolwich Arsenal in June 1906. In his two seasons at the club he served the south eastern league side well, his first team duties being restricted because of the consistency of Roddie McEachrane. In 1906-07 he played in only three league games (all of which were lost), his debut being a home fixture versus Sunderland, 1st December 1906. In 1907-08 his whole season was restricted to reserve team action, and when in September 1908 the position had not altered, he returned to Scotland to play for Partick Thistle.

	Games	Goals
League	3	0
Other Senior Matches	1	0
Friendly Matches	21	0
London League Reserves	30	1

	Games	Goals
South Eastern League	53	2
Total	**108**	**3**

Honours:
Two South Eastern League Championship
Medals 1906-07,1907-08
London League Reserve Championship
Medal 1906-07

LOW, Thomas 1900-01

Birth Place: Cambuslang, Lanarkshire
Date of Birth: 3rd October 1874

☛Thomas "Boy" Low (boy being his nickname because of his slight stature) began his career with Parkhead F C. Before joining Glasgow Rangers (whilst on trial with Blackburn Rovers) in November 1896. He had a meteoric rise to fame in that 1896-97 season, winning a Scottish Cap versus Northern Ireland and a Scottish FA Cup Winners Medal. He spent three seasons with Rangers before joining Dundee in July 1899. Tranferred to Woolwich Arsenal in May 1900. In his one and only season at the Manor Field he was the club's regular outside right, playing in twenty four league games. His Arsenal league debut was on the opening day of the season in a home fixture versus Gainsborough Trinity 1st September 1900. Thomas returned to Scotland during the summer of 1901 when he linked up with Abercorn and later played for Renton where he won a Scottish FA Cup Finalists Medal, 1904-05.

	Games	Goals
League	24	1
FA Cup	2	1
Kent League	1	0
Friendly Matches	7	2
London League Reserves	5	1
Total	**39**	**5**

Honours:
(WITH RANGERS)
1 Scottish Cap
1 Scottish League Cap
Scottish FA Cup Winners Medal 1896-97
(WITH RENTON)
Scottish FA Cup Finalists Medal 1904-05

McAULEY, James 1897-1898

Birth Place: Scotland

☛ James McAuley was yet another Scotsman who played for Woolwich Arsenal during the early years of the club. He signed from Greenock Morton in May 1897. McAuley was a right back who in his only season with the club 1897-98 played in twenty three out of thirty league games played. His debut being on the opening day of the season at home to Grimsby 1st September 1897.

Returned to Scotland in the summer of 1898.

	Games	Goals
League	23	1
FA Cup	4	1
United League	7	1
Friendly Matches	4	0
Total	**38**	**3**

McAVOY, Francis 1895-98

Birth Place: Ayr, Scotland
Date of Birth: 1876

☛Francis McAvoy was transferred to Woolwich Arsenal from the Scottish junior side Ayr in May 1895. An outside left, in his first season with the club he tussled with Peter Mortimer for the left wing spot, playing in eleven league games, which included his debut versus Lincoln at the Manor Field, 21st September 1895. In 1896-97 he played in several different roles which included left wing, inside right, centre forward, inside left and both wing half positions. Finished the season playing in eighteen of the club's thirty league games. In season 1897-98, he started well, scoring three times in four games from the wing half position, however, (in March 1898) was suspended by the club for misdemeanours. Joined Brighton United in the summer of 1898 and later returned to Scotland and rejoined Ayr.

	Games	Goals
League	44	8
FA Cup	3	2
United League	17	1
Kent League	17	20
Freindlys	50	35
Total	**131**	**66**

Honours:
Kent League Championsip Medal 1896-97

McAVOY, John 1898-99

Birth Place: Scotland
Date of Birth: 1878

☛John McAvoy was a full back playing for Glasgow Celtic reserve side when signing for Woolwich Arsenal in October 1898. In that 1898-99 season (after making his league debut at Loughborough Town, 12th November 1898) he remained everpresent whilst playing in both full back positions. However, after the signing of fellow full back James Jackson from Newcastle United, John's first team chances were limited. This resulted in him being transferred to Grimsby Town in December 1899. He spent two seasons with the Mariners before returning to Scotland.

	Games	Goals
League	25	0
FA Cup	1	0

	Games	Goals
United League	10	0
Kent League	13	0
Friendly Matches	10	0
Southern Combination	2	0
Other Youth Matches	3	0
Total	**64**	**0**

McBEAN, John 1888-1892

Birth Place: Kirkcaldy, Fife
Date of Birth: 1868

☛John McBean, like several other players of that generation, joined Royal Arsenal from Scottish junior side Kirkcaldy Wanderers in December 1888. John was a left back who served the club well in the senior side in the pre league days, making his senior first class debut in the first ever FA Cup tie versus Lyndhurst, 5th October 1889. After leaving Royal Arsenal in 1892, he like many others, played for and worked at the Royal Ordanance. John was empolyed there for over forty years, receiving in 1932 a long service medal from King George V. Died January 1954 aged 85.

	Games	Goals
FA Cup	6	0
Other Senior Matches	111	1
Other Reserve Matches	5	0
Total	**122**	**1**

Honours:
London Senior Cup Winners Medal 1890-91
London Senior Cup Finalist Medal 1889-90
London Charity Cup Winners Medal 1889-90
Kent Senior Cup Winners Medal 1889-90

McCONNELL, Alexander 1897-99

Birth Place: Glenbuck, Scotland
Date of Birth: 1875

☛ Alex McConnell was playing Scottish junior football for his home club side when spotted by Everton whom he joined in 1895. He spent two seasons at Goodison Park (without getting a first team chance) before joining Woolwich Arsenal in November 1897, was plunged straight in to league action deputising for the injured John Caldwell, making his league debut in a home encounter versus Blackpool 27th November 1897. Alex played in seventeen of the last eighteen league games. In 1898-99 he was still the club's regular left back until an injury forced him to miss three months of that season, in which time John McAvoy had staked a claim for the left back birth. McConnell was transferred to Queens Park Rangers during the summer of 1899. He spent two seasons with them before finishing his career with Grimsby Town 1901-05, where he played in nearly one hundred first team games.

	Games	Goals
League	37	1
FA Cup	1	0
United League	25	0
Kent League	1	0
Friendly Matches	13	0
Other Youth Matches	1	0
Total	**78**	**1**

McCOWIE, Andrew   1899-1900

Birth Place: Scotland
Date of Birth: 1876

☛ Andrew McCowie had served Liverpool for three seasons, 1896-99, being a regular inside forward, in their team during the 1897-98 season. But, with competition from fellow inside forwards Becton and Walker in 1898-99, he was allowed to leave the club and joined Woolwich Arsenal in May 1899. In his one full season at Plumstead he enjoyed reasonable success when playing in twenty five league games and scoring seven goals. Andrew played in the first three league games of the season 1900-01, his inconsistent form resulted in him beimg transferred to Middlesborough in October 1900, where he stayed for one season before finishing his career.

	Games	Goals
League	28	7
FA Cup	5	0
Friendly Matches	10	4
Southern Combination	9	4
Total	**52**	**15**

McDONALD, Duncan   1909-11

Birth Place: Bo'ness, Scotland

☛ Duncan McDonald joined Woolwich Arsenal from his home club Townside in April 1909. A right full back, he was virtually everpresent in the Woolwich side from making his debut at Manchester United 30th October 1909. He found himself a regular, because Joe Shaw had switched to left back, which enabled McDonald to to fill in at right back for the, out of sorts Archibald Gray. However, in 1910-11 the roles were reversed, Gray coming back in to favour which resulted in him only playing in one league game. Transferred to West Hartlepool in the summer of 1911.

	Games	Goals
League	26	0
FA Cup	1	0
Other Senior Matches	1	0
Friendly Matches	15	2
London League Reserves	1	0
South Eastern League	33	1
Total	**77**	**3**

McDONALD, Hugh 1906, 1908-10, 1912-13

Birth Place: Kilwinning, Ayrshire
Date of Birth: 1884

☛ Hugh Laughlan McDonald is one of only a handful of players to have played for Arsenal football club in three different periods. Hugh had played Scottish junior football for a host of clubs including Ayr Westerlea, Maypole, Ayr Academical and Beith, before joining Woolwich Arsenal in January 1906. In his first short stay with the club he was goalkeeping understudy to Jimmy Ashcroft and played in two league games in 1905-06 of which his league debut was at the Manor Field versus Blackburn Rovers 17th February 1906. Released during the summer of 1906 when he joined Brighton. He spent two seasons at the Goldstone Ground before rejoining Woolwich Arsenal in May 1908. On his return to the club he became, at that stage, only the third goalkeeper (after Ord and Ashcroft) to remain everpresent in a season, 1908-09. Hugh missed only two games the following season before leaving the club once again to join Oldham Athletic in July 1910. He spent one season at the newly promoted Lancashire outfit and one season at Bradford before rejoining Woolwich Arsenal for the third time in December 1912. In that doomed 1912-13 season he stepped in to replace Harold Crawford when playing in eighteen of the last twenty one league games. McDonald left the club for the last time in November 1913, later playing for Bristol Rovers 1914-15. Died August 1920 aged 36.

	Games	Goals
League	94	0
FA Cup	9	0
Other Senior Matches	2	0
Friendly Matches	9	0
South Eastern League	2	0
London FA Challenge Cup	4	0
Total	**120**	**0**

McEACHRANE, Rod   1902-15

Birth Place: Inverness, Scotland
Date of Birth: 1878

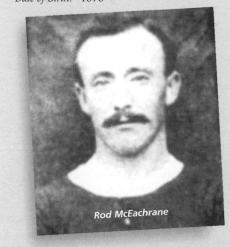
Rod McEachrane

☛ Rod McEachrane played in more games for Arsenal football club than any other player (with out ever winning a major or international honour) and although it is eighty years since he played for the club, only nineteen players have ever figured in more than his three hundred and thirteen league games. McEachrane, a left half, began his footballing career with Thames Ironworks 1898 (later West Ham) making over one hundred appearances, before joining Woolwich Arsenal in May 1902, this after moving down from Scotland to live in Canning Town and working for the Thames Iron Works Shipbuilders. His thirteen year romance with the club began in 1902-03 when he helped the team to their then highest ever league position (third in division two). He missed only six league games that season of which his Arsenal league debut was on the opening day of that campaign at Preston North End 6th September 1902. In 1903-04 Rod missed only one league game during the club's promotion winning season. Playing in the first division for the first time, he adapted well when playing in the majority of the club's league games. In seasons 1905-06 and 1906-07 he was ever reliable helping the club to two succesive FA Cup Semi Finals. In 1907-08 his remarkable consistency was shown when remaining ever present. McEachrane missed only two league games in 1908-09. Between 1909-1911 he remained a stalwart for the club before, in 1911 -12, losing his place to Angus Mckinnon. In his final three seasons with the club he provided a solid back up to the first choice McKinnon. What is very unusual with Rod's league career is that all of his three hundred and forty six first class games for Arsenal he wore the number six shirt on every occasion The outbreak of world war one brought his career to an end. Died November 1952, Aged 74.

	Games	Goals
League	313	0
FA Cup	33	0
Other Senior Matches	8	0
Kent League	1	0
Friendly Matches	31	0
London League	14	0
London League	17	0
South Eastern League	84	0
London FA Challenge Cup	5	0
Total	**506**	**0**

Honours:
Southern Professional Charity Cup Finalists
   Medal   1903-04

MACFARLANE, Alex   1896-97

Birth Place: Airdrie, Scotland
Date of Birth: 1877

🏴 Alex Macfarlane began life playing his football for the Scottish junior team, Baillieston, before joining Airdrie in 1895. He was transferred to Woolwich Arsenal in November 1896, Alex's duration at the club was only six months in which time he played in five league games in four different positions, his debut being at the Manor Fiald versus Grimsby Town 28th November 1896. His potential at the club was not seen which resulted in him being transferred back to Airdrie during the summer of 1897. 'Sandy' moved back over the border to join Newcastle United in October 1898. He spent three seasons on Tyneside when becoming the club's first choice inside left. He returned to Scotland in November 1901 when joining Dundee. Alex enjoyed a twelve year stay at the club helping the side to a Scottish Cup Final victory versus Clyde in 1910 (this after two drawn games) as well as winning the first of his five Scottish Caps versus Wales in 1903-04. He also represented the Scottish League on three occassions. Alex moved to Stamford Bridge to play for Chelsea in 1913, playing in just four league games for them up to the outbreak of World War One. He later managed Dundee 1919 - 25 guiding the club to the 1925 Scottish Cup Final. Charlton Athletic enticed him back down south to become their manager in 1925. He stayed for two seasons at the Valley before returning to Dundee in December 1927. He spent only seven months back at Dens Park before packing his bags to return to Charlton, spening four and a half years at the club. 1928 - 32 in which time, in his first full season back at the Valley he led the club to the Third Division South Championship. Macfarlane finished his managerial career with Blackpool 1933 - 1935.

	Games	Goals
League	5	0
United League	2	1
Kent League	10	9
Friendly Matches	10	5
Total	27	15

Honours:
(WITH DUNDEE)
5 Scottish Caps
3 Scottish League Caps
Scottish Cup Winners Medal   1909-10
(WITH ARSENAL)
Kent League Championship Medal   1896-97

McGEOCH, Craig   1897-1899

Birth Place: Scotland

🏴 Craig McGeoch came down from Scotland to join Woolwich Arsenal from junior side Dunblane in May 1897. McGeoch

for some reason could not establish himself as a first team regular in 1897-98 although when he did play he did very well scoring eight times in nine games, this included two hat tricks in home games versus Gainsborough Trinity and Walsall. Having already made his league debut on the opening day of the season versus Grimsby Town. However, in 1898-99 although establishing himself as a regular, his goalscoring form dried up, scoring only five goals in twenty six matches. This loss of form subsequently resulting in him returning to Scotland when he linked up with Dundee.

	Games	Goals
League	35	13
FA Cup	4	1
United League	23	6
Kent League	8	5
Friendly Matches	29	20
Other Youth Matches	4	3
Total	103	48

McGIBBON, Charles   1905 & 1909-10

Birth Place: Portsmouth
Date of Birth: 1880

🏴 Charles McGibbon originally joined Woolwich Arsenal as an amateur in August 1905. He was yet another army man to play for the club, at this time, and in fact was a sergeant in the Royal Artillery throughout his playing career. In his early career he played amateur football for Eltham and New Brompton. He played for Crystal Palace 1907, and rejoined Woolwich Arsenal from Southampton in 1909. He made his league debut for the club (scoring the only goal of the game) versus Chelsea at Stamford Bridge 28th March 1910. Charles followed this up by scoring crucial goals at home to Aston Villa and away at Tottenham. He was not retained and eventually transferred to Leyton in August 1910. His son, Douglas, played for many years with Southampton. Charles played county cricket for Hampshire his only first class game being in 1919 at the age of thirty nine. Died May 1954 aged 73.

	Games	Goals
League	4	3
London League Reserves	2	1
Total	6	4

McKELLAR, Matthew   1909-10

Birth Place: Campsie, Stirlingshire
Date of Birth: 1887

🏴 Matthew McKellar was a centre forward playing in Scottish junior football for Kirkintilloch Harp when signing for Woolwich Arsenal in November 1909. He spent the remainder of that season as deputy for resident centre forward William Buckenham. He played in three league games during this period which

included his debut at Hillsborough versus Sheffield Wednesday 13th November 1909. He finished his league career in fine style by scoring in a 1-1 draw with Liverpool at Manor Field.

	Games	Goals
League	3	1
FA Cup	2	1
Friendly Matches	1	1
South Eastern League	11	2
Other Youth Matches	1	0
Total	18	5

McLAUGHLAN, Joseph   1911-13

Birth Place: Edinburgh, Scotland
Date of Birth: 1891

🏴 Joseph McLaughlan was transferred to Woolwich Arsenal from the Scottish junior side Bathgate in September 1911. In 1911-12 he was the club's reserve centre forward to John Chalmers and Alf Common. He played in three league games that term which included his debut at Meadow Lane versus Notts County 23rd December 1911. However, at the start of 1912-13 season he found himself as first choice centre forward, playing in ten of the clubs first fourteen games (scoring 3 goals). Joe lost his position in December 1912 and at no other stage was able to regain it. He joined the forces in wartime, after he had been transferred to Watford in June 1913.

	Games	Goals
League	16	3
Other Senior Matches	2	2
Friendly Matches	11	20
South Eastern League	32	17
London FA Challenge Cup	1	0
Other Youth Matches	1	0
Total	63	42

McNAB, William   1893-1894

Birth Place: Scotland

🏴 William McNab played in thirteen league games for Burnley (scoring five goals) in 1892-93. In 1893-94 he lost his place to P Turnbull and joined Woolwich Arsenal in December 1893. In his only season at the Manor Field he was understudy to Walter Shaw and managed to play in only two league games of which his debut was in a 6-0 home victory versus Northwich Victoria 23rd March 1894 and the other game seeing him score in a 1-4 home defeat versus Small Heath (now Birmingham City). He joined Royal Ordnance FC during the summer of 1894, later returning to Scotland.

	Games	Goals
League	2	1
Friendly Matches	5	4
Total	7	5

McNICHOL, Duncan   1899-1903

Birth Place: Alexandria, Dumbarton

☞ Duncan was a young full back who played junior football for St Bernards before joining Woolwich Arsenal in June 1899. In his first season at the Manor Field, 1899-00, he became an automatic choice for the club at right back playing in thirty league games which included his league debut versus Leicester Fosse 2nd September 1899, as well as featuring in the club's record 12-0 league victory versus Loughborough. In 1900-01 he was as consistent as ever when missing only four league games. In 1901-02 he missed just one league game before, in 1902-03, switching to the right back berth so the club could accomodate James Jackson at left back. He lost his way due to inconsistency and injury and was transfer listed in October 1903 and he linked up with Aberdeen. In 1905 he was forced to retire from the game through injury.

	Games	Goals
League	101	1
FA Cup	11	0
Other Senior Matches	3	0
Friendly Matches	24	0
London League	9	0
London League Reserves	3	0
Southern Combination	11	0
Total	162	1

McPHEE, John   1898-99

☞ John McPhee was a Scottish junior international full back who had played for Glasgow and Perth before joining Woolwich Arsenal in May 1898. In his only season at the club he played in just seven league games after making his debut against Burton Swifts at the Manor Field 22nd October 1898.

	Games	Goals
League	7	0
FA Cup	1	0
United League	6	0
Kent League	14	0
Friendly Matches	23	1
Other Youth Matches	1	0
Total	52	1

McQUILKIE, J   1892-1893

Birth Place: Scotland

☞ J McQuilkie was a Scottish full back who joined Royal Arsenal in their pre-league days from Scottish side Renton in October 1892. He fluctuated between senior and reserve team football, in his only season with the club. He played in two FA Cup ties of which his senior debut was versus the Highland Light Infantry, 15th October 1892.

	Games	Goals
FA Cup	2	0
Other Senior Matches	10	0
Other Reserve Matches	11	0
Total	23	0

MAIN, Alexander   1899-1903

Birth Place: Scotland

☞ Alex had begun his career with Scottish junior side West Calder before joining Hibernian, being on the books when they reached the Scottish FA Cup Final of 1895-96. An inside forward, he was transferred to Woolwich Arsenal in November 1899. In that 1899-1900 season he was a regular understudy to Paddy Logan and Andrew McCowie. He played in (when scoring twice) Arsenal's record ever league victory, 12-0 versus Loughborough Town, after making his league debut in a 0-5 defeat at Lincoln on Christmas day 1899. In 1900-01 Alex played in the majority of the league games, scoring six goals. In 1901-02 season he enjoyed his best spell at the club, missing only six of the teams thirty four league games, scoring five times. In the 1902-03 season he lost his place to Maurice Connor and only played in the league side seven times whilst deputising for the injured John Dick at centre half. Returned to Scotland in October 1903 when he joined Motherwell, who had just won promotion to the Scottish First Division. He later played for Watford 1904-07.

	Games	Goals
League	63	14
FA Cup	6	0
Other Senior Matches	3	0
Kent League	12	2
Friendly Matches	19	11
London League	10	1
London League Reserves	17	14
Southern Combination	6	3
Other Youth Matches	2	0
Total	138	45

Honours:
Kent League Championship Medal   1902-03

MAXWELL, James   1908-09

Birth Place: Kilmarnock, Scotland
Date of Birth: 1882

☞ James Maxwell was an outside right who served Kilmarnock (1901-07) before being transferred to Sheffield Wednesday in March 1907. In 1907-08 he shared the right wing birth at Hillsborough with Harry Chapman (brother of the legendary Herbert Chapman later, of course, to become Arsenal's manager). He joined Woolwich Arsenal in May 1908, making his Arsenal league debut versus Everton on the opening day of the season 2nd September 1908. After this result he lost his place to David Greenaway and played in only one other league game versus Sunderland at Roker Park before returning to Scotland to play for Galstone. James was killed whilst on active service during World War One.

	Games	Goals
League	2	0
Friendly Matches	3	0
London League Reserves	14	1
South Eastern League	26	5
Total	45	6

MEADE, Thomas   1893-97

Birth Place: Plumstead, London
Date of Birth: 14th May 1877

☞ Thomas Meade, an explosive centre forward, joined Woolwich Arsenal as an amateur in November 1893, turning professional one year later. He made his Arsenal league debut at Leicester Fosse 7th January 1895. He played in only three league games that season, spending much of the time in the reserve side. In 1895-96 his action was only seen in reserve and friendly matches at the club. Thomas managed to play in eleven first team matches (scoring six times) . In 1896-97, before being transferred to Tottenham Hotspur in the summer of 1897. He moved on to Fulham in 1900 spending four seasons at Craven Cottage where he was leading scorer in each season and helped them to two Southern League Division Two Championships. In all competitions his goalscoring ratio remains one of the highest in the club's history.

	Games	Goals
League	11	5
FA Cup	3	2
United League	3	3
Kent League	28	31
Friendly Matches	76	58
Other Youth Matches	1	0
Total	122	99

Honours:
(WITH FULHAM)
2 Southern League Championship
Medals   1901-02, 1902-03
(WITH ARSENAL)
Kent League Championship
Medal   1896-97

MEGGS, James   1889-91

James Meggs was an inside forward who was transferred to Royal Arsenal from City Ramblers in September 1889. In his two seasons in the club's non league days he was a consistent member of the senior side and he played in five FA Cup Ties during this period in which his senior debut was versus Lyndhurst 5th October 1889, Meggs scoring twice in an 11-0 victory.

	Games	Goals
FA Cup	5	4
Other Senior Matches	21	14
Total	**26**	**18**

Honours:
Kent Senior Cup Winners Medal	1889-90
London Senior Cup Finalists Medal	1889-90

MILLS, Samuel   1895-96

Birth Place: Derby
Date of Birth: 1871

Samuel Mills had played junior football for Derby Midland before joining Derby County in June 1891. In 1891-92 he missed only two of Derby's twenty six league games and was a regular again in 1892-93. Samuel went on to play at Leicester Fosse 1893-94 and Loughborough Town 1894-95 before joining Woolwich Arsenal in June 1895. In his one season with Woolwich he was a regular in the first team at outside right playing in twenty four of the club's thirty league games which included his Arsenal league debut at Lincoln City 14th September 1895. At the start of the following campaign, 1896-97, new signing James Brock occupied the right wing berth which resulted in Samuel wanting away. He moved on to Heanor Town in November 1896.

	Games	Goals
League	24	3
FA Cup	1	0
Kent League	5	3
Friendly Matches	15	6
Total	**45**	**12**

MITCHELL, Andrew   1898-99

Birth Place: Scotland
Date of Birth: 1879

Andrew Mitchell was an outside left who was transferred to Woolwich Arsenal from Albion Rovers in May 1898. During his one season at the club he had to be content with sharing the left wing position with Hugh Dailly and Herbert Shaw. He played in ten league games of which his debut was on the opening day of the season at the Excelsior, Dallow Lane versus Luton, a game in which Arsenal won 1-0 with Mitchell scoring the winning goal.

	Games	Goals
League	10	2
United League	8	2
Kent League	14	4
Friendly Matches	14	8
Other Youth Matches	1	0
Total	**47**	**16**

MOIR, James   1898-1900

Birth Place: Inverbervie, Kincardineshire
Date of Birth: 7th January 1874

James Moir had played Scottish junior football for Kirkintilloch Rob Roy and Gowan Athletic before joining Sunderland where he spent his time as a reserve wing half. James was transferred to Woolwich Arsenal in May 1898. In 1898-99 he became the club's automatic choice at right half playing in twenty nine out of thirty four league games, his debut was at Burslem Port Vale 5th September 1898. In 1899-1900 he lost his place to the newly signed Joseph Murphy and managed to play in only twelve league games which included playing in the club's record league victory, 12-0 versus Loughborough Town. Later played for Gravesend United 1900-01, Fulham 1901-02 and became assistant trainer at Chelsea 1908-12. Died January 1953 aged 79.

	Games	Goals
League	41	0
FA Cup	4	0
United League	15	1
Kent League	9	0
Friendly Matches	20	2
Southern Combination	7	0
Other Youth Matches	3	0
Total	**99**	**3**

MONTEITH, James   1897

Birth Place: Ireland

James Monteith was an outside left who was transferred to Woolwich Arsenal from Glasgow Celtic in May 1897. He played in the first five league games of season 1897-98 of which his debut (when scoring) was in a 4-1 home victory versus Grimsby 1st September 1897. However, he lost his place to firstly Adam Haywood and later William White. He only played in one more league game before moving on to Belfast Distillery.

	Games	Goals
League	6	1
Friendly Matches	8	2
Total	**14**	**3**

MORDUE, John   1907-08

Birth Place: Edmondsley, Co. Durham
Date of Birth: 1897

Barnsley Town have over the years produced many footballing legends which include Eric Brook, George Robledo, Danny Blanchflower and Tommy Taylor, and although "Jackie" Mordue could never be classed in the same bracket as the aformentioned, he was still a very fine winger, good enough to play for England twice. John began his career in junior football with Sacriston and Spennymoor United, before joining the Oakwell Unit in 1906. Woolwich Arsenal paid Barnsley £450 for his services in April 1907, linking up with his brother-in-law Jimmy Ashcroft. He spent one full season at Manor Field playing in twenty three league games, after playing in the last three league games of the 1906-07 season of which his Arsenal league debut was a home encounter versus Birmingham City 13th April 1907. With Mordue being one of the club's best assets, it came as no surprise when a £750 offer from "The Bank of England Team", Sunderland was accepted in May 1908. John had a glittering eight season career at Roker Park, playing in over two hundred and eighty first class games scoring nearly eighty goals, helping them win the League Championship in 1912-13, as well as, in the same season, to a losing FA Cup Final appearance versus Aston Villa. He won the first of his two England Caps versus Ireland in 1911-12. He also represented the football league on three occasions. Mordue's best years were probably lost to the first Word War, However, he played for a further season at Sunderland before being transferred to Middlesbrough in May 1920, spending two seasons there before finishing his career with Hartlepool 1922-23, and player manager with Durham City 1923-24. Died December 1957 aged 70.

	Games	Goals
League	26	1
FA Cup	2	0
Other Senior Matches	1	0
Friendly Matches	14	7
London League Reserves	4	2
South Eastern League	12	2
Total	**59**	**12**

Honours:
(WITH SUNDERLAND)
2 England Caps	
3 Football League Caps	
League Championship Medal	1912-13
FA Cup Finalists Medal	1912-13

(WITH ARSENAL)
South Eastern League Championship Medal	1907-08

MORTIMER, Peter   1894-96

Birth Place: Calton, Glasgow, Scotland
Date of Birth: 17th August 1875

Peter Mortimer was a utility forward who played for many junior Glasgow sides between 1889-94, before joining Woolwich Arsenal from Leith Athletic in April 1894. In the 1894-95 season Peter finished the season as the club's leading marksman with fourteen goals in twenty two games, after scoring on his league debut in a 2-5 away defeat at the newly opened Sincil Bank ground on the opening day of the season versus Lincoln City 1st September 1894. In 1895-96 he again was a regular playing at either inside right or outside left when scoring nine times in twenty seven of the club's thirty league games. (this included a hat trick in a 7-0 home victory versus Crewe). For unknown political reasons he was transferred to Chatham in May 1896. Died 1951 aged 76.

	Games	Goals
League	49	23
Kent League	4	2
Friendly Matches	62	48
Total	**115**	**73**

MURPHY, Joseph   1899-1900

Birth Place: Stockton on Tees, North Yorks
Date of Birth: 1873

Joseph "Judge" Murphy was a wing half or inside forward who served Hibernian well 1892-97 helping the club to the Scottish Second Division Championship in 1894-95 and to the Scottish FA Cup Final of 1896. Joined Stoke City in 1897, was a regular for them for two seasons and joined Woolwich Arsenal in April 1899. In his only season at the club he was a consistent member of the side, playing in twenty seven of thirty four league games of which his debut was on the opening day of the season at home to Leicester Fosse. Was transferred to Raith Rovers during the summer of 1900.

	Games	Goals
League	27	0
FA Cup	5	0
Friendly Matches	16	0
Total	**48**	**0**

MURRELL, Harry   1898-1900

Birth Place: Hounslow, Middlesex
Date of Birth: 19th November 1879

"Joe" as he was affectionately known was a full back who had played junior football in the Kent and Middlesex areas before joining Woolwich Arsenal in October 1898. In his first season for the club 1898-99 he was a regular in the Kent league side (mainly playing outside left). However, in 1899-1900 his first team chance came when injuries to both full backs David McNichol and James Jackson resulted in Harry playing in six of the club's last seven league games of that season in which his debut was away to Small Heath (now Birmingham City) 31st March 1900. He was transferred to Clapton Orient during the summer of 1900. A noted cricketer, Murrell played county crisket for twenty seven years for both Kent and Middlesex which included, when between 1905 and 1926 he hardly missed a game behind the stumps for the latter county, when helping them to the County Championship in 1920 and 1921. A position which a future Arsenal player, Leslie Compton, would take over less than twelve years later. For a good many years after his retirement he was the scorer for Middlesex C.C. Died August 1952 aged 72.

	Games	Goals
League	6	0
Kent League	23	5
Friendly Matches	11	1
Southern Combination	1	0
Total	**41**	**6**

NEAVE, David   1904-12

Birth Place: Arbroath, Scotland
Date of Birth: 1883

David Neave was an outside left when playing for Scottish clubs Forfar and Montrose before joining Woolwich Arsenal from Arbroath in March 1904, spending the rest of that season in the reserve eleven. In the club's first ever Division One campaign 1904-05 he was left wing understudy to Satterthwaite and Templeton. He only played three league games that term of which his league debut was at Small Heath (now Birmingham City) 3rd December 1904. In May 1905, David left for Leyton but returned to Plumstead seven months later, when becoming first choice on the left wing in the club's league side. In 1906-07 he was an automatic choice and helped Woolwich Arsenal to the 1907 FA Cup Semi Final. In seasons 1907-08 and 1908-09 he again was a regular selection playing in thirty five and twenty five games respectively. In 1909-10, although playing in just over half of the club's league fixtures, he was joint top league scorer with five goals. However, in his last two seasons at the club he had to be content in sharing the left wing position with Charles Lewis. Transferred to Merthyr Town in July 1912. His younger brother Andrew was also, at some time, on the club's books.

	Games	Goals
League	154	30
F A Cup	14	2
Other Senior Matches	6	0
Friendly Matches	25	7
London League	2	0
London League Reserves	21	12
South Eastern League	58	14
London FA Challenge Cup	3	0
Other Youth Matches	1	0
Total	**284**	**65**

Honours:
Southern Professional Charity Cup Winners
  Medal   1905-06
Southern Professional Charity Cup Finalists
  Medal   1903-04

NORMAN, James   1914-19

Birth Place: Hackney Wick, London
Date of Birth: 1893

James Norman joined Arsenal from local East London side Walthamstow Grange in May 1914. He was one of many players whose career was disturbed by the First World War. In his one season with the club, he was a regular member of the club's South Eastern League side. He managed to play in four consecutive league games in November 1914 (taking over from 'Tiny' Winship but losing his place to Charles Lewis) his debut being versus Birmingham City at St Andrews 7th November 1914.

	Games	Goals
League	4	0
Other Senior Matches	1	0
Friendly Matches	4	2
London League Reserves	7	1
South Eastern League	29	3
London FA Challenge Cup	1	0
Wartime	4	0
Total	**50**	**6**

O'BRIEN, Patrick   1894-97

Birth Place: Scotland
Date of Birth: 1875

Patrick O'Brien was a diminutive inside forward who started in junior football in Scotland with Elm Park and Glasgow Northern, before joining Woolwich Arsenal in April 1894. In the first of his three seasons with the club, "Paddy" played in twenty seven league games scoring eleven goals,(including a hat trick versus Burslem Port Vale on Christmas day 1894), this after making his debut in a home match versus Grimsby Town 10th September 1894. A serious injury in the opening day of the 1895-95 season resulted in O'Brien missing four months action until returning to the side in late January 1896. He regained his first team inside left position in 1896-97 when he was the club's leading league goal scorer with fourteen in twenty six appearances. He was transferred to Bristol City during the summer of 1897. Died 1951 aged 76.

	Games	Goals
League	63	27
FA Cup	4	2
United League	12	5

	Games	Goals
Kent League	14	3
Friendly Matches	80	53
Total	**173**	**90**

OFFER, Henry   1889-91

Birth Place: Devizes, Wiltshire
Date of Birth: 1871

Henry Offer joined Royal Arsenal in September 1889 from Swindon Town. Henry was the regular full back in the pre league days for the senior side. His first class debut was in an FA Cup Qualifying game versus Norwich Thorpe 26th October 1889. In later years he played for Southampton St Marys. Died January 1947 aged 75.

	Games	Goals
FA Cup	4	1
Other Senior Matches	52	16
Other Reserve Matches	1	0
Total	**57**	**17**

Honours:
London Charity Cup Winners Medal 1889-90
London Senior Cup Winners Medal 1890-91
London Senior Cup Finalist Medal 1889-90
Kent Senior Cup Winners Medal   1889-90

OLIVER, Harold   1909-10

Birth Place: Holloway, London

Harold Oliver was an amateur centre forward who joined Woolwich Arsenal from Great Eastern Rovers in September 1909. He played predominantely for the clubs South Eastern League side. Managed to play in one league game in 1909-10 in a home fixture versus Nottingham Forest 9th October 1909.

	Games	Goals
League	1	0
Friendly Matches	12	13
South Eastern League	19	15
Other Youth Matches	1	0
Total	**33**	**28**

ORD, Roger   1897-1900

Birth Place: Northumberland
Date of Birth: 1871

Roger Ord joined Woolwich Arsenal in 1897 from Middlesbrough Ironopolis, having previously played for Northumberland Juniors and Hebburn Argyle. In his initial season with the club, 1897-98, he became the first goalkeeper in Arsenal's history to remain everpresent in a league campaign, this after making his debut in a game at the Manor Ground versus Grimsby Town 1st September 1897. In 1898-99 he kept up his consistent form when missing only one of the thirty four league games. In 1899-1900 he played in the first twenty six league games of the season which included an appearance in the record ever league victory versus Loughborough Town. However, after a 1-3 away defeat in the next league game at Sheffield Wednesday he lost his place to Thomas Hamilton. When Jimmy Ashcroft joined the club in June 1900 Roger's first team days were over and he was transferred to Southern League side Luton Town in September 1900, where he stayed for three seasons.

	Games	Goals
League	89	0
FA Cup	10	0
United League	34	0
Kent League	3	0
Friendly Matches	24	0
Southern Combination	7	0
Other Youth Matches	3	0
Total	**170**	**0**

OWENS, Isaac   1901-02

Birth Place: Darlington, Durham
Date of Birth: 1881

Isaac Owens was an inside forward who had played amateur football for Bishop Auckland and Crook before joining Woolwich Arsenal in October 1901. In his one season at the club he could not command a regular place although he did manage to play in nine of Arsenal's ten league games played between mid October and Christmas 1901. This included a scoring debut away at Gainsborough Trinity 12th October 1901. He returned to amateur football and later played for Plymouth Argyle 1904-06, Bristol Rovers 1907, Crystal Palace 1907, Grimsby Town 1908 and Darlington 1909.

	Games	Goals
League	9	2
FA Cup	2	0
Kent League	8	5
Friendly Matches	6	4
London League	3	1
London League Reserves	7	5
Total	**35**	**17**

Honours:
London League Reserve Championship
    Medal   1901-02
Kent League Championship Medal   1901-02

PAYNE, George   1912-13

Birth Place: Hitchen, Herts
Date of Birth: 17th February 1887

George Payne was a utility forward playing in Southern League football for Crystal Palace before joining Tottenham Hotspur in 1906. He moved on to Leyton FC and was transferred to Sunderland in 1910. He spent two seasons at Roker Park playing in only three league games. George returned south when joining Woolwich Arsenal in June 1912. In his only season at the club (the last season when the club was known as Woolwich Arsenal), although being a consistent performer in the South Eastern League side, he played in only three league games (all of which were heavy defeats) which included his debut in a home fixture versus Aston Villa 16th September 1912. No details can be obtained about him leaving the club. Died August 1932 aged 45.

	Games	Goals
League	3	0
Friendly Matches	2	0
South Eastern League	16	9
Total	**21**	**9**

PEACHEY, C B   1891-92

C B Peachey was an amateur outside left who had a short spell with Royal Arsenal when joining the club from Chiswick Park. His only first class appearance was in an FA Cup Tie versus Small Heath (now Birmingham City) 16th January 1892.

	Games	Goals
FA Cup	1	0
Other Senior Matches	3	2
Total	**4**	**2**

PLACE, Walter   1900-02

Birth Place: Burnley, Lancashire
Date of Birth: 1875

Walter joined his home town club, Burnley, in 1894. He spent six seasons with them playing in nearly two hundred first team games. A wing half or inside forward, Walter enjoyed mixed emotions at the club helping them to the Second Division Championship in 1897-98, the season after he had been involved in their relegation from Division one. Place was again in their relegated side of 1899-1900 before joining Woolwich Arsenal in May 1900. In 1900-01 he established himself in the side at Plumstead when playing in twenty five league games of which his debut was on the opening day of the season in a home encounter versus Gainsborough Trinity 1st September 1900. In 1901-02 he played in seventeen league games when helping the club to their then highest ever league position (fourth in Division Two). He later left the club after his contract was cancelled.

	Games	Goals
League	42	6
FA Cup	3	1
Kent League	3	1

	Games	Goals
Friendly Matches	9	2
London League	7	0
London League Reserves	4	1
Total	**68**	**11**

Honours:
(WITH BURNLEY)
Division Two Championship Medal 1897-98

POWELL, Joseph   1892-96

Birth Place: Bristol
Date of Birth: 1870

Joseph Powell's story can only be described as, possibly, the greatest tragedy in Arsenal's long history. Born in Bristol in 1870. Joseph was in the Walsall 80th Staffordshire Regiment when Royal Arsenal bought him out of the army to play professional football in December 1892. In his first season with the club, 1892-93 (the club's last pre league season) he was a main stay in the senior side. In 1893-94 he became the club's first captain in league football, missing only two league games of which his debut was in the first ever game in the Football League at home to Newcastle on 2nd September 1893. In 1894-95 he missed the first three league games of the season before returning to the side when remaining everpresent to the end of the season. His consistency was shown yet again in 1895-96 when he missed just five of the thirty league games, in which time he scored his one and only league goal in a 5-0 home victory versus Loughborough Town. At the start of the 1896-97 season, everything started brightly with Joseph having played in eight of the first ten league encounters, when tragedy struck. In a United League match versus Kettering Town on the 23rd November 1896 he fell akwardly breaking an arm and contracted blood posioning and tetanus. The arm was later amputated but he died within a week when just twenty six years of age.

	Games	Goals
League	86	1
FA Cup	6	1
Other Senior Matches	30	0
United League	4	0
Kent League	1	0
Friendly Matches	76	5
Total	**203**	**7**

PRATT, Thomas   1903-04

Birth Place: Fleetwood, Lancashire
Date of Birth: 28th August 1875

Thomas Pratt began his career in junior football with his home town club, Fleetwood Rangers (1892-95). He moved on to Grimsby Town during the summer of 1895 where he scored sixteen goals in twenty nine league games. He was transferred to Preston in 1896 and in his first spell at the club he played in seventy one league games, scoring twenty one goals. Thomas then spent one season in the Southern League with Tottenham Hotspur 1899-1900 when helping the club to the Southern League Championship before rejoining Preston the following May. During the next three seasons he again was a regular at Deepdale scoring twenty league goals in seventy three games. Pratt was transferred to Woolwich Arsenal in August 1903. In his one season at Woolwich Arsenal he could never command a regular position, deputising in only eight games for either John Coleman or Tommy Shanks. His Arsenal league debut being on the opening day of the season in a home fixture versus Blackpool 5th September 1903. Having helped Arsenal to promotion to Division One for the first time in their history he moved on to Fulham in August 1904 spending less than one season at Craven Cottage before finishing his career at the back end of the 1904-05 season with Blackpool. Died August 1935 aged 59.

	Games	Goals
League	8	2
FA Cup	2	0
Other Senior Matches	2	3
Friendly Matches	2	2
London League	7	7
London League Reserves	1	1
South Eastern League	3	3
Total	**25**	**18**

Honours:
(WITH TOTTENHAM)
Southern League Championship
   Medal   1899-1900

QUAYLE, James   1907,1908, 1910-11

Birth Place: Charlton, London
Date of Birth: 1890

James Quayle originally joined Woolwich Arsenal as an amateur full back in August 1907, after he had played junior football for Old Charlton and Woolwich Polytechnic. He left the club but rejoined as an amateur in June 1908. He joined Northfleet in the later half of 1908 and served them for two seasons. James continued his career with Woolwich Arsenal for the third time in October 1910, when turning professional. He made his one and only league appearance when he deputised for the injured Joe Shaw versus Sheffield Wednesday 12th November 1910. He was severely injured which resulted in him being carried off, and finished his career.

	Games	Goals
League	1	0
Friendly Matches	6	0
London League Reserves	5	0
South Eastern League	21	0
Total	**33**	**0**

RANDALL, Charles   1911-14

Birth Place: Burnopfield, Durham
Date of Birth: 1887

Charles Randall, a centre forward, had scored over fifty goals for Northern Junior side Hobson Wanderers in 1907-08, before being snapped up by Newcastle United in May 1908. He spent three seasons with United before being transferred to Woolwich Arsenal for £400 in September 1911. In 1911-12 he was a consistent member of the side, playing in twenty seven league games scoring eight goals which included a hat trick versus Sunderland, after making his Arsenal league debut at Burnden Park versus Bolton Wanderers 7th October 1911. In Arsenal's relegation term, 1912-13, Randall had eight different periods in the side when playing in only fifteen league games, this inconsistency resulted in him playing in only one league game in 1913-14. He moved on to North Shields in the summer of 1914.

	Games	Goals
League	43	12
FA Cup	1	0
Friendly Matches	5	1
London League Reserves	7	2
South Eastern League	30	13
London FA Challenge Cup	2	1
Total	**88**	**29**

RANKIN, Andrew   1891-1893

Birth Place: Glasgow
Date of Birth: 1869

Andrew was a Scottish full back who had played in Scottish junior football for Maryhill, Cowlairs, Airdrie and Glasgow Northern before joining Royal Arsenal in September 1891. In his two seasons with the club he was a key member of the seniors defence. His first class debut was versus Millwall Athletic in an FA Cup Qualifying game on the 19th November 1892. His last senior appearance was in a 0-6 drubbing at Roker Park versus Sunderland in the first round of the FA Cup in 1892-93.

	Games	Goals
FA Cup	3	0
Other Senior Matches	74	2
Other Reserve Matches	13	0
Total	**90**	**2**

RANSOM, Frank   1900-05

Birth Place: Ireland

☛ Frank Ransom was a magnificent servant for Woolwich Arsenal, between joining the club in August 1900, to his departure for Southend United in June 1905. During those five years Frank played in just one first team game, being quite satisfied in being a stalwart for the junior and reserve sides. His solitary league game was versus Leicester Fosse away on Boxing day 1903. He later played in the Southern League with Crystal Palace.

	Games	Goals
League	1	0
Other Senior Matches	2	0
Kent League	36	4
Friendly Matches	36	2
London League	7	0
London League Reserves	91	11
South Eastern League	44	3
Other Youth Matches	4	1
Total	**221**	**21**

Honours:
Kent League Championship
    Medals   1900-01, 1901-02, 1902-03
Two London League Championship
    Medals   1901-02, 1903-04
South Eastern League Championship
    Medal   1903-04
Kent Charity Cup Winners Medal   1904-05

RAYBOULD, Samuel   1908-09

Birth Place: Chesterfield, Derbyshire
Date of Birth: 1875

☛ Samuel Raybould was a young outside right who played for various Derbyshire youth teams. These included Chesterfield Town and Ilkeston Town, before joining Derby County in 1894-95. He played in only four league games for the club, subsequently released spending the following four seasons back in Derbyshire Junior football with Poolsbrook United,a second spell with Ilkeston Town and Bolsover Collier. New Brighton Tower spotted his potential in 1899 and within four months Raybould had been snapped up by Liverpool. At the age of twenty five Samuel had made his breakthrough. Liverpool switched him from outside right to centre forward, with Raybould accepting the challenge with glee. In the following eight seasons at Anfield he played in two hundred and eleven league games scoring one hundred and twenty one league goals, of which his thirty one league goals in 1902-03 stood as a Liverpool record for twenty eight years. He won two League Championship Medals

in 1900-01 and 1906-07, a Second Division Championship Medal in 1904-05 and three Football League Caps. Samuel moved on to Sunderland in 1907, spending one season at Roker Park before joining Woolwich Arsenal in May 1908. In his final season in League football he scored six times (which included a hat trick versus Bury) playing in twenty six league games of which his Arsenal league debut was on the opening day of the season at the Manor Field versus Everton.

	Games	Goals
League	26	6
FA Cup	4	1
Other Senior Matches	1	0
Friendly Matches	1	1
London League Reserves	1	1
South Eastern League	1	2
London FA Challenge Cup	3	0
Total	**37**	**11**

Honours:
(WITH LIVERPOOL)
2 League Championship
    Medals   1900-01, 1906-07
Division Two Championship Medal   1904-05
3 Football League Caps

REECE, George   1895

☛ George Reece spent only a matter of weeks with Woolwich Arsenal after joining the club from the Birmingham junior side, Soho Villa. He played in only two games of which one was in the league when he deputised for Paddy O'Brien at Burslem Port Vale 19th January 1895.

	Games	Goals
League	1	0
Friendly Matches	1	0
Total	**2**	**0**

RIPPON, Willis   1910-11

Birth Place: Beighton, Nr Sheffield, Yorks
Date of Birth: 15th May 1886

☛ Willis Rippon had played junior football for several Sheffield youth sides before joining Bristol City. He spent three seasons at Ashton Gate. Willis was transferred to Woolwich Arsenal in July 1910. In that 1910-11 season he started as the clubs number one centre forward scoring in each of the first two league matches of the season of which his debut was versus Manchester United at Manor Field 1st September 1910. Soon after he lost his place to newly signed John Chalmers. Not happy with reserve team football, he was subsequently transferred

to Brentford in October 1911. He later played for Hamilton Academical, Grimsby Town and Rotherham Town. Died 1956 aged 60.

	Games	Goals
League	9	2
Other Senior Matches	1	1
Friendly Matches	4	6
South Eastern League	23	9
London FA Challenge Cup	2	2
Total	**39**	**20**

ROBERTSON, Alexander   1891-92

☛ Alex was transferred to Woolwich Arsenal in October 1891 from Preston North End. Whilst with Preston he had helped the club to the first ever League Championship of 1888-89. Unfortunately he missed out on winning the double when he was not selected for the FA Cup Final versus Wolverhampton Wanderers. In 1889-90 and 1890-91 he was only regarded as the clubs reserve right half. In his one season at the Invicta Ground he was a stalwart in the senior side. He played in just one FA Cup Tie versus Small Heath 16th January 1892.

	Games	Goals
FA Cup	1	0
Other Senior Matches	29	1
Total	**30**	**1**

ROBERTSON, Hope   1889-90

Birth Place: Glasgow

☛ Hope Robertson was a prolific goal scoring inside forward who joined Royal Arsenal from Scottish junior side Westburn in September 1889. He was a consistent performer in his only season with the club helping the seniors to three Cup Finals. He scored twice on his senior debut versus Lyndhurst in an FA Cup Qualifying game 5th October 1889. He later served Walsall for three seasons 1892-95.

	Games	Goals
FA Cup	4	4
Other Senior Matches	27	24
Other Reserve Matches	1	3
Total	**32**	**31**

Honours:
London Charity Cup Winners
    Medal   1889-90
Kent Senior Cup Winners
    Medal   1889-90
London Senior Cup Finalists
    Medal   1889-90

RODGER, James

1907-08

Birth Place: Scotland

James Rodger was an outside left who had served Paisley, St Mirren and Renton before joining Woolwich Arsenal in June 1907. He was a regular in the club's South Eastern League side of 1907-08 helping them to the League Championship. He played in only one league game, (due to the consistent form on the left flank of David Neave), against Preston 25th January 1908.

	Games	Goals
League	1	0
Friendly Matches	1	1
London League Reserves	11	1
South Eastern League	21	1
Total	**34**	**3**

Honours:
South Eastern League Championship
Medal   1907-08

ROOSE, Dr Leigh

1911-12

Birth Place: Holt, Nr Wrexham, Wales
Date of Birth: 27th November 1877

Leigh Roose was for many years Wales' most capped goalkeeper, playing twenty four times for them between 1900-11. An amateur throughout his career, he started off with Aberystwyth in 1899, followed by London Welsh. Leigh then spent three seasons at Stoke City before moving on to Everton 1904-05. He returned to Stoke for the 1905-06 season, linking up with Sunderland for the seasons 1907-11. This followed moves to Huddersfield Town 1910-11 and Aston Villa, during the summer of 1911. Roose was transferred to Woolwich Arsenal in December 1911 and in his only season at the club he played in thirteen league games. His Arsenal league debut was versus Middlesborough 16th December 1911. A Doctor of bacteriology, Leigh Richmond Roose was described as the most discussed goalkeeper of the time, spectacular and brave, Leslie Knighton the Huddersfield Town manager, said of Roose, "The most notorious practical joker the game had ever seen as well as being the game's most unorthodox goalkeeper". He died in action in France on the 7th October 1916 aged 38.

	Games	Goals
League	13	0
Total	**13**	**0**

Honours:
24 Welsh Caps.

RUSSELL, Albert

1895-1896

Albert Russell, a goalkeeper, who joined Woolwich Arsenal on Boxing Day 1895 after he had played junior football for White Hart, Dartford and New Brompton (now Gillingham) and in the Southern League for Luton and Bristol Rovers. He was signed when the club had a goalkeeping crisis, playing in just one first team game, an FA Cup First Round Tie at Turf Moor versus Burnley which resulted in a 1-6 defeat (one of the club's biggest in FA Cup history) 1st February 1896.

	Games	Goals
FA Cup	1	0
Friendly Matches	2	0
Total	**3**	**0**

RUSSELL, John

1896-97

Birth Place: Carstairs, Lanarks, Scotland
Date of Birth: 29th December 1872

John Russell began his career with the Scottish junior side Glasgow Thistle. Was transferred to Leith Athletic and played for St Mirren 1894-96. He joined Woolwich Arsenal from St Mirren in June 1896. In his one season at the club he took over the left wing position from Frank McAvoy making his league debut in a 3-0 home win versus Burton. He eventually went on to play in twenty three of the last twenty five league games of that season. However, he was transferred to Bristol South East (now Bristol City) during the summer of 1897. Was later on Blackburn Rovers books (but never appeared for the league side). Died August 1905 aged 32.

	Games	Goals
League	23	4
FA Cup	2	0
United League	9	5
Friendly Matches	19	14
Total	**53**	**23**

SANDERS, Moses

1899-1900

Birth Place: Lancashire
Date of Birth: 26th September 1873

Moses Sanders began his footballing career with Crewe Alexandra before moving on to football league outfit Accrington Stanley in 1890. Moved on to Preston in 1891 and in his eight seasons with the club Moses played in well over two hundred first team games, helping them to Division one runners-up in 1891-92 and 1892-93 as well as to the FA Cup Semi Final in that latter season. Sanders joined Woolwich Arsenal in May 1899. His stay was less than eight months, in which

time this talented wing half or inside forward played in only four league games, his Arsenal league debut was on the opening day of the season, a home encounter with Leicester Fosse 2nd September 1899. He later played in the Southern League with Dartford. Died April 1941 aged 67.

	Games	Goals
League	4	1
Kent League	7	1
Friendly Matches	5	1
Southern Combination	3	0
Total	**19**	**3**

SANDS, Percy

1902-19

Birth Place: Norwood, London
Date of Birth: 1881

Percy Sands was one of Arsenal's greatest ever servants in his seventeen years at the club in which time Percy witnessed both the changing of Arsenal's name and ground. His total of three hundred and twenty seven league games was a club record which stood for nearly fifteen years before being broken by Bob John. He started his football career with St Pauls Teachers Training College in Cheltenham and Cheltenham Town before joining Woolwich Arsenal as an amateur in December 1902 (Sands not turning professional until August 1906). This was because he wanted to combine his teacher training with professional football. In 1903-04 he stepped straight in to the first team centre half position when playing in thirty two of the thirty four league games in that promotion winning season. His league debut being on the opening day of the season versus Blackpool 5th September 1903. In the club's first ever season in the top flight, Percy missed only three league games. In 1905-06 and 1906-07 he again was a consistent member of the side helping Arsenal to the 1905-06 FA Cup Semi Final versus Newcastle. In 1907-08 and 1908-09 he again was "Mr Reliable", this being the case right up to the 1913-14 season. In 1914-15 his first team days were virtually finished, his dominance of the number five jersey over the last eleven seasons had been lost to James Buchan. He stayed on the club's books during the wartime period, playing the occassional match. He served his country as a sargeant in the RAMC in France. On the rerurn of peacetime he joined Southend United in the summer of 1919. Percy captained Arsenal on many occassions and during his long career managed to win one major honour, a football league cap in 1905, after he played in England Trial matches between 1903 and 1905. Died December 1965 aged 84.

Percy Sands

	Games	Goals
League	327	10
FA Cup	23	2
Other Senior Matches	2	2
Kent League	3	0
Friendly Matches	10	0
London League	1	0
London League Reserves	1	0
South Eastern League	19	0
London FA Challenge Cup	1	0
Other Youth Matches	1	0
Wartime	19	0
Total	**407**	**14**

Honours:
Southern Professional Charity Cup
   Winners Medal   1905-06
1 Football League Cap

SATTERTHWAITE, Charles   1904-10

Birth Place: Cockermouth, Cumberland
Date of Birth: 1877

Charles was a utility forward who had played junior football for Black Diamond and Workington in the Cumberland League. He then played league football for Bury 1896-97 and Burton Swifts 1897-99. He was transferred to Liverpool in late 1899, spending three seasons with them during which time he helped them to the League Championship in 1900-01. Charles then moved on to New Brompton in the summer of 1902, before joining West Ham in the Southern League for the 1903-04 season. He spent one season with the Hammers, linking up with Woolwich Arsenal in April 1904, joining the club soon after the end of their promotion campaign. In the club's first ever First Division season, Charles finished as the leading goalscorer with eleven goals in thirty games. He holds the record of scoring Arsenal's first ever first division goal at Newcastle, 3rd September 1904, on his debut. In the same season he was good enough to be picked for England Trial Matches. In 1905-06 Charles, noted for his ferocious shooting, played in only eighteen league games, but still found the net on ten occassions. In 1906-07 he enjoyed his most successful season, not only was he ever present, but he again was Arsenal's leading scorer with seventeen goals as well as helping the club to the 1906-07 FA Cup Semi Final. In seasons 1907-08 and 1908-09 his consistency diminished, resulting in him playing in only fifty per cent of first team fixtures. He retired during the summer of 1910. Died May 1948, aged 70.

	Games	Goals
League	129	45
FA Cup	12	3
Other Senior Matches	6	1
Friendly Matches	39	30
London League Reserves	10	8
South Eastern League	35	32
London FA Challenge Cup	4	1
Other Youth Matches	2	0
Total	**237**	**120**

Honours:
(WITH LIVERPOOL)
League Championship Medal   1900-01
(WITH ARSENAL)
Southern Professional Charity Cup
   Winners Medal   1905-06

SATTERTHWAITE, Joseph   1906-08

Birth Place: Cockermouth, Cumberland
Date of Birth: 1885

Joe was playing junior football for Workington when he joined his brother Charles at Woolwich Arsenal in December 1906. Whilst at Manor Field, although being a regular in the club's South Eastern League side, he could never claim a permanent place in the league side. In fact, he had to wait fifteen months after joining the club before making his league debut, versus Manchester United, 21st March 1908. He enjoyed a run of five league appearances, two of them, versus Manchester United and Bolton Wanderers, he was partnered in the forward line by his brother Charles (only the Clapton and Compton brothers have since achieved this distinction). However, after the signing of Samuel Raybould from Sunderland in May 1908, his first team chances were limited, resulting in him moving to Grimsby in November 1908, where he spent one season.

	Games	Goals
League	5	1
Friendly Matches	8	9
London League Reserves	30	35
South Eastern League	44	24
Total	**87**	**69**

Honours:
South Eastern League Championship
   Medals   1906-07, 1907-08
London League Reserve Championship
   Medal   1906-07

SCOTT, W   1888-90

Birth Place:
Date of Birth:

W. Scott was the club's first team choice on the left wing for two seasons, having joined Woolwich Arsenal from Forfar Athletic in September 1888. He played in three FA Cup Qualifying games which included his first team baptism when scoring a hat trick in the 11-0 defeat of Lyndhurst, 5th October 1889.

	Games	Goals
FA Cup	3	4
Other Senior Matches	39	14
Other Reserve Matches	10	5
Total	**52**	**23**

SHANKS, Thomas   1903-1904

Birth Place: Wexford, Ireland
Date of Birth: 1880

Thomas Shanks started out on his footballing career with his home town club, Wexford. He linked up with Derby (West) End before joining Derby County in April 1898. In his three seasons at the baseball ground he could never command a regular first team spot, despite doing well when called upon (scoring five times in twenty seven league games). Thomas moved to Brentford in October 1901. Shanks was transferred to Woolwich Arsenal in January 1903 and during the rest of that 1902-03 season he held down a first team place playing at either inside right or left, of which his Arsenal league debut was at Burslem Port Vale on the 10th January 1903. His Arsenal form had been noted by the Irish selectors and he won the first of his three Irish caps, versus Scotland. In 1903-04, during the club's promotion campaign, he became the first ever Arsenal player to score twenty or more league goals in a season. His total of twenty four was a club record for eleven years and it included four hat tricks versus Leicester Fosse, Lincoln City, Burnley and four versus Grimsby. To the dismay of all the club followers he was transferred to Brentford in May 1904. Thomas later played for Leicester Fosse 1906-09 (for whom he helped to promotion to Division one in 1907-08). Finished his career back in London, with Leyton 1909 and Clapton Orient 1911.

	Games	Goals
League	44	28
FA Cup	4	1
Other Senior Matches	2	0
Friendly Matches	4	2
London League	10	7
Total	**64**	**38**

Honours:
(WITH ARSENAL AND BRENTFORD)
3 Irish Caps

(WITH ARSENAL)
Southern Professional Cup Finalists
Medal   1903-04

SHARP, James   1905-08

Birth Place: Alyth, Perthshire, Scotland
Date of Birth: 11th October 1880

James Sharp

☛ Jimmy Sharp was probably the finest left back the club had had up to the outbreak of World War One. He began his career with Dundee youth side East Craigie before joining Dundee during the 1899-1900 season. James spent five seasons at Dens Park, 1899-1904, helping the club to the Scottish Championship runners-up position in 1902-03, winning the first of his five Scottish caps versus Wales in 1903-04 and two Scottish League caps. He moved South of the border when joining Fulham, in the Southern League for the 1904-05 season. James was transferred to Woolwich Arsenal in June 1905. In 1905-06 he missed only three league games as well as helping the club to the 1905-06 FA Cup Semi Final, his Arsenal league debut being on the opening day of the season versus Liverpool, 2nd September 1905. In the following term Sharp played in thirty six of the club's thirty eight league games as well as making another FA Semi Final appearance, versus Sheffield Wednesday. This sturdy little full back played in a further thirty two league games and won three more Scottish caps, in 1907-08, before being transferred to Glasgow Rangers for £400 in April 1908. His stay at Ibrox was only nine months, Fulham paying £1,000 for his services in January 1909. He spent the best part of four seasons back at Craven Cottage before joining neighbours Chelsea (after a short spell in the USA) for £1,750 in late 1912. Sharp enjoyed three seasons at Stamford Bridge before the outbreak of World War One. He officially retired during the war, returning to Fulham as trainer in 1919. However, when Fulham's inside left Harold Crockford, missed the clubs bus to an away game at Bury in 1920, James

filled in at the helm, and at the age of forty, he scored his one and only goal for the Craven Cottage outfit. He later coached at Walsall and Cliftonville. Died November 1949 aged 69.

	Games	Goals
League	103	4
FA Cup	13	1
Other Senior Matches	6	1
Friendly Matches	7	0
Total	**129**	**6**

Honours:
(WITH ARSENAL AND DUNDEE)
5 Scottish Caps
(WITH DUNDEE)
2 Scottish League Caps
(WITH ARSENAL)
Southern Professional Charity Cup Winners
Medal   1905-06

SHARPE, William   1894-95

☛ William Sharpe was yet another inside left who was playing for Loughborough Town when signing for Woolwich Arsenal in May 1894. He made his league debut on the opening day of the season at the newly built Sincil Bank Ground versus Lincoln City, 1st September 1894, which resulted in a 2-5 defeat in front of a 2,000 crowd. He had to be content that season in sharing the left wing position with Peter Mortimer, eventually playing in thirteen league games and scoring four goals. He departed for pastures new in August 1895 when he joined Glossop North End.

	Games	Goals
League	13	4
FA Cup	1	0
Friendly Matches	22	6
Other Youth Matches	2	0
Total	**38**	**10**

SHAW, Bernard   1891-92

Birth Place: Sheffield, Yorkshire
Date of Birth: 1866

☛ Bernard Shaw had appeared for three clubs that at this stage had not reached league status, Sheffield Wednesday, Wolverhampton Wanderers and Sheffield United, from whom he joined Woolwich Arsenal in September 1891. In his one and only season at the club, Bernard was a prolific goalscoring forward for the senior side. He made just one first class appearance in a Round One FA Cup Tie versus Small Heath (now Birmingham City) 16th January 1892.

	Games	Goals
FA Cup	1	0
Other Senior Matches	42	23
Other Reserve Matches	6	5
Total	**49**	**28**

SHAW, Herbert   1898-1900

☛ Herbert Shaw was a utility forward who joined Woolwich Arsenal from the junior club side, Haverton Hill, of Durham in December 1898. He gained the left wing position (from Mitchell and Dailly) making his league debut in a 6-2 home win versus Luton Town on New Years Eve 1898. He did well scoring seven goals in sixteen appearances including braces versus Burton and Barnsley. However, after the signing of James Tennant in May 1899, Herbert's league appearances were limited, even though he scored twice in his first game of the 1899-90 season versus Middlesbrough. Finished up playing in ten league games that season and was released from his contract during the summer of 1900.

	Games	Goals
League	26	9
FA Cup	4	0
United League	6	3
Kent League	12	5
Friendly Matches	14	0
Southern Combination	4	0
Other Youth Matches	2	0
Total	**68**	**17**

SHAW, Walter   1893-1895

Birth Place: Small Heath, Birmingham
Date of Birth: 1870

☛ Walter Shaw was transferred to Woolwich Arsenal from junior side Birmingham St Georges in January 1893. He made his league debut in the club's first ever league match, versus Newcastle United at the Manor Field on the 2nd September 1893. He holds the distinction of having scored the club's first ever league goal, in a season, when he finished joint top league goalscorer with James Henderson, scoring eleven times in seventeen league appearances. This included a hat trick at Lynthorpe Road versus Middlesbrough in a 6-3, victory 24th February 1894. In 1894-95 he was left out in the cold after the summer signings of fellow forwards (Boyd, Buchanan and O'Brien). He was released at the end of the 1894-95 season when he returned to Birmingham.

	Games	Goals
League	19	11
FA Cup	5	1
Other Senior Matches	23	16
Friendly Matches	41	39
Other Reserve Matches	1	1
Other Youth Matches	3	2
Total	**92**	**70**

SHORTT, Matthew   1910

Birth Place: Dumfries, Scotland
Date of Birth: 5th February 1889

☛ Matthew Shortt's career with Woolwich Arsenal is ironically, one of the shortest on record, for it lasted less than seven weeks. He joined the club from Dumfries in November 1910. In his short stay he played in four league games (all defeats) as an inside forward. His debut was versus Newcastle United at the Manor Field 26th November 1910. He returned to Scotland in January 1911, when he joined Kilmarnock. He gave them thirteen years fantastic service, switching to the centre half position. He died in his home town in June 1974 aged 85.

	Games	Goals
League	4	0
South Eastern League	4	1
Total	**8**	**1**

SHREWSBURY, Thomas   1896-1900

☛ Thomas Shrewsbury was transferred to Woolwich Arsenal from Darwen during the summer of 1896. He had appeared in three league games at half back with them in the previous season. Although Thomas spent four seasons with the club, he managed to play in only three league games, playing for the reserves in the Kent League and Friendly Games. He played in two league games in 1896-97, his debut being versus Notts County at the Manor Field 26th September 1896. This was followed in 1897-98 when he appeared in just one league game. In his final two seasons with the club he did not appear in the league side.

	Games	Goals
League	3	0
FA Cup	3	0
United League	6	0
Kent League	47	0
Friendly Matches	61	1
Southern Combination	1	0
Other Youth Matches	2	0
Total	**123**	**1**

Honours:
Kent League Championship Medal   1896-97

SINCLAIR, Finlay   1896-97

Birth Place: Glasgow
Date of Birth: 18th June 1871

☛ Finlay Sinclair was Glasgow Rangers reserve full back when he joined Woolwich Arsenal in June 1896. He had

previously played junior football for Elderslie and Linthouse. At the Manor Field he blossomed as the club's first choice left back in 1896-97. He made his league debut at Hyde Road versus Manchester City on the opening day of the season, 5th September 1896. He played in twenty six of thirty league games. He surprisingly left the club during the summer of 1897 when he linked up with Bristol City.

	Games	Goals
League	26	0
FA Cup	2	0
United League	11	0
Friendly Matches	16	0
Total	**55**	**0**

SLADE, Donald   1913-14

Birth Place: Southampton, Hampshire
Date of Birth: 26th November 1888

☛ Donald Slade was a centre forward who began his career in the Southern League with Southampton (1910-1912), later joining Lincoln City (1912-13) before being transferred to to the newly named Arsenal for £1,000 in December 1913. The fee was not well spent in the sense that his twelve league games for the side cost the club nearly £100 for each appearance. His Arsenal league debut being a local derby at Clapton Orient, 13th December 1913. He moved on to Fulham in May 1914. Later playing for Dundee. Died in March 1980 aged 91.

	Games	Goals
League	12	4
Friendly Matches	1	1
London League Reserves	8	2
South Eastern League	8	5
Total	**29**	**12**

SPICER, Thomas   1900-01

☛ Thomas Spicer had played junior football for Sheppey United (now Fisher Athletic) when he joined Woolwich Arsenal from Brighton United in April 1900. A goalkeeper, he was signed as reserve team cover for Thomas Hamilton to understudy for the injured first team keeper Roger Ord. His first two league games for the club are quite unique, in that they were over only a three day period playing home and away to Grimsby Town. In 1900-01 he started the season as the club's first choice keeper playing in the first two league games versus Gainsborough Trinity and Walsall. However, it was not long before, new signing, Jimmy Ashcroft became the club's

number one custodian. Spicer finding himself, doomed to reserve team football for the rest of the season. Was released in the summer of 1901. He later played for Leyton and Brentford.

	Games	Goals
League	4	0
Kent League	9	0
Friendly Matches	12	0
London League Reserves	18	0
Total	**43**	**0**

Honours:
Kent League Championship Medal   1900-01

STEVENS, Andrew   1897-98

Birth Place: Scotland

☛ Andrew Stevens was transferred to Woolwich Arsenal from the Scottish junior side Bathgate FC in May 1897. An inside right, he made his league debut when scoring in the home game versus Grimsby Town on the opening day of the season, 1st September 1897. He played in the first five games of the season before losing his place after two heavy defeats at Newcastle and Burnley. He was not chosen again for first team duties and it came as no surprise when he moved on to Dartford in January 1898.

	Games	Goals
League	5	1
FA Cup	1	1
Friendly Matches	8	3
Total	**14**	**5**

STEVENS, Robert   1909-10

Birth Place: Maryhill, Glasgow
Date of Birth: 1886

☛ Robert Stevens, a utility forward, was signed by Woolwich Arsenal from Glasgow Rangers in November 1909. He made his league debut within twenty four hours of signing for the club at Hillsborough versus Sheffield Wednesday, 13th November 1909. He kept his place for the following three league games but lost it to Charles Lewis. He played in a further three league games that season. With an abundance of inside forwards on the clubs books, he was released during the summer of 1910.

	Games	Goals
League	7	1
Friendly Matches	5	0
South Eastern League	12	2
Other Youth Matches	1	0
Total	**25**	**3**

STEVENSON, Robert — 1894-95

Birth Place: Barrhead, Glasgow, Scotland
Date of Birth: 1869

Robert Stevenson had been on the books of Third Lanark when joining Woolwich Arsenal in May 1894. In his one and only season with the club, 1894-95, he alternated between all three half back positions in his and the club's first seven league games of the season his debut being away at Lincoln City (on the opening day of the season 1st September 1894). He was released by the club in March 1895 when he joined Thames Iron Works (now West Ham United).

	Games	Goals
League	7	0
Friendly Matches	19	4
Total	**26**	**4**

STEWART, William — 1889-1893

Birth Place: Dundee, Scotland
Date of Birth: 1867

William Stewart had played Scottish junior football in Edinburgh and Dundee before coming south when he linked up with Kidderminster Harriers. He joined Royal Arsenal in October 1889 and in his four (pre-league) seasons with the club he was a mainstay of the defence in the senior side. His first class debut was in an FA Cup Qualifying match versus Swifts 7th December 1889. When he left the club he, like so many others of the time, worked and played for the Royal Ordanance.

	Games	Goals
FA Cup	2	0
Other Senior Matches	58	2
Other Reserve Matches	33	5
Total	**93**	**7**

Honours:
London Senior Cup Winners Medal 1890-91

STONLEY, Stephen — 1913-14

Birth Place: Sunderland
Date of Birth: 1891

Stephen Stonley was playing junior football in the North Eastern League with Newcastle City when joining Woolwich Arsenal in February 1913. Within twenty four hours of joining the club he made his Arsenal league debut in a home fixture versus Oldham 8th February 1913. In that relegation season he finished up playing in eleven of the club's last twelve league games. The club, now back in Division two, with a new name and playing at a new ground, found Stephen in that 1913-14 season as the club's leading marksman in the football league with thirteen goals in twenty eight matches, this including a hat trick at Bradford Park Avenue on Christmas Day 1913. He was surprisingly transferred to Brentford in June 1914.

	Games	Goals
League	38	14
FA Cup	1	0
Other Senior Matches	1	1
Friendly Matches	2	6
London League Reserves	3	2
South Eastern League	7	11
London FA Challenge Cup	2	0
Total	**54**	**34**

STORER, Harry — 1894-95

Birth Place: Butterley, Derbyshire
Date of Birth: 24th July 1870

Harry Storer came from a very famous football and cricketing family. Harry played football for Gainsborough Trinity, Loughborough Town Woolwich Arsenal and Liverpool, playing cricket for Derbyshire. His brother William played football for Derby County, Loughborough Town and Glossop North End, playing cricket for Derbyshire and England. Harry's son Harry Junior played football for Grimsby Town, Derby County, Burnley and England. He later managed Coventry City (twice), Birmingham City and Derby County also playing county cricket for Derbyshire. Harry had joined Woolwich Arsenal from Loughborough Town in May 1894, a goalkeeper, he was the first player to win representative honours whilst on Arsenal's books a football league cap in 1895. Missed only two league games in 1894-95, his Arsenal league was debut versus Lincoln City 1st September 1894. Storer played in the first twelve league games of the 1895-96 season before being suspended by the club for four weeks in November 1895 for a breach of discipline. He was eventually transferred to Liverpool in December 1895, playing in over one hundred first team games for the club between 1895-1900, helping them to the Second Division Championship in 1895-96 and to the First Division runner-up position in 1898-99. Harry died of comsumption in April 1908 aged 37.

	Games	Goals
League	40	0
FA Cup	1	0
Kent League	1	0
Friendly Matches	35	0
Other Youth Matches	1	0
Total	**78**	**0**

Honours:
(WITH ARSENAL)
1 Football League Cap
(WITH LIVERPOOL)
Second Division Championship
Medal 1895-96

STORRS, J A — 1893-95

J A Storrs was yet another soldier who played for Woolwich Arsenal having joined them from the Lincolnshire Regiment in August 1893. He had a rapid rise to fame winning himself a regular first team spot at left back after making his league debut in the club's fourth match of the season at home to Grimsby Town 25th September 1893. He played in eleven consecutive league games, but after a run of disastrous results which included 0-6 at Newcastle, 1-4 at Small Heath, 0-5 at home to Liverpool and 2-6 at Burton Swifts, he found himself back in the reserve team. In 1894-95 with new signing John Caldwell being everpresent at left back, Storrs was reduced to playing in only reserve team friendly matches. He left the club in the summer of 1895.

	Games	Goals
League	12	0
FA Cup	4	0
Friendly Matches	53	2
Other Youth Matches	3	0
Total	**72**	**2**

STUART, James — 1897

Birth Place: Coatbridge, Scotland

James Stuart was a centre forward who forced himself in to the Blackburn Rovers team in 1894-95, scoring four goals in thirteen league games. However, after Rovers signed Turnbull during the summer of 1895, he found himself in the wilderness for the following two seasons. Transferred to Woolwich Arsenal in September 1897, his stay was of less than three months. He played in two league games, scoring on his debut at home to Luton Town 9th October 1897. He was released from his contract in December when he joined New Brompton (now Gillingham).

	Games	Goals
League	2	1
United League	1	0
Friendly Matches	4	4
Total	**7**	**5**

SWANN, Andrew — 1901

Birth Place: Dalbeattie, Scotland
Date of Birth: 1878

Andrew Swann was a prolific scoring centre forward who made his name with Lincoln City in 1989-98 when scoring ten times in only thirteen league games. With a pay restraint being placed on football league players Andrew moved in to the Southern League to play for New Brompton (now Gillingham) in 1899-1900. In 1900-01 he returned to the Football League to play for Barnsley when he had an exceptional season finishing as Division two's leading goalscorer with eighteen goals. This made Woolwich Arsenal take note of his prowess in front of goal and within a week of the end of the 1900-01 season Arsenal had captured the man who they thought would end their goalscoring crisis (their leading scorer in that previous season had been Gaudie with only eight goals). However, although scoring on his Arsenal league debut in the opening game of the season versus Barnsley the move did not suit either player or club and within seven months of joining them he had moved on to Stockport County. Later played for Tottenham Hotspur back in the Southern League.

	Games	Goals
League	7	2
Kent League	1	1
Friendly Matches	1	0
London League	1	0
London League Reserves	2	2
Total	**12**	**5**

TALBOT, Arthur   1896-97

🖙 Arthur Talbot signed for Woolwich Arsenal from the Staffordshire side Hednesford Town in November 1896 as goalkeeping cover for the club's first choice goalkeepers, William Fairclough and John Leather. Poor Arthur Talbot was on the receiving end, in only his second league game, of the club's biggest ever league defeat in history, 0-8 away at Loughborough Town. His debut was a happier affair with Arsenal winning 3-2 at Sincil Bank versus Lincoln 5th December 1896. It came as no surprise (after conceding sixteen goals in only five games) that he was demoted back to the Kent League side.

	Games	Goals
League	5	0
United League	1	0
Kent League	5	0
Friendly Matches	7	0
Total	**18**	**0**

TENNANT, James   1899-1901

Birth Place: Glasgow, Scotland
Date of Birth: 1878

🖙 James had played junior football in Scotland for Linton Villa, Parkhead and St Bernards before joining Woolwich Arsenal in May 1899. In 1899-1900 he was a key

TEMPLETON, Robert   1904-06

Birth Place: Ayrshire, Scotland
Date of Birth: 22nd June 1879

Robert Templeton

🖙 Robert Bryson Templeton was one of the great personalities of British football. A showman, known as the "Edwardian Dandy" or "The Prince of Dribblers". The quotes, which have been used to describe Templeton, have been, "A Tactical Genius", "Brilliant", "He had everything, speed, control, shooting and centring ability", "Amazing dribbler", "Wonderful winger", "Mercurial", on the other hand, "Temperamental", "Erratic", "Selfish", "Moody", "Wayward and "Irresponsible". To put Robert Templeton in a nutshell, he is best described by William Pickford, who wrote in 1905, "Bobby is the delight and the despair of thousands, to watch Templeton at his best was a sight for the gods to watch him at his worst was to see at a glance the frailty of things human". Robert began his footballing career with Kilmarnock in 1895 before being transferred to Hibernian in 1897. He joined Aston Villa in March 1899 playing in one league game in Villa's 1898-99 championship winning season. In 1899-1900 he just qualified for a league championship

medal when playing in eleven league games. He spent a further three seasons at Villa Park winning the first of his eleven Scottish caps versus England 1901-02 before being transferred to Newcastle United for £400 in February 1903. In 1904-05 he missed out on a league championship medal when playing only ten league games. He signed for Woolwich Arsenal from Newcastle for £375 in December 1904 making his Arsenal league debut at Notts County (in a 5-1 victory) 17th December 1904. In his two seasons at Manor Field he played in only thirty four of the clubs seventy six league games but was a member of the side that reached the 1906 FA Cup Semi Final versus Newcastle. Robert returned North of the border in May 1906 when he joined Glasgow Celtic for £250, and was a member of that great Celtic side which won the league and cup double that season. He then moved back home when joining Kilmarnock in October 1907. Templeton stayed six seasons with his home town club before returning south when joining Fulham in June 1913. He spent two seasons at Craven Cottage before the outbreak of world war one. He returned to Kilmarnock in 1915. The last legacy which can be attributed to Robert Bryson Templeton, that it has often been claimed that he was the indirect cause of "The Ibrox disaster" in 1902 after the crowd swayed, attempting to see one of his amazing dribbles. Died November 1919 aged 40.

	Games	Goals
League	33	1
FA Cup	8	0
Other Senior Matches	2	0
Friendly Matches	8	0
Total	**51**	**1**

Honours:
Eleven Scottish Caps.
(WITH KILMARNOCK)
3 Scottish League Caps.
(WITH ASTON VILLA)
League Championship Medal   1899-1900
(WITH CELTIC)
Scottish League Championship
  Medal   1906-07
Scottish Cup Winners Medal   1906-07

member of the Woolwich side playing in twenty six of the club's thirty four league games, in which he scored two goals, in the record 12-0 league victory versus Loughborough Town after making his league debut at home to Leicester Fosse 2nd September 1899. In 1900-01 he retained his first team place on the left wing. However, three days after the end of that 1899-1900 season Arsenal could not resist a £180 transfer bid for Tennant and Peter Turner from Middlesborough where he spent one season helping the club to promotion from Division Two, playing in

sixteen league games scoring eight goals. He later played for three seasons in 1902-05 for Watford, helping them to the Southern League Second Division Championship in 1903-04.

	Games	Goals
League	51	8
FA Cup	3	2
Kent League	3	3
Friendly Matches	16	7
London League Reserves	3	2
Southern Combination	12	5
Total	**88**	**27**

THEOBALD, Stephen   1900-1909

Birth Place: Plumstead, London
Date of Birth:

☛ Stephen Theobald was a magnificent servant for Woolwich Arsenal during nine seasons at the turn of the century. Stephen, a centre half, played in only twenty four league games during his time with the club, being quite content as a reserve to a succession of fine pivots which included John Dick, Percy Sands and Thomas Hynds. He originally joined Woolwich Arsenal from junior side St Andrews (Woolwich) in October 1900. He had to wait over two years before his league baptism versus Burton United on Christmas Day 1902. Stephen played in only one other league game that season, before enduring another two years wait for his next senior opportunity. The 1905-06 season was definitely Theobald's most productive fourteen outings for the first team. However, in his last three seasons at the Manor Field he was confined to reserve team action barring the odd first team call up. His loyalty was rewarded by a succession of junior and reserve team honours.

	Games	Goals
League	24	0
Other Senior Matches	8	0
Kent League	18	1
Friendly Matches	48	3
London League	5	0
London League Reserves	100	5
South Eastern League	108	6
London FA Challenge Cup	3	0
Other Youth Matches	2	0
Total	**316**	**15**

Honours:
Southern Professional Charity Cup
 Winners Medal   1905-06
4 South Eastern League Championship Medals
        1903-04, 1905-06, 1906-07, 1907-08
3 London League Reserve Championship
 Medals   1901-02, 1903-04, 1906-07
2 Kent League Championship
 Medals   1901-02, 1902-03
Kent Charity Cup Winners Medal   1904-05

THOMSON, Matthew   1908-14

Birth Place: Maryhill, Glasgow
Date of Birth: 1887

☛ Matthew Thomson was on his home town club's books, Maryhill FC. when joining Woolwich Arsenal in June 1908 after he had played whilst on trial in the club's summer Scottish tour of 1908. In his first season at Manor Field he had to be content in being deputy to the ever reliable Percy Sands, playing in only three league games which included his league debut in a home fixture with Middlesbrough 17th March 1909.

In 1909-10 he won a regular place in the side when he played in thirty league games (taking over from Sands) However, in the following season Sands bounced back and Matthew, in that 1910-11 season had to be satisfied in playing in only half of the club's league encounters. Much was the same in 1911-12, when Sands strengthened his hold, Thomson playing in just seven league games. After the departure of Andy Ducat, he switched from the number five to the number four shirt and partnered his rival in the majority of league games in that relegation season of 1912-13. In 1913-14, after the club had moved to Highbury, he found himself out in the cold again after the signing of George Jobey from Newcastle United and at the end of that season in May1914, he was transferred to Swindon Town.

	Games	Goals
League	89	1
FA Cup	5	0
Other Senior Matches	6	1
Friendly Matches	29	5
London League Reserves	16	1
South Eastern League	83	0
London FA Challenge Cup	8	0
Other Youth Matches	1	0
Total	**237**	**8**

THORPE, Harold   1903-04

Birth Place: Barrow Hill, Derbyshire
Date of Birth: 1880

☛ Harold Thorpe began his career in Derbyshire Junior Football, before joining his local League club Chesterfield in 1900. He spent three seasons there of which two were as the club's regular left back. He moved on to Woolwich Arsenal in April 1903. His stay at the Manor Field was of just one season, the 1903-04 promotion season in which Harold played in ten league games making his debut on the opening day of the campaign in a 3 - 0 home victory versus Blackpool 5th September 1903. But his appearances were being restricted because of the emergence after injury of "Archie" Cross. He was transferred to Fulham during the summer of 1904 where he helped them to Southern League Championship in 1906-07. He later played for Leicester Fosse 1907, died September 1908 aged 29.

	Games	Goals
League	10	0
Other Senior Matches	2	0
Friendly Matches	2	0
London League	8	0
London League Reserves	1	0
South Eastern League	5	0
Total	**28**	**0**

Honours:
(WITH FULHAM)
Southern League Championships   1906-07

TURNER, Peter   1900-01

Birth Place: Scotland

☛ Peter Turner, like his close friend James Tennant, had played Scottish Junior Football for Parkhead and St. Bernards before joining James at Woolwich Arsenal in May 1900. In his one season at the club 1900-01 Peter missed just one league game whilst playing in virtually every forward position, his league debut, playing alongside Tennant to form the club's left wing, versus Gainsborough Trinity on the opening day of the season 1st September 1900, (Turner scoring the opening goal in a 2-1 victory). He was transferred to Middlesbrough with James Tennant in a package deal in May 1901, and in his only season at the club 1901-02 he helped Middlesbrough to promotion to Division One when playing in twenty three league games scoring six goals. He later played in the Southern league for Luton Town 1902-04 before teaming up again with James Tennant at Watford in May 1904. He finished his career playing with Leyton and Doncaster.

	Games	Goals
League	33	5
FA Cup	3	0
Friendly Matches	9	2
Total	**45**	**7**

VAUGHAN, John   1900-03

☛ John Vaughan joined Woolwich Arsenal from North London local football in November 1900, signing league forms the following month. In his three seasons with the club he was a permanent fixture in the club's London League Reserve and Kent League teams. Managed to play in only one first team game, an FA Cup Supplementary Round match at home to Luton 14th December 1901. He later played for Millwall.

	Games	Goals
FA Cup	1	0
Other Senior Matches	1	0
Kent League	31	13
Friendly Matches	17	9
London League	2	1
London League Reserves	48	17
Other Youth Matches	3	0
Total	**103**	**40**

Honours:
Three Kent League Championship
Medals   1900-01, 1901-02, 1902-03
London League Reserve Championship
Medal   1901-02

WARD, Allen   1895-96

Birth Place: Parkgate, Barnsley, Yorks
Date of Birth: 1872

Allen Ward had played junior football for Barnsley St Peters before playing for Sheffield Wednesday (1893-94) and Burton Wanderers (1894-95) from whom he joined Woolwich Arsenal in May 1895. He immediately gained a first team place at left half playing in the first seven league games of the 1895-96 season, which included his league debut versus Grimsby Town at home 2nd September 1895. However, he was suspended by the club for a breach of discipline for six months in November 1895 and was released from his contract at the end of the season.

	Games	Goals
League	7	0
Friendly Matches	5	0
Total	**12**	**0**

WATSON, Robert   1903-05

Birth Place: Middlesbrough
Date of Birth: 1883

Robert began his league career with his home town club Middlesbrough in 1902 after he played junior football for South Bank. He could not command a regular place at Lynthorpe Road (during Middlesbrough's last season there before moving to Ayresome Park) and was subsequently transferred to Woolwich Arsenal in June 1903. In his two seasons at the club, (of which 1903-04 was Woolwich Arsenal's promotion season), Robert had to be content in playing only nine league games, six in 1903-04 and three in 1904-05. His Arsenal league debut being versus Bolton Wanderers at home 26th March 1904. Not happy with reserve team football, he joined Leeds City in July 1905. He stayed there for three seasons playing in nearly one hundred first team games before finishing his career playing with Rochdale, Exeter and Stallybridge Celtic. He will be remembered in his Woolwich Arsenal days for scoring seven times in a 26-1 victory versus Paris Eleven at Plumstead in December 1904.

	Games	Goals
League	9	1
FA Cup	1	0
Other Senior Matches	2	0
Friendly Matches	11	9
London League	7	1

London League Reserves	21	15
South Eastern League	24	15
Total	**75**	**41**

Honours:
Southern Professional Charity Cup
Finalists Medal   1903-04
South Eastern League Championship
Medal   1903-04
London League Reserves Championship
Medal   1903-04

WHITE, William   1897-1899

Birth Place:
Date of Birth:

William White joined Woolwich Arsenal in May 1897 from the Scottish club Heart of Midlothian. An inside forward, William was pressed straight into league duties when making his debut on the opening day of the season, when scoring in a 4-1 victory at the Manor Field versus Grimsby Town 1st September 1897. William played in twenty three league games that season scoring six goals. In 1898-99, although doing well scoring ten times in sixteen games (this including a hat trick versus Newton Heath, (now Manchester United) He was transferred to New Brompton (now Gillingham) in March 1899. White later played for Queens Park Rangers 1900-01 and Liverpool 1901-02, making a sensational league debut for them when scoring in the second minute of a Merseyside Derby at Goodison Park versus Everton.

	Games	Goals
League	39	16
FA Cup	3	0
United League	22	11
Kent League	4	4
Friendly Matches	10	5
Other Youth Matches	1	1
Total	**79**	**37**

WHITFIELD, Job   1896-1897

Job Whitfield joined Woolwich Arsenal from the junior side Houghton-Le-Ware in December 1896. He spent less than three weeks at the club in which time he filled in at right back when the club had hit a defensive crisis. His debut started on a bright note which was a home encounter versus Blackpool 19th December 1896. However, his second league game was in a 1-4 away defeat at Darwen. He left the club soon after.

	Games	Goals
League	2	0
Total	**2**	**0**

WILLIAMS, Charles   1891-94

Birth Place: Welling, Kent.
Date of Birth: 19th November, 1873

Charles Williams was a goalkeeper who played junior football for Phoenix and Erith in local Kent leagues before joining Royal Arsenal in November 1891, signing league forms eighteen months later in June 1893. In his first two seasons with the club (in the pre-league days) he alternated between reserve and senior side football. In the club's first ever football league season Charles was mainly the regular goalkeeper, playing in nineteen league games and although doing well in most, he was on the end of some considerable defeats, none more so than in a three game period when the club lost 0-6 at Newcastle, 1-4 at Small Heath and in a miserable 0-5 home reverse versus Liverpool, this after making his league debut in the club's first ever league match versus Newcastle 2nd September 1893. With the club not happy with the goal keeping position, they signed Loughborough Town's goalkeeper Harry Storer in May 1894. This resulted in Williams being transferred to Manchester City in June 1894. This proved to be a mistake by the Woolwich club, Charles Williams over the following eight seasons developed into one of the top goalkeepers in the country. Whilst with City he played in nearly two hundred and fifty first team games (missing only one league game in seasons 1898-99 and 1900-01 and being everpresent in 1899 -1900). Whilst at Hyde Road he won a Second Division Championship medal 1898-99 and a football league cap against the Irish in 1899. He saved his claim to fame when becoming one of the first goalkeepers to score with a huge clearance at Roker Park, versus Sunderland on the 14th April 1900. He left the club after the relegation season of 1901-02. He later played for Tottenham Hotspur 1902-05, Norwich City and Brentford before becoming Manager with the French club Lille. He died whilst living in South America in 1952 aged 78.

	Games	Goals
League	19	0
FA Cup	4	0
Other Senior Matches	29	0
Friendly Matches	32	0
Other Reserve Matches	3	0
Total	**87**	**0**

Honours:
(WITH MANCHESTER CITY)
Division Two Championship Medal   1898-99
1 Football League Cap

WILLIAMS, Edward — 1889-90

☛ Edward Williams spent just one season at Royal Arsenal in 1889-90. He played spasdmodically for the club this included his only first team outing, an FA Cup qualifying game versus Swifts 7th December 1889.

	Games	Goals
FA Cup	1	0
Other Senior Matches	6	4
Other Reserve Matches	9	4
Total	**16**	**8**

WILLIAMS, Walter — 1893-95

☛ Walter Williams joined Woolwich Arsenal from junior side Bostal Rovers a an amateur in November 1893. He did not sign professional until the following November. A utility forward, he was quite happy to play mainly friendly games for the reserves, although he did have one opportunity in the league side in the club's first season in the league when he played inside left in a home encounter versus Crewe Alexandra on the 10th February 1894.

	Games	Goals
League	1	0
Kent League	10	7
Friendly Matches	49	19
Other Youth Matches	3	2
Total	**63**	**28**

WILSON, Jack — 1896-97

☛ Jack Wilson was a versitile player who could play admirably at either left back or outside right. In his only season at the club he played in the majority of his matches for the Kent League side. However, he did play in one FA Cup Tie when the club fielded five reserves in a fourth round qualifying tie at home to Leyton 12th December 1896. This was the same day that the alleged Arsenal first team were being beaten 8-0 at Loughborough Town. He later played and coached at Watford.

	Games	Goals
FA Cup	1	0
Kent League	9	3
Friendly Matches	6	3
Total	**16**	**6**

Honours:
Kent League Championship Medal 1906-07

WILSON, Oliver — 1912-13

☛ Oliver Wilson was a goalkeeper who was yet another player who joined the club from the East London junior side Leyton, this being in, September 1912. In 1912-13 he was the clubs regular custodian in the South Eastern League side. With the presence of fellow goalkeepers (Crawford and McDonald) his chances in the league side were limited and he played in only the last game of the season (the last ever home game at the Manor Field) in a 1-1 draw versus Middlesbrough 26th April 1913.

	Games	Goals
League	1	0
Friendly Matches	2	0
South Eastern League	21	0
London FA Challenge Cup	1	0
Total	**25**	**0**

WINSHIP, Thomas — 1910-13 & 1913-15

Birth Place: Wallsend, Newcastle-upon-Tyne
Date of Birth: 1890

☛ Thomas Winship was a diminutive outside left standing only five feet four inches and was affectionately known as both "Tiny" and "Wee". Thomas joined Woolwich Arsenal in November 1910 from the Northern junior side Wallsend Park Villa, making rapid progress when selected for his league debut at Manchester United on Boxing Day 1910. He had a six game spell in the side before losing his place to Charlie Lewis. In 1911-12 much was the same with "Tiny" finding himself third choice left winger to John Flanagan and Lewis. In the club's dreadful 1912-13 relegation campaign, Winship scored twice in fourteen games before moving on to Fulham in March 1913. Resigned for the club in August 1913. He was one of the last players to leave the Manor Field and then became one of the first to join the club at Highbury, making his return league debut in the first ever league game at the ground versus Leicester Fosse 6th September 1913. Eventually figured in fourteen league games that season. After another twelve league appearances in 1914-15. The club lost contact with Thomas during the years of the First World War but after hostilities finished he resumed his career with Darlington 1919-1926, helping them win Division 3 North in 1924-25 season.

	Games	Goals
League	55	7
FA Cup	1	0
Other Senior Matches	2	0
Friendly Matches	10	13
London League Reserves	9	1
South Eastern League	52	8
London FA Challenge Cup	3	2
Other Youth Matches	1	0
Total	**133**	**31**

Honours:
(WITH DARLINGTON)
Division Three North Championship
Medal 1924-25

WOLFE, George — 1900-03

Birth Place: East London

☛ George Wolfe was a centre half who had played junior football for Northfleet and Folkestone before joining Woolwich Arsenal in March 1900. In his three seasons with the club he was a regular member of the clubs reserve teams of that era. His league opportunities were restricted by the dominance, in that position, of John Dick. However, he did manage to play in three league games in 1900-01 which included his debut versus Burslem Port Vale at the Manor Field 8th December 1900. George spent all of season 1901-02 playing reserve team football before returning to league action to replace the injured James Jackson at left back in December 1902. Wolfe left the club to play Southern League Football for Swindon Town during the summer of 1903. Later joined Nottingham Forest during the summer of 1905 serving them well for six seasons playing in over one hundred and twenty league games, winning a Second Division Championship Medal in 1906-07. However, his career finished on a sour note when the club were relegated to Division Two in 1910-11.

	Games	Goals
League	5	0
Other Senior Matches	1	0
Kent League	32	3
Friendly Matches	25	5
London League	6	0
London League Reserves	45	2
Other Youth Matches	2	0
Total	**116**	**10**

Honours:
(WITH NOTTINGHAM FOREST)
Division Two Championship
Medal 1906-07
(WITH ARSENAL)
Three Kent League Championship
Medals 1900-01, 1901-02, 1902-03
London League Reserve Championship
Medal 1901-02

WOOD — 1892

Mr Wood is one of Arsenal football club's statisticians nightmares, no one seems to know his christian name! However, we do know he was yet another soldier who appeared for the club at the time. He appeared in one first team game for Royal Arsenal as a goalkeeper in a FA Cup qualifying game versus City Ramblers 29th October 1892.

	Games	Goals
FA Cup	1	0
Other Senior Matches	5	0
Total	**6**	**0**

WORRALL, Arthur — 1894

Arthur Worrall began his footballing career with Wolverhampton Wanderers in 1889 being a first team choice at centre forward scoring nine goals in twenty league games and helping the club to the FA Cup semi final versus Blackburn Rovers. In 1890-91 he could not command a regular place and was subsequently transferred to Burton United in 1891. Arthur Worrall spent two seasons there before joining Woolwich Arsenal in January 1894. Arthur spent only three months at the club (playing in the first ever season in the football league) in just four league games of which his Arsenal league debut was at Lincoln City 3rd February 1894. Not being content at being Walter Shaw's deputy he was transferred to Nelson during the summer of 1894.

	Games	Goals
League	4	1
Friendly Matches	18	13
Total	**22**	**14**

James Jackson

For James Jackson biography, see page 30.

AUGUST 5th, 1936:
With the football season in sight at last,
the Arsenal team has gone into strict
training for their opening matches.
Long walks through the streets of
Tufnell Park, form an important part of
the training programme.
Pictured (from left to right):
Copping, Moss, Drake and James.

1919-1939

Members of the Wartime Cup winning side of 1943 pose for the camera

BAKER, Alfred — 1919-31

Birth Place: Ilkeston, Derbyshire
Date of Birth: 27th April 1898

☛ Alf "Doughy" Baker was possibly the finest utility player the club have ever had. He played in every position for Arsenal including goalkeeper. His favourite and most frequent position, however, was at right half. Alf began his career playing in Derbyshire junior football before appearing for Chesterfield, Crystal Palace and Huddersfield during World War One. Alf joined Arsenal in May 1919, making his league debut on the opening day of the season at Highbury v. Newcastle on 30th August 1919. In his opening season with the club he played in seventeen league games. In 1920-21 Alf missed only five league games, this consistency resulted in him playing in the first of three England trials. He played in thirty-two, twenty-nine and twenty-one league games respectively in the following three seasons. In 1924-25 he was made captain of the club, won the first of his two Football League Caps, played for the professionals versus the amateurs in that season's F.A. Charity Shield and played in 32 league games (mainly at right back). Baker followed this by scoring six times in thirty-one league games in 1925-26. In 1926-27 he enjoyed one of his finest seasons when helping Arsenal to their first ever F.A. Cup Final appearance versus Cardiff City as well as playing in further England trials. In 1927-28 Alf missed only five league games and deservedly won a full England Cap versus Wales. "Doughy" was again a pillar of strength in the side, 1928-29. In his final full season at the club, although only playing in 19 league games, he reached the three hundred league game milestone versus Leeds at Elland Road on 28th December 1929 to

become at that time, only the fifth Arsenal player to reach the 300. Alf finished his career on a winning note when being in the Arsenal side which won the F.A. Cup for the first time in 1930 versus Huddersfield Town. He played in just one league game in 1930-31 before retiring. Alf later scouted for the club. He died in April 1955 aged 56.

	Games	Goals
League	310	23
F.A. Cup	41	3
Other Senior Matches	5	0
Friendly Matches	23	7
Tours	8	5
Combination League	43	6
London Challenge Cup	18	2
London Midweek League	5	0
Total	**453**	**46**

Honours:
One England Cap
Two Football League Caps
F.A. Cup Winners Medal — 1929-30
F.A. Cup Finalists Medal — 1926-27
Northampton Charity Shield Winners Medal — 1929-30
(for professionals)
F.A. Charity Shield Winners Medal — 1924-25
London F.A. Challenge Cup Winners Medal — 1921-22
London F.A. Challenge Cup Finalists Medal — 1925-26

BARLEY, John — 1925-29

Birth Place: Staveley, Derbyshire
Date of Birth: 30th October 1904

☛ "J.C." Barley began life in footballing terms with Derbyshire Youth sides Poolsbrook, Lowgates Juniors and Staveley Town, after captaining North-East Derbyshire schoolboys. John joined Arsenal as an amateur in October 1925, turning professional in the same month. In his first season with the club, 1925-26, he was a regular member of the Football Combination team. Barley eventually got his League opportunity versus Leeds Utd. at Highbury on the 12th Feb., 1927. The only other two League games he played in that season were of stark contrast, a 0-7 away defeat at West Ham and a 3-2 away victory at Villa Park (with John scoring the winning goal). Barley played in the 6th round F.A. Cup tie home victory versus Wolves, which helped the club to their first ever Wembley Cup Final in 1927. He played in only two, and three League games respectively during the following two seasons when deputising for the ever consistent Bob John. Not happy at twenty-five years of age with permanent reserve team football he was transferred to Reading in May 1929, giving the Elm Park outfit eight solid seasons at wing half, playing in over two hundred first team games for the

Alf Baker

1919-1939

club. His son, Derek, was on Arsenal's books in the early 1950's. Died September 1962, aged 57.

	Games	Goals
League	8	1
F.A. Cup	2	0
Friendly Matches	22	6
Combination League	135	14
London Challenge Cup	1	0
Total	**168**	**21**

Honours:
3 London Combination Championship
Medals — 1926-27, 1927-28, 1928-29

BASTIN, Cliff — 1929-46

Birth Place: Exeter, Devon
Date of Birth: 14th March, 1912

☛ A schoolboy prodigy, Cliff Bastin's name was paramount in football supporters discussions of the 1930's. "Arbiter" (the late Frank Carruthers of the Daily Mail) once wrote "Bastin is one of the most brilliant footballers of modern times". Cliff's career began while playing for Exeter schools and his prodigious skills were soon to be seen when he was selected to play for England Schoolboys versus Wales when only fourteen. Soon after he joined his local side, Exeter City, and made his league debut for them when aged only fifteen. Cliff had scored six goals in seventeen league games, when, as a seventeen year old, Herbert Chapman signed him for Arsenal for £2,000 in May 1929. Bastin made his league debut for Arsenal at inside right (later converting to his famous left wing position) versus Everton at Goodison Park on 5th October 1929. By the end of his initial season at the club Cliff had featured in twenty-one league games, scoring seven times. In that 1929-30 season he was at the time, at the age of eighteen years and forty-three days, the youngest player ever to appear in a F.A. Cup Final when helping Arsenal to victory against Huddersfield Town. In Arsenal's first league championship season of 1930-31 his legendary partnership with Alex James on the left flank soon started to flourish. Not only was Bastin ever present (the youngest at the age of eighteen/nineteen to be so for the club) but he contributed with no less than twenty-eight league goals. This included a hat trick at Highbury versus Derby and also included three penalties. How many eighteen year olds would be their club's penalty taker today ? In 1931-32 he won the first of his twenty-one England Caps versus Wales on

Cliff Bastin

half when filling in for Jack Crayson. In his fifth League Championship campaign of 1937-38, he reverted back to his original outside left position in November of that season and finished it by scoring fifteen times in thirty-eight league appearances. In the season leading up to the Second World War a long term injury to his right leg reduced him to playing in only twenty-three league games. On the 4th February 1939 he scored his one hundred and fiftieth League goal when playing against Sunderland. During the War his deafness meant he was exempt from active service and he played in nearly two hundred and fifty games scoring seventy goals during this period. On the resumption of peace time and at the age of thirty-four he played in a further six league games before the leg injury which had hindered him prior and during the Second World War finally took its toll and he announced his retirement in January 1947. Nearly fifty years after playing his last game for the club, Cliff Bastin still holds the record of scoring more first team goals for Arsenal (one hundred and seventy-six), most league goals for Arsenal (one hundred and fifty) and by a long way, most F.A. Cup goals for the club (twenty-six). Cliff Bastin is not only a legend in Arsenal's history but will be remembered as a football immortal. He died in December 1991 aged 79.

	Games	Goals
League	350	150
F.A. Cup	42	26
Charity Shield	4	2
Other Senior Matches	6	4
Friendly Matches	13	6
Tours	14	8
Combination League	22	15
Combination Cup	1	0
London Challenge Cup	2	1
War Time	244	71
London Midweek League	3	0
Total	**701**	**283**

Honours:

21 England Caps
4 Football League Caps
5 League Championship Medals   1930-31, 1932-33, 1933-34, 1934-35, 1937-38
3 War time South Championship Medals   1939-40, 1941-42, 1942-43
2 F.A. Cup Winners Medals 1929-30, 1935-36
1 F.A. Cup Finalists Medal   1931-32
1 Football League War time Cup Winners Medal   1942-43
1 Football League War time Cup Finalists Medal   1940-41
3 F.A Charity Shield Winners Medals   1930-31, 1931-32, 1934-35
1 F.A Charity Shield Finalists Medal 1935-36
1 Combination Championship Medal   1929-30
2 Sheriff of London Charity Shield Winners Medals   1930-31, 1932-33
3 Northampton Charity Shield Winners Medals   1929-30, 1930-31, 1931-32

18th November 1931 and at the age of nineteen years and two hundred and forty-nine days became (and still is) the youngest player to win an England Cap, League Championship and F.A. Cup Winners Medal and therefore, after this, was known as "Boy Bastin" because he had done everything in the game when still a boy. Also in that season he appeared for Arsenal in the Cup Final versus Newcastle, was a member of the Charity Shield winning team versus W.B.A. and he missed only two league games when scoring fifteen goals, including a hat trick at Bloomfield Road versus Blackpool. In 1932-33 Bastin set a record, which undoubtedly will stand for all time, when from the outside left position he scored a staggering thirty-three League goals. No other winger in the history of the game, before or since, has come remotely close to equalling this total. Without saying, he was the club's leading scorer, when again ever present. This total included only one hat trick in a 9-2 home victory over Sheffield Utd. His consistency was proved when scoring in twenty-three of those forty-two league games (only one penalty). The reason that Bastin was so deadly was that unlike any other winger, he stood at least ten yards in from the touch line so that his alert football brain could thrive on the brilliance of James threading through defence splitting

passes with his lethal finishing completing the job. It became abundantly clear that he was having problems with his hearing and in not so many years to follow he was virtually deaf. In 1933-34 he secured his third League Championship medal when missing only four games and finishing as equal top scorer with thirteen goals. However, no other player was more distressed than Bastin when, on the 6th January 1934, he heard of the death of Herbert Chapman, his mentor and the man he absolutely idolised. The hat trick of Championships was duly completed in 1934-35 when Cliff found the net on twenty occasions in thirty-six league appearances. The 1935-36 season saw the club drop to sixth place. This was partly due to the fact that George Allison was in a quandary as to whom was to replace Alex James when unavailable, and in that season, in over two thirds of the games he played, Bastin played in the alien position of inside forward. However his contribution in helping Arsenal win the F.A. Cup versus Sheffield United was immense, scoring six times in seven ties. 1936-37 must have seemed strange to Bastin for it was the first time in eight seasons with the club that he was not involved in domestic honours. In a matter of only two seasons he had switched from outside left to inside forward and had now been converted to right

BEASLEY, Albert 'Pat'   1931-36

Birth Place: Stourbridge, Worcestershire
Date of Birth: 27th July 1913

☛ Albert began his long career in junior football in Kidderminster after playing for Birmingham Schoolboys. He joined his home town club Stourbridge and was transferred to Arsenal as a seventeen year old for £550 in May 1931. For most of the 1931-32 season he was a regular in the reserve and youth sides before Herbert Chapman gave him his league debut at Roker Park versus Sunderland on 6th April 1932. Finishing that season playing in three of the club's last seven games. At this stage of his career he was primarily a winger who could play on either flank and in 1932-33 he was restricted to just reserve team football because of the consistency of Hulme and Bastin. But in 1933-34 he scored ten times in twenty-three league games when helping Arsenal to the League Championship. In 1934-35 he won his second League Championship medal after playing in twenty league games. In 1935-36 he unfortunately missed out on not being selected for the F.A.Cup Final versus Sheffield United, despite playing in four of the previous six ties. "Pat" played in seven of the first eight league games in 1936-37 before being transferred to Huddersfield Town for £750 in October 1936. In the three seasons leading up to the Second World War, Beasley played in over one hundred league games for Huddersfield, being a member of their 1937-38 F.A.Cup Final team (beaten by Preston) as well as winning a full England cap (scoring the winning goal versus Scotland in 1938-39). During the War he guested for Arsenal, won two war time caps as well as working at the Royal Mint. He signed for Fulham in December 1945, when by this time he was playing a more influential role at wing half or inside forward. In his four seasons at Craven Cottage Albert was made club captain , playing in over one hundred and fifty league games for the club and helping them to the Second Division Championship in 1948-49. He became player manager of Bristol City in August 1950, spending two seasons at Ashton Gate before finishing his playing career. "Pat" later managed Birmingham City, 1958-60 and Dover. He died in March 1986 aged 72.

	Games	Goals
League	79	19
F.A. Cup	10	5
Other Senior Matches	1	1
Friendly Matches	14	6
Tours	1	0
Combination League	112	73
London Challenge Cup	12	7
War Time	18	2
London Midweek League	12	4
Total	**259**	**117**

Honours:
(WITH ARSENAL)
2 League Championship Medals
                        1933-34, 1934-35
London Combination Championship Medal
                        1933-34
Northampton Charity Shield Winners Medal
                        1931-32
London Midweek League Champ'ship Medal
                        1931-32
(WITH HUDDERSFIELD)
1 England Cap
2 Wartime Caps
F.A. Cup Finalists Medal   1937-38
(WITH FULHAM)
Division 2 Championship Medal   1948-49

BIGGS, Arthur   1933-37

Birth Place: Wootton, Bedfordshire
Date of Birth: 26th May 1915

☛ Arthur Biggs was yet another talented, goalscoring inside forward whose first team chances were very limited due to the fantastic array of International inside forwards on the club's books at this time. Arthur had originally joined Arsenal as an amateur in October 1933, turning professional two months later. He had to wait nearly three and a half years before being given his League debut at Stoke City on the 29th March 1937, after he had smashed the Club's Football Combination goal-scoring record, scoring forty-one times in forty-four

Arthur Biggs

games. Arthur played in only two League games at the start of the 1937-38 season, before being transferred to Hearts for £2,500 in December 1937 and was on their books when they finished as Scottish League Runners-up in 1937-38.

	Games	Goals
League	3	0
Tours	3	3
Friendly Matches	13	5
Combination League	106	60
London Midweek League	8	3
London Challenge Cup	10	3
Total	**143**	**74**

Honours:
3 London Combination Championship
Medals   1934-35, 1936-37, 1937-38
London F.A. Challenge Cup Winners 1935-36
London F.A. Challenge Cup Finalists 1936-37

BIRKETT, Ralph   1933-35

Birth Place: Torquay, Devon
Date of Birth: 9th January 1913

☛ R. J. E. Birkett was playing junior football for Dartmouth United before joining Torquay United in 1929. He spent four years with his home town club and played in nearly one hundred League games for them. Ralph was transferred to Arsenal in April 1933 as a fast and direct winger and in his first season at Highbury he won a League Championship Medal when playing in fifteen league games and scoring five goals. His Arsenal league debut was at Hillsborough versus Sheffield Wednesday on the 2nd September 1933. Also, in that 1933-34 season, he won an F.A. Charity Shield Medal when scoring twice in a 3-0 victory versus Everton. Birkett had originally been signed to replace the ageing Joe Hulme, however, with Hulme resurrecting his career and with young Albert Beasley showing promise as well as Alf Kirchen who had joined the club from Norwich City in March 1935, Ralph's first team opportunities were limited. This resulted in him being transferred to Middlesbrough in March 1935 for £2,000. In his near four seasons at Ayresome Park he matured into one of the finest right wingers of the late 1930's. His form in the 1935-36 season, when scoring twenty-one league goals, earned him a full England cap versus Northern Ireland. He finished his career with Newcastle in 1938-39 and retired from football during the War.

	Games	Goals
League	19	7
F.A.Cup	2	1
Charity Shield	2	3
Friendly Matches	4	1
Combination League	43	27
London Midweek League	2	1
London Challenge Cup	2	4
Total	**74**	**44**

Honours:
(WITH MIDDLESBROUGH)
1 England Cap
2 Football League Caps
(WITH ARSENAL)
League Championship Medal   1933-34
2 F.A. Charity Shield Winners Medals
                                1933-34, 1934-35
2 London Combination Championship
    Medals   1933-34, 1934-35
London F.A. Challenge Cup Winners 1933-34
(WITH NEWCASTLE)
1 England War-time Cap

BLACK, Thomas   1931-33

Birth Place: Mossend, Glasgow
Date of Birth: 1st December 1908

☛Thomas Black career at Highbury can
only be described as one of the most
unfortunate and undistinguished of any
player in the club's history. He had joined
Arsenal from Strathclyde in July 1931
spending the best part of his two years at the
club as left back reserve to the legendary
Eddie Hapgood. However, in January 1933
Arsenal were drawn to play Walsall in the
3rd round of the F.A.Cup. Hapgood and
Hulme were injured and Bob John, Lambert
and Coleman were victims of a flu epidemic.
Three players, which included Black, were
thrown in by Herbert Chapman for their first
team debut. Thomas had such a miserable
experience, mainly due to nerves in this most
famous of all F.A.Cup upsets, Herbert
Chapman showed his derision by selling
Black to Plymouth Argyle six days later. He
served Argyle well for six seasons before
finishing his career with Southend United in
1939.

	Games	Goals
F.A.Cup	1	0
Friendly Matches	9	0
London Combination League	26	1
London Midweek League	17	0
London Challenge Cup	2	0
Total	**55**	**1**

Honours:
London Midweek League Championship
    Medal   1931-32

BLYTH, William   1914-29

Birth Place: Dalkeith, Midlothian
Date of Birth: 17th June 1895

☛William began his career in Scottish
junior football with Wemyss Athletic, after
winning two Scottish junior caps. He was on
Manchester City's books when joining
Arsenal in May 1914. In the penultimate
season leading up to World War One, 1914-
15, he played in twelve league games of

which his Arsenal debut was at Leeds Road
versus Huddersfield on 21st November 1914.
During the War he served in the R.A.S.C. in
France before returning to Highbury on the
cessation of hostilities in 1919-20. William
had described football as being "the greatest
happiness of his life." He was determined to
make good at the game in spite of his parents
plans for him to follow another career. In
1919-20 he played in twenty-nine league
games, scoring five goals. William missed
only two league games in 1920-21 and over
the next four seasons he played in one
hundred and two of the club's one hundred
and sixty-eight league games, mainly at
either inside left or left half. This happy go
lucky, courageous, midfield dynamo was
made club captain in 1925-26 when playing
in all but two of Arsenal's forty-two league
games. In 1926-27 he played in thirty-three
league games as well as helping the club to
their first ever F.A. Cup Final versus Cardiff
City. In 1927-28 he figured in thirty-nine
league games followed by finishing his
Arsenal career in 1928-29 by playing in
twenty-one league games of which his three
hundredth league appearance (becoming
only the fourth Arsenal player to achieve this
total) was in a 4-4 home draw versus
Liverpool on 27th October 1928. William was
transferred to Birmingham City in May 1929
where he spent one season before retiring.
He died in July 1968 aged 73.

William Blyth

	Games	Goals
League	314	45
F.A.Cup	29	6
Other Senior Matches	6	2
Friendly Matches	25	12
Tours	16	0
London Combination League	37	6
London Challenge Cup	18	1
War time	3	1
South Eastern League	19	7
London League Reserves	13	7
Total	**480**	**87**

Honours:
F.A. Cup Finalists Medal   1926-27
London F.A. Challenge Cup Winners Medal
                                1921-22, 1923-24
London F.A. Challenge Cup Finalists Medal
                                      1925-26

BOREHAM, Reg   1921-25

Birth Place: Wycombe, Buckinghamshire

☛Reg Boreham was an England Amateur
International with Wycombe Wanderers
when joining Arsenal in July 1921. In his
initial season at the club he won a first team
place when taking over from James Hopkins
in December 1921, finishing that season
scoring ten times in twenty-two League
games. His debut was at Burnden Park versus
Bolton Wanderers on 12th December 1921.
In 1922-23 he played in twenty-seven
League games scoring eight times. However,
in his final two seasons at Highbury he had
to be content with virtual reserve football,
his contract being cancelled in May 1925. He
was later secretary of Wycombe Wanderers
for thirteen years (1937 to 1950). He died
March 1976.

	Games	Goals
League	51	18
F.A.Cup	2	0
Other Senior Matches	1	0
Friendly Matches	5	2
Combination League	15	5
London Challenge Cup	1	0
Total	**75**	**25**

Honours:
London F.A. Challenge Cup Winners 1921-22
England Amateur International.

BOULTON, Frank   1936-38

Birth Place: Chipping Sodbury, Gloucs.
Date of Birth: 12th August 1917

☛Frank Preece Boulton began his
goalkeeping career with Bristol City in
November 1934. He was not retained by
them, moving to Bath City in the summer of
1936. After several brilliant displays by
Frank, Arsenal were encouraged to sign him
in October 1936. He played in the club's last
twenty-one League games in 1936-37, taking
over from George Swindin, of which his
debut was at Deepdale versus Preston North
End on 28th December 1936. In 1937-38 he
just qualified for a League Championship
Medal when playing in fifteen league games.
However, at the start of the 1938-39 season
with George Swindin and Alex Wilson at the
helm and with also the young George Marks
on their books, Arsenal transferred Frank to
Derby County in August 1938. He was
Derby's regular keeper in that last season

before the outbreak of World War Two. On the return of first class football in 1945-46, Frank was very unfortunate, when having played in all of Derby's six F.A.Cup ties he was badly injured in a clash with Swansea's Trevor Ford in a League South game and missed the 1946 F.A.Cup Final versus Charlton Athletic. All this after he had served with the R.A.F. in West Africa. Frank later played for Swindon Town, Crystal Palace and Bedford Town. He died in June 1987 aged 69.

	Games	Goals
League	36	0
F.A.Cup	6	0
Other Senior Matches	1	0
Friendly Matches	3	0
Tours	6	0
Combination League	12	0
London Challenge Cup	1	0
War Time	11	0
Total	**76**	**0**

Honours:
League Championship Medal 1937-38
Bath Coronation Cup Winners Medal
1936-37

Frank Boulton

BOWDEN, Edward Raymond 1933-37

Birth Place: Looe, Cornwall
Date of Birth: 13th September, 1909

Christened Edwin, Bowden was better known throughout his football career as Ray. He first came to prominence when scoring ten times in a match for his native town, Looe, versus Tavistock. This drew the attention of Football League clubs and he signed for Plymouth Argyle in 1926. In seven seasons at Home Park, Ray played in nearly one hundred and fifty league games for the club, scoring eighty-three goals. He was the club's leading league scorer in 1928-29 and 1931-32. Ray won a Third Division South Championship Medal in 1929-30 and took part in the F.A. tour of Canada in 1931. Bowden was transferred to Arsenal for £4,500 in March 1933, playing in seven of the club's last eleven league games (not enough appearances for him to qualify for a Championship medal). His Arsenal league debut (when scoring) was at Highbury versus Wolves on 18th March 1933. In his four and a half years with the club he played in all three inside forward berths, being described by Charlie Buchan as "a great player with the ball, a player full of grace and style". In his first full season at the club he was joint top league scorer (with Cliff Bastin) with thirteen in thirty-two league games whilst helping Arsenal to the League Championship and also winning a F.A. Charity Shield medal in a 3-0 victory versus Everton. 1934-35 was Ray's finest season, he won the first of his six England caps versus Wales, represented the Football League and added another League Championship Medal to his collection when playing twenty-four League games and scoring fourteen goals. This included a hat trick in an 8-1 victory at Highbury versus Liverpool. In 1935-36 he contributed greatly (playing in every tie) when helping Arsenal win the F.A. Cup for the second time in their history by defeating Sheffield United. However, by this time his career was being interrupted by constant ankle injuries and in that 1935-36 season he played in only twenty-two league games scoring just six times although this did include his second league hat trick for the club in a 5-1 victory at Highbury versus Blackburn. Ray followed this up by playing in twenty-eight league games in 1936-37 and ten appearances at the start of the 1937-38 season before being transferred to Newcastle for £5,000 in

Raymond Bowden

November 1937, playing two seasons at St. James Park before retiring at the outbreak of the Second World War.

	Games	Goals
League	123	42
F.A. Cup	13	5
Charity Shield	2	1
Other Senior Matches	1	1
Friendly Matches	3	1
Tours	2	1
Combination League	14	4
Total	**158**	**55**

Honours:
(WITH ARSENAL)
6 England Caps
2 Football League Caps
2 League Championship Medals
1933-34, 1934-35
F.A. Cup Winners Medal 1935-36
F.A.Charity Shield Winners Medal 1933-34
F.A. Charity Shield Finalists Medal 1936-37
Bath Coronation Cup Winners Medal
1936-37

(WITH PLYMOUTH)
Division 3 South Championship Medal
1929-30

BOWEN, Edward   1926-28

Birth Place: Goldthorpe, Yorkshire
Date of Birth: 1st July 1903

☛ Edward was playing junior football for Wath Athletic when Arsenal signed him for £500 in February 1926. Bowen was yet another player of this era whose opportunities at Highbury were limited. In his instance due to the goal scoring prowess of Brain and Lambert. In Edward's two years at the club his goal scoring capabilities were seen when scoring no less than ten hat-tricks in reserve team and friendly matches, his only League opportunity coming in a 2-3 away defeat at Bury on the 4th March 1927. With no chance of first team football he was transferred to Northampton in February 1928. Over the next five seasons at the Cobblers he plundered nearly one hundred and twenty goals in only just over one hundred and sixty games, being the club's leading league scorer for four consecutive seasons 1928-32. He finished his career with Bristol City in 1932-33 when scoring twenty-seven times (and being their leading scorer) in thirty-nine League games. Bowen's thirty-five League goals for Northampton in 1928-29 stood as a Northampton Town record for thirty-three years until beaten by an ex-Arsenal player, Cliff Holton, in 1961-62.

	Games	Goals
League	1	0
Friendly Matches	11	21
Combination League	60	56
Total	**72**	**77**

Honours:
2 London Combination Championship
Medals   1926-27 & 1927-28

BRADSHAW, Frank   1914-23

Birth Place: Sheffield, Yorkshire
Date of Birth: 31st May 1884

☛ Frank Bradshaw played for Sheffield Schoolboys and was a product of Sheffield Sunday School football. Frank joined Sheffield Wednesday as an amateur before turning professional in 1904. In his near twenty year footballing career, he began as a centre forward , moved to inside right and finished it as a full back. In his six seasons at Hillsborough (as a centre forward) he scored thirty-eight first team goals in ninety-four games. He went into dispute with the club when refused a pay increase in 1906. Frank was a member of the 1907 F.A.Cup winning team versus Everton as well as winning a full England Cap when scoring a hat trick versus Austria in June 1908 and it was his bad luck, that when selected to play against Ireland in February 1909, he had to cry off with injury and was never chosen again. A frequent

knee injury looked to be the ending of his career when Southern League side, Northampton Town brought him for £250 in 1910. Frank was transferred to Everton in 1911, staying three seasons at Goodison Park helping them to the Division One runners-up spot in 1911-12. Bradshaw joined Arsenal in June 1914 and in the last season before the outbreak of World War One he played in twenty-six league games scoring ten goals. His Arsenal league debut was on the opening day of the season (when scoring) in front of a 7,000 crowd at Highbury versus Glossop on 1st September 1914. During the War he played in nearly one hundred and thirty games for the club, before in 1919-20, (when mainly reverting to the left back position) he played in thirty-three league games. He followed this when making twenty-one, thirty-two, and seventeen league appearances in the next three seasons before retiring in May 1923, aged 39. Frank later became the manager of Aberdare Athletic.

	Games	Goals
League	132	14
F.A.Cup	10	0
Other Senior Matches	5	0
Friendly Matches	8	0
Tours	4	1
Combination League	20	0
London Challenge Cup	12	1
War Time	129	12
South Eastern League	2	1
London League Reserves	3	1
Total	**325**	**30**

Honours:
(WITH SHEFFIELD WEDNESDAY)
1 England Cap
2 Football League Caps
F.A. Cup Winners Medal   1906-7
(WITH ARSENAL)
London Combination Championship Medal
1922-23
London F.A. Challenge Cup Winners Medal
1921-22
London F.A. Challenge Cup Finalists Medal
1914-15

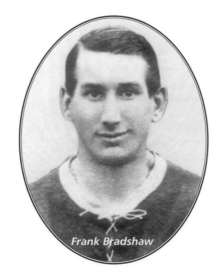
Frank Bradshaw

BRAIN, James   1923-31

Birth Place: Bristol, Gloucestershire
Date of Birth: 11th September 1900

☛ Jimmy Brain was one of the most prolific goalscorers in Arsenal's history and he was the first player ever to score one hundred League goals for the club. This he achieved in only his one hundred and thirty-third game (only Ted Drake has achieved this target in less games). The one hundredth goal being his third in a home fixture versus Liverpool on 7th March 1928. James Brain had had an unsuccessful trial with Cardiff City before joining Arsenal at the age of twenty-three from Ton Pentre in August 1923. He spent his first season at Highbury in the club's London Combination team before making his league debut when scoring the only goal in a 1-0 victory at Highbury versus North London rivals Tottenham in front of a 51,000 crowd on 25th October 1924. The rest of that season he scored twelve League goals in twenty-eight appearances in which he scored a hat trick versus Burnley at Highbury and four times versus Leeds. In 1925-26, he rewrote the Arsenal record books when scoring thirty-four league goals in forty-one games (this record of league goals in a season for the club stood for five years until beaten by Jack Lambert in 1930-31). In Brain's record breaking season he scored four hat tricks, home and away versus Everton, and at Highbury versus Cardiff and Bury. This form earning him an England trial. In 1926-27, this brilliant opportunist centre forward scored thirty-one league goals which included a hat trick on New Years' Day versus Cardiff (again) - the club that had turned him down, and he scored four goals in the home fixtures versus Sheffield Wednesday and Burnley. During that season he was the main inspiration when helping the club to the F.A.Cup Final versus Cardiff City. In 1927-28 James was as prolific when scoring twenty-five times in thirty-nine league games. This included a further two hat tricks, both at Highbury, versus Derby and Liverpool. He followed this up when scoring nineteen times in thirty-seven league appearances in 1928-29. However in 1929-30, with loss of form and stiff competition from Jack Lambert and Dave Halliday for the inside right or centre forward position he played in only six league games. In 1930-31, he qualified for a League Championship Medal when playing in sixteen league games (four goals) scoring his last hat trick for the club in a 7-1 home victory versus Blackpool. Brain was transferred to Tottenham on the eve of his 31st birthday in September 1931. Brain played for Tottenham 1931-34 (forty-five league games, ten goals), Swansea Town 1934-37 (fifty-one league games, twenty-five goals), and Bristol City 1937-39 (thirty-two league games, nine goals). On his retirement he managed Kings Lynn and when manager of Cheltenham he recommended Peter Goring to Arsenal before retiring from the football scene in 1948. Died 1971, aged 70.

	Games	Goals
League	204	125
F.A. Cup	27	14
Charity Shield	1	0
Friendly Matches	17	10
Tours	14	8
Combination League	93	56
London Challenge Cup	11	11
London Midweek League	2	2
Total	**369**	**226**

Honours:

League Championship Medals	1930-31
F.A. Cup Finalists Medal	1926-27
F.A. Charity Shield Winners Medal	1930-31
Combination League Championship Medals	
	1929-30, 1930-31
London F.A. Challenge Cup Winners Medal	
	1930-31
London F.A. Challenge Cup Finalists Medal	
	1925-26

James Brain

BREMNER, Gordon   1937-46

Birth Place: Glasgow
Date of Birth: 12th November 1917

☛ Gordon Hutton Bremner was one of many footballers who lost their best years of their career due to the Second World War. Gordon, a very talented inside forward, had moved South of the Border to join Arsenal from Glasgow junior side Cartha Athletic in March 1937. He spent his first season at the club, 1937-38, as a dependable member of the Combination team making his league debut at Elland Road versus Leeds United

(scoring in the last minute) on 9th April 1938. In the last season before hostilities, 1938-39, Gordon shared the first team inside right position with Bryn and Leslie Jones as well as George Drury, scoring three times in thirteen games. He served in the Army during the War and was good enough to play in two War time Internationals for Scotland versus England in 1942 and 1943. Gordon's brother Thomas played for Motherwell, and after being demobbed from the Army in 1946, he also linked up with Motherwell.

	Games	Goals
League	15	4
Friendly Matches	9	4
Tours	3	1
Combination League	43	15
London Challenge Cup	5	0
War Time	25	6
Southern League	4	3
Total	**104**	**33**

Honours:
2 Scottish War-time Caps
2 London Combination Championship
  Medals   1937-38, 1938-39

BUCHAN, Charles   1909-10 & 1925-28

Birth Place: Plumstead, London
Date of Birth: 22nd September 1891

☛ Charles Buchan was one of the first breed of thoroughbred footballers. Tall, elegant, a craftsman of his trade, and at his peak, 1911-14, he was described as the best footballer in England. Within footballing terms his name became an institution not only for his feats on the football field but later in the football journalistic world when he was editor of Charles Buchan's Football Monthly between 1949-60. Charles began his career playing with the Plumstead St Nicholas Church at Woolwich Polytechnic before joining Arsenal as an amateur on Boxing Day 1909 from Plumstead F.C. He scored three times in four Eastern Counties league games but when negotiations with the then Arsenal manager, George Murrell, over a professional contract collapsed, owing to non-agreement of his salary, Charles left the club and joined Northfleet in 1910. This is one of the greatest blunders by any manager in the history of the club. Charles later moved to Leyton where his performances caught the eye of the Sunderland management and he duly signed for them in March 1911 for £1250. Over the following fourteen years Charles Buchan became idolised by the whole of Wearside. He helped the club to the League Championship in 1912-13 and to the F.A.Cup Final of the same season when losing 0-1 to Aston Villa. He won six England caps and was the club's leading league scorer in 1912-13 and for six consecutive seasons

(peacetime) 1914-15 - 1923-24 and was the First Division's leading scorer in 1922-23. In total Charles played three hundred and seventy league games scoring two hundred and nine goals. Seventy years on his total of two hundred and nine league goals is still a Sunderland record. During the First World War he had served with the Grenadier Guards and was with the Sherwood Foresters. He was awarded the Military Medal for his bravery in pulling Lewis Guns out of a burning ammunition dump in France. In July 1925, Arsenal's new manager, Herbert Chapman, required a player with leadership qualities, so a meeting was set up with the Sunderland Manager, Robert Kyle, to discuss the possibility of Arsenal signing Charles Buchan. Kyle put a £4,000 asking fee on Buchan's head, and Chapman stated that no way was he going to pay £4,000 for a player approaching his 34th birthday. After deliberation, Chapman, thinking that Buchan might be over the hill, offered £2,000 plus £100 per goal. As it turned out Buchan scored twenty goals and Arsenal had to pay £4,000. Chapman made Buchan captain in the first season of the new offside rule and he allied his footballing brain to that of Chapman to create the "third back" style of play. Charles made his Arsenal debut on the opening day of the season in front of an audience of 53,000 against North London rivals, Tottenham, at Highbury on 29th August 1925. In 1926-27 he scored fourteen league goals in thirty-three games and captained Arsenal to their first ever F.A. Cup Final versus Cardiff City. Then in his 36th year, the 1927-28 season was to be his last even though he still managed to score sixteen league goals in thirty outings. Charles's last league game being in a 3-3 draw versus Everton at Goodison Park on the 5th May 1928. This was the match in which Dixie Dean scored a hat trick and thus reached sixty league goals for the season, beating George Campsell's record of fifty-nine. Charles will be remembered for his style, deft touches and his complete command of the game. His total of two hundred and fifty-eight league goals (remembering he lost four seasons due to World War One) all in Division One, has been bettered by few. On retirement he was a journalist with the Daily News / News Chronicle 1925-56, he edited his own football magazine and was a B.B.C. broadcaster. Without doubt Charles Buchan was a footballing immortal who died whilst on holiday in Monte Carlo in June 1960 aged 68.

	Games	Goals
League	102	49
F.A. Cup	18	7
Friendly Matches	3	2
Tours	6	3
London Challenge Cup	1	0
South Eastern League	4	3
Total	**134**	**64**

Honours:
(WITH SUNDERLAND)
6 England Caps
9 Football League Caps
League Championship Medal   1912-13
F.A. Cup Finalists Medal   1912-13
(WITH ARSENAL)
F.A. Cup Finalists Medal   1926-27
1 Football League Cap

BUCKLEY, Christopher   1914-21

Birth Place: Urmston, Manchester, Lancs
Date of Birth: 9th November 1888

Chris Buckley served his football apprenticeship (after finishing his educational studies at the Xaverian College, Manchester) with the Manchester Catholic Collegiate Institute, The Ship Canal F.C. and Manchester City Reserves. A centre half, he joined Brighton in the Southern League in 1905 before moving to Aston Villa in August 1906. In his initial season at Villa Park he played in twenty league games, sharing the position with Arthur Boden. However, Christopher broke an ankle in the opening fixture of the 1907-8 season at Villa Park versus Manchester United which kept him out of the game for over a year. In his six seasons at Villa Park he played in nearly one hundred and fifty first team games winning a League Championship Medal in 1909-10. Christopher Sebastian Buckley was transferred to Arsenal in July 1914 and in that last season before hostilities began, he played in twenty-nine league games. His Arsenal league debut (along with King and Bradshaw) was versus Glossop on the opening day of the season, at Highbury on 1st September 1914. On the declaration of peacetime he played in twenty-three league games in 1919-20, before losing his place to Alex Graham in 1920-21 when playing in only four league games after breaking a leg. His brother, the legendary Major Frank Buckley managed Wolves 1927-44 and in 1936 Christopher was elected to the Aston Villa board, where he served the club as director and chairman for thirty-one years until retiring in 1967. Died January 1974, aged 85.

	Games	Goals
League	56	3
F.A. Cup	3	0
Other Senior Matches	1	0
Friendly Matches	1	0
Combination League	2	0
London Challenge Cup	3	0
War time	33	1
Total	**99**	**4**

Honours:
(WITH ASTON VILLA)
League Championship Medal   1909-10

BURGESS, Daniel   1919-22

Birth Place: Goldenhill, Staffordshire
Date of Birth: 23rd October 1896

Daniel Burgess had served in the Royal Field Artillery during World War One when joining Arsenal from the Army in May 1919. In his three seasons with the club, whilst hitting the net consistently for the reserves, he played in only thirteen League games when normally deputising for the injured Henry White. His best run in the League side was at the start of the 1919-20 season when he played in seven consecutive League fixtures in September & October. His debut was in a 3-2 victory at Anfield versus Liverpool on 1st September 1919. Daniel, with his limited capabilities could never command a regular first team place so he joined West Ham in June 1922. He later played for Aberdare and Q.P.R.

	Games	Goals
League	13	1
Other Senior Matches	1	0
Friendly Matches	20	9
Combination League	78	41
London Challenge Cup	1	0
Total	**113**	**51**

BUTLER, John 'Jack'   1914-30

Birth Place: Colombo, Ceylon
Date of Birth: 14th August 1894

Jack was a proud man, tall and slim with athletic features, strong yet gentle and kind and a keystone of the famous half back line, Baker, Butler, and Blyth which virtually picked itself throughout the 1920's. Butler started his career in junior football with Dartford and Fulham Wednesday before joining Arsenal in March 1914. In that season, prior to the outbreak of war, he was a regular member of the club's South Eastern League side. He served in the Royal Field Artillery in France during the war before returning to Highbury in 1919. Butler made his league debut at Burnden Park versus Bolton Wanderers on 15th November 1919 when sharing the centre half position with Chris Buckley, playing in twenty-one league games in that 1919-20 season. Over the course of the next four seasons Jack started to establish himself in the side, playing in seventy-three league games. In 1924-25, although Arsenal had an unsatisfactory season (just avoiding relegation), Jack was the pillar of the defence, missing only three games. This consistency gained him an England cap versus Belgium in December 1924. In the following season, 1925-26, he played in forty-one league games before, in 1926-27 playing in all 7 F.A.Cup ties when helping Arsenal to reach their first F.A. Cup Final versus Cardiff City. Jack was a key member of the side in 1927-28 and 1928-29 before losing his place to Herbie Roberts in 1929-30 and at the end of that season he was transferred to Torquay United for £1,000 in June 1930. Butler became coach to the Belgium club, Royal Daring F.C., in 1932 and to the Belgium national side. Jack was trainer/coach at Leicester City from 1940-46 and managed Torquay United 1946-47, Crystal Palace 1947-49. Coached in Denmark, again in Belgium 1949-53, finally

Jack Butler

managing Colchester United 1953-55. He died in January 1961, aged 66.

	Games	Goals
League	267	7
F.A. Cup	29	1
Other Senior Matches	2	0
Friendly Matches	20	3
Tours	18	1
Combination League	62	3
South Eastern League	18	4
London Challenge Cup	16	2
War time	2	4
London League Reserves	8	2
London Midweek League	1	0
Total	**443**	**27**

Honours:
1 England cap
F.A. Cup Finalist Medal   1926-27
London Combination League Championship Medal   1929-30
London F.A. Challenge Cup Winners Medal   1921-22
London F.A. Challenge Cup Finalists Medal   1925-26

CARR, Edward — 1935-40

Birth Place: Shadforth, Durham
Date of Birth: 3rd October 1917

☛ Edward was a young, sturdily built seventeen year old centre forward when joining Arsenal in February 1935. He went straight to Margate (Arsenal's nursery) before returning to Highbury in August 1937. Edward played in eleven league games (seven goals) at the end of Arsenal's 1937-38 League Championship season. In those eleven games he was not on the losing side once. His league debut being at Maine Road versus Manchester City on 16th February 1938. Carr played in just one league game in 1938-39 before suffering a serious knee injury which looked as if it would finish his career. During the War he returned to Wheatley Colliery to work down the pits and at the end of hostilities he joined Huddersfield Town in October 1945. He later played for Newport County 1946-49, Bradford City 1949-53, and Darlington 1953-54. Edward later managed Darlington 1960-64 and scouted for Newcastle United.

Edward Carr

	Games	Goals
League	12	7
Other Senior Matches	1	0
Friendly Matches	4	1
Tours	1	0
Combination League	38	15
London Challenge Cup	5	4
War Time	1	1
Southern League	7	4
Total	**69**	**32**

CARTWRIGHT, Sydney — 1931-46

Birth Place: Kiverton Park, Sheffield
Date of Birth: 25th June 1910

☛ Sydney Cartwright was an outstanding servant to Arsenal F.C. Shown in the fact that in fifteen years at Highbury he played in only sixteen league games, mainly when deputising at wing half for either Jack Crayston or Wilf Copping. Syd had been at the club for over five years and was nearly twenty-six years old before making his League debut, Cartwright being quite content in being a stalwart to the Combination side with whom he won no less than five Championship Medals during that period. Cartwright had begun his career with Sheffield junior side, High Moor, before joining Arsenal as an amateur in April 1931, turning professional the following month. During the War he served in the Army before finishing his career with the club in 1946-47. He died in December 1953 aged 43.

	Games	Goals
League	16	2
Other Senior Matches	1	0
Friendly Matches	30	3
Tours	3	0
Combination League	192	2
London Challenge Cup	21	0
London Midweek League	33	1
Southern League	3	0
War Time	3	0
Total	**292**	**8**

Honours:
5 London Combination Championship
   Medals   1933-34, 1934-35, 1936-37,
                          1937-38, 1938-39
London F.A. Challenge Cup Winners Medal
                          1935-36
London F.A. Challenge Cup Finalists Medal
                          1936-37

CLARK, Archie — 1927-28

Birth Place: Shoreham, Kent
Date of Birth: 4th April 1904

☛ Archie began his career with Kent junior side Grays, joining Brentford in March 1927. He had played only one League game for the Bees before being transferred to Arsenal in May 1927. Although Archie was primarily a half back, he did play at centre forward with success for the combination side. In his eighteen months at Highbury, although a mainstay in the reserves, he managed to play in only one League game, in a heavy 1-4 defeat at Ewood Park versus Blackburn Rovers on Guy Fawkes day 1927. Clark moved to Luton in November 1928 where he spent three seasons. This was followed by a five year spell at Goodison Park with Everton, where in his first season (1931-32) he played

in thirty-nine games when helping them to the League Championship. In his last four seasons at Goodison, 1932-36, he managed to play in only two League games due to the Toffee men's brilliant England wing-halfs, Cliff Britton and Joe Mercer. Archie moved across the Mersey to join Tranmere Rovers in March 1936, helping them to the Third Division North Championship in 1937-38. He later became the manager of Gillingham, a post he held for nearly twenty years, 1939-58. Archie being the manager when Gillingham were re-elected to the Football League in 1950-51. He re-joined his old friend Joe Mercer as chief scout at Sheffield United in late 1958. Died January 1967 aged 62.

	Games	Goals
League	1	0
Friendly Matches	12	2
Combination League	56	13
Total	**69**	**15**

Honours:
(WITH EVERTON)
League Championship medal   1931-32
(WITH TRANMERE)
Third Division North Championship Medal
                          1937-38
(WITH ARSENAL)
2 London Combination Championship
   Medals   1927-28 & 1928-29

CLARK, John — 1923-26

Birth Place: Renfrewshire, Scotland
Date of Birth: 4th March 1900

☛ John Clark was transferred to Arsenal from the then Scottish 2nd Division outfit Bo'ness in March 1923. John made his League debut soon after at Villa Park, 7th April 1923. Clark played in only two League games in each of his three seasons at Highbury, this owing to the stiff right-wing competition, firstly from Rutherford and Patterson and then Hoar and Hulme. He was allowed to leave the club in August 1926 when he signed for Luton Town.

	Games	Goals
League	6	0
Friendly Matches	14	4
Combination League	76	14
London Challenge Cup	2	0
Total	**98**	**18**

Honours:
London F.A. Challenge Cup Winners medal
                          1923-24

COCK, Donald   1925

Birth Place: Hayle, Cornwall
Date of Birth: 10th July 1896

☞ Although Donald Cock was a prodigious goalscorer in his own right, he had to live in the shadows of his brother Jack, who was a goal scoring phenomenon playing for Huddersfield Town, Chelsea, Everton and England. Donald was playing for Brentford during World War 1 before joining Fulham in the summer of 1919. In his three seasons at Craven Cottage he averaged a goal every other game, being their leading goalscorer in 1919-20 and 1920-21. Donald was transferred to Notts County in October 1922 and in three seasons at Meadow Lane he played in just under one hundred first team games, scoring nearly forty goals. He was leading League goal scorer in 1922-23 and 1923-24, as well as helping County to the Second Division Championship in 1922-23. Arsenal broke their transfer record paying £4,000 for Cock in March 1925. Donald made his Arsenal League debut at Highbury versus Bolton Wanderers on 7th March 1924. However, the following Saturday, in his second League game for the club, playing against his former club, Notts County at Meadow Lane, he was tackled heavily and broke a leg. This put him out of action for five months and after recovery he played in just one more League game for the club before being transferred to Clapton Orient for £1,500 in Oct. 1925. Donald was leading League scorer at Homerton in both his seasons at the club, 1925-26 and 1926-27 and finished his career when playing three League games for Wolves in 1927. Donald is one of only a handful of players to have been three different club's leading League goal scorer in two or more seasons. He died in August 1974, aged 78.

	Games	Goals
League	3	0
Combination League	4	2
London Challenge Cup	1	1
Total	**8**	**3**

Honours:
(WITH NOTTS COUNTY)
Division Two Championship medal   1922-23

COLEMAN, Ernie 'Tim'   1932-34

Birth Place: Blidworth, Nottinghamshire
Date of Birth: 4th January 1908

☞ Ernie Coleman had played junior football for Hucknall before being turned down by Nottm Forest after a trial. Ernie joined Halifax Town in 1927 and scored five goals for them in nineteen league appearances. Coleman was transferred to Grimsby Town in March 1929 and at the back end of that 1928-29 season he scored seven times in eight league appearances, helping the club to promotion to Division One. In the following three seasons at Blundell Park "Tim" was the club's leading league scorer in 1930-31 (with thirty-five, a new club record) and in 1931-32. In his total career at Grimsby he scored fifty-seven league goals in only eighty-five games. Ernie Coleman was brought to Arsenal by Herbert Chapman in March 1932, but the way the transfer came about was a strange affair. At a chance meeting, the Grimsby chairman, Mr George Pearce, said to Herbert Chapman "Why not sign our boy, Ernie Coleman? We could do with the money." It was arranged that they would travel to Grimsby as soon as the specialist had made his examination. Which they did. On arrival at Grimsby, Mr Pearce, hurriedly called his directors together, and Mr Chapman told the Arsenal chairman, Sir Samuel Hill-Wood, over the phone, about his change of mind. He added : "Pearce wants £8,000 but I won't go beyond £7,500." Said the chairman, "Put him on," said Hill-Wood and he said to George, "I'll toss you for £7,750 or £7,500." "Right," said George, "I'll call heads to you". Heads it was. Whereupon the sporting Grimsby chairman said, "You can have him for £7,500 – and if you are satisfied send us on the extra £250." Ernie Coleman was yet another centre forward who was brought to supposedly replace Jack Lambert. Coleman made his Arsenal league debut versus Leicester City at Highbury on 5th March 1932 and finished the season playing in six league games. In his one full season at Highbury, Coleman did remarkably well scoring, twenty-four times in only twenty-seven games, helping Arsenal to the League Championship in 1932-33. He scored two hat tricks, one at Bolton and in a 8-0 home victory versus Blackburn Rovers, earning Ernie an England trial. However, in 1933-34, he scored only once in twelve league games and after the signing of Ted Drake in March 1934 he realised his first team days were over. Coleman was transferred to Middlesbrough in August 1934, spending three seasons at Ayresome Park scoring twenty-one goals in eighty-five league appearances. Ernie finished his career with Norwich City, 1937-39. After the war he managed Linby Colliery and Notts County. Died Jan. 1984 aged 76.

	Games	Goals
League	45	26
F.A. Cup	1	0
Charity Shield	1	0
Other Senior Matches	1	5
Friendly Matches	3	0
Combination League	26	14
London Challenge Cup	2	0
Total	**79**	**45**

Honours:
League Championship Medal   1932-33
F.A. Charity Shield Winners Medal   1933-34

London Comb. Champ'ship Medal   1933-34
Sheriff of London Winners Medal   1932-33

COLLETT, Ernie   1933-49

Birth Place: Sheffield, Yorkshire
Date of Birth: 17th November 1914

☞ Ernie Collett can only be described as one of Arsenal's greatest ever servants, who for forty-six years served Arsenal as player, coach and assistant chief scout. Ernie was playing in Sheffield junior football with Oughtibridge Working Mens Club and his decision to join Arsenal in April 1933 was due to the fame of the club. Over the next sixteen seasons, his love of Arsenal was shown (although good enough to be a regular member of most First Division teams) when he played in only twenty league games. A wing half, he had to wait nearly four and a half years before making his league debut at the Victoria Ground versus Stoke City on 23rd October 1937. In 1938-39 he managed to play in nine league games when deputising for Wilf Copping at left half. During World War Two he played in nearly two hundred games for the club and assisted Brentford when playing in the 1941-42 War time Cup Final. On the resumption of peace, Ernie played in six league games in 1946-47 and assisted the reserve side 1947-49 before retiring aged thirty-four, in the summer of 1949. Ernie then became assistant coach to the youngsters under George Male before becoming chief assistant scout and scout 1963-79. He died in tragic circumstances when knocked over by a Fire Engine in April 1980 aged 65.

	Games	Goals
League	20	0
F.A. Cup	1	0
Other Senior Matches	2	0
Friendly Matches	34	4
Tours	6	0
Combination League	218	7
Combination Cup	8	0
London Challenge Cup	19	0
War Time	189	1
London Midweek League	2	0
Eastern Counties League	4	0
Total	**503**	**12**

Honours:
6 London Combination Championship
Medals   1933-34, 1934-35, 1936-37,
                1937-38, 1938-39, 1946-47
2 War time South Championship Medals
                1939-40, 1940-41
1 Football League War time Cup Finalist
Medal   1940-41
2 London F.A. Challenge Cup Winners
Medals   1933-34, 1935-36
London F.A. Challenge Cup Finalists Medal
                              1936-37

COMPTON, Denis   1932-50

Birth Place: Hendon, Middlesex
Date of Birth: 23rd May 1918

☛ Whether on the cricket pitch or the football field, Denis Compton was the most popular sportsman in England in the 1940's. A natural at both games, his colourful and bucaneering style captured and held the public's imagination. Although the statistics do not show him as the great all-rounder he undoubtedly was, the vivid memories he left with football and cricket supporters of the immediate post war years will long remain a tribute to the wonderful entertainment he gave. Denis Compton had began his footballing career playing for Golders Green, Hampstead Town and Nunhead before joining Arsenal as a fourteen year old amateur in September 1932. In his first four seasons at Highbury he was a regular on the club's left wing when playing in junior and reserve team football. Denis made his league debut (when scoring) in front of a 61,500 crowd versus Derby at Highbury on 26th September 1936 and in that season he played in fourteen league games, sharing the left wing position with John Milne, after he turned professional in May 1935. In 1936-37, Denis twice scored five goals in a game when hitting blistering form for the London Combination side. However, in the seasons 1937-38 and 1938-39 he managed to play in only eight league games. During the war he was in the Army serving in India, but still managed the time to feature in over one hundred and twenty games for the club (seventy-four goals). This form won Denis twelve War time International caps for England and without doubt if it had not been for the war he would have become a fully fledged double international. Denis was powerful, quick, and rather unorthodox with a superb left foot and was good in the air. On the resumption of league football in 1946-47, he was stricken with a leg injury which resulted in him making only one league appearance. It was not until February 1948 that Denis gained a regular place in the Arsenal league side. He played in the last fourteen league games of that season when his enthusiastic style helped Arsenal to the League Championship. In 1948-49 a recurrence of the leg injury limited Denis to just six league games and it was not until January 1950 that he regained full fitness and his position in the team. It was Denis's corner which his brother Leslie headed home for Arsenal's equalising goal in the 2-2 draw versus Chelsea in the first semi-final of the F.A. Cup in March 1950. Denis Compton finished his career on a high note when he helped Arsenal to beat Liverpool in that season's F.A. Cup Final. Although many critics thought that Denis was a better footballer than cricketer, it was on the cricket pitch that Denis made a name for himself. The word great must be used in describing Denis's cricketing ability. In a first class career which spanned twenty-two years, 1936-58, he scored nearly 39,000 runs with a batting average of nearly 52, he played in 78 tests for England and of his many achievements all are dwarfed by Compton's incredible season of 1947 when scoring 3,816 runs at an average of 91 with 18 centuries. Thus he created new records both for the most runs in first class cricket in a season and most centuries. The famous "Brylcream boy" was awarded the C.B.E. in 1958 and later became a football and cricket reporter with The Sunday Express and a cricketing commentator on television with the B.B.C. Denis Charles Scott Compton was a schoolboy hero to millions. As a sporting hero only a handful of sportsmen have received the adulation that he inspired.

	Games	Goals
League	54	15
F.A. Cup	5	1
Charity Shield	1	0
Other Senior Matches	4	1
Friendly Matches	16	10
Combination League	137	92
Combination Cup	8	2
London Challenge Cup	13	7
War Time	127	74
Southern League	4	5
London Midweek League	13	0
Total	**382**	**207**

Honours:
12 England Wartime caps
League Championship Medal   1947-48
F.A. Cup Winners Medal   1949-50
F.A.Charity Shield Finalists Medal   1936-37
3 Combination League Championship
   Medals   1936-37, 1937-38, 1938-39
London F.A. Challenge Cup Winners Medal
                 1935-36
London F.A. Challenge Cup Finalists Medal
                 1936-37
3 Football League South Championship
   Medals   1939-40, 1941-42, 1942-43
1 Football League War Time Cup Winners
   Medal   1942-43
1 Football League War Time Cup Finalists
   Medal   1940-41
Bath Challenge Cup Winners Medal 1936-37

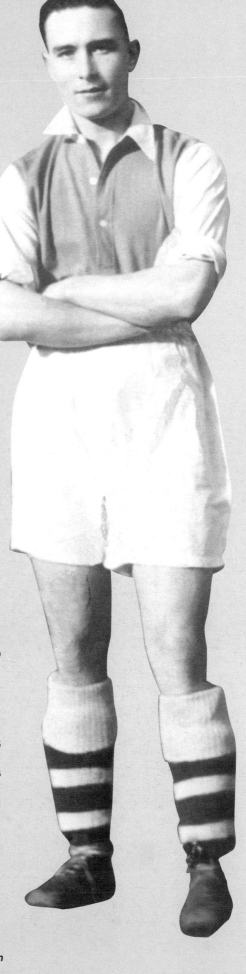

Denis Compton

Leslie Compton

COMPTON, Leslie 1930-53

Birth Place: Woodford, Essex
Date of Birth: 12th September 1912

☛ In all of Arsenal's long and illustrious years no player in the history of the club has served them for such a long period as Leslie Compton and, in fact, his twenty-three years service for the club has been bettered by only a few in the history of the Football League. Leslie had played for Middlesex schools and Bell Lane Old Boys before joining Arsenal as an amateur in August 1930 from Hampstead Town. Over the next twenty-three years he served in literally every position. In his first eighteen months at Highbury his appearances were limited to junior football. Signing professional in February 1932, within two months he had made his League debut in a 1-1 at Villa Park versus Aston Villa on 25th April 1932. He finished that season (deputising for Tom Parker) featuring in four league games. At the beginning of Arsenal's 1932-33 League Championship winning season he played in four league games before losing his place to Tom Parker and then to the newly converted right back George Male. At this stage of his career his positional play was lacking and he was slow on the ground, hence in 1933-34 Leslie reverted to total

reserve team football when understudy to George Male and Eddie Hapgood. In season 1934-35 he figured in only five league games and in 1935-36 twelve games. However, in 1936-37, he had his longest stretch in the league side when playing in fifteen league games and although still mainly a reserve for Arsenal he played in the first of two England trials. Many players would have been disillusioned of being reserve to one England full back let alone two and after playing in only nine league games in 1937-38, the season prior to the 2nd World War was his most fruitful when appearing in eighteen league games and winning an F.A. Charity Shield Medal against Preston. By the time war was declared in September 1939, Compton was twenty-seven years of age and because of the brilliance of Male and Hapgood had yet to take part in more than

seventy league games. However, during this period he had the consolation of winning five Football Combination Championship Medals. During the War years he served in the Army and whilst on leave played in one hundred and thirty games for the club scoring ninety-three goals (after he had been converted to centre forward). Leslie won five war time caps and in a game against Leyton Orient in February 1941, he scored ten times (six with his head). When hostilities finished the loyal, dependable Compton missed only six league games in 1946-47 when converted to the centre half position. By this time his game was made up of grace and style when distributing the ball and he was a tower of strength at the centre of the defence when captain. In the 1947-48 League Championship campaign he missed the first six games owing to his cricket commitments but still played in thirty-five of the club's last thirty-six League games. By this time he was affectionately known as either as "Big Leslie" or "Big 'ead". In 1948-49, he missed only two league games when given the Arsenal captaincy, but after a short period of time he had requested Tom Whittaker, the Arsenal manager, to restore Mercer as captain. In 1949-50 he was unflappable when scoring one of Arsenal's most important goals when, in the 1950 F.A.Cup semi-final he headed the equalising goal from his brother's corner versus Chelsea, after Joe Mercer, his Arsenal captain, had demanded he stay back. At the age of thirty-six he won a F.A.Cup winners medal versus Liverpool. Compton, virtually unbeatable in the air, rugged and powerful won the first of his two England caps versus Wales in November 1950, and at the age of thirty-eight years and two months he became, and still is, the oldest ever debutant for England in a full international. In 1951-52, he played in only four league games before retiring at the end of the season. He later became coach/scout, 1953-56, and was Middlesex wicket keeper 1938-56. Leslie had a foot amputed in 1982. He died December 1984 aged 72.

	Games	Goals
League	253	5
F.A. Cup	17	1
Charity Shield	3	0
Other Senior Matches	6	0
Friendly Matches	36	3
Tours	16	1
Combination League	226	31
Combination Cup	1	0
London Challenge Cup	21	2
War Time	133	93
London Midweek League	10	0
Total	**722**	**136**

Honours:
2 England Caps
5 England Wartime caps
League Championship Medal   1947-48
F.A. Cup Winners Medal   1949-50
F.A.Charity Shield Winners Medals
                        1938-39, 1948-49
F.A.Charity Shield Finalists Medal 1936-37
5 Combination League Championship
   Medals   1933-34, 1934-35, 1936-37,
                        1937-38, 1938-39
2 London F.A. Challenge Cup Winners
   Medals   1933-34, 1935-36
1 London F.A. Challenge Cup Finalists Medal
                                   1936-37
3 Football League South Championship
   Medals   1939-40, 1941-42, 1942-43
1 Football League War Time Cup Winners
   Medal   1942-43
1 Football League War Time Cup Finalists
   Medal   1940-41
Bath Coronation Cup Winners Medal
                                   1936-37
1 Northampton Charity Shield Medal
                                   1931-32

COPE, Horace   1926-33

Birth Place: Treeton, nr Sheffield, Yorks
Date of Birth: 24th May 1899

☞ Horace began his career with his Home town club Treeton United before joining Notts County in 1920. In six seasons at Meadow Lane he played in one hundred and twenty-six league games in which time he was selected to play for England but withdrew through injury, and he also won a Second Division Championship medal in 1922-23. Cope was transferred to Arsenal for £3,125 from Notts County in December 1926 making his Arsenal league debut at Ninian Park versus Cardiff on 27th December 1926. In that same season he played in an England trial and missed the 1927 F.A. Cup Final versus Cardiff because of an injury picked up in a home game three weeks before the final versus Huddersfield Town. Horace was a left back who established himself in seasons 1927-28 and 1928-29 when playing in twenty-four and twenty-three league games respectively. However, after the signing of Eddie Hapgood his league opportunities in 1929-30 were restricted to one. In his last three seasons at Highbury he played in only six league games when deputising for Hapgood, in the meantime he won a host of honours with the reserve side before being transferred to Bristol Rovers for £1,500 in July 1933. Horace later became trainer at Norwich City 1934-37, Southampton and Blackburn Rovers. Died October 1961, aged 62.

	Games	Goals
League	65	0
F.A. Cup	11	0
Friendly Matches	9	0
Combination League	149	10
London Challenge Cup	12	2
Total	**246**	**12**

Honours:
(WITH ARSENAL)
3 Combination League Championship Medals
                1928-29, 1929-30, 1930-31
London F.A. Challenge Cup Winners Medal
                                   1930-31
(WITH NOTTS CO.)
Division 2 Championship Medal   1922-23

COPPING, Wilf   1934-39

Birth Place: Middlecliffe, Barnsley, Yorks
Date of Birth: 17th August 1909

☞ Wilf started his football career playing in Yorkshire junior football with Dearn Valley Old Boys, Middlecliffe and Darfield Rovers before failing to impress the Barnsley management as a trialist. Little did they know that Copping would become one of the most talked about and respected players of the 1930's. Although never cautioned or sent-off during his ten year career he had the legendary reputation of being more than forceful in the tackle, this gave him the nickname of "The Ironman". Although Wilf was the first to admit that he was temperamental and fiery his bone-jarring tackles were mainly timed to perfection and fair. His famous quote was "The first man in a tackle never gets hurt". What added to his misconceived manner on the field was that he never shaved on match days, which gave him a mean blue stubble and more than a fearsome appearance. Copping signed for Leeds in March 1929 and in his first full season at the club, 1930-31, he was ever present when appearing in the formidable Edwards-Hart-Copping half back line. During his first stint with Leeds, 1929-34, he played in over one hundred and sixty league games, represented the Football League twice and won six England caps. Wilf was transferred to Arsenal in June 1934 for £8,000, making his Arsenal league debut on the opening day of the 1934-35 season at Fratton Park versus Portsmouth on the 25th August 1934. During that League Championship winning season he was virtually ever present up until March 1935 missing only two league games, before receiving a hideous knee injury at Goodison Park versus Everton. In the same season he had added two more England caps to his collection (which at the end of his career totalled twenty) one of which was being one of seven Arsenal players (still a record) to represent England in the Battle of "Highbury" versus the world champions Italy, in November 1934. Wilf was a superstitious player who always put his left boot on first and insisted on being the sixth (his left half number) out of the dressing room. In 1935-36, he played a further 33 league games and helped the club in winning the 1936 F.A. Cup Final versus Sheffield United. In the following campaign, 1936-37, he missed only four league games as he did in 1937-38, when helping Arsenal to another League Championship. In 1938-39 Copping was still an England regular, he was a member of the F.A. Charity Shield team versus Preston, and had played in twenty-six league games up until March 1939 when, as a regular member of Tom Whittaker's treatment room he confided in Tom " I am going to ask for a transfer". Whittaker replied " Why ?". Copping replied " I feel war is coming and I want to get my wife and kids back up North before I join the army ". There was no reply to that. Copping rejoined Leeds United in March 1939. During the War he was a C.S.M.I. in the army in North Africa. He later coached in Belgium with Royal Beerschot as well as the Belgium national team returning to England to train/coach at Southend, Bristol City (where he linked up with his old Arsenal colleague "Pat" Beasley and Coventry City 1956-59. He died June 1980 aged 70.

Wilf Copping

	Games	Goals
League	166	0
F.A. Cup	19	0
Charity Shield	4	0
Other Senior Matches	2	0
Friendly Matches	3	0
Tours	9	0
Combination League	1	0
London Challenge Cup	1	0
War Time	3	0
Total	**208**	**0**

Honours:
(WITH LEEDS UNITED)
7 England Caps
2 Football League Caps
(WITH ARSENAL)
13 England Wartime caps
2 League Championship Medals
            1934-35, 1937-38
F.A. Cup Winners Medal   1935-36
F.A.Charity Shield Winners Medals
            1934-35, 1938-39
F.A.Charity Shield Finalists Medals
            1935-36, 1936-37
Bath Coronation Cup Winners Medal
            1936-37

COUPLAND, Walter   1920-23

Birth Place: Sheffield, Yorkshire
Date of Birth: 1st March 1900

☛ Walter was enjoying playing junior football for Sheffield youth side Birley Carr when joining Arsenal in January 1920. During his three year stay at the club, although being a key member of the reserve side on the left wing, he played in just one League encounter (when filling in for the injured Toner) in an away fixture at Aston Villa on the 11th February 1920. With no first team football on the horizon he was transferred to Exeter City in February 1923. Coupland later played for Aberdare.

	Games	Goals
League	1	0
Friendly Matches	37	9
Combination League	46	11
Total	**84**	**20**

COWNLEY, Francis   1919-23

Birth Place: Scunthorpe, Lincolnshire
Date of Birth: 17th December 1896

☛ Francis began with his home town club Scunthorpe United and was on the club books of Nottm Forest during the First World War when joining Arsenal as a young right back in May 1919. He made his League debut for the club in a 3-2 home victory versus Oldham Athletic on the 7th February 1920. Francis enjoyed a four game run in the side before losing his place to first choice custodian Joe Shaw. In 1920-21 he played in just one League game when again being reserve to Shaw and Frank Bradshaw. Francis did, however, manage to play in ten League games in 1921-22. Cownley, who had served with the Royal Field Artillery in World War One, was sidelined by injury during 1922-23 and subsequently left the club.

	Games	Goals
League	15	0
Friendly Matches	19	1
Combination League	64	1
London Challenge Cup	1	0
Total	**99**	**2**

COX, George Junior   1933-36

Birth Place: Warnham, Nr Horsham
Date of Birth: 23rd August 1911

☛ George was playing junior football for Horsham when joining Arsenal as an amateur in November 1933, turning professional a month later. George was a prolific goal scoring centre forward for the reserves before being given his league baptism at Filbert Street versus Leicester City on 8th March 1934. In Arsenal's championship winning season of 1934-35 he was reserve centre forward to the legendary Ted Drake without playing. However in 1935-36 he had five league outings when replacing the injured Drake. With limited first team opportunities, Cox was transferred to Fulham for £150 in May 1936, finishing his footballing career with Luton in 1937. The love of his life though, was undoubtedly cricket (his father, George senior, had played for thirty-three years for Sussex between 1895-1928). George junior joined Sussex in 1931 and played for them for twenty-nine years until 1960. He later coached Sussex from 1960-64. He died in March 1985 aged 73.

	Games	Goals
League	7	1
Other Senior Matches	1	0
Friendly Matches	10	18
Combination League	75	53
London Midweek League	2	3
London Challenge Cup	6	5
Total	**101**	**80**

Honours:
2 London Combination Championship
  Medals   1933-34, 1934-35
London F.A. Cup Challenge Cup Winners
  Medal   1933-34

CRAYSTON, Jack   1934-43

Birth Place: Grange-over-sands, Lancs
Date of Birth: 9th October 1910

☛ Jack was a product of Barrow schools and Ulverston Town before joining Barrow in 1928. He spent two seasons at the ex-League club and played in seventy-seven league matches. Jack signed for yet another ex-league club, Bradford in 1930 and in four seasons with them he developed into one of the finest right halfs in the lower leagues. He played in nearly one hundred and twenty league games for Bradford before being transferred to Arsenal for £5,250 in May 1934. This was surprising though, because in his last season at Bradford, 1933-34, he broke both a wrist and a leg. A non-smoker and a tee-totaller, "Gentleman Jack" made his Arsenal league debut (when scoring) in a 8-1 victory against Liverpool at Highbury on 1st September 1934. Crayston, full of grace, an excellent ball player, strong in the tackle and brilliant in the air had started to make the international selectors take note of his performances and he was selected to play for England against the Anglo-Scots and he also won Football League representative honours. Although having stiff competition from Frank Hill, Jack played in thirty-seven league games during that 1934-35 League Championship season. In 1935-36 league campaign he won the first of his eight England caps, against Germany in December 1935. He played in thirty-six league games and was instrumental, with his sterling displays when helping Arsenal win the 1935-36 F.A. Cup Final versus Sheffield United. The dignified Crayston was known, on away trips, to carry the bible so that he could read his favourite psalms. This must have seemed strange as he had a very dry and wicked sense of humour. In 1936-37, no honours came his way before winning a second League Championship Medal when playing in thirty-one league games in 1937-38. In the last season, prior to the Second World War, Jack was still a regular in the side when playing in thirty-four league games and like so many others, he, in footballing terms, at his peak (twenty-nine years of age). Jack carried on his footballing career during the war playing in nearly one hundred games for the club but unfortunately a serious knee injury sustained in a match versus West Ham at Highbury in December 1943 curtailed his career. At this time Jack was seeing service as a flight-lieutenant in the R.A.F. On demobilisation he was appointed onto the coaching staff at Highbury. In June 1947, at the tender age of thirty-six he became assistant manager to Tom Whittaker and on the death of Tom he was appointed Arsenal manager in November 1956. For the first time in over thirty years the secretary/manager role was split. With the secretary's job going to Bob Wall. In his first season as manager 1956-57, he was quite pleased with the club's performance when finishing fifth in the league and reaching the Quarter-finals of the F.A. Cup. In 1957-58, with no money being available for transfers, Arsenal slipped to 12th place in the league which was the club's lowest position for thirty-eight years. To make matters worse the club suffered a shock F.A.Cup defeat at Northampton and although "gentleman Jack" realised the position of the club, he became disillusioned in the way the club seemed to be heading and in a boardroom meeting in May 1958 he tendered his resignation. In July 1958 he became manager of Doncaster Rovers until retiring from football in March 1961. He died in December 1992 aged 82.

Jack Crayston

	Games	Goals
League	168	16
F.A. Cup	16	1
Charity Shield	3	0
Other Senior Matches	4	0
Friendly Matches	4	0
Tours	13	4
Combination League	7	2
War Time	97	26
Total	**312**	**49**

Honours:
8 England Caps
1 Football League Cap

1 England Wartime cap
2 League Championship Medals
  1934-35, 1937-38
F.A. Cup Winners Medal 1935-36
F.A.Charity Shield Winners Medal 1938-39
F.A.Charity Shield Finalists Medals
  1935-36, 1936-37
Bath Coronation Cup Winners Medal
  1936-37
3 Football League South Championship
  Medals 1939-40, 1941-42, 1942-43
War Time F.A. Cup Winners Medal 1942-43
War Time F.A. Cup Finalists Medal 1940-41

CREEGAN, Walter   1921-23

Birth Place: Manchester, Lancashire
Date of Birth: 4th January 1902

🎺 Walter Creegan was a young outside right when joining Arsenal as an amateur in January 1921, turning professional in March the same year. Walter spent just over two years at Highbury in which he played in five League games (all in the 1921-22 season) making his League debut versus Chelsea on the 14th January 1922. He left the club during the summer of 1923 after which no trace can be found of him playing any first class football.

	Games	Goals
League	5	0
F.A.Cup	1	0
Other Senior Matches	1	0
Friendly Matches	20	7
Tours	4	0
Combination League	44	5
London Challenge Cup	1	0
Total	**76**	**12**

CUMNER, Horace   1938-46

Birth Place: Aberdare, Wales
Date of Birth: 31st March 1918

🎺 Horace joined Arsenal as a young 18 year old outside left and was immediately sent by the club to Margate, to learn the rudiments of the game. He was then loaned by Arsenal from Margate to Hull City in January 1938 returning to Highbury in May 1938. In the last season leading up to World War Two, 1938-39, Horace not only broke into the Arsenal league side, playing in twelve games when replacing Cliff Bastin, but he also won three Welsh Caps. His Arsenal League debut was when he scored the only goal in a 1-0 victory at Molineux versus Wolves. During the War this ex-Welsh schoolboy International served with the Royal Marines, receiving severe burns whilst in action. During this time he played in ten War-time Internationals for Wales. In August 1946 he was transferred to Notts County in part exchange for Ian McPherson. Cumner later played for Watford,

Scunthorpe and Bradford City.

	Games	Goals
League	12	2
F.A.Cup	1	1
Charity Shield	1	0
Other Senior Matches	1	0
Friendly Matches	3	1
Combination League	13	7
War Time	31	6
Southern League	7	2
Total	**69**	**19**

Honours:
3 Welsh Caps
10 Welsh War time Caps
F.A. Charity Shield winners medal 1938-39

CURTIS, George   1936-47

Birth Place: West Thurrock, Essex
Date of Birth: 3rd December 1919

🎺 George Frederick Curtis was a young seventeen year old inside forward when signing for Arsenal from Essex junior side Anglo (Purfleet) in December 1936, as an amateur. He then joined Margate, Arsenal's nursery, turning professional in April 1937 before returning to Highbury in February 1938. George played in two league games in the 1938-39 season of which his debut was a home fixture versus Blackpool on 10th April 1939. During the War he served in India as a corporal in the R.A.F. After the resumption of league football in 1946-47 he played in eleven league games before being transferred to Southampton for £8,000 in part exchange for Don Roper. Curtis was tall and willowy and made ball control look easy but lacked devil and drive. He stayed five seasons at the Dell, playing in nearly two hundred first team games. Curtis then played for French club, Valenciennes 1952-53, before returning to England as player coach at Chelmsford City. He, by this time, had become a qualified coach and over the following twenty years held many positions in coaching. These included Stevenage Town, Grays Ath., Sunderland, Brighton, England Youth team, The Sudan and coach to the Norwegian National team.

	Games	Goals
League	13	0
F.A.Cup	1	0
Friendly Matches	12	2
Combination League	76	10
Combination Cup	5	2
War Time	51	6
London Challenge Cup	3	1
Southern League	8	3
Total	**169**	**24**

Honours:
London Comb. Champ'ship Medal 1938-39
Football Comb. Champ'ship Medal 1946-47
Football Comb. Cup Finalist Medal 1946-47

DAVIDSON, Robert 1935-37

Birth Place: Lochgelly, Fifeshire
Date of Birth: 23rd April 1913

☛ Robert Trimming Davidson had played for Cowdenbeath and District Schoolboys before playing junior football for Bowhill Juniors and St. Bernards, linking up with St. Johnstone in March 1933. He was a regular for them for two seasons in which time Davidson won Scottish League Representative Honours. He came South of the Border when joining Arsenal in February 1935 as the new "Alex James". Robert made his league debut versus Stoke City at Highbury on 20th February 1935. Unfortunately his eleven appearances that season were not enough for him to win a championship medal. In 1935-36 he started the season as first choice inside right but lost his place to Ray Bowden and finished the season playing in thirteen league games. In the following term, 1936-37, he switched to inside left when replacing the ageing Alex James playing in twenty-eight league games scoring nine goals. This included the highlight of his Highbury career when scoring four times in a 5-1 victory at Fratton Park versus Portsmouth on 12th December 1936. Although he scored twice in five games at the beginning of the 1937-38 season he was transferred to Coventry City (in exchange for Leslie Jones) in November 1937. He finished his career playing non league football for Hinckley and Redditch before becoming player-manager of Rugby Town (when in his forty-first year). Robert later managed Redditch. Died October 1988, aged 75.

	Games	Goals
League	57	13
F.A.Cup	4	2
Charity Shield	2	0
Other Senior Matches	1	0
Friendly Matches	2	2
Tours	7	2
Combination League	36	18
London Challenge Cup	4	0
Total	**113**	**37**

Honours:
(WITH ST. JOHNSTONE)
2 Scottish League Caps
(WITH ARSENAL)
2 F.A. Charity Shield Finalists Medals
1935-36, 1936-37
London F.A. Challenge Cup Winners Medal
1935-36
Bath Coronation Cup Winners Medal
1936-37

DOUGALL, Peter 1933-37

Birth Place: Denny, Stirlingshire
Date of Birth: 21st March 1909

☛ Peter Dougall was yet another inside forward who was on the club's books who could never quite achieve the breakthrough into the league side in those halcyon days of the mid-1930's. Peter began his league career playing six league games for Burnley as an eighteen year old in 1927-28. He then tried his luck North of the Border with Clyde 1928-30, returning South to join Southampton for the end of the 1929-30 season. Dougall spent the best part of four seasons at the Dell playing in less than twenty league games before becoming one of Herbert Chapman's last signings for the club in October 1933 (this after a month's trial). Bernard Joy wrote in "Forward Arsenal". At ball control Dougall was superior to James and I have seen him do incredible things with the ball on the practice ground. In a match, however, he failed to harness that ability to the realities of the situation and he did not know, as James did, the right moment to pass. Peter never qualified for a League Championship Medal in 1933-34 but he filled in on five occasions for the injured Alex James. His Arsenal league debut was at Middlesbrough 10th February 1934. In 1934-35 he again was James's understudy when playing in eight league fixtures. The 1935-36 season saw Peter in the same situation, although he did manage to have an eight game stint in the side in January - March 1936. Side-lined for the whole of the 1936-37 season he moved on to Everton in August 1937 making his league debut for the club versus Blackpool in September 1937. He was in a forward line with Dixie Dean and Tommy Lawton as well as the youngest player to figure in a first division game (Albert Geldard). Dougall finished his career with Bury in 1938-39. He died in June 1974 aged 65.

	Games	Goals
League	21	4
F.A.Cup	2	1
Other Senior Matches	1	0
Friendly Matches	7	2
Tours	2	1
Combination League	80	14
London Challenge Cup	7	1
Total	**120**	**23**

Honours:
2 London Combination Championship
Medals 1933-34, 1934-35
London F.A. Challenge Cup Winners Medal
1933-34

DRAKE, Ted 1934-45

Birth Place: Southampton, Hampshire
Date of Birth: 16th August 1912

☛ The word legend is often used lightly and a person being described as a legend is seldom worthy of that claim. However, in Edward Joseph Drake's case, he was, he is, and always will be an Arsenal legend. Ted's career began when he was playing for Southampton Gasworks F.C. He later played for Winchester City before joining Southampton in November 1931. Ted scored a hat trick on his Saints league debut, and in total scored forty-eight league goals in seventy-two league games (1931-34), before joining Arsenal for £6,500 in March 1934, making his Arsenal league debut (when scoring the first goal) in a 3-2 home victory versus Wolves. Ted just missed out on qualifying for a League Championship Medal when playing in ten games and scoring seven goals, in 1934-35. He wrote himself into the Arsenal record books (probably for all-time) when he broke Jack Lambert's individual goal scoring record, scoring forty-two league goals in forty-one games. In this tally were three hat tricks versus Liverpool, Tottenham and Leicester City and four, four goal hauls against Birmingham, Chelsea, Wolves and Middlesbrough. These goals helped Arsenal to the League Championship and gained Drake international recognition when he won the first of only five England caps as one of seven Arsenal players to play against the Italians in the "Battle of Highbury" in November 1934. At this stage of his career, he was one of the most feared centre forwards in English football. Drake's main attributes were his powerful dashing runs, his great strength combined with terrific speed and a powerful shot. Ted was also brilliant in the air but above all, so unbelievably fearless. In fact many would say that he was too brave for his own good. This is shown by the fact that in his five seasons at Highbury there was no less than twenty-two occasions when he was out of the side due to injury. It was one of these injuries that put him out of action for ten weeks and nearly prevented him playing in the 1936 Cup Final. This no-nonsense, lion hearted, human dynamo thrived on the long through passes from James or Bastin and in 1935-36 he again wrote himself into the Arsenal and Football League record books when on the 14th December 1935 he equalled James Ross's goal scoring record in scoring seven times in a First Division League game. Plus bandages, minus James, Drake is allegedly known to have had eight shots at the Villa goal, the other hitting the bar. Drake claiming it was over the line, the referee waved aside his appeals and he said to Ted "Don't be greedy, isn't six enough". After the game the Villa players signed the ball and it

was the only souvenir he had at the time of his death. This was because all his caps, medals etc., were stolen when his house was burgled some years ago. Aston Villa, at this time, must have been sick of the sight of Ted Drake because later on in that 1935-36 season, in his come back match to try and prove his fitness for the forthcoming F.A. Cup Final, Ted scored the only goal against them in the corresponding match at Highbury which sent Aston Villa down to the Second Division for the first time in their history. Although not match fit, Ted played and scored the only goal in the 1935-36 final. Drake was the club's leading league goalscorer in each of his five seasons at the club, this included 1936-37 when he scored twenty times in twenty-six league appearances of which four were in a 5-0 victory at Burnden Park versus Bolton Wanderers. At this point in time you would have been thinking of Odeon Cinemas with Tracey and Hepburn, of young ovaltinies and the thousands of cigarette cards which sported Ted Drake's head. In 1937-38, he won a further League Championship Medal when scoring seventeen times in twenty-eight games, this included his only hat trick that season on the opening day at Goodison Park versus Everton. In the last season before the War he seemed to have fought off his injury problems when missing only four league games, scoring fourteen goals. An excellent all round sportsman, Ted adapted to most, and was good enough to play County Cricket for Hampshire. In one County game against Notts he had to face three balls from the awesome Frank Larwood. During the war, Ted was still seen in Arsenal colours when scoring eighty-six goals in one hundred and twenty-eight games, as well as being a flight-lieutenant in the R.A.F. However, Ted's career was brought to a premature end when he received a serious spinal injury, in a game at Reading in 1945. He became manager of Hendon in 1946, and then Reading between 1947-52, before being appointed Chelsea's manager in June 1955. In 1955, he guided Chelsea to their still one and only League Championship. Ted thus becoming the first person in football league history to play for and manage a Division One League Championship winning combination. In his nine seasons at Stamford Bridge, he , along with scout Jimmy Thompson produced players of the calibre of Peter Bonetti, Jimmy Greaves and Terry Venables. His son, Bobby, played for Fulham 1963-67. It was with Fulham where Ted's footballing days finished when he was reserve team manager and chief scout, later becoming a member of the board and then life president. He died May 1995 aged 82.

Ted Drake

	Games	Goals	Honours:
League	168	124	5 England Caps
F.A. Cup	14	12	2 League Championship Medals
Charity Shield	2	3	1934-35, 1937-38
Other Senior Matches	2	0	F.A. Cup Winners Medal 1935-36
Friendly Matches	4	8	F.A.Charity Shield Winners Medals
Tours	8	6	1934-35, 1938-39
Combination League	4	4	2 Football League South Championship
War Time	130	91	Medals 1941-42, 1942-43
Total	**332**	**248**	War Time F.A. Cup Winners Medal 1942-43
			War Time F.A. Cup Finalists Medal 1940-41

DRURY, George — 1938-46

Birth Place: Hucknall, Nottinghamshire
Date of Birth: 22nd January 1914

George had played junior football for Heanor Town and Loughborough Town before joining Sheffield Wednesday as a young, up and coming inside forward in September 1934. However, in four seasons at Hillsborough he played in less than fifty league games. Arsenal, surprisingly, paid £7,000 for his services in March 1938, George playing in the club's last eleven league games in that 1937-38 season. His Arsenal league debut was at Middlesbrough on 12th March 1938, in 1938-39 he played in twenty-three league games. George, fair haired, stocky and hard working was unfortunately temperamental and moody and therefore inconsistent. During the War George served in the R.A.F. before returning to Highbury when playing in four league games at the start of the 1946-47 season. He was then transferred to West Bromwich Albion in October 1946. Drury later played for Watford 1948-50 and in non-league circles with Darlaston and Linby Colliery. He died in 1972 aged 58.

George Drury

	Games	Goals
League	38	3
F.A.Cup	2	0
Other Senior Matches	3	3
Friendly Matches	2	2
Tours	8	6
Combination League	20	17
Combination Cup	2	1
War Time	24	10
London Challenge Cup	3	2
Southern League	1	1
Total	**103**	**45**

Honours:
London Comb. Champ'ship Medal 1938-39

DUNN, Steven — 1919-25

Birth Place: Darlaston, Staffordshire
Date of Birth: 31st January 1893

At five foot eight inches, Steven Dunn was one of the club's shortest ever goalkeepers. An army man, Steven had served with the Gloucestershire regiment in India, when joining Arsenal from the army in May 1919. In that first season at the club he deputised for E.C. Williamson on sixteen occasions in the League of which his debut was in a 3-2 victory at Goodison Park on the 11th October 1919. During the following two seasons 1921-23 he played in only ten League games due to the consistency of Williamson. After Ernest had conceded fourteen goals in the opening five games of the 1922-23 season, Steven was given the chance to show his ability, playing in seventeen consecutive games (the last two were heavy defeats at Huddersfield and Bolton). Steven had not grabbed his opportunity and so third choice keeper, Jock Robson, filled the breach. In his last two seasons at Highbury, with the presence of Robson and the newly signed Dan Lewis, Steven's football consisted totally of reserve team duties. He retired during the summer of 1925 when he became a businessman in the Bristol area.

	Games	Goals
League	43	0
F.A.Cup	1	0
Other Senior Matches	3	0
Friendly Matches	32	0
Tours	12	0
Combination League	143	0
London Challenge Cup	2	0
Total	**236**	**0**

DUNNE, Jimmy — 1933-36

Birth Place: Dublin, Ireland
Date of Birth: 3rd September 1905

James Dunne had a thirteen season league career, 1925-38 in which time, although being a reserve for five of those seasons whilst with Sheffield United and Arsenal, he amassed the amazing total of one hundred and seventy-six league goals in just two hundred and fifty-nine league games. A legend in Sheffield United's history, where only three players have bettered his total of one hundred and forty-three goals, 65 years on he still holds the club's individual scoring record in a season (forty-six in 1930-31, which included nine hat tricks). His league scoring rate at Bramall Lane was an incredible 83%. James began his career with Shamrock Rovers in 1923 and crossed the Irish sea in 1925 to join New Brighton where his goalscoring ability was soon to be seen when he scored six times in only eight league games at the start of the 1925-26 season. This resulted in him catching the eye of 1st Division clubs and he subsequently moved on to Sheffield United in February 1926 Dunne won the first of his twenty-three Irish caps in 1927-28 as well as being the club's leading scorer for four consecutive seasons 1929-33. These goalscoring exploits tempted Arsenal into paying £8,250 for his services in September 1933 making his Arsenal league debut in a 6-0 victory at Highbury versus Middlesbrough on 30th September 1933. He scored nine goals in twenty-three league games in that 1933-34 season helping Arsenal win the League Championship although at the end of that season he lost his place to the newly signed Ted Drake. In Drake's record breaking season of 1934-35, James managed to play in only one league game, and he was being described as the most expensive reserve player in the history of English League football. Dunne faired no better in 1935-36, playing in only six league games and he was transferred to Southampton (at a £6,250 loss) for £2,000 in July 1936. Bernard Joy wrote of him "Fair-haired, he was brilliant in the air and had a short striding run with great balance". Another quote "Dunne seemed to be bewildered by the magnificence of Highbury". But Cliff Bastin described Dunne as "One of the best five centre forwards he had seen". Jimmy spent 2 seasons at the Dell being their leading league scorer in 1936-37 (before returning home to Ireland to firstly play and then coach at Shamrock Rovers). Jimmy later joined Bohemians as a coach in 1942 before returning to Shamrock Rovers for a third time in 1947. He died December 1949 aged 44.

	Games	Goals
League	28	10
F.A. Cup	4	3
Charity Shield	1	0
Friendly Matches	2	1
Tours	1	0
Combination League	48	42
Total	**84**	**56**

Honours:
22 Irish Caps
2 Irish Football League Caps
League Championship Medal 1933-34
F.A. Charity Shield Finalists Medal 1935-36
London Combination Championship Medal
1934-35

EARLE, Stanley — 1922-24

Birth Place: Stratford, London
Date of Birth: 6th September 1897

Stanley was the son of Harry Earle who had been a centre half for Clapton, Millwall and Nott'm Forest. An England schoolboy

International, he was on the books of Clapton where he won three amateur caps as well as an F.A. Amateur Cup Winners Medal in 1924. At the same time he was also an amateur on Arsenal's books from March 1922-July 1924. He played in four League games for Arsenal (three goals) spread over three seasons of which his League debut was at Villa Park versus Aston Villa on the 18th March 1922. A creative six foot plus inside right, he must have impressed the West Ham management team when scoring twice against them at Highbury in September 1923. During this period Stan twice represented the F.A. eleven versus the Army. He signed as an amateur for West Ham in August 1924 (later turning professional). Over the following eight seasons he struck up a fine understanding when scheming many goals for the prolific Vic Watson. He played in over two hundred and fifty League games for the Hammers: his consistency winning him a full England cap versus Ireland 1927. Stan finished his career with Clapton Orient (1932-33) and later had spells as the Walthamstow Avenue coach and manager of Leyton. He died in September 1971 aged 74.

	Games	Goals
League	4	3
Combination League	1	0
Total	**5**	**3**

Honours:
(WITH CLAPTON)
F.A. Amateur Cup Winners Medal   1923-24
3 England Amateur Caps
(WITH WEST HAM)
1 England Cap

ELVEY, John   1922-23

Birth Place: Luton, Bedfordshire
Date of Birth:

☛ John had played junior football in the Luton area before playing for Luton Town and Millwall during World War One. Whilst at Luton he won unofficial England honours in South Africa in 1920. In 1920-21 he joined Bolton Wanderers playing the first three games of the season before losing his place to Herbert Baverstock. Disillusioned with reserve team football at Burnden Park , Elvey decided to try his luck with Arsenal in September 1922. Unfortunately for him his opportunities were scarce with Bradshaw and Mackie preferred for the right back position. John's only game for the club was at Highbury versus Preston North End on 14th April 1923.

	Games	Goals
League	1	0
Other Senior Matches	1	0
Friendly Matches	16	0
Combination League	9	0
Total	**27**	**0**

FARR, Andrew   1937-40

Birth Place: Larkhall, Motherwell
Date of Birth: 7th August 1911

☛ Andrew had moved South of the Border to join Arsenal's nursery club, Margate, from Scottish junior side Yoker Athletic in December 1937. At five foot four and a half inches, Andrew is one of the smallest players to have appeared for the club. In the two seasons leading up to the 2nd World War he was a key member, at inside forward, in the club's reserve and junior sides. Andrew was given two league opportunities in the last two games of the 1938-39 season getting off to a dream start when scoring the first goal in a 2-1 victory at the Baseball Ground versus Derby County on 29th April 1939. During the War he served in munition factories in Scotland after he had been transferred to Airdrieonians in August 1940.

	Games	Goals
League	2	1
Friendly Matches	4	3
Combination League	31	15
War time	1	0
Southern League	28	7
Total	**66**	**26**

Honours:
London Combination Championship Medal
1937-38

FIELDS, Alf   1936-52

Birth Place: Canning Town, London
Date of Birth: 15th November 1918

☛ Alf had played for West Ham schoolboys and a West Ham youth club before joining Arsenal as an amateur in January 1936, after serving a mandatory "apprenticeship" at Margate. Alf turned professional in May 1937. Like his close friend, Ernie Collett, HE was to become one of Arsenal's greatest servants when serving the club as a player, coach and trainer over a course of forty-seven years. Prior to the Second World War, he had to be content in being reserve to Bernard Joy and Leslie Compton, although he did play in three league games in 1938-39 of which his league debut was at Blackpool on 7th April 1939 (this being because Bernard Joy had broken his nose against Middlesbrough on April Fools Day). Alf later stated that " One of my biggest thrills in life was playing in the same side as Eddie Hapgood and George Male". During the war he served with the Royal Artillery in Africa and Italy winning the British Empire Medal. On his return to Highbury , 1946-47, he played in eight league games at the start of Arsenal's League Championship campaign of 1947-48. He had figured in all of the club's

first six league fixtures (when deputising for Leslie Compton who was finishing his cricketing season) when disaster struck. Fields collided with George Swindin in a game versus Bolton at Highbury and damaged both knee ligaments which virtually ended his playing career. Alf stayed on the club's books for a further four seasons helping the youngsters in the reserve and youth sides. By this time, arthritis had set into his injured leg and he was advised to retire. Whilst serving the club over the following thirty-one years he gained an F.A. trainers certificate and took up physiotherapy before retiring three days after his 65th birthday in November 1983.

	Games	Goals
League	19	0
Other Senior Matches	2	0
Friendly Matches	24	0
Tours	15	0
Combination League	87	0
Combination Cup	23	0
War time	9	0
Eastern Counties League	29	0
Southern League	3	0
London Challenge Cup	7	0
London Midweek League	4	0
Total	**222**	**0**

Honours:
London Combination Championship Medal
1938-39
Football Combination Championship Medal
1946-47

GRAHAM, Alexander   1911-24

Birth Place: Hurlford, Ayrshire, Scotland
Date of Birth: 11th July 1890

☛ Alex was playing in junior football in Lanarkshire with Larkhall United before joining Arsenal on a month's trial in December 1911, turning professional in January 1912. Alex spent the best part of a year playing in reserve and youth team football before making his Arsenal league debut on Christmas Day 1912 in a home fixture at Manor Field versus Notts County. Graham finished that season playing in twelve league games. In 1913-14, he deputised thirteen times in the league for Angus McKinnon at left half back before, in 1914-15, he won a regular place in the league side (when playing in all three half back positions). During the war he returned North of the Border and in 1919-20 Alex came back to Highbury to play in 22 league games. In 1920-21 he defended his position as centre half when playing in thirty league games, scoring five goals (all penalties) and won a Scottish Cap versus Ireland. In 1921-22, Graham lost his centre half position to Jack Butler at the beginning of the season, even though playing in twenty-one league games. In the following season, Alex played in seventeen league games, before, in 1923-24, he finished his career at Highbury scoring once in twenty-five league matches. Graham was transferred to Brentford in December 1924 staying for a season at the club before becoming assistant manager in December 1925. He died in 1943, aged 52.

	Games	Goals
League	166	17
F. A. Cup	13	3
Other Senior Matches	6	0
Friendly Matches	13	4
Tours	3	3
Combination League	47	13
War time	5	1
London League Reserves	13	2
South Eastern League	60	13
London Challenge Cup	13	2
Total	**339**	**58**

Honours:
1 Scottish Cap
London F.A. Challenge Cup Winners Medal
1923-24
London F.A. Challenge Cup Finalists Medal
1914-15

GREENAWAY, David   1908-21

Birth Place: Coatdyke, Lanark, Scotland
Date of Birth: 1889

🐦 David joined Woolwich Arsenal from Scottish junior side Shettleston F.C. (Glasgow) in May 1908. This then nineteen year old outside right, settled straight into the league side and in that first season at Manor Field, David missed only two league games. David's debut was at Meadow Lane versus Notts County September 1908. During the following four seasons, Greenaway developed into one of the league's most respected wingers, playing in thirty-six, twenty-two, twenty-three, and twenty-seven league matches during that period 1909-13. However, he lost his place to the veteran Jock Rutherford in 1913-14 and 1914-15 playing in only fourteen league games in these two seasons. During the 1st World War David served with the Royal Field Artillery and in the two seasons 1919-21 after the resumption of peacetime he had to be content with reserve team football. He was released on a free transfer during the summer of 1921.

	Games	Goals
League	161	13
F. A. Cup	9	0
Other Senior Matches	5	0

Friendly Matches	28	9
Tours	1	0
Combination League	41	4
London League Reserves	20	3
South Eastern League	57	11
London Challenge Cup	11	0
Total	**333**	**40**

GRIFFITHS, William 'Mal'   1936-38

Birth Place: Merthyr, Wales
Date of Birth: 8th March 1919

🐦 Mal Griffiths was playing in the local leagues in his home town when joining Arsenal as an amateur in September 1935. He spent seven months at Highbury before going to Margate, Arsenal's nursery, in May 1936 returning to Arsenal and signing professional in February 1937. He was the club's regular reserve team right winger before replacing Alf Kirchen in nine league games at the end of the 1937-38 league championship season. His league debut was versus Leicester City (the club he was to serve for over eighteen years) on 2nd February 1938. The £800 which City paid Arsenal must have been one of the best investments made by any club. Mal played in over 400 first team games for the club as well as winning eleven Welsh Caps (his debut was Northern Ireland 1946-47). He also helped City to win the Second Division Championship in 1953-54 and he scored Leicester's only goal in the 1-3 defeat by Portsmouth in the 1948-49 F.A. Cup Final. He finished his career with Burton Albion. He died in April 1969 aged 50.

	Games	Goals
League	9	5
Other Senior Matches	1	0
Friendly Matches	8	3
Combination League	38	18
London Challenge Cup	3	0
Southern League	2	0
Total	**61**	**26**

Honours:
(WITH LEICESTER)
11 Welsh Caps
F.A. Cup Finalists Medal   1948-49
Division 2 Championship Medal   1953-54

GROVES, Frederick   1912-21

Birth Place: Shadwell (Stepney), London
Date of Birth: 13th January 1891

🐦 Frederick was a utility forward playing as an amateur with Glossop when joining Arsenal in August 1912, turning professional fourteen months later in October 1913. He played in three League games in 1912-13 (All defeats in Arsenal's disastrous relegation campaign) of which his debut was at the

Baseball Ground, Derby on the 7th Decmber 1912. In 1913-14, with Arsenal back in Division Two, Frederick played in a further three League games (all defeats) followed by two League games in 1914-15. Groves was not on the winning side until his eighth League match versus Wolves. Fred played over one hundred and thirty games for the club during the War years and resumed his League career when playing in twenty-nine League games in 1919-20. Frederick finally left Highbury in August 1921, joining Brighton for £500. Groves later played for Charlton in the 1924-25 season.

	Games	Goals
League	50	6
F.A.Cup	3	1
Other Senior Matches	2	0
Friendly Matches	18	4
Combination League	18	2
London Challenge Cup	2	2
War time	133	31
South Eastern League	72	17
London League Reserves	19	6
Total	**317**	**69**

HADEN, Samson   1922-27

Birth Place: Royston nr Barnsley, Yorks
Date of Birth: 17th July 1903

🐦 Samson Haden was a young coal miner playing for Castleford Town when joining Arsenal as an amateur in March 1922, turning professional the following month. In his first full season at Highbury he featured permanently for the reserve side (on either wing) when helping the club in winning their first ever London Combination Championship. Haden broke through into the League side when replacing Joe Toner versus West Ham at Upton Park on the 27th August 1923 finishing that season playing in thirty-one League games. However, Toner replaced Haden for the first six months of the 1924-25 season, Samson though, regained the left wing berth to play in the last fifteen League games. In the 1925-26 season Haden and Toner were still battling it out for the left wing position with Haden victorious, playing in twenty-five consecutive League games until, unfortunately, breaking a leg in a League encounter with Burnley at Highbury on the 3rd February 1926. He recovered to play in seventeen League games in 1926-27. His new rival at the club was Sid Hoar who eventually succeeded in gaining Herbert Chapman's confidence when playing in the club's first ever F.A.Cup final against Cardiff City. He left Highbury in October 1927 to join Notts County. Samson later managed Peterborough United. Died February 1974, aged 70.

	Games	Goal
League	88	10
F.A.Cup	5	1
Friendly Matches	32	20

Tours	10	2
Combination League	67	23
London Challenge Cup	8	2
Total	**210**	**58**

Honours:

London Combination Championship Medal
1922-23
London F.A. Challenge Cup Winners Medal
1923-24
London F.A. Challenge Cup Finalists Medal
1925-26

HALLIDAY, David   1929-30

Birth Place: Dumfries, Scotland
Date of Birth: 11th December 1897

☞ David Halliday would not be one of the first footballers mentioned by a football supporter discussing great goalscorers, but in reality, he was one of the top six strikers in the history of British football, when between 1919-35 David scored an incredible 347 English and Scottish league goals in only 464 games. David was working as a motor mechanic when he was given the chance to join his local side, Queen of the South, where from the outside left position he showed his goalscoring abilities when in that 1919-20 season he scored thirteen goals in nineteen league games. Halliday moved to St. Mirren in 1920 staying there a season before joining Dundee in 1921-22. At Dens Park he was converted to centre forward where his ability to snap up half chances enabled him to set a new club scoring record (which still stands today) when scoring thirty-eight league goals in 1923-24. This form earned him a Scottish League cap and he also helped Dundee (when losing) to the 1925 Scottish Cup Final. By the summer of 1925, he had scored ninety-one league goals in only one hundred and twenty-five games for Dundee and it came as no surprise when (the bank of England club) Sunderland paid £4,000 to obtain his services. Halliday repaid them well being ever present in 1925-26, scoring 38 goals and in 1926-27 was again the club's leading scorer with thirty-six goals in thirty-three games. This included him scoring four against Manchester Utd. 1927-28 saw him score in each of the first eight league games and he went on to score thirty-six times in thirty-eight games. However, he surpassed this in 1928-29 and scored in twenty-four of the forty-two league games when scoring forty-three league goals, in 1995, this still remains a Sunderland record. At the beginning of the 1929-30 season and with having the record of scoring one hundred and sixty-two goals in only one hundred and seventy-five league and cup games (virtually a goal a game) David was transferred to Arsenal (as a supposed replacement for Jack Lambert) for £6,500 in November 1929,

making his Arsenal league debut in a 3-2 win at St. Andrews versus Birmingham on 9th November 1929. In the remainder of that season he played in 15 league games scoring eight league goals which included four at Filbert Street in the famous 6-6 draw with Leicester City. However, he missed being selected for the 1930 F.A. Cup Final versus Huddersfield. In 1930-31 Jack Lambert regained his first team place and without getting a sniff of first team football, Halliday was transferred to Manchester City for £5,700 in November 1930. In the best part of three seasons at Maine Road he kept up his formidable scoring rate when scoring forty-seven times in seventy-four games, but he missed out on City's F.A. Cup Final appearances of 1933 and 1934. David finished his playing career with Clapton Orient 1933-35, being their leading scorer in each season. Halliday became player-manager of Yeovil and Petters Utd. in the Southern League in 1935 before becoming manager of Aberdeen in December 1937. Over the following 18 years he guided the Dons to a Scottish League Championship in 1954-55, to three Scottish Cup Finals, a win versus Hibernian in 1947 and two defeats versus Rangers in 1953 and Celtic in 1954. A Scottish League Cup Final, when losing to Rangers in 1947. Halliday then managed Leicester City 1955-58, guiding them to the Second Division Championship in 1956-57. Even though Hughie Gallagher was the Scottish selectors choice of centre forward at the time, a serious question can be asked. Why was David Halliday never selected to play for Scotland?. He died January 1970 aged 72.

	Games	Goals
League	15	8
Friendly Matches	1	4
Combination League	29	39
London Challenge Cup	3	3
Total	**48**	**54**

Honours:

(with Dundee) 1 Scottish League Cap
Scottish Cup Finalists Medal   1924-25
(with Arsenal) Two London Combination
Championship Medals   1929-30, 1930-31

HAPGOOD, Eddie   1927-45

Birth Place: Bristol, Gloucestershire
Date of Birth: 27th September 1908

☞ Eddie Hapgood was undoubtedly Arsenal's greatest ever left back and he was affectionately known as the "ambassador of football". Including war time internationals, Eddie played forty-three times for England of which he captained his country, on a then record, thirty-four occasions. Added to this he played in five England trial games and won four Football League Caps between

1932 -45. The names of Male and Hapgood were so inter-linked that their names rolled off the tongue as have Marks and Spencers and Morecambe and Wise. In that time they played in excess of three hundred games for Arsenal and England. However, Eddie's career did not get off to a blistering start for he was turned down by Bristol Rovers after a trial and he was playing for Kettering Town when Herbert Chapman signed him for £1,000, in October 1927. At this juncture of his career he was so frail at nine st six lbs that he used to get knocked out almost everytime he headed the ball. It was discovered that he was a vegetarian and to help build his physique, Arsenal trainer Tom Whittaker, put him on a diet which consisted almost entirely of steak. By doing so, it built Hapgood into being a fine figure of a man and by January 1929 he was the club's regular left back. Eddie had made his league debut when deputising for Horace Cope at St. Andrews, Birmingham on the 19th November 1927. Hapgood's many splendid attributes included, being technically exceptional, he showed shrewd anticipation and he was elegant, polished, unruffled and calm. But above all Chapman and Whittaker

Eddie Hapgood

developed him into a footballing full back. Eddie Hapgood was also a courageous player, this was not better exemplified than when he broke his nose in "the battle of Highbury" in November 1934 versus Italy. Between 1928-39, he played in nearly four hundred and fifty first team games for the club and in this period, January 1928 to the outbreak of War, Eddie missed only forty-seven out of four hundred and thirty-seven league games played by the club. This consistency was rewarded, for he won five League Championship Medals, played in three F.A. Cup Finals as well as playing in six F.A. Charity Shield Finals. Unfortunately, like so many other players of the time, he was at the peak of his career when war came (being only 30). During hostilities he served as a flying officer in the R.A.F. though he did manage to find time to play in over one hundred games for the club between 1939-45. Hapgood retired in December 1945. Unfortunately, Eddie left highbury in unhappy circumstances and for political and personal reasons it is not for anyones benefit they are recorded. After the war he managed Blackburn Rovers, was player coach for a period at Shrewsbury Town and later managed Watford 1948-50, and Bath City 1950-56. Eddie Hapgood's name will live on, a football immortal, the prince of all full backs. He died April 1973 aged 64.

	Games	Goals
League	393	2
F.A. Cup	41	0
Charity Shield	6	0
Other Senior Matches	9	0
Friendly Matches	21	0
Tours	22	0
Combination League	50	3
London Challenge Cup	1	0
War Time	102	1
Total	**645**	**6**

Honours:
30 England Caps
13 England Wartime Caps
4 Football League Caps
5 League Championship Medals   1930-31
        1932-33, 1933-34, 1934-35, 1937-38
2 F.A. Cup Winners Medal 1929-30, 1935-36
1 F.A. Cup Finalists Medal   1931-32
2 Wartime Football League South
    Champ'ship Medals   1939-40, 1940-41
1 F.A. Cup Wartime Finalists Medal 1940-41
4 F.A Charity Shield Winners Medals
        1930-31, 1931-32, 1933-34, 1934-35
2 F.A Charity Shield Finalists Medals
                    1935-36, 1936-37
2 London Combination Championship Medal
                    1927-28, 1928-29
2 Sheriff of London Charity Shield Winners
    Medals   1930-31, 1932-33
3 Northampton Charity Shield Winners
    Medals   1929-30, 1930-31, 1931-32
Bath Coronation Cup Winners Medal
                    1936 -37

HARDINGE, Harold 'Wally'   1913-21

Birth Place: Greenwich, London
Date of Birth: 25th February 1886

H.T.W. Hardinge was an inside forward who had played junior football for Eltham, Tonbridge and Maidstone when joining Newcastle in May 1905. In his two and a half years at St. James's Park, he played in only nine league games, this due to the great depth of inside forwards on the club's books at the time. Wally was transferred to Sheffield United for £350 in December 1907 and in his six seasons at Bramall Lane he matured into one of the trickiest inside forwards in the game. Hardinge scored nearly fifty league goals in nearly 150 league games, and was their leading scorer in 1908-9 and 1912-13 and he deservedly won an England cap in April 1910 versus Scotland. Harold returned South when joining Arsenal for £500 in June 1913. Wally made his Arsenal league debut in the first ever league match to be played at Highbury v. Leicester Fosse 6th September 1913. In that season he scored four times in twenty-nine league games. Hardinge scored seven league goals in only twelve league games at the start of the 1914-15 season before being called up to serve his country as a chief petty officer in both the Royal Navy and Air Force during World War One. On his return to Highbury in 1919-20 he played in thirteen games but in his last season at the club he never appeared in the league side having to be content with reserve team football. He retired in the summer of 1921. Although a very good footballer, he was an even better cricketer, in a 31 year career, 1902-33, he played in over 600 first class matches for Kent scoring nearly 34,000 runs and became one of the select band of double Internationalists (at the same time as Andy Ducat) when chosen to represent England versus Australia at Headingley in 1921. Wally was later manager/coach to Tottenham reserve team in 1935 and was an employee of John Wisden (sports outfitters) for a long period. He died in May 1965, aged 79.

	Games	Goals
League	54	14
F. A. Cup	1	0
Other Senior Matches	2	0
Friendly Matches	7	8
Combination League	22	8
War time	70	37
London League Reserves	3	0
South Eastern League	4	3
London Challenge Cup	9	6
Total	**172**	**76**

Honours:
(WITH SHEFFIELD UTD)
1 England Cap
(WITH ARSENAL)
London F.A. Challenge Cup Finalists Medal
                    1914-15

HARPER, William   1925-27, 1930-31

Birth Place: Tarbrax, Lanarks, Scotland
Date of Birth: 19th January 1898

Bill Harper began his goalkeeping career in Scottish junior football with Winchburgh Thistle and Edinburgh Emmett during World War 1. During the war he was also a heavyweight boxing champion with the 5th Brigade Scots Guards who served in France. In September 1921 he signed for Hibernian, spending four full seasons at Easter Road, playing in over one hundred Scottish league matches, winning two Scottish Cup Finalists Medals, and being capped nine times by Scotland winning two Scottish League caps. Bill became one of Herbert Chapman's first signings when joining Arsenal for £4,000 in November 1925. Bill replaced both "Jock" Robson and Dan Lewis as the club's number one custodian playing in nineteen league games of which his Arsenal league debut was in a 6-1 victory at Highbury versus Bury on 14th November 1925. Harper also played in two further internationals for Scotland versus England and Northern Ireland. Harper began the 1926-27 season, playing in twenty league games but caught the wrath of Herbert Chapman after a 2-4 home defeat in front of a 50,000 home crowd versus Tottenham. William only played in a further three games that season before leaving the club in the summer of 1927 when he emigrated to the U.S.A., he stayed for three years playing for Fall River F.C. On his return to England, Herbert Chapman surprisingly resigned him in September 1930 and in his first season back at the club he overtook Keyser and Preedy as the first choice keeper playing in nineteen league games, helping Arsenal win their first ever League Championship in 1930-31. However he played in just the first two league games of 1931-32 (losing his place to Preedy) and after the signing of Frank Moss in November 1931 his league career with Arsenal was over. Harper left Highbury for the second time in December 1931 when he was transferred to Plymouth Argyle. Although he played in less than one hundred league games for the Pilgrims he served them well for eight seasons before retiring in the summer of 1939, aged 41. William worked at Rosyth Dockyard during the 2nd World War before returning to Plymouth where he served as trainer, 1945-50, groundsman 1950-64, and as club helper into his 70's. Bill was granted a testimonial by Plymouth in the early 1980's and it was fitting that Arsenal was the opposition. He will be remembered by his ex-colleagues for his cigar smoking and for the enormous length of his goal kicks. He died in April 1989 aged 91.

	Games	Goals
League	63	0
F.A. Cup	10	0
Other Senior Matches	2	0
Friendly Matches	1	0
Tours	7	0
Combination League	26	0
London Challenge Cup	3	0
London Midweek League	6	0
Total	**118**	**0**

Honours:
(WITH HIBERNIAN)
9 Scotland Caps
2 Scottish Football League Caps
2 Scottish F.A. Cup Finalists Medals
1922-23, 1923-24
(WITH ARSENAL)
2 Scotland Caps
League Championship Medals   1930-31
London Combination Championship Medal
1926-27
Sheriff of London Charity Shield Winners
Medal   1930-31
Northampton Charity Shield Winners Medal
1930-31

HAYNES, Alf   1928-33

Birth Place: Oxford
Date of Birth: 4th April 1907

Alf Haynes was a fine servant for the best part of six seasons when playing for the club in any of the half back positions when deputising for the likes of Bob John and Herbie Roberts at the start of the club's golden era. Alf had originally joined Arsenal from his home town club, Oxford City, in May 1928. He played in only twenty-nine league games during the course of his career at Highbury of which his best spell was playing in thirteen league games in 1929-30 just after making his debut versus Liverpool on 21st December 1929. For the reserves, he won a host of honours as well as playing in the 1-0 defeat of West Bromwich in the 1931-32 F.A. Charity Shield. Having reached the age of 26 and with the club's half back line of Hill, Roberts and John looking as solid as ever, Haynes was transferred to Crystal Palace, (where he stayed for three seasons) in November 1933. He died in June 1953 aged 48.

	Games	Goals
League	29	0
F.A.Cup	1	0
Charity Shield	1	0
Other Senior Matches	3	0
Friendly Matches	22	0
Tours	4	0
Combination League	174	4
London Challenge Cup	9	0
London Midweek	8	0
Total	**251**	**4**

Honours:
F.A. Charity Shield Winners Medal   1931-32
Two Sheriff of London Shield Winners
Medals   1930-31, 1932-33
Northampton Charity Shield Winners Medal
1931-32
Three London Combination Championship
Medal   1928-29, 1929-30, 1930-31

HENDERSON, William   1921-23

Birth Place: Carlisle, Cumberland
Date of Birth: 11th January 1899

Arsenal paid Carlisle United £1,000 for William Henderson's services in October 1921. He initially was a centre forward, who in the 1921-22 season played in five League games when deputising for Henry White or Andrew Young making his League debut in a 0-2 defeat at Leeds Road, Huddersfield on the 22nd October 1921. In the 1922-23 season he moved out to the right wing but could only muster two League matches in his newly found position. He was allowed to leave the club to join Luton Town in March 1923. He had a short spell with the Hatters before enjoying a five year stint with Southampton (1923-28) where he played in nearly two hundred first team games. He finished his career with Coventry City 1928-30. Died January 1934 aged 35.

	Games	Goals
League	7	0
Other Senior Matches	1	0
Friendly Matches	15	6
Combination League	34	13
London Challenge Cup	4	1
Total	**61**	**20**

Honours:
London Combination Championship Medal
1922-23
London F.A. Challenge Cup Winners Medal
1921-22

HILL, Frank   1932-36

Birth Place: Forfar, Scotland
Date of Birth: 21st May 1906

Frank began his career with Scottish Second Division side Forfar 1924-28. Transferred to Aberdeen in the summer of 1928 where he stayed for a further four seasons playing in over one hundred league games, and from the right half position Frank won three Scottish caps and a Scottish Football League Cap. Frank "Tiger" Hill (nicknamed because of his tigerish tackling) was transferred to Arsenal for £3,000 in May 1932. In his four seasons at Highbury although under strong competition from his fellow wing-halfs (Charlie Jones, Bob John, Wilf Copping and Jack Crayston) Hill still managed to win the approval of managers Chapman and Allison when winning three League Championship Medals. In 1932-33, he played in twenty-six league games when basically sharing the right half position with Charlie Jones. The following season, 1933-34, Frank played in twenty-five league games which were shared between left and right half and occasionally on the right wing. He also appeared in Arsenal's 3-0 victory in the 1933-34 F.A. Charity Shield versus Everton. In the following campaign 1934-35 he had strong competition for a wing half place from Copping and Crayston although he deputised for both of them when playing in fifteen league games. However, the England internationals held such a stranglehold on their positions, Hill was reduced to playing in only ten league games in 1935-36. It was inevitable that this Scottish international wanted away and he was transferred to Blackpool in June 1936. Frank helped the "Seasiders" when captain, to promotion and was ever present in 1936-37. Hill joined Southampton in September 1937 and played for them in the two seasons up to the Second World War. During the war he became assistant trainer to Preston North End and was a flight lieutenant in India with the R.A.F. Hill later became player-manager of Crewe Alexandra (July 1944 - Sept. 1948) making his final league appearance when in his forty-second year. He went on to manage Burnley, 1948-54, Preston North End, 1954-56, and became coach in Iraq in Jan. 1957 before returning to England to manage Notts County 1958-61, guiding them to promotion in the Third Division 1959-60. Frank then went on to manage Charlton Athletic 1961-65 and finished his long career in football in his sixtieth year when he was scouting for Manchester City. He died in June 1993 aged 87.

	Games	Goals
League	76	4
F.A. Cup	2	0
Charity Shield	3	0
Other Senior Matches	2	0
Friendly Matches	7	0
Tours	4	2
Combination League	53	5
London Challenge Cup	3	2
Total	**150**	**13**

Honours:
(WITH ABERDEEN)
3 Scotland Caps
1 Scottish Football League Cap
(WITH ARSENAL)
3 League Championship Medals
1932-33, 1933-34, 1934-35
2 F.A. Charity Shield Winners Medal
1933-34, 1934-35
F.A. Charity Shield Finalists Medal
1935-36
Sheriff of London Charity Shield Winners
Medal   1932-33

HOAR, Sidney　　　　1924-29

Birth Place:　Leagrave, Nr Luton, Beds
Date of Birth:　28th November 1895

Sidney was a winger who could operate on either flank. He joined Luton Town as a fifteen year old from local junior side, Luton Clarence in 1911. In the four seasons leading up to the First World War he was only seen playing in the club's reserve and junior teams. During hostilities he suffered a German poisonous gas attack whilst in action in Northern France which put his footballing career in jeapordy. However, he gained full recovery and returned to Kenilworth Road serving them well for five seasons playing in over one hundred and fifty league games before joining Arsenal for £3,000 in November 1924. In that 1924-25 season he played in nineteen league games of which his Arsenal league debut was at Ninian Park versus Cardiff on 29th November 1924. Hoar also played in one England trial match. In 1925-26 he began the season as the club's first choice right wing but lost it midway through the season to Herbert Lawson and later to the newly signed Joe Hulme. In the first five months of the 1926-27 season Hoar was left in the cold with Hulme and Haden occupying the wing positions. However he returned to the league side on the left wing playing in fifteen consecutive games before being injured in a home fixture versus Aston Villa. This put in doubt whether he would pass a fitness test for the 1927 F.A. Cup Final versus Cardiff City. He came through the test alright but had a miserable time when facing Cardiff's right back Jimmy Nelson. Sidney enjoyed his finest season at the club in 1927-28 when missing only four league games (nine goals). When Welsh international Charlie Jones was signed in May 1928 Sid's first team chances were limited and he played in only six league games in 1928-29 before being transferred to Clapton Orient for £1000 in September 1929. He served them for one season before retiring in the summer of 1930. Died May 1967, aged 71.

	Games	Goals
League	100	16
F.A. Cup	17	2
Friendly Matches	8	1
Tours	5	1
Combination League	34	3
London Challenge Cup	4	0
Total	**168**	**23**

Honours:
F.A. Cup Finalists Medal　　　　1926-27
London F.A. Challenge Cup Finalists Medal
　　　　　　　　　　　　　　1925-26
London Combination Championship Winners
　Medal　　　　　　　　　　　1926-27

HOPKINS, James　　　　1919-23

Birth Place:　Belfast, Northern Ireland
Date of Birth:　12th July 1901

James was a young eighteen year old inside forward playing for Belfast United when joining Arsenal soon after the First World War in September 1919. In his first season at the club, 1919-20, he became a regular member of the reserve side before breaking through to make his League debut (when scoring) in a 4-3 victory at The Hawthorns versus West Bromwich Albion on the 29th March 1921. In 1921-22 his career was affected by terms of injury and illness although he did manage to play in eleven League games. James appeared in just two League games (scoring in both) at the beginning of the 1922-23 season before being transferred to Brighton in January 1923. James spent six seasons at the Goldstone ground playing in over two hundred League games scoring nearly seventy goals as well as winning a Northern Ireland Cap versus England in 1925-26. He finished his career with Aldershot.

	Games	Goals
League	21	7
F.A. Cup	1	0
Other Senior Matches	2	0
Friendly Matches	14	9
Tours	1	0
Combination League	47	9
London Challenge Cup	3	0
Total	**89**	**25**

Honours:
(WITH BRIGHTON)
One Northern Ireland Cap

HUGHES, Joseph　　　　1925

Birth Place:　Manchester, Lancashire
Date of Birth:　4th June 1902

Joseph was a promising centre forward who had played junior football in Manchester for Gorton and New Cross. He was at some stage, on the books of both Bolton Wanderers and Chelsea before joining Guildford Town in 1924-25. Joseph was transferred to Arsenal in March 1925. He made rapid progress when being selected for the League side (only a month after joining the club) versus West Bromwich at the Hawthorns on the 13th April 1925. However, in a London Combination League match at Southend United on Christmas Day 1925 he received a horrific knee injury which brought a premature end to his footballing career. Died October 1978, aged 76.

	Games	Goals
League	1	0
Friendly Matches	2	3
Combination League	5	2
Total	**8**	**5**

HULME, Joe　　　　1926-38

Birth Place:　Stafford
Date of Birth:　26th August 1904

Joe Hulme's long footballing career began whilst playing for Stafford Y.M.C.A. before joining York City in their pre-league days during 1923. Joe moved on to Blackburn Rovers in February 1924 for £250 and for the best part of three seasons at Ewood Park, he made seventy-four league appearances, scoring six goals. In February 1926, Hulme became one of Herbert Chapman's first major signings with Arsenal paying Blackburn £3,500 for his services and on the following day after his transfer he made his Arsenal league debut at Elland Road versus Leeds United on 6th February 1926. By the end of that first season Hulme's startling pace had become his trade mark, his main trick being to push the ball past the opposing full back then tear past him as if he never existed and in that initial season at Highbury he won the first of many honours when he was picked for the Football League Representative Side. Joe was an amazingly brilliant all round sportsman, he played county cricket for Middlesex from 1929 to 1939. He was nearly chosen to represent England and also played golf, snooker, table tennis and billiards. He was later to put that down to not drinking or smoking. In 1926-27, his lightning speed and astonishing ball control were rewarded when he won the first of his nine England caps, against Scotland, in April 1927. Joe scored eight goals in thirty-seven league appearances as well as playing an important role in helping the club to the 1927 F.A. Cup Final. Over the next two seasons, 1927-29, he was a permanent fixture on the club's right wing when missing only seven league games. However, it was not until the 1929-30 season that Joe came into his own, for Alex James, making full use of both Hulme and Bastin's speed with powerfully hit cross field balls for both of them to run on to. In 1928-29, Joe scored only six league goals but with the service that James provided, Hulme's goal tally more than doubled in 1929-30 when scoring fourteen times in thirty-seven appearances and at the end of that season he won his first F. A. Cup winners medal as a member of the victorious Arsenal side versus Huddersfield Town. In Arsenal's record breaking league championship side of 1930-31 the Arsenal forward line of Hulme, Jack, Lambert, James and Bastin virtually picked itself and between them they scored a staggering one hundred and sixteen league goals of which many of Lambert's goals were provided by excellent crosses on the run by Hulme. Now known as the practical joker within the club, Hulme, for the third consecutive season hit fourteen league goals in 1931-32 when missing only two league games and he played in his third

Joe Hulme

F.A. Cup Final versus Newcastle. In the first of the hat-trick of championships in 1932-33, the two Arsenal wing men, Hulme and Bastin, scored the unbelievable total of fifty-three league goals of which Hulme's contribution was twenty, this included two hat tricks against Sunderland at Highbury and at Middlesbrough. However, in 1933-34 Joe was plagued by injuries and managed to play in only eight league games. In season, 1934-35, he won a further League Championship Medal, although by this time he was not an automatic choice due to the occasional loss of form and injury. In 1935-36, he played in only half of the club's league games but was ever present in the club's F.A. Cup run and he won his second winners medal , in that years final against Sheffield United, thus becoming the only Arsenal player to play in all of the club's first four F.A. Cup Finals. By this time Joe was getting to the veteran stage, he made only three league appearances in 1936-37 and seven at the beginning of the 1937-38 season before being transferred to Huddersfield Town in January 1938. His last senior appearance was in the 1938 F.A. Cup Final versus Preston when he became the first player ever to appear in five Wembley F.A. Cup Finals. During the Second World War he was a reserve policeman and in February 1944 became assistant secretary of Tottenham Hotspur, becoming manager in October 1945 until May 1949. He later became a well known journalist. Joe Hulme's name will live on in the memory of Arsenal Football Club. He died in September 1991 aged 87.

	Games	Goals
League	333	107
F.A. Cup	39	17
Charity Shield	2	1
Other Senior Matches	4	4
Friendly Matches	14	8
Tours	11	4
Combination League	48	26
London Challenge Cup	6	2
London Midweek League	4	1
Total	**461**	**170**

Honours:
(WITH ARSENAL)
9 England Caps
6 Football League Caps
3 League Championship Medals
   1930-31, 1932-33, 1934-35
2 F.A. Cup Winners Medal 1929-30, 1935-36
2 F.A. Cup Finalists Medal 1926-27, 1931-32
2 F.A Charity Shield Winners Medals
                  1930-31, 1931-32
2 Sheriff of London Charity Shield Winners
   Medals   1930-31, 1932-33
2 Northampton Charity Shield Winners
   Medals   1929-30, 1930-31
(WITH HUDDERSFIELD)
F.A. Cup Finalists Medal   1937-38

HUMPISH, Albert 1930

Birth Place: Newcastle, Durham
Date of Birth: 2nd April 1903

Albert had played in Newcastle junior football as a young wing half before joining Bury in 1923-24. He signed for Wigan Borough during the summer of 1925 giving the club five seasons excellent service in which time he played in over one hundred and seventy first team games being ever-present in 1928-29. With Alf Baker coming to the end of his career and with Herbert Chapman not too happy with the up and coming Alf Haynes, Arsenal signed Albert in January 1930. His potential though, was not fulfilled, playing in only three League games for the club which included a disastrous debut at the Baseball ground in a 1-4 defeat versus Derby on the 19th February 1930. At the start of the 1930-31 season Arsenal found the answer to their right half position when Chapman decided to switch the Welsh outside left, Charlie Jones, to the right half position in order to find a place for the young boy wizard, Cliff Bastin. Humpish was transferred to Bristol City in December 1930, and was with Stockport County 1933-35. He was later trainer at Rochdale.

	Games	Goals
League	3	0
Friendly Matches	1	0
Combination League	21	0
London Midweek League	2	0
Total	**27**	**0**

Honours:
London Combination Championship
Medal 1929-30

HUNT, George 1937-38

Birth Place: Barnsley, Yorkshire
Date of Birth: 22nd February, 1910

George Hunt was a slight built, inside or centre forward who began his career in junior football in local Barnsley leagues. He had trials with Barnsley and Sheffield United who cast him off before he joined Chesterfield in February 1929 and in his only season at the club , he showed as a nineteen year old, his potential goal scoring prowess when netting nine times in only fourteen league games. Tottenham Hotspur drew him to the capital in June 1930 and over the following seven years he became an idol of the White Hart Lane crowd. His goalscoring record with Tottenham was quite phenomenal (one hundred and twenty-five goals in only one hundred and eighty-five league games). He was leading scorer in 1931-32 and 1933-34 and without doubt his best season at the club was in 1932-33 when he was not only top marksman with thirty-

two goals in forty-one appearances he also helped Tottenham to promotion to Division One and won three England caps. In 1935-36 and 1936-37 George's career had somewhat nose-dived, injuries, inconsistency and lack of confidence were mainly responsible, but even taking these facts into consideration, the whole of the North London footballing fraternity were shocked and stunned when as a replacement for the injured Ted Drake, he signed for Arsenal on the 1st October 1937. George made his Arsenal league debut, watched by a 68,500 crowd, versus Manchester City at Highbury on the 2nd October 1937. In his first away match for the club an audience of 76,000 watched him in action at Chelsea. In the history of league football no player had or has been watched by as many spectators in their first two games for a club. In his only season at Highbury he scored just three league goals in eighteen league games helping Arsenal to the League Championship. Unfortunately he had to make way for the now fully fit Ted Drake and after less than six months at the club he was transferred to Bolton Wanderers in March 1938. His career at Burnden Park spanned the war years where at the beginning he re-found his true form when finishing as their leading league goalscorer

George Hunt

(twenty-three) in thirty-seven appearances in 1938-39. George moved on to Sheffield Wednesday in November 1946 where he finished his career in 1948. In his total career his scoring percentage of nearly 60% has been bettered by few. Hunt was later coach and trainer at Bolton for over twenty years.

	Games	Goals
League	18	3
F.A. Cup	3	0
Tours	1	1
Combination League	1	1
Total	**23**	**5**

Honours:
(WITH TOTTENHAM)
3 England caps
(WITH ARSENAL)
League Championship Medal 1937-38

HUTCHINS, Arthur 1916-23

Birth Place: Bishops Waltham
Date of Birth: 15th September 1890

Arthur, a left back, had guested for Arsenal in over one hundred games during World War One. He signed for Arsenal for £50 from the Southern league side, Croydon Common, in April 1919 and in his last season at the club Hutchins created a remarkable goal scoring record when finishing that season as the club's leading goalscorer with seven goals (all penalties). In 1919-20, he eventually became first choice left back when playing in eighteen league games taking over from Frank Bradshaw who had moved to inside forward. His league debut being at Roker Park versus Sunderland on 13th September 1919. His consistency was shown, in 1920-21, when he missed only three league games and he was invited along to participate in an England trial game. Thirty-seven league games were played by Arthur in 1921-22, but unfortunately he lost his place to Andrew Kennedy, playing in only ten league games in 1922-23. Hutchins was transferred to Charlton Athletic in July 1923, staying three seasons at the Valley before retiring in 1926. He died in 1948 aged 57.

	Games	Goals
League	104	1
F.A. Cup	4	0
Other Senior Matches	3	0
Friendly Matches	8	0
Tours	4	1
Combination League	26	5
London Challenge Cup	6	1
War time	102	2
Total	**257**	**10**

Honours:
London Combination Championship League
Medal 1922-23
London F.A. Challenge Cup Winners Medal
1921-22

JACK, David   1928-34

Birth Place: Bolton, Lancashire
Date of Birth: 3rd April 1899

Footballing records are set to be broken. Some players achieve the odd record and a player from another generation then obliterates him from the records, his name removed for ever. In David Bone Nightingale Jack's case he holds three records which will remain untouched as long as football is played.
1) He was the first player ever to score a goal in a Wembley F.A. Cup Final.
2) He was the first player to play for two different clubs in two Wembley Cup Finals.
3) The first player to be transferred for a five-figure fee. David Jack was arguably, the most stylish, elegant and sophisticated footballer Arsenal have ever had on their books. His tall, willowy figure and nonchalant approach to the game added to his unbelievable body swerve and the cool, clinical manner in which he poached his goals, made him into the near perfect inside forward. David Jack's career began with Plymouth Presbyterians and the Royal Navy before joining his father, Robert , at Plymouth Argyle in 1919. He spent just over two seasons at Home Park before Bolton Wanderers paid out their record transfer fee of £3,500 to obtain David's services in December 1920. His father had once managed Bolton and his two brothers, Rolo and Donald also played for them. In eight seasons at Burnden Park, 1920-28, David Jack and Joe Smith formed one of the most lethal goalscoring partnerships in the land and in that time they plundered over three hundred league and F.A. Cup goals. David was the club's leading scorer in five of those seasons when he scored one hundred and forty-four goals in two hundred and ninety-five league games. He scored the first goal in Bolton's 1923 F.A. Cup Final victory versus West Ham and the only goal in the 1926 Cup Final when beating Manchester City. Jack also won the first of his nine England caps in March 1924. At the beginning of the 1928-29 season the Bolton manager, Charles Foweraker had put virtually all of Bolton's first team squad up for sale. However, this did not include David Jack. The Arsenal manager, Herbert Chapman, got wind of the situation, and arranged a meeting with the Bolton management to discuss a possible transaction involving David Jack. The former Arsenal secretary, Bob Wall, in his book "Arsenal from the heart" described the meeting:
A few months after I joined the staff of Arsenal Football Club as his personal assistant, Herbert Chapman, then secretary-manager, summoned me to his office.
"Young Wall come with me today. I'll show you how to conduct a transfer," he said. "We are going to sign David Jack, the England

David Jack

inside forward, from Bolton Wanderers. We are meeting their chairman and manager at the Euston Hotel. You are to sit with me , listen and not to say a word. I'll do all the talking. Is that clear?"
I nodded assent and hurried away to order him a taxi. We arrived at the hotel half an hour before our appointment. Chapman immediately went into the lounge bar. He called the waiter, placed two pound notes in his hand and said. "George. This is Mr Wall, my assistant. He will drink whisky and dry ginger. I will drink gin and tonic. We shall be joined by guests. They will drink whatever they like. But I want you to be careful of one thing. See that our guests are given double of everything, but Mr Wall's whisky and dry ginger will contain no whisky and my gin and tonic no gin."
When the Bolton pair arrived, Chapman ordered the drinks. We quickly downed ours and he called for the same again. The drinks continued to flow and our guests were soon in gay mood.
Finally, when Chapman decided the time was opportune for talking business, they readily agreed to letting him sign Jack - and for £10,890, which we considered a bargain !!
David had been signed to replace the retired Charles Buchan and the fee which Arsenal had splashed out smashed the existing transfer fee record by nearly £4,500. David made his Arsenal league debut in a 3-0 victory at Newcastle on 20th October 1928 and in his first season at the club he finished as top league goalscorer with twenty-five goals from thirty-one appearances, this included scoring four versus Bury. Although not so prolific in 1929-30 it was his goal in the semi-final replay versus Hull City which helped

Arsenal reach Wembley and to win the F.A. Cup against Huddersfield. In the ultimate season of 1930-31, David was a consistent member of that prodigious forward line and he contributed thirty-one league goals in thirty-five games. These included two hat tricks versus Chelsea and Blackpool and four versus Grimsby Town. In 1931-32, he was just as prolific, (twenty-one goals in thirty-four league appearances) and he returned to Wembley for his fourth F.A. Cup Final versus Newcastle. An old fable of David Jack was that he was a loner and very aloof and that was the reason why he had his own room on away trips. However, this was not the case. The reason being was that the other players could not put up with his compulsive smoking, so he had to skulk off in his own room to smoke. A second League Championship Medal came his way in 1932-33 when he scored eighteen times in thirty-four games. Now in the twilight of his career he finished his last season with the club playing in fourteen league games (five goals) just qualifying for a third League Championship Medal. David retired on the 5th May 1934 and four days later was appointed manager of Southend United where he stayed until August 1940. David later managed Middlesbrough, 1944-52, and Shelbourne, 1953-55. He died in September 1958 aged 59.

	Games	Goals
League	181	113
F.A. Cup	25	10
Charity Shield	2	1
Other Senior Matches	4	2
Friendly Matches	7	5
Tours	8	6
Combination League	5	2
London Challenge Cup	2	0
Total	**234**	**139**

Honours:
(WITH BOLTON)
2 F.A. Cup Winners Medals 1922-23, 1925-26
(WITH ARSENAL & BOLTON)
9 England Caps
5 Football League Caps
(WITH ARSENAL)
3 League Championship Medals
        1930-31, 1932-33, 1933-34
F.A. Cup Winners Medal   1929-30
F.A. Cup Finalists Medal   1931-32
2 F.A Charity Shield Winners Medals
        1930-31, 1931-32
2 Sheriff of London Charity Shield Winners
    Medals   1930-31, 1932-33
2 Northampton Charity Shield Winners
    Medals   1929-30, 1930-31

JAMES, Alex   1929-37

Birth Place: Mossend, Lanarkshire
Date of Birth: 14th September 1901

The famous cliché "Every picture tells a story", is without doubt highlighted in a famous photograph which was taken at 3.46 p.m. on the 13th October, 1934, which shows Alex James in control of the ball having tormented the Manchester City defence of which the three international defenders (Busby, Bray and Cowan) are left looking bemused, bewildered and open mouthed at the sheer genius which had been displayed by the Scottish maestro. Alex Wilson James is unquestionably, the greatest player in Arsenal's long history to have worn the famous red and white jersey, for in between the two wars no footballer, other than perhaps "Dixie" Dean, was discussed or was in the media's attention more than Alex. James was born in Mossend, Lanarkshire on the 14th September 1901 and was brought up in the tiny village of Bellshill which was a mining and industrial area deeply affected by the ravages of the First World War and in this time of deep depression Alex counted himself lucky when finding a job at the local steelworks. Alex began his footballing career in local junior football with Brandon Amateurs, Orbiston Celtic and Ashfield of Glasgow. His close friend, at this time, was Hughie Gallagher who, like James, would later become a football immortal, and both of them were idols of Patsy Gallagher who was of the same build and was the great play maker of the Celtic side of the day. Before joining Ashfield, when only nineteen years old, he was playing for Orbiston Celtic who were a small village side in which the area consisted of only thirty-two homes and a young ten year old named Matt Busby was the "bag boy" who absolutely idolised Alex. However, it was while at Ashfield that his talents were spotted by a Raith Rovers director, a Mr Morrison, who signed him for the club in the close season of 1922. After a shaky start, Alex settled into their side in the 1922-23 season and whilst at Starks Park he played in one hundred Scottish league games, in 1925 he was invited to play in a Scottish trial game along with his close friend Hughie Gallagher. At the beginning of the 1925-26 season, transfer speculation was rife and eventually he signed for Preston North End for a £3,000 fee. In his stay at Deepdale Alex scored fifty-three goals in one hundred and forty-seven league games, winning the first of his eight Scottish Caps in October 1926 versus Wales and was a member of the legendary "Wembley Wizards" when he scored twice in a 5-1 victory against England in April 1928. His relationship with Mr Alex Gibson, the Preston manager, had turned sour when he was refused to be released for a Scottish international at the end of the

1928-29 season and a meeting with the Arsenal manager, Herbert Chapman, was arranged. He signed for the Gunners in June 1929 for a fee of £8,750. Playing in the Second Division had taken its' toll, and the Arsenal trainer, Tom Whittaker was amazed when he examined Alex's legs, for his ankles were so badly bruised and battered that a specialist was required to treat him. Alex was seen by Chapman as the final cog in his well oiled machine and when taking the field for the first time on his Arsenal league debut versus Leeds United in August 1929 he was being seen by the Highbury crowd for the first time in his famous "baggy pants" which he had adopted while at Preston after seeing a cartoon of himself by Tom Webster of the Daily Mail with "shorts" down to his knees - and so Alex decided to live up to the caricature and there after wore baggy pants that reached down almost to the top of his stockings. However, after a not too brilliant start at the club, he started to relish his new deep lying midfield position providing the likes of Hulme and Bastin on the wings and Lambert through the middle with tantalising passes which, often resulted in breakaway goals. In his first season at Highbury, his magical displays were paramount when helping the club to the 1930 F.A. Cup Final against Huddersfield Town. James scoring the second goal in a 2-0 victory. To try to portray Alex James's importance to Arsenal Football Club during those glory years of the 1930's is a different task. However, to demonstrate his influence on the side is shown in the remarkable statistic that in the two hundred league appearances he made for Arsenal, between August 1930 and May 1937, he was on the losing side in only thirty-six games. In the 1930-31 season, Alex missed only two league fixtures when steering the club to their first ever League Championship. Alex was a happy-go-lucky, self confident, humourist who realised that he was at the top of his profession and that top artists in other fields were commanding larger fees than himself and because of this he went on a one man strike during the summer of 1931, when demanding a pay increase. In Herbert Chapman's reign as manager, the only player who caused him any grief was Alex, and Chapman realising the "wee man" was the star of his glorious team arranged a two year contract of £250 per annum with Selfridges's, in return for promotional work, as part of the original deal when signing him from Preston. In 1931-32, his full array of tricks were again on display when playing in thirty-two of the club's first thirty-three league games. However, he was injured in a league encounter at Upton Park versus West Ham in March 1932 resulting in him missing the last nine league games and was deemed to be very doubtful to play in that season's F.A. Cup Final against Newcastle. Herbert Chapman ordered Alex and Joe Hulme to

Brighton for last minute fitness tests. Hulme was passed fit as was Alex but unfortunately James broke down after he was involved in a freak accident at a late photocall for a national newspaper. In Arsenal's three consecutive League Championship campaigns, Alex James was undoubtedly the king pin in the side which Chapman had built and in these seasons, his regular fellow forwards, who consisted of Hulme and Bastin on the wings, Jack, Bowden and Beasley at inside forward and Lambert, Coleman and Drake through the centre, between them amassed the incredible total of nearly two hundred and fifty goals. It is, of course, impossible to view Arsenal out of historical perspective. The thirties were, for most of provincial Britain, arguably the worst decade for almost a century. In many of the textile towns unemployment reached a third of the workforce; in some places like Jarrow, literally the whole town was on the dole for years on end. To these towns, Arsenal came to represent the wealth, the affluence, and the unfair advantage that London seemed to have stolen from the rest of the country. It was not too unrealistic to see Arsenal as a symbol of the wealth earned in the North but spent and enjoyed in the South. With the football ground being almost the only entertainment outlet available to the working classes, it is not surprising that Arsenal became a subject of fierce emotional commitment of which James was the inspiration in all aspects of this derision. However, in 1935-36, although helping the club when captaining the side to victory in the F.A. Cup Final versus Sheffield United, James's position in the side was not secure due to many injuries and at times, loss of form and at the end of the following season, at the age of thirty-five, he retired from the game. In retirement he became a journalist, tried to start a pools competition (which was frowned upon by the F.A.) and just prior to the war was offered a coaching contract in Poland. During hostilities he served in the Royal Artillery as a gunner and later returned to Highbury in January 1949 as a coach to the junior sides. However, on the 1st June 1953 (the day before Queen Elizabeth's Coronation) Alex James passed away, he was just fifty-one years of age. For as long as football is played, the life and times of Alex James will be forever discussed and three legends of the game described their thoughts of the man. Ted Drake - "A great player, thrilling to behold." Matt Busby - "One of the all-time greats." and Tom Finney - "Pure magic." The last sentiment should be left to Alan Hoby, journalist, who, in the Arsenal Supporters Club magazine "Gunflash", suggested "In all humanity it would be nice to see a bust of Alex adorning the main entrance at Highbury alongside that splendid sculpture of Herbert Chapman, or failing that, what about Alex James' gate?"

For mere memories of Alex James are not sufficient, something should be produced in stone or brass to perpetuate the memory of the greatest Gunner of them all.

	Games	Goals
League	231	26
F.A. Cup	28	1
Charity Shield	2	0
Other Senior Matches	3	0
Friendly Matches	4	1
Tours	7	1
Combination League	7	1
Total	**282**	**30**

Honours:
(WITH PRESTON)
4 Scottish Caps
(WITH ARSENAL)
4 Scottish Caps
4 League Championship Medals
     1930-31, 1932-33, 1933-34, 1934-35
2 F.A. Cup Winners Medals
     1929-30, 1935-36
2 F.A Charity Shield Winners Medals
     1931-32, 1933-34
Sheriff of London Charity Shield Winners
  Medal   1930-31
Northampton Charity Shield Winners
  Medal   1929-30
Bath Coronation Cup Winners Medal
     1936 -37

ALEX. JAMES

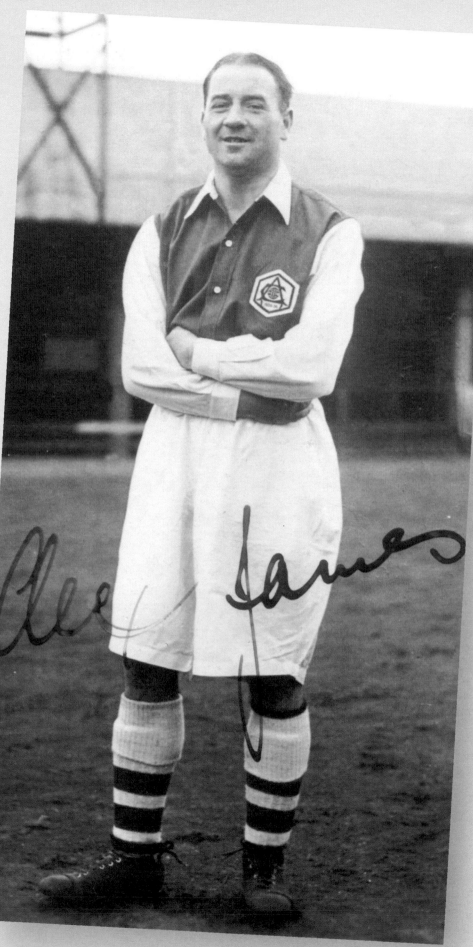

Alex James

JOHN, Bob   1922-37

Birth Place: Barry Dock, South Wales
Date of Birth: 3rd February 1899

Bob John had put in many startling displays for Barry Town and Caerphilly and was sought after by numerous clubs (including Cardiff City) when joining Arsenal in January 1922. Over the following fifteen years Bob John was instrumental in many of the club's successes. In 1921-22 he settled down at left half in Arsenal's reserve side before, in 1922-23, he won the first of his fifteen Welsh caps versus Scotland whilst still a reserve player. Bob's other fourteen caps were spread over a fourteen-year period. Bob made his Arsenal league debut at Highbury versus Newcastle on 28th October 1922 and he eventually took over the left half position from Tom Whittaker when playing in 24 league games. Surprisingly he played in only fifteen league games in 1923-24 when he had stiff opposition from Bill Blyth and Andrew Young. Noted for his fine distribution as well as being a prodigious ball winner, Bob missed only three league games in 1924-25 when helping Arsenal stave off relegation. He was converted to the left back position (taking over from Andrew Kennedy) by Herbert Chapman in 1925-26, playing in twenty-nine league games. He followed this in 1926-27, switching from left back to left half and missed only one league game as well as appearing in the losing F.A. Cup Final versus Cardiff. It was the unobtrusive Bob John who was the first to turn to the distraught Dan Lewis when he retrieved the goalkeeper's thrown away loser's medal and said to him, "Never mind Dan you will get another chance". This did not materialise. Cool and calm Bob won a further two Welsh caps in 1927-28 when again being as consistent as ever when missing only three league games. By this time he had made the left back position his own playing in thirty-four league games in both the 1928-29 and 1929-30 seasons. Alex James had now joined the club and it was Alex who stated that Bob John had guided him as much as any other player in his early days at Highbury. However, he only got the nod to play in the 1930 F.A. Cup Final versus Huddersfield Town when Charlie Jones was injured. In 1930-31 he helped the club to their first League Championship when playing in forty league games and was also a member of the F.A. Charity Shield winning side versus Sheffield Wednesday. Runners-up in the league, 1931-32, when Bob's consistency knew no bounds and he played in thirty-eight league games and broke Percy Sands three hundred and twenty-seven league appearances record versus Chelsea on 2nd April 1932. (He later went on to play in four hundred and twenty-one

league games, a record he held for forty-two years until surpassed by George Armstrong in November 1974). Described by Cliff Bastin as "The most unassuming man I have ever met", in that 1931-32 season he scored Arsenal's only goal in the famous "over the line" Cup Final versus Newcastle. He won a further League Championship Medal, 1932-33, when missing only five league games. Bob won his third League Championship Medal in 1933-34 when playing in a further thirty-one league games. However, now at the age of 35 and after the signing of Wilf Copping he was still good enough to play for Wales. In his last three seasons at Highbury , 1934-37, he played only occasionally for the league side. Unspectacular, Bob John never got the praise he deserved. The biggest compliment paid to him was by Eddie Hapgood who said. "He was the best player I ever played behind". He retired during the summer of 1938 and later was coach at West Ham in 1938 and after the war he was trainer and manager at Torquay, trainer of Crystal Palace and coach and scout for Cardiff City. He died in July 1982 aged 83.

	Games	Goals
League	421	12
F.A. Cup	46	1
Charity Shield	3	0
Other Senior Matches	8	2
Friendly Matches	29	0
Tours	28	1
Combination League	85	2
London Challenge Cup	9	0
London Midweek League	1	1
Total	**630**	**19**

Honours:
15 Welsh Caps
3 League Championship Medals
                    1930-31, 1932-33, 1933-34
F.A. Cup Winners Medal   1929-30
2 F.A. Cup Finalists Medals 1926-27, 1931-32
3 F.A Charity Shield Winners Medals
    1930-31, 1933-34, 1934-35
2 London Combination Championship Medal
    1922-23, 1936-37
London F.A. Challenge Cup Finalists Medal
    1925-26
2 Sheriff of London Charity Shield Winners
    Medals   1930-31, 1932-33
3 Northampton Charity Shield Winners
    Medals   1929-30, 1930-31, 1931-32

JOHNSTONE, William   1929-31

Birth Place: Fife, Scotland
Date of Birth: 18th May 1900

William Johnstone was yet another promising inside forward of the early 1930's whose chances were restricted due to the brilliance of the likes of Jack and James. William began his career just after the First

World War with Scottish junior sides Fife, Rosyth Juniors and Kings Park before entering Scottish League football with Dundee United and Clyde. Johnstone moved South when joining Reading in September 1926. He spent three seasons at Elm Park where he was the club's leading goalscorer with nineteen goals in 1928-29. This alerted Herbert Chapman to sign him for Arsenal in May 1929 for a small fee. However, he played in only seven league games during that 1929-30 season scoring three goals, two in a 8-1 home victory versus Sheffield United. This after making his Arsenal league debut versus Sheffield Wednesday on 7th September 1929. In Arsenal's first ever League Championship season he only played in two league games when deputising for the injured Alex James. Although William never played in a losing Arsenal league side, he was eventually transferred to Oldham Athletic for £2,130 in January 1931. He served them well for five seasons and was their leading league goalscorer in 1931-32. William returned to Scotland when joining Clyde in 1935.

	Games	Goals
League	9	4
Friendly Matches	4	3
Combination League	40	21
London Challenge Cup	1	1
London Midweek League	7	1
Total	**61**	**30**

Honours:
Two London Combination Championship
    Medals   1929-30, 1930-31

JONES, Bryn   1938-49

Birth Place: Merthyr Tydfil, Wales
Date of Birth: 14th February 1912

Bryn Jones had played junior football for Merthyr Amateurs, Glenavon (Ireland, 1931), and Aberaman before joining Wolves in 1933. Whilst at Molineux he made one hundred and sixty-three league appearances and won the first of his seventeen Welsh caps versus Northern Ireland in 1934-35. Although Arsenal had won the League Championship in 1937-38 the club management, under the scrutiny of George Allison, were not happy, for they could not find a ready replacement for Alex James even though, in that 1937-38 season, Davidson, Leslie Jones, as well as Bremner and Drury, were all given chances. In August 1938, just prior to the start of the season, George Allison shocked the footballing world by breaking the British record transfer fee when paying £14,000 to Wolves for the services of Brynmor Jones. To show how staggering the fee was, people have got to remember that this broke the existing transfer fee by nearly £4,000. This being when Arsenal had paid Bolton Wanderers,

Bryn Jones

ten years earlier, £10,895 for David Jack. Taking everything into account the equivalent in 1995 would be a player transferring for £11,500,000 ! No player up to that point had been under such media attention and immediately the press, unkindly described him as "the new James". What Bryn, and millions like him, did not know, was that war was just around the corner and so, in that 1938-39 season, the dark crinkly haired little Welshman had little time to show his true talents. Having said that, his Arsenal league debut got off to a dream start when he scored the first goal in a 2-0 home victory in front of a 55,000 crowd versus Portsmouth. He followed this by scoring twice in the next three league games. The Arsenal public realised that the club had not signed a second Alex James (for Alex hardly ever scored). The truth of the matter being that they were two completely different players. At the end of that season he had scored four goals in thirty league appearances. To lay blame on Bryn Jones for the club's lack of success that season was unfair, for in a nutshell, the quiet, modest, self evasive, lonely figure could not cope with the intense pressure of the media spotlight even though his good positional awareness and splendid ball control were there for everyone to behold. During the war Bryn was posted to Italy and North Africa whilst serving with the Royal Artillery. On his return to Highbury (now aged 34) for the 1946-47 season, Bryn seemed to show more confidence and it was as if the seven year gap had helped to ease the burden of his former memories, playing in twenty-six league games. However, in the 1947-48 championship winning season he lost his place (playing in only seven league games) to Jimmy Logie and in 1948-49, although he played and scored in the 4-3 victory versus Manchester United in the Charity Shield, he played in only eight league games. His Arsenal career finished whilst on the summer tour of Brazil in 1949 when unfortunately in a game against Vasco

de Gama spectators kept running on the pitch and accidently or not he was hit on the head by a Brazilian policeman. In 1950, on doctors advice, he was recommended to retire from the game. Like so many other players oh! what could have been if it had not been for Hitler. He died in October 1985 aged 73.

	Games	Goals
League	71	7
F.A. Cup	3	0
Charity Shield	2	1
Other Senior Matches	3	0
Friendly Matches	10	1
Tours	11	0
Combination League	2	1
Combination Cup	7	2
War time	28	6
Total	**137**	**18**

Honours:

(with Wolves and Arsenal) 17 Welsh Caps
(with Arsenal)   8 wartime Welsh caps
2 F.A Charity Shield Winners Medals
    1938-39, 1948-49
Football League South Championship Medal
    1942-43

JONES, Charlie   1928-34

Birth Place: Troedyrhiw, South Wales
Date of Birth: 12th December 1899

☞ Charlie Jones started his footballing career as a neat tricky outside left with Cardiff City in 1920-21. He failed to make the grade at Ninian Park and was allowed to leave the club in the summer of 1921 when he linked up with Stockport County. In his one full season at Edgeley Park he helped County to the Third Division North Championship in 1921-22. Charlie's next move was to Boundary Park, Oldham in March 1923 but at the end of that 1922-23 season he suffered the indignity of being in their side relegated to Division Two. Jones spent a further two seasons at the club before joining Nottm Forest during the summer of 1925, and in his three seasons with the club he played in one hundred league games as well as winning the first of seven Welsh caps versus England at Selhurst Park. In this game he caught the attention of the footballing public with a "dazzling display" in his country's 3-1 victory. Charlie was transferred from Nottm Forest to Arsenal in May 1928 for a four-figure sum. In his first season at Highbury, 1928-29, Jones scored six times when missing only three of the club's forty-two league games of which his Arsenal league debut was on the opening day of the season in an away fixture versus Sheffield Wednesday on 25th August 1928. In the following campaign, 1929-30, he added two Welsh caps to his collection, played in thirty-one league games and was unfortunate when

missing out on being selected for the 1930 F.A. Cup Final versus Huddersfield Town (this after Alex James declared himself fit for the Final). In Arsenal's first League Championship season, 1930-31, Jones had moved to the orthodox right half position where his terrier-like tackles, tenacious play and never-say-die attitude brought inspiration to the club and when Alex James never turned up at the Championship banquet it was Jones who received the trophy. At this time in Arsenal's history, Charlie was an important cog in Chapman's machine-like side, and in 1931-32 he missed only five league games, won further international honours when captaining his country and helped the club to the famous "over the line final" versus Newcastle United. He also featured in the F.A. Charity Shield victory against W.B.A. at Villa Park. After the signing of Frank Hill in the summer of 1932 (and at the age of 33) Charlie's first team place seemed not so secure, however, he won a second League Championship Medal when playing in sixteen league games. At this time, it was his creative tactical brain, which thought up the man to man marking, and he often fed Herbert Chapman with new ideas, which kept him in the side and in 1933-34 (his last season at the club) he won his third League Championship Medal when playing in twenty-nine league games. Charlie retired in the summer of 1934 and became manager of Notts County, where he spent only a matter of months before turning his back on football and later became a very successful businessman who died in April 1966 aged 66.

	Games	Goals
League	176	8
F.A. Cup	17	0
Charity Shield	2	0
Other Senior Matches	3	0
Friendly Matches	7	1
Tours	5	1
Combination League	24	8
London Challenge Cup	5	1
London Midweek League	3	0
Total	**242**	**19**

Honours:

(WITH STOCKPORT)
Division 3 North League Championship
    Medal   1921-22
(WITH ARSENAL & NOTT'M FOREST)
8 Welsh Caps
(WITH ARSENAL)
3 League Championship Medals
            1930-31, 1932-33, 1933-34
1 F.A. Cup Finalists Medal   1931-32
2 F.A Charity Shield Winners Medals
            1931-32, 1933-34
London Comb. Champ'ship Medal   1930-31
1 Sheriff of London Charity Shield Winners
    Medal   1930-31
2 Northampton Charity Shield Winners
    Medals   1930-31, 1931-32

JONES, Fred   1923-24

Birth Place: Clerkenwell, London
Date of Birth: 17th May 1900

Frederick Jones was an inside forward who joined Arsenal from the Royal Navy in June 1923. He spent just one season at Highbury playing predominately for the reserve side although he did manage to play in the last two League games of the 1923-24 season of which his debut was in a 1-4 defeat at Turf Moor versus Burnley on the 28th April 1924. Jones later had short spells playing for Aberdare Athletic, Charlton and Blackpool

	Games	Goals
League	2	0
Friendly Matches	10	6
Combination League	27	6
Total	**39**	**12**

JONES, Leslie   1937-46

Birth Place: Aberdare, Wales
Date of Birth: 1st July 1911

Leslie Jones could never be considered as a household name in English football although his career which, if you include the war years, spanned nearly twenty years. A clever inside forward, he began his career with his home town club Aberdare before joining Cardiff City in 1929. Leslie spent four and a half seasons at Ninian Park scoring over thirty league goals in nearly one hundred and forty league games. He won the first of eleven Welsh caps versus France in 1932-33. Leslie was transferred to Coventry City in January 1934 and in nearly five years with them he scored at a rate of a goal in every other game (seventy in one hundred and thirty-eight). Leslie gained a further five Welsh caps and a Division Three South League Championship Medal in 1935-36. Jones joined Arsenal (in part exchange for Robert Davidson) in November 1937. In his first season at Highbury he played in twenty-eight league games (three goals) of which his Arsenal league debut (when scoring) was in a 1-2 defeat at Grimsby Town on 6th November 1937. He had helped Arsenal to the League Championship and won three Welsh caps. In the last season before the war, he played in eighteen league games and won an F.A. Charity Shield winners medal versus Preston. During hostilities Leslie made a further sixty-eight appearances for the club, won five war time caps and served in the R.A.F. On the return of peacetime, and nearing 35, Jones was granted a free transfer and so he moved on to Swansea Town as player coach in May 1946. His stay at Vetch Field was short lived and he became player-manager of Barry Town before returning to League football with Brighton where he

finished his long career in 1948-49. Jones scouted and coached for the club 1949-50 and became manager of newly elected League side, Scunthorpe United, in June 1950 where he was in charge for just one season. He died January 1981 aged 69.

Leslie Jones

	Games	Goals
League	46	3
F.A. Cup	3	0
Charity Shield	1	0
Other Senior Matches	4	0
Friendly Matches	2	0
Tours	6	0
Combination League	9	6
War time	71	10
Total	**142**	**19**

Honours:
(WITH CARDIFF, COVENTRY & ARSENAL)
11 Welsh caps
(WITH COVENTRY)
Division 3 South League Championship
   Medal   1935-36
(WITH ARSENAL)
League Championship Medal   1937-38
F.A Charity Shield Winners Medal 1938-39
Football League South Championship Medal
                                  1939-40
War time F.A. Cup Winners Medal   1940-41
5 War time caps

JOY, Bernard   1935-46

Birth Place: Fulham, London
Date of Birth: 29th October 1911

Bernard Joy studied at London University and started his centre half footballing career by playing for them all throughout his distinguished career. Bernard then played for the great amateur side Corinthian Casuals, Southend 1931-33 and Fulham 1933. He was permanently on the books of Casuals (1931-

48) and whilst there he won ten England Amateur caps, captained them to a 2-0 victory versus Ilford in the 1936 F.A. Amateur Cup Final as well as captaining the British team in the 1936 Olympic Games. By this time, Bernard had joined Arsenal , this being in May 1935. He played for them in two league games in 1935-36 when replacing Herbie Roberts of which his Arsenal league debut was in a home fixture against Bolton Wanderers on April Fools Day 1936. Bernard was actually classed as being on the books of Casuals when he won a full England cap on the 9th May 1936 versus Belgium (the last amateur to win a full cap for England). In 1936-37 he deputised six times in the league when nagging injuries were getting the better of Herbie Roberts. In the summer of 1937 he went with the England Amateur side on a tour of Australasia. After the tragic injury to Herbie Roberts in October 1937, Bernard filled the breach admirably when playing in twenty-six of the club's last twenty-nine league games. This helping Arsenal to the League Championship that season. In 1938-39 he was a member of the F.A. Charity Shield winning side versus Preston and although still an amateur, he missed only three league games in that campaign. How Bernard Joy's career would have turned out without the intervention of the Second World War no one knows. However, during the war years he played in over two hundred games for the club, winning an England wartime cap as well as being a flight lieutenant in the R.A.F. He returned to Highbury at the start of the 1946-47 season and played in the first thirteen league fixtures of which twelve were in unaccustomed positions when deputising for either Laurie Scott or Walley Barnes. Now aged 35 and thinking ahead to later years, he announced his retirement in December 1946. By this time he had become a schoolmaster in Hounslow. In 1952 he became author of the marvellous book, Forward Arsenal, and later became a leading journalist for many years with The Evening Standard and Sunday Express, retiring in 1976. Like so many players past and present, Bernard Joy's love of Arsenal never diminished and up to his death in July 1984 aged 72, he was still known to be singing the club's praises.

	Games	Goals
League	86	0
F.A. Cup	6	0
Charity Shield	3	0
Other Senior Matches	2	0
Friendly Matches	6	0
Tours	4	0
Combination League	33	0
War time	208	0
Total	**348**	**0**

Honours:
(WITH CORINTHIAN CASUALS)
10 England Amateur Caps
F.A. Amateur Cup Winners Medal   1935-36

(WITH ARSENAL)

1 England cap

1 England Wartime cap

League Championship Medal 1937-38

F.A Charity Shield Winners Medal 1938-39

F.A Charity Shield Finalists Medals

1935-36, 1936-37

London Combination Championship Medal

1936-37

3 Football League South Championship

Medals 1939-40, 1941-42, 1942-43

War time F.A. Cup Winners Medal 1942-43

War time F.A. Cup Finalists Medal 1940-41

Bernard Joy

KEMPTON, Arthur   1914-21

Birth Place: West Thurrock, Essex
Date of Birth: 29th January 1892

☛ Playing for Hastings and St. Leonards in Sussex junior football, Arthur Kempton pursued his goalkeeping career when joining leading North London amateur side, Tufnell Park. His capabilities were apparent when joining Arsenal in October 1914, turning professional the following month. He had little time to prove his ability before the outbreak of World War One although he had

one first team opportunity when playing for Arsenal in an F.A. Cup 1st round match versus Merthyr Tydfil on 9th January 1915. During the war Arthur served in the R.A.F. before returning to Highbury where he spent two more years as third choice goalkeeper to Dunn and Williamson. Kempton was released on a free transfer in June 1921 when he joined Reading.

	Games	Goals
F.A.Cup	1	0
Friendly Matches	13	0
Combination League	27	0
War time	30	0
South Eastern League	22	0
London League Reserves	8	0
Total	**101**	**0**

KENNEDY, Andy   1922-28

Birth Place: Belfast, Ireland
Date of Birth: 1st September 1897

☛ Andrew Kennedy had played Irish junior football for Belfast Celtic before joining Glentoran during the First World War. He crossed the Irish Sea when joining Crystal Palace in 1920 and played in one League game for them in 1920-21 when they won the Third Division South Championship. He could never gain a first team place when Arsenal signed him in August 1922 as left back cover for Arthur Hutchins. However, after a 2-3 home defeat versus Sunderland Andy took over the left back position from Hutchins when making his Arsenal League debut at St. Andrews, Birmingham on the 2nd December 1922. Andrew finished that season playing in twenty-four of the club's last twenty-five League games as well as winning the first of his two Irish Caps versus Wales. In 1923-24, he missed thirteen League games due to first, injury then secondly, after being dropped after a 1-6 defeat at Huddersfield Town on 22nd December 1923. In 1924-25 he missed only two League games when helping Arsenal avoid relegation to Division Two. In Herbert Chapman's first season with the club, 1925-26, Andrew played in the first thirteen League games before making way for Bob John after a 0-4 defeat at Sheffield United. Although playing in only eleven League games in 1926-27, Andrew's luck changed for the better, when not having played in any of the previous ties, he was selected to take the place of the injured Horace Cope to play in the infamous 1927 F.A. Cup Final versus Cardiff City. He played in just two League games at the start of the 1927-28

season (1-5 at Bury, 0-4 at Derby) before Chapman lost his patience and he was transferred to Everton in January 1928 where he was understudy (when not playing) to the consistent O'Donnell in the team's 1927-28 League Championship campaign. Andrew finished his career with Tranmere Rovers in 1930. He died in December 1963 aged 66.

	Games	Goals
League	122	0
F.A. Cup	7	0
Other Senior Matches	1	0
Friendly Matches	12	0
Tours	7	0
Combination League	80	0
London Challenge Cup	3	0
Total	**232**	**0**

Honours :

(WITH ARSENAL)

Two Irish Caps,

F.A. Cup Finalists Medal 1926-27

London Combination Championship Medal

1926-27

KEYSER, Gerald   1930-31

Birth Place: Holland
Date of Birth: 1910

☛ Gerald Peiter Keyser was a Dutch born goalkeeper, daring, spectacular and reckless, who had been on the books of Millwall and Margate before joining Arsenal as an amateur in August 1930, turning professional in May 1931. Gerald played in the first twelve league games of the club's first league championship campaign of 1930-31 (Arsenal winning eight and drawing three of these games) including his league debut at Blackpool on August 30th 1930. He also played in the 2-1 victory at Stamford Bridge versus Sheffield Wednesday in the 1930-31 F.A. Charity Shield. However, with stiff competition from Bill Harper and Charlie Preedy he was never selected again and was transferred to Charlton in July 1931. Gerald later played for Q.P.R. Died 1980, aged 70.

	Games	Goals
League	12	0
Charity Shield	1	0
Combination League	9	0
London Midweek League	1	0
Total	**23**	**0**

Honours :

F.A. Charity Shield Winners Medal 1930-31
2 Caps for Holland

KING, Henry   1914-19

Birth Place: Evesham, Worcestershire
Date of Birth: 1886

☛ Henry King was a fine centre forward whose career was badly interrupted by the First World War. He had begun his career with Worcester before playing for Birmingham, Crewe Alexandra and Northampton Town before joining Arsenal in April 1914. In his one solitary season for the club, 1914-15, before the outbreak of war he broke Tommy Shank's record of the most goals in a League season (twenty-six). A record which stood for twelve seasons until beaten by Jimmy Brain in 1925-26. His twenty-six goals included hat-tricks versus Grimsby Town and Merthyr Tydfill in the F.A. Cup and he scored four goals at Highbury versus Wolves and Nottm Forest. Henry served with the Royal Garrison Artillery in Italy before returning to Highbury in the summer of 1919. However, at the age of 33, the club decided to release him and in the following month he joined Leicester City.

	Games	Goals
League	37	26
F.A.Cup	2	3
Other Senior Matches	2	5
Friendly Matches	1	2
Combination League	6	5
London Challenge Cup	5	4
War time	37	26
South Eastern League	1	1
Total	**91**	**72**

Honours :

London F.A. Challenge Cup Finalists Medal
                                    1914-15

KIRCHEN, Alf   1935-43

Birth Place: Shouldham, Norfolk
Date of Birth: 26th August, 1913

☛ Alf appeared for Kings Lynn Schoolboys gaining Norfolk County Honours and later played for his local village, Shouldham. The former Arsenal full back and captain, then manager of Norwich City, Tom Parker, signed Alf at the end of the 1933-34 season. He had scored seven goals in only fourteen league games, when George Allison signed him for Arsenal in March 1935 for £6,000. In the 1934-35 championship campaign Alf never had the time to qualify for a championship medal although he played in seven league games as the successor to Joe Hulme's right wing position. His league debut could not have got off to a better start when scoring twice at White Hart Lane versus Tottenham Hotspur in a 6-0 victory 6th March 1935 , this after Spurs had tried to buy him. In 1935-36, Hulme regained his outside right first team position and Kirchen only played

Alf Kirchen

in six league games. However, in 1936-37, the roles were reversed when Alf played in thirty three league games scoring eighteen goals, this included a hat trick at Grimsby Town in February 1937. His form impressing the England selectors and he won three England caps on the Scandinavian tour of 1936-37. In 1937-38 he played in nineteen league games when helping Arsenal to the league championship in that season and in the last season prior to the Second World War he was a member of the side which beat Preston in the F.A. Charity Shield and scored nine goals in twenty seven league appearances. During the war he served in the R.A.F. as a physical training instructor and played in nearly one hundred and twenty games for the club (eighty goals). This fast sharp shooting and very dangerous winger with a terrific shot had to retire at the early age of twenty eight, when a severe leg injury, in a war time game in 1943 versus West Ham United, ended his career. Kirchen had a short spell as trainer at Norwich City before becoming a director at the club. He showed his all round sporting abilities when winning England honours at clay pigeon shooting and was also a fine bowls player.

	Games	Goals
League	92	38
F.A. Cup	7	6
Charity Shield	2	1
Other Senior Matches	2	0
Friendly Matches	2	1
Tours	10	5
Combination League	31	25
London Challenge Cup	3	5
War time	116	81
Southern League	4	5
Total	**269**	**167**

Honours:
3 England caps
3 England war time caps
League Championship Medals1937-38
F.A Charity Shield Winners Medal   1938-39
F.A Charity Shield Finalists Medal   1936-37
London F.A. Challenge Cup Winners Medal
    1935-36
3 Football League South War time
Championship Medals
    1939-40, 1941-42, 1942-43
F.A. Cup Wartime Winners Medal1942-43
F.A. Cup Wartime Finalists Medal1940-41

LAMBERT, Jack   1926-33

Birth Place: Greasborough, Yorkshire
Date of Birth: 22nd May, 1902

☛ Jack Lambert was Arsenal's big hearted and broad shouldered centre forward at the start of the club's halcyon days in the late 1920's and early 1930's. Whilst at Highbury Jack's robust , dash and punch, approach reaped ninety-eight goals in only one hundred and forty-three league games. It seemed though, that Herbert Chapman was never quite satisfied and that he was looking for a more skilful and accomplished centre forward. Three times Herbert plunged into the transfer market to replace "Honest Jack" and he spent over £22,000 on Halliday, Coleman and Dunne in trying to do so! In the end only the latter outlasted Lambert. Described by Cliff Bastin as the best uncapped centre forward, Jack's career did not get off to the best of starts for he was turned down by Sheffield Wednesday after a trial. His next port of call was Rotherham County , 1922, where he scored in his only league game for the club. Jack moved onto Leeds without success in November 1922 before joining Doncaster Rovers in January 1925. He scored fourteen league goals in forty-four games and was transferred to Arsenal for £2,000 in June 1926. Jack made his Arsenal league debut at Burnden Park versus Bolton Wanderers on 6th September 1926 and in his initial season at the club scored only once in sixteen league appearances and missed out on being selected for the 1927 F.A. Cup Final versus Cardiff. Over the next two seasons he was the club's reserve centre forward to Jimmy Brain whilst scoring only four goals in twenty-two appearances. However, in 1929-30, he started to show his goalscoring ability when netting eighteen times in only twenty appearances. This included three hat tricks in home fixtures versus Grimsby Town, Everton and Sheffield United. It seemed the newly signed Alex James had helped Lambert in turning his career around. Jack also scored Arsenal's first goal in the 1930 F.A. Cup Final versus Huddersfield Town. In Arsenal's League Championship campaign of

Jack Lambert

1919-1939

team chances were restricted and he was transferred to Fulham for £2,500 in October 1933. Lambert spent two seasons at Craven Cottage before returning to Highbury and Margate (Arsenal's nursery club) in January 1936. In 1938 he became the coach to the sides 'A' team. Jack was tragically killed in a road accident in Enfield, North London in December 1940 aged 38.

	Games	Goals
League	143	98
F.A. Cup	16	11
Charity Shield	2	0
Other Senior Matches	4	6
Friendly Matches	17	19
Tours	11	15
Combination League	141	110
London Challenge Cup	6	5
London Midweek League	1	0
Total	**341**	**264**

Honours:
2 League Championship Medals
   1930-31, 1932-33
1 F.A. Cup Winners Medal 1929-30
1 F.A. Cup Finalists Medal 1931-32
2 F.A Charity Shield Winners Medals
   1930-31, 1931-32
4 London Combination Championship Medal
   1926-27, 1927-28, 1928-29, 1929-30
Sheriff of London Charity Shield Winners
Medal   1930-31
3 Northampton Charity Shield Winners
Medals   1929-30, 1930-31, 1931-32

LAWSON, Herbert   1924-27

Birth Place: Luton, Bedfordshire
Date of Birth: 12th April, 1905

Herbert joined Arsenal as an amateur in October 1924 turning professional the following month. This after he had begun his career in Bedfordshire junior football with Frickers Athletic and Luton Clarence. Herbert spent the first sixteen months of his career at Highbury as the reserve team's outside right before being given his League debut in a home fixture versus Burnley on the 3rd February 1926 and then played in thirteen of Arsenal's last sixteen games of the season. With the signing of Joe Hulme, who had switched to the right wing position at the start of the 1926-27 season, Lawson's first team chances were numbered. He eventually left the club in March 1927 joining Brentford who he served for three seasons.

	Games	Goals
League	13	2
F.A.Cup	3	0
Friendly Matches	16	6
Tours	1	0
Combination League	42	5
Total	**75**	**13**

LEE, John   1926-28

Birth Place: Blyth, Northumberland
Date of Birth: 1904

John Lee was a stocky built outside left who had spent much of his footballing career playing in the North East of England with Blackhall Wesleyans and Hartlepool United as an amateur before joining Arsenal in May 1926 from Horden Athletic. In his two seasons at the club he played in only seven League games, all of which were in the 1926-27 season. This included his League debut at Burnden Park versus Bolton Wanderers on 6th September 1926. With no opportunities forthcoming John was transferred to Chesterfield in June 1928. Lee spent five seasons with them scoring over forty goals in over one hundred and fifty first team games, helping them to win the Third Division North Championship in 1930-31. John finished his career with Aldershot 1933-35.

	Games	Goals
League	7	0
Friendly Matches	11	8
Tours	5	1
Combination League	52	23
Total	**75**	**32**

Honours:
(WITH ARSENAL)
2 London Combination Championship
   Medals   1926-27, 1927-78
(WITH CHESTERFIELD)
Division Three North Championship
   Medal   1930-31

LEWIS, Charles   1907-21

Birth Place: Plumstead, London
Date of Birth: 15th August 1886

Charles, during his long career at Woolwich Arsenal/Arsenal was used in every forward position. This after beginning his career in junior football with Eltham before joining Maidstone United. Charles was transferred to Arsenal in May 1907. In the 1907-8 season he finished as joint top league goal scorer with eight in only thirteen appearances of which his Arsenal league debut (when scoring twice) was in a home fixture versus Sunderland on 28th December 1907. In the next two seasons, he was in and out of the first team due to different reasons, while playing in fifty one of the club's seventy six league games (1908-10).

1930-31, Jack really came into his own, when scoring thirty-eight league goals smashing Jimmy Brain's record of thirty-four league goals. Included in Jack's total were seven hat tricks, two at home versus Middlesbrough and Grimsby, and a possible record five away, at Birmingham, Bolton, Leicester, Middlesbrough and Sunderland. The following season, 1931-32, he kept up his goalscoring record netting twenty-two times in thirty-six appearances. One hat trick was scored in a 6-0 home victory against Liverpool. He also helped Arsenal by scoring four times in five ties when reaching the F.A. Cup Final versus Newcastle. In 1932-33 he was selected to play in only twelve league games but he still managed to score fourteen league goals when becoming the first player in Arsenal's history to score five times in a league match. This being in a 9-2 home victory versus Sheffield United. However, after the signing of Jimmy Dunne his first

In 1910-11, he played in every forward role when playing in thirty-four league games. Lewis was never a regular scorer for the first team but provided for others and he was a consistent member of the side up to the First World War. This included, scoring a hat trick in front of a 6,000 crowd at Highbury versus Leicester Fosse on Boxing Day 1914. Lewis played in additional matches for the club during World War One before returning to Highbury for the 1919-20 season.. Now aged thirty-three he had to be content to serve in a reserve role, playing in only five league games. In his last season with the club, 1920-21, his appearances were all in the reserve team. This resulted in him being given a free transfer during the summer of 1921 when he joined Margate. He died in 1967 aged 70.

	Games	Goals
League	206	30
F.A. Cup	14	4
Other Senior Matches	7	2
Friendly Matches	30	12
Tours	5	2
Combination League	28	3
London Challenge Cup	12	6
London League Reserves	18	10
South Eastern League	61	28
War time	43	8
Total	**424**	**105**

Honours:
South Eastern League Championship Medal
1907-8
London F.A. Challenge Cup Finalists Medal
1914-15

LEWIS, Dan   1924-31

Birth Place: Mardy, South Wales
Date of Birth: 11th December 1902

☛ Dan Lewis had played junior football for his home town club Mardy before moving to London to join Clapton Orient. Joining Arsenal in August 1924, Daniel made his Arsenal league debut in a 3-2 victory at Goodison Park versus Everton on 15th November 1924 and in that 1924-25 season he played in a run of fourteen league games before losing his place to Jock Robson (this after a 0-5 home defeat versus Huddersfield). In Herbert Chapman's first season at the club Lewis had to share the goalkeeping duties with Robson and Harper finishing the season playing in fourteen league games. In that fateful 1926-27 season Dan was good enough to win the first of his three Welsh caps against England. Bill Harper had played in twenty-three league games compared to Lewis's seventeen but it was Dan who Chapman constantly gave the nod to during the club's run up to the 1927 F.A. Cup Final versus

Cardiff. The goal which Dan let in, in Arsenal's 0-1 defeat has been described as one of the most tragic ever goalkeeping disasters seen at the famous stadium. Ferguson, the Cardiff forward, seemed to hit a tame shot which Lewis looked to have well covered but the ball squirmed underneath his body and rolled gently into the net. Although, partly fable, it was later stated, that Dan's new shiny shirt had not helped the situation. However, no Arsenal keeper in Cup Finals since, have worn a new jersey. Dan was later to describe the goal to the Daily Mail.

"I got down to it and stopped it. I can usually pick up a ball with one hand, but as I was laying over the ball, I had to use both hands to pick it up, and already a Cardiff forward was rushing down on me. The ball was very greasy. When it touched Parker it had evidently acquired a tremendous spin, and for a second it must have been spinning beneath me. At my first touch it shot away over my arm. I sent my hand after it and touched it. I may have sent it quicker over the goal line with this touch but I think it would have reached it in any case."

After the game Dan was so distraught with his performance he threw away his losers medal (retrieved by Bob John). Herbert Chapman stuck by him and in the following three seasons he was the club's regular goalkeeper when playing in nearly one hundred league games. However, in Arsenal's first League Championship season of 1930-31, he unbelievably, within a few months, went from first choice to fourth choice (behind Keyser, Harper and Preedy) and in his last season at Highbury his appearances were restricted to just Football Combination matches. Desperate Dan, disillusioned with his position, transferred to Gillingham in May 1931 where he played in just six league games. Ironically, although playing in six of the seven ties leading up to the 1930 F.A. Cup Final versus Huddersfield Town, Herbert Chapman decided not to take the risk with Lewis so selected Preedy. He died in July 1965 aged 62

	Games	Goals
League	142	0
F.A. Cup	25	0
Friendly Matches	16	0
Tours	12	0
Combination League	63	0
London Challenge Cup	4	0
War time	1	0
Total	**263**	**0**

Honours:
3 Welsh caps
F.A. Cup Finalists Medal   1926-27
London Combination Championship Medal
1926-27

LEWIS, Reg   1935-53

Birth Place: Billston, Staffordshire
Date of Birth: 7th March 1920

☛ Reg Lewis holds the record of scoring most goals for the Arsenal in all competitions in the club's history (three hundred and ninety-two), scored in only four hundred and fifty-one games. He alone scored one hundred and forty-three times in only one hundred and thirty appearances in war time games and if it had not been for the war Reg's name would have been at the very top of the all time Arsenal greats. His ability and knack of scoring goals were attributed to his fine positional sense when finding space in the box as well as being cool, calm and collected. Reg Lewis had played for South London Schools and London Schools (also at cricket) and had played for Nunhead and Dulwich Hamlet Juniors, before joining Arsenal as a fifteen year old from the club's nursery side, Margate. This as an amateur in May 1935, turning professional, soon after his seventeenth birthday in March 1937. In 1937-38, he made his league debut (scoring the first goal) on New Years Day 1938 at Highbury versus Everton, he finished that season playing in four league games (two goals). In 1938-39, he not only created a club record by scoring forty three times in thirty one appearances for the reserves, including six in a game versus Reading, but he also played in fifteen league games (seven goals) and this resulted in the great Ted Drake having to move to the right wing position to accommodate the young Lewis. During the war he served with B.A.O.R. in Germany as well as finding time to play in the 1943 war time Cup Final, when he scored four times in Arsenal's 7-1 demolition of Charlton Athletic. A brilliant ball player, he got off to a good start in the first post war season of 1946-47. Reg scored six goals in the first Arsenal trial, played for England versus Scotland in the "Bolton Disaster Match" and scored nine out of Arsenal's ten goals in the first six league games. He finished with twenty-nine league goals (leading scorer) in only twenty-eight games, this included a hat trick versus Preston and four versus Grimsby Town. In 1947-48, although having to play second fiddle to the goal scoring exploits of Ronnie Rooke. He still helped Arsenal to the league championship when making twenty eight league appearances scoring fourteen goals, this included scoring another four times versus Charlton Athletic. However, by this stage (still only twenty eight) a succession of injuries were hindering his career but he still managed to score sixteen league goals in only twenty five games (when again being leading goal scorer in 1948-49). The 1949-50 season was Reg's season, he played twice for England B team, scored a further nineteen league goals in thirty one starts and was the

Reg Lewis

hero of the 1950 F.A. Cup Final when scoring both of Arsenal;s goals in the 2-0 victory over Liverpool. However, constant injuries were affecting Lewis's career and in seasons 1950-51 and 1951-52 he mustered only twenty three league appearances although he still managed to maintain his great goal scoring ability (sixteen goals). In 1952-53, the injuries finally took their toll and at the end of that season he announced his retirement from the game.

	Games	Goals
League	154	103
F.A. Cup	21	13
Charity Shield	1	2
Other Senior Matches	4	1
Friendly Matches	22	24
Tours	23	17
Combination League	80	77
Combination Cup	5	5
London Challenge Cup	11	7
War time	130	143
Total	**451**	**392**

Honours:
2 England B caps
League Championship Medal   1947-48
F.A. Cup Winners Medal   1949-50
F.A Charity Shield Winners Medal   1948-49
2 London Combination Championship
   Medals   1937-38, 1938-39
London F.A. Challenge Cup Finalists Medal
     1936-37
3 Football League Sth Wartime Champ'ship
   Medals   1939-40, 1941-42, 1942-43
F.A. Cup Wartime Winners Medal   1942-43

LIDDELL, Edward   1914-20

Birth Place: Sunderland, Tyne & Wear
Date of Birth: 27th May 1878

☛ Edward Liddell was a centre half who played for Southampton in the Southern League 1905-6, Gainsborough Trinity 1906-7, Clapton Orient and Southend, before joining Arsenal (when 36) in September 1914. In that season prior to the outbreak of World War One he played in just two league games when deputising for the injured Chris Buckley. His league debut being in an away fixture at Hull City on 2nd April 1915. During the war, Edward worked in the shipyards. On the return of League Football in 1919-20, he spent the season at the club as reserve cover (at the age of 41 and not playing) to Voysey, Buckley and later Jack Butler. Edward left Highbury in November 1920 and over the following forty-five years (up until his 87th birthday) his whole life was devoted to football. He managed Southend 1920, Q.P.R. 1920-25, Fulham 1929-31, and Luton 1935-38. In between these appointments up until 1945 he served as a scout for West Ham, Chelsea, Portsmouth and Brentford and from 1945-65 he was a scout for Tottenham Hotspur. He died in November 1968 aged 90.

	Games	Goals
League	2	0
Other Senior matches	1	0
Friendly Matches	4	0
Combination League	2	0
London Challenge Cup	2	0
South Eastern League	26	1
London League Reserves	13	1
War time	67	1
Total	**117**	**3**

MACKIE, John   1921-28

Birth Place: Monkstown, Co Antrim
Date of Birth: 23rd February 1903

☛ John Mackie was a young right back who played for Monkstown F.C., The Royal Irish Rifles (wartime) and was with Forth River F.C. (Belfast) when joining Arsenal in February 1922 (after a month's trial). John, making his league debut for the club a year later when replacing Frank Bradshaw against Birmingham City at Highbury on 9th December 1922. He established himself in the side for the rest of the season (twenty-three league games) and won the first of his three Irish caps versus Wales. In 1923-24 he was consistent when missing only eleven games. However, in the following campaign he picked up a series of injuries which were to plague him for the rest of his Highbury career. In 1925-26 Mackie resumed full fitness, playing in thirty-five league games. After the signing of Tom Parker in March 1926, John had to endure two seasons playing reserve team football, before being transferred to Portsmouth in June 1928. Having completely recovered from an injury which looked like ending his career, John spent seven remarkable seasons at Fratton Park playing in over two hundred and fifty league games (ever-present 1930-31 and 1931-32), winning two more Irish caps and he played in two losing F.A. Cup Finals against Bolton (0-2) 1929 and Manchester City (1-2) 1934. John finished his long career with Northampton Town (1936-38) and Sittingbourne 1938. He died in June 1984 aged 81.

	Games	Goals
League	108	0
F.A. Cup	10	1
Other Senior matches	1	0
Tours	10	0
Friendly Matches	26	0
Combination League	58	1
London Challenge Cup	12	1
Total	**225**	**3**

MALE, George   1929-48

Birth Place: West Ham, London
Date of Birth: 8th May 1910

☛ George Male had played for West Ham schoolboys when he signed for Clapton F.C. as an amateur where he played alongside Denis Hill-Wood, father of the present Arsenal chairman, Peter Hill-Wood. George joined Arsenal as an amateur in November 1929 turning professional on his twentieth birthday on May 8th 1930. The quiet, retiring, modest Male made his league debut at left half in a 7-1 victory versus Blackpool at Highbury on 27th December 1930 and in Arsenal's first ever League Championship season he appeared in three league games when deputising for either Eddie Hapgood or Bob John. In the following season , 1931-32, the outlook was the same and he played in only nine league games when filling in for either Charlie Jones or Bob John. However, to his utter surprise he was handed the number 6 shirt (after the side had been shuffled around to compensate for the loss of Alex James) and he played in his first ever Cup tie in the 1932 "over the line final" versus Newcastle United. At the beginning of the 1932-33 season Leslie Compton had not looked the part and the ageing Tom Parker had been recalled (but later left for Norwich City). Arsenal had a right back dilemma, and George later told how he came to switch from one position

George Male

McKINNON, Angus   1908-22

Birth Place: Paisley, Scotland
Date of Birth: 8th December 1886

Angus McKinnon

Angus McKinnon was a left half back who served Woolwich Arsenal/Arsenal magnificently over fourteen years. Angus had had a trial with Heart of Midlothian before joining Scottish junior side Petershill F.C. (Glasgow). He was transferred to Woolwich Arsenal in May 1908 (after spending a month on trial). McKinnon played in just two league games in 1908-9 and only eight and ten games respectively in the following two seasons when being left half understudy to Roddy McEachrane. His league debut for the club was in a 1-4 defeat at Bradford City on 12th December 1908. In 1911-12, Angus finally took over from the veteran when playing in twenty-two league games. In the club's relegation season of 1912-13 he battled on bravely for the club but could not thwart the inevitable consequences. In the two seasons leading up to World War One he was hampered by a series of injuries, one of which put him out of action (March-November 1914). During the War he served in France as a driver in the Royal Field Artillery and when peace time resumed (at the age of 32) he was a stalwart in the club's defence of 1919-20 when missing only one league game, followed by, in 1920-21, when again being a mainstay in the side (thirty-seven league games played). However, although starting the season 1921-22 as automatic choice, he lost his place to young Tom Whittaker. McKinnon was released in the summer of 1922 when he joined Charlton Athletic where he ended his career. For one season he was manager of Wigan Borough and for twenty-seven years (1935-62) he was trainer/coach at New Brighton. Died May 1968 aged 81.

	Games	Goals
League	211	4
F.A. Cup	6	0
Other Senior matches	11	0
Friendly Matches	30	1
Tours	3	1
Combination League	12	0
London Challenge Cup	14	0
South Eastern League	101	5
London League Reserves	18	2
War time	49	0
Total	**455**	**13**

Honours:
London F.A. Challenge Cup Finalists Medal
1914-15

to the other, making another Herbert Chapman story.

On an autumn day in 1932 Mr Chapman suddenly decided that Arsenal needed a new right back. Tom Parker was at the end of his tether, and obviously needed to be replaced. Chapman had young George Male - he was twenty-two years old , at the time - sent up to his office , and dropped yet another one of his bombshells. "George" he announced, "you are going to become a right back." Before George could open his mouth in a gasp, Chapman had already begun to give him a strong dose of the hypnotic eloquence which has never seen equalled, before or since. "By the time I got out of that room," George said afterwards, "I wasn't only convinced I was a full-blown right back, I knew without doubt that I was the best right back in the country!"
Arsenal's new right back was that good, that within five months he had had England trials in his new position. He played in thirty-five league games when helping the club to the League Championship. In his newly found position George was ever present in that 1933-34 title winning side. By this time, George Male had developed into the finest right back in the country and in 1934-35 he helped Arsenal to their third consecutive League Championship and won the first of his nineteen England caps versus Scotland, later to captain England on occasions. George now, was supremely confident and was being talked of as the best right back in the world. In 1935-36, he missed only seven league games, added two Football League caps to his honours collection and was ever present when helping Arsenal beat Sheffield United in the 1936 F.A.Cup Final. He was still a permanent fixture in the side in 1936-37, before winning his fourth League Championship Medal in 1937-38. Male had played in a further twenty-eight league games in 1938-39 before the outbreak of war. Aged 29, he was then at his peak. During the War he made over one hundred and eighty appearances for the club as well as serving in Palestine with the R.A.F. When League Football resumed in 1946-47 he was unfortunately past his best. He did, however, play in fifteen league games that season. In 1947-48 he became the first player in League history to take part in six League Championship seasons and even fifty years on, this record has only been equalled or bettered by a handful of Liverpool players. George bowed out on a high note when in his last league game for the club in May 1948 Arsenal beat Grimsby Town 8-0. George was not lost to Arsenal for over the next twenty-seven years he served them in many capacities in coaching, in training the youth and reserve teams, in administrative positions and as a scout (discovered Charlie George). He retired after forty-five years with the club in May 1975. He will be remembered by all at Highbury as a great player and a wonderful servant.

	Games	Goals
League	285	0
F.A. Cup	29	0
Charity Shield	4	0
Other Senior Matches	5	0
Friendly Matches	20	2
Tours	14	1
Combination League	83	1
Combination Cup	1	0
London Challenge Cup	9	0
War time	184	2
London Midweek League	1	0
Total	**635**	**6**

Honours:
19 England caps
2 Football League caps
4 League Championship Medals
          1932-33, 1933-34, 1934-35, 1937-38
F.A. Cup Winners Medal   1935-36
F.A. Cup Finalists Medal   1931-32
3 F.A Charity Shield Winners Medals
          1933-34, 1934-35, 1938-39
F.A Charity Shield Finalists Medals   1935-36
London Comb. League Champ'ship Medal
                                 1930-31
London F.A. Challenge Cup Winners Medal
                                 1930-31
Sheriff of London Charity Shield Winners
   Medal   1932-33
Northampton Charity Shield Winners Medal
                                 1931-32
3 Football League South War time Champ.
   Medals   1939-40, 1941-42, 1942-43
F.A. Cup Wartime Winners Medal   1942-43

MARKS, George   1936-46

Birth Place: Figheldean, Wiltshire
Date of Birth: 9th April 1915

☛ No player's career, in Arsenal's history, was more dramatically interrupted by the Second World War than that of George Marks. The record books show George as having played in only two League games in goal for the club. Hidden behind these facts is the statistic that he made eight appearances for England during the War years when he was considered to be the best goalkeeper in the League and the tragedy of the story is that at 31 he was deemed too old at the resumption of peace time football. George began his footballing career in junior football with Salisbury Corinthians, joining Arsenal as an amateur in March 1936, turning professional two months later. He was then shipped out to Margate, Arsenal's nursery, before returning to Highbury in May 1938. His two League games were the final two of the last full season played by Arsenal (1938-39) before the War. His debut was at the Baseball Ground versus Derby County on 29th April 1939. He served his country in the R.A.F. in Northern Ireland and on the resumption of peacetime George was transferred to Blackburn Rovers for £5,000 in August 1946. Marks later played for Bristol City in 1948 and Reading from 1948-53. Whilst at Elm Park he helped the club to the Division Three South Runners-up position in 1948-49 and 1951-52. He went on to be trainer/coach at the club.

	Games	Goals
League	2	0
Other Senior Matches	2	0
Friendly Matches	1	0
Tours	7	0
Combination League	18	0
London Challenge Cup	3	0
War time	129	0
Southern League	15	0
Total	**177**	**0**

Honours:
8 England War-time Caps
2 Football League South Championship
   Medals   1939-40 & 1942-43
1 War-time F.A.Cup Winners Medal 1942-43
1 War-time F.A.Cup Finalists Medal 1940-41
London Combination Championship Medal
                     1938-39

MARSHALL, Dr. James   1934-35

Birth Place: Avonbridge, Stirling, Scotl'd
Date of Birth: 3rd January 1908

☛ James had begun his career with Scottish junior side, Shettlestone, before

joining Glasgow Rangers as a seventeen year old in June 1925. In his nine years at Ibrox he scored one hundred and thirty-eight goals in two hundred and fifty-seven games and he won a glittering array of honours which included three Scottish caps (all versus England), six Scottish Championship Medals as well as playing in four Scottish F.A. Cup Finals. His career followed a remarkably similar path to that of Archie MacAulay for it was the latter who took over Marshall's role in the Rangers team and did the same later on when replacing James in the West Ham side. They also both played for Arsenal and Scotland. James obtained his medical degree in October 1933 before joining Arsenal in July 1934. In his only season at the club, 1934-35, he scored one of the goals in the 4-0 defeat of Manchester City in the 1934 F.A. Charity Shield. However, he played in only four league games in Arsenal's 1934-35 Championship campaign of which his debut was at Blackburn Rovers on 17th December 1934. He was transferred to West Ham for £2,000 in March 1935 where he spent two seasons before announcing his premature retirement (aged 29) in 1937. He died in December 1977 aged 69.

	Games	Goals
League	4	0
Charity Shield	1	1
Friendly Matches	3	1
Tours	1	0
Combination League	26	7
London Challenge Cup	1	0
Total	**36**	**9**

Honours:
(WITH GLASGOW RANGERS)
3 Scottish Caps
1 Scottish League Cap
6 Scottish League Championship Medals
       1926-27, 1928-29, 1929-30, 1930-31
                 1933-34, 1934-35
3 Scottish F.A.Cup Winners Medals
           1929-30, 1931-32, 1933-34
1 Scottish F.A.Cup Finalists Medal   1928-29
(WITH ARSENAL)
F.A. Charity Shield Winners Medal   1934-35
London Combination Championship Medal
                     1934-35

MAXWELL, Thomas   1921

Birth Place: Dunfermline, Scotland

☛ Thomas Maxwell must hold the club record for the shortest ever known career at Highbury, for it seems it lasted less than three weeks in which time Thomas played three times for the club including a League appearance in a 1-3 home defeat versus Huddersfield Town on October 29th 1921. Joined Arsenal on free transfer from

Dunfermline 20th October 1921.

	Games	Goals
League	1	0
Combination League	2	1
Total	**3**	**1**

MAYCOCK, William   1928-31

Birth Place: Burton-on-Trent, Derbyshire
Date of Birth: 1906

☛ William had begun his footballing career in the Derbyshire area playing junior football for Burton Town and Gresley Rovers before joining Arsenal in March 1928. For three seasons William served the reserve team well, whilst playing mainly in both wing forward positions. During this time he won three London Combination Championship Medals. His first team chances were restricted due to the consistency of firstly Sid Hoar and then later Charlie Jones and Cliff Bastin. His one first team game for the club was at Highbury in a fifth round F.A.Cup replay versus Swindon on 20th February 1929. William unfortunately had to retire through injury during the close season of 1931.

	Games	Goals
F.A. Cup	1	0
Friendly Matches	16	6
Combination League	79	27
London Challenge Cup	1	0
London Midweek League	7	3
Total	**104**	**36**

Honours:
3 London Combination Championship
   Medals   1928-29, 1929-30, 1930-31

McKENZIE, Alexander   1920-23

Birth Place: Leith, Edinburgh
Date of Birth: 5th March 1896

☛ Alexander was playing for Armiston Rangers in Scottish junior football when invited South of the border for trials at Arsenal in November 1920, signing professional forms in January 1921. He was given his League opportunity soon after when making his debut at Highbury versus West Bromwich on 28th March 1921. In 1921-22 he played in three League games followed by seven in 1922-23. With his first team chances restricted Alex was transferred to Blackpool in May 1923.

	Games	Goals
League	15	2
Other Senior Matches	1	1
Friendly Matches	11	4
Combination League	45	16
Total	**72**	**23**

Honours:
London Combination Championship Medal
                     1922-23

MILNE, John   1935-37

Birth Place: Stirling, Scotland
Date of Birth: 25th March 1911

John Vance Milne was a tricky wing forward who began his career in Scottish junior football with Glasgow Ashfield before joining Blackburn Rovers in February 1932. He spent three seasons at Ewood Park before being transferred to Arsenal for a four figure sum in June 1935. His signing was seen to be as replacement for the evergreen Joe Hulme and although John played in fourteen league games scoring six goals (which included a hat trick versus Grimsby) he missed out in the team selection for the 1936 F.A. Cup Final versus Sheffield United. This after making his Arsenal League debut at Highbury versus Sunderland on 31st August 1935. He did considerably well in 1936-37 when scoring nine goals in nineteen league appearances. In Arsenal's 1937-38 League Championship campaign, J.V. Milne played in sixteen of the club's first nineteen league games (which earned him a championship medal) before being surprisingly transferred to Middlesbrough in December 1937. His consistent form for his new club gaining him the first of his two Scottish caps versus England at the back end of the 1937-38 season. However, his playing career came to an end during World War Two.

	Games	Goals
League	49	19
F.A. Cup	3	0
Charity Shield	2	0
Friendly Matches	5	1
Tours	6	5
Combination League	21	7
London Challenge Cup	3	2
Total	**89**	**34**

John Milne

Honours:
(WITH MIDDLESBROUGH)
2 Scottish Caps
1 War time Cap
(WITH ARSENAL)
League Championship Medal   1937-38
2 F.A. Charity Shield Finalists Medals
          1935-36, 1936-37
London F.A. Challenge Cup Winners Medal
          1935-36

MILNE, William   1921-27

Birth Place: Buckie, Banffshire, Scotland
Date of Birth: 24th November 1895

Billy Milne was a true Highlander who was playing for his hometown club, Buckie Thistle, when joining Arsenal in September 1921. (This after spending a month on trial). A wing half, he made his Arsenal league debut at Ninian Park versus Cardiff City on 27th December 1921 and played in four league games that season. Over the next four seasons he became the club's regular right half when playing in over one hundred league games. However, at the beginning of the 1925-26 season he was injured in a league encounter with Liverpool which resulted in him losing his place to Alf Baker. A broken leg received in a match versus Huddersfield Town at Highbury in April 1927 curtailed his career and in that same year, at the age of 32, he was appointed assistant trainer to Tom Whittaker. This after George Hardy had left for Tottenham Hotspur. During World War One Bill served with the Seaforth Highlanders in France and won the Distinguished Conduct Medal in March 1918 after he had entered an occupied enemy dugout, single-handed with just a gun and bayonet. His valuable work behind the scenes helped the club's reserve side win nine championships in twelve seasons. As a player Billy had been described as "a tireless and enthusiastic wing half. A glutton for work." These were the qualities that Billy Milne showed when assisting Whittaker up to the outbreak of the Second World War. During the war, he was an air raid warden at Highbury and was there one night when one hundred and twenty-four incendiary devices exploded. These set the the goal posts on fire and it was Billy's brave efforts that prevented serious damage to the stadium. After the war he became first team trainer 1947-60. Bill was a very popular personality in his years at Highbury, who believed in physical perfection but God help any scrimshanker caught on the hop from training. It was Bill's healing of aches and pains in the treatment room where many Arsenal victories were won. His strong character made him in to a father-like figure to many of the players and indeed it was

Billy who was at Alex James's death bed. Milne retired in 1960 after giving the club thirty-nine magnificent years service during which he served England on several occasions as trainer. His son, William junior, was on the club's books as a junior. He died in July 1975 aged 79.

	Games	Goals
League	114	1
F.A. Cup	10	2
Other Senior Matches	2	0
Friendly Matches	20	1
Tours	13	0
Combination League	109	9
London Challenge Cup	8	0
Total	**276**	**13**

Honours:
London Combination League Championship
   Medal   1926-27
London F.A. Challenge Cup Winners Medal
          1923-24

MOODY, John   1925-28

Birth Place: Heeley, near Sheffield, Yorks
Date of Birth: 1st November 1904

John was a goalkeeper playing in the Sheffield Amateur League when joining Arsenal in August 1925. In 1925-26, with Robson, Harper and Lewis all on the club's books, Moody's appearances were restricted to reserve team football. His first League opportunity came in the penultimate game of the 1926-27 season versus Bury at Gigg Lane on 4th May 1927. He also played in the last game of the season in a 4-0 victory at White Hart Lane ! John played in just four League games in 1927-28 when deputising for the injured Dan Lewis, his last being in an amazing 4-6 defeat at Bramall Lane versus Sheffield United. He later played for Bradford 1928-30, Doncaster 1930-31 before joining Manchester United in 1930-31 (where he was ever-present in 1932-33). He spent the last six seasons of his career with Chesterfield 1933-39; being ever-present in three of those seasons as well as helping them to the Third Division North Championship in 1935-36.

	Games	Goals
League	6	0
Friendly Matches	16	0
Combination League	38	1
Total	**60**	**1**

Honours:
(WITH ARSENAL)
London Combination Championship Medals
          1927-28
(WITH CHESTERFIELD)
Division Three North Championship Medal
          1935-36

MOSS, Frank   1931-37

Birth Place: Leyland, Lancashire
Date of Birth: 5th November 1909

If his career at the age of 27 had not been curtailed through injury, Frank Moss's name, in goalkeeping terms, would have been mentioned, with the likes of Banks, Shilton and Jennings. Even so, apart from Harry Hibbs of Birmingham City, he was considered to be the most complete and confident goalkeeper of the 1930's. Moss was brave, agile with an uncanny sense of anticipation and kicked well with both feet. Frank had begun his goalkeeping career at junior level with Leyland Motors and Lostock Hall before joining Preston in February 1928. He played twenty-four league games for them before joining Oldham Athletic in 1929. Frank had played in twenty-nine league games for the Boundary Park outfit, mainly as reserve to England goalkeeper Jack Hacking, before Herbert Chapman spotted his obvious potential and he signed for Arsenal for £3,000 in November 1931. Moss made his Arsenal league debut (when taking over from

Charlie Preedy) at Stamford Bridge versus Chelsea on 21st November 1931. Frank, who made goalkeeping look easy, played in the last twenty-seven league games of that season and helped the club to the 1932 F.A.Cup Final versus Newcastle United. This form gaining him Football League honours. Over the next three seasons in which Arsenal won a hat trick of Championships, Frank missed only fifteen of the club's one hundred and twenty-six league games. This resulted in him winning 4 England caps. The first being against Scotland in 1934. However, in a match at Goodison Park versus Everton in March 1935, he suffered a dislocated shoulder and was forced to play on the left wing for the remainder of the game. He always thought that he was good enough to be an outfield player and he proved this when scoring Arsenal's first goal in the aforementioned match. Frank managed to play in five league games in 1935-36, but was plagued by this recurring injury and he was finally advised to retire from the game in March 1937 when he was appointed

manager of Heart of Midlothian. He died in February 1970 aged 60.

	Games	Goals
League	143	1
F.A. Cup	16	0
Charity Shield	2	0
Friendly Matches	12	2
Tours	3	0
Combination League	7	0
Total	**183**	**3**

Honours:
4 England caps
2 Football League caps
3 League Championship Medals
         1932-33, 1933-34, 1934-35
F.A. Cup Finalists Medal   1931-32
2 F.A Charity Shield Winners Medals
         1933-34, 1934-35
Sheriff of London Charity Shield Winners
   Medal   1932-33
Northampton Charity Shield Winners Medal
         1931-32

Frank Moss (third from left)
in 'training' prior to the 1936-37 season. From left to right:
Whittaker (trainer), Copping (behind), Moss, Drake and James.

NEIL, Andrew   1924-26

Birth Place: Kilmarnock, Scotland
Date of Birth: 18th November 1895

🦅 Andrew Neil began his footballing career with his home town club Kilmarnock, before joining Brighton soon after the end of the First World War. Andrew spent four seasons at the Goldstone Ground playing in nearly one hundred and fifty first team games (being ever-present in 1922-23). Arsenal paid £3,000 for his services in March 1924, he made his debut at Nottm Forest on 15th March 1924. In 1924-25 he began the season as the club's regular inside right, playing the first roving schemers roll for the club - a position later adopted by Alex James, before losing his place to Jimmy Brain. In Arsenal's then, best ever season in the Football League when being First Division Runners-up in 1925-26, Andrew played in twenty-seven league fixtures before losing his place once again (to James Ramsay). He subsequently returned to Brighton in March 1926. Andrew finished his career (when playing in nearly one hundred league games) with Q.P.R. 1927-30.

	Games	Goals
League	54	10
F.A. Cup	3	0
Friendly Matches	3	0
Tours	6	0
Combination League	18	3
London Challenge Cup	4	2
Total	**88**	**15**

Honours:
London F.A. Challenge Cup Finalists Medal 1925-26

NELSON, David   1936-46

Birth Place: Douglas Water, Scotland
Date of Birth: 3rd February 1918

🦅 David was a versatile wing half or forward who began his footballing career with his home town club before joining Scottish Second Division side, St. Bernards during the summer of 1935, moving South to join Arsenal in May 1936. David played in eight league games in 1936-37 of which his league debut (when scoring) was at Deepdale versus Preston North End on 28th December 1936. In 1937-38 all of his appearances were confined to reserve team football. He made a return to league action in 1938-39 when playing in nine league games. During the War , although serving as a sergeant in the army, he managed to play in over one hundred and fifty games for the club. In the first season after the War, 1946-47, he played in a further ten league games before being transferred with Cyril Grant to Fulham in part exchange for the legendary Ronnie

Rooke. David later played for Brentford, 1947-50, Q.P.R. 1950-52, and Crystal Palace. In 1954 he became player-manager of Ashford Town. He emigrated to the U.S.A. in 1955 where he died in September 1988 aged 70.

David Nelson

	Games	Goals
League	27	4
F.A. Cup	2	0
Other Senior Matches	3	0
Friendly Matches	10	7
Tours	7	5
Combination League	94	26
Combination Cup	1	0
London Challenge Cup	12	3
War Time	164	29
Southern League	3	1
Total	**323**	**75**

Honours:
Three London Combination Championship Medals   1936-37, 1937-38, 1938-39
London F.A. Challenge Cup Finalists Medal 1936-37
Bath Coronation Cup Winners Medal 1936-37
Three Football League South War Time Championship Medals 1939-40, 1941-42, 1942-43

NORTH, Ernest 'Joe'   1919-22

Birth Place: Burton-upon-Trent, Staffs
Date of Birth: 23rd September 1895

🦅 During World War One "Joe" North served as a lieutenant in the Army winning the coveted Military Medal and during the War years was on the books of Sheffield United before joining Arsenal as an amateur in November 1919, turning professional the following month. In his first season at

Highbury, 1919-20, he was reserve centre forward to both Henry White and Fred Pagnam, playing in only four League games of which his debut (when scoring the first goal) was in a home fixture versus Oldham Athletic on the 7th February 1920. In 1920-21 Ernest played in only eight League games followed by, in 1921-22, when he played in just eleven League games. Realising he could not obtain first team football he was transferred to Reading in May 1922. North later played for Gillingham 1923-24, Norwich City 1925-26 and Watford 1926-27. Ernest later became coach to Northfleet in 1927. "Joe" played County Cricket for Middlesex 1923-27 and later became a Minor Counties Umpire. He died in August 1955 aged 59.

	Games	Goals
League	23	6
Other Senior Matches	1	0
Friendly Matches	11	7
Combination League	57	29
London Challenge Cup	1	0
Total	**93**	**42**

PAGNAM, Fred   1919-21

Birth Place: Poulton Le Fylde, Lancs
Date of Birth: 4th September 1891

🦅 Fred Pagnam was a prolific goalscoring inside or centre forward who had played junior football for Lytham and Blackpool Wednesday before joining Huddersfield Town in 1910. He spent two seasons at Leeds Road without playing a League game. He joined Southport Central in the summer of 1912 before returning to Football League service with Blackpool in February 1913, making no significant progress before joining Liverpool in the summer of 1914. In that last season, prior to the outbreak of World War One, he was Liverpool's leading scorer when netting twenty-four times in twenty-nine League games. He continued this form for the first two seasons during World War One, 1915-17, when scoring forty-two goals in forty-eight games. Fred joined Arsenal for £1,500 in October 1919 and in his first season at the club he scored twelve League goals in twenty-five games. His Arsenal League debut was at Highbury versus Bradford City on 25th October 1919. In 1920-21, although only playing in twenty-five League games (and being transferred to Cardiff City for £3,000 in March 1921), he still finished as the club's leading League scorer with fourteen goals. Pagnam spent just nine months at Ninian Park before Watford paid out their first ever four figure fee to sign him in December 1921. He stayed five seasons at Vicarage Road, playing in over one hundred and fifty first team games, scoring over seventy-five goals, in which time he was the leading League goal scorer in Division Three South in 1922-23. Fred later managed Watford (1926-29) as well as coaching in Turkey and Holland. He died in March 1962 aged 70.

	Games	Goals
League	50	26
F.A. Cup	3	1
Friendly Matches	2	0
London Challenge Cup	2	3
War time	20	14
Total	**77**	**44**

Fred Pagnam

PARKER, Tom   1926-33

Birth Place: Woolston, Hampshire
Date of Birth: 19th November 1897

Tom Parker will be remembered as the first of Arsenal's great captains. A right back, he began his career playing junior football in the Hampshire Leagues before joining Southampton (then Southern League) in 1919. In seven seasons at the Dell, he played in over two hundred league games, helping them to the Third Division South Championship in 1921-22 and also to the 1924-25 F.A.Cup semi-final. Tom was unfortunate to be a contemporary of Goodall and Cooper, if not he would have have won many more England caps. As it was, he played in three England trials but won just one full cap versus France in 1925. The cool calm, balding Parker was transferred to Arsenal in March 1926 and was later given the captain's job. This was because Herbert Chapman realised that Tom was a born leader who led by example. Tom made his Arsenal league deput versus Blackburn Rovers at Highbury, 3rd April 1926. This starting a run of one hundred and fifty consecutive first team games for the club which lasted up to 28th December 1929. The utterly reliable Parker played in Arsenal's first ever F.A. Cup

Final, versus Cardiff City in 1927. Tom's amazing stamina saw him miss only one league game in 1929-30 and he made history when becoming the first Arsenal captain to hold aloft the F.A. Cup at Wembley after the 2-0 defeat of Huddersfield Town. In his time at the club he was Arsenal's expert penalty taker (twelve converted). In 1930-31, Arsenal's first ever league championship season, Tom was ever reliable when missing only one league game. He was a mainstay in the side during 1931-32, when he captained Arsenal to a second F.A. Cup Final, versus Newcastle United, but after George Male was converted to right back, by Herbert Chapman, his league appearances, in 1932-33, were restricted to just five. Tom will be affectionately remembered for his great loyalty to the club. Tom Parker was granted a free transfer in March 1933 when he became manager of Norwich City. Later managed Southampton , 1937-39 and during the war he worked for the Ministry of Transport. Tom had a second spell as manager of Norwich City 1955-57 before returning home, becoming chief scout at Southampton. Died

November 1987 aged 87.

	Games	Goals
League	258	17
F.A. Cup	34	0
Charity Shield	2	0
Other Senior Matches	3	0
Friendly Matches	8	1
Tours	14	1
Combination League	5	0
London Challenge Cup	4	3
London Midweek League	3	0
Total	**331**	**22**

Honours:
WITH ARSENAL

League Championship Medal   1930-31
F.A.Cup Winners Medal   1929-30
F.A. Cup Finalists Medals   1926-27, 1931-32
2 F.A Charity Shield Winners Medals
                        1930-31, 1931-32
Sheriff of London Charity Shield Winners
    Medal   1930-31
Northampton Charity Shield Winners Medals
                        1930-31

WITH SOUTHAMPTON
1 England cap
Division Three Championship Medal 1921/22

Tom Parker

PARKIN, Ray   1928-36

Birth Place: Crook, County Durham
Date of Birth: 11th February 1911

➤ Ray Parkin was yet another reserve team player at the club during the 1930's who was content to deputise for Arsenal at either wing half or inside forward when the likes of Jack, Brain and Lambert at inside forward were injured, and later on, occasionally at wing half for Charlie Jones. His loyalty was shown in the fact that he played in only twenty-five league games in eight years at Highbury. Raymond had played for Durham schools and was an England Schoolboy International when joining Arsenal from the North East junior side Esh Winning in January 1928. He made his league debut on New Years Day 1929, when scoring in a 1-5 defeat at Roker Park versus Sunderland. Whilst at the club he appeared in two League Championship winning campaigns playing in five league games in 1932-33 and five in 1933-34. Ray won five London Combination Championship Medals as well as representing the London Combination versus Diables Rouges in 1935. After eight years of outstanding service he was transferred to Middlesbrough in January 1936, spending two seasons there, playing in only a handful of league games. After nearly ten years, he won a regular first team position with Southampton in the last two seasons prior to the outbreak of World War Two. He died in July 1971 aged 60.

	Games	Goals
League	25	11
F.A. Cup	1	0
Other Senior Matches	2	1
Friendly Matches	26	20
Tours	4	2
Combination League	232	60
London Challenge Cup	14	1
London Midweek League	19	10
Total	**323**	**105**

Honours:
Five London Combination Championship
  Medals   1928-29, 1929-30, 1930-31,
                      1933-34, 1934-35
London F.A. Challenge Cup Winners Medal
                                     1930-31
Sheriff of London's Shield Winners Medal
                                     1932-33

DR. PATERSON, James   1920-26

Birth Place: London
Date of Birth: 9th May 1891

James had been on the books of Glasgow Rangers before joining Queens Park as an amateur. This was while he was qualifying as a doctor at the Bellahouston Academy and during World War One he was a medical officer

in the London Scottish, winning the prized Military Cross for his deeds whilst in action in France. James took up his medical practice in Clapton and joined Arsenal as an amateur in October 1920 making his debut on the club's left wing at Highbury versus Derby County on 30th October 1920. He made history that season when becoming the only Scotsman (although being born in London) to represent the Football League in an Inter League game. In 1921-22 he played in just two League games but played more regularly in 1922-23 (twenty-six League games) followed by twenty-one League games in 1923-24. James retired from football at the end of the 1923-24 season to concentrate on his medical practice. However, he was recalled out of retirement to play in one final League match (when scoring his only League goal) in a 3-0 victory at Highbury versus Newcastle United in February 1926.

	Games	Goals
League	70	1
F.A. Cup	7	1
Other Senior Matches	1	0
Friendly Matches	4	0
Combination League	13	0
London Challenge Cup	2	1
Total	**97**	**3**

Honours:
1 Football League Cap

PATERSON, William   1928-29

Birth Place: Dunfermline, Scotland
Date of Birth: 1902

➤ William, standing six foot three inches and weighing fourteen and a half stone, was a goalkeeper with immense physical presence. He came South of the border to join Arsenal from Dundee United in 1928 as cover to Dan Lewis and John Moody. He played in five League games that 1927-28 season, of which his Arsenal League debut

Dr Paterson

was in a 3-4 home defeat versus Derby County on 4th February 1928. In 1928-29 he deputised ten times for Lewis before being given a free transfer when he returned to Scotland to join Airdrie in July 1929.

	Games	Goals
League	15	0
Friendly Matches	1	0
Combination League	47	0
Total	**63**	**0**

Honours:
2 London Combination Championship
  Medals   1927-28, 1928-29

PATTISON, George   1920-22

Birth Place: North Shields, Tyneside
Date of Birth: 28th February 1898

➤ George was playing junior football for North East side Wallsend when joining Arsenal as an amateur in May 1920, turning professional three months later. The club had signed him because of a centre half crisis when both Buckley and Butler were injured. Unbelievably, George made his debut only hours after signing for the club on the 1st May 1920 versus Bradford. In his other two seasons at the club he was virtually a permanent reserve to Baker and McKinnon playing in only six League games in 1920-21 and just two in 1921-22. Pattison moved to West Ham in May 1922.

	Games	Goals
League	9	0
F.A. Cup	1	0
Other Senior Matches	2	0
Friendly Matches	22	1
Combination League	43	1
London Challenge Cup	1	0
Total	**78**	**2**

PEART, John   1910-14 & 1919-21

Birth Place: Tewkesbury, Gloucs
Date of Birth: 1887

➤ J.C. Peart, a full back, joined Woolwich Arsenal as an amateur in December 1910, turning professional in January 1911. John made his League debut for the club in the third League game of the 1911-12 season (replacing Archie Gray at left back) versus Newcastle at Highbury on the 16th September 1911. He enjoyed rapid progress during that season when playing in thirty-four League games. However, he lost his place in the side after a 0-4 home defeat versus Manchester City in November 1912, appearing in fourteen League games that 1912-13 relegation season. His appearances were limited to just reserve team football in 1913-14 and John was granted a free transfer in the summer of 1914 when he joined

Croydon Common. During the First World War he served with the RASC before rejoining Arsenal in 1919. John played in only six League games over the following two seasons when deputising for the injured Joe Shaw. Peart was released for the second time on a free transfer when he joined Margate during the summer of 1921.

	Games	Goals
League	63	0
F.A. Cup	3	0
Other Senior Matches	2	0
Friendly Matches	20	0
Tours	8	1
Combination League	36	2
London Challenge Cup	4	0
South Eastern League	64	0
London League Reserves	9	0
Total	**209**	**3**

PEEL, Harold   1926-29

Birth Place: Bradford, Yorkshire
Date of Birth: 26th March 1900

 Harold Peel's Football League career spanned fifteen years, 1921-36, playing for Bradford, Arsenal and Bradford City, in which time he played in over four hundred and fifty League and F.A. Cup games. Harold had begun playing in the Bradford League with junior side, Calverley, before joining Bradford in 1921. He spent five seasons at Park Avenue before being transferred to Arsenal for £1,750 in December 1926 to replace the out of form Samson Haden. However, Peel played in just nine league games up to the end of that season and missed out on being selected for the 1927 F.A. Cup Final team. In 1927-28 he found himself as understudy to Sid Hoar and played in only thirteen league games. In the following campaign, 1928-29, he fared better when moving to the inside left position and scored five times in twenty-four league games. The signing of Alex James in June 1929 saw Harold's first team chances diminish. This resulted in him returning to Bradford to play for City in December 1929, for £1,000. He gave them seven years excellent service before retiring in 1936. Died January 1976, aged 75.

	Games	Goals
League	47	5
F.A. Cup	5	1
Friendly Matches	10	4
Tours	3	1
Combination League	76	19
London Challenge Cup	1	0
London Midweek League	1	0
Total	**143**	**30**

Honours:
3 London Combination Championship
    Medals   1926-27, 1927-28, 1928-29

PLATT, Ted   1938-53

Birth Place: Romford
Date of Birth: 26th March 1921

 Ted Platt joined Arsenal from the then Southern League club Colchester United in December 1938, as an amateur, turning pro in January 1939. Over the following fifteen years he was reserve team goalkeeper, being kept out of the league side by first George Swindon and then Jack Kelsey. During season 1938-39 he won a regular place in the reserve side before the outbreak of the war in 1939. He spent the following six years as a Royal Fusilier, seeing service in North Africa and Egypt. After the war he made his league debut versus Leeds, 16th November 1946. Played in only four league matches that season and in 1947-48 spent the whole season in the reserve side. During 1948-49 and 1949-50 he played in a total of twenty-nine league matches, followed by seventeen in season 1950-51. During the following seasons (1951-52 and 1952-53) he played in only, three league games, eventually being transferred to Portsmouth in September 1953. Later played for Aldershot and Worcester City. Ted Platt will be remembered as one of Arsenal's great servants.

	Games	Goals
League	53	0
F.A. Cup	4	0
Friendly Matches	19	0
Tours	4	0
Combination League	75	0
Combination Cup	42	0
London Challenge Cup	2	0
War time	34	0
Southern League	15	0
Eastern Counties League	1	0
Total	**249**	**0**

Honours:
London Combination League Championship
    Medal   1946-47
London F.A. Challenge Cup Finalist Medal
                            1946-47

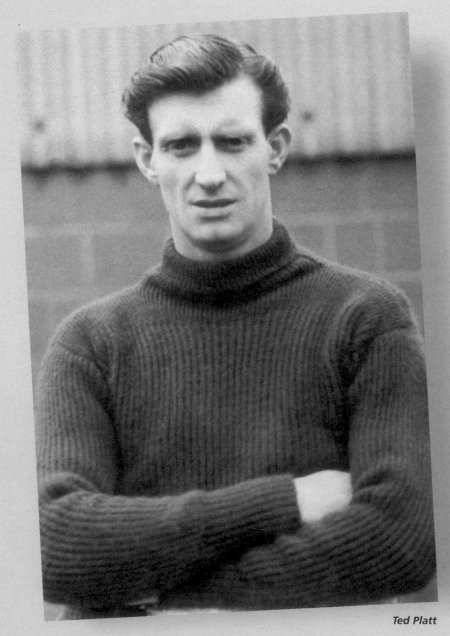

Ted Platt

PREEDY, Charles — 1929-33

Birth Place: Neemuch, India
Date of Birth: 11th January 1903

☞ C.J.F. Preedy had played for several junior sides before joining Charlton Athletic in December 1922. Charles spent five seasons at the Valley being the club's regular goalkeeper, 1924-28. He spent one season at Wigan Borough, 1928-29, before being transferred to Arsenal in May 1929. In his first full season at the club, Charles made his Arsenal league debut in the third game of the season at Sheffield Wednesday on 7th September 1929. However, after his fifth league game, he was dropped in favour of Dan Lewis, after being in an Arsenal side which lost 2-5 at Aston Villa. Preedy was left out in the cold for virtually the rest of that season when suddenly his fortunes changed for the better. A week before Arsenal's 1930 F.A. Cup Final tie versus Huddersfield Town, the club took part in the highest ever score draw in the history of the Football League, a 6-6 with Leicester City. Herbert Chapman dropped Lewis in favour of Preedy for that particular final. Chapman also remembered Lewis' blunder in the 1927 final. Charles stood up in the coach travelling to Wembley and said " Boys, I know you think I'm the worst goalkeeper in the world, I probably am, but today I'm going to play like the best . Nothing is going to get past Charles Preedy this afternoon ". In Arsenal's League Championship winning side of 1930-31 Charles missed out on a medal when playing in only eleven league games. In his penultimate season with the club, 1931-32, although taking over from Bill Harper in the third game of the season (making thirteen league appearances) he lost his place to new signing Frank Moss in November 1931. In his final eighteen months at Highbury he had to be content in being the permanent deputy to Frank Moss. He was transferred to Bristol Rovers in July 1933 together with Horace Cope in an exchange deal which saw R.C. Green joining Arsenal in a transaction worth £3,000. Preedy later played for Luton Town, 1934-35, finishing his career with Margate. He died February in 1978 aged 75.

	Games	Goals
League	37	0
F.A. Cup	2	0
Charity Shield	1	0
Other Senior Matches	1	0
Friendly Matches	6	0
Tours	2	0
Combination League	116	0
London Challenge Cup	7	0
London Midweek League	8	0
Total	**180**	**0**

Honours:
F.A. Cup Winners Medal	1929-30
F.A. Charity Shield Winners Medal	1931-32
2 London Combination Championship Medals	1929-30, 1930-31
London F.A. Challenge Cup Winners Medal	1930-31
Northampton Charity Shield Winners Medal	1929-30

PRYDE, David — 1935-46

Birth Place: Newtongrange, Scotland
Date of Birth: November 10th 1913

☞ David was one of many footballers whose career was severely interrupted by the war years. David was on the books of Margate when joining Arsenal in May 1935, returning to Margate (Arsenal's nursery) until September 1937. He was a regular in the Combination side (wing half) in the two seasons leading up to the outbreak of war. David managed to play in four consecutive League games (February 1939) of which his debut was versus Sunderland at Highbury on 4th February 1939. He remained on the club's books throughout the war in which time he served with the R.A.F. in India and Burma. He left Highbury in October 1946 when linking up with Torquay United.

	Games	Goals
League	4	0
Combination League	53	0
Combination Cup	3	0
London Challenge Cup	7	0
War time	23	0
Southern League	15	1
Total	**105**	**1**

Honours:
2 London Combination Championship Medals	1937-38, 1938-39

PUGH, Sidney — 1936-39

Birth Place: Dartford, Kent
Date of Birth: 10th October 1919

☞ Sidney Pugh was one of several young players who lost their lives in the defence of their country in the Second World War. This whilst as a flying officer with the R.A.F. in April 1944. Sidney had played for Nunhead as a junior wing half before joining Arsenal's nursery team, Margate. He signed amateur forms for Arsenal in April 1936, turning professional two years later. He played in one League game for the club in a 2-1 victory at St. Andrews versus Birmingham City on 8th April 1939. Died April 1944 aged 24.

1919-1939

	Games	Goals
League	1	0
Friendly Matches		2
0 Combination League	11	0
London Challenge Cup	1	0
Southern League	21	1
Total	**36**	**1**

RAMSAY, James — 1924-26

Birth Place: Clydebank, Glasgow
Date of Birth: 7th August 1898

☞ James was a stylish inside forward who began his footballing career in Scottish junior football with Moor Park and Arthurlie before joining Renfrew in 1919, this was after serving in France with the Seaforth Highlanders during World War One. James moved on to Kilmarnock during the 1919-20 season which saw the club winning the Scottish F.A. Cup Final versus Albion Rovers. He moved South of the border when joining Arsenal in February 1924, playing in eleven of Arsenal's last thirteen League fixtures and making his debut versus Liverpool at Highbury on 1st March 1924. At the start of the 1924-25 campaign he played in all of the club's first twenty-six fixtures before losing his place to William Blyth. After the opening game of the 1925-26 season (a 0-1 home defeat versus Tottenham) James lost his place to Andrew Neil before returning to the side in February 1926. He then played in sixteen League games when helping Arsenal to the League Championship Runners-up spot. Ramsay had played in twelve League games at the start of the 1926-27 season before returning to Scotland when he linked up again with Kilmarnock in December 1926. He died in January 1969 aged 70.

	Games	Goals
League	69	11
F.A. Cup	6	0
Friendlies	6	3
Tours	8	1
Combination League	37	14
London Challenge Cup	5	1
Total	**131**	**30**

ROBERTS, Herbie   1926-37

Birth Place: Oswestry, Shropshire
Date of Birth: 19th February 1905

☞ Of all the Arsenal players of the 1930's, only Alex James and possibly Cliff Bastin were talked about and discussed more than Herbie Roberts. The footballing public believed that Herbert Chapman had created a monster when turning Roberts into the pillar of his third back system. Charles Buchan and Chapman had conceived the idea when the offside law was changed in favour of the forward player, and so in Chapman's eyes the footballing centre half was dead. His idea being that a tall domineering centre half was required to defend the middle ground at the back of the defence and in Herbie Roberts he basically had the ready made article. Off the field Herbie was a gentleman, shy and unassuming, on the field he was known as "Policeman Roberts" whose main aim was to blot out and stop the opponents' centre forward and these policies made him into one of the most unpopular players the length and breadth of the country. Whether it be at Portsmouth or Sunderland the unruffled red haired Roberts was abused and barracked when ever he played away. He was later to say "that this never disturbed his cool, calm approach to the game". Herbert Roberts had began his footballing career with his home town club Oswestry in 1922. He spent four years there before joining Arsenal for £200 in December 1926. Herbie made his league debut at Villa Park versus Aston Villa 18th April 1927 (at right half). In his first two seasons at the club he played in only five league games. By now, Herbie had been converted to centre half, taking over from Jack Butler, when playing in twenty league games in 1928-29. In 1929-30, an injury picked up at Upton Park versus West Ham in March 1930 resulted in him having to miss that years Cup Final versus Huddersfield. 1930-31 was Herbie's season, he missed only two league games when helping Arsenal to their first League Championship, won an F.A.Charity Shield Winners Medal and his only England cap versus Scotland. In the following campaign he was a member of the losing F.A.Cup Final team versus Newcastle United whilst still being the kingpin in Arsenal's defensive formation. In Arsenal's hat trick of League Championships, 1932-35, he played in thirty-six, thirty, and thirty-six league games respectively. Not everything was a bed of roses however, for in a league game at Highbury versus Derby County in October 1932 he had the misfortune of scoring in his own goal, twice (The only Arsenal player ever to do so) In 1935-36, he was a member of the F.A.Cup winning team versus Sheffield United. In 1936-37, there was seven periods where he missed league games due to niggling injuries. In Arsenal's 1937-38 season, he had played in the first thirteen league games when, in that unlucky thirteenth match he collided with a Middlesbrough forward which left his leg dead. This injury resulting in Herbie's premature retirement. If he had played in just one more league game he would have qualified for his fifth League Championship Medal. On retirement George Allison gave him the job as trainer to Arsenal's Southern League team 1938-39. During the War he served as a lieutenant in the Royal Fusilliers. He died tragically from Erysipelas in June 1944 aged 39.

	Games	Goals
League	297	4
F.A. Cup	36	1
Charity Shield	2	0
Other Senior Matches	2	0
Friendly Matches	14	0
Tours	7	0
London Challenge Cup	5	0
Combination League	63	0
Total	**426**	**5**

Honours:
1 England cap
4 League Championship Medals
        1930-31, 1932-33, 1933-34, 1934-35
F.A. Cup Winners Medal   1935-36
F.A. Cup Finalists Medal   1931-32
2 F.A Charity Shield Winners Medals
        1930-31, 1931-32
London Combination Championship Winners
    Medal   1927-28
Northampton Charity Shield Winners Medals
        1930-31

Herbie Roberts

ROBSON, John 'Jock' 1921-26

Birth Place: Innerleithen, Scotland
Date of Birth: 15th April 1899

☛ John Hardy Robson, standing just five feet eight and a half inches, must be one of the shortest custodians ever to have pulled on an Arsenal goalkeeper's jersey. John had come to Highbury from his home town club, Innerleithen, in November 1921. This was after he had served in France during World War One with the Sixth Seaforth Highlanders. At the start of his first full season at the club, 1922-23, (after spending the latter half of 1921-22 season in the reserves) he started as the club's third choice keeper behind Williamson and Dunn. However, Williamson was dropped for Dunn after a 1-4 defeat at Burnley and Robson replaced Dunn after a 1-4 defeat at Bolton. Jock made his League debut in the return game versus Bolton (Arsenal winning 5-0) on Boxing Day 1922. John kept his place for the remainder of the season keeping twelve clean sheets in twenty games. This form made him automatic choice and he was ever present in the 1923-24 season. Robson lost his place to Dan Lewis in the middle of the 1924-25 season (later to regain it) when he played in twenty-six League games. However in 1925-26, with Scottish International Harper and Welsh International Lewis both on the club's books, Robson's first team days were numbered and was subsequently transferred to Bournemouth and Boscombe Athletic in Aug. 1926.

	Games	Goals
League	97	0
F.A. Cup	4	0
Other Senior Matches	1	0
Friendlies	27	0
Combination League	34	0
London Challenge Cup	9	0
Total	**172**	**0**

Honours:
London F.A. Challenge Cup Winners Medal
1923-24
London F.A. Challenge Cup Finalists Medal
1925-26

ROE, Archibald 1922-23

Birth Place: Hull, Yorkshire
Date of Birth: 9th December 1893

☛ Young Archibald was playing in Yorkshire junior football for Castleford Town when he joined Arsenal in 1922. He received his first chance of League action when the club made five changes after a disastrous 0-7 defeat at West Bromwich Albion in October 1922. Roe making his debut the following Saturday at St. James Park versus Newcastle. He finished that season playing in four League games, scoring once. In 1923-24,

with Turnbull and Young ahead of him in the centre forward pecking order he moved on to Sincil Bank to try his luck with Lincoln City in November 1923. Archibald finished his career with Rotherham United. Died 1947, aged 53.

	Games	Goals
League	4	1
Friendly Matches	7	7
Combination League	37	23
London Challenge Cup	2	1
Total	**50**	**32**

Honours:
London Combination Championship Medal
1922-23

ROE, Arthur 1925

Birth Place: Derbyshire
Date of Birth: 1896

☛ Arthur Roe had spent six seasons at Kenilworth Road with Luton Town (1919-25) playing in just over one hundred first team games for the club. Arthur was released by them at the back end of the 1924-25 season and signed for Arsenal in May 1925. He played in just one League game for the Gunners in the last fixture of the season at Gigg Lane versus Bury. Roe's contract with the club was cancelled nine days later.

	Games	Goals
League	1	0
Total	**1**	**0**

ROGERS, Ehud 'Tim' 1935-36

Birth Place: Chirk, Wales
Date of Birth: 15th October 1912

☛ Ehud Rogers was one of many forwards brought in to Highbury (supposedly to replace ageing stars) during the 1930's, whose move to the club, like many of his counterparts, bore little fruition. His sixteen league games for the club were spread over two seasons. In the Championship winning campaign of 1934-35, he played in the last five league fixtures and possibly made Arsenal history when he made his debut for the club in an 8-0 thrashing of Middlesbrough at Highbury on 19th April 1935 (Rogers scoring twice). In his only other season at the Arsenal he played in eleven league games. The £3,000 that Arsenal had invested in him (to replace the ageing outside right, Joe Hulme) had not paid off. This was all after, Tim, had had a meteoric rise to fame with Wrexham in 1934-35. After starting out in Welsh junior football with several teams including Oswestry Town, Ehud was transferred to Newcastle United for £2,500 in June 1936, finishing his career with Swansea Town in 1939, where he won two War-time Welsh Caps to add to the ones he had won as an amateur.

	Games	Goals
League	16	5
Friendly Matches	7	6
Combination League	27	9
London Challenge Cup	3	0
Total	**53**	**20**

Honours:
London F.A. Challenge Cup Winners Medal
1935-36
(WITH SWANSEA)
2 Welsh War-time Caps

RUTHERFORD, John 'Jock' 1913-26

Birth Place: Percy Main, Northumberland
Date of Birth: 12th October, 1884

☛ Jock Rutherford became a footballing legend in his own life time. In a playing career which lasted nearly twenty-five years he played in nearly six hundred league and F.A. Cup games (this would have been nearer eight hundred if not for the loss of four seasons during World War One). His footballing league career began in January 1902, when Newcastle United acquired his services from the junior side Willington Athletic. Over the next ten years, this blond, right winger could be seen tormenting defenders all over the country with his speed and magnetic ball control as well as his ability to make near perfect crossfield passes. During Jock's career at St James's Park, "the Newcastle flyer", played in three hundred and thirty-four first team games (92 goals). He won the first of his eleven England caps v. Wales 1904, three League Championship Medals and played in five F.A. Cup Finals. (1905 v. Aston Villa, 1906 v. Everton, 1908 v. Wolves, 1910 v. Barnsley and 1911 v. Bradford City). However, at the beginning of the 1913-14 season he went into dispute with Newcastle over payments and was subsequently transferred to Arsenal for £800 in October 1913. In his first season at Highbury he played in twenty-one league games (six goals) of which his Arsenal league debut (when scoring twice) was versus Nottm Forest at Highbury on 1st November 1913. Jock followed this in the last season prior to the War playing in twenty-six league games (three goals). Rutherford played in nearly one hundred games for Arsenal during the War years. In 1919-20 and 1920-21 he was as consistent as ever when playing in thirty-six and thirty-two games respectively. Over the next four seasons he remained a mainstay in the league side. However, at the age of thirty-eight he was tempted into management with Stoke City in April 1923. But his stay at the Victoria Ground was less than four months and he returned to Highbury as a player, in September 1923. But in 1923-24 he played in a further twenty-two league games (two goals). Twenty league games were played by

Jock in 1924-25, before retiring in the summer of 1925. Still feeling the urge to play in top flight football, he came out of retirement and resigned for Arsenal in January 1926. Seventy years on Jock Rutherford still holds the record as being the oldest player to represent Arsenal in a League match (forty one years, one hundred and fifty-nine days) when playing against Manchester City at Highbury on 20th March 1926. Jock was transferred to Clapton Orient in Aug. 1926 where he spent one season before finally retiring during the summer of 1927. John's two brothers, Sep and Bob, both played League football and his son, John Jnr, also played for Arsenal. He died in April 1963 aged 78.

	Games	Goals
League	222	25
F.A. Cup	10	2
Other Senior Matches	5	2
Friendly Matches	11	2
Tours	6	0
London Challenge Cup	11	0
Combination League	16	2
War time	91	29
South Eastern League	1	0
Total	**373**	**62**

Honours:
(WITH NEWCASTLE)
11 England caps
1 Football League cap
3 League Championship Medals
1904-5, 1906-7, 1908-9
F.A. Cup Winners Medal   1909-10
4 F.A. Cup Finalists Medals
1904-5, 1905-6, 1907-8, 1910-11
(WITH ARSENAL)
London F.A. Challenge Cup Winners Medal
1923-24
London F.A. Challenge Cup Finalists Medal
1914-15

RUTHERFORD, John 'J.J.'   1924-27

Birth Place: South Shields, Durham
Date of Birth: 4th March 1907

☛ J.J. Rutherford and his father Jock set a record unprecedented in Arsenal's history when in the 1925-26 season they, as father and son, they played in a League match together. Young John had joined Arsenal as an amateur from Ilford soon after his 17th birthday in April 1924, after he had represented the Isthmian League. It was not until January 1927 that he turned professional, after he had played in his only League game v. Bury at Highbury on 14th Nov. 1925, with dad. John was granted a free transfer in June 1927 when he joined West Ham Utd.

	Games	Goals
League	1	0
Friendly Matches	2	2
Combination League	14	3
Total	**17**	**5**

SCOTT, Laurie   1937-51

Birth Place: Sheffield
Date of Birth: 23rd April 1917

☛ Laurie Scott joined Bradford City as an amateur when only fourteen years old in 1931, after playing for Sheffield schoolboys. He turned professional three years later in 1934. He played in thirty-nine league games for Bradford before joining his ex-team mate George Swindin at Highbury in February 1937 in exchange for Ernest Tuckett. Pre-war he spent two seasons in the reserve side making over eighty appearances. Unfortunately the war came, in which he served as a P.T. Instructor in the R.A.F., at a time when Laurie Scott was making a name for himself. During those years he developed into one of the country's finest full backs, winning sixteen England war time international caps between 1941-45. He made his league debut (at the age of twenty-nine) on the opening day of the 1946-47 season against Wolves. During that season he played in twenty-eight league matches and won the first of his seventeen England caps (all consecutively between 1946-49), against Scotland. He missed only three league games during Arsenal's championship season of 1947-48, but from then on was unfortunately dogged by injury for the rest of his career. He had an appendicitis operation during the summer of 1948 followed by a serious knee injury sustained in an international match versus Wales. He managed to play in only twelve league matches during the 1948-49 season and on his return to the league side during 1950-51, a recurrence of the injury resulted in him playing in only seventeen league matches, having to share the right back position with Wally Barnes, while Lionel Smith was the regular left back. With his first class career coming to a close, he was transferred to Crystal Palace as player/manager in October 1951, taking over from another ex-Arsenal player, Ronnie Rooke. Had it not been for the war years, Laurie Scott would surely have had a longer and more distinguished career. Even so, he will be remembered as one of the finest full backs the club has had, for his speed over 10 yards and his ability to turn quickly. These attributes, added to his fine distribution and positional sense made him the complete full back. He was later quoted to have said "I was fortunate to go all over the world - it was a wonderful life - Arsenal were *the* team".

	Games	Goals
League	115	0
F.A. Cup	11	0
Other Senior Matches	1	0
Friendly Matches	19	0
Tours	16	0
Combination League	86	0
Combination Cup	2	0
London Challenge Cup	9	0
War time	191	0
Southern League	7	0
Total	**457**	**0**

Honours:
17 England caps
16 England Wartime caps
4 England B Caps
5 Football League Caps
League Championship Medal   1947-48
F.A. Cup Winners Medal   1949-50
2 London Combination Championship
Winners Medal   1937-38, 1938-39
2 Football League South Wartime
Championship Medals   1941-42, 1942-43
F.A. Cup Wartime Winners Medal   1942-43
F.A. Cup Wartime Finalists Medal   1940-41

Laurie Scott

SEDDON, William — 1924-32

Birth Place: Clapton, London
Date of Birth: 28th July 1901

☛ Bill Seddon had played in junior football, in North West London, for Villa Athletic before playing for Gillingham as an amateur and having trials with Aston Villa. William joined Arsenal as a twenty-three year old in Dec. 1924. A consistent member of the London Comb. side during his near eight years at Highbury, he was captain when the club reserves won five consecutive titles 1927-31. Seddon had to wait sixteen months after joining the club before making his League debut (when deputising for Alf Baker) in an away fixture at Roker Park versus Sunderland on 10th April 1926. Bill played in 17 league games in 1926-27, but missed out on being selected for the 1927 F.A.Cup Final versus Cardiff City. By then, 1927-28, the half back line, Baker-Butler-John virtually picked itself and he played in only four league games that season. Even worse was to follow, in 1928-29, when his position looked hopeless as he was reduced to playing in only reserve team football. However in 1929-30, his fortunes changed when at the beginning of the season he alternated with Alf Baker for the right half position, but when Herbie Roberts was injured in a league encounter at Upton Park versus West Ham, he switched to centre half, playing in twelve of the club's last fourteen league games, as well as appearing for Arsenal in the 1930 F.A.Cup Final versus Huddersfield Town. Seddon helped Arsenal to their first ever League Championship in 1930-31 (reverting to right half) when playing in eighteen games. In his last season at Highbury, 1931-32, Charlie Jones held a stranglehold on the right half position, resulting in Bill making only five league appearances. William Charles Seddon was one of the many players who were loyal to the club at the beginning of it's halcyon days. He was transferred to Grimsby for £2,500 in March 1932, spending two seasons at Blundell Park before finishing his career with Luton Town in 1933-34. Seddon was later trainer at Notts County (joining his great friend and rival Charlie Jones) and later served Romford in the same capacity. During the War he served in the Army in West Africa before returning to Romford as groundsman up until his retirement in August 1966, when Arsenal provided the opposition in his benefit match at Brooklands. He died in January 1993 aged 91.

	Games	Goals
League	69	0
F.A. Cup	6	0
Charity Shield	1	0
Other Senior Matches	1	0
Friendly Matches	23	6
Tours	13	1
Combination League	201	2
London Challenge Cup	5	0
London Midweek League	2	0
Total	**321**	**9**

Honours:
League Championship Medal 1930-31
F.A. Cup Winners Medal 1929-30
F.A.Charity Shield Winners Medal 1930-31
5 London Combination Championship Winners Medal 1926-27, 1927-28, 1928-29, 1929-30, 1930-31
F.A. London Challenge Cup Winners Medal 1930-31
Northampton Charity Shield Winners Medal 1929-30

SHAW, James — 1926-30

Birth Place: Goldenhill, Staffordshire
Date of Birth: 1904

☛ James was a young inside forward who had played at junior level for his home town club before joining Frickley Athletic in 1925. The Arsenal scouts got word of his potential and James eventually joined the club in April 1926. In his four seasons at Highbury, although being a prolific marksman in the reserve side, his League opportunities were limited owing firstly, to Charles Buchan and then David Jack. In 1926-27 he had five League outings which included a terrible experience in his League debut. A 0-7 defeat at Upton Park versus West Ham on 7th March 1927. In his next two League games James fared better, playing in a 1-6 defeat at Newcastle and a 1-5 defeat at Sunderland ! However, this was because Arsenal were resting most of the first team squad leading up to the 1927 F.A. Cup Final versus Cardiff City. In 1927-28 he played in six League games scoring three goals. In 1928-29 and 1929-30, the seasons leading up to the great era, James was only seen in reserve team action. Shaw was transferred to Brentford in May 1930.

	Games	Goals
League	11	4
Friendlies	23	17
Tours	1	0
Combination League	92	57
London Challenge Cup	1	0
London Midweek League	8	5
Total	**136**	**83**

Honours:
3 London Combination Championship Medals   1926-27, 1927-28, 1928-29

SHAW, Joe — 1907-23

Birth Place: Bury, Lancashire
Date of Birth: 7th May 1883

☛ Joe Shaw came to prominence with his home town club Bury, helping them win the Lancashire Amateur Cup and he was with Accrington Stanley, where he had been a member of their side when they won the

Lancashire Combination and reached the Lancashire Cup Final, when joining Woolwich Arsenal in May 1907. Joe made his Arsenal league debut at Deepdale versus Preston North End on 28th September 1907 and in that first season at the club he was reserve left back to James Sharp. A member of the Players Union, Joe held down the left back position for the following seven seasons up to the outbreak of World War One. He was the captain of the side and he had the distinction of being the only ever present in the club's worst ever season of 1912-13 as well as playing in every league game in 1914-15. Shaw played regularly for Arsenal during the First World War and afterwards he remained the first choice right back for two seasons 1919-21 and at this time he became only the third Arsenal player to reach the milestone of three hundred league appearances for the club. This being against Newcastle United at Highbury on 23rd April 1921. In 1921-22 (in his thirty-eighth year), Joe lost his place to the two Franks, Cownley and Bradshaw. He assisted the reserves, in 1922-23, before retiring and becoming manager of the Arsenal reserve side. Shaw was Arsenal's acting manager for a short period after the death of Herbert Chapman in 1934. Under the influence of Joe Shaw and Billy Milne the reserve side won nine championships in twelve seasons. After the Second World War, this excellent tactician became a famous Arsenal personality, known the world over when becoming Arsenal's general assistant manager and he also assisted the club as head coach and chief representative. This well known member of Arsenal's boot room of the 1930's retired in the summer of 1956, after forty-nine years service to the club. Joe Shaw, truly one of Arsenal's all-time greats, died in September 1963 aged 80

	Games	Goals
League	309	0
F.A. Cup	17	0
Other Senior Matches	14	0
Friendly Matches	25	1
Tours	1	0
Combination League	21	1
London Challenge Cup	18	0
War time	68	0
South Eastern League	36	1
London League Reserves	16	0
Total	**525**	**3**

Honours:
F.A. London Challenge Cup Finalists Medal 1914-15
South Eastern League Championship Medal 1907-08

SIDEY, Norman — 1929-39

Birth Place: London
Date of Birth: 31st May 1907

☛ Norman spent ten loyal seasons at Highbury as centre half understudy to Herbie Roberts and Bernard Joy. He joined Arsenal from Nunhead (Isthmian League) as an amateur in March 1929, turning professional two years later in February 1931. It was not until the 27th December 1932 that he made his league debut, versus Leeds United at Elland Road, in front of their record league crowd of 56,796. Between 1932-39, Norman played in only forty league games, although he did play in two winning F.A. Charity Shield sides in 1933 and 1934. Instead he was quite content in plying his trade in the reserves (over two hundred and fifty games) winning four London Combination Championship Medals and twice representing the London Combination against the Central League. Norman at one stage had offers from at least eleven other First Division clubs, but he refused to leave Highbury. Manager Allison and captain Hapgood both regarded him as one of the best footballers at the club during this time. Norman retired during the War when he served his country in the R.A.F. as a pilot officer. Died December 1969, aged 62.

	Games	Goals
League	40	0
F.A. Cup	3	0
Charity Shield	2	0
Friendly Matches	21	0
Tours	11	1
Combination League	228	22
London Challenge Cup	20	0
War time	1	0
Southern League	3	0
London Midweek League	13	7
Total	**342**	**30**

Honours:
2 F.A.Charity Shield Winners Medal
1933-34, 1934-35
4 London Combination Championship
Winners Medal 1933-34,
1934-35, 1936-37, 1937-38
2 London Challenge Cup Winners Medals
1933-34, 1935-36
London Challenge Cup Finalists Medal
1936-37

Norman Sidey

SMITH, James — 1920-21

Birth Place: Preston, Lancashire
Date of Birth: 27th March 1887

☛ James Smith was one of those players who, if you briefly flick through the record books, would appear to have had a short and undistinguished career. In fact, his career spanned the best part of twenty years, which included four lost seasons to the First World War. James began his footballing life with Bury in the same year as the Lancashire side last won the F.A. Cup, 1903. He stayed at Gigg Lane until 1906 when he joined Stalybridge Rovers. He then had a short stay at Accrington Stanley before moving on to Chorley in September 1908. James scored thirty-eight goals for them in the 1908-9 season. This alerted Fulham scouts and he signed for them in March 1909. In his six seasons at Craven Cottage, up to the outbreak of World War One, James played in nearly two hundred first team games for the "Cottagers" and was the club's leading League scorer in 1911-12. On the resumption of League football in 1919, Smith found himself out in the cold at Craven Cottage but experienced an Indian summer when Leslie Knighton signed Smith at the age of thirty-three in June 1920. James played in ten League games for the club, making his debut on the opening day of the season at Villa Park in a 0-5 defeat versus Aston Villa on the 28th August, 1920. The strange thing was that he lost his place to thirty-seven year old Jock Rutherford.

	Games	Goals
League	10	1
Friendly Matches	3	0
Combination League	15	2
Total	**28**	**3**

SMITH, Lionel — 1939-54

Birth Place: Mexborough, Yorkshire
Date of Birth: 23rd August 1920

☛ Lionel Smith joined Arsenal as an amateur in April 1939, turning professional in the August, after he had been playing junior football with Mexborough Albion Juniors, Yorkshire Tar Distillers and Denaby United. Unfortunately for Lionel, War was declared within weeks of him turning professional. During the conflict he was injured in a crane accident when he was a sapper in the Army. At the resumption of League Football, 1946-47, (and at the age of 26) Lionel was made captain of the Combination League side. However, with Scott and Barnes holding down the full back positions, his league chances were few but he eventually made his league debut at centre half (when deputising for Leslie Compton, who was playing cricket for Middlesex) in an 8-0 victory versus Grimsby Town on 1st May, 1948. (This also happened to be George Male's last league game for Arsenal.) In 1948-49, Laurie Scott was plagued with a series of injuries and so Barnes switched to right back with Lionel filling in at left back. In that season, when playing thirty-two league games, he was fast becoming one of the best left backs in the country. Lionel's passing ability, for a full back, was exceptional, he was good in the air (6' 1") and he was quick on the recovery. In fact Eddie Hapgood once said of him "That he was faster than Stanley Matthews". Smith held his place in the league side in 1949-50, playing in thirty-one league games. In 1950-51 his outstanding form deservedly won him the first of his six England caps against Wales. During the 1951-52 season, he played in a further twenty-eight league games, won Football League honours and was a member of the F.A.Cup Final team versus Newcastle United. In Arsenal's League Championship campaign of 1952-53, Lionel played in thirty-one league games. He played in only seven league games in 1953-54 and in June 1954 he was granted a free transfer when joining Watford, spending one season at Vicarage Road. He later managed Gravesend and Northfleet, 1955-60. If it had not been for the War, Lionel Smith may have pushed Eddie Hapgood in being the club's finest ever left back. He died in November 1980 aged 60.

	Games	Goals
League	162	0
F.A. Cup	18	0
Charity Shield	1	0
Friendly Matches	25	0
Tours	13	0
Combination League	50	0
Combination Cup	14	0
London Challenge Cup	5	0
War time	17	0
Southern League	2	0
Total	**307**	**0**

Honours:
6 England Caps
3 Football League Caps
League Championship Medal   1952-53
F.A. Cup Finalists Medal   1951-52
F.A.Charity Shield Winners Medal 1948-49
Football Combination Cup Finalists
    Medal   1946-47

SPITTLE, William   1912-19

Birth Place: Southfields, London
Date of Birth: 19th March 1894

☛ Billy Spittle was a demunitive inside forward who was playing junior football for his local side when joining Woolwich Arsenal as an amateur in August 1912, turning professional the following month. This

eighteen year old had made his League debut within two months versus Manchester City at Highbury on 2nd November 1912. William finished that disastrous 1912-13 campaign playing in six League games. His last league game for the club was in a 2-5 reverse at Lincoln City in February 1914. During World War One he was a Lance Corporal in the 17th Middlesex Regiment, being wounded in action in Northern France. Arsenal had kept his registration and he was transferred to Leicester City in October 1919.

	Games	Goals
League	7	0
Other Senior Matches	1	0
Friendlies	8	6
Combination League	1	0
London Challenge Cup	1	1
War Time	27	7
South Eastern League	70	32
London League Reserves	18	2
Total	**133**	**48**

STOCKILL, Reg   1931-34

Birth Place: York
Date of Birth: 24th November, 1913

☛ Reg was an England Schoolboy International who made his league debut for York City versus Wigan Borough in August 1929, becoming one of the youngest ever league debutants, before or since, at the tender age of fifteen years and two hundred and eighty days. He also, in that match, became possibly the youngest player to score in a league match. Reg played in only one more league game for the club before joining non-league Scarborough in 1930. Arsenal signed him from the seaside town club in May 1931, when still six months away from his eighteenth birthday. Stockill played in the last three league games of the 1931-32 season of which his debut was at Leeds Road versus Huddersfield Town on 27th April 1932. Reg played in the first two league games at centre forward in the 1932-33 season (scoring in both) before making way for new signing Ernie Coleman. He played in just a further two league games that season of which his last league game for the club was whilst scoring in an 8-0 home victory versus Blackburn Rovers. Reg spent the whole of the 1933-34 season in the reserves before being transferred to Derby County for £2,000 in September 1934. County outbidding Huddersfield, Liverpool and Newcastle for his signature. Reg was an immediate success at the Baseball Ground before being carried off with a severely injured right knee versus Wolves on Boxing Day 1934. This injury kept him out of the game for fifteen months but, unfortunately, on his return he was never the same player again. He finished his career with Luton Town in 1939.

	Games	Goals
League	7	4
Other Senior Matches	1	0
Friendly Matches	11	16
Combination League	89	56
London Challenge Cup	7	6
London Midweek League	17	13
Total	**132**	**95**

Honours:
London Combination Championship Medal
                                1933-34
London F.A. Challenge Cup Winners Medal
                                1933-34
Northampton Charity Shield Winners Medal
                                1931-32

SWINDIN, George   1936-54

Birth Place: Campsall ,Yorkshire
Date of Birth: 4th December 1914

☛ George Hedley Swindin began his goalkeeping career with Rotherham Y.M.C.A. and New Stubbin Colliery before joining Rotherham United as an amateur. He then joined Bradford City in 1934, this was after having England schoolboy trials in 1929. In his two years at Bradford he made twenty-six league appearances before being transferred to Arsenal for £4,000 in April, 1936. George made his Arsenal league debut versus Brentford on 3rd September 1936. In his first season he played in nineteen league games. At this early stage of his career he was inconsistent and excitable, nervous and highly strung. George was also hesitant and lacked confidence and his kicking was poor. However, the club stood by him and he won the first of his three League Championship Medals in 1937-38 when playing in the last seventeen league games of the season (conceding only thirteen goals). In the last season up to hostilities, he played twenty-one league games. During the war, George was in the army as a P.T. Instructor. On the resumption of League Football, in 1946-47, he became the club's first choice goalkeeper. This after George Marks had not been able to get leave to play in an F.A.Cup tie versus West Ham the previous January. In the League Championship season of 1947-48 George was ever present when conceding only thirty-two league goals (at this time a new Division One defensive record). George had now developed into an excellent keeper (with John Lukic, he must be regarded as the best uncapped goalkeeper Arsenal have ever had) and undoubtedly he would have been capped but for the brilliance of Frank Swift and then Bert Williams. His confidence at cutting out high balls increased due to the aerial command of Leslie Compton. George played in a further thirty-two league games in 1948-49, followed by twenty-three in 1949-50, when he won an F.A. Cup winners medal versus Liverpool, 1950. George, a strong member of the P.F.A. Union played in only half of the club's league games in 1950-51 when sharing the position with Ted Platt. However, he bounced back and was ever present in 1951-52 and helped the club to the 1952 F.A. Cup Final versus Newcastle United. In Arsenal's record breaking seventh League Championship side, George just qualified for a medal when playing in fourteen games. By this time, 1953-54, and in his fortieth year, the young Jack Kelsey had taken over his mantle. In February 1954 he joined Peterborough as player manager and it was George's sterling work at "The Posh", initially ,that helped Peterborough later gain League status. He returned to Highbury as manager in August 1958. In his four seasons in charge of the Gunners it seemed that he made too many changes too quickly and a settled side was never achieved. Arsenal's mediocre showing and the emergence "up the road" of the great Tottenham Hotspur double winning side, meant George Swindin was in a deep dilemma and although he delved into the transfer market in buying the likes of Docherty, Eastham and McLeod, he was criticised in not buying big. The biggest flack he ever took was when Arsenal had agreed a £50,000 fee with Manchester City to buy Denis Law and Denis turned down Arsenal because Swindin had sent his deputy, Ron Greenwood, to sign him. Law later stating that if the manager cannot be bothered to come up here to sign me then I can't be bothered to sign for him. It came as no surprise when George Swindin offered his resignation in May 1962. George later managed Norwich City for five months until October 1962, finishing with Cardiff City October 1962 - April 1964.

George Swindin

	Games	Goals
League	271	0
F.A. Cup	23	0
Charity Shield	3	0
Other Senior Matches	2	0
Friendly Matches	19	0
Tours	31	0
Combination League	75	0
Combination Cup	12	0
London Challenge Cup	5	0
War time	46	0
Southern League	4	0
Total	**491**	**0**

Honours:
3 League Championship Medal
1937-38, 1947-48, 1952-53
F.A. Cup Winners Medal   1949-50
F.A. Cup Finalists Medal   1951-52
F.A.Charity Shield Winners Medal
1938-39, 1948-49
F.A.Charity Shield Finalists Medal   1936-37
London Combination Championship Medal
1936-37, 1937-38

THOMPSON, Leonard   1928-33

Birth Place: Sheffield, Yorkshire
Date of Birth: 18th February 1901

☛ Leonard had played for Sheffield and England Schoolboys just prior to the outbreak of World War One before joining Barnsley as an amateur in 1917. He turned professional when moving to Birmingham City in 1918. Leonard spent three seasons at St. Andrews before being transferred to Swansea Town in 1922. He spent six seasons at Vetch Field playing in nearly two hundred first team games, scoring almost one hundred goals in which time he was the club's leading league goalscorer (with twenty-six in 1926-27) as well as helping the club to the Third Division South Championship in 1924-25. Arsenal paid the "Swans" £4,000 for his services in March 1928. A lot of critics at the time believed that Thompson had enough ability to be another Alex James but unfortunately in his five years at Highbury he was consistently plagued with a severe knee injury which later required an operation. He made his league debut for the Gunners in a 0-2 home defeat versus Portsmouth on 28th March 1928. In 1928-29 he shared the inside left position with Harold Peel when playing in seventeen league games. Thompson was Arsenal's penalty king, and his method of taking the kick was most unusual. He described it himself: "I just run up, do a dog's leg half turn and hit it the way the goalkeeper thinks it can't come." He gave a full account of the method to a newspaper and when he arrived at Highbury one rainy day for the match against Sheffield United, he found placards "How I take penalty kicks,

by Len Thompson" together with action pictures. Sure enough a penalty was awarded midway through the first half and as Thompson walked up, the photographers rushed behind the goal and the crowd hushed expectantly. Thompson missed miserably, slicing the greasy ball nearer the corner flag than the goal 'right out of the picture' in fact! It says much for his temperament that he survived the shattering experience to score many other penalties for Arsenal. However, over the next four seasons, although a mainstay in the Combination side, he played in only eight league games. Leonard was transferred to Crystal Palace in June 1933 before retiring from football a year later. Thompson later assisted Tottenham Hotspur as their reserve team manager and he was later a scout for Arsenal.

	Games	Goals
League	26	6
F.A. Cup	1	0
Friendly Matches	10	7
Tours	4	1
Combination League	160	86
London Challenge Cup	10	4
London Midweek League	6	0
Total	**217**	**104**

Honours:
(WITH SWANSEA)
Division 3 South League Championship
Medal   1924-25
(WITH ARSENAL)
3 London Combination Championship Medal
1928-29, 1929-30, 1930-31
London F.A. Challenge Cup Winners Medal
1930-31

TONER, Joseph   1919-26

Birth Place: Castlewellan, County Down
Date of Birth: 30th March 1894

☛ Joseph Toner was yet another player whose footballing career was badly disrupted by the First World War. Joseph ventured over to England to join Arsenal from Belfast United in August 1919 and was good enough to be seen in League action when making his debut on the club's left wing versus Everton at Goodison Park on 11th October 1919. He played in only twelve League games in 1920-21 before regaining his first team position (twenty-four League games) in 1921-22 and he won the first of his eight Irish Caps versus Wales. However he played in only five and three games in 1922-23 and 1923-24. Joseph at this time was having a running battle for the club's outside left position with Dr James Paterson and Samson Haden. Toner was restored to the first team at the start of the 1924-25 campaign, playing in twenty-six of the first twenty-eight league fixtures. He was dropped from the side after a 0-5 home defeat versus Huddersfield Town. Joseph played in just two more league games at the start of the 1925-26 season before being transferred to St. Johnstone in January 1926. Whilst there a broken leg ended his career, although he did come out of retirement for a short spell when assisting Colraine. He died in November 1954 aged 60.

	Games	Goals
League	89	6
F.A. Cup	11	0
Other Senior Matches	3	2
Friendly Matches	20	1
Combination League	89	7
London Challenge Cup	9	0
Total	**221**	**16**

Honours:
(WITH ARSENAL)
London Combination Championship Medals
1922-23
(WITH ARSENAL & ST. JOHNSTONE)
8 Irish Caps

TOWNROW, Frank 1921-26

Birth Place: West Ham, London
Date of Birth: 27th November 1902

☛ Frank was an England Schoolboy International when joining Arsenal as an amateur in March 1921, turning professional the following month. In his first full season at Highbury he established himself playing all along the front line in the reserve side before being given his first League opportunity at Bramall Lane versus Sheffield United on the 2nd October 1922. In 1923-24, Frank filled in on seven occasions in the league side and scored Arsenal's equalising goal in a 1-1 home draw with Tottenham in front of a 50,000 audience. However, he had to play second fiddle to the likes of Neil, Brain and Buchan in seasons 1924-25 and 1925-26 when limited to reserve team duties. Frank was transferred to Dundee during the summer of 1926, spending four years at Dens Park before returning South to finish his career in Bristol, with City, 1930-31, and Rovers, 1931-32. His brother John played for Clapton Orient, Chelsea and England.

	Games	Goals
League	8	2
F.A. Cup	1	0
Friendly Matches	45	25
Tours	2	0
Combination League	115	34
London Challenge Cup	3	0
Total	**174**	**61**

Honours:
London Combination Championship Medals
1922-23

TRICKER, Reg 1927-29

Birth Place: Karachi, India
Date of Birth: 5th October 1904

☛ Reg Tricker is one of only two players in the club's League history to have been born in India. His family returned to Suffolk, England in 1908, that was where Reg began his footballing career in junior football with Beccles Town and at the same time was a fine athlete, winning the one hundred and twenty yard hurdles in the Norfolk and Suffolk Championships. He joined Luton Town as an amateur in 1924, keeping the same status when joining Charlton Athletic in the summer of 1925. Reg was a regular member of their league side at inside forward during the following two seasons before turning professional in early 1927, this enabling Tricker to join Arsenal in March 1927. He made his Arsenal League debut four days after joining the club versus Everton at Highbury on the 19th March, 1927. He became a folk hero at Highbury when scoring twice (in only his fourth game) versus Tottenham at White Hart Lane in the last League game of the 1926-27 season. However, like so many others, with an abundance of talented inside forwards on the books during the seasons 1927-28 and 1928-29, his league outings were restricted to only eight. At the age of twenty-four Reg required first team football and was subsequently transferred to Clapton Orient in February 1929, serving them well for five seasons and being their leading scorer for three consecutive seasons, 1930-33. He later trained at Borough Road Training College, Isleworth to become a school master.

	Games	Goals
League	12	5
Friendly Matches	4	3
Combination League	40	10
Total	**56**	**18**

Honours:
London Combination Championship Medal
1927-28

TRIM, Reg 1933-37

Birth Place: Portsmouth, Hampshire
Date of Birth: 1st October 1913

☛ Reg was the England Schoolboy Captain in 1928 before joining Bournemouth and Boscombe in April 1931. He had played in only twenty league games for them when Herbert Chapman signed him for Arsenal for a four figure fee in April 1933. Trim spent over 4 years at Highbury, where his position was the unenviable one of left back understudy to the legendary Eddie Hapgood. Although

playing in nearly two hundred reserve games, Reg managed to play in just the one league game, in the last encounter of Arsenal's 1934-35 Championship winning season at Highbury versus Derby County on 4th May 1935. He was transferred to Nottm Forest in July 1937, where he was a regular in the last two seasons prior to the Second World War. Reg signed for Derby County in December 1943 and finished his career with Swindon in 1946-47. Trim was later trainer at Leyton Orient, 1948-49.

	Games	Goals
League	1	0
Friendly Matches	15	0
Combination League	155	0
London Challenge Cup	12	0
Total	**183**	**0**

Honours:
Three London Combination Championship
  Medals   1933-34, 1935-36, 1936-37
London F.A. Challenge Cup Winners Medal
  1933-34
London F.A. Challenge Cup Finalists Medal
  1936-37

TUCKETT, Ernest 1932-37

Birth Place: Lingdale, Yorkshire
Date of Birth: 1st March 1914

☛ Ernest began his footballing career with local junior side Scarborough in 1931, joining Arsenal in July 1932 as an amateur. This followed a spell at Arsenal's nursery club, Margate, 1934-36, before returning to Highbury when turning professional in March 1936. Ernest made his league debut soon after, as a centre half replacement for Herbie Roberts in a 2-2 draw at Molineux versus Wolves on 28th March 1936. However, with no chance of first team football, Ernest was transferred to Bradford City in part exchange for Laurie Scott in February 1937. Tuckett later played for Fulham 1938-39 with whom he was with, when killed in active service in May 1945 aged 31.

	Games	Goals
League	2	0
Friendly Matches	11	2
Combination League	40	11
London Challenge Cup	1	0
London Midweek League	24	16
Total	**78**	**29**

Honours:
London Combination Championship Medal
  1936-37

TURNBULL, Robert — 1921-24

Birth Place: Dumbarton, Scotland
Date of Birth: 22nd June 1894

☛ Robert was working in the Signal Corps with the Royal Engineers when joining Arsenal as an amateur in January 1921, turning professional in September of the same year. He played in five league games in 1921-22, when replacing Arthur Hutchins at left back. His league debut was at Ninian Park versus Cardiff City on the 27th December 1921. At the beginning of the 1922-23 season, Robert had played in eight of the club's first fifteen League games of which the club won only four and scored only seventeen goals in the process. With a definite goal scoring problem on their hands (and with no cash available) the Arsenal manager, Leslie Knighton, turned to Turnbull in this moment of crisis. Robert took up the challenge and from centre forward blasted in twenty-one goals in twenty-eight games, which included scoring fourteen in a ten game period from mid November to the end of December 1922. Included in his tally was a hat trick versus Middlesbrough and two four goal hauls versus Bolton and at Blackpool. Thus he became the first player in Arsenal's history to score four goals in an away League fixture. In 1923-24 the goals dried up when he scored only six times in eighteen League games. In 1924-25 he lost his place to Henry Woods and subsequently was transferred to Charlton in November 1924. He spent only three months at the Valley before being transferred to Chelsea in February 1925. In the twilight of his career, he repaid the club by scoring fifty-eight times in only eighty-seven first team games. Robert later played briefly for Clapton Orient and Southend United before finishing his career at the age of 38 with Crystal Palace in 1932-33 where he was trainer for many years. He died in 1946 aged 52.

	Games	Goals
League	59	26
F.A. Cup	7	2
Other Senior Matches	2	0
Friendlies	18	13
Tours	9	19
Combination League	56	20
London Challenge Cup	5	0
Total	**156**	**80**

Honours:
London F.A. Challenge Cup Winners Medal
1921-22

VOYSEY, Clement — 1919-26

Birth Place: New Cross, London
Date of Birth: 27th December 1898

☛ Clement was an apprentice craftsman linked to the Royal Naval Air Service during World War One before joining Arsenal as an amateur in March 1919, turning professional a month later. Clement played in the first five League games (at centre half) of the 1919-20 season but unfortunately, a serious knee injury put him out of the game for twenty months (Sept. 1919 - May 1921). Clement had made his league debut at Highbury versus Newcastle United on the 30th August 1919. He played in just two League games between May 1921 and August 1922, before playing in eighteen League games in 1922-23. Voysey moved to the inside right position at the start of the 1923-24 season. His form being so good that he was selected as a reserve to play for England versus Belgium. However it seems that a succession of niggling and serious injuries brought about a premature ending of his career in May 1926. He died in January 1989 aged 90.

	Games	Goals
League	35	6
F.A. Cup	2	0
Other Senior Matches	2	0
Friendly Matches		30
5 Combination League	91	13
London Challenge Cup	2	1
War Time	9	0
Total	**171**	**25**

Clem Voysey

WALDEN, Harold — 1920-21

Birth Place: Manchester, Lancashire
Date of Birth: 10th October 1890

☛ Harold was a centre forward who had began his career with Halifax Town before joining Bradford City in December 1911. (Just seven months after City had won the F.A. Cup). Henry spent four seasons with them being leading League goal scorer in 1911-12, when scoring eleven times in seventeen games as well as being a member of the British team that won the 1912 Olympic Games Football Tournament. He saw active service during World War One before joining Arsenal in October 1920. In his one season at Highbury, Harold played in two League encounters, both versus Oldham Athletic. His debut was at Boundary Park on the 12th February 1921. He was transferred to Bradford during the summer of 1921.

	Games	Goals
League	2	1
Other Senior Matches	1	0
Friendly Matches	3	2
Combination League	2	0
Total	**8**	**3**

Honours:
(WITH BRADFORD CITY)
1912 Olympic Games Football Gold Medal

WALLER, Henry — 1937-47

Birth Place: Ashington, Northumberland
Date of Birth: 20th August 1917

☛ Henry, a wing half, joined Arsenal from his home town club in October 1937. He then spent seven months with Arsenal's nursery team, Margate, before returning to Highbury in May 1938. Waller's career, like so many others, was disrupted by The War, during which he served in The Army in Sicily and Italy. On the resumption of peace time he played in eight league games in 1946-47. His debut was versus Blackburn Rovers on the 4th September, 1946. He was transferred to Leyton Orient in July 1947. He later linked up with North Eastern teams Ashington and Consett.

	Games	Goals
League	8	0
F.A. Cup	1	0
Friendly Matches	5	0
Combination League	21	0
Combination Cup	3	0
War Time	12	0
Southern League	36	0
Total	**86**	**0**

Honours:
Football Combination Championship Medal
1946-47
Football Combination Cup Finalists 1946-47

WALLINGTON, Edward 1923-24

> Edward was a young right winger with Herts junior club, Rickmansworth, when joining Watford as an amateur in 1914, turning professional when the club achieved League status in 1920. Edward played in over fifty League games for the "Hornets" before being transferred to Arsenal on a free transfer in August 1923. In Wallington's only season at Highbury, he played in just one league game at Newcastle on the 1st September 1923. He was released during the summer of 1924.

	Games	Goals
League	1	0
Friendly Matches	7	1
Combination League	2	0
Total	**10**	**1**

WALSH, Charles 1930-33

Birth Place: London
Date of Birth: 27th October 1910

> Charles was playing for Hampstead Town before joining Arsenal as an amateur in August 1930, turning professional in May 1931. A reserve understudy to Jack Lambert while at Highbury, his only first team game for the club was in the famous 0-2 defeat at Walsall on 14th January 1933, in the 3rd Round of the F.A. Cup. Herbert Chapman, so distressed with the result, transferred Walsh to Brentford within two weeks.

	Games	Goals
F.A. Cup	1	0
Friendly Matches	9	13
Combination League	32	18
London Challenge Cup	2	2
London Midweek League	19	9
Total	**63**	**42**

WALSH, Wilfred 1935-39

Birth Place: Pontlottyn, South Wales
Date of Birth: 29th July 1917

> Wilfred was an outside right who joined Arsenal as an amateur in May 1935, turning professional a year later in May 1936. He spent the following two years at Arsenal's nursery club, Margate, before returning to Highbury in August 1938. He played three league games for the Gunners in 1938-39 which included his debut versus Preston at Highbury on 22nd October 1938. Walsh was transferred to Derby County for £2000 in June 1939 just prior to the outbreak of World War Two. He later played for Walsall and managed non-league clubs Redditch Town and Hednesford Town. He died in 1977 aged 59.

	Games	Goals
League	3	0
Friendlies	2	0
Tours	1	0
Combination League	16	4
London Challenge Cup	4	3
Southern League	24	9
Total	**50**	**16**

Honours:

London Combination Championship Medals
1938-39

WARNES, William 1925-33

Birth Place: Rotherhithe, London
Date of Birth: 14th November 1907

> William was a tricky amateur English International when joining Arsenal from Woking in May 1925 after beginning his career with Nunhead. Warnes not turning professional until June 1929. In his eight years at Highbury, although being a regular for the reserves, he played in only one first team game for the club when stepping in for the injured Joe Hulme in the infamous F.A. Cup defeat at Walsall in January 1933. Herbert Chapman subsequently sold him to Norwich City in May 1933. He enjoyed four seasons with the club, scoring nearly fifty league goals in just under one hundred and twenty games, helping City to the 3rd Division South Championship in 1933-34. A career which never reached its heights, Eddie Hapgood described Warnes as "the winger who gave me the most trouble". His father Rube was an amateur boxing champion.

	Games	Goals
F.A. Cup	1	0
Friendly Matches	9	6
Combination League	89	37
London Challenge Cup	7	0
London Midweek League	3	3
Total	**109**	**46**

Honours:

(WITH WOKING)
England Amateur International
(WITH ARSENAL)
London Combination Championship Medal
1928-29
London FA. Challenge Cup Winners Medal
1930-31
(WITH NORWICH)
3rd Division South Championship Medal
1933-34

WESTCOTT, Ronald 1935-36

Birth Place: Wallasey, Cheshire
Date of Birth: 30th September 1910

> Ronnie was a young centre forward who joined Arsenal from Banbury Spencer in July

1935 as an amateur, turning professional six months later. Ronnie had scored ten times in eighteen reserve games before being given his league debut v. Wolves on 28th March 1936 (The club his brother Dennis served well). In his second league game v. Bolton on April Fools Day 1936 he suffered a severe injury which resulted in him retiring from football.

	Games	Goals
League	2	1
Friendly Matches	2	3
Combination League	17	9
London Challenge Cup	1	1
Total	**22**	**14**

WHITE, Henry 1919-23

Birth Place: Watford, Hertfordshire
Date of Birth: 17th April 1892

> Henry White was an inside or centre forward who had been an amateur on Brentford's books during the First World War as well as serving his country in the Royal Fusiliers. He joined Arsenal in July 1919, making his Arsenal debut on the opening day of the season at Highbury versus Newcastle United on the 30th August 1919. In that first season at the club, Henry finished as Arsenal's top marksman with fifteen goals in thirty games which included a hat trick versus Sunderland at Highbury. This form gaining him an England trial match. In 1920-21 he scored ten times in twenty-six league games followed in 1921-22, by again being the club's leading scorer with nineteen first team goals in forty-one games. However, he lost his place in the side in November 1922 and was subsequently transferred to Blackpool in March 1923. Henry's all-round sporting abilities were shown when he played eight County Cricket matches for Warwickshire in 1923. White later played for Fulham, 1925-26, Walsall 1926-27, and Nelson 1927-29 finishing his career with Thames Association. His father, Harry White, was for many years, the Ground Superintendent at Lords cricket ground. He died in November 1972 aged 80.

	Games	Goals
League	101	40
F.A. Cup	8	5
Other Senior Matches	6	4
Friendly Matches	17	18
Combination League	18	8
London Challenge Cup	7	4
Total	**157**	**79**

Honours:

London F.A. Challenge Cup Winners Medal
1921-22

WHITTAKER, Tom   1919-25

Birth Place: Aldershot, Hampshire
Date of Birth: 21st July 1898

No Arsenal book has ever been written without the name of Thomas James Whittaker being mentioned, for Tom (other than Herbert Chapman) was Mr "Arsenal" and in the history of football only a handful of men have been more respected for their all round knowledge of the game more than Tom Whittaker. In his fifty-eight years he was a soldier, sailor, airman, marine engineer, and trainer to Arsenal and England as well as trainer to England's Davis Cup Tennis team, player and manager. Nicknamed "The man with the magic hands" he rubbed shoulders with statesmen, famous sportsmen, business men, personalities of stage and screen and even royalty. People, who he treated, included famous sports stars of the day such as Steve Donoghue, Jack Parker, Gubby Allen and Fred Perry, and even the Indian Maharajah. The son of a soldier, Tom began his footballing career in junior football in the North East of England with Newcastle United Swifts and at this time he was qualifying as a marine engineer. During World War One he served in the Army as an ordnance engineer. In November 1919, Tom joined Arsenal from the Army, playing in only one league game, in 1919-20, (at centre forward) against West Bromwich Albion at the Hawthorns on 6th April 1920. In 1920-21, he was converted to a wing half, playing in only five league games when deputising for either Baker or McKinnon. However, in 1921-22, his footballing career started to blossom when missing only six league games over the period of the next three seasons, 1922-25. His progress was dampened through lack of form and injuries, spending the majority of the time in reserve team football. At the end of the 1924-25 season, Tom was invited to tour Australia with the F.A. Touring team, but tragically his footballing career came to a premature end when cracking a knee socket. Over the course of the next year, 1925-26, Tom studied physiotherapy and Herbert Chapman appointed Whittaker as assistant trainer in 1926. During a match at Highbury in February 1927, the then Arsenal trainer, George Hardy, shouted a tactical switch to the players from his bench on the touchline. Herbert Chapman was furious at these antics, and after the game duly dismissed him. On the following Monday morning he summoned Whittaker to his office and told him he was now first team trainer. Tom was dumfounded and at the age of twenty-eight with no practical experience, he was younger than players such as Charlie Buchan, Tom Parker and Jock Rutherford. Whittaker then proceeded to change the whole concept of footballing injuries, and brought about the end of the bucket and sponge era in first class football. Into his treatment room came sunray lamps and electrical equipment of all kinds. This accompanied with his strong but gentle hands enabling him to become a household name within his field. Tom was modest and retiring but within the dressing room he was the master. Tom expected everyone to give one hundred percent in training for which he devised road walks, installed a shooting box for practice and was the mastermind of head tennis which is still commonly played today and Chapman, whom Whittaker absolutely idolised (only ever calling him Mister), was happy leaving him to the discipline and training of the players and Whittaker was later reduced to tears when hearing of his mentor's death in January 1934. Former Arsenal centre half, Bernard Joy, described Tom as the kindest, almost humble, man he had ever met and if any players had any problems the first person they went to was "Uncle Tom". During his career as Arsenal's trainer, the club won five League Championships and appeared in four F.A.Cup Finals and was England's trainer on seven continental tours between 1930 and 1946. At least twenty-five players whom he trained and furthered their footballing education later became managers of Football League sides. These included Tom Parker, Ted Drake, Jack Crayston, George Swindin and Joe Mercer. During World War Two he served in the R.A.F. as a squadron leader on secret missions in connection with D-Day and for his sterling work was awarded the M.B.E. in 1947. This was after he had become England's first ever manager in 1946. A post he later handed over to Walter Winterbottom, and became Arsenal's assistant manager in the same year. In that first season after the War, 1946-47, the signing by George Allison and Whittaker of "two old boys", Joe Mercer (thirty-two) and Ronnie Rooke (thirty-five) helped cast off relegation fears. When Allison announced his retirement in May 1947, Tom, with nearly thirty years service with the club, was appointed secretary-manager, and in his first season in his new position, he guided the club to the League Championship (when setting a new defensive record). He later managed Arsenal when reaching the F.A. Cup Finals of 1950 and 1952 and to a further League Championship in 1953. Tom thus became the only person in the club's history to be connected with Arsenal whilst winning the seven League Championships as well as six F.A. Cup Finals. Between 1947 and 1955, he would not allow the likes of Jack Crayston, Bob Wall and Billy Milne to take responsibility for certain tasks, however, his beloved Arsenal were not the side they once were. Average home attendances had plummeted from an average of 55,000 in 1947-48 to 42,000 in 1955-56, this, added to his inability to attract to Highbury star names (he tried unsuccessfully to capture both Jack Froggatt and Stanley Matthews) brought about mounting pressure and to alleviate the situation and to take weight off his shoulders, Alec Stock was appointed assistant manager. Whittaker was not happy with this because he wanted to carry the burden of the club on his own and when told that this was too much for him his reply was. "Someone has to drive himself too hard for Arsenal. Herbert Chapman worked himself to death for Arsenal and if that is my fate I am happy to accept it." His words were prophetic for on the 24th October 1956, Thomas James Whittaker passed away after having a heart attack in a London hospital, aged 57. No other person, with the exception of Herbert Chapman, has ever made such a massive contribution to Arsenal Football Cub. The efforts of others pale into insignificance in comparison.

	Games	Goals
League	64	2
F.A. Cup	6	0
Other Senior Matches	2	0
Friendly Matches	41	4
Tours	5	0
Combination League	117	19
London Challenge Cup	10	0
Total	**245**	**25**

Honours:
London Combination Championship Medal
        1922-23
2 London F.A. Challenge Cup Winners Medal
        1921-22, 1923-24

WILLIAMS, Joseph   1929-32

Birth Place: Rotherham, Yorkshire
Date of Birth: June 1902

"J.J." Williams was a short, stocky, dynamic wing forward who began his footballing career with his hometown club, Rotherham County, in 1921-22. He spent three years with the club (ever present 1923-24) when playing in over one hundred first team games. Herbert Chapman spotted his potential and signed him for Huddersfield Town for £1,800 during the summer of 1924. Huddersfield, the then league champions, went on to complete a hat trick of championships of which Williams was a key member. In the 1924-25 championship campaign he played in thirty-five league games followed in 1925-26, by playing in twenty-three league games before being transferred to Stoke City in March 1926. He thus became, the only player in Football League history to win a Championship Medal and be relegated in the same season. Joseph stayed for just over three seasons at the Victoria Ground, winning unofficial England caps on a South African tour as well as helping Stoke to the Third Division North Championship in 1926-27.

Herbert Chapman signed him for a second time when "J.J." joined Arsenal in September 1929 for £3000 and soon after he played in the 1929 Charity Shield for the professionals versus the amateurs. In his first season at Highbury, 1929-30, he gained a regular first team spot after making his Arsenal League debut in a 2-5 defeat at Aston Villa on 25th September 1929. However, after helping the club to the 1930 F.A. Cup Final "J.J." was injured in an away match versus Newcastle on 5th April 1930, hence he missed the final. In Arsenal's first League Championship campaign, he just failed to qualify for a third Championship Medal when playing in nine league games. By this time Hulme and Bastin had made the wing positions their own and after just one more league game in 1931-32,

he was transferred to Middlesbrough in March 1932, where he stayed for four seasons before finishing his career at Carlisle 1935-36

	Games	Goals
League	22	5
F.A. Cup	4	0
Friendly Matches	3	0
Tours	7	2
Combination League	65	21
London Challenge Cup	3	0
London Midweek League	4	2
Total	**108**	**30**

Honours:
(WITH HUDDERSFIELD)
2 League Championship Medals
1924-25, 1925-26
(WITH STOKE)
3 Unofficial England Caps
3rd Division North Championship Medal
1926-27
(WITH ARSENAL)
2 London Combination Championship
Medals 1929-30, 1930-31
London F.A. Challenge Cup Winners Medal
1930-31

WILSON, Alex   1933-41

Birth Place: Wishaw, Lanarkshire
Date of Birth: 29th October 1908

☛ Alex Wilson was a young Scottish goalkeeper playing junior football for Overton Athletic when joining Greenock Morton in 1927-28. He spent six seasons at Greenock, helping them win promotion to the Scottish First Division in 1928-29. Alex was transferred to Arsenal in May 1933. In his first season at Highbury he played in only five league games when deputising for the injured Frank Moss making his debut in a 3-2 home win versus Aston Villa on 10th March, 1934. The picture was the same in 1934-35, when Wilson played in the last nine league games of the season after Moss had been injured in a match versus Everton. These nine appearances were not enough to gain Alex a Championship Medal. In 1935-36 he was the club's regular custodian, for the only time in his career, when playing in thirty-seven league games and helping the club win the 1936 F.A. Cup Final versus Sheffield United. In 1936-37, with strong opposition from Frank Boulton and George Swindin, he played in only two league games. In Arsenal's 1937-38 Championship season, Alex played in just ten league games, becoming probably the only player in league history to feature in three championship winning seasons without winning a medal. However, in the last season prior to hostilities he shared the goalkeeping position with George Swindin when playing in nineteen league games. Alex was transferred to St. Mirren (where he finished his career) in January 1941. This after becoming Kent County Cricket Club's physiotherapist in 1939. Up to his departure to the United States in 1967 he had periods as trainer/coach/physio at Brighton, Birmingham, Sunderland and Blackpool. Wilson later trained Boston Beacons in the N.A.S.L. He died in April 1971 aged 62.

Alex Wilson

	Games	Goals
League	82	0
F.A. Cup	7	0
Charity Shield	1	0
Other Senior Matches	1	0
Friendly Matches	10	0
Tours	1	0
Combination League	139	0
London Challenge Cup	14	0
War Time	9	0
Southern League	2	0
London Midweek League	2	0
Total	**268**	**0**

Honours:
F.A. Cup Winners Medal 1935-36
F.A. Charity Shield Finalists Medal 1935-36
5 London Combination Championship
Medals 1933-34, 34-35, 36-37,
37-38, 38-39
2 London F.A. Challenge Cup Winners Medal
1932-33, 1935-36
London F.A. Challenge Cup Finalists Medal
1936-37

WILLIAMSON, Ernest 1919-23

Birth Place: Murton, County Durham
Date of Birth: 24th May 1890

☛ Ernest began his goalkeeping career in North Eastern junior football with Murton Red Star and Wingate Albion before moving down to London to join Croydon Common in June 1913. Ernest guested in over one hundred and twenty matches for Arsenal during World War One, as well as serving in the R.A.S.C. He officially signed for Arsenal for £150 in April 1919. In the 1919-20 season he played in twenty-six league games and in 1920-21, thirty-three league games. The following season, 1921-22, he missed one solitary game. This consistency led him in becoming Arsenal's first England International after the First World War when he won two caps versus Sweden. However, after conceding fourteen goals in five league games at the start of the 1922-23 season he lost his place to Stephen Dunn and later John Robson and was subsequently transferred to Norwich City in June 1923. Williamson stayed there for two seasons before retiring. He died in April 1964 aged 73.

	Games	Goals
League	105	0
F.A. Cup	8	0
Other Senior Matches	3	0
Friendly Matches	19	0
Tours	4	0
Combination League	26	0
London Challenge Cup	10	0
War Time	122	0
Total	**297**	**0**

Honours:
2 England Caps
1 Victory International Cap
London Combination Championship Medal
1922-23
London F.A. Challenge Cup Winners Medal
1921-22

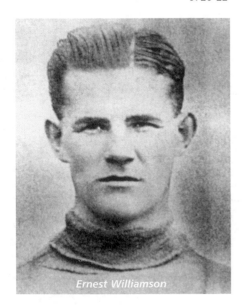
Ernest Williamson

WOODS, Henry 1923-26

Birth Place: St. Helens, Lancashire
Date of Birth: 14th March 1894

☛ Henry Woods began his career with his home town club, St. Helens, before joining Norwich City in their Non-League days in 1912. Woods moved back up North at the end of the First World War after serving in the Tank Corps in France when joining South Shields in August 1919. His talented displays for them caught the eye of Newcastle United which resulted in the "Magpies" paying the astronomical sum of £2,600 in January 1922. But in eighteen months with them he played in just sixteen first team games. He was transferred to Arsenal for £750 in July 1923. Henry, a centre forward, made his Arsenal League debut at Highbury versus his previous club, Newcastle on 25th August 1923 (After, unbelievably, he had made his Newcastle League debut versus Arsenal) and finished the season as the club's top League goal scorer with nine in thirty-six games. In 1924-25 he was again top scorer with twelve league goals in thirty-two games which included a hat trick versus Preston at Highbury. However, in 1925-26 his opportunities were limited and he eventually left the club when joining Luton Town in August 1926. Henry served them well for four seasons before finishing his career back home with North Shields in 1930-31.

	Games	Goals
League	70	21
F.A. Cup	5	1
Friendly Matches	7	0
Tours	3	3
Combination League	34	8
London Challenge Cup	8	4
Total	**127**	**37**

Honours:
London F.A. Challenge Cup Winners Medal
1923-24
London F.A. Challenge Cup Finalists Medal
1925-26

YOUNG, Andrew 1922-27

Birth Place: Darlington, Co. Durham
Date of Birth: 17th September 1896

☛ Andrew was a young centre forward playing for Blyth Spartans when Aston Villa signed him in 1919. In his three seasons at Villa Park he was generally understudy to the legendary Billy Walker but never let the club down when scoring eleven times in twenty-six league games. With his first team chances limited, he was transferred to Arsenal in March 1922 and played in nine of the club's last eleven League games of which his League debut was in a home fixture in the Tuesday afternoon fixture of March 22nd 1922 versus Liverpool, in front of a crowd of just 10,000 (The lowest ever attendance for an Arsenal v. Liverpool fixture since World War One). Andrew played in the first eleven League games of the 1922-23 season before being one of five players to be dropped following a 0-7 defeat at the Hawthorns versus West Bromwich Albion. In 1923-24 he was converted into an orthodox wing half when playing in twenty league games. However, in his last three seasons at the club, he played in a total of only twenty-one league games, mainly when deputising for either Billy Milne or Alf Baker. At the age of thirty, Andrew was not content with reserve team football and finally, in June 1927, he was transferred to Bournemouth and Boscombe Athletic.

	Games	Goals
League	68	9
F.A. Cup	3	0
Other Senior Matches	1	0
Friendly Matches	23	6
Tours	3	0
Combination League	102	13
London Challenge Cup	7	7
Total	**207**	**35**

Honours:
London Combination Championship Medals
1922-23, 1926-27
London F.A. Challenge Cup Winners Medal
1923-24

Andy Young

1945-1985

A quintet of Gunners goalies (l-r) Gary Lewin, Rhys Wilmot, Nicky Sullivan, Paul Barron and Pat Jennings

Wembley joy – Charlie George and Frank McLintock Celebrate with the FA Cup in 1971

ADAMS, Ernie   1964-67

Birth Place: Dagenham, Essex
Date of Birth: 17th January 1948

☞ Ernie Adams signed for Arsenal as an apprentice goalkeeper in February 1964, turning professional in January 1965. Was Arsenal's regular youth team goalkeeper in 1964-66 helping them to many youth honours. However, with a surplus of goalkeepers on the books was not retained after the 1966-67 season. Was released on a free transfer in July 1967 when he joined Colchester United. Later played for Crewe and Darlington.

	Games	Goals
Friendly Matches	9	0
Combination League	5	0
Combination Cup	1	0
Metropolitan League	44	0
Metropolitan Cup	6	0
South East Counties League	44	0
Youth Cup	18	0
Other Youth Cups	13	0
Youth Tour Matches	22	0
Total	**162**	**0**

Ernie Adams

Honours:
FA Youth Cup Winners Medal	1965-66
FA Youth Cup Finalists Medal	1964-65
South East Counties League Championship Medal	1964-65
South East Counties League Cup Winners Medal	1963-64
Southern Junior Floodlight Cup Winners Medal	1965-66
London Minor Challenge Cup Finalists Medal	1964-65

ADAMS, Vince   1962-65

Birth Place: Chesterfield, Derbyshire
Date of Birth: 16th October 1946

☞ Vince Adams joined Arsenal as an apprentice in June 1962, after winning England schoolboy caps as a promising wing half. Showed early promise in the South East

Counties youth side before turning professional in October 1963. Was a member of Arsenal's FA Youth Cup Finalist's team in 1964-65. Was released on a free transfer in November 1965 when he joined Chesterfield.

	Games	Goals
Friendly Matches	14	1
Combination League	11	0
Metropolitan League	52	4
Metropolitan Cup	10	0
South East Counties League	46	3
Youth Cup	8	2
Other Youth Cups	12	0
Youth Tour Matches	15	0
Total	**168**	**10**

Vince Adams

Honours:
FA Youth Cup Finalists Medal	1964-65
Metropolitan League Professional Cup Winners	1962-63
South East Counties League Cup Winners Medal	1963-64
Southern Junior Floodlight Cup Winners Medal	1962-63
London Minor Challenge Cup Finalists Medal	1964-65

ADDISON, Colin   1966-67

Birth Place: Taunton, Somerset
Date of Birth: 18th May 1940

☞ Colin Addison started his league career with York City in May 1957. Nottingham Forest snapped him up in January 1961, for £15,000. He was a regular at Forest for five years, playing in nearly one hundred and sixty league games before joining Arsenal in September 1966 for £45,000. Unfortunately for Arsenal and Addison, his brief stay at Highbury (fifteen months) was not enough to show his full potential. Subsequently transferred to Sheffield United in December 1967 for £40,000. He finished his playing career as player/manager of Hereford United. Later managed Durban City in South Africa, assisted Notts County and West Bromwich as assistant manager as well as managing Newport County

(two spells) and Derby County. Later managed Celta Virgo and Athletico Madrid in Spain before returning to England to manage Hereford United 1990 - 91.

Colin Addison

	Games	Goals
League	28	9
FA Cup	2	0
League Cup	2	1
Friendly Matches	5	3
Tour Matches	5	2
Combination League	7	1
Total	**49**	**16**

ALLEN, Clive   1980

Birth Place: Stepney, London
Date of Birth: 20th May 1961

☞ Clive Allen will go down in history as the only player to be bought for £1,000,000, never to play for the club who spent all that money on him. He joined QPR as an English schoolboy international in the summer of 1977, turning professional in September 1978, after having won six England youth caps, and made his debut during season 1978-79. It was the following season. though, that Allen took the English football scene by storm, when he finished as the country's leading goalscorer with thirty goals. At under nineteen years of age, he was the youngest player since Jimmy Greaves to top the scoring charts. By now the 'giants' were looking at this goalscoring sensation, and it was Arsenal who snapped him up in June 1980 for £1,200,000. However, within six weeks and after only three friendly matches, he left Arsenal with George Wood to join Crystal Palace in a deal which took Kenny Sansom to Arsenal. His stay at Palace was not of much longer duration. This meant that Allen, still only twenty, had been transferred for £1,000,000 or more three times in less than a year, this time back to his old club QPR. This surely was home to him and slowly but surely his form returned. He helped QPR to the FA Cup Final in1981-82 and to the second division championship the following season, as well as regaining his England under - 21 place. He joined Tottenham in August 1984, just after winning the first of his five England caps versus Brazil in June 1984. During his four seasons at White Hart Lane he helped Tottenham to the 1987 FA Cup Final versus Coventry and in the same season, was the country's leading goalscorer and became Spurs' record all time individual goalscorer in a season (forty nine). He was transferred to Bordeaux (France) in May 1988 for £1,000,000 returning to England in August 1989 joining Manchester City for £1,000,000. Later played for Chelsea 1991 £250,000, West Ham 1992, £275,000 and Millwall 1994, £75,000. In total Clive Allen's nine transfer moves have cost clubs nearly £7 million pounds. Clive's father, Les, played for Tottenham, his uncle Dennis played for Reading, his cousin Martin for QPR and West Ham, his younger brother Bradley for QPR and his cousin Paul for West Ham, Tottenham and Southampton. He is the only player to have played for as many as seven London League clubs.

	Games	Goals
Friendly Matches	3	0
Total	**3**	**0**

Clive Allen

Honours:
(QPR AND WITH TOTTENHAM)
FA Cup Finalist Medal   1981-82, 1986-87
Second Division Championship
    Medal   1982-83
3 Full England caps
13 England Under 21 caps
5 England youth caps
Footballer of the Year   1986-87
PFA Footballer of the Year   1986-87
PFA Award Division One   1987

ALLEN, Russell   1969-71

Birth Place: Birmingham
Date of Birth: 9th January 1954

➤ Joined Arsenal as an apprentice in April 1969. Was a regular member of the youth team for two seasons before his contract was cancelled in April 1971 after a youth tour in Portugal. Joined WBA the following month but never settled there, later moving to Tranmere and Mansfield. Son of Ronnie Allen former WBA player.

	Games	Goals
Friendly Matches	11	6
Combination League	4	4
Combination Cup	2	0
Metropolitan League	6	1
South East Counties League	46	29
Youth Cup	11	4
Other Youth Cups	9	3
Youth Tour Matches	3	2
Total	**92**	**49**

Honours:
Combination Cup Winners Medal   1969-70
South East Counties League Cup
    Winners Medal   1970-71

AMOS, Keith   1949-54

Birth Place: Walton-on-Thames, Surrey
Date of Birth: 13th January 1932

➤ Keith Amos was a goalkeeper with Walton and Hersham whilst on amateur terms with Arsenal. He had originally joined Arsenal as an amateur during 1949, but it was not until May 1952, when he was released from national service that he signed professionally for them. Although a regular in the Eastern Counties League side during 1952-53, he was eventually granted a free transfer in August 1954 when he joined Aldershot. Later played for Fulham.

	Games	Goals
Friendly Matches	7	0
Combination League	1	0
Combination Cup	1	0
Eastern Counties League	27	0
Eastern Counties Cup	5	0
London Midweek League	13	0
Total	**54**	**0**

Honours:
London Midweek League Championship
    Medal   1952-3

ANDERSON, Terry   1959-65

Birth Place: Woking, Surrey
Date of Birth: 11th March 1944

➤ Terry Anderson joined Arsenal's ground staff in July 1959 as a schoolboy winger,

progressing to professional status in August 1961. By this time he was a key member of what was probably Arsenal's most successful youth team ever. He won England youth caps during 1961-62, followed in 1962-63 by his league debut versus West Ham on 2nd March 1963. Unfortunately with other top class wingers on the books (Armstrong, Macleod and Skirton) Anderson's first team chances were limited, and he was eventually allowed to leave Arsenal in February 1965, when he joined Norwich City for £15,000. Served Norwich well for nine seasons, winning a second division championship medal and a league cup finalist medal. Ultimately finished his career in the lower divisions with Colchester, Scunthorpe, Crewe and Bournemouth, before his untimely death at the age of thirty-five in 1979.

	Games	Goals
League	25	6
UEFA Cup	1	1
Friendly Matches	33	27
Tour Matches	1	0
Combination League	55	25
London Challenge Cup	4	1
Metropolitan League	54	16
Metropolitan Cup	16	3
South East Counties League	20	19
Youth Cup	11	7
Other Youth Cups	17	17
Youth Tour Matches	19	6
Total	**256**	**128**

Terry Anderson

Honours:
Football Combination Champions   1962-63
London FA Challenge Cup Winners   1962-63
Metropolitan League Champions   1960-61
Metropolitan League Professional
    Cup Winner   1960-61, 1961-62
Metropolitan League Cup Winner   1960-61
South East Counties League Cup
    Winner   1960-61
2 Youth England Caps   1961
(WITH NORWICH)
2nd Division Championship Medal   1971-72
League Cup Finalists Medal   1972-73

ARBER, Bobby — 1967-70

Birth Place: Poplar, London
Date of Birth: 13th January 1951

Bobby Arber joined Arsenal as an apprentice during the close season of 1967, turning professional in March 1968. Was a regular member of the South East Counties League side then the Metropolitan team. Was released on a free transfer to Orient in July 1970.

	Games	Goals
Friendly Matches	3	1
Metropolitan League	21	0
Metropolitan Cup	5	0
Youth Cup	2	0
Other Youth Cups	7	1
Youth Tour Matches	8	1
Total	46	3

Honours:
London Youth Challenge Cup Winners
Medal   1966-67
Southern Junior FloodLight Cup Finalists
Medal   1967-68

ARMSTRONG, George — 1961-77

Birth Place: Hebburn, Durham
Date of Birth: 9th August 1944

"Geordie" Armstrong was one of Arsenal's greatest ever servants. In a playing career which spanned sixteen seasons at Highbury, he played in over nine hundred competitive games for the club (902), a figure only bettered by David O'Leary. His skill, speed, stamina and work rate on either flank was there for everyone to behold (none more so than in the double season 1970-1971 when he must have covered every blade of grass on the Highbury pitch). George signed for Arsenal firstly as an amateur and then as a professional in the same month of August 1961. This being from the North East Boys Club of Hawthorne Leslie. His progress was so swift that within six months of joining the club he had made his league debut versus Blackpool, 24th February 1962. During that season he won three England Youth Caps. Little did he know that he would keep his place in the side, virtually unchallenged for fifteen seasons, despite opposition from the likes of Skirton, Macleod, Robertson and Marinello. In 1963-64 he played in twenty eight league matches. Predominantly on the left wing, progress was steadily made in 1964-65 when he missed out just two league matches and won the first of his five England Under 23 Caps. Unfortunately for George, during this period the England Manager, Alf Ramsey, had dispensed with wingers, so he must rate as one of the finest players never to wear an England Jersey. In Arsenal's,

George was always a player that rolled his sleeves up and got on with the job.

"Slumber Seasons", 1965-66, 1966-67 he missed only five of eighty four league matches, in which he did his best to pull a very poor side around. However, in 1967-68, not only was he ever present, but he helped Arsenal to their first major cup final for fifteen years against Leeds in the League Cup. At the start of the 1968-69 he was at loggerheads with the club but eventually came back into the side and helped the Gunners back to Wembley for the disastrous League Cup Final versus Swindon. Although missing much of th 1969-70 season, he was still a member of Arsenal's victorious Inter-Cities Fairs Cup Triumph against Anderlecht of Belgium. Without doubt, George's greatest success was the double winning season of 1970-71, not only playing in all sixty two first class games, but he was also voted Arsenal Player of the Year 1970. In 1971-72 he was again everpresent whilst helping Arsenal to the 1971-72 Cup Final versus Leeds. Over the following five seasons, 1972-77, he was still a regular in the Arsenal set up. However, after a disagreement with the manager, Terry Neill (an ex playing team mate for eight seasons), he left Highbury when he joined Leicester City for £15,000 in September 1977. At that stage he had played in five hundred league games and six hundred and twenty one first team games. (These were both Arsenal records) until they were overhauled by David O'Leary . He finished his playing career with Stockport in 1979. Later coached at various clubs including Fulham, Aston Villa, Middlesbrough and QPR and in Norway and Kuwait. Returned "home" to Highbury as reserve Team Coach during the summer of 1990. If you asked any Arsenal follower who had supported the club over the last thirty years - to name their favourite Arsenal player - many would say "George Armstrong".

George Armstrong

	Games	Goals
League	500	53
FA Cup	60	10
League Cup	35	3
European Cup	9	1
UEFA Cup	17	1
Friendly Matches	76	18
Tour Matches	70	21
Combination League	95	27
London Challenge Cup	13	3
Metropolitan League	4	2
Metropolitan Cup	12	4
Youth Cup	3	2
Other Youth Cups	4	2
Youth Tour Matches	4	1
Total	**902**	**148**

Honours:
League Championship Medal	1970-71
F A Cup Winners Medal	1970-71
Inter Cities Fairs Cup Winners Medal	1969-70
FA Cup Finalist Medal	1971-72
2 League Cup Finalist Medals	1967-68
	1968-69

5 England Under-23 Caps
3 England Youth Caps
Football Combination Championship
Medal   1969-70

ARMSTRONG, Paul   1975-78

Birth Place: London
Date of Birth: October 1959

☛ Paul Armstrong was a wing half who served the reserve and youth teams well for two seasons before being released in May 1978.

	Games	Goals
Friendly Matches	8	0
Combination League	56	7
South East Counties League	39	2
Youth Cup	11	2
Other Youth Cups	8	3
Total	**122**	**14**

ARPINO, Joe   1946-52

Birth Place: London
Date of Birth: December 1929

☛ Joe Arpino joined Arsenal as an amateur during 1946 from the amateur side Chase of Chertsey. A right back or wing half, Arpino turned professional two years later in August 1948. Spent two years in HM Forces 1949-51, reducing his football appearances. Spent most of his career at Highbury playing youth friendlies and Eastern Counties League games. Released on a free transfer during the 1951-52 season.

	Games	Goals
Friendly Matches	3	0
Eastern Counties League	25	1
Eastern Counties Cup	6	0
London Midweek League	15	1
Other Youth Cups	15	0
Total	**64**	**2**

ASHBERRY, Alan   1959-61

Birth Place: Boston, Lincolnshire
Date of Birth: November 1940

☛ Alan Ashberry joined Arsenal from Boston United in October 1959 after a months' trial. Was a regular member of Arsenal's Metropolitan League side for two seasons as a hard-working wing half. Released on a free transfer in June 1961, when he emigrated to Canada to play for Toronto Blizzards.

	Games	Goals
Friendly Matches	11	0
Combination League	5	0
Metropolitan League	55	3
Metropolitan Cup	9	1
Total	**80**	**4**

Honours:
Metropolitan League Championship Medal	1960-61
Metropolitan League Cup Winners Medal	1960-61
Metropolitan League Professional Cup Winners Medal	1960-61

ATKINSON, Phillip   1950-52

Birth Place: Idle, Yorkshire
Date of Birth: May 1928

Phillip Atkinson

☛ Phil Atkinson joined Arsenal from the Bradford side Thackley, in February 1950. Was a reliable left back in the Eastern Counties side for two seasons before being released on a free transfer in September 1952.

	Games	Goals
Friendly Matches	2	0
Combination League	3	0
Combination Cup	1	0
Eastern Counties League	28	0
Eastern Counties Cup	2	0
London Midweek League	28	0
Other Youth Matches	1	0
Total	**65**	**0**

BABES, John — 1947-50

Birth Place: Lurgan, Northern Ireland
Date of Birth: 20th November 1929

John Babes

☛ John Babes joined Arsenal from Glentoran as a promising amateur wing half in December 1947, turning professional the following month. Was a member of the first Arsenal youth teams of 1947-48, before winning a place in Arsenal's Eastern Counties team during 1949-50. Transferred to Scunthorpe on a free transfer in September 1950.

	Games	Goals
Eastern Counties League	46	1
Eastern Counties Cup	3	0
London Midweek League	9	0
Other Youth Matches	21	1
Total	**79**	**2**

BACCUZI, Dave — 1958-64

Birth Place: Islington, London
Date of Birth: 12th October 1940

☛ Signed for Arsenal as an amateur from Eastbourne in April 1958, turning professional in May 1959. Made his league debut versus WBA, 18th February 1961. He played in thirteen league matches in 1960-61, and in 1961-62 he shared the right back position with Jimmy Magill, playing in twenty-two league games. However, he played in only six league matches in 1962-63 and only a further five in 1963-64 before being transferred for £40,000 to Manchester City in April 1964, after the signing of Don Howe from West Brom. Later played for Reading. His father Joe, played for Fulham.

	Games	Goals
League	46	0
FA Cup	2	0
Friendly Matches	44	1
Tour Matches	1	0
Combination League	93	1

London Challenge Cup	13	0
Metropolitan League	50	0
Metropolitan Cup	4	0
South East Counties League	7	0
Youth Cup	6	0
Other Youth Cups	5	0
Youth Tour Matches	3	0
London Midweek League	1	0
Total	**275**	**2**

Dave Baccuzi

Honours:
7 England Youth Caps
Football Combination Champions   1962 - 63
London FA Challenge Cup
   Winners   1961-62, 1962-63
Metropolitan League Champions
                   1958-59, 1960-61
(WITH MANCHESTER CITY)
Division Two Championship Medal   1964-65

BAKER, Doug — 1963-66

Birth Place: Lewisham, London
Date of Birth: 8th April 1947

☛ Joined Arsenal as an apprentice in December 1963, turning professional in May 1964. Was a prolific goalscoring centre forward in the youth team, scoring fifty-six goals in 1964-65. Never realised full potential and was given a free transfer to Millwall in June 1966.

	Games	Goals
Friendly Matches	10	6
Combination League	31	20
London Challenge Cup	3	2
Metropolitan League	42	36
Metropolitan Cup	5	1
South East Counties League	15	18
Youth Cup	10	13
Other Youth Cups	8	7
Youth Tour Matches	14	2
Total	**138**	**105**

Honours:
FA Youth Cup Finalists Medal   1964-65
South East Counties League Cup
   Winners Medal   1963-64

1945-1985

BAKER, Joe — 1962-66

Birth Place: Liverpool, Lancashire
Date of Birth: 17th July 1940

☛ In the early and mid 1960's, for four seasons, Joe Baker captivated the Highbury audience like only Charlie George, Malcolm MacDonald and Ian Wright have since. In fact, only Ian Wright's goal ratio compares to Joe's one hundred goals in one hundred and fifty six first team games. He began his career with Hibernian in 1957 and in four seasons at Easter Road he scored one hundred and two league goals in only one hundred and seventeen games. This form winning him the first of his eight England Caps versus Northern Ireland in November 1959. Thus becoming the first English man to play for his country whilst with a Scottish club. What his new England team mates found amusing was his broad Scottish accent. In the summer of 1961 he decided to join Jimmy Greaves and his good friend Denis Law in Italy. Unfortunately, his spell at Torino was short lived, which resulted in him becoming Billy Wright's first signing for a new record Arsenal transfer fee of £72,500, in July 1962. In his first season at Highbury he was easily the club's leading scorer with twenty nine league goals (which included two hat tricks versus Wolves and Fulham) in thirty nine games. The following season, he was joint leading scorer (with Geoff Strong) on twenty six league goals. In 1964-65 he was ever present in the league and again leading scorer with twenty five league goals and after a five year break, he won back his England place. In 1965-66, he was leading scorer but, with Arsenal having one of their poorest seasons for many years he opted to join Nottingham Forest in March 1966 for £65,000. Whilst at Forest he was picked, but not selected, in the original forty for England's 1966 World Cup squad. Joe was transferred to Sunderland in 1969, returning to Hibernian in 1971 and finishing his career with Raith Rovers 1972-74. In a career spanning sixteen seasons in English and Scottish football, he scored an incredible two hundred and ninety four league goals in less than five hundred games. His older brother Gerry played for Manchester City, Ipswich Town and Coventry City.

Joe Baker

	Games	Goals
League	144	93
FA Cup	10	4
UEFA Cup	2	3
Friendly Matches	19	6
Tour Matches	11	17
Total	**186**	**123**

Honours:
8 England Caps
6 Under-23 Caps
1 Football League Cap

BALDWIN, Tommy   1962-66

Birth Place: Gateshead, Tyne and Wear
Date of Birth: 10th June 1946

☛ Tommy Baldwin was a prodigious goalscoring inside forward for Arsenal's youth and third teams in the early 1960's. He joined Arsenal as an amateur in September 1962 and turned professional in December of the same year. Made his league debut versus Birmingham, 6th April 1965. Although he scored eleven goals in only twenty first team games (which included Arsenal's first ever goal in the League Cup competition versus Gillingham), he never settled at Highbury and was transferred to Chelsea in September 1966, for £25,000 in a deal which took George Graham to Arsenal. He was a regular over the following eight seasons during which time he helped Chelsea to two FA Cup Finals(1967, 1970). He later played for Millwall and Manchester United on loan periods and Brentford as a non contract player, where he went on to join the coaching staff.

	Games	Goals
League	17	7
League Cup	3	4

Friendly Matches	25	15
Tour Matches	5	3
Combination League	60	41
London Challenge Cup	8	5
Metropolitan League	49	20
Metropolitan Cup	11	12
South East Counties League	16	9
Youth Cup	3	0
Youth Tour Matches	10	4
Total	**207**	**120**

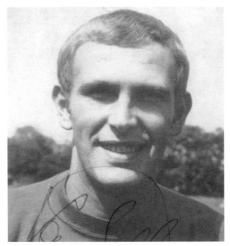

Tommy Baldwin

Honours:
(WITH ARSENAL)
London FA Challenge Cup
    Runners-up   1965-66
(WITH CHELSEA)
2 England Under-23 Caps
FA Cup Winners Medal   1969-70
FA Cup Finalists Medal   1966-67
European Cup Winners Cup Winners Medal
                                1970-71

BALL, Alan   1971-76

Birth Place: Farnworth, Lancashire
Date of Birth: 12th May 1945

☛ Alan Ball will rank as one of the great midfield players of the post war period. His career spanned over twenty years and over seven hundred league games. The son of Alan Ball senior, he joined Blackpool in May 1962, and spent four seasons at Bloomfield Road and whilst there he won the first of his seventy two England caps versus Yugoslavia just four days after his twentieth birthday. In July 1966 he was the youngest member of England's world cup winning team and it came as no surprise the following month when he joined Everton for a then British record fee of £110,000. He played in more than two hundred league games in five years at Goodison Park. With Howard Kendall and Colin Harvey he was part of the midfield trio which helped Everton to the 1968 FA Cup Final versus West Brom and the league championship in 1969-70. He was sensationally transferred to Arsenal for a new British record

fee of £220,000 in December 1971. Alan made his Arsenal league debut versus Nottingham Forest, 29th December 1971, and in his first season at Highbury helped guide Arsenal to the 1972 FA Cup Final versus Leeds. In 1972-73 he missed only two league matches and chipped in with ten goals from midfield. In 1973-74 he was the club's leading goalscorer with thirteen goals. He was a regular in the following two seasons 1974-75, 1975-76, but playing in possibly Arsenal's poorest ever side, he was transferred to Southampton in December 1976, for £60,000. Alan was a regular at The Dell for four seasons before trying his luck in the American soccer league with Philadelphia Fury and Vancouver Whitecaps. Returned to England as player/manager of Blackpool in July 1980, parting company in March 1981. He returned to Southampton as a player in the same month. He had two seasons at The Dell when in 1982, he moved to Hong Kong. Bally joined Bristol Rovers in January 1983 and became manager between 1984-88, of Portsmouth. Had a short spell as coach with Colchester under Jock Wallace. Became Stoke City manager 1989, Exeter 1991 and Southampton 1994 and was appointed Manchester City boss in the summer of 1995.

Alan Ball

	Games	Goals
League	177	45
FA Cup	28	7
League Cup	12	0
Friendly Matches	12	4
Tour Matches	12	1
Combination League	2	1
Total	**243**	**58**

Honours:
World Cup Winners Medal   1966
2 FA Cup Finalist Medals   1967-68, 1971-72
League Championship Medal   1969-70
League Cup Finalist Medal   1977-78
72 England Caps
8 Under-23 Caps
5 Football League Caps

Alan Ball in action

BARLEY, Derek   1951-53

Birth Place: Highbury, London
Date of Birth: 20th March 1932

☛ Derek Barley signed for Arsenal from Maidenhead United in December 1951. The son of Charlie Barley, an ex - Arsenal player of the 1920's, Barley played most of his football at Highbury for the third team as an inside forward. Granted a free transfer in May 1953 when he joined QPR. Later played for Aldershot.

	Games	Goals
Friendly Matches	7	1
Combination League	3	0
Eastern Counties League	20	3
London Midweek League	20	4
Total	**50**	**8**

Honours:
2 England Youth Caps
London Midweek League Championship
  Medal   1952-53
East Anglian Cup Finalists Medal   1951-52

BARNES, Walley   1943-56

Birth Place: Brecon, Wales
Date of Birth: 16th January 1920

☛ Walley Barnes was one of the greatest full backs Arsenal have ever had. He was spotted while playing as an amateur inside forward for Southampton. Arsenal signed him in June 1943 and during the war years he played in every position except centre forward, including a match in goal against Brighton. After the end of the war he damaged his knee in a PT display and it was thought his career was over. However, with guts and courage he forged his way back to full fitness, so making his full league debut versus Preston on 9th November 1946. He was at this stage nearly twenty six years old. Almost immediately he won a regular place in the league side, won a Championship medal as well as the first of his twenty - two Welsh caps during 1947 - 48. Switched from left back to right back following an injury to Laurie Scott. During

1949 - 50 he captained Wales for the first time, as well as winning an FA Cup winners medal. The following season 1950 - 51 he missed only one league game. Unfortunately, during the FA Cup Final versus Newcastle the following season, he suffered a severe leg injury which kept him out of action for the whole of season 1952 - 53. Was appointed Wales team manager in May 1954, before retiring in October 1956, to become the BBC football advisor. Served the BBC in many capacities up to his untimely death at the age of fifty five in September 1975.

	Games	Goals
League	267	11
FA Cup	25	1
Charity Shield	2	0
Friendly Matches	30	1
Tour Matches	20	0
Combination League	5	0
Combination Cup	5	0
London Challenge Cup	1	0
Wartime Appearances	40	3
Total	**395**	**16**

Walley Barnes

Honours:

League Championship Medal	1947-48
FA Cup Winners Medal	1949-50
FA Cup Finalist Medal	1951-52
FA Charity Shield Winners Medal	
	1948-49, 1953-54

22 Welsh Caps
2 Wartime Caps.

BARNETT, Geoff   1969-76

Birth Place: Northwich, Cheshire
Date of Birth: 16th October 1946

Geoff Barnett

☞ Spent five seasons at Everton as reserve keeper to Gordon West before being transferred to Arsenal in October 1969 for £30,000. Made his debut versus Coventry 4th October 1969. Could never gain a regular

place because of the brilliance of Bob Wilson, but spent seven years at Highbury where he was a regular in the reserves. Given a free transfer in January 1976 and finished his career playing in the United States, with Minnesota Kicks.

	Games	Goals
League	39	0
FA Cup	3	0
League Cup	5	0
UEFA Cup	2	0
Friendly Matches	20	0
Tour Matches	16	0
Combination League	172	0
Combination Cup	11	0
London Challenge Cup	8	0
Total	**276**	**0**

Honours:

FA Cup runners up Medal	1971-72
Football Combination Cup	
Winners	1969-70

BARNWELL, John   1955-64

Birth Place: Newcastle, Durham
Date of Birth: 24th December 1938

John Barnwell

☞ John Barnwell was playing as an amateur with Bishop Auckland when Arsenal signed him as an amateur in September 1955. Showed great promise and turned professional in November 1956. Played ten times for the England youth team and was a regular in Arsenal's successful youth team the following season. Was called up for his national service in 1957, just after he had made his league debut versus Sunderland on the 13th April

1957. Did not gain a regular place in the league side until 1959-60. In the following season, 1960-61, held a first team place as well as winning an England under 23 cap. Barnwell lost his place the following season, 1961-62, after being unsuccessfully switched from inside forward to the wing half position. Lost form the following season and was subsequently transferred to Nottingham Forest in March 1964 for a fee of £40,000. Served Nottingham Forest well for six seasons before finishing his career with Sheffield United in 1971. Later coached and then managed Peterborough United (1973 - 78). Became Wolves manager in 1978 where he stayed for four years, guiding them to the League Cup Final in 1980. Later managed A E K Athens, Greece, Notts County, Walsall and Northampton Town.

	Games	Goals
League	138	23
F A Cup	10	0
UEFA Cup	3	1
Friendly Matches	35	18
Tour Matches	7	2
Combination League	78	18
London Challenge Cup	13	2
Southern Floodlight Cup	4	1
Eastern Counties Cup	3	0
London Midweek League	4	1
Metropolitan League	5	0
South East Counties League	10	1
Youth Cup	7	4
Other Youth Cups	5	0
Youth Tour Matches	9	0
Total	**331**	**71**

Honours:

1 England Under - 23 Cap
10 England Youth Caps
Southern Junior Floodlight Challenge Cup
  Winners Medal   1958-59

BARR, Bill   1952-56

Birth Place: Wallasey, Cheshire
Date of Birth: 7th June 1935

☞ Bill Barr joined Arsenal as an amateur in July 1952, turning professional a year later. Spent a year in the Eastern Counties League side before being called up for national service in August 1953. On resuming his football career in August 1955, he spent a year playing for the London Midweek League side. Was given a free transfer in May 1956.

	Games	Goals
Friendly Matches	6	4
Combination League	2	1
Eastern Counties	14	4
Eastern Counties Cup	1	0
London Midweek League	15	5
Total	**38**	**14**

BARR, Ray — 1949-52

Birth Place: Dromore, Northern Ireland
Date of Birth: 27th October 1930

Ray Barr

☞ Ray Barr joined Arsenal from the Northern Ireland youth side Dromore in July 1949 as a promising young full back. Spent three seasons in Arsenal's Eastern Counties League side. Granted a free transfer in May 1952.

	Games	Goals
Friendly Matches	5	0
Combination League	3	0
Combination Cup	4	0
Eastern Counties League	57	1
Eastern Counties Cup	7	0
London Midweek League	40	1
Other Youth Matches	2	0
Total	**118**	**2**

Honours:
East Anglian Cup Finalists Medal   1951-52

BARRATT, Dave — 1954-58

Birth Place: London
Date of Birth: 2nd October 1938

☞ Dave Barratt joined Arsenal's ground staff in June 1954. An England schoolboy international, he later turned professional in May 1956. A regular member of Arsenal's South East Counties League Championship side of 1956 - 57. A consistent goalscorer in the youth side, scoring eighteen and twenty goals in seasons 1954 - 55 and 1955 - 56, and then a post - war club record up to then of fifty - seven goals in forty one youth matches in 1956 - 57. Upgraded to the reserve team in 1957 - 58 but unfortunately his potential was not realised and was given a free transfer to Guildford in June 1958.

	Games	Goals
Friendly Matches	11	5
Combination League	2	1
Eastern Counties Cup	3	4
London Midweek League	12	4
South East Counties League	65	70
Youth Cup	8	2
Other Youth Cups	7	11
Youth Tour Matches	9	6
Total	**117**	**103**

Honours:
South East Counties League Championship
    Medal   1955-56

BARRON, Paul — 1978-80

Birth Place: Woolwich, London
Date of Birth: 16th September 1953

☞ Started his career with Slough Town. Joined Plymouth in July 1976, spending two seasons there before being transferred to Arsenal in July 1978 for £40,000, as goalkeeper cover for Pat Jennings. Made his league debut versus Manchester City, 22nd August 1978. After two years in the reserves he wanted first team football and in August 1980 was transferred to Crystal Palace for £200,000 with Clive Allen in the deal which took Kenny Sansom to Arsenal. Later played for West Bromwich, Crystal Palace, Stoke, QPR and then to non league with Cheltenham and Welling.

Paul Barron

	Games	Goals
League	8	0
Friendly Matches	6	0
Tour Matches	3	0
Combination League	60	0
Total	**77**	**0**

BATSFORD, Allen — 1947-55

Birth Place: London
Date of Birth: July 1931

☞ Allen Batsford joined Arsenal as an amateur in June 1947, turning professional in July 1949. Allen served Arsenal for eight years, and although never once playing in the first team, was a regular member of the reserve team in season 1953 - 54. The rest of his playing days were spent in the third team as a tireless wing half. Left Highbury in May 1955.

Allen Batsford

	Games	Goals
Friendly Matches	8	2
Combination League	24	0
Combination Cup	10	0
Eastern Counties	103	3
Eastern Counties Cup	6	0
London Midweek League	52	4
Other Youth Matches	9	0
Total	**212**	**9**

Honours:
London FA Challenge Cup Winners
    Medal   1953-54
Eastern Counties League Championship
    Medal   1954-55
London Midweek League Championship
    Medal   1952-53

BATSON, Brendon — 1969-74

Birth Place: Grenada, West Indies
Date of Birth: 6th February 1953

☞ Signed as apprentice in July 1969, turning Professional in January 1971. Was a regular member of Arsenal's successful youth team of 1970 - 71. Made league debut versus Newcastle (as substitute), 11th March 1972 becoming Arsenal's first black player. Could never maintain a regular place due to the consistency of Rice, McNab, Storey and Nelson and was transferred to Cambridge

Untied in January 1974 for £5,000. Later played for West Bromwich Albion, retiring through injury in 1983. He is now Assistant Secretary of the Professional Footballers Association.

	Games	Goals
League	10	0
Friendly Matches	32	2
Tour Matches	1	0
Combination League	104	4
Combination Cup	2	1
London Challenge Cup	8	0
Metropolitan League	4	1
Metropolitan Cup	1	1
South East Counties League	15	2
Youth Cup	6	0
Other Youth Cups	8	2
Youth Tour Matches	14	1
Total	**205**	**14**

Honours:
Football Combination Cup Winners 1969-70
FA Youth Cup winners
                                   1970-71
South East Counties League Cup
   Winners   1970-71

BEAN, Warwick   1974-76

Birth Place: Tadworth, Surrey
Date of Birth: 13th March 1958

☛ Signed as apprentice in June 1974, turning professional in December 1975. In the two seasons he spent at Highbury he was very highly thought of as a very promising midfield player and although during this period he was a regular in the youth team, he was plagued by injury and eventually had to retire in 1976.

	Games	Goals
Friendly Matches	10	5
Combination League	5	1
South East Counties League	24	13
Youth Cup	2	0
Other Youth Cups	4	1
Youth Tour Matches	2	0
Total	**47**	**20**

BENNETT, David   1954-58

Birth Place: Southampton, Hampshire
Date of Birth: 5th March 1939

☛ Dave Bennett joined Arsenal as an apprentice in June 1954 already being an England schoolboy international winger, turning professional in May 1956. Was a consistent member of Arsenal's first successful youth squad of that period. Eventually won England youth caps before graduating to the reserve side. Was released by Arsenal on free transfer in June 1958 when he was signed by Portsmouth. Later played for Bournemouth.

	Games	Goals
Friendly Matches	9	7
Combination League	8	0
London Challenge Cup	1	0
Eastern Counties Cup	2	0
London Midweek League	17	2
South East Counties League	59	20
Youth Cup	7	3
Other Youth Cups	10	1
Youth Tour Matches	9	2
Total	**122**	**35**

Honours:
3 England Youth Caps
South East Counties League Championship
   Medal   1955-56

BENNETT, Don   1950-59

Birth Place: Wakefield, Yorkshire
Date of Birth: 18th December 1933

☛ Don Bennett was one of the loyalist players Arsenal have had in the post - war period. In nine years at Highbury he played in well over three hundred matches but not one of them in the league side. Bennett joined Arsenal's ground staff in September 1950. Played three times for the England youth side during April 1951, before becoming a professional in August 1951. Originally started life as a winger, but later he settled down as a regular and consistent member of Arsenal's reserve team (1953 - 59) as a full back. Left highbury on a free transfer in September 1959, when he joined Coventry City, whom he served well for three seasons. Was a Middlesex county cricketer for eighteen years (1950 - 68).

Don Bennett

	Games	Goals
Friendly Matches	30	11
Combination League	126	6
Combination Cup	23	1
London Challenge Cup	13	0
Southern Floodlight Cup	2	0
Eastern Counties League	65	19
Eastern Counties Cup	10	0
London Midweek League	49	6
Metropolitan League	8	0
Total	**326**	**43**

Honours:
3 England Youth Caps
London FA Challenge Cup Winners
   Medal   1957-58
London Midweek League Championship
   Medal   1952-53

BIGGS, Tony   1956-58

Birth Place: Greenford, Middlesex
Date of Birth: 17th April 1936

Tony Biggs

☛ Tony Biggs was an England amateur International with Hounslow serving in the armed forces when he signed for Arsenal in August 1956. Was a prolific goalscorer in Arsenal's reserve team 1956 - 58, scoring forty - six goals in seventy - two games. Made his league debut versus Wolves on the 8th April 1958. Eight months later he was transferred to Leyton Orient as part of the deal which took Len Julians to Highbury. Later played for Guildford and Hereford.

	Games	Goals
League	4	1
Friendly Matches	7	4
Combination League	64	43
London Challenge Cup	8	3
London Midweek League	1	1
Metropolitan League	1	0
Total	**85**	**52**

Honours:
Three England Amateur Caps
London FA Challenge Cup Winners
   Medal   1957-58

BLACK, John   1961-64

Birth Place: Blackburn, Lancashire
Date of Birth: 4th November 1945

Goalkeeper. Became an apprentice in August 1961, turning professional in February 1963. Won Welsh schoolboy caps although being born in Blackburn. Was a regular member of Arsenal's successful youth team of that time, before being given a free transfer to Swansea in December 1964.

John Black

	Games	Goals
Friendly Matches	12	0
Combination League	14	0
Metropolitan League	23	0
Metropolitan Cup	9	0
South East Counties League	47	0
Youth Cup	9	0
Other Youth Cups	21	0
Youth Tour Matches	6	0
Total	**141**	**0**

Honours:
Combination Championship Medal   1962-63
Metropolitan League Championship
  Medal   1962-63
South East Counties League Cup Winners
  Medal   1961-62,1963-64
Southern Junior Floodlight Cup Winners
  Medal   1962-63
London Minor Challenge Cup Finalists
  Medal   1961-62

BLOCKLEY, Jeff   1972-75

Birth Place: Leicester
Date of Birth: 12th September 1949

Jeff Blockley began his career with Coventry City in 1968 and played in nearly one hundred and fifty league games, also

winning England Under 23 honours, before being transferred to Arsenal for £200,000 in October 1972. Unfortunately his short stay at the club was not a happy one. This was mainly due to the fact that he was brought as a long term successor for the beloved Frank McLintock (which did not go down too well with the Highbury faithful), his inconsistent form, which in Jeff's defence was caused by many niggling injuries, and finally a never to be forgotten blunder in the disastrous FA cup semi final defeat by Sunderland in 1973. His Highbury career had, however, started so differently. He made his league debut versus Sheffield United 7th October 1972 and was even good enough at that stage to win a full England cap versus Yugoslavia only seven days after joining the club. But with a crop of young central defenders awaiting in the wings ie;Matthews, Powling and O'Leary he was allowed to depart to Leicester City for £100,000 in January 1975. He later played for Notts County 1978 - 80.

Jeff Blockley

	Games	Goals
League	52	1
FA Cup	7	0
League Cup	3	0
Friendly Matches	5	0
Tour Matches	3	0
Combination League	16	0
Total	**86**	**1**

Honours:
1 England Cap
1 Football League Cap
10 England Under - 23 Caps.

BLOOMFIELD, Jimmy   1954-60

Birth Place: Kensington, London
Date of Birth: 15th February 1934

Jimmy Bloomfield started his football career with Hayes before signing for Brentford in October 1952. During the

summer of 1954, Arsenal required a player to replace the ageing Jimmy Logie and Bloomfield fitted the bill, so after the completion of his national service, Arsenal paid Brentford £8,000 for his services in July 1954. In his first season at Highbury he played in nineteen league games including his debut versus Everton on the 25th August 1954. Bloomfield became a regular in the first team the following season 1955 - 56 and was ever present in the side during 1956 - 57. Around this time he represented the England under - 23 side and won football league representative honours. In all, held a first team place regularly up to his transfer to Birmingham for £15,000 in November 1960, after the arrival of George Eastham. Jimmy Bloomfield spent three seasons at Birmingham before returning to Brentford in June 1964. Spent a short time at both West Ham United and Plymouth before finishing his playing career at Orient. Managed Orient 1969 - 71, Leicester 1971 - 77 and Orient again 1977 - 81. Was still scouting for Luton Town when he suddenly died at the relatively young age of forty nine in April 1983.

Jimmy Bloomfield

	Games	Goals
League	210	54
FA Cup	17	2
Friendly Matches	42	14
Tour Matches	11	2
Combination League	10	2
Combination Cup	11	5
London Challenge Cup	3	1
Southern Floodlight Cup	9	3
Total	**313**	**83**

Honours:
2 England Under 23 Caps
1 Football League Cup
Inter Cities Fairs Cup Finalist Medal 1956-58
League Cup Winners Medal   1962-63

BLOOMFIELD, Ray   1960-64

Birth Place: Kensington, London
Date of Birth: 15th October 1944

Ray Bloomfield was a nephew of Jimmy Bloomfield and represented West London Schools and England at schoolboy level. Signed for Arsenal as an apprentice in May 1960, becoming a professional soon after his seventeenth birthday in November 1961. Bloomfield was a valuable member of the Arsenal Youth team of that period as well as winning England Youth honours. Played predominantly in the Metropolitan League for Arsenal during his period at the club before being transferred to Chelsea for £5,000 in May 1964. Later played for Aston Villa.

Ray Bloomfield

	Games	Goals
Friendly Matches	15	1
Combination League	33	10
London Challenge Cup	2	0
Metropolitan League	44	17
Metropolitan Cup	13	2
South East Counties League	18	5
Youth Cup	12	6
Other Youth Cups	15	5
Youth Tour Matches	14	7
Total	**166**	**53**

Honours:
7 England Youth Caps
London FA Challenge Cup Winners
   Medal   1962-63
Metropolitan League Professional Cup
   Winners Medal   1961-62
South East Counties League Cup
   Medal   1960-61, 1961-62
Southern Junior Floodlight Cup Winners
   Medal   1962-63
London Minor Challenge Cup Finalist
   Medal   1960-61

BOOT, Micky   1963-67

Birth Place: Leicester
Date of Birth: 17th December 1947

Joined Arsenal as an apprentice in June 1963, turning professional in December 1964. Was very versatile, playing at full back, wing half and inside forward for the youth team. Scored on his league debut versus Newcastle, 8th October 1966. Was given a free transfer in March 1967 and emigrated to South Africa where he joined Durban City.

Micky Boot

	Games	Goals
League	4	2
League Cup	1	0
Friendly Matches	22	8
Combination League	44	8
Combination Cup	7	0
London Challenge Cup	3	1
Metropolitan League	29	14
Metropolitan Cup	6	0
South East Counties League	31	13
Youth Cup	18	3
Other Youth Cups	19	5
Youth Tour Matches	36	8
Total	**220**	**62**

Honours:
FA Youth Cup Winners   1965-66
   runners up   1964-65
South East Counties League Cup
   WInners   1963-64
   runners up   1965-66

BOWDEN, Norman   1943-49

Birth Place: Glossop, Derbyshire
Date of Birth: May 1923

Norman Bowden was an RAF pilot who, during the war, signed for Arsenal as an amateur in June 1943, and turned professional in December 1943. After the war he settled in Arsenal's reserve and youth teams, predominantly as an inside forward. Unfortunately a succession of injuries forced his early retirement in January 1949.

	Games	Goals
Friendly Matches	1	0
Combination League	14	3
Combination Cup	4	1
London Challenge Cup	4	0
Eastern Counties League	8	5
Eastern Counties Cup	1	0
Other Youth Matches	30	11
Wartime	5	2
Total	**67**	**22**

BOWEN, Dave   1950-59

Birth Place: Maesteg, Wales
Date of Birth: 7th June 1928

Dave Bowen signed for Arsenal from Northampton Town in July 1950 as an under study to Joe Mercer. The Welshman made his league debut versus Wolves on the 24th March 1951. He had to wait until the end of the 1954 - 55 season before winning a regular place in Arsenal league side, by this time he had won the first of his 18 Welsh caps against Yugoslavia in September 1954. Was a consistent member of the Arsenal league side from 1955 until his departure back to Northampton Town in July 1959, where he became player/manager. A fine servant to Arsenal who captained Wales during the 1958 World Cup series. In later years served Northampton as manager, at one point guiding them from the Fourth Division to the First in five seasons. His son Keith Bowen played league football for Brentford, Northampton and Colchester. Dave sadly passed away in September 1995.

Dave Bowen

	Games	Goals
League	146	2
FA Cup	16	0
Friendly Matches	33	2
Tour Matches	20	2
Combination League	90	7
Combination Cup	29	1
London Challenge Cup	13	0
Southern Floodlight Cup	5	0
Total	**352**	**14**

Honours:
18 Welsh Caps
Southern Floodlight Challenge Cup
   winners   1958-59
Football Combination champions   1950-51
Football Combination Cup winners   1952-53
London FA Challenge Cup winners   1953-54

1927 F.A. Cup Final
Arsenal versus.
Cardiff City.

C. M. BUCHAN
ARSENAL.

E. HAPGOOD (ARSENAL)

C. BASTIN

WILLS'S CIGARETTES

B. JONES (ARSENAL)

J. CRAYSTON

E. J. DRAKE

CARRERAS CIGARETTES

ALEX. JAMES
ARSENAL (1ST DIVISION)

DAVID JACK
ARSENAL

CARRERAS CIGARETTES

J. HULME
ARSENAL (1ST DIVISION)

1950 FA CUP WINNERS. Back row (l to r): Whittaker (manager), Compton (L), Scott, Swindin, Barnes, Milne (trainer). Front: Forbes, Cox, Logie, Mercer, Goring, Lewis and Compton (D).

STARS OF THE FIFTIES

Doug Lishman

Cliff Holton

Derek Tapscott

J. Kelsey

Vic Groves

Jack Kelsey

...he Arsenal dressing room, five minutes to ...ck-off. All strangers are asked to leave while ...om Whittaker tells his secret – the plan of ...ampaign to be fought out before 60,000 spec-...tors. Yates Wilson, who picture illustrates the ...ene, reported that there was a surprising ...ck of dramatic tension. "Due," he said, "to ...e remarkable hamrony and confidence ...Whittaker has managed to build." The key plan ...entifies everyone present: 1 Ronald Rooke, 2 ...eslie Compton, 3 Archie Macaulay, 4 James ...ogie, 5 Walley Barnes, 6 Reginald Lewis, 7 ...alter Sloan, 8 George Male, 9 Bryn Jones, 10 ...on Roper, 11 George Swindin, 12 Tom ...hittaker, 13 Billy Milne and 14 Denis ...ompton, "who, this time, just turned up to ...atch."

Golden Gunners

Leslie Compton and
(inset) Denis Compton

Arsenal

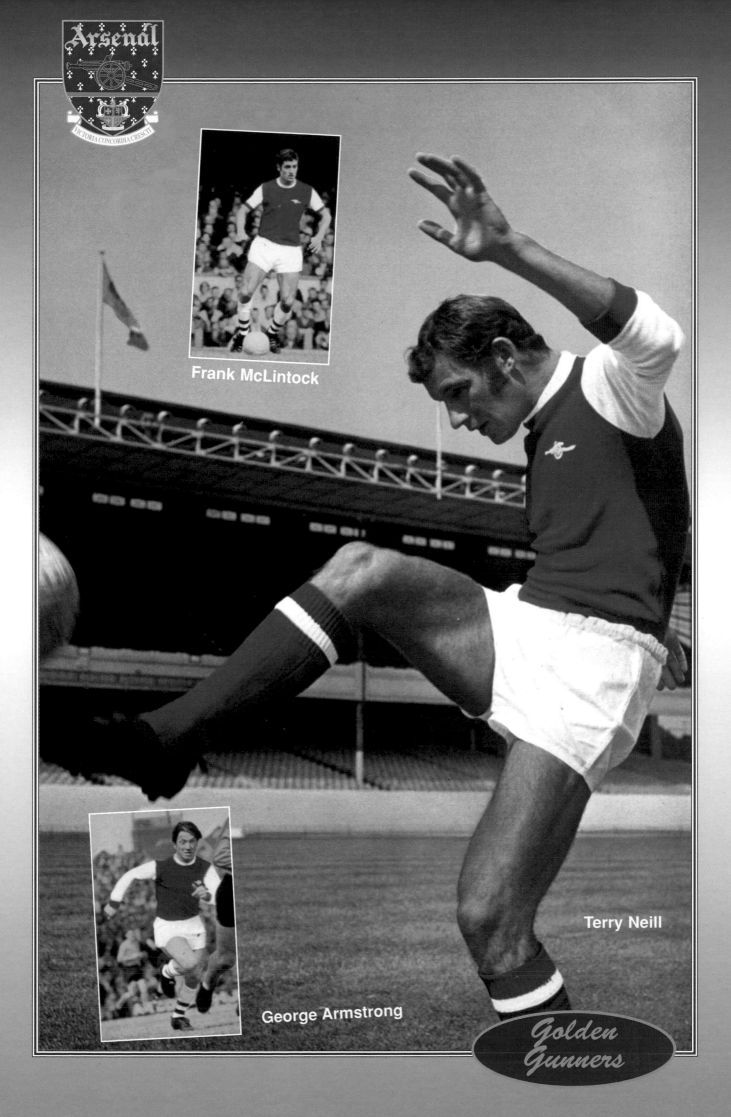

Frank McLintock

George Armstrong

Terry Neill

Golden Gunners

Strikers John Radford and Ray Kennedy show off the FA Cup after victory over Liverpool in 1971 to complete the famous double.

The 1971 First Division champions and FA Cup double winners.
Back row, left to right: Pat Rice, Sammy Nelson, Peter Marinello.
Middle: Bob McNab, Peter Simpson, Charlie George, Geoff Barnett,
Bob Wilson, John Roberts, Ray Kennedy, Peter Storey.
Front: Trainer George Wright, George Armstrong, Eddie Kelly, John Radford, manager Bertie Me
captain Frank McLintock, George Graham, Jon Sammels and coach Don Howe.

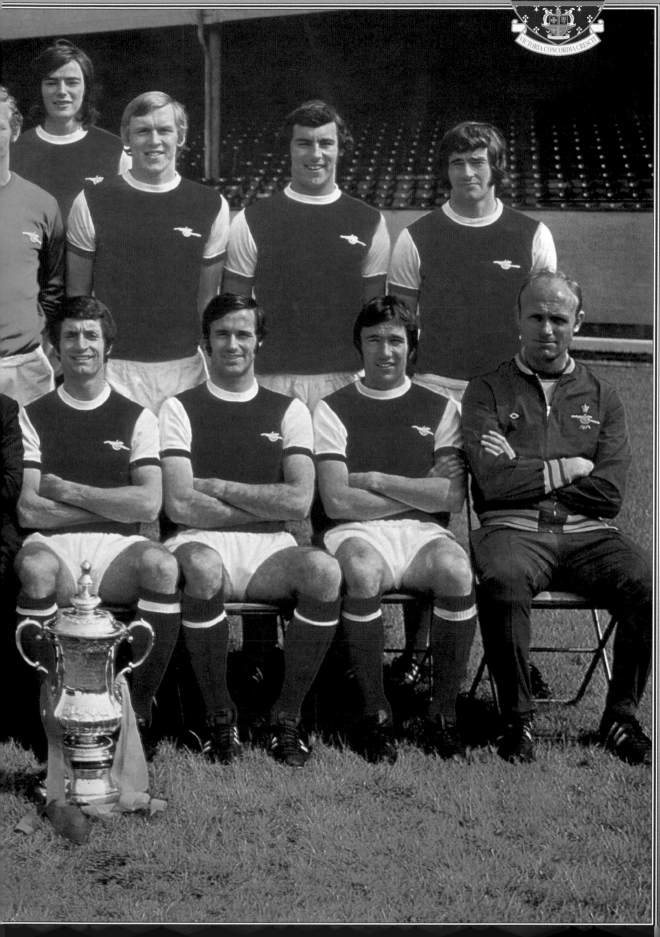

Malcolm Macdonald

Liam Brady

Alan Ball

Charlie George

Pat Jennings

Arsenal

David O'Leary
FA Cup & Coca-Cola Cup
winner 1993

Golden Gunners

Champions of England, 1991. Back row, left to right: Coach Stewart Houston, manager George Graham, Lee Dixon, Steve Bould, Paul Merson, Tony Adams, Andy Linighan, Alan Smith, Perry Groves and physio Gary Lewin.
Front: Michael Thomas, Kevin Campbell, Nigel Winterburn, David Rocastle, Anders Limpar, David Seaman, David O'Leary, Paul Davis, David Hillier.

Kings of Europe. Manager George Graham, skipper Tony Adams and match-winner Alan Smith parade the European Cup Winners' Cup through the streets of Islington after the 1-0 victory over Parma of Italy in May 1994.

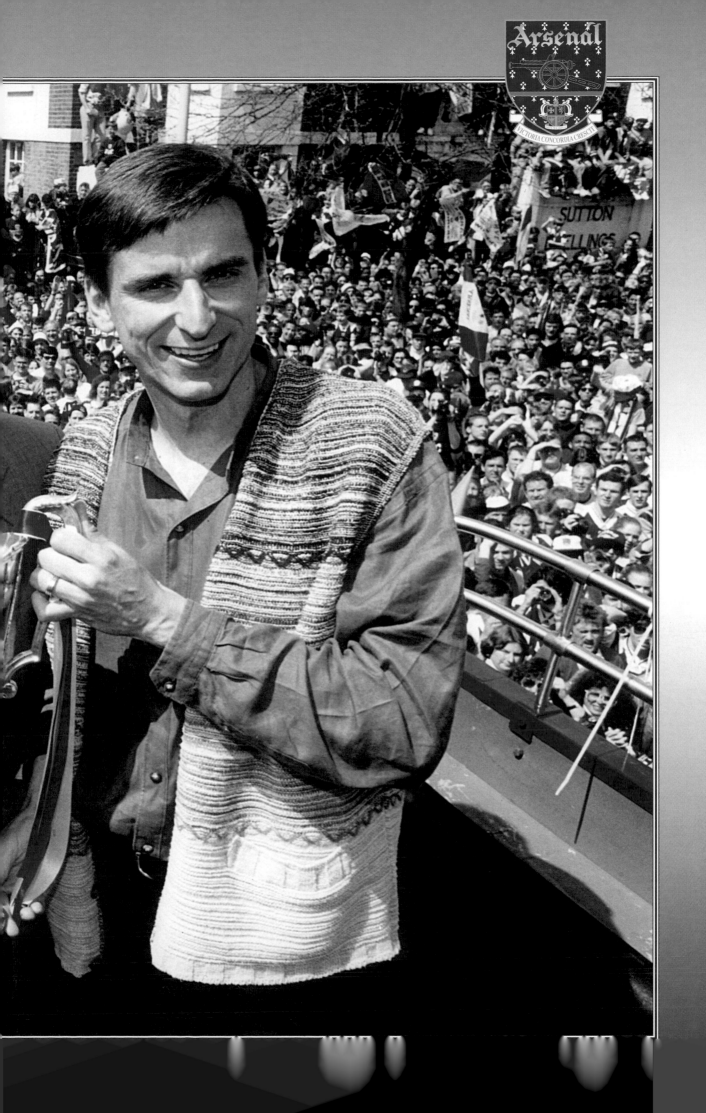

Ian Wright

Arsenal

BRADY, Liam — 1971-80

Birth Place: Dublin
Date of Birth: 13th February 1956

Without any doubt, Liam Brady must rank as one of the greatest players ever to pull on the famous red and white shirt of Arsenal. In his seven seasons at Highbury his influence over the rest of the side has only been matched by Alex James, Joe Mercer, Frank McLintock and later Tony Adams. Of all the Arsenal players to benefit from Brady's brilliance none gained more than Frank Stapleton. In fact if one produced a survey of how Frank's goals were scored a great percentage of them were set up or assisted by "Chippy". Liam joined Arsenal as an apprentice in June 1971, turning professional in July 1973, he made his Arsenal league debut versus Birmingham City, as a substitute, on 6th October 1973. Became a regular in the side in 1974-75 as well as winning the first, of his seventy two, Republic of Ireland caps, versus Russia. He was ever present in 1975-76 and in 1976-77 was instrumental in feeding Macdonald and Stapleton for many of the goals they scored that season .In 1977-78 he was a regular in the Arsenal side which reached the league cup semi-final and the FA Cup Final. In 1978-79 he was back at Wembley with Arsenal when he gave one of the greatest individual performances seen in a Cup Final helping Arsenal to a last minute victory over Manchester United. Played in his third consecutive F A Cup Final in 1979-80, Arsenal losing 1-0 to West Ham. The newly crowned P F A Footballer of the Year was also a member of Arsenal's European Cup Winners Cup side which lost on penalties to Valencia. After much speculation and to the derision of the Highbury faithful he was transferred to Juventus of Italy in July 1980 for the ludicrously low sum of £514,000. He spent two seasons in Turin playing fifty seven Serie A matches helping them to win the Italian Championship in both seasons. Transferred to Sampdoria in 1982, he spent a further two seasons there before joining Inter Milan in 1984. He had two seasons with Inter before finishing his Italian honeymoon with Ascoli in 1986-87. Returned to England to play for West Ham in March 1987 playing in over one hundred first team games for the Hammers before announcing his retirement during the summer of 1990. He later managed Celtic 1991-92, and Brighton 1993-95. His two older brothers Pat and Ray played league football for Millwall and QPR. The word 'great' is too often applied to many who have not earned this eminence, however, having seen Liam on many occasions he fully deserves the accolade.

	Games	Goals
League	235	43
FA Cup	35	2
League Cup	23	10
Cup Winners Cup	9	2
UEFA Cup	4	2
Charity Shield	1	0
Friendly Matches	46	9
Tour Matches	25	5
Combination League	62	9
London Challenge Cup	4	0
South East Counties League	38	12
Youth Cup	15	7
Other Youth Cups	12	3
Youth Tour Matches	6	1
Total	**515**	**105**

Honours:
(WITH ARSENAL)
72 Eire Caps
PFA Footballer of the Year — 1978-79
FA Cup Winners Medal — 1978-79
FA Cup Finalist Medals — 1977-78, 1979-80
European Cup Winners Cup Finalist
   Medal — 1979-80
11 Eire Youth Caps
South East Counties League Champions
   — 1971-72
South East Counties League Cup
   runners up — 1971-72
(WITH JUVENTUS)
Italian Serie A Championship
   Medals — 1980-81, 81-82

Liam Brady

Liam Brady in action

BRASTED, Gordon   1953-56

Birth Place: Burnham, Essex
Date of Birth: 30th June 1933

☛ Gordon Brasted joined Arsenal as an amateur from his home town Burnham Ramblers in March 1953. Turned professional in November 1953. Brasted played mainly in the Eastern Counties League for Arsenal during his three years at the club where he was a prolific goalscorer. Released on free transfer in July 1956 when he joined Gillingham.

	Games	Goals
Friendly Matches	10	13
Combination League	1	1
London Challenge Cup	1	0
Eastern Counties League	42	35
Eastern Counties Cup	2	1
London Midweek League	33	18
Total	**89**	**68**

Honours:
Eastern Counties League
   Championship Medal   1954-55

BREWER, William   1952-56

Birth Place: Peckham, London
Date of Birth: May 1933

☛ Bill Brewer joined Arsenal as a professional in August 1952 after a private trial. An inside forward, his career at Highbury was hindered by two years national service, and his apprenticeship in the printing trade. However was a fine member of Arsenal's Eastern Counties team of that time before being granted a free transfer during the summer of 1956.

	Games	Goals
Friendly Matches	8	1
Eastern Counties League	32	1
Eastern Counties Cup	3	0
London Midweek League	20	5
Total	**63**	**7**

Honours:
London Midweek League
   Championship Medal   1952-53

BRIGNALL, Steve   1976-79

Birth Place: Ashford, Kent
Date of Birth: 12th June 1960

☛ Signed as an apprentice in February 1976, and turned professional in May 1978. Made his one and only first team appearance as substitute versus Liverpool 7th April 1979. In November of the same year was granted a free transfer and went to play in Norway. Returned to England in 1980 to play for Hastings and Luton and then on to Tonbridge, Gravesend, Ashford and Hythe Town in non league.

	Games	Goals
League	1	0
Friendly Matches	8	0
Combination League	79	3
South East Counties League	47	0
Youth Cup	7	0
Other Youth Cups	6	0
Total	**148**	**3**

BRISTOW, Ray   1964-66

Birth Place: London
Date of Birth: 17th June 1948

☛ Joined Arsenal as an apprentice in May 1964. Was a winger in the youth team for two seasons before being given a free transfer to QPR in September 1966.

	Games	Goals
Friendly Matches	8	1
Combination League	8	2
Combination Cup	2	0
Metropolitan League	34	9
Metropolitan Cup	4	1
South East Counties League	25	7
Youth Cup	12	1
Other Youth Cups	12	2
Youth Tour Matches	11	1
Total	**116**	**24**

Honours:
F A Youth Cup Winners
   Medal   1965-66
Metropolitan League Challenge Cup
   Winners Medal   1965-66
South East Counties League
   Championship Medal   1964-65
Southern Junior Floodlight Cup
   Winners Medal   1965-66
London Minor Challenge Cup
   Winners Medal   1964-65

BROWN, Eddie   1954-57

Birth Place: Choppington,
                 Northumberland
Date of Birth: August 1936

☛ Turned professional for Arsenal in August 1954 just before call up for national service. Was not regularly available for two years, and when demobbed, spent a season fighting injuries before being released on a free transfer in June 1957.

	Games	Goals
Friendly Matches	3	1
Combination League	5	2
Eastern Counties Cup	2	2
London Midweek League	18	9
Total	**28**	**14**

BROWN, Laurie   1961-64

Birth Place: Shildon, Durham
Date of Birth: 22nd August 1937

☛ Laurie Brown started his footballing career as an amateur with Woking Town and Bishop Auckland and represented England in the 1960 Olympic Games in Rome, on his return he signed professional forms for Northampton Town in October 1960. Was the Club's leading goal scorer (1960 - 61) with twenty one goals, during this period he switched from a goal scoring centre forward to a deep lying wing half, this position he held when joining Arsenal in August 1961 for £35,000. In his three seasons at Highbury he was a first team regular playing in forty one league matches, 1961 - 62, thirty eight in 1962 - 63 and twenty two in 1963 - 64, before his departure to Tottenham for £40,000 in April 1964. Transferred to Norwich in 1966 and later became player manager of Bradford Park Avenue 1968 - 69 before their demise from the Football League.

Laurie Brown

	Games	Goals
League	101	2
FA Cup	5	0
UEFA Cup	3	0
Friendly Matches	15	2
Tour Matches	3	1
Combination League	8	3
London Challenge Cup	6	0
Metropolitan League	2	2
Total	**143**	**10**

Honours:
14 England Amateur Caps
London FA Challenge Cup
   winners   1961-62

BURNS, Tony 1963-66

Birth Place: Edenbridge, Kent
Date of Birth: 27th March 1944

☛ Tony Burns joined Arsenal in March 1963, from Non league club Tonbridge United. He made great progress through the junior ranks over the following eighteen months before making his league debut versus Burnley, 17th October 1964. He played in twenty four consecutive league games (Oct 1964 - Mar 1965) conceding forty seven goals, thus losing his place, to Jim Furnell, he was sold to Brighton for £5,000 in July 1966. He later played for Charlton 1969 Durban United (South Africa) 1970, Crystal Palace 1973 and Plymouth 1978.

Tony Burns

	Games	Goals
League	31	0
FA Cup	2	0
Friendly Matches	16	0
Tour Matches	5	0
Combination League	23	0
London Challenge Cup	3	0
Metropolitan League	52	0
Metropolitan Cup	6	0
South East Counties League	7	0
Youth Cup	2	0
Youth Tour Matches	14	0
Total	**161**	**0**

Honours:
London FA Challenge Cup
  Runners - up 1965-66

BURTON, Terry 1968-71

Birth Place: Islington, London
Date of Birth: 16th June 1953

☛ Joined Arsenal as an apprentice in July 1968 turning professional in July 1970. Was a wing half in Arsenal's Youth Team 1970 - 71 when he helped them win the FA Youth Cup and South East Counties League. Was given a free transfer by Bertie Mee in June 1971. He soon after became player coach to Isthmian League side Ilford. Also coached Holloway and Islington Schools, returned to Highbury as youth team coach in 1979 becoming reserve team coach in 1982. In July 1984, at the tender age of twenty nine Terry was appointed first team coach after he had become Don Howe's assistant after the departure of Terry Neill. However, after the appointment of John Cartwright as first team coach in July 1985 he returned to his former position with the reserves. He briefly resumed first team duties in April 1986 after Don Howe had left and Steve Burtenshaw was appointed caretaker manager. Reverted back to the reserves after the appointment of George Graham before leaving Highbury in 1987. Later held coaching positions at Wimbledon and is currently Assistant Manager at Wimbledon.

Terry Burton

	Games	Goals
Friendly Matches	25	0
Combination League	27	2
Combination Cup	2	0
London Challenge Cup	2	1
Metropolitan League	27	0
Metropolitan Cup	4	0
South East Counties League	30	1
Youth Cup	13	1
Other Youth Cups	9	0
Youth Tour Matches	14	2
Total	**153**	**7**

Honours:
Football Combination Cup Winners
  Medal 1969-70
FA Youth Cup Winners Medal 1970-71
South East Counties League Cup Winners
  Medal 1970-71

1945-1985

BUTCHER, Bernard 1951-55

Birth Place: Birmingham
Date of Birth: October 1935

☛ Bernard Butcher signed for Arsenal from the Birmingham league side Pheasey in November 1951, but had little chance to prove his worth when he was called up for two year's national service in February 1952. A wing half, who on his return to Highbury in February 1954, found his form had deserted him and was released on a free transfer in the close season of 1955.

	Games	Goals
Friendly Matches	3	0
Eastern Counties League	26	0
Eastern Counties Cup	3	0
London Midweek League	22	2
Total	**54**	**2**

Honours:
Eastern Counties League Championship
  Medal 1954-55
East Anglian Cup Finalists Medal 1951-52

CALVERLEY, Alf 1947

Birth Place: Huddersfield, Yorkshire
Date of Birth: 24th November 1917

☛ When Arsenal had a problem with the outside left position in the first season after the war, they spent £5,000 on purchasing Calverley from Mansfield in March 1947. Made his league debut versus Preston 15th March 1947 making ten further appearances that season. Spent only four months at Highbury before being transferred to Preston in July 1947. Later played for Doncaster.

	Games	Goals
League	11	0
Friendly Matches	1	0
Total	**12**	**0**

CANT, Cliff 1976-79

Date of Birth: November 1959

☛ Joined Arsenal as an apprentice in July 1976. Turned professional in December 1977 after which he settled down as a regular in Arsenal's reserve team as an inside forward. Was granted a free transfer in November 1979. Later played in Norway before emigrating to Australia, whom he represented against England during the summer of 1983. On his return to England Cliff played for various non league sides including Carshalton, Crawley, Welling, Horsham and Gravesend.

	Games	Goals
Friendly Matches	11	1
Combination League	109	11
South East Counties League	39	9
Youth Cup	8	1
Other Youth Cups	6	3
Total	**173**	**25**

CARMICHAEL, Jackie 1967-71

Birth Place: Newcastle
Date of Birth: 11th November 1948

☛ Signed from Possilpark YMCA in May 1967 and for the next four seasons was a stalwart defender in the reserve team. Never made the first team and was eventually sold to Peterborough in January 1971 for £5,000. Served Peterborough well for over ten years.

Jackie Carmichael

	Games	Goals
Friendly Matches	28	0
Combination League	93	3
Combination Cup	36	0
London Challenge Cup	9	1
Metropolitan League	5	0
Metropolitan Cup	1	0
Youth Tour Matches	4	0
Total	**176**	**4**

Honours:
Football Combination Championship
  Medals   1968-69, 1969-70
Football Combination Cup Winners
  Medals   1967-68, 1969-70
London Challenge Cup Winners
  Medal   1969-79

CARSON, Charles 1949-55

Birth Place: Edinburgh
Date of Birth: 21st April 1932

☛ Joined Arsenal as a professional in September 1949. His career was hindered by two year's national service. A centre forward who spent most of his six years with Arsenal in the third team. Given free transfer to Stockport in June 1955.

Charles Carson

	Games	Goals
Friendly Matches	7	2
Combination League	2	0
Combination Cup	5	4
Eastern Counties League	84	31
Eastern Counties Cup	10	5
London Midweek League	30	13
Total	**138**	**55**

Honours:
Eastern Counties League Championship
  Medal   1954-55
London Midweek League Championship
  Medal   1952-52

CHAMBERS, Brian 1973-74

Birth Place: Newcastle
Date of Birth: 31st October 1949

☛ Joined Arsenal from Sunderland in June 1973 for £20.000. He played his one and only game versus Birmingham City on 6th October 1973. Although being a regular in Arsenal's reserve team of that season he became unsettled and was transferred to Luton Town in March 1974 for £10,000. Later played for Millwall, Bournemouth and Halifax and non league for Poole, Salisbury, Dorchester and Swanage.

	Games	Goals
League	1	0
League Cup	1	0

	Games	Goals
Friendly Matches	5	0
Tour Matches	3	0
Combination League	37	9
London Challenge	3	0
Total	**50**	**9**

CHAPMAN, Lee 1982-83

Birth Place: Lincoln
Date of Birth: 5th December 1959

☛ Lee Chapman started his long career with Stoke City in June 1978. Became a regular for the Potters in 1979 - 80 and was the leading goal scorer for City in 1980 - 81 and 1981 - 82. This form winning him an England under 21 cap versus Eire. However, although Stoke, in Chapman, Paul Bracewell, Adrian Heath and Steve Bould held great potential, the break up of the side was inevitable. He was transferred to Arsenal in August 1982 after a tribunal had set the fee at £500,000. Ironically making his league debut against his old club on the opening day of the season, 28th August 1982. Unfortunately, as he was settling in to the side he was injured in training and a cartilage operation was required. He spent the first half of the 1982 - 83 season in the reserves and became unsettled and wanted away. His wish was granted and in December 1983, when he joined Sunderland for £200,000. Over the next ten seasons he became a footballing nomad, joining Sheffield Wednesday, £100,000 August 1984; Niort (France) £350,000 1988; Nottingham Forest October 1988, for £350,000 and during his two seasons at the City ground helped Forest to win the League Cup in 1988 - 89 and the Simod Cup in the same season; Leeds £400,000 January 1990, where he achieved even greater success helping them to win the Second Division title in 1989 - 90 and ultimately the League Championship in 1991 - 92. Has since played for Portsmouth 1993, £250,000, West Ham 1993 - 95, £250,000, Southend on loan 1995 and Ipswich Town 1995, £50,000. His brother Jon and his father Roy also played league football. Up to the end of the 1994 - 95 season, Lee Chapman has been involved in transfers totalling nearly £2.5 Million pounds and has scored over two hundred league goals in over five hundred league appearances.

	Games	Goals
League	23	4
FA Cup	1	0
League Cup	2	0
UEFA Cup	2	2
Friendly Matches	9	7
Tour Matches	8	3
Combination League	28	23
Total	**73**	**39**

Lee Chapman

Honours:
(WITH STOKE)
1 England Under 21 Cap
(WITH NOTTINGHAM FOREST)

League Cup Winners Medal	1988-89
Simod Cup Winners Medal	1988-89

(WITH LEEDS)
One England B Cap

League Championship Medal	1991-92
Charity Shield Medal	1992
Division Two Championship Medal	1989-90

CHARLES, Mel   1959-62

Birth Place: Swansea, Wales
Date of Birth: 14th May 1935

Mel Charles signed professional forms for Swansea Town in May 1952 and over the following seven seasons he played in over two hundred and fifty first team games as well as winning twenty one Welsh caps including playing in the 1958 World Cup Finals. Like his brother John, he became much sought after, and in March 1959 Arsenal believed they had pulled off a transfer coup when he became their record buy at £40,000 (plus David Dodson and Peter Davies). Charles made his league debut for Arsenal at centre-half, versus Sheffield Wednesday, 22nd August 1959. In that first season at Highbury he played in twenty league games alternating between centre half and centre forward, before a cartilage operation in September 1959 hindered his progress. In 1960 - 61 a second cartilage operation was required which resulted in him playing in only nineteen league matches. In 1961 - 62 he started the season as the club's first choice centre forward playing in sixteen of the first eighteen league matches (scoring eleven goals). However, he lost his place to the up and coming Geoff Strong in February 1962, and within the same month

was transferred to Cardiff City for £20,000. Later played for Port Vale 1967. His son, Jeremy, played league football for Swansea City, QPR, Oxford United and Wales.

Mel Charles

	Games	Goals
League	60	26
FA Cup	4	2
Friendly Matches	9	2
Tour Matches	8	3
Combination League	14	5
London Challenge Cup	4	2
Southern Floodlight Cup	2	3
Metropolitan League	2	1
Metropolitan Cup	1	0
Total	**104**	**44**

Honours:
31 Welsh Caps

Southern Floodlit Challenge Cup Winners	1958-59
London FA Challenge Cup Winners	1961-62
Runners up	1960-61

CHARLTON, Stan   1955-58

Birth Place: Exeter, Devon
Date of Birth: 28th June 1929

Stan Charlton was an amateur with Bromley and won four England amateur caps as well as playing in the 1952 Olympic games in Helsinki. He joined Leyton Orient as a professional in November 1952 and was virtually everpresent over the following three years playing in over one hundred and fifty league games. Transferred to Arsenal with Vic Groves for £30,000 in November 1955. He made his right back position his own taking over from Len Wills after making his Arsenal league debut versus Chelsea 24th December 1955. In 1956 - 57 he played in forty out of Arsenal's forty two league games and thirty six in 1957 - 58, however, after a three - one home defeat by Burnley in

September 1958 he lost his place to the man he was brought to succeed - Len Wills. Transferred back to Leyton Orient in December 1958, he gave them excellent service over the following seven seasons. Helping the club in to the First Division for the one and only time in 1962 - 63. In a league career which spanned thirteen seasons, Stan Charlton played in four hundred and sixty two league matches. Later became secretary - manager of Weymouth 1965 - 72.

Stan Charlton

	Games	Goals
League	99	0
FA Cup	11	3
Friendly Matches	17	1
Tour Matches	5	0
Combination League	18	0
London Challenge Cup	2	0
Southern Floodlight Cup	4	0
Total	**156**	**4**

Honours:
4 England Amateur Caps

CHENHALL, John   1944-53

Birth Place: Bristol, Avon
Date of Birth: 23rd July 1927

Signed as an amateur for Arsenal in October 1944 and as a professional in November 1945. Like a host of other players in that period, John Chenhall was for nine years a most reliable and loyal reserve. He played full back on only sixteen occasions for the first team during that period, which included his league debut versus Charlton, 20th October 1951. Transferred to Fulham in July 1953, where he was everpresent in his first season at Craven Cottage. He later played for Gravesend. His brother, Ray was also on Arsenal's books as an amateur.

John Chenhall

	Games	Goals
League	16	0
Friendly Matches	25	0
Tour Matches	5	0
Combination League	109	1
Combination Cup	62	0
London Challenge Cup	9	0
Eastern Counties League	10	0
Eastern Counties Cup	1	0
London Midweek League	2	0
Youth Tour Matches	17	1
Wartime	5	0
Total	**261**	**2**

Honours:
Football Combination Champions	1950-51
Football Combination Cup winners	1952-53
runners up	1950-51

CLAMP, Eddie   1961-62

Birth Place: Coalville, Leicestershire
Date of Birth: 14th September 1934

Eddie Clamp's career began in April 1952 when he signed for Wolverhampton Wanderers, after being on the ground staff as a junior. His enjoyable eight year stint at Molineux playing with such players as Bert Williams, Billy Wright, Johnny Hancocks and Ron Flowers etc., helped Clamp to become an English International in his own right. During this period 1953 - 61 he won four England caps (all won during the 1958 World Cup Finals) and helped Wolves to win the Division One championship in 1957 - 58 and 1958 - 59 as well as the FA Cup in 1959 - 60. He had played in over 200 league matches for Wolves when, in November 1961, he was transferred to Arsenal for £30,000. Arsenal had hoped that his experience would guide the younger players within the squad. However, after only ten months and twenty two league games, which included his league debut versus Nottingham Forest, 18th November 1961, he was transferred to Stoke City for £15,000. In

his first season in the Potteries he helped the club win the Second Division title playing in thirty two league games (1962 - 63). Transferred to Peterborough in October 1964 and later played non - league football for Worcester City.

Eddie Clamp

	Games	Goals
League	22	1
FA Cup	2	0
Friendly Matches	5	0
Tour Matches	6	0
Combination League	1	0
London Challenge Cup	1	0
Total	**37**	**1**

Honours:
(WITH WOLVES)
4 England Caps
2 Football League Caps
FA Cup Winners Medal	1959-60
Division One Championship Medals	1957-58, 1958 - 59

(WITH STOKE)
Division Two Championship Medal	1962-63

(WITH ARSENAL)
London FA Challenge Cup Winners	1961-62

CLAPTON, Dennis   1957-61

Birth Place: Hackney, London
Date of Birth: 12th October 1939

Signed for Arsenal as an amateur in August 1957 and became a professional in August 1958. Was a consistent member of Arsenal's first successful youth team either playing on the wing or at centre forward. Made his league debut versus Burnley, 19th March 1960. Could never hold down a regular place and was finally given a free transfer to Northampton in August 1961.

	Games	Goals
League	4	0
Friendly Matches	21	13
Combination League	54	16
London Challenge Cup	4	1

CLAPTON, Danny   1953-62

Birth Place: Stepney, London
Date of Birth: 22nd July 1934

Danny Clapton was an amateur with Leytonstone when he joined Arsenal in August 1953. He was a regular in Arsenal's Eastern Counties League and Football Combination sides, before making his league debut versus Chelsea on Christmas Day 1954, in February 1955 he won a regular position on the Arsenal right wing, taking over from Arthur Milton. Over the following two seasons, 1955 - 56, 1956 - 57 he missed only six of Arsenal's eighty four league matches. He was not as consistent in 1957 - 58 but in 1958 - 59 he helped Arsenal to their highest league position (third) for twelve seasons, playing in thirty nine league games as well as winning his solitary England Cap versus Wales in November 1958. In 1959 - 60 season he had to be content with sharing the right wing berth with the newly signed Jackie Henderson. In 1960 - 61 his place was still not secure, sharing it again with Henderson and Alan Skirton. He lost his place in the side all together after the signing of Johnny MacLeod during the summer of 1961. A career which had looked so promising had petered out shortly after his twenty eighth birthday.

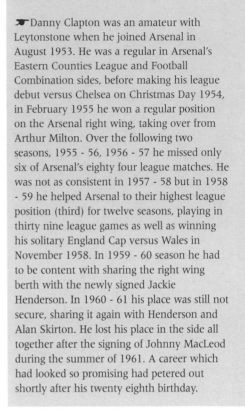

Southern Floodlight Cup	1	0
London Midweek League	1	1
Metropolitan League	44	37
Metropolitan Cup	7	2
South East Counties League	16	8
Youth Cup	9	10
Other Youth Cups	5	4
Total	**166**	**92**

Dennis Clapton

Honours:
Metropolitan League Champions	1958-59
Metropolitan League Cup Winners	1960-61
Metropolitan League Professional Cup winners	1960-61
Southern Floodlight Cup runners up	1957-58
2 England Youth Caps	1958

Transferred to Luton for £6,000 in September 1962. Later played in Australia for Corinthians of Sydney before returning to England in 1970. His younger brother Denis also played league football with Arsenal. Died in tragic circumstances June 1986, aged 51 years.

	Games	Goals
League	207	25
FA Cup	18	2
Friendly Matches	45	5
Tour Matches	21	6
Combination League	51	12
Combination Cup	12	3
London Challenge Cup	4	0
Southern Floodlight Cup	8	3
Eastern Counties League	30	6
Eastern Counties Cup	1	0
London Midweek League	10	5
Metropolitan League	8	2
Metropolitan Cup	2	1
Total	**417**	**70**

Honours:
1 England Cap
1 Football League Cap
Southern Floodlight Challenge Cup
  winners   1958-59
Eastern Counties League Champions 1954-55
Metropolitan League Cup Winners   1960-61
Metropolitan League Professional Cup
  winners   1960-61

Danny Clapton

CLARKE, Colin   1963-65

Birth Place: Penilee, Scotland
Date of Birth: 4th April 1946

☛ Signed for Arsenal from Glasgow junior club Arthurlie in October 1963. Spent two seasons as youth team wing-half before being given a free transfer to Oxford United in July 1965. Spent thirteen years at Oxford where he made nearly five hundred first team appearances. Later played for Plymouth and Los Angeles, USA.

	Games	Goals
Friendly Matches	9	5
Combination League	13	3
Metropolitan League	34	2
Metropolitan Cup	7	0
South East Counties League	2	0
Youth Cup	3	1
Other Youth Cups	4	2
Youth Tour Matches	10	1
Total	**82**	**14**

Honours:
South East Counties League Cup
  Winners Medal   1963-64

CLARKE, Freddie   1960-65

Birth Place: Kilpike, County Down, Northern Ireland
Date of Birth: 4th November 1941

☛ Freddie Clarke signed for Arsenal from the Irish club Glenavon for £5,000 in November 1960. He was a consistent member of Arsenal's reserve side during the early part of the 1960's when he was left back understudy to Billy McCullough. He played in twenty six league games for Arsenal, including his league debut versus Aston Villa 31st March 1962. Although a Northern Ireland amateur, Inter League and Under 23 International, his days at Highbury were numbered with the breakthrough of a young and up and coming Peter Storey. He rejoined Glenavon on a free transfer in November 1965.

	Games	Goals
League	26	0
FA Cup	2	0
Friendly Matches	22	0
Combination League	103	1
London Challenge Cup	8	0
Metropolitan League	22	1
Metropolitan Cup	9	0
Youth Tour Matches	3	0
Total	**195**	**2**

Honours:
4 Irish Under 23 Caps
Irish Inter-League and Amateur
  International Caps
Football Combination Cup winners   1962-63
London FA Challenge Cup winners   1962-63
  runners up   1960-61
Metropolitan League Professional Cup
  winners   1960-61
Metropolitan League Cup winners   1960-61
Sheriff of London Shield winners   1964-65

Freddie Clarke

CLAYTON, Ronnie   1958

Birth Place: Hull, Yorkshire
Date of Birth: 18th January 1937

☛ Signed for Arsenal with Freddie Jones from Hereford in January 1958. Played two first team friendlies but never made the league side. Transferred eight months later to Brighton.

	Games	Goals
Friendly Matches	3	3
Combination League	11	1
London Midweek League	1	1
Metropolitan League	2	1
Total	**17**	**6**

CLELLAND, Dave   1946-48

Birth Place: Larkhall, Lanarkshire, Scotland
Date of Birth: 18th March 1924

☛ Signed for Arsenal in August 1946. Was a regular in Arsenal's reserve team before his transfer to Brighton in January 1948. Later played for Crystal Palace and Scunthorpe.

	Games	Goals
Friendly Matches	2	1
Combination League	24	13
Combination Cup	3	1
London Challenge Cup	2	0
Youth Tour Matches	9	2
Total	**40**	**17**

Honours:
Football Combination Championship
   Medal   1946-47

CLOSE, Brian   1950-52

Birth Place: Rawden, Yorkshire
Date of Birth: 24th February 1931

☛ Transferred to Arsenal in August 1950 from Leeds United. His promising career in football never really materialised due to his commitments on the cricket scene. Spent only two years at Highbury before being transferred to Bradford City in October 1952. Retired from football the following year at the tender age of twenty two to pursue a long and illustrious cricket career, playing over forty tests for England.

	Games	Goals
Friendly Matches	2	1
Combination League	5	2
Combination Cup	3	1
Eastern Counties League	19	11
Eastern Counties Cup	1	0
London Midweek League	6	2
Total	**36**	**17**

Honours:
2 England Youth Caps

Brian Close being shown the ropes.

COAKLEY, Tommy 1966-67

Birth Place: Bellshill, Lanarkshire
Date of Birth: 2nd May 1947

☛ Tommy Coakley joined Arsenal on a free transfer from Motherwell in May 1966, making his league debut versus Aston Villa on the 27th August 1966. During his eighteen months at Highbury he could never command a regular place in the first team, playing in only thirteen first team games. Was granted a free transfer in December 1967, when he went to America to play for Detroit Cougars. Returned to play for Morton and later played for Chelmsford City. Managed non league Bishops Stortford and later Walsall 1986 - 88.

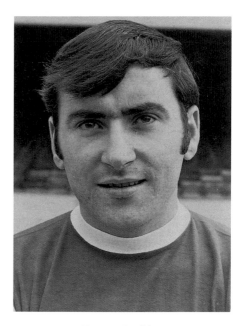

Tommy Coakley

	Games	Goals
League	9	1
League Cup	4	1
Friendly Matches	15	2
Tour Matches	6	1
Combination League	33	7
Combination Cup	8	3
London Challenge Cup	1	0
Metropolitan Cup	2	1
Total	**78**	**16**

COE, Norman 1957-60

Birth Place: Pentrewyth, Wales
Date of Birth: 6th December 1940

☛ Joined Arsenal's ground staff in July 1957 and turned professional in August 1958. Was Arsenal's regular youth team goalkeeper for two seasons before being released on a free transfer to Northamptom in July 1960.

	Games	Goals
Friendly Matches	6	0
Combination League	2	0
Southern Floodlight Cup	1	0
London Midweek League	5	0
Metropolitan League	15	0
South East Counties League	27	0
Youth Cup	19	0
Other Youth Cups	13	0
Youth Tour Matches	3	0
Total	**91**	**0**

Norman Coe

Honours:
Metropolitan League Championship
   Medal   1958-59
Southern Junior Floodlight Cup
   Winners Medal   1958-59
Southern Junior Floodlight Cup
   Finalists Medal   1957-58

COMMON, Bob   1951-54

Birth Place: Northumberland
Date of Birth: November 1933

☛ Signed as a professional in May 1951 but soon after was called up for two years national service. He never really established himself and it was no surprise when he was given a free transfer to Hartlepool in June 1954.

	Games	Goals
Friendly Matches	3	0
Eastern Counties League	16	0
Eastern Counties Cup	2	0
London Midweek League	22	0
Total	**43**	**0**

Honours:
London Midweek League Championship
   Medal   1952-53

COOK, Reuben   1951-56

Birth Place: Gateshead, Durham
Date of Birth: 9th March 1933

☛ A wing half, joined Arsenal in November 1951 from Tow Law. His career was hindered by two years national service. Played regularly in Arsenal's third team of that period before being transferred to Leyton Orient in January 1956.

Reuben Cook

	Games	Goals
Friendly Matches	5	0
Combination League	18	1
Combination Cup	7	0
Eastern Counties League	63	2
Eastern Counties Cup	8	0
London Midweek League	7	1
Total	**108**	**4**

Honours:
Eastern Counties League Championship
   Medal   1954-55
East Anglian Cup Finalists Medal   1951-52

CORR, Johnny   1965-67

Birth Place: Glasgow
Date of Birth: 18th December 1946

☛ Signed for Arsenal from Possilpark YMCA in July 1965. An outside right who served the youth team well for two seasons before being given a free transfer to Exeter City in July 1967.

	Games	Goals
Friendly Matches	5	0
Combination League	20	5
Combination Cup	2	1
London Challenge Cup	3	1
Metropolitan League	42	19
Metropolitan Cup	7	2
Youth Tour Matches	7	1
Total	**86**	**29**

Honours:
London FA Challenge Cup Finalists
   Medal   1965-66
Metropolitan League Challenge Cup
   Winners Medal   1965-66

COURT, David   1959-70

Birth Place: Mitcham, Surrey
Date of Birth: 1st March 1944

☛ David Court joined Arsenal's ground staff as an amateur in April 1959, soon after his fifteenth birthday. He became an apprentice in July 1960, turning professional in January 1962. He started his career as a prolific scoring inside/centre forward in the club's youth and metropolitan league sides. Later progressing to the reserve team before making his league debut versus Aston Villa, 10th September 1962. He played six league games in that initial season, followed in 1963 - 64 with just another eight appearances. In 1964 - 65 his career took a turn for the better when the late Billy Wright switched him in a league match versus Everton to an orthodox wing half position. He became a regular, playing in thirty three league games. Such was David Court's versatility that by the end of the 1965 - 66 season he found himself as Arsenal's regular right back. Over the next three seasons he played for Arsenal in every position bar goalkeeper, including helping the club to the 1969 League Cup Final versus Swindon Town. However, in July 1970 the club he had supported and worshipped since a boy decided to accept Luton Town's £30,000 offer. Finished his career with Brentford 1972 - 73.

COX, Eric   1951-58

Birth Place: Kent
Date of Birth: September 1935

☛ Joined ground staff as an amateur in February 1951 and turned professional in September 1952. Was a regular third team full back in his seven years at Highbury, never once getting the chance to play in the first team. Granted a free transfer in March 1958.

	Games	Goals
Friendly Matches	16	0
Combination League	9	0
Combination Cup	8	0
London Challenge Cup	1	0
Eastern Counties League	44	1
Eastern Counties Cup	12	0
London Midweek Challenge	43	1
Total	**133**	**2**

Honours:
London Midweek League
   Championship Medal   1952-53
East Anglian Cup Finalists
   Medal   1951-52

	Games	Goals
League	175	17
FA Cup	10	0
League Cup	11	1
UEFA Cup	8	0
Friendly Matches	60	15
Tour Matches	29	7
Combination League	90	42
Combination Cup	13	2
London Challenge Cup	8	4
Metropolitan League	46	30
Metropolitan Cup	15	7
South East Counties League	35	22
Youth Cup	15	10
Other Youth Cups	15	4
Youth Tour Matches	21	1
Total	**551**	**172**

Honours:
Football League Cup
  runners up   1968-69
Football Combination
  Champions   1969-70
London FA Challenge Cup
  Winners   1962-63
Metropolitan League Champions   1960-61
Metropolitan League Professional
  Cup Winners   1961-62
South East Counties League Cup
  Winners   1959-60, 1960-61, 1961-62

David Court

COX, Freddie   1949-53

Birth Place: Reading, Berkshire
Date of Birth: 1st November 1920

Freddie Cox signed professional forms for Tottenham in 1938, just prior to the outbreak of the second world war. During those war years, 1939 - 45, he served his country in the RAF as a flight lieutenant. After the war he continued with Tottenham for three seasons before being allowed to make the short journey to Highbury in September 1949, for £12,000, making his league debut versus West Bromwich, 7th September 1949. He was a regular in the league side that season, playing in thirty two league matches. Freddie Cox then decided to write his name in the Arsenal record books, possibly for all time, when in March 1950, in the semi final of the FA Cup versus Chelsea, he scored the first goal in the first game in a two all draw and he scored the only goal in the replay at White Hart Lane, thus helping Arsenal to the FA Cup Final versus Liverpool. Not content with that feat, virtually two years later in April 1952, again in the semi final versus Chelsea at White Hart Lane scored Arsenal's only goal in a one all draw. In the replay, two days later, at the same ground, he scored twice in Arsenal's three nil victory. Arsenal then met Newcastle United in the Final. In 1952 - 53 he managed to play in only nine league games due to the meteoric rise of Arthur Milton. Transferred to West Brom in July 1953 on a free transfer where he later became player coach. He had become a qualified coach which enabled him to move in to management, with Bournemouth 1956, Portsmouth 1958, Gillingham 1962 and again with Bournemouth 1965. Died in August 1973 aged 52.

	Games	Goals
League	79	9
FA Cup	15	7
Friendly Matches	10	1
Tour Matches	8	0
Combination League	30	8
Combination Cup	17	5
London Challenge Cup	4	0
London Midweek League	1	0
Total	**164**	**30**

Honours:
FA Cup Winners Medal   1949-50
FA Cup Finalist Medal   1951-52
Football Combination Cup
  Winners   1952-53

Freddie Cox

CROPLEY, Alex — 1974-76

Birth Place: Aldershot, Hampshire
Date of Birth: 16th January 1951

➤ Alex Cropley started his footballing career with Hibernian in July 1968. He spent six and a half years at Easter Road playing in over one hundred league matches as well as helping the club to the 1974 Scottish League Cup Final. He was already a Scottish International when he joined Arsenal for £150,000 in December 1974. The winning of these Scottish honours was only possible because his father was a Scotsman. His brief twenty month spell at Highbury was littered with niggling and serious injuries which included, in 1974 - 75, a broken leg which was first diagnosed a day after playing at Middlesbrough. Unfortunately, within a few weeks of his comeback, he broke a leg again. Alex had made his Arsenal league debut versus Carlisle 7th December 1974. In his short period of time at the club, he only played, due to these injuries only thirty league games, but even so, had become a Highbury favourite with his tough tackling and his never say die attitude. He was transferred to Aston Villa for £125,000 in September 1976, where he spent four seasons helping them to win the League Cup in 1977. However, in December 1977 he broke a leg for a third time in a match against West Brom at Villa Park. This subsequently (although later playing for Toronto Blizzards in Canada and Portsmouth) finished his career at the age of thirty.

Alex Cropley

	Games	Goals
League	30	5
FA Cup	2	0
League Cup	2	1
Friendly Matches	4	1

Tour Matches	11	2
Combination League	15	1
Total	**64**	**10**

Honours:
Two Scottish Caps
Four Under 23 Caps
(WITH HIBERNIAN)
Scottish League Cup Finalist Medal 1973-74
(WITH ASTON VILLA)
Football League Cup Winners Medal 1976-77

CROUCH, Bobby — 1953-57

Birth Place: Sussex
Date of Birth: July 1935

➤ Signed for Sheppey United in August 1953 as a centre forward, later being converted to a wing half. During his time at Arsenal he also spent two years in the armed forces. Given a free transfer in May 1957.

	Games	Goals
Friendly Matches	9	3
Combination League	7	0
London Challenge Cup	2	0
Eastern Counties League	19	2
Eastern Counties Cup	6	0
London Midweek Challenge	29	6
Total	**72**	**11**

Honours:
Eastern Counties League Championship
   Medal   1954-55

CRUSE, Pat — 1972-73

Birth Place: Camden, London
Date of Birth: 10th January 1951

➤ Joined Arsenal from Slough Town in April 1972, along with John Ritchie. Was a regular in Arsenal's reserve team of 1972 - 73 but was never given a chance in the first team. Was subsequently given a free transfer to Luton Town in July 1973. Later played for Shrewsbury on Loan.

	Games	Goals
Friendly Matches	7	2
Combination League	38	8
London Challenge Cup	1	0
Total	**46**	**10**

Honours:
5 England Amateur Caps

CUMMING, Gordon — 1964-69

Birth Place: Renfrew, Scotland
Date of Birth: 23rd January 1948

➤ Came to Highbury for trials in 1964 and joined Arsenal as a professional in January 1965 from Glasgow United. Was a regular in Arsenal's youth team during seasons 1965 - 66 and 1966 - 67. In the seasons 1967 - 68 and 1968 - 69 was in the reserve team as a goalscoring inside forward. Was transferred to Reading in December 1969, where he played over 300 first team games.

Gordon Cumming

	Games	Goals
Friendly Matches	27	14
Combination League	74	37
Combination Cup	22	4
London Challenge Cup	7	2
Metropolitan League	53	35
Metropolitan Cup	9	3
South East Counties League	13	2
Youth Cup	9	7
Other Youth Cups	11	9
Youth Tour Matches	9	2
Total	**234**	**115**

Honours:
FA Youth Cup Winners
   Medal   1965-66
Football Combination
   Championship Medal   1968-69, 1969-70
Football Combination Cup
   Winners Medal   1968-69
Metropolitan League Challenge
   Cup Winners Medal   1965-66
South East Counties League
   Cup Finalists Medal   1965-66
Southern Junior Floodlight Cup
   Winners Medal   1965-66
London Minor Challenge Cup
   Finalists Medal   1964-65

D
1945-1985

DANIEL, Ray 1946-53

Birth Place: Swansea
Date of Birth: 2nd November 1928

☛Ray Daniel was an amateur with Swansea when he signed for Arsenal in October 1946, just before his eighteenth birthday. Called up for national service in January 1947, before making his league debut versus Charlton on the 7th May 1949. His first five seasons at Highbury were spent as reserve centre half to Leslie Compton before making the position his own in season 1951 - 52. Daniel won the first of his twenty one caps for Wales during the 1950 - 51 season versus England while still an Arsenal reserve. Was a regular again in the Arsenal team during 1952 - 53, missing only one match during Arsenal's Championship season. Was transferred to Sunderland in June 1953 for a record £30,000. Daniel spent four seasons at Roker Park before finishing his career with Cardiff and then Swansea. Later managed Hereford Town. His elder brother Bobby played for Arsenal but was killed in the second world war.

Ray Daniel

	Games	Goals
League	87	5
FA Cup	12	0
Friendly Matches	14	2
Tour Matches	15	0
Combination League	50	0
Combination Cup	26	0
London Challenge Cup	5	0
Eastern Counties League	15	1
Eastern Counties Cup	1	0
London Midweek League	1	0
Other Youth Matches	14	1
Total	**240**	**9**

Honours:
21 Welsh Caps
FA Cup Finalist Medal 1951-52
League Championship Medal 1952-53
Football Combination Championship
   Medal 1950-51

DAVIDSON, Roger 1964-69

Birth Place: Islington, London
Date of Birth: 27th October 1948

☛Roger Davidson signed for Arsenal as an apprentice in July 1964. Turned professional in October 1965, a day after his seventeenth birthday. Davidson was a regular member of the successful Arsenal youth team of that period, 1964 - 66. Was a valuable member of the reserve team for two seasons 1967 - 69, during which time he played his only league game for Arsenal as substitute versus Wolves at Highbury on the 16th March 1968. Transferred to Portsmouth in June 1969 on a free transfer. He later played for Fulham, Lincoln and Aldershot.

Roger Davidson

	Games	Goals
League	1	0
Friendly Matches	30	17
Combination League	48	6
Combination Cup	20	3
London Challenge Cup	1	0
Metropolitan League	54	25
Metropolitan Cup	5	3
South East Counties League	27	9
Youth Cup	11	6
Other Youth Cups	13	7
Youth Tour Matches	15	4
Total	**225**	**80**

Honours:
Football Combination Cup winners 1967-68
Football Combination champions 1968-69
South East Counties League
   Champions 1964-65
South East Counties League Cup Finalist
   Medal 1965-66

DAVIES, Edmund 1948-50

Birth Place: Oswestry, Shropshire
Date of Birth: 5th June 1927

☛Edmund Davies joined Arsenal from Liverpool in August 1948 as a promising young centre forward, where he played as an amateur. Spent two seasons at Highbury as the Eastern Counties League side centre forward. His potential was never fulfilled and he was given a free transfer in April 1950 when he joined QPR. Later played for Crewe Alexandra.

	Games	Goals
Combination League	11	2
Combination Cup	1	0
Eastern Counties League	34	16
Eastern Counties Cup	1	0
London Midweek League	6	1
Other Youth Matches	11	4
Total	**64**	**23**

DAVIES, Paul 1969-72

Birth Place: St. Asaph, Flint
Date of Birth: 10th October 1952

☛Paul Davies joined Arsenal as an apprentice in January 1969, being already a Welsh schoolboy international, turning professional in October of the same year. In his first two seasons was a valuable goalscoring asset to Arsenal's youth team, helping them win the FA Youth Cup in 1970 - 71. Became a regular in the reserve team the previous year. Played in seventy two out of Arsenal's eighty four reserve games between 1970 - 72, this form gaining him his league debut versus Newcastle on the 9th October 1971. With no chance of maintaining a regular first team place Paul was transferred to Charlton for £8,000 in August 1972. His elder brother Ron was a prolific scoring Welsh international centre forward.

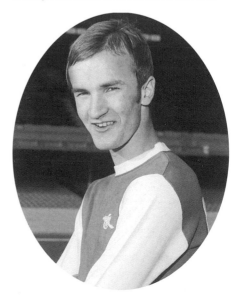

Paul Davies

	Games	Goals
League	1	0
European Cup	1	0
Friendly Matches	38	18
Combination League	90	27
Combination Cup	7	1
London Challenge Cup	9	2
Metropolitan League	12	5
Metropolitan Cup	1	0
South East Counties League	9	2
Youth Cup	10	5
Other Youth Cups	7	2
Youth Tour Matches	10	5
Total	**195**	**67**

Honours:

Football Combination champions	1969-70
FA Youth Cup winners	1970-71
South East Counties League Cup winners	1970-71
5 Wales Youth Caps	1971-72

DAVIES, Peter 1957-59

Birth Place: Llanelli
Date of Birth: 8th March 1936

☛ Peter Davies joined Arsenal from his home town club, Llanelli in November 1957, immediately winning a regular place in the reserve side. Due to injuries and loss of form, he lost his reserve team place the following season and played regularly in the third team. Was transferred to Swansea in March 1959 where he was a regular for five seasons. Later joined Brighton

	Games	Goals
Friendly Matches	3	0
Combination League	27	1
London Challenge Cup	3	0
Metropolitan League	20	0
Metropolitan Cup	1	0
Total	54	1

Honours:

London FA Challenge Cup Winners Medal	1957-58
Metropolitan League Championship Medal	1958-59

DAVIS, Len 1949-54

Birth Place: Cork, Eire
Date of Birth: 31st July 1931

☛ Len Davis joined Arsenal as a professional in November 1949, after a three month trial. Served two years in HM services before returning to Highbury. During his five seasons at Arsenal he was the third team's leading scorer in 1950 - 51 and 1951 - 52 and was a regular in that side for four seasons, playing the odd reserve game in between. Granted a free transfer in February 1954 when he joined Walsall.

	Games	Goals
Friendly Matches	9	15
Combination League	10	3
Combination Cup	2	1
Eastern Counties League	78	55
Eastern Counties Cup	11	8
London Midweek League	36	25
Other Youth Matches	5	2
Total	**151**	**109**

Honours:
East Anglian Cup Finalists Medal   1951-52

DE GARIS, Jim 1968-71

Birth Place: Worcester
Date of Birth: 9th October 1952

☛ Jim De Garis joined Arsenal as an apprentice straight from school in April 1968. Turned professional in October 1969 after winning himself a place in Arsenal's Metropolitan side. The year 1970 - 71 was his finest season, being a member of Arsenal's Youth Cup and South East Counties League Cup winning side as well as being in the Combination Cup Final winning side against West Ham. However, his form lacked consistency and he was allowed to leave Highbury in September 1971, on a free transfer to Bournemouth. Later played for Torquay. Returned to Highbury in December 1983 as youth coach.

Jim De Garis

	Games	Goals
Friendly Matches	21	6
Combination League	47	3
Combination Cup	10	0
London Challenge Cup	4	1
Metropolitan League	31	3
Metropolitan Cup	8	1
South East Counties League	10	0
Youth Cup	13	1
Other Youth Cups	7	1
Youth Tour Matches	24	1
Total	**175**	**17**

Honours:

Football Combination Championship Medal	1969-70
Football Combination Cup Winners Medal	1969-70
FA Youth Cup Winners Medal	1970-71
South East Counties League Cup Winners Medal	1970-71
Southern Junior Floodlight Cup Finalists Medal	1967-68

DELANEY, Louis 1939-49

Birth Place: Uddington, Lanarkshire
Date of Birth: 28th February 1921

☛ Louis Delaney joined Arsenal as an amateur full back in June 1939 from the Scottish junior side Nunhead. Gained good experience during the war when he toured South East Asia with the services side. On his return to Highbury after the war he was a consistent member of the reserve side for three seasons, but never made the league side. Was given a free transfer to Crystal Palace in November 1949

Louis Delaney

	Games	Goals
Friendly Matches	2	0
Combination League	48	0
Combination Cup	15	0
London Challenge Cup	2	0
Eastern Counties League	1	0
London Midweek League	2	0
Other Youth Matches	11	1
Wartime	2	0
Total	**83**	**1**

Honours:
Football Combination Championship
    Medal   1946-47

DEVINE, John   1974-83

Birth Place: Dublin
Date of Birth: 11th November 1958

John Devine joined Arsenal in November 1974 as an apprentice, being already an Eire schoolboy international full back. Almost immediately won a regular place in Arsenal's reserve side. In fact, he spent seven of his ten seasons at Highbury as a member of the reserve side. Turned professional in October 1976 after winning Eire Youth honours and five full caps. Was a fine understudy to Pat Rice and Sammy Nelson, and it was not until they left the club that Devine won himself a regular place in the side during 1980 - 81. A season after he helped Arsenal to the FA Cup Final versus West Ham. However, he lost his place to John Hollins the following season, resulting in Arsenal surprisingly giving him a free transfer to Norwich in June 1983. Later played for Stoke City and for Bengal in India.

John Devine

	Games	Goals
League	89	0
FA Cup	6	0
League Cup	8	0
Cup Winners Cup	5	0
UEFA Cup	3	0
Friendly Matches	38	5
Tour Matches	13	1
Combination League	165	8
South East Counties League	38	5
Youth Cup	12	0
Other Youth Cups	9	0
Youth Tour Matches	11	0
Total	**397**	**19**

Honours:
FA Cup Finalist Medal   1979-80
12 Eire Caps
2 Eire Under 21 Caps
5 Eire Youth Caps.

DICKSON, Bill   1953-56

Birth Place: Lurgan, Northern Ireland
Date of Birth: 15th April 1923

Bill Dickson started his league career with Notts County before being transferred to Chelsea in the deal which took Tommy Lawton to Meadow Lane in November 1947. Stayed at Chelsea for six years, playing in over one hundred league games for them as well as winning nine caps for Northern Ireland. Was transferred to Arsenal in October 1953 for £15,000. Unfortunately, his three year stay at Highbury was littered with injuries, including a dislocated shoulder, appendicitis, a poisoned knee and torn ligaments. These injuries restricted him to only twenty nine league games in those three years. Added three more Northern Ireland caps to his total whilst at Highbury before being transferred to Mansfield in July 1956.

Bill Dickson

	Games	Goals
League	29	1
FA Cup	2	0
Friendly Matches	6	0
Tour Matches	2	0
Combination League	16	0
London Challenge Cup	1	0
Eastern Counties League	1	0
Total	57	1

Honours:
12 Northern Ireland Caps

DICKSON, Gordon   1963-64

Birth Place: Sidcup, Kent
Date of Birth: January 1945

Gordon Dickson was a Metropolitan police cadet, and it was while playing for the police that Arsenal spotted him and signed him as a professional in March 1963. However, he spent only one full season at Highbury, mainly playing in the Metropolitan

League, before being given a free transfer in May 1964.

	Games	Goals
Friendly Matches	2	0
Metropolitan League	19	14
Metropolitan Cup	1	0
South East Counties League	2	0
Total	**24**	**14**

DIXON, Bob   1957-58

Birth Place: Felling, County Durham
Date of Birth: 11th January 1936

Bob Dixon joined Arsenal from the famous amateur side Crook Town, in August 1957 as a tricky winger. Spent fifteen months at Highbury where he played only a handful of reserve team games. Given a free transfer in November 1958, when he joined the now defunct league side, Workington Town. Later played for West Bromwich.

	Games	Goals
Friendly Matches	9	7
Combination League	7	0
London Midweek League	8	4
Metropolitan League	8	3
Metropolitan Cup	1	0
Total	**33**	**14**

DIXON, Ken   1954-57

Birth Place: Hackney, London
Date of Birth: January 1937

Ken Dixon joined Arsenal as a professional in March 1954. As a schoolboy played for Islington and London schools. Spent only one full season playing for Arsenal's youth team before being called up for national service in November 1954. Was demobbed in November 1956, but was released on a free transfer at the end of the 1956 - 57 season.

	Games	Goals
Combination League	2	0
Eastern Counties League	6	0
London Midweek League	9	3
South East Counties League	14	9
Total	**31**	**12**

DIXON, Wilf   1965-69

Birth Place: Wood Green, London
Date of Birth: 2nd February 1950

Wilf Dixon joined Arsenal as an associated schoolboy during the summer of 1965. He signed as an apprentice the following year before being offered professional terms in May 1968. Spent four years at Highbury as a sturdy full back in the youth teams and the Metropolitan side. Was granted a free transfer in July 1969, when he joined Reading. Wilf Dixon spent the next twelve seasons in the lower leagues playing in over four hundred league matches for Reading, Swindon and Aldershot.

	Games	Goals
Friendly Matches	12	6
Combination League	9	1
Combination Cup	2	0
Metropolitan League	45	3
Metropolitan Cup	10	4
South East Counties League	37	6
Youth Cup	4	1
Other Youth Cups	8	0
Youth Tour Matches	19	3
Total	**146**	**24**

Honours:
Football Combination Cup Winners
  Medal   1967-68
Southern Junior Floodlight Cup Finalists
  Medal   1967-68
London Youth Challenge Cup Winners
  Medal   1966-67

DOCHERTY, Tommy   1958-61

Birth Place: Glasgow
Date of Birth: 24th August 1928

Tommy Docherty joined Celtic after being demobbed from the army in July 1948. Was only considered a reserve whilst at Celtic, which caused him to leave in November 1949 to join Preston. Whilst at Deepdale, enjoyed remarkable consistency missing only eleven league games in seven seasons, apart from season 1953 - 54 when he missed a third of the season due to a broken ankle. He won a Second Division Championship Medal in 1950 - 51 and an FA Cup Finalists Medal in 1953 - 54 as well as nineteen caps for Scotland. Joined Arsenal in August 1958 for £30,000. Played in thirty eight league matches in his first season, but unfortunately broke a leg when playing against Preston in October 1959. While at Highbury won a further six Scottish caps. Played in twenty one league games in season 1960 - 61 before being appointed player/coach at Chelsea in April 1961. Managed Chelsea for five years (1962 - 67) before going on a managing merry - go - round the like of which football had never seen before. Rotherham (1967), QPR (1968), Aston Villa (1969 - 70), Porto of Portugal (1971), Hull City assistant manager (1971 - 72), Scottish team manager (1972 - 74), Manchester United (1973 - 77), Derby County (1977 - 79), QPR (1979), Sydney Australia (1980 - 81), Preston (1981 - 82). Melbourne Australia (1982 - 83), Wolves (1984 - 85). His son Michael has also played for and managed league clubs. Tommy is a BBC radio personality on Five Live, and an accomplished aftre dinner speaker.

	Games	Goals
League	83	4
FA Cup	7	0
Friendly Matches	19	2
Tour Matches	9	0
Combination League	3	0
London Challenge Cup	1	0
Southern Floodlight Cup	4	1
Total	**126**	**7**

Honours:
(WITH PRESTON & ARSENAL)
Second Division Championship
  Medal   1950-51
FA Cup Finalist Medal   1953-54
25 Scottish Caps
Southern Floodlight Challenge Cup Winners
  Medal   1958-59

Tommy Docherty

DODGIN, Bill   1952-61

Birth Place: Wardley, County Durham
Date of Birth: 4th November 1931

Bill Dodgin started his league career with Fulham in September 1949. He had to wait two years until he made his league debut during season 1951 - 52. However, after thirty five league games for Fulham, was transferred to Arsenal in December 1952 for £8,000 plus Fulham receiving Arsenal's reserve full back Bill Healey. Played well in Arsenal's reserve team for the rest of the season and also made his league debut versus Bolton in April 1953. With the departure of Ray Daniel to Sunderland in June 1953, Dodgin made the centre half spot his own the following season. He missed only three league matches and won an England under - 23 cap versus Italy in January 1954. However, his form deserted him and he had to be content to share the centre half spot with Jim Fotheringham during seasons 1954 - 55 and 1955 - 56. Dodgin won back his first team place the following season 1956 - 57 and was the regular centre half for three seasons before being given a free transfer back to Fulham in March 1961. After his playing days were over, he coached and scouted for several teams as well as managing QPR, Fulham, Northampton and Brentford. His father Bill Dodgin senior also managed several clubs, including Brentford, Bristol Rovers and Fulham.

Bill Dodgin

	Games	Goals
League	191	0
FA Cup	16	1
Charity Shield	1	0
Friendly Matches	43	0
Tour Matches	11	0
Combination League	91	0
Combination Cup	23	0
London Challenge Cup	10	0
Southern Floodlight Cup	8	0
Eastern Counties League	1	0
Metropolitan League	1	1
Total	**396**	**2**

Honours:
1 England Under - 23 Cap
FA Charity Shield Winners Medal   1953-54
Southern Floodlight Challenge Cup
  Winners Medal   1958-59
London FA Challenge Cup Winners
  Medal   1954-55
London FA Challenge Cup Finalists
  Medal   1960-61
Football Combination Cup Winners
  Medal   1952-53

DODSON, David   1955-59

Birth Place: Gravesend, Kent
Date of Birth: 20th January 1940

Dave Dodson joined Arsenal's ground staff in May 1955. A winger, he played for Kent schools as well as being an England schoolboy trialist. Turned professional in November 1957 and was a member of Arsenal's successful youth team in 1956 - 57, scoring thirty two goals for them as well as winning six England youth caps in the same season. Scored thirty eight goals in youth football in season 1957 - 58 and forty four goals the following season before, surprisingly, being given a free transfer in July 1959 when he joined Swansea Town. Later played for Portsmouth and Aldershot.

	Games	Goals
Friendly Matches	9	10
Combination League	18	6
London Challenge Cup	3	1
Eastern Counties League	2	1
London Midweek League	12	4
Metropolitan League	23	31
Metropolitan Cup	1	0
South East Counties League	47	38
Youth Cup	15	14
Other Youth Cups	16	12
Youth Tour Matches	10	4
Total	**156**	**121**

Honours:
6 England Youth Caps
Metropolitan League Championship
    Medal   1958-59
South East Counties League Championship
    Medal   1955-56
Southern Junior Floodlight Cup Finalists
    Medal   1957-58

DONALDSON, Dave   1970-73

Birth Place: Islington, London
Date of Birth: 12th November 19954

Dave Donaldson signed for Arsenal as an apprentice in May 1970 after playing for Islington and England schoolboys. He played in over fifty youth team matches during 1970 - 71, helping Arsenal win the South East Counties League as well as the FA Youth Cup. During the following season he won two England youth caps as well as a place in Arsenal's reserve side. However, did not make the improvement which at first looked inevitable and was transferred to Millwall in June 1973 for £5,000. Donaldson spent seven seasons at Millwall before joining Cambridge United in February 1980. His son David joined Arsenal, as a trainee in the summer of 1995.

	Games	Goals
Friendly Matches	22	0
Combination League	73	1
London Challenge Cup	2	0

South East Counties League	30	1
Youth Cup	18	1
Other Youth Cups	16	1
Youth Tour Matches	20	0
Total	**181**	**4**

Honours:
2 England Youth Caps
FA Youth Cup Winners Medal   1970-71
South East Counties League Cup Winners
    Medal   1970-71
South East Counties League Cup Finalists
    Medal   1971-72

DOOLER, George   1954-58

Birth Place: North Tidworth, Hampshire
Date of Birth: 1937

George Dooler joined Arsenal as a young amateur full back in May 1954, Turning professional in August of the same year. Spent a full season as a regular in Arsenal's youth team 1954 - 55, before being called up for national service in November 1957. Was granted a free transfer soon after.

	Games	Goals
Friendly Matches	13	0
Eastern Counties League	1	0
London Midweek League	17	0
South East Counties League	28	0
Total	**59**	**0**

DOUGHTY, Eric   1951-58

Birth Place: Radstock, Somerset
Date of Birth: 9th April 1932

Eric Doughty played for Somerset Youth before joining Arsenal as a promising wing half from Radstock in May 1951. He spent one full season at Highbury before commencing his national service in 1952. On his release he immediately won a regular place in Arsenal's reserve team during season 1953 - 54, but over the following four seasons interchanged between reserve and Eastern Counties football. Served Arsenal well for seven seasons before being given a free transfer in July 1958, when he joined Plymouth.

	Games	Goals
Friendly Matches	15	1
Combination League	115	0
Combination Cup	16	0
London Challenge Cup	11	0
Eastern Counties League	55	1
Eastern Counties Cup	4	0
London Midweek League	25	0
Total	**241**	**2**

Honours:
London FA Challenge Cup Winners
    Medal   1954-55
Eastern Counties League Championship
    Medal   1954-55

DOVE, Henry   1950-58

Birth Place: Stepney, London
Date of Birth: 11th March 1932

Henry Dove was an apprentice Thames Lighterman when signing for Arsenal in August 1950 as a part time professional. Signed full professional terms two years later. Dove, like so many other players during that period, was quite happy spending his time at Arsenal playing in the third team and reserve side. A wonderfully loyal centre half who after eight years at Highbury, without ever playing in the first team, was granted a free transfer in April 1958 when he joined Millwall. His brother Terry, also played for Arsenal.

Henry Dove

	Games	Goals
Friendly Matches	16	0
Combination League	44	0
Combination Cup	5	0
London Challenge Cup	9	0
Eastern Counties League	104	0
Eastern Counties Cup	16	0
London Midweek League	84	0
Total	**278**	**0**

Honours:
Eastern Counties League Championship
    Medal   1954-55
East Anglian Cup Finalists Medal 1951-52

DOVE, Terry   1951-57

Birth Place: Bow, London
Date of Birth: July 1934

Terry Dove was a promising young goalkeeper when signing for Arsenal as an amateur in July 1951, having played for South East Essex schools as a schoolboy. He turned professional in June 1954, although in November 1954 was called up for his two years national service. Was demobbed in

November 1956 when he spent a short spell as the Eastern Counties keeper for Arsenal. Was released on a free transfer in August 1957.

	Games	Goals
Friendly Matches	5	0
Combination League	4	0
Combination Cup	1	0
London Challenge Cup	1	0
Eastern Counties League	13	0
Eastern Counties Cup	2	0
London Midweek League	17	0
Total	**43**	**0**

DRUMMY, Dermot   1976-80

Birth Place: Hackney, London
Date of Birth: 16th January 1961

☛ Dermot Drummy joined Arsenal as an apprentice during the summer of 1976. Was a regular in Arsenal's youth team as a promising wing half during seasons 1976 - 77 and 1977 - 78. During the latter season also won four Irish youth caps, before winning a regular place in Arsenal's reserve side during 1978 - 79. Turned professional in January 1979. He was an automatic choice for the reserves during 1979 - 80 before being loaned to Blackpool in March 1980. On his return to Highbury was given a free transfer in May 1980, when he linked up with Hendon. Over the next ten seasons he played for a number of non league clubs including Enfield, Chesham, Finchley, St Albans, Boreham Wood and Wealdstone.

	Games	Goals
Friendly Matches	7	0
Combination League	63	7
South East Counties League	47	2
Youth Cup	11	0
Other Youth Cups	4	0
Total	**132**	**9**

Honours:
4 Irish Youth Caps

DUFFY, Bill   1948-50

Birth Place: Ireland

☛ Bill Duffy was another of Arsenal's many Irishmen who played for them over the years. Served the Gunners well for two seasons as a goalscoring inside forward. Released on a free transfer in May 1950.

	Games	Goals
Combination League	12	6
Combination Cup	2	0
London Challenge Cup	2	3
Eastern Counties League	24	12
London Midweek League	6	3
Other Youth Matches	10	12
Total	**56**	**36**

Bill Duffy

DUFFY, Bobby   1974-77

Birth Place: Dublin
Date of Birth: 1958

☛ Bobby Duffy joined Arsenal straight from school as an apprentice during the summer of 1974. He was already an Irish schoolboy international when joining Arsenal and later added an Eire youth international cap to his honours during the season of 1975 - 76. Unfortunately injuries plagued his career while at Highbury and was released in June 1977.

	Games	Goals
Friendly Matches	3	0
Combination League	3	0
South East Counties League	28	8
Youth Cup	1	2
Other Youth Cups	5	1
Youth Tour Matches	6	2
Total	**46**	**13**

Honours:
1 Eire Youth Cap

DUNKLEY, George   1948-54

Birth Place: Ipswich, Suffolk
Date of Birth: 1926

☛ George Dunkley signed for Arsenal as a cover goalkeeper in May 1948. Played originally for Millwall (1943 - 47). Served Arsenal well for six seasons, playing regularly in the reserve and Eastern Counties teams. Released on a free transfer in June 1954.

	Games	Goals
Friendly Matches	7	0
Combination League	21	0
Combination Cup	32	0
London Challenge Cup	6	0
Eastern Counties League	85	0
Eastern Counties Cup	16	0
London Midweek League	20	0
Other Youth Matches	26	0
Total	**213**	**0**

George Dunkley

Honours:
East Anglian Cup Finalists Medal   1951-52

EASTHAM, George   1960-66

Birth Place: Blackpool, Lancashire
Date of Birth: 23rd September 1936

George Eastham

☛ George Eastham was one of the finest midfield players Arsenal have had since World War II. Eastham was signed from the Irish club Ards by Newcastle, for £8,000 in May 1956. Was a regular at St James's Park for four seasons, gaining Football League honours as well as winning six England under - 23 caps in 1959 - 60. Eastham refused to sign a new contract during the summer of 1960, causing one of the longest

and prolonged transfers in the history of the game. Finally, in October 1960, he signed for Arsenal who paid a new club record fee of £47,500. Made his debut versus Bolton in November 1960 and scored twice. He won the first of his nineteen England caps during season 1962 - 63, and was a member of England's World Cup squads in both 1962 and 1966. During his stay with Arsenal, he was a great inspiration to the club, and captained them for three seasons. However, after Arsenal's worst season (1965 - 66) for many years he could not agree new terms, and was transferred to Stoke City in August 1966 for £30,000. He spent eight seasons at Stoke, helping them win their first major honour, the League Cup in 1971 - 72. Finally retired in May 1974. He later coached and managed Stoke City. Eastham's father, George senior and his uncle Henry, also played league football. Awarded the OBE in 1973. Now lives in South Africa.

	Games	Goals
League	207	41
FA Cup	13	0
UEFA Cup	3	0
Friendly Matches	31	20
Tour Matches	9	6
Combination League	11	8
London Challenge Cup	6	3
Total	**280**	**78**

Honours:
19 England Caps
3 Football League Caps
6 England Under - 23 Caps
League Cup Winners Medal   1971-72
London FA Challenge Cup Winners
  Medal   1961-62
  Runners - up   1960-61
PFA special Merit Award.

*George Eastham leading
the Gunners out*

EDINGTON, John　　1943-48

Birth Place:　Wealdstone, Middlesex
Date of Birth:　November 1925

🎯 John Edington signed for Arsenal as an amateur in September 1943, turning professional on Christmas Eve 1943. Played in the reserve team as full back, serving the club well for two seasons 1946 - 48, before being released in the summer of 1948.

John Edington

	Games	Goals
Friendly Matches	2	0
Combination League	18	2
Combination Cup	8	0
Other Youth Matches	27	4
Wartime	8	0
Total	**63**	**6**

Honours:
Football Combination Championship
　Medal　　　　　　　　　　　1946-47

EVANS, Chris　　1979-81

Birth Place:　Rhondda, Wales
Date of Birth:　13th October 1962

🎯 Chris Evans joined Arsenal as an apprentice in May 1979, turning professional in June 1980. Played regularly at full back in Arsenal's South East Counties team for two seasons before being given a free transfer in May 1981 when he joined Stoke City. Later played for York City.

	Games	Goals
Friendly Matches	3	0
Combination League	12	0
South East Counties League	53	5
Youth Cup	5	0
Other Youth Cups	10	0
Youth Tour Matches	1	0
Total	**84**	**5**

Honours:
South East Counties League Cup Winners
　Medal　　　　　　　　　　　1979-80
Presidents Cup Winners Medal　1979-80

EVANS, Dennis　　1951-63

Birth Place:　Ellesmere Port, Cheshire
Date of Birth:　18th May 1930

🎯 Dennis Evans joined Arsenal from his home town club, Ellesmere Port, in January 1951. Graduated from Arsenal's Eastern Counties side to the reserve side during 1952 - 53 followed by his full league debut versus Huddersfield on the 22nd August 1953, playing ten games that season. His progress continued the following season (1954 - 55) when he played twenty three league games at left back. During the next three seasons (1955 - 58) was virtually a permanent fixture in Arsenal's side, although he did lose his place for ten matches to Len Wills at the end of the 1957 - 58 season. However, he regained his place the following season before breaking a leg playing against Wolves in August 1959, and played only half a dozen league games that season. Dennis Evans showed great courage in trying to resume his career at the top level and although he stayed at Highbury for a further three years, assisting the reserve and junior teams, never played for the first team again up to his retirement in May 1963. Dennis Evans will be remembered as probably scoring the most bizarre own goal ever recorded. Playing against Blackpool at Highbury in December 1955, with only a couple of minutes left and Arsenal leading four nil, Evans had possession of the ball when a spectator blew a whistle in the crowd. Dennis, thinking play was over, hammered the ball back past a bemused Con Sullivan in the Arsenal goal!

	Games	Goals
League	189	10
FA Cup	18	2
Friendly Matches	49	2
Tour Matches	15	0
Combination League	78	5
Combination Cup	28	0
London Challenge Cup	13	1
Southern Floodlight Cup	6	1
Eastern Counties League	36	6
Eastern Counties Cup	4	0
London Midweek League	25	1
Metropolitan League	27	11
Metropolitan Cup	1	0
Total	**489**	**39**

Honours:
Football Combination Cup
　Winners　　　　　　　　　　1952-53
London FA Challenge Cup
　Winners　　　　1953-54, 1957-58
Metropolitan League
　Champions　　　　　　　　　1962-63
East Anglian Cup
　Runners-Up　　　　　　　　　1951-52

Dennis Evans

EVERITT, Mick 1956-61

Birth Place: Weeley, Essex
Date of Birth: 16th January 1941

☛ Mick Everitt joined Arsenal's ground staff during the summer of 1956, turning professional in February 1958. Was a regular member of Arsenal's first ever successful youth side of 1956 - 57 as a left winger, before converting to a wing half for the third team and reserve side. Everitt finally made his league debut versus Fulham on the 15th April 1960, playing in the last five league games of that season. He could not regain his place the following season and was subsequently transferred to Northampton Town in February 1961. He helped them rise from the Fourth Division to the First within four years. Served Northampton well for six years before being transferred to Plymouth in March 1967. Finished his career with Brighton the following year. Later managed Wimbledon and Brentford.

Mick Everitt

	Games	Goals
League	9	1
Friendly Matches	21	19
Combination League	36	9
London Challenge Cup	2	0
London Midweek League	9	3
Metropolitan League	42	14
Metropolitan Cup	6	7
South East Counties League	45	15
Youth Cup	20	5
Other Youth Cups	16	3
Youth Tour Matches	4	0
Total	**210**	**76**

Honours:

Metropolitan League	
Champions	1958-59
Southern Junior Floodlight Cup	
runners - up	1957-58

FARQUHAR, Doug 1944-50

Birth Place: Methil, Scotland
Date of Birth: 11th June 1921

☛ Doug Farquhar joined Arsenal from St Andrews Athletic in April 1944. During the war he guested for the Irish side Distillery. However, after the war, he served the Arsenal reserve side well for four seasons, originally as a centre forward, then as a wing half. Was granted a free transfer in September 1950 when he joined Reading.

Doug Farquhar

	Games	Goals
Friendly Matches	3	0
Combination League	62	4
Combination Cup	34	2
London Challenge Cup	1	0
Eastern Counties League	19	0
Eastern Counties Cup	2	0
London Midweek League	3	0
Other Youth Matches	24	6
Wartime	48	15
Total	**196**	**27**

Honours:

Football Combination Championship	
Medal	1946-47

FERRY, Gordon 1960-65

Birth Place: Sunderland
Date of Birth: 22nd December 1943

☛ Gordon Ferry joined Arsenal as an apprentice in July 1960 after playing for Sunderland schoolboys. He became a full time professional in January 1961, during which time he became the regular centre half in Arsenal's successful youth side of that period. He graduated from Arsenal's Youth and Metropolitan teams to become a regular in the reserve side during 1962 - 63 and 1963 - 64, this consistent form earning

1945-1985

him his league debut versus Sheffield Wednesday on 2nd September 1964. He played in eleven consecutive league matches before being dropped after a 4 - 0 defeat at Sheffield United in October 1964. Gordon Ferry spent the rest of that season in the reserve side before being transferred to Leyton Orient for £5,000 in May 1965. Gordon later played in USA and for Barnet.

Gordon Ferry

	Games	Goals
League	11	0
Friendly Matches	27	1
Combination League	70	0
London Challenge Cup	5	0
Metropolitan League	60	0
Metropolitan Cup	18	0
South East Counties League	22	0
Youth Cup	11	0
Other Youth Cups	8	0
Youth Tour Matches	17	0
Total	**249**	**1**

Honours:

London FA Challenge Cup	
Winners	1962-63
Sheriff of London Shield	
Winners	1964-65
Metropolitan League	
Champions	1962-63
Metropolitan League Cup	
Winners	1960-61
Metropolitan League Professional	
Cup Winners	1961-62
South East Counties League	
Cup Winners	1960-61

FLANAGAN, Denzil — 1955

Denzil Flanagan was an amateur international inside forward with Walthamstow Avenue when Arsenal invited him to Highbury for trials in August 1955. Unfortunately the gap between First Fivision and amateur football was too great and within two months was released to return to amateur circles.

	Games	Goals
Friendly Matches	2	1
Combination League	5	1

Denzil Flanagan

Total	7	2

Honours:
3 England Amateur Caps

FORBES, Alex — 1948-56

Birth Place: Dundee
Date of Birth: 21st January 1925

Ale Forbes was a Scottish hockey international who started his football career with Dundee North End during the war. Signed for Sheffield United in 1944 and was a regular member of their side during the first two seasons after the war, his consistency winning him the first of his fourteen Scottish caps. Was transfer - listed by Sheffield United after he had been side - lined by an appendix operation in February 1948. It was his great friend, Archie Macaulay, the Arsenal wing half, who persuaded Forbes to join Arsenal in February 1948 for £15,000. Ironically, it was Forbes who later kept Macaulay out of the 1949 - 50 FA Cup Final side. Ale Forbes made his Arsenal league debut versus Wolves on 6th March 1948 scoring in a 5 - 2 victory. He was the regular wing half in Arsenal's first team during the following seven seasons, in which time he played nearly three hundred first team games. However, after a cartilage operation kept him out of the side during the 1955 - 56 season, he transferred to Leyton Orient in August 1956. He spent a season with Orient before finishing his career with Fulham. Later returned to Highbury in the early Sixties to coach the reserve and junior teams. Later coached and managed in South Africa.

Alec Forbes

	Games	Goals
League	217	20
FA Cup	22	0
Charity Shield	1	0
Friendly Matches	35	3
Tour Matches	25	5
Combination League	21	4
Combination Cup	1	0
London Challenge Cup	4	0
Total	**326**	**32**

Honours:
14 Scottish Caps
League Championship
   Medals   1947-48, 1952-53
FA Cup Winners Medal   1949-50
FA Cup Finalist Medal   1951-52
FA Charity Shield Winners Medal   1953-54

FOSTER, Tony — 1965-66

Birth Place: Dublin
Date of Birth: 13th February 1949

Tony Foster joined Arsenal as an apprentice during 1965, turning professional soon after his seventeenth birthday in February 1966. But with a strong nucleus of young wing halves on their books, Arsenal released him on a free transfer in September 1966 when he joined Oldham.

	Games	Goals
South East Counties League	7	0
Total	**7**	**0**

FOTHERINGHAM, Jim — 1949-59

Birth Place: Hamilton, Scotland
Date of Birth: 19th December 1933

Jim Fotheringham played for Northamptonshire schoolboys before going to Highbury for trials in October 1949. Later joined the Arsenal ground staff before turning professional in March 1951. Served two years in HM Forces 1951 - 53. Gained a regular place in Arsenal's reserve side during 1953 - 54. Was drafted in to Arsenal's league side for his debut versus Bolton on the 6th November 1954 and kept his place during that season, playing in twenty seven league matches. He played in twenty five league matches the following season 1955 - 56, when he shared the centre half position with Bill Dodgin. During season 1956 - 57 he lost his place to Dodgin and played reserve team football for the whole of that season. During 1957 - 58 he re-discovered his form and played in nineteen league matches, being regarded as a possible for Scotland's 1958 World Cup squad. Figured in only one league match during 1958 - 59 and was subsequently transferred to Hearts in April 1959. Finished his playing career with Northampton in 1960, who were managed by his former Arsenal teamate, Dave Bowen. Died in September 1977 at the age of forty three.

Jim Fotheringham

	Games	Goals
League	72	0
FA Cup	4	0
Friendly Matches	27	0
Tour Matches	4	0
Combination League	123	1
Combination Cup	29	0
London Challenge Cup	15	0
Southern Floodlight Cup	3	0
Eastern Counties League	31	0
Eastern Counties Cup	4	0
London Midweek League	7	0
Metropolitan League	3	0
Total	**322**	**1**

1945-1985

1945-1985

Honours:
London FA Challenge Cup Winners 1953-54

FREEMAN, Neil   1972-74

Birth Place: Northampton
Date of Birth: 16th February 1955

➤ Neil Freeman played for Northamptonshire schoolboys prior to joining the Army after leaving school in 1971. Was recommended to Arsenal by Ted Drake whilst playing for the army side at Arbofield and joined the Gunners in June 1972. Freeman spent nearly two years at Highbury playing for the youth and reserve teams before being granted a free transfer in March 1974 when he joined Grimsby Town. Later played for Southend, Birmingham, Walsall, Huddersfield, Peterborough and Northampton before retiring from league football in 1983 to join the police force.

	Games	Goals
Friendly Matches	13	0
Combination League	11	0
South East Counties League	10	0
Youth Cup	2	0
Other Youth Cups	3	0
Total	**39**	**0**

FURNELL, Jim   1963-68

Birth Place: Clitheroe, Lancashire
Date of Birth: 23rd November 1937

➤ Jim Furnell signed for Burnley soon after his seventeenth birthday in November 1954. Due to the consistency of first Colin McDonald then Adam Blacklaw, Furnell's chances at Turf Moor were restricted to just two league matches in eight seasons before being transferred to Liverpool in February 1962. His term at Anfield was of just over eighteen months in which time he helped Liverpool to the Second Division Championship. Was transferred to Arsenal for £15,000 in November 1963, making his league debut the following day, versus Blackpool. Over the next five seasons Furnell was Arsenal's regular goalkeeper, being ever present in season 1966 - 67. A tragic goalkeeping error by Furnell versus Birmingham at Highbury in March 1968 caused him to lose his first team place, and after spending the rest of that season in Arsenal's reserve team, was transferred to Rotherham in September 1968, for £8,000. He spent two years at Millmoor before being transferred to Plymouth in December 1970. Served Plymouth well for a further five seasons before retiring in 1976, twenty two years after starting his career. Later coached Plymouth.

	Games	Goals
League	141	0
FA cup	13	0

Jim Furnell

	Games	Goals
League Cup	12	0
UEFA Cup	1	0
Friendly Matches	23	0
Tour Matches	19	0
Combination League	32	0
Combination Cup	7	0
Metropolitan League	1	0
Metropolitan Cup	1	0
Total	**250**	**0**

Honours:
League Cup Finalist Medal   1967-68
Football Combination Cup Winners   1967-68

GARRETT, Len   1954-58

Birth Place: Hackney, London
Date of Birth: 14th May 1936

➤ Len Garrett joined Arsenal as an amateur in February 1954, turning professional in May of the same year. Before joining Arsenal had represented London youth, England amateur boys club as well as winning three England youth caps. His career was hindered, however, when he was called up for national service in September 1954. After his return served Arsenal's Eastern Counties team well before being released on a free transfer to Ipswich in May 1958.

	Games	Goals
Friendly Matches	10	0
Combination League	4	0
Eastern Counties League	12	0
Eastern Counties Cup	4	0
London Midweek League	18	0
Total	**48**	**0**

Honours:
3 England Youth Caps
Eastern Counties League Championship
  Medal   1954-55

GATTING, Steve   1975-81

Birth Place: Park Royal, London
Date of Birth: 29th May 1959

➤ Steve Gatting represented Brent district schools and Middlesex boys before joining Arsenal as an apprentice in July 1975. Almost immediately gained a regular place in Arsenal's youth team of that period. He turned professional in February 1977, by which time he had won himself a regular place in Arsenal's reserve team. He made his Arsenal league debut versus Southampton on 21st October 1978. He consolidated his position for the rest of that season. During the next two seasons he was a valuable member of Arsenal's first team squad which reached three consecutive F.A. cup finals. However, due to the signing of Brian Talbot, his first team appearances at Highbury were restricted, resulting in Gatting being transferred to Brighton in September 1981 for £180,000. His elder brother Mike Gatting plays cricket for Middlesex and England. Later played for Charlton.

Steve Gatting

	Games	Goals
League	58	5
FA Cup	10	1
League Cup	4	0
European Cup Winners Cup	4	0
Friendly Matches	36	4
Tour Matches	4	0
Combination League	146	19
South East Counties League	35	2
Youth Cup	8	0
Other Youth Cups	8	0
Youth Tour Matches	8	0
Total	**321**	**31**

Honours:
(WITH BRIGHTON)
FA Cup Finalist Medal   1982-83

GEORGE, Charlie   1966-75

Birth Place: Islington, London.
Date of Birth: 10th October 1950

Charlie George will always be remembered as the long haired, twenty year old youth who scored Arsenal's winning goal in the 1971 Cup Final, taking the double to Highbury. Charlie George represented Islington schoolboys before joining Arsenal as an apprentice in May 1966. Even at that early age, Arsenal realised they had discovered a potentially great goalscoring talent. By the time he turned professional in February 1968, he was already a regular in Arsenal's reserve team. He eventually made his league debut in August 1969 on the opening day of the season, against West Bromwich. In his first season in the league side, he helped Arsenal win their first major honour for seventeen years when they won the Inter Cities Fairs Cup. However, in the opening game of the following season, George sustained a broken ankle versus Everton at Goodison Park, resulting in him missing the first five months of the season. After recovering, Charlie was a vital member of Arsenal's great double winning side. During the next four seasons, he only managed to play on average half of Arsenal's first team matches due to injuries, loss of form and disciplinary reasons. By this time Charlie George became disillusioned with the team he had supported as a boy, and after another disciplinary disagreement with manager Bertie Mee, was placed on the transfer list at the bargain price of £100,000. Eventually, in July 1975, he was transferred to Derby County. He spent three and a half seasons at the Baseball Ground before being transferred to Southampton in December 1978. After two seasons there, which included a loan period at Nottingham Forest, Charlie George went to the USA and Hong Kong, before coming home to try his luck with Dundee United, Bournemouth and Coventry. Is now curator of the Arsenal Museum at Highbury.

	Games	Goals
League	133	31
FA Cup	22	11
League Cup	8	2
European Cup	8	1
UEFA Cup	8	4
Friendly Matches	49	44
Tour Matches	17	13
Combination League	77	52
Combination Cup	14	8
London Challenge Cup	3	2
Metropolitan League	19	10
Metropolitan Cup	7	2
South East Counties League	21	12
Youth Cup	5	2
Other Youth Cups	7	5
Youth Tour Matches	12	7
Total	**410**	**206**

A triumphant Charlie George holding the FA Cup with Frank McLintock.

Charlie George

Honours:

(WITH ARSENAL)
5 England Under 23 Caps
League Championship Medal   1970-71
FA Cup Winners Medal   1970-71
FA Cup Finalists Medal   1971-72
Inter Cities Fairs Cup Winners
    Medal   1969-70
Football Combination
Champions   1968-69
Football Combination Cup
    Winners Medals   1967-68, 1969-70
London FA Challenge Cup
Winners   1969-70
Southern Junior Floodlight Cup
    Runners - up   1967-68

(WITH DERBY)
1 England Cap

(WITH NOTTINGHAM FOREST)
European Super Cup Winners
    Medal   1978-79

GERBALDI, Mark   1981-83

Birth Place: London
Date of Birth: 1965

☛Mark Gerbaldi joined Arsenal straight from school in April 1981, turning professional in September 1982. During his two seasons at Highbury he served the South East Counties team well, before being granted a free transfer in May 1983. Later played for Charlton and Dartford.

	Games	Goals
Friendly Matches	3	4
Combination League	16	4
South East Counties League	51	11
Youth Cup	4	2
Other Youth Cups	8	2
Youth Tour Matches	2	0
Total	**84**	**23**

GILLIBRAND, Ian   1964-1967

Birth Place: Blackburn, Lancashire
Date of Birth: 24th November 1948

☛Ian Gillibrand joined Arsenal as an apprentice in April 1964, turning professional as an up - and - coming wing half in December 1965. In his four seasons at Highbury was a regular member of Arsenal's youth and metropolitan teams. He was granted a free transfer in December 1967 when he joined Wigan Athletic, who were then in the Northern Premier Division. Was still a Wigan player ten years later when the Lancastrians obtained league status.

Ian Gillibrand

	Games	Goals
Friendly Matches	22	6
Combination League	17	0
Combination Cup	7	0
London Challenge Cup	1	0
Metropolitan League	34	7
Metropolitan Cup	4	0
South East Counties League	53	2

Youth Cup	11	1
Other Youth Cups	16	1
Youth Tour Matches	13	1
Total	**178**	**18**

Honours:
FA Youth Cup Winners Medal   1965-66
South East Counties League Championship
  Medal   1964 -65
Southern Junior Floodlight Cup Winners
  Medal   1965-66
South East Counties League Cup Finalists
  Medal   1965-66
London Youth Challenge Cup Winners
  Medal   1966-67

GOODCHILD, Gary   1974-76

Birth Place: Chelmsford, Essex
Date of Birth: 27th January 1958

☛Gary Goodchild joined Arsenal as an apprentice in May 1974, after representing Chelmsford and England schoolboys. He turned professional in January 1975. In his two seasons at Highbury, was Frank Stapleton's goalscoring partner in the Arsenal youth team, but was surprisingly granted a free transfer during the summer of 1976 when he joined Hereford United. Later played for Reading, Crystal Palace and Sheffield Wednesday.

	Games	Goals
Friendly Matches	19	7
Combination League	36	7
South East Counties League	31	14
Youth Cup	7	6
Other Youth Cups	10	5
Youth Tour Matches	12	3
Total	**115**	**42**

GORING, Peter   1948-60

Birth Place: Bishops Cleve, Gloucestershire
Date of Birth: 2nd January 1927

☛Peter Goring joined Arsenal from Cheltenham Town in January 1948. He came to the fore during Arsenal's Brazilian tour of 1948, settling down to reserve team football during 1948 - 49 before making his league debut versus Chelsea, in August 1949. In his first season in the league side, incredibly finished as the club's leading league goalscorer, with twenty - one goals in twenty - nine games as well as winning an FA Cup winner's medal versus Liverpool. Although he kept his place as centre forward in the Arsenal first team the following season, in 1951 - 52 he lost his place to Cliff Holton. He scored ten goals the following season when helping the club to the League Championship, but during 1953 - 54 he lost form altogether, resulting in him playing only nine league matches. It was during this

period that Peter Goring was about to start on the second half of his career as a constructive wing half; and it was in this position that during seasons 1954 - 55 and 1955 - 56 he missed only six league matches. During 1955 the FA picked him for their side to tour the West Indies. In his final four seasons at Highbury (1956 - 59) he figured in only twenty - five league matches, being quite happy to help Arsenal's young reserve team of that period, later played for Boston. Died December 1994, aged 67.

Peter Goring

	Games	Goals
League	220	51
FA Cup	20	2
Friendly Matches	50	15
Tour Matches	18	9
Combination League	117	20
Combination Cup	28	11
London Challenge Cup	6	0
Southern Floodlight Cup	4	0
Eastern Counties League	3	9
Eastern Counties Cup	1	0
London Midweek League	2	0
Metropolitan League	11	1
Other Youth Matches	13	3
Total	**493**	**121**

Honours:
League Championship Medal   1952-53
F A Cup Winners Medal   1949-50
Football Combination Cup Runners Up
  Medal   1950-51

GORMAN, Paul   1979-84

Birth Place: Dublin
Date of Birth: 6th August 1963

☛Paul Gorman joined Arsenal as an apprentice during the summer of 1979. In his first full season with the club he was a consistent member of the youth side, before turning professional in September 1981. During the three seasons (1980 - 83), he was a regular of the reserve side, playing in well over one hundred Combination League matches. He did break into the league side for four matches during the 1981 - 82 season, which included his debut versus Manchester City at Maine Road in March 1982, but he had to wait nearly twenty months for his next opportunity in league football, when he came on as substitute at Ipswich in November 1983. Was granted a free transfer in May 1984 when he joined Birmingham City. Later played for Carlisle, Shrewsbury and Carlisle again.

Paul Gorman

	Games	Goals
League	6	0
Friendly Matches	47	7
Combination League	139	10
South East Counties League	38	15
Youth Cup	8	1
Other Youth Cups	18	4
Youth Tour Matches	3	0
Total	**259**	**37**

Honours:
21 Eire Youth Cap
1 Eire Under 21 Cap
Football Combination
  Champions   1983-84
South East Counties League
  Cup winners   1979-80
President's Cup winners   1980-81

GOULD, Barry   1960-64

Birth Place: Ammanford, South Wales
Date of Birth: 18th January 1944

Barry Gould joined Arsenal's ground staff during January 1960, after representing

Slough schoolboys. He was offered apprenticeship terms in July 1960, later turning professional in November 1961. During his five seasons at Highbury he was a regular, first in the youth side as a free scoring inside forward and later in the Metropolitan team as a wing half. Was granted a free transfer in February 1964 when he joined Chelsea. He stayed eighteen months at Stamford Bridge without getting a first team chance and was subsequently transferred to Peterborough in July 1965.

Barry Gould

	Games	Goals
Friendly Matches	16	6
Combination League	32	11
London Challenge Cup	3	1
Metropolitan League	66	33
Metropolitan Cup	19	8
South East Counties League	36	11
Youth Cup	10	15
Other Youth Cups	11	10
Youth Tour Matches	15	5
Total	**208**	**100**

Honours:
Football Combination Championship
  Medal   1962-63
Metropolitan League Championship
  Medals   1960-61, 1962-63
Metropolitan League Professional Cup
  Winners Medals   1960-61, 1961-62
Metropolitan League Cup Winners
  Medal   1960-61
South East Counties League Cup Winners
  Medals   1959-60, 1960-61, 1961-52

GOULD, Bobby   1968-70

Birth Place: Coventry, Warwickshire
Date of Birth: 12th June 1946

Bobby Gould had already made his league debut for Coventry as a sixteen year old apprentice when he turned professional in June 1964. He spent four seasons at Highfield Road, playing in eighty league games and scoring forty goals, being their leading goalscorer during their promotion season of 1966 - 67. Arsenal signed him in February 1968 for a record fee of £90,000. He played in fifteen league matches during the rest of that season, although he had to miss Arsenal's League Cup Final versus Leeds due to being cup tied. During the next two seasons was in and out of Arsenal's first team, playing in only a further fifty league matches before being transferred to Wolves in June 1970. He later played for West Brom 1971 - 72, Bristol City 1972 - 73, West Ham 1973 - 75, Wolves 1975 - 77, Bristol Rovers 1977 - 78, Hereford 1978 - 79, Wimbledon 1979 - 80, Aldershot 1980, before going on to coach Chelsea and manage Bristol Rovers 1981 - 83 and Coventry 1983 - 84. Bristol Rovers again 1985 - 87, Wimbledon 1987 - 90, WBA 1991 and later assistant manager and manager at Coventry. Appointed Welsh National Team Manager July, 1995.

Bobby Gould

	Games	Goals
League	65	16
FA Cup	7	3
League Cup	9	3
UEFA Cup	2	1
Friendly Matches	4	7
Tour Matches	12	5
Combination League	15	16
Combination Cup	9	16
London Challenge Cup	1	2
Total	**124**	**69**

Honours:
League Cup Finalists Medal   1968-69
Combination Champions   1969-70
London FA Challenge Cup winners 1969-70

GOULDEN, Roy   1953-61

Birth Place: Ilford, Essex
Date of Birth: 22nd September 1937

☛ Roy Goulden joined Arsenal as an amateur in May 1953. Turned professional in September 1954. Before joining Arsenal had represented Ilford, London and England schoolboys. Roy Goulden was a member of Arsenal's first successful youth team during the mid 1950's. However, during his eight years at Highbury, which included two years national service 1956 - 58, he never fulfilled his true potential, playing in only one league match versus Leeds in November 1959. Was granted a free transfer in May 1961 when he joined Southend. His father Len Goulden played for West Ham, Chelsea and England.

Roy Goulden

	Games	Goals
League	1	0
Friendly Matches	34	19
Combination League	85	22
London Challenge Cup	7	3
Southern Floodlight Cup	1	0
Eastern Counties League	5	0
Eastern Counties Cup	5	0
London Midweek League	29	7
Metropolitan League	28	11
Metropolitan Cup	7	0
South East Counties League	38	36
Youth Cup	5	2
Other Youth Cups	2	3
Youth Tour Matches	5	2
Total	**252**	**105**

Honours:
Metropolitan League Champions   1960-61
Metropolitan League Cup Winners   1960-61
Metropolitan League Professional Cup
   Winners   1960-61
South East Counties Champions   1955-56
South East Counties League Cup
   Winners   1955-56

GOY, Peter   1954-60

Birth Place: Beverley, Yorkshire
Date of Birth: 8th June 1938

☛ Peter Goy joined Arsenal's goundstaff in March 1954 after representing Lincolnshire at football, cricket and athletics. He turned professional in June 1955, having already established himself as Arsenal's first choice youth goalkeeper during seasons 1954 - 55 and 1955 - 56. Unfortunately, as his career was blossoming, he was called up for National Service in April 1956. On resumption of his football career, spent three seasons as third choice goalkeeper, although he did play in two league matches due to injuries to Kelsey and Standen in season 1958 - 59. Left Highbury on a free transfer in October 1960 when he joined Southend. Later played for Watford and Huddersfield, later played in South Africa.

Peter Goy

	Games	Goals
League	2	0
Friendly Matches	25	0
Combination League	45	0
London Challenge Cup	2	0
Eastern Counties Cup	2	0
London Midweek League	21	0
Metropolitan League	42	0
Metropolitan Cup	5	0
South East Counties League	47	0
Youth Cup	6	0
Other Youth Cups	4	0
Youth Tour Matches	5	0
Total	**206**	**0**

Honours:
Metropolitan League Champions   1958-59
South East Counties League Champions
   and League Cup Winners   1955-56

GRAHAM, George   1966-72

Birth Place: Bargeddie, Scotland
Date of Birth: 30th November 1944

☛ George Graham was a Scottish Schoolboy and Youth International when he signed for Aston Villa in December 1961. He spent three seasons at Villa Park, playing in only eight league matches, although he did appear for Villa in the 1962 - 63 League Cup Final versus Birmingham. Tommy Docherty signed George for Chelsea in July 1964 for a bargain £8,000 and he repaid them by scoring thirty five league goals in seventy two games during his two year spell at the club. Arsenal, having sold Joe Baker to Nottingham Forest in March 1966, required a top class centre forward and in Graham they knew they had their man, so in October 1966 Graham joined Arsenal in a deal worth £75,000 with Tommy Baldwin going in the opposite direction, being valued at £25,000. During his first two seasons at Highbury, he was Arsenal's leading goalscorer, and helped Arsenal to League Cup Finals in 1967 - 68 and 1968 - 69. During this period, Arsenal's backroom boys realised that George Graham's skills were being wasted as a centre forward, so John Radford switched to orthodox centre forward, with Graham switching to a deeper position at inside forward. This turned out to be a master stroke; not only did Arsenal win the Fairs Cup in 1969 - 70 but also the Double, the following season. Graham won the first of his twelve Scottish caps in 1971 - 72 as well as helping Arsenal reach Wembley again the same season. Unfortunately, after the arrival of Alan Ball midway through the 1971 - 72 season, Graham's position in the Arsenal team was not certain. In December 1972 he was transferred to Manchester United for £120,000. He spent two years at Old Trafford before finishing his career with Portsmouth and Crystal Palace. Later coached Crystal Palace and QPR and was appointed manager of Millwall in December 1982. He instantly saved them from relegation to the Fourth Division that season and guided the club to a Football League trophy win in 1983, followed by promotion to the Second Division 1985. Later Millwall attained First Division status for the first time. A success which George Graham had founded. After Arsenal's interest in Terry Venables as a successor to Don Howe, wained, George Graham was appointed Manager of Arsenal in May 1986. In his first season back at the club 1986 - 87 he guided Arsenal to a memorable Littlewood's Cup Final victory versus Liverpool. In 1987 - 88 George with Arsenal were back at Wembley in the same final this time disappointingly losing to Luton. In 1988 - 89 he achieved his greatest success, with Arsenal winning the League Championship in the last minute of the final game against fellow title contenders

Liverpool. Arsenal repeating this feat with the Championship title win in 1990 - 91 and in1992 - 93, George steered Arsenal to becoming the first team ever to win the FA Cup and League Cup double. Even greater success was to follow in 1993 - 94 with Arsenal, against all odds, winning the European Cup Winners Cup versus Parma. George Graham had written himself in to the record books as the first person to play for, and manage European cup winning sides. Departed company with his beloved Arsenal in February 1995 after speculation of transfer irregularities. George Graham had created a Highbury dynasty which had not been seen at the club since the days of Herbert Chapman, what a crying shame that it had to end in such circumstances.

	Games	Goals
League	227	59
FA Cup	27	2
League Cup	29	9
European Cup	6	1
UEFA Cup	19	6
Friendly Matches	17	4
Tour Matches	23	1
Combination League	11	4
Combination Cup	3	1
London Challenge	1	0
Total	**363**	**87**

Honours:

AS A PLAYER
(WITH ASTON VILLA)
League Cup Finalist Medal	1962-63
4 Scottish Youth Caps	

(WITH CHELSEA)
League Cup Winners Medal	1964-65
2 Scottish Under - 23 Caps	

(WITH ARSENAL)
8 Scottish Caps	
League Championship Medal	1970-71
FA Cup Winners Medal	1970-71
League Cup Finalist Medal	1967-68, 1968-69
Inter Cities Fairs Cup Winners Medal	1969-70
FA Cup Finalist Medal	1971-72

(WITH MANCHESTER UNITED)
4 Scottish Caps	
2nd Division Championship Medal	1974-75

Honours:

AS MANAGER OF ARSENAL
League Champions	1988-89, 1990-91
FA Cup Winners	1992-93
League Cup Winners	1986-87, 1992-93
League Cup Finalists	1987-88
European Cup Winners Cup Winners	1993-94
European Super Cup Finalist	1995
Manager Of The Year	1988-89, 1990-91

George Graham

George Graham in action for the Gunners

GRANT, Cyril   1946-47

Birth Place: Wath, Yorkshire
Date of Birth: 10th July 1920

☛ Cyril Grant started his football league career with Lincoln during the war. He was transferred to Arsenal in 1946 as a possible replacement at centre forward for Ted Drake. Spent only five months at Highbury, playing in two league matches before being transferred to Fulham in January 1947. (In the Ronnie Rooke deal). Later served Southend well for several seasons.

	Games	Goals
League	2	0
Friendly Matches	2	3
Combination League	9	6
Combination Cup	5	2
Total	**18**	**11**

GRAY, Jimmy   1946-51

Birth Place: Southampton, Hampshire
Date of Birth: 19th May 1926

☛ Jimmy Gray signed for Arsenal as an amateur from Salisbury in August 1946, turning professional a year later. Was a regular member of Arsenal's youth and reserve teams as a full back during his stay at the club. Around this time he was establishing himself as a cricketer with Hampshire, and it came as no great surprise when he retired from football to concentrate on his cricketing career in 1951.

Jimmy Gray

	Games	Goals
Friendly Matches	1	0
Combination League	5	0
Combination Cup	2	0
Eastern Counties League	49	0
Eastern Counties Cup	1	0
London Midweek League	27	0
Other Youth Matches	20	0
Total	**105**	**0**

GREENWOOD, Roy   1953-56

Birth Place: London
Date of Birth: 1937

☛ Roy Greenwood signed for Arsenal as an amateur during his national service in December 1953, turning professional in July 1956. Spent three seasons at Highbury, establishing himself as a full back in Arsenal's youth team. Released on a free transfer during the summer of 1956.

	Games	Goals
Friendly Matches	9	0
Combination League	4	0
Eastern Counties League	21	0
Eastern Counties Cup	5	0
London Midweek League	36	0
Total	**75**	**0**

Honours:
Eastern Counties League Champions 1954/55.

GRIFFITHS, Arfon   1961-62

Birth Place: Wrexham
Date of Birth: 23rd August 1941

☛ Arfon Griffiths joined Wrexham straight from school in May 1959. He was transferred to Arsenal for £15,000 in February 1961. He made his debut in a 5 - 1 defeat versus Wolves in April 1961, and represented Wales at under - 23 level. The following season, 1961 - 62, he played in fourteen league matches predominantly as a scheming inside forward. The following September, however, he was unable to maintain his first team place and was subsequently transferred back to his old club Wrexham for £8,000. Arfon Griffiths was a faithful servant to Wrexham for seventeen seasons, playing in well over six hundred first team matches as well as winning seventeen caps for Wales. Later managed Wrexham and Crewe and was awarded the MBE for his services to football.

	Games	Goals
League	15	2
Friendly Matches	9	6
Tour Matches	6	0
Combination League	24	10
Metropolitan League	2	0
Youth Tour Matches	3	1
Total	**59**	**19**

Honours:
17 Welsh Caps
2 Welsh Under - 23 Caps

GRIFFITHS, Brian   1949-54

Birth Place: Lincoln
Date of Birth: 1931

☛ Brian Griffiths represented Lincolnshire Schoolboys before signing for Arsenal as an amateur in January 1949. Turned

professional in May 1949, but unfortunately a year later was called up for his two years National Service. Returned to Arsenal in July 1952, spending a further two years as an inside forward, playing mainly in Arsenal's

Brian Griffiths

Eastern Counties League side.

	Games	Goals
Friendly Matches	4	2
Eastern Counties League	63	9
Eastern Counties Cup	9	4
London Midweek League	35	15
Other Youth Matches	7	1
Total	**118**	**31**

Honours:
London Midweek League Championship
   Medal   1952-53

GRIMSHAW, Colin   1947-52

Birth Place: Betchworth, Surrey
Date of Birth: 16th September 1925

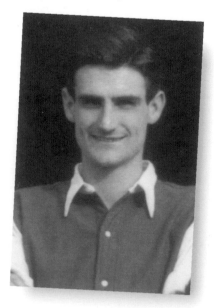

Colin Grimshaw

☛Colin Grimshaw joined Arsenal from Redhill in November 1947 as an amateur, turning professional in June 1948. He toured Brazil with Arsenal's first team on the summer tour of 1950. Throughout his five seasons at Highbury, was a regular in the reserve side as an inside forward or wing half. Was released on a free transfer in October 1952 when he joined Crystal Palace.

	Games	Goals
Friendly Matches	9	6
Tour Matches	2	0
Combination League	53	14
Combination Cup	41	12
London Challenge Cup	1	0
Eastern Counties League	49	8
Eastern Counties Cup	5	1
London Midweek League	8	3
Other Youth Matches	14	1
Total	**182**	**45**

GROVES, Vic   1955-64

Birth Place: Stepney, London
Date of Birth: 5th November 1932

☛Vic Groves started his football career with Leytonstone and Walthamstow Avenue as an amateur. He joined Leyton Orient as a professional in June 1954, spending eighteen months at Brisbane Road as a goalscoring inside forward. Transferred to Arsenal with Stan Charlton in November 1955 for £30,000. Made his league debut versus Sheffield United on the 12th November 1955. He played in only fifteen league matches that season due to a leg injury. A back injury sustained in April 1956 did not respond to treatment, resulting in Groves playing in only five league matches that season and in thirty three league games during 1958 - 59, scoring ten goals. During the following season, 1959 - 60, was switched to wing half back where he stayed for the rest of his career. He lost his place in the first team during 1961 - 62, playing his last league game for Arsenal during 1963 - 64. Later played in the southern league with Canterbury after being released by Arsenal in May 1964. Vic Groves will be remembered for his loyal service to Arsenal and, but for his unfortunate injuries would have achieved greater honours. His nephew Perry Groves later played for Arsenal.

	Games	Goals
League	185	31
FA Cup	16	6
UEFA Cup	2	0
Friendly Matches	47	11
Tour Matches	12	10
Combination League	62	19
London Challenge Cup	10	2
Southern Floodlight Cup	7	1
Metropolitan League	2	0
Total	**343**	**80**

Vic Groves

Honours:
1 England Under - 23 Cap
3 England Amateur Caps
3 England Youth Caps
1 Football League Cap
Southern Floodlight Cup
    Winners   1958-59
London FA Challenge Cup
    Winners   1962-63
Inter Cities Fairs Cup Final
    Medal (For combined London XI)   1958

GUDMUNDSSON, Albert   1946-47

Birth Place: Iceland
Date of Birth: 5th October 1923

☛Albert Gudmundsson was an Icelandic International inside forward who came to play in England for Arsenal as an amateur immediately after the war. He played in two league matches for them in October 1946 versus Stoke and Chelsea. Albert was not granted a work permit to turn professional in English football so he signed for AC Milan in 1947. Later played in France for Nancy, Racing De Paris and FC Nice returning to play in Iceland in 1957. Became president of the Icelandic Football Association and later became the countries Finance Minister. Died May 1994, aged 70.

	Games	Goals
League	2	0
Friendly Matches	3	0
Tour Matches	6	1
Combination League	12	7
Combination Cup	2	0
Total	**25**	**8**

Honours:
Iceland Full Caps

GUTHRIE, Ralph   1952-56

Birth Place: West Hartlepool, Durham
Date of Birth: 13th September 1932

☛Ralph Guthrie joined Arsenal as an amateur goalkeeper from Tow Law Town in December 1952, turning professional in May the following year. During his four seasons at Highbury he figured mainly in the Eastern Counties side although he did make two league appearances during the 1954 - 55, including his debut versus Manchester City at Maine Road in September 1954. Was not retained at the end of the 1955 - 56 season and subsequently joined Hartlepool in July 1956, playing for them for two seasons.

Ralph Guthrie

	Games	Goals
League	2	0
Friendly Matches	9	0
Combination League	25	0
Combination Cup	6	0
Eastern Counties League	30	0
Eastern Counties Cup	3	0
London Midweek League	20	0
Total	**95**	**0**

Honours:
London FA Challenge Cup
    Winners   1953-54
Eastern Counties League
    Champions   1954-55

HANCOCK, Peter   1949-52

Birth Place: Doncaster, Yorkshire
Date of Birth: 1928

☞ Peter Hancock joined Arsenal as a professional in October 1949, soon after his release from HM Forces. He had previously played for Edgware Town, Portsmouth and Boreham Wood. He spent three seasons at Highbury as wing half in Arsenal's reserve and Eastern Counties sides.

Peter Hancock

	Games	Goals
Friendly Matches	4	0
Combination League	11	0
Combination Cup	2	0
Eastern Counties League	28	5
Eastern Counties Cup	3	0
London Midweek League	27	3
Total	**75**	**8**

Honours:
Football Combination Championship
Medal   1950-51

HANKIN, Ray   1981-82

Birth Place: Wallsend, Durham
Date of Birth: 2nd February 1956

☞ Ray Hankin joined Burnley, turning professional in February 1973. Spent four seasons at Turf Moor, scoring thirty seven goals in one hundred and twelve league games as well as winning three England under - 23 caps. He was transferred to Leeds United in September 1976 for £200,000. Unfortunately his spell at Elland Road was not the happiest, and in four seasons he played in only eighty three league matches scoring thirty two goals. He then went to the USA for two years and played for Vancouver Whitecaps in the N.A.S.L. In November 1981, Arsenal bought Hankin for £400,000, to be paid only if Hankin proved himself. After

only five matches he was released to go back to the USA. Eventually he came back to England to play for Middlesbrough, Peterborough and Wolves.

Ray Hankin

	Games	Goals
League Cup	2	0
Friendly Matches	1	0
Combination League	2	1
Total	**5**	**1**

Honours:
(WITH BURNLEY)
3 England Under - 23 Caps
6 England Youth Caps

HARDING, Bobby   1969-75

Birth Place: Wanstead, London
Date of Birth: July 1953

Bobby Harding

☞ Bobby Harding joined Arsenal as an apprentice in August 1969, turning professional in July 1970. Within two years at Highbury, he became a regular in Arsenal's

reserve team as a promising winger. However, a succession of injuries, including a serious back injury sustained early in his career, reduced his appearances to only nine in 1972 - 73, six in 1973 - 74 and nine in 1974 - 75. Later played in non league football for Ilford, Enfield, Harlow, Bishop Stortford and Hayes.

	Games	Goals
Friendly Matches	19	7
Combination League	68	14
Combination Cup	4	0
London Challenge Cup	4	0
Metropolitan League	3	0
South East Counties League	27	5
Youth Cup	9	3
Other Youth Cups	5	1
Youth Tour Matches	4	1
Total	**143**	**31**

Honours:
Football Combination Cup Winners
Medal   1969-70

HARRISON, David   1979-82

Birth Place: Leeds, Yorkshire
Date of Birth: 1st December 1963

☞ David Harrison joined Arsenal as an apprentice in March 1979, turning professional in July 1981. In his three year spell at Highbury he became a regular in Arsenal's South East Counties League side as a versatile defender/midfield player, although during his first season 1979 - 80 he was sidelined through injury. Was released on a free transfer in May 1982.

	Games	Goals
Friendly Matches	2	0
Combination League	16	2
South East Counties League	49	11
Youth Cup	4	1
Other Youth Cups	10	2
Youth Tour Matches	2	0
Total	**83**	**16**

HARVEY, Jimmy   1977-80

Birth Place: Lurgan
Date of Birth: 2nd May 1958

☞ Jimmy Harvey joined Arsenal from the Northern Ireland side Glenavon in August 1977 for £30,000. At that time he was regarded as one of the finest young players to have emerged from Northern Ireland for many years. In fact he was voted the Young Player of the Year for season 1976 - 77. However, during his three years at Highbury, only managed to play in three league matches including his debut versus Derby County in May 1978. Was a regular in the reserve side before being granted a free transfer to Hereford United in March 1980.

Later played for Bristol City, Wrexham (loan), Tranmere and Crewe Alexander. In a career spanning fifteen years he totalled nearly five hundred league matches.

	Games	Goals
League	3	0
UEFA Cup	1	0
Friendly Matches	8	0
Tour Matches	1	0
Combination League	97	7
Total	**110**	**7**

Honours:
1 Northern Ireland Under - 21 Cap
6 Division Four PFA Awards   1984, 1985, 1986, 1987, 1989, 1990
(won while with Hereford, Tranmere and Crewe)

HAVERTY, Joe   1954-61

Birth Place: Dublin
Date of Birth: 17th February 1936

☛ Joe Haverty was already an Eire youth international when he joined Arsenal from the Eire side St Patrick's in July 1954. Within a month of coming to Highbury he made his league debut versus Everton at Goodison Park. Played in six league matches during 1954 - 55 and eight league matches in 1955 - 56, during which season he won the first of his thirty two Republic of Ireland caps. During 1957 - 58 Joe Haverty, playing at left wing, played in twenty eight league matches. Lost his place the following season but regained it in 1959 - 60, scoring eight goals in thirty five league matches. During 1960 - 61 he decided to ask for a transfer after sharing the left wing position with Alan Skirton. Blackburn paid Arsenal £25,000 for Haverty in August 1961. Spent only one season with the Lancastrians before finishing his career in the lower divisions with Millwall and Bristol Rovers.

Joe Haverty

Later played for Shelbourne in Ireland and for Chicago Spurs in America.

	Games	Goals
League	114	25
FA Cup	8	1
Friendly Matches	40	9
Tour Matches	7	1
Combination League	86	21
London Challenge Cup	9	6
Southern Floodlight Cup	6	2
Eastern Counties League	7	1
London Midweek League	9	4
Metropolitan League	1	1
Total	**287**	**71**

Honours:
32 Eire Caps
One Eire Youth Cap
London FA Challenge Cup
    Winners Medals   1954-55, 1957-58
    Runners up Medal   1960-61

HAWLEY, John   1981-83

Birth Place: Withernsea, Yorkshire
Date of Birth: 8th May 1954

☛ John Hawley spent the first four years of his playing career as an amateur with Hull City before turning professional in July 1976. Joined Leeds United in April 1978 for £140,000, but his stay at Elland Road was of only eighteen months duration, playing in thirty three league matches before joining Sunderland for £80,000 in October 1979. However, his stay there was also short lived, because in September 1981, John was transferred to Arsenal for £40,000. He played in fourteen league matches during 1981 - 82 and six league matches during 1982 - 83 before being released on a free transfer in May 1983 when he joined Bradford City. Later played for a season with Scunthorpe United.

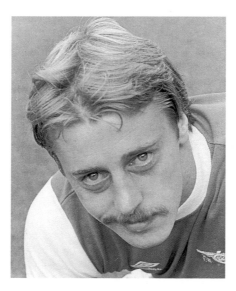

John Hawley

1945-1985

	Games	Goals
League	20	3
League Cup	1	0
Friendly Matches	6	1
Tour Matches	5	1
Combination League	31	10
Total	**63**	**15**

HEAD, David   1959-60

Birth Place: Midsommer Norton, Wiltshire
Date of Birth: 11th August 1940

☛ David Head joined Arsenal from Swindon Town in March 1959. Unfortunately he never fulfilled his promise, spending only fifteen months at Highbury playing in the Metropolitan league. Was granted a free transfer in July 1960 when he joined Reading. His father Bert Head played league football for Torquay and Bury and later managed Swindon and Crystal Palace.

	Games	Goals
Friendly Matches	6	4
Combination League	1	0
Metropolitan League	31	18
Metropolitan Cup	3	3
Total	**41**	**25**

HEALEY, Bill   1949-52

Birth Place: Liverpool
Date of Birth: 22nd May 1926

☛ Bill Healey joined Arsenal from Chorley FC in May 1949. Sustained a leg injury during a practice match in July 1949 and was laid off for half the 1949-50 season. He played in ten reserve matches during 1950 - 51 and eighteen matches in 1951 - 52. Although never playing for the first team, Bill served Arsenal well for over three years before being transferred to Fulham in December 1952 in the part exchange deal which took Bill Dodgin to Highbury. Finished his career with Hartlepool.

	Games	Goals
Friendly Matches	5	0
Combination League	42	0
Combination Cup	7	0
London Challenge Cup	3	0
Eastern Counties League	40	0
London Midweek League	21	1
Total	**118**	**1**

Honours:
Football Combination Championship
    Medal   1950-51

HEELEY, Mark   1977-80

Birth Place: Peterborough
Date of Birth: 8th September 1959

☛ Mark Heeley joined Arsenal from Peterborough in September 1977 for £40,000. He made his league debut versus Birmingham as substitute on 29th October 1977. Played in four league matches during 1977 - 78 and eleven league matches during 1978 - 79. However, he did not get a chance in the league side during 1979 - 80 and was loaned to Northampton before eventually joining them on a free transfer in March 1980.

Mark Heeley

	Games	Goals
League	15	1
UEFA Cup	5	0
Friendly Matches	8	1
Combination League	73	19
Youth Cup	3	0
Other Youth Cups	3	2
Total	**107**	**23**

HENDERSON, Jackie   1958-62

Birth Place: Glasgow
Date of Birth: 17th January 1932

☛ Jackie Henderson started his football career with Portsmouth in January 1949. He made his league debut during the 1951 - 52 season and played regularly in all forward line positions for seven seasons 1951 - 57. During this period he won the first of his seven Scottish caps versus Sweden in 1952 - 53. Moved to Wolves for £30,000 in March 1958 making only nine league appearances for them before being transferred to Arsenal for £30,000 in October 1958. Made his Arsenal debut versus West Brom at Highbury on the 4th October 1958, scoring twice. He played in only twenty one league matches due to injury in 1958 - 59 but played in thirty one and thirty nine matches respectively during seasons 1959 - 60 and 1960

- 61. He played in a further twelve league matches during season 1961 - 62 before being transferred to Fulham for £15,000 in January 1962, spending two seasons there before retiring from league football.

Jackie Henderson

	Games	Goals
League	103	29
FA Cup	8	0
Friendly Matches	22	18
Tour Matches	12	5
Combination League	13	13
London Challenge Cup	5	6
Southern Floodlight Cup	5	1
Total	**168**	**72**

Honours:
9 Scottish Caps
2 Scottish B Caps
Southern Floodlight Challenge Cup Winners
  Medal   1958-59

HENLEY, Les   1940-46

Birth Place: Lambeth, London
Date of Birth: 26th September 1922

☛ Les Henley joined Arsenal during the summer of 1940 as an England Schoolboy international. An inside forward who, after the war, played in Arsenal's reserve side during season 1946 - 47 before being transferred to Reading in December 1946. He spent seven seasons at Elm Park, playing at inside forward in their Third Division South Side. Les later managed Wimbledon.

	Games	Goals
Friendly Matches	1	0
Combination League	9	4
Combination Cup	13	1
Wartime	92	15
Total	**115**	**20**

Honours:
Wartime South League Championship
  Medal   1943-44

HERD, David   1954-61

Birth Place: Hamilton, Scotland
Date of Birth: 15th April 1934

☛ David Herd was the son of Alex Herd, the Scottish International who won an FA Cup Winners Medal with Manchester City in 1934. David Herd signed for Stockport just after his seventeenth birthday in April 1951, and played in the same forward line as his father. During his four years at Stockport, he played in only sixteen league matches due to being called up for two years national service. Arsenal showed interest in him after he was demobbed in August 1954 and eventually signed him for £10,000. He spent most of his first season in the reserves, although making his league debut versus Leicester at Highbury in February 1955. He played regular first team football the following season, 1956 - 57, scoring ten goals in twenty two league matches, followed by twenty four and fifteen goals respectively in seasons 1957 - 58 and 1958 - 59, winning the first of his five Scottish caps versus Wales during the latter season. He had an outstanding 1960 - 61 season, scoring twenty nine league goals (including four hat tricks) the largest number by an Arsenal player since Ronnie Rookes` thirty three in 1947 - 48. Became disillusioned by Arsenal's poor form, and was transferred to Manchester United for £35,000 in July 1961. David Herd spent seven seasons at Old Trafford, scoring 114 league goals in 202 games, helping them to two League Championships and an FA Cup Final victory. Was later transferred to Stoke in July 1968, where he finished his career. Herd is one of only a dozen players who have scored over two hundred league goals, all in the First Division. Later managed Lincoln City.

	Games	Goals
League	166	97
FA Cup	14	10
Friendly Matches	26	15
Tour Matches	12	11
Combination League	67	34
Combination Cup	8	3
London Challenge Cup	10	9
Southern Floodlight Cup	5	2
Metropolitan League	1	1
Total	309	182

Honours:
(WITH ARSENAL)
Five Scottish Caps
London FA Challenge Cup Winners
  Medal   1954-55
(WITH MANCHESTER UNITED)
FA Cup Winners Medal   1962-63
Two League Championship
  Medals   1964-65, 1966-67

David Herd

HINTON, Billy   1963-66

Birth Place: Islington, London
Date of Birth: October 1947

☛ Billy Hinton joined Arsenal as an apprentice in May 1963. Already an England schoolboy international full back when turning professional in November 1964. He was a regular member of Arsenal's youth team of 1963 - 64 and 1964 - 65. Progressed to the Metropolitan league side during 1965-66, but never fulfilled his potential, and was subsequently given a free transfer in May 1966.

Billy Hinton

	Games	Goals
Friendly Matches	5	0
Combination League	2	0
Metropolitan League	34	0
Metropolitan Cup	5	0
South East Counties League	56	1
Youth Cup	11	0
Other Youth Cups	13	0
Youth Tour Matches	32	0
Total	**158**	**1**

Honours:

FA Youth Cup Finalists Medal	1964-65
Metropolitan League Challenge Cup Winners Medal	1965-66
South East Counties League Championship Medal	1964-65
South East Counties League Cup Winners Medal	1963-64
London Minor Challenge Cup Finalist Medal	1964-65

HINTON, Terry   1958-60

Birth Place: London
Date of Birth: 1940

☛ Terry Hinton joined Arsenal as an amateur in November 1958, but continued to play for Hastings United, his old club, until he turned professional in May 1959. He

played in only five FA Youth Cup matches during 1958 - 59, and in 1959 - 60 became regular inside forward in Arsenal's Metropolitan league side. Was granted a free transfer in May 1960 when he joined Watford.

	Games	Goals
Friendly Matches	5	1
Combination League	2	0
Metropolitan League	22	10
Metropolitan Cup	3	1
Youth Cup	4	2
Total	**36**	**14**

HITCHEN, Gordon   1954-57

Birth Place: Wiltshire
Date of Birth: 1936

☛ Gordon Hitchen joined Arsenal from Chippenham Town in November 1954 after playing for Wiltshire County as a youth. An outside left, he played for Arsenal juniors during his first season at the club. Was called up for two years National Service in July 1955, and in the course of the next two seasons, played in only two Midweek League matches. Demobbed in the summer of 1957 when he was released on a free transfer.

	Games	Goals
London Midweek League	10	1
South East Counties League	4	1
Total	**14**	**2**

HODGES, Cyril   1944-46

Birth Place: Hackney, London
Date of Birth: 18th September 1919

☛ Cyril Hodges joined Arsenal in February 1944 as an amateur, signing as a professional in April 1945, but it was not until 1946-47 season that he had the chance of league football. Played in two league matches at outside left versus Blackburn Rovers and Blackpool. Transferred to Brighton 1946, where he later became assistant trainer and then trainer for many seasons. Died 1980 aged 60.

	Games	Goals
League	2	0
Friendly Matches	2	0
Combination League	7	7
Combination Cup	3	1
Wartime	9	3
Total	**23**	**11**

HOLLAND, Edward   1945-51

Birth Place: Canning Town, London
Date of Birth: 1927

☛ Edward Holland joined Arsenal as an amateur in April 1945, turning professional

in August of the same year. During his five seasons at Highbury he never got the chance of first team football, although he played regularly for the reserves as a goalscoring inside forward. Released on a free transfer during the 1950 - 51 season.

Edward Holland

	Games	Goals
Friendly Matches	3	0
Combination League	50	10
Combination Cup	26	6
London Challenge Cup	2	0
Eastern Counties League	15	4
Eastern Counties Cup	1	0
London Midweek League	17	2
Other Youth Matches	16	4
Wartime	8	2
Total	**138**	**28**

HOLLINS, John   1979-83

Birth Place: Guildford, Surrey
Date of Birth: 16th July 1946

☛ John Hollins came from a family of four brothers, three of them played league football, as did his father and grandfather. John Hollins joined Chelsea as a fifteen year old during the summer of 1961, turning professional on his seventeenth birthday in July 1963. Almost immediately won a regular place at wing half in Chelsea's great young side of the Sixties. Served them with great distinction for twelve seasons, taking part in all Chelsea's successes during that period. After Chelsea's relegation, was transferred to QPR in June 1975 for £80,000 after playing in over five hundred league matches. His first season saw him play a major part in helping QPR attain First Division runners up spot. Served QPR well for a further four seasons before surprisingly being transferred to Arsenal for £40,000 in July 1979. Was signed originally as a defensive cover player but, in his four seasons at Highbury, never played less than twenty three league matches in any one season. Made his Arsenal debut versus Liverpool in the FA Cup Charity Shield of 1979. He had settled in the side as a full back, although occasionally reverting back to his old position of wing half. John Hollins was still playing well at the age of thirty six when Arsenal granted him a free transfer in May 1983. After twenty consecutive seasons playing in the First Division, rejoined Chelsea in June 1983 to taste Second Division football for the first time and helped them to promotion in his first season back at Stamford Bridge. Retired at the end of 1983 - 84 season when appointed first team coach. Awarded the MBE for his services to football in 1981. Later became manager of Chelsea 1985 - 88.

John Hollins

	Games	Goals
League	127	9
FA Cup	12	0
League Cup	19	3
Cup Winners Cup	7	0
UEFA Cup	6	1
Charity Shield	1	0
Friendly Matches	10	1
Tour Matches	17	1
Combination League	22	1
Total	**221**	**16**

Honours:
(WITH CHELSEA AND ARSENAL)
1 England Cap
12 England Under - 23 Caps
6 England B Caps
4 Football League Caps
8 England Youth Caps

FA Cup Winners Medal	1969-70
FA Cup Finalist Medal	1966-67
League Cup Winners Medal	1964-65
League Cup Finalist Medal	1971-72
European Cup Winners Medal	1970-71
European Cup Winners Cup Finalist Medal	1979-80
FA Charity Shield Finalist Medal	1979-80

HOLTON, Cliff — 1947-58

Birth Place: Oxford
Date of Birth: 29th April 1929

☞ Cliff Holton will be remembered for having one of the most ferocious shots of any centre forward since the war. His total of two hundred and ninety two league goals has only been bettered since the war by Rowley, Greaves and Atyeo. He also holds the distinction, with Jimmy Greaves, of holding two clubs' seasonal records, forty two goals for Watford in 1959 - 60 and thirty six goals for Northampton in 1961 - 62. Both of these still remain club records. Cliff Holton joined Arsenal from Oxford City as a full back in October 1947. Converted to centre forward with great success in April 1950, after spending the previous two years on National Service. In 1950 - 51 he scored twenty seven reserve team goals in thirty games, and he made his league debut versus Stoke City on Boxing Day 1950. Played regularly as centre forward for the next three seasons, scoring fifty three goals in eighty one league games, helping Arsenal to the League Championship in 1952 - 53. Lost his place during the 1954 - 55 season and became a wing half during the 1955 - 56 season. During the next two seasons he played in all half back positions as well as at centre and inside forward. Was transferred to Watford for £9,000 in October 1958. Spent the rest of his career in the lower divisions with Watford, Northampton, Crystal Palace, Charlton and Orient before retiring at the age of thirty nine in 1968.

	Games	Goals
League	198	83
FA Cup	18	5
Charity Shield	1	0
Friendly Matches	33	28
Tour Matches	12	3
Combination League	95	72
Combination Cup	25	26
London Challenge Cup	7	8
Southern Floodlight Cup	3	1
Eastern Counties League	13	1
London Midweek League	5	0
Other Youth Matches	8	2
Total	**418**	**229**

Honours:

League Championship Medal	1952-53
FA Cup Finalist Medal	1951-52
FA Charity Shield Winners Medal	1953-54
Football Combination Champions	1950-51
London FA Challenge FA Cup Winners	1954-55

Cliff Holton

HORN, Graham   1969-73

Birth Place: Westminster, London
Date of Birth: 23rd August 1954

☛Graham Horn joined Arsenal as an apprentice straight from school in 1969. In his first season at Highbury, 1970 - 71, was the regular youth team goalkeeper in Arsenal's FA Youth Cup and South East Counties League Championship sides. He kept his place the following season but in 1972 - 73, for most of the season was loaned to Portsmouth, and on his return to Highbury was transferred to Luton in February 1973. Later played for Brentford. Los Angeles Aztecs, Charlton, Kettering, Southend, Aldershot and Torquay.

	Games	Goals
Friendly Matches	18	0
Combination League	10	0
London Challenge Cup	1	0
South East Counties League	70	0
Youth Cup	18	0
Other Youth Cups	17	0
Youth Tour Matches	18	0
Total	**152**	**0**

Honours:
FA Youth Cup Winners Medal   1970-71
South East Counties League Championship
   Medal   1971-72
South East Counties League Cup Winners
   Medal   1970-71
South East Counties League Cup Finalist
   Medal   1971-72

HORNSBY, Brian   1970-76

Birth Place: Peterborough
Date of Birth: 10th September 1954

☛Brian Hornsby joined Arsenal as an apprentice in May 1970, turning professional in September 1971. Had already represented England as a schoolboy international. In his first season at Highbury was a regular member of Arsenal's FA Youth Cup winning side and the South East Counties League Championship team, playing in fifty four matches and scoring nineteen goals as an inside forward. He played regularly for the reserves in season 1971-72 and during the following season, 1972-73, made his league debut in Arsenal's last game of the season at Leeds in May 1973. Also during that season he became a regular in England's youth team winning six caps. During the next three seasons could not forge a regular first team place, playing in nine, eleven and four league matches respectively. Was transferred to Shrewsbury for £40,000 in June 1976. He spent two seasons with them before moving to Sheffield Wednesday in March 1978. Brian had four seasons at Hillsborough and a further two seasons at Carlisle. Also played in USA and for Chesterfield.

Brian Hornsby

	Games	Goals
League	26	6
Friendly Matches	35	12
Tour Matches	9	1
Combination League	120	27
London Challenge Cup	3	2
South East Counties League	43	16
Youth Cup	19	9
Other Youth Cups	15	5
Youth Tour Matches	19	4
Total	**289**	**82**

Honours:
6 England Youth Caps
FA Youth Cup Winners   1970-71
South East Counties League
   Champions   1971-72
South East Counties League Cup
   Winners   1970-71
   runners - up   1971-72

HORSFIELD, Alex   1939-51

Birth Place: Selby, Yorkshire
Date of Birth: 1921

☛Alex Horsfield joined Arsenal as an amateur from Selby Town in August 1939, but had to wait until after the war before turning professional in November 1946. Started his career as a wing half switching eventually to inside forward. Served the reserve team well for five seasons, playing in over one hundred Combination matches without ever getting a first team chance. Released on a free transfer during the 1950 - 51 season.

	Games	Goals
Friendly Matches	2	0
Combination League	93	44
Combination Cup	42	15
London Challenge Cup	4	0
London Midweek League	2	0

Other Youth Cups	17	5
Wartime	7	2
Total	**167**	**66**

Honours:
Football Combination Championship
   Medal   1950-51

HOWARD, Pat   1976-77

Birth Place: Dodworth, Yorkshire
Date of Birth: 7th October 1947

☛Pat Howard started his league career with Barnsley, turning professional in October 1965. He spent seven seasons at Oakwell, playing in over two hundred first team games. Transferred to Newcastle in September 1971 for £30,000. He spent a further five season there, helping them to the 1974 FA Cup Final. Transferred to Arsenal in September 1976 for a fee of £40,000, and in his first season at Highbury played in sixteen league matches, his debut was at West Ham on 11th September 1976. After less than a year at Highbury was transfer listed, and eventually moved to Birmingham City in August 1977. Moved to Bury in July 1979 spending the last three seasons of his career there. Altogether played in well over five hundred league games.

Pat Howard

	Games	Goals
League	16	0
League Cup	4	1
Friendly Matches	6	0
Tour Matches	3	0
Combination League	16	2
Total	**45**	**3**

Honours:
(WITH NEWCASTLE)
FA Cup Finalist Medal   1973-74

HOWE, Don   1964-67

Birth Place: Wolverhampton
Date of Birth: 12th October 1935

Don Howe

☛ Don Howe joined West Bromwich Albion as a professional soon after his seventeenth birthday in October 1952. It was not until 1955 that he made his league debut, gaining a regular place soon afterwards. He spent nearly twelve years at the Hawthorns, playing in nearly three hundred and fifty league games. Won twenty three England caps and played in the 1958 World Cup series. Transferred to Arsenal for £40,000 (then a record fee for a full back) in April 1964, just in time to tour South Africa with the Arsenal first team. During 1964 - 65 was made club captain, and played in all of Arsenal's first twenty nine league games. During a game versus Blackpool at Highbury in March 1966, he unfortunately broke a leg. Over the next two years, tried unsuccessfully to regain full fitness, although he did play regularly for the reserve side during 1966 - 67. Became reserve team coach and when Dave Sexton left for Chelsea, was promoted to first team coach during 1968. Was the mastermind behind Arsenal's double winning side of 1970 - 71, after he had become assistant manager in March 1969. He left Arsenal amidst great controversy to join West Bromwich Albion in July 1971. After spells at Galatasary, Turkey and Leeds as coach he rejoined Arsenal as chief coach in August 1977. At this time he took on the role of coach to the England national team. Don became caretaker manager of Arsenal after

the departure of Terry Neill in December 1983, and full time manager in April 1984. In his two years as manager of Highbury Don must be given credit for the players which later helped George Graham to succeed, ie Tony Adams, David Rocastle, Martin Keown, Niall Quinn and Martin Hayes. Was released from his contract at his own request in March 1986. Later coached at Wimbledon and QPR as well as managing QPR and Coventry. Has just been appointed technical coaching advisor in the new England international set up.

	Games	Goals
League	70	1
FA Cup	3	0
League Cup	1	0
Friendly Matches	21	4
Tour Matches	21	3
Combination League	35	0
Combination Cup	6	0
London Challenge Cup	3	0
Metropolitan League	2	0
Total	**162**	**8**

Honours:
(WITH WEST BROMWICH)
23 England Caps
6 England Under - 23 Caps
1 England B Cap
3 Football League Caps

HUDSON, Alan   1976-78

Birth Place: Chelsea, London
Date of Birth: 21st June 1951

☛ Alan Hudson will rank with players such as Stan Bowles, Charlie George, Rodney Marsh, Tony Currie and Frank Worthington as one of the great enigma's of English football over the last twenty years, all of them brilliant, but often inconsistent and controversial. Alan Hudson started his football career with Chelsea, turning professional on his seventeenth birthday in June 1968. He soon became a regular in the Chelsea side, and during the early seventies was ranked as the young golden boy of English football. However, his short and controversial career at Chelsea ended in January 1974 when he was transferred to Stoke City for £200,000. During his four seasons at Stoke, was mainly responsible for the most successful period in the club's history. Arsenal signed him in December 1976, for £200,000 and in his first full season at Highbury was a member of Arsenal's FA Cup Final team against Ipswich. It was during Arsenal's Australia trip in June 1978 that Hudson's career at Highbury turned sour. He was sent home in disgrace after a so called "booze up" with Macdonald and Armstrong. Hudson was never to play for Arsenal again. In October 1978, Seattle Sounders paid Arsenal £100,000 for him, and

despite many rumours concerning his return, Hudson remained in America for a long period, although he did play for Chelsea on a week to week basis at the beginning of the 1983 - 84 season. Resigned by Stoke in January 1984. One day he will possibly look back on what could have been.

Alan Hudson

	Games	Goals
League	36	0
FA Cup	7	0
League Cup	4	0
Friendly Matches	2	0
Tour Matches	7	0
Combination League	9	1
Total	**65**	**1**

Honours:
(WITH CHELSEA AND ARSENAL)
2 England Caps
10 England Under - 23 Caps
European Cup Winners Cup Medal   1970-71
League Cup Finalist Medal   1971-72
FA Cup Finalist Medal   1977-78

HUGHES, John   1959-60

Birth Place: Llandudno, Wales
Date of Birth: 1940

☛ John Hughes joined Arsenal for a small fee from Bangor City in March 1959, being already a Welsh amateur, and youth international, and he played in the last five reserve matches of that season. However, after a further season playing in Arsenal's reserve team, he retired from first class football the following year to take up a career in chartered accountancy.

	Games	Goals
Friendly Matches	5	0
Combination League	17	0
Metropolitan League	10	0
Total	**32**	**0**

Alan Hudson in flight for Arsenal during the
1978 F.A. Cup final versus Ipswich Town.

JENKINS, David — 1962-68

Birth Place: Bristol
Date of Birth: 2nd September 1946

David Jenkins joined Arsenal as an apprentice in July 1962, turning professional in October 1963. In his first two seasons at Highbury was a consistent member of Arsenal's youth side, playing either at wing half or inside forward. During 1964-65 he was a member of Arsenal's F A Youth Cup and London Minor Challenge Cup Finalist teams. After being a regular in the Metropolitan League side for three seasons (1963 - 65), was drafted into the reserve side during 1966-67 and made his first team debut versus Gillingham in the League Cup in September 1966. In 1967 - 68 he figured in only two league matches, but did play in the League Cup Final of that season versus Leeds, due to Bobby Gould being cup - tied. Became a regular in the league side during the first half of the 1968 - 69 season, before being transferred to Spurs in October 1968 for £50,000, in the deal which took Jimmy Robertson to Highbury. Later played for Brentford, Hereford, Newport, Shrewsbury and Workington.

David Jenkins

	Games	Goals
League	17	3
F A Cup	2	1
League Cup	6	5
Friendly Matches	33	10
Tour Matches	9	8
Combination League	63	10
Combination Cup	16	8
London Challenge Cup	4	2
Metropolitan League	76	19
Metropolitan Cup	15	2
South East Counties League	36	16
Youth Cup	14	9
Other Youth Cups	14	4
Youth Tour Matches	31	6
Total	**336**	**103**

Honours:

League Cup Finalists Medal	1967-68
Football Combination Cup winners	1967-68
London F A Challenge Cup runners - up	1965-66
F A Youth Cup runners - up	1964-65
Metropolitan League Challenge Cup winners	1965-66
Southern Junior Floodlight Cup winners	1962-63
London Minor Challenge Cup runners - up	1964-65

JOHNSON, Glenn — 1968-70

Birth Place: Barrow, Cumbria
Date of Birth: 7th March 1952

Glenn Johnson joined Arsenal as an apprentice in August 1968, turning professional in June 1969. His first season at Highbury was spent as the regular youth team goalkeeper. Unfortunately during 1969 - 70 was replaced by Malcolm Webster, although he was still good enough to win an England youth cap versus Eire. Was granted a free transfer during the summer of 1970 when he joined Doncaster. Later joined Aldershot, where he played for ten seasons before retiring through injury in 1983.

Glenn Johnson

	Games	Goals
Friendly Matches	11	0
Combination League	13	0
Combination Cup	2	0
London Challenge Cup	3	0
Metropolitan League	23	0
Metropolitan Cup	5	0
South East Counties League	6	0
Youth Cup	2	0
Other Youth Cups	2	0
Youth Tour Matches	7	0
Total	**74**	**0**

Honours:
1 England Youth Cap
London Challenge Cup Winners Medal 1969-70

JOHNSON, Laurie — 1951-55

Birth Place: Liverpool
Date of Birth: 1933

Laurie Johnson joined Arsenal as a professional in June 1951 after representing Liverpool and England at schoolboy level. Spent two years in HM Services (1951 - 53) before returning to Highbury in 1953 - 54, when he captained the Eastern Counties team for two seasons before being released on a free transfer during the summer of 1955.

	Games	Goals
Friendly Matches	4	0
Combination Cup	8	0
Eastern Counties League	69	0
Eastern Counties Cup	11	0
London Midweek League	17	0
Total	**109**	**0**

Honours:
Eastern Counties League Championship Medal — 1954-55

JOHNSON, Robbie — 1977-81

Birth Place: London
Date of Birth: 30th March 1962

Robbie Johnson joined Arsenal as an apprentice in July 1977, turning professional in February 1980. Spent four seasons at Highbury, two as a regular in the Arsenal youth team at full back (1977 - 79), then progressed to the reserve team (1979 - 81). Was granted a free transfer in March 1981 when he joined Brentford. Later played in non league football for Hayes, Harrow Borough, Enfield and Slough.

	Games	Goals
Friendly Matches	10	1
Combination League	56	0
South East Counties League	52	0
Youth Cup	8	0
Other Youth Cups	14	0
Youth Tour Matches	1	0
Total	**141**	**1**

Honours:

South East Counties League Cup Winners Medal	1979-80
Presidents Cup Winners Medal	1979-80

JOHNSTON, George — 1967-69

Birth Place: Glasgow
Date of Birth: 21st March 1947

George Johnston spent three years at Cardiff City before joining Arsenal in March 1967 for £30,000. Made his league debut versus Stoke in August 1967, and played in seventeen league matches that season. Could not maintain a regular place during the following season, and played in the reserve side scoring twenty five goals in twenty nine games. Transferred to Birmingham for £15,000 in May 1969. Later played for Walsall, Fulham, Hereford and Newport.

George Johnston

	Games	Goals
League	21	3
League Cup	4	0
Friendly Matches	14	10
Tour Matches	4	2
Combination League	47	27
Combination Cup	10	7
London Challenge Cup	1	0
Metropolitan Cup	1	0
Total	**102**	**49**

Honours:
Football Combination Champions 1968-69
Football Combination Cup
  Winners 1967-68

JONES, David — 1966-68

Birth Place: Brixham, Devon
Date of Birth: 18th May 1950

David Jones joined Arsenal as an apprentice in April 1966, turning professional in February 1968. In two seasons at Highbury, David Jones played regularly in Arsenal's youth team either at wing half or inside forward. Was granted a free transfer in October 1968 when he joined Oxford United. Later played for Torquay.

	Games	Goals
Friendly Matches	8	2
Combination League	3	0
Combination Cup	6	0
Metropolitan League	22	2
Metropolitan Cup	7	1
South East Counties League	18	2
Youth Cup	5	1
Other Youth Cups	11	3
Youth Tour Matches	16	2
Total	**96**	**13**

Honours:
Southern Junior Floodlight Cup
  Finalist Medal 1967-68
London Youth Challenge
  Winners Cup 1966-67

JONES, Freddie — 1958

Birth Place: Caerphilly, Wales
Date of Birth: 11th January 1938

Fred Jones joined Arsenal with Ronnie Clayton from Hereford United in January 1958. He spent only nine months at Highbury as a winger in the reserve side, although he did play in a first team friendly match versus Eintracht Frankfurt in February 1958. Was transferred to Brighton in September 1958 where he spent three seasons, winning two Welsh under - 23 caps in 1959 - 60. Later played for Swindon, Grimsby and Reading.

	Games	Goals
Friendly Matches	3	0
Combination League	14	5
London Midweek League	1	0
Total	**18**	**5**

Honours:
2 Welsh Under - 23 Caps

JONES, Ivor — 1949-50

Birth Place: Rhondda, Wales
Date of Birth: 1st April 1925

Ivor Jones joined Arsenal from Crystal Palace in December 1949, having started his career with them in the war years. He spent only ten weeks at Highbury during which time he played in only three matches for the third team. Was transferred to Reading in February 1950.

	Games	Goals
Friendly Matches	1	0
Eastern Counties League	1	0
London Midweek League	1	0
Total	**3**	**0**

JONES, Syd — 1939-48

Birth Place: Rothwell, Yorkshire
Date of Birth: 15th February 1921

Syd Jones joined Arsenal from Kippax juniors as an amateur in March 1939, turning professional in May 1939. Played in only seven southern league games during that season before the outbreak of World War Two. On the resumption of league football in 1946-47, Syd spent two seasons as full back in Arsenal's reserve team before being transferred to Walsall in August 1948.

	Games	Goals
Friendly Matches	2	0
Combination League	37	1
Combination Cup	21	0
London Challenge Cup	3	0
Southern League	7	0
Total	**70**	**1**

Honours:
Football Combination Championship
  Medal 1946-47

JULIANS, Len — 1958-60

Birth Place: Tottenham
Date of Birth: 19th June 1933

Len Julians started his football career with Leytonstone before joining Leyton Orient in June 1955. Spent three seasons at Brisbane Road, joining Arsenal in December 1958 for £12,000, and during the remainder of that season scored five league goals in ten games. However, during 1959-60 could not maintain a regular first team place, playing in only eight league games. Not content with reserve team football, Len was transfer listed, subsequently joining Nottingham Forest in June 1960 for £10,000. Spent four seasons at Forest, playing in fifty nine league matches, scoring twenty four goals. Later moved to

Len Julians

Millwall where he spent four seasons before finishing his career in the United States. Died December 1993, aged 60.

	Games	Goals
League	18	7
FA Cup	6	3
Friendly Matches	7	9
Tour Matches	1	0
Combination League	27	17
London Challenge Cup	1	2
Southern Floodlight Cup	3	1
Total	**63**	**39**

KANE, Peter   1960-63

Birth Place: Petershill, Scotland
Date of Birth: 4th April 1939

Peter Kane started his football career with the Scottish club Queens Park. Joined Northampton in October 1959 and scored sixteen goals in twenty eight league games before being transferred to Arsenal for £8,000 in July 1960. Made his league debut versus Manchester City in September 1960. Was called up for national service in November 1960, but still managed to play in twenty one reserve matches, scoring fifteen goals. Over the next two seasons he never regained a first team place, although he served the reserve team well during that period. Transferred back to Northampton Town in September 1963, where he again played under former Gunner Dave Bowen. Finished his career with Crewe and then at St. Mirren.

Peter Kane

	Games	Goals
League	4	1
Friendly Matches	11	10
Combination League	54	37
London Challenge Cup	5	7
Metropolitan League	28	23
Metropolitan Cup	8	10
Total	**110**	**88**

Honours:
Football Combination Champions	1962-63
Metropolitan League Champions	1962-63
Metropolitan League Cup Winners	1960-61
Metropolitan League Professional Cup Winners	1960-61
Scotland Youth and Amateur Caps	

KAY, John   1980-84

Birth Place: Sunderland
Date of Birth: 29th January 1964

John Kay joined Arsenal as an apprentice in April 1980, turning professional in July 1981. Started his career in the Arsenal youth team during 1980-81 as a skilful midfield player, but was converted to full back after promotion to the reserve team in 1981-82. His progress continued the following season when making his league debut versus West Bromwich in February 1983, playing in seven league matches that season. Played in a further seven league matches in 1983-84 before being surprisingly released on a free transfer to Wimbledon in June 1984. Had a two month loan period at Middlesborough in 1984-85. Joined Sunderland in 1987.

John Kay

	Games	Goals
League	14	0
Friendly Matches	32	4
Combination League	80	7
South East Counties League	49	8
Youth Cup	5	1
Other Youth Cups	8	1
Youth Tour Matches	1	0
Total	**189**	**21**

Honours:
Football Combination Championship Medal	1983-84

KELLY, Eddie   1966-76

Birth Place: Glasgow
Date of Birth: 7th February 1951

Eddie Kelly joined Arsenal from the Scottish club Possilpark in July 1966, turning professional in February 1968. Was a regular member of Arsenal's youth team for two seasons, 1966 - 68, and played at wing half in the reserve side during 1968 - 69, as well as winning five Scottish youth caps. His progress continued the following season when he played in sixteen league games, his debut coming versus Sheffield Wednesday in September 1969. Played in Arsenal's Inter Cities Fairs Cup - winning side, scoring one of the goals in the 2-leg final versus Anderlecht. Played in thirty four first team games during the Double season of 1970 - 71 and scored the first goal in the FA Cup Final versus Liverpool. That season also saw him winning the first of his three Scottish under - 23 caps versus England. Over the next two seasons he played in only fifty out of a possible eighty four league games, due to a series of injuries and suspensions. However, missed only five league matches during 1974-75, when he was made club captain, becoming, at the age of twenty three, one of the youngest captains Arsenal have ever had. Became unsettled during 1975-76 when he made several transfer requests due to the loss of his first team place. Finally, in September 1976, his request was granted and he joined QPR for £80,000. Later served Leicester and Notts County (both clubs being promoted to

Eddie Kelly

the First Division while he was playing for them). Later played for Bournemouth and Torquay.

	Games	Goals
League	175	13
FA Cup	17	4
League Cup	15	0
European Cup	3	1
UEFA Cup	12	1
Friendly Matches	60	11
Tour Matches	20	0
Combination League	97	9
Combination Cup	17	2
London Challenge Cup	5	1
Metropolitan League	13	0
Metropolitan Cup	1	0
South East Counties League	29	3
Youth Cup	5	0
Other Youth Cups	4	0
Youth Tour Matches	6	0
Total	**479**	**45**

Honours:
3 Scottish Under - 23 Caps
5 Scottish Youth Caps
Inter Cities Fairs Cup Winners
  Medal   1969-70
League Championship Medal   1970-71
FA Cup Winners Medal   1970-71
Football Combination Champions
              1968-69, 1969-70
Football Combination Cup Winners 1967-68
London FA Challenge Cup Winners 1969-70
(WITH LEICESTER)
Division Two Championship Medal 1979-80

KELLY, Noel   1947-50

Birth Place: Dublin
Date of Birth: 28th December 1921

Noel Kelly joined Arsenal from the Irish club Glentoran in October 1947. Settled down in Arsenal's reserve team during 1947-48, playing in twenty three games and a further thirty four games in 1948-49. Made his one and only league appearance versus Everton at Goodison Park in February, 1950. Could never establish a first team place at Highbury and subsequently joined Crystal Palace in March 1950. Later played for Nottingham Forest (where he won his one Irish Cap versus Luxembourg in 1954) and Tranmere, where he became player - manager, 1955-57.

	Games	Goals
League	1	0
Friendly Matches	1	0
Combination League	47	11
Combination Cup	26	5
London Challenge Cup	1	0
London Midweek League	2	0
Other Youth Matches	10	2
Total	**88**	**18**

Honours:
1 Eire Cap

KELSEY, Jack   1949-63

Birth Place: Llansamlet, Wales
Date of Birth: 19th November 1929

Jack Kelsey joined Arsenal from the Welsh side Winch Wen in September 1949. Almost immediately won a regular place in the reserve side, playing in thirteen matches during 1949 - 50. Kept his place during 1950 - 51 and made his first team debut versus Charlton at Highbury in February 1951. Unfortunately, this game resulted in Arsenal's heaviest home defeat, 2-5, for twenty two years. Thirty seven games in the reserves the following season, gave Kelsey the confidence and experience needed for league football and he returned to the league side for twenty nine first team matches during 1952 - 53, helping Arsenal to their seventh League Championship. Became Arsenal's regular first choice goalkeeper in 1953 - 54, missing only three league matches. Also won the first of his forty one Welsh caps. Played for Arsenal and Wales during the next eight seasons, appeared in well over three hundred and fifty first team games for Arsenal. Tragically his footballing career ended after sustaining a serious injury versus Brazil during the 1962 World Cup series, and although many attempts were made to rectify the injury, he finally announced his retirement in May 1963. Later served Arsenal in public relations and as commercial manager. Jack Kelsey will be remembered as one of the great goalkeepers of modern times. Died March 1992 aged 62.

	Games	Goals
League	327	0
FA Cup	24	0
Charity Shield	1	0
Friendly Matches	55	0
Tour Matches	15	0
Combination League	68	0
Combination Cup	24	0
London Challenge Cup	6	0
Southern Floodlight Cup	4	0
Eastern Counties League	12	0
London Midweek League	8	0
Other Youth Matches	4	0
Total	**548**	**0**

Honours:
41 Welsh Caps
League Championship
  Medal   1952-53
F A Charity Shield Winners
  Medal   1953-54
Football Combination
  Champions   1950-51
Football Combination Cup
  Winners   1952-53
London FA Challenge Cup
  Winners   1961-62
Inter Cities Fairs Cup Final
  Medal   1956

Jack Kelsey

KENNEDY, Ray 1968-74

Birth Place: Seaton Delavel, Northumberland
Date of Birth: 28th July 1951

Ray Kennedy joined Arsenal as an apprentice in April 1968, after having been rejected by Port Vale and going to work in a sweet factory. At that time little did he realise he was to become the most honoured player (in terms of medals won) in the history of English football. Turned professional in November 1968. Spent two seasons in Arsenal's reserve team, making his league debut versus Sunderland in February 1970. Shot to fame when he scored one of Arsenal's goals in the 2-leg 1969-70 European Fairs Cup Final. Became a regular in the league side the following season. Was Arsenal's leading scorer with twenty six goals in sixty three games, as well as being selected for England's Under 23 side and winning the Rothmans Young Player of the Year award. Formed one of the league's deadliest goalscoring partnerships with John Radford. Spent a further three seasons at Highbury, winning an FA Cup Finalists medal in 1971 - 72 and six Under 23 caps. Was Arsenal's leading scorer during seasons 1971 - 72 and 1973 - 74. Transferred to Liverpool for £200,000 in July 1974, being Bill Shankly's last signing. Spent eight seasons at Anfield, during which time he switched from striker to midfield. Won many further honours, including seventeen England caps. Released by Liverpool in 1981 to join Swansea. Later played for Hartlepool. Tragically in the late 1980's was struck down with Parkinson's Disease, and has since become the Parkinson Disease Society's cause célèbre by virtue of his work for the charity. Ray put his huge haul of medals and trophies up for auction at Christies in 1993.

	Games	Goals
League	158	53
FA Cup	27	6
League Cup	11	4
European Cup	6	4
EUFA Cup	10	4
Friendly Matches	38	23
Tour Matches	11	3
Combination League	51	24
Combination Cup	11	8
London Challenge Cup	4	3
Metropolitan League	9	1
Metropolitan Cup	2	2
Youth Cup	3	4
Other Youth Cups	2	0
Youth Tour Matches	14	5
Total	**357**	**144**

Ray Kennedy with left, George Armstrong and right, Alan Ball and Charlie George in the wall for Arsenal.

Ray Kennedy

Honours:
(WITH ARSENAL AND LIVERPOOL)
17 England Caps
6 England Under - 23 Caps
1 Football League Cap
6 League Championships Medals
      1970-71, 1975-76, 1976-77, 1978-79,
                1979-80, 1981-82
FA Cup Winners Medal   1970-71
Two FA Cup Finalists Medals   1971-72,
                        1976-77
League Cup Winners Medal   1980-81
League Cup Finalist Medal   1977-78
3 European Cup Winners Medals
        1976-77, 1977-78, 1980-81
Inter Cities Fairs Cup Winners
   Medal   1969-70
UEFA Cup Winners Medal   1975-76
European Super Cup Winners Medal 1977-78
European Super Cup Finalists
   Medal   1978-79
World Club Championship Finalist
   Medal   1981-82
5 FA Charity Shield Winners Medals
        1974-75, 1976-77, 1977-78,
                1979-80, 1980-81
Rothmans Young Player of the Year 1970-71
Football Combination Champions
               1968-69, 1969-70
London FA Challenge Cup
   Winners   1969-70
Southern Junior Floodlight Cup
   Runners up   1967-68

KIDD, Brian   1974-76

Birth Place: Manchester, Lancashire
Date of Birth: 29th May 1949

☛ Brian Kidd rose to fame as one of the last of the "Busby Babes", being the

youngest member of Manchester United's European Cup winning team of 1968 (scoring one of the goals in the Final versus Benfica on his Nineteenth Birthday). Spent eight seasons at Old Trafford, scoring over fifty league goals in two hundred and three league games. Won two England caps and was a member of England's 1970 World Cup squad. Signed by Arsenal for £100,000 in July 1974, as a replacement for Ray Kennedy, and in his first season at Highbury was the club's leading goalscorer with twenty two goals. Added a further eleven goals in thirty seven games during 1975 - 76. Became homesick and was allowed to join Manchester City in July 1976 for £100,000. Served City for three seasons before moving on to Everton in March 1979. Spent fifteen months at Goodison Park before moving to Bolton in May 1980. Left Bolton in November 1981 when he moved to the United States. Returned to England in 1984 when he became player/manager of Barrow. Managed Preston in 1986 before moving back to Manchester United as coach, and Assistant Manager.

	Games	Goals
League	77	29
FA Cup	9	3
League Cup	4	1
Friendly Matches	9	7
Tour Matches	11	5
Total	**110**	**45**

Honours:
(WITH MANCHESTER UNITED)
2 England Caps
10 England Under - 23 Caps
7 England Youth Caps
3 Football League Caps
League Championship Medal   1966-67
European Cup Winners Medal   1967-68
FA Charity Shield Winners Medal 1967-68

Brian Kidd

KINSELLA, Tom   1962-63

Birth Place: Dublin
Date of Birth: 1943

☛ Tom Kinsella joined Arsenal from the Irish club Drumcondra in January 1962. Played regularly as a winger in Arsenal's reserve side during the second half of the 1961 - 62 season. In 1962-63 he inter-changed between the reserve and Metropolitan league sides. Released on a free transfer in May 1963.

	Games	Goals
Friendly Matches	9	3
Combination League	20	4
London Challenge Cup	1	0
Metropolitan League	25	8
Metropolitan Cup	5	1
Total	**60**	**16**

Honours:
Football Combination Championship
   Medal   1962-63
Metropolitan League Championship
   Medal   1962-63

KOSMINA, John   1978-79

Birth Place: Adelaide, Australia
Date of Birth: 17th August 1956

☛ John Kosmina became Arsenal's first ever foreign signing when he joined them from the Australian league side Polonia, for £40,000 in February 1978. Was already an experienced Australian international when Terry Neill decided to sign him during the preparation for the club's proposed summer Australian tour. His career at Highbury lasted only fifteen months, during which time he played regular reserve team football. Played in only one league game versus Leeds (as substitute) in August 1978. Later returned to play in Australia (whom he represented during England's 1983 summer tour).

	Games	Goals
League	1	0
UEFA Cup	3	0
Friendly Matches	2	1
Tour Matches	2	0
Combination League	38	12
Total	**46**	**13**

Honours:
60 Australian Caps

LAW, Nicky   1977-81

Birth Place: Greenwich, London
Date of Birth: 8th September 1961

☛ Nicky Law joined Arsenal as an apprentice during the summer of 1977, turning professional in July 1979. Spent season 1977-78 as captain of Arsenal's South East Counties Youth side before being promoted to the reserve side in 1978-79.

Played over eighty Combination matches during 1978-80, without ever getting a first team chance. Was granted a free transfer during the close season of 1981, when he joined Barnsley. Later went on a merry - go - round in the lower leagues playing for Blackpool, Plymouth, Notts County, Scarborough, Rotherham and Chesterfield.

Nicky Law

	Games	Goals
Friendly Matches	13	0
Combination League	74	0
South East Counties League	53	4
Youth Cup	4	1
Other Youth Cups	16	0
Youth Tour Matches	3	0
Total	**163**	**5**

Honours:
South East Counties League Cup Winners
1979-80
Presidents Cup Winners 1979-80

LAWTON, Tommy   1953-56

Birth Place: Bolton, Lancashire
Date of Birth: 6th October 1919

☛Tommy Lawton will be regarded as one of the greatest centre forwards of all time. In fifteen playing seasons Lawton scored two hundred and thirty one league goals in less than four hundred league games (these totals would have been greater if it had not been the loss of seven seasons owing to the war). Joined Burnley as a groundstaff boy in 1934. By the time he was sixteen he was already spearheading Burnley's attack, scoring a hat - trick on his debut versus Spurs. Scored eleven goals in eighteen games for Burnley during the first half of the 1936-37 season, when Everton paid a staggering £6,500 for the seventeen year - old in December 1936. At first Lawton appeared at inside forward to accommodate the great "Dixie" Dean, settling down at centre forward the following season. Scored sixty two

goals in seventy seven games for Everton during the two seasons before the war. Helped Everton win the league title in 1938-39, as well as being the country's top league goalscorer with thirty four goals and winning the first of his England caps. All this and he was still only nineteen years old. After the war Lawton became involved in a dispute with Everton,which led to his being transferred to Chelsea in November 1945. Spent two years at Stamford Bridge before being transferred to Notts County for the then British record fee of £20,000. During his five seasons at Meadow Lane, helped Notts County win promotion to the Second Division in 1949-50 as well as scoring ninety league goals in one hundred and fifty one games. His next move was to Brentford in March 1952, but after only eighteen months was transferred to Arsenal in September 1953 for £10,000, plus James Robertson. Although now in the twilight of his career, Tommy Lawton spent two years at Highbury, scoring thirteen goals in thirty five games. Left Gunners in October 1955 when he joined Kettering Town as player/manager. Later managed Notts County. Undoubtedly one of the greatest centre forwards of all time.

Tommy Lawton

	Games	Goals
League	35	13
FA Cup	2	1
Charity Shield	1	1
Friendly Matches	9	3
Tour Matches	2	1
Combination League	2	5
Combination Cup	1	3
Total	**52**	**27**

Honours:
(WITH EVERTON / NOTTS COUNTY / ARSENAL)
23 England Caps
22 England Wartime Caps
Division One Championship Medal   1938-39
Division Three Championship Medal 1949-50
FA Charity Shield Winners Medal   1953-54

1945-1985

LE ROUX, Daniel   1957-58

Birth Place: Port Shepstone, Natal,
South Africa
Date of Birth: 25th November 1933

☛Daniel Le Roux joined Arsenal from the South African side, Queens Park, in February 1957. Already a South African international (fourteen caps) he spent the rest of the 1956-57 season playing in the reserve side. Played either on the wing or at centre forward, Le Roux showed his potential at the beginning of the 1957-58 season, scoring eleven goals in sixteen reserve matches. Made the first of his five league appearances versus Burnley at Turf Moor in December 1957. Left Highbury in April 1958, when he returned to South Africa.

Daniel Le Roux

	Games	Goals
League	5	0
Friendly Matches	3	1
Combination League	25	12
London Challenge Cup	5	5
Eastern Counties Cup	1	0
Total	**39**	**18**

Honours:
14 South African Caps

LEVEN, Neil   1963-67

Birth Place: Glasgow
Date of Birth: 17th November 1947

☛Neil Leven joined Arsenal as an apprentice in July 1963, turning professional on his seventeenth birthday in November 1964. Played in the final of the FA Youth Cup in 1964 - 65. Was a regular member of the Metropolitan side for three seasons before being granted a free transfer in February 1967.

Neil Leven

	Games	Goals
Friendly Matches	14	4
Combination League	19	3
Combination Cup	1	0
Metropolitan League	68	10
Metropolitan Cup	9	1
South East Counties League	31	6
Youth Cup	22	5
Other Youth Cups	24	4
Youth Tour Matches	25	3
Total	**213**	**36**

Honours:
FA Youth Cup Winners Medal 1965-66
FA Youth Cup Finalist Medal 1964-65
Metropolitan League Challenge Cup Winners
    Medal 1965-66
South East Counties League Cup Winners
    Medal 1963-64
South East Counties League Cup Finalist
    Medal 1965-66
Southern Junior Floodlight Cup Winners
    Medal 1965-66

LEWIN, Gary   1980-82

Birth Place: London
Date of Birth: 16th May 1964

☛ Gary Lewin was never offered professional terms with Arsenal, so, in that sense, he should not actually be appearing in this book, but it would be an injustice to his modest self not to mention him. His contribution as first team physiotherapist since 1987 has been immense. His inspirational, motivating and healing

techniques during Arsenal's last eight successful seasons have been invaluable. This must have been seen by George Graham when he appointed Gary to his current position in 1987, at the tender age of twenty three. This was after he had served his apprenticeship as physiotherapist to the reserves. Everything might have been different if a promising goalkeepers career had not been severed by injury. He originally joined Arsenal as an apprentice in April 1980. Was Arsenal's regular youth team keeper 1980 - 82. Later played non league football before returning to Highbury in 1984.

	Games	Goals
Friendly Matches	3	0
Combination League	3	0
South East Counties League	55	0
Youth Cup	2	0
Other Youth Cups	7	0
Total	**70**	**0**

Gary Lewin

LISHMAN, Doug   1948-56

Birth Place: Birmingham
Date of Birth: 14th September 1923

☛ Doug Lishman joined Arsenal for £10,500 (as a replacement for Reg Lewis) from Walsall in May 1948. He had originally joined Walsall in August 1946 and had scored twenty - six goals in fifty nine games for them. Made his league debut for Arsenal in September 1948, versus Sheffield United. Played in twenty three league matches that season, scoring twelve goals. A series of injuries and loss of form reduced his appearances to only fourteen league matches during 1949 - 50 and when re - establishing himself in the side during 1950-51, he unfortunately broke a leg versus Stoke in December 1950. Fully recovered for the opening of the 1951-52, season he struck top form, scoring three successive hat-tricks versus Fulham, West Brom and Bolton, resulting in him being picked for the England B side versus France in October 1951. Finished as Arsenal's leading scorer for five consecutive seasons, 1950-54, scoring one hundred goals in one hundred and seventy four league matches. Was transferred to Nottingham Forest in March 1956, where he finished his career. Lishman's total of one hundred and sixty three goals puts him second only to John Radford as Arsenal's most prolific goalscorer since the war. Overall, only Cliff Bastin has scored more than his one hundred and twenty five league goals for Arsenal. Died December 1994, aged 71.

	Games	Goals
League	226	125
FA Cup	17	10
Charity Shield	1	2
Friendly Matches	38	22
Tour Matches	21	18
Combination League	34	13
Combination Cup	6	1
London Challenge Cup	5	4
Total	**348**	**195**

Doug Lishman

Honours:
League Championship Medal	1952-53
F A Cup Finalist Medal	1951-52
F A Charity Shield Winners Medal	1953-54
1 England B Cap	
1 Football League Cap	

LOGIE, Jimmy — 1939-1955

Birth Place: Edinburgh
Date of Birth: 23rd November 1919

Jimmy Logie joined Arsenal in June 1939 from the Scottish junior side, Lochore Welfare. Five weeks later he was called up and joined the navy where he spent the following seven war years. Made his Arsenal debut on the opening day of the 1946-47 season versus Wolves at Molineux. Over the next nine seasons he consistently masterminded the Arsenal attack, playing in two hundred and eighty three out of a possible three hundred and thirty six league matches between 1946-54. A great mystery was why he won only one Scottish cap, versus Northern Ireland in October 1952. During his spell at Highbury, he guided Arsenal to two League Championships and an FA Cup Final victory in 1950. Also Captained Arsenal during the latter years of his career when Joe Mercer was not available. In years to come, people will see and read about Jimmy Logie and think that because he only won one Scottish cap he was merely an average player. In fact, that could not be further from the truth. On leaving Highbury in February 1955 he joined Gravesend as player/manager before settling down in business as a newsagent. Died in April 1984 aged sixty four.

	Games	Goals
League	296	68
FA Cup	30	8
Charity Shield	2	0
Friendly Matches	29	7
Tour Matches	29	5
Combination League	3	1
London Challenge Cup	2	0
War Time	9	3
Total	**400**	**92**

Honours:
1 Scottish Cap
2 League Championship Medals
          1947-48, 1952-53
FA Cup Winners Medal   1949-50
FA Cup Finalists Medal   1951-52
2 FA Charity Shield Winners
    Medals   1948-49, 1953-54

Jimmy Logie

MACAULAY, Archie — 1947-50

Birth Place: Falkirk, Scotland
Date of Birth: 30th July 1915

Archie Macaulay began his football career with Glasgow Rangers, winning Scottish league and cup winners medals. Was transferred to West Ham for £6,000 in 1937. In 1940 he played for West Ham in the first war time FA Cup Final and also played in seven Scottish internationals during the war. Brentford signed him for £7,500 in October 1946, but were relegated at the end of that season. Against strong competition, Arsenal signed him for £10,000 in July 1947. In his first season at Highbury, Archie won a league championship medal and played in forty league matches. He played in thirty nine league games the following season and a further twenty four in 1949 - 50 (a total of one hundred and three league matches for Arsenal). Was unfortunate not to win the only honour to elude him (FA Cup Winners Medal) because after playing in the semi final replay, versus Chelsea, Alex Forbes was preferred for the 1950 FA Cup winning team. Joined Fulham in June 1950, where he finished his career in 1953. Later managed Guildford City, Norwich, WBA and Brighton. Died June 1993, aged 77.

	Games	Goals
League	103	1
FA Cup	4	0
Charity Shield	1	0
Friendly Matches	6	0
Tour Matches	13	0
Combination League	1	0
Combination Cup	1	0
Total	**129**	**1**

Archie Macaulay

Honours:
7 Scottish Caps
7 Scottish War-Time Caps
(WITH GLASGOW RANGERS)
Scottish League Championship
    Medal   1936-37
Scottish Cup Winners Medal   1935-36
(WITH ARSENAL)
League Championship Medal   1947-48
FA Charity Shield Winners Medal   1948-49

McCALL, Alex — 1965-67

Birth Place: Glasgow, Scotland
Date of Birth: 3rd September 1948

Alex McCall joined Arsenal in September 1965 on his seventeenth birthday, after having previously played for the Scottish junior side Glasgow United. Played regularly in first the youth side during 1965-66, then for the metropolitan team in 1966 - 67. Was released on a free transfer in January 1967.

Alex McCall

	Games	Goals
Combination Cup	1	1
Metropolitan League	21	13
Metropolitan Cup	2	1
South East Counties League	19	8
Youth Cup	1	1
Other Youth Cups	6	1
Youth Tour Matches	9	2
Total	**59**	**27**

Honours:
Southern Junior Floodlight Cup Winners
    Medal   1965-66

McCLELLAND, Jack   1960-64

Birth Place: Lurgan, Northern Ireland
Date of Birth: 19th May 1940

Jack McClelland joined Arsenal from the Irish club, Glentoran, in October 1960. He played in four league matches during the 1960 - 61 season, including his debut versus Spurs in January 1961. By this time he had won the first of his six Northern Ireland caps, although McClelland still could not wrest the regular goalkeeping position in the Arsenal team from Jack Kelsey. In 1961-62, he played in only four league matches, but when Kelsey's career ended during the World Wup series of 1962, he grabbed his chance and the following season became Arsenal's regular goalkeeper, playing thirty - three league games. He suffered a serious injury in the following September (broken collar bone) resulting in him being out of action for four months. After regaining full fitness he found himself back in the reserve side due to the consistency of Arsenal's new goalkeeper, Jim Furnell. Never regained his first team place and was transferred to Fulham for £5,000 in December 1964. Spent four seasons at Craven Cottage, including a loan period at Lincoln City, and drifted in to non league football with Barnet during the early 1970's. About this time his health deteriorated, and it was a great shock when he died in March 1976, at the age of thirty five.

Jack McClelland

	Games	Goals
League	46	0
FA Cup	3	0
Friendly Matches	22	0
Tour Matches	4	0
Combination League	51	0
London Challenge Cup	2	0
Metropolitan League	10	0
Metropolitan Cup	4	0
Total	**142**	**0**

Honours:
6 Northern Ireland Caps
1 Irish League Cap
London FA Challenge Cup
    runners - up   1960-61
Metropolitan League Professional Cup
    winners   1961-62

McCREEVEY, Brian   1953-57

Birth Place: Prestwich, Lancashire
Date of Birth: 29th September 1935

Brian McCreevey joined Arsenal as an amateur in September 1953, after having been on Preston's books. He spent six months at Hendon Town, but returned to Highbury in March 1954, when he turned professional. Called up for National Service in June 1954, reducing his appearances to only nine during the two seasons, 1954-56. Demobbed in May 1956 and spent a further nine months at the club, playing mainly for the London Midweek side. Released on a free transfer in March 1957 when he joined Stockport.

	Games	Goals
Friendly Matches	4	2
Combination League	9	0
Combination Cup	1	1
Eastern Counties League	10	1
Eastern Counties Cup	2	1
London Midweek League	10	1
Total	**36**	**6**

McCULLOUGH, Billy   1958-66

Birth Place: Woodburn,
            Northern Ireland
Date of Birth: 27th July 1935

Billy McCullough joined Arsenal from the Irish side Portadown in September 1958. Played regularly at left back for the reserve side during 1958 - 59. He made his league debut versus Luton Town in December 1958, playing ten league matches that season. In the 1959-60 season, Len Wills switched to right back, enabling McCullough to play thirty six league matches that season at left back. He missed only one league match in the 1960 - 61 season and won the first of his ten Northern Ireland caps versus Italy. During the next two seasons, he missed only two of Arsenal's eighty four league matches and was the club's most consistent player around the time. In 1963 - 64 he was again a regular member of the side, playing in forty league matches and winning further Irish caps. He played in thirty league games in 1964 - 65 and a further seventeen in 1965 - 66, before losing his place to the up and coming Peter Storey. Transfer listed during the summer of 1966, and joined Millwall for £8,000 in August 1966. Later played for

Bedford Town, Cork Celtic and Derry City. Billy McCullough will be remembered as one of the most consistent full back's the club has had, playing in all, nearly three hundred first team games.

Billy McCullough

	Games	Goals
League	253	4
FA Cup	11	0
UEFA Cup	4	1
Friendly Matches	51	0
Tour Matches	30	1
Combination League	46	1
London Challenge Cup	10	2
Southern Floodlight Cup	5	0
Total	**410**	**9**

Honours:
10 Northern Ireland Caps
1 Northern Ireland B Cap
Southern Floodlight Challenge Cup
    winners   1958-59
London FA Challenge Cup
    winners   1961-62
    runners - up   1965-66

McDERMOTT, Brian   1977-84

Birth Place: Slough, Berkshire
Date of Birth: 8th April 1961

Brian McDermott joined Arsenal as an apprentice in January 1977, turning professional in February 1979. He won a regular place in Arsenal's reserve team in the 1977-78 season. Was the reserve's leading goalscorer in 1978-79 and won the first of his five England youth caps. Made his league debut (as substitute) versus Bristol City in March 1979. Was again the top scorer for the reserves with twenty six in 1979-80, but played in only one league match that season. Won a regular place in the league side during 1980-81 playing in twenty three games. Played in only thirteen games in 1981 - 82 and nine in 1982 - 83. In 1983 - 84 he still could not command a regular place in the first team. In the seven seasons he spent at Highbury he can consider himself unlucky to have played in only seventy first team matches. However, he was a valuable member of the reserve side. Went on loan to Fulham, March 1983, and IFK Norrkoping

Brian McDermott

April to October 1984. In December 1984, when he left Highbury for Oxford United for a fee of £40,000, he had played over one hundred and seventy reserve games. Whilst at Oxford United, Brian had a loan period at Huddersfield Town, November 1986, before being transferred to Cardiff. Later played for Exeter and non league Yeovil Town.

	Games	Goals
League	61	12
FA Cup	1	0
League Cup	4	0
Europe	4	1
Friendly Matches	42	15
Tour Matches	13	2
Football Combination	174	81
South East Counties League	40	10
Youth Cup	6	1
Other Youth Cups	6	3
Youth Tours	4	4
Total	**355**	**129**

Honours:
5 England Youth Caps
Football Combination Championship
  Medal   1983 - 84

MACDONALD, Malcolm   1976-79

Birth Place: Fulham, London
Date of Birth: 7th January 1950

Malcolm Macdonald began his football career as a full back with Tonbridge. Joined Fulham in August 1968 and was switched with great success to centre forward. He spent only one season at Craven Cottage, being transferred to Luton Town for £30,000 in July 1968. In two seasons with Luton he averaged well over a goal every other game, scoring forty nine goals in eighty eight league matches. By this time the larger clubs had taken note of the twenty one year old goalscoring sensation. Eventually Newcastle United signed him for £180,000 in May 1971. On Tyneside he became the greatest idol since the days of Jackie Milburn. In one of his first matches for the club he scored a hat trick versus Liverpool and finished each of his five seasons with Newcastle as leading scorer, scoring well over one hundred first team goals for the club during those five seasons. Scored five goals in one match for England versus Cyprus (to equal the individual match scoring record). Also scored in every round of the FA Cup when Newcastle reached the FA Cup Final in 1973 - 74. In August 1976 all Geordie supporters were stunned when 'Supermac' was allowed to leave the club. Macdonald joined Arsenal for £333,333 (at that time the largest fee Arsenal had ever paid). He repaid some of the fee in his first season when he scored twenty nine first team goals (twenty five league), and finished the season as the First Division's leading goalscorer. In 1977 - 78 he scored a further twenty six goals and helped Arsenal to the FA Cup Final of that year versus Ipswich. The following season was only four games old when Macdonald suffered a serious leg injury in a League Cup match at Rotherham. He tried with no success to regain full fitness, playing in only two further matches that season (versus Red Star Belgrade as substitute and Chelsea). Eventually, in July 1979, at the age of twenty nine, it was announced that Malcolm Macdonald would retire. In little over two seasons at Highbury he had scored fifty seven goals in one hundred and seven first team matches. Malcolm Macdonald will be remembered as one of the most prolific goalscorers of the 1970's. Later became manager of Fulham, and also Huddersfield Town 1987 - 88.

	Games	Goals
League	84	42
FA Cup	9	10
League Cup	14	5
EUFA Cup	1	0
Friendly Matches	14	3
Tour Matches	10	15
Combination League	13	5
Total	**145**	**80**

Honours:
(WITH NEWCASTLE AND ARSENAL)
14 England Caps
4 England Under 23 Caps
2 Football League Caps
2 FA Cup Finalist
  Medals   1973-74, 1977-78
PFA Division One Team Award   1973-74

Malcolm Macdonald

Malcolm Macdonald with
his eyes firmly on the ball

McGILL, Jimmy　　1965-67

Birth Place:　Glasgow
Date of Birth:　27th November 1946

🔫 Jimmy McGill joined Arsenal from the Scottish youth side Possil Park in July 1965. During his two seasons at Highbury he was a valuable member of the reserve side, playing either at full back, wing half, or inside forward. Made his league debut versus Leeds, at Highbury in May 1966 (the night when the attendance of only 4,600 was Arsenal's lowest ever at Highbury). Played in eight league matches during 1966 - 67. Transferred to Huddersfield Town in September 1967 for £8,000. Spent four seasons there, and a further five seasons at Hull City. Finished his career with Halifax in 1976 - 77.

Jimmy McGill

	Games	Goals
League	10	0
League Cup	2	0
Friendly Matches	17	0
Tour Matches	1	0
Combination League	39	7
Combination Cup	3	0
London Challenge Cup	2	0
Metropolitan League	24	1
Metropolitan Cup	7	0
Total	**105**	**8**

Honours:
Metropolitan League Challenge Cup
　winners　　1965-66

McKECHNIE, Ian　　1958-64

Birth Place:　Bellshill, lanark, Scotland
Date of Birth:　4th October 1941

🔫 Ian McKechnie joined Arsenal's groundstaff in October 1958, turning professional in April 1959. Originally joined the staff as an outside left, but soon switched to goalkeeper. He won a regular place in Arsenal's youth team during 1959 - 60, making his reserve team debut in 1960 - 61, and was the first choice reserve team goalkeeper in 1961 - 62 when he was drafted in to the league side for his debut versus Blackburn in October 1961, playing in three league matches that season, followed by eight in 1962 - 63. In 1963 - 64 he played in a further eleven league games, but with Burns, Furnell, McClelland and Wilson on the books as goalkeepers, his first team chances were limited. Arsenal released him on a free transfer in March 1964 and McKechnie spent weeks writing to clubs for a chance to prove himself. Eventually, in May 1964, moved to Southend where he spent two seasons before joining Hull City in August 1966, he spent eight successful seasons at Boothferry Park and played in nearly three hundred first team games. Later became manager of Sligo Rovers, Ireland.

Ian McKechnie

	Games	Goals
League	23	0
UEFA Cup	2	0
Friendly Matches	27	0
Tour Matches	5	0
Combination League	43	0
London Challenge Cup	6	0
Southern Floodlight Cup	1	0
Metropolitan League	36	0
Metropolitan Cup	15	0
South East Counties League	33	3
Youth Cup	5	0
Other Youth Cups	5	0
Youth Tour Matches	5	0
Total	**206**	**3**

Honours:
Football Combination Champions	1962-63
London FA Challenge Cup Winners	1962-63
Metropolitan League Champions	1960-61
Metropolitan League Challenge Cup	
Winners	1960-61
Metropolitan League Professional Cup	
Winners	1960-61
South East Counties League Cup	
Winners	1959-60

MACKENZIE, Angus　　1966-68

Birth Place:　Glasgow, Scotland
Date of Birth:　30th November 1949

🔫 Angus Mackenzie joined Arsenal from the Scottish youth side, Drumchapel A F C, in December 1966. Established himself as a wing half in Arsenal's youth side during the 1966 - 67 season. In the 1967 - 68 season he played in over fifty matches, though not regularly for any of Arsenal's reserve or youth sides. Released on a free transfer in May 1968.

	Games	Goals
Friendly Matches	21	3
Combination League	12	0
Combination Cup	3	0
Metropolitan League	18	0
Metropolitan Cup	8	0
South East Counties League	18	2
Youth Cup	7	0
Other Youth Cups	11	1
Youth Tour Matches	17	2
Total	**115**	**8**

Honours:
London Youth Challenge Cup Winners
　Medal　　1966-67
Southern Junior Floodlight Cup Finalists
　Medal　　1967-68

McKINNON, David　　1972-76

Birth Place:　Glasgow
Date of Birth:　23rd May 1956

🔫 David McKinnon joined Arsenal as an apprentice in May 1972, after previously playing for Glasgow United, the Scottish junior side. He had also played in trials for the Scottish Schoolboy international side. Served the youth team well for two seasons, turning professional in January 1974. Played regularly for the reserve side as a wing half during season 1974 - 75. Retained his place during the first half of the following season before being granted a free transfer in February 1976. Later played for Dundee and Partick before joining Glasgow Rangers in 1982 for £30,000. David played in nearly one hundred and fifty first team games for Rangers, before joining Airdrie in 1986.

	Games	Goals
Friendly Matches	22	2
Combination League	51	1
South East Counties League	48	3
Youth Cup　5	0	
Other Youth Cups	6	0
Youth Tour Matches	19	0
Total	**151**	**6**

MACLEOD, Johnny   1961-64

Birth Place: Edinburgh, Scotland
Date of Birth: 23rd November 1938

➤ Johnny Macleod began his career with Hibernian in 1957, playing in eighty five league matches for the Edinburgh club between 1957 - 61. During this time he won five Scottish caps. Joined Arsenal in July 1961 for £40,000 (at that time the highest fee ever paid for a winger). Played regularly for Arsenal in a period spanning three seasons and made over one hundred league appearances. With the young George Armstrong pushing for Macleod's first team place, he accepted a transfer to Aston Villa in September 1964 for £35,000. Played regularly at Villa Park for four seasons. Later played in Belgium with KV Mechelen 1968 - 71 before returning to Scotland with Raith Rovers.

Johnny Macleod

	Games	Goals
League	101	23
FA Cup	8	4
EUFA Cup	3	1
Friendly Matches	13	2
Tour Matches	11	3
Combination League	5	2
London Challenge Cup	5	1
Total	**146**	**36**

Honours:
5 Scottish Caps
1 Scottish Under 23 Cap
2 Scottish League Caps
London FA Challenge Cup winners 1961-62

McLEAN, Desmond   1949-52

Birth Place: Glasgow, Scotland
Date of Birth: July 1931

➤ Desmond McLean joined Arsenal as a promising goalkeeper in August 1949, having previously played for Celtic and Queens Park as an amateur. Called up for National Service within three weeks of joining the club.During the following two seasons managed to play in only a handful of games. Was released on a free transfer, after being demobbed in February 1952.

	Games	Goals
Friendly Matches	2	0
Eastern Counties League	10	0
London Midweek League	14	0
Other Youth Matches	2	0
Total	**28**	**0**

McLINTOCK, Frank MBE   1964-73

Birth Place: Glasgow, Scotland
Date of Birth: 28th December 1939

➤ Frank McLintock will be remembered as the man who captained Arsenal to the double during the 1970 - 71 season. Started his football career with Leicester City in January 1957, making his league debut in the 1959 - 60 season. During his seven seasons at Filbert Street, played in over two hundred first team games, and won the first of his nine Scottish caps. He played in two FA Cup Finals in 1961 and 1963, and a League Cup Final in 1964, always playing on the losing side. Transferred to Arsenal for £80,000 in October 1964, at that time a record fee for a wing half. It was also the highest amount Arsenal had ever paid. Made his league debut the same month versus Nottingham Forest. During the following nine seasons, McLintock became the driving force at either wing half or centre half. In his first three seasons at the club (1964 - 67) he was probably the most consistent of all the Arsenal players, playing in a side which was the poorest for many years. In 1967-68, he became team captain and guided Arsenal to the League Cup Final versus Leeds. In 1968-69, Arsenal finished fourth in the league, the club's highest position in the league for fifteen seasons, and he played in the League Cup Final versus Swindon. At the beginning of the 1969 - 70 season, McLintock asked for a transfer due to the lack of success at Highbury. Fortunately for both him and the club, he was persuaded to stay. In that season Arsenal won their first major honour for seventeen years, winning the Inter Cities Fairs Cup. In 1970-71, he became only the second player this century to captain a Double winning side (Danny Blanchflower with Spurs in 1960 - 61 being the other). Was voted Footballer of the Year that season. In 1971-72 he captained Arsenal to the FA Cup Final versus Leeds, returning to Wembley for his sixth major final. In 1972-73 he led Arsenal to second place in the First Division. After nine years service, he was surprisingly transferred to QPR in June 1973 for £20,000, where he spent four seasons before retiring in 1977. During a career which spanned twenty years, he played in well over six hundred league matches. Later managed, without much success, Leicester City. In 1981 - 82 he became a member of Radio 2's football commentary team. Was appointed manager of Brentford in February 1984. And later became assistant manager at Millwall. Awarded the MBE for his services to football in 1972. Now a regular commentator on Capital Gold Radio.

Frank McLintock

	Games	Goals
League	314	26
FA Cup	36	1
League Cup	34	4
European Cup	5	1
UEFA Cup	14	0
Friendly Matches	33	7
Tour Matches	24	4
Combination League	10	0
London Challenge Cup	2	0
Total	**472**	**43**

Honours:
9 Scottish Caps
1 Scottish Under - 23 Cap
Footballer of the Year   1970-71
League Championship Medal   1970-71
FA Cup Winners Medal   1970-71
Three FA Cup Finalist Medals   1960-61, 1962-63, 1971-72
Three League Cup Finalists Medals   1963-64, 1967-68, 1968-69
Inter Cities Fairs Cup Winners   1969-70
London FA Challenge Cup Winners Medal   1969-70

McNAB, Bob
1966-75

Birth Place: Huddersfield, Yorkshire
Date of Birth: 20th July 1943

Bob McNab

	Games	Goals	Honours:
League	278	4	4 England Caps
FA Cup	39	0	1 Football League Cap
League Cup	27	2	League Championship
European Cup	2	0	Medal 1970-71
UEFA Cup	19	0	FA Cup Winners Medal 1970-71
Friendly Matches	26	2	FA Cup Finalist Medal 1971-72
Tour Matches	20	2	Inter Cities Fairs Cup Winners
Combination League	23	0	Medal 1969-70
London Challenge Cup	2	0	2 League Cup Finalist
Total	**436**	**10**	Medals 1967-68, 1968-69

☛Bob McNab joined Arsenal from Huddersfield Town as a replacement for Billy McCullough in October 1966. Arsenal payed £50,000 for him, which at the time, was the highest fee ever paid for a full back. He immediately won a regular place in the first team, and over the next nine seasons was the club's first choice left back, although for several of those seasons, he suffered many niggling injuries. During seasons 1967-68 and 1968-69 he played a major part in helping Arsenal reach two League Cup Finals. In 1969-70 he won the first of his four England caps and helped Arsenal to win the Inter Cities Fairs Cup. He was also named in England's World Cup Squad for the 1970 World Cup Series. In the Double season of 1970-71, McNab played in sixty two of the sixty four first team games, winning League and FA Cup winners medals. In 1971-72 he missed half the season through injury, leaving Sammy Nelson to deputise. He did, however, play in the Cup Final side versus Leeds. In 1972-73, when Arsenal finished as league runners up, he was back to his consistent best and played regularly throughout that season. In the next two seasons, 1973-74 and 1974-75, a succession of injuries and loss of form resulted in him playing in only twenty three and eighteen league matches respectively. With Sammy Nelson showing great promise, Arsenal gave McNab a free transfer in June 1975. He joined Wolves the following month where he spent one season before finishing his career in the United States. Played for Barnet in 1977 before becoming coach to Vancouver Whitecaps, Canada. Now lives in California, USA, where he runs his own executive recruitment agency.

McPHERSON, Ian — 1946-51

Birth Place: Glasgow
Date of Birth: 26th July 1920

Ian McPherson joined Arsenal from Notts County for £10,000 in August 1946 after having previously played, pre war, for Glasgow Rangers. Reg Cumner, the Welsh International departing to Notts County in part exchange. In his first season at Highbury, McPherson played in thirty seven league matches mainly on the right wing. In the championship season of 1947-48, he was switched to the left wing after an injury to Dennis Compton. Played regularly (eighty six league matches) over the following three seasons (1948-51), returning to Notts County in August 1951. Ian McPherson possessed a terrific shot as well as great speed and strength, but was something of an enigma whilst at Highbury, at times brilliant, at others very mediocre. Finished his league career with Brentford in 1953-54. Later played for Bedford Town 1954 and Cambridge United 1954-55. Died March 1983 aged 62.

Ian McPherson

	Games	Goals
League	152	19
FA Cup	11	2
Friendly Matches	23	14
Tour Matches	18	0
Combination League	14	5
London Challenge Cup	3	1
Combination Cup	7	4
Total	**228**	**45**

Honours:
League Championship Medal   1947-48
Football Combination Cup
   runners - up   1950-51

MADDEN, David — 1983-84

Birth Place: Stepney, London
Date of Birth: 6th January 1963

David Madden joined Arsenal on a free transfer from Southampton during the summer of 1983 after playing in a trial match versus Gillingham at the end of the 1982 - 83 season. He played regularly for the reserves during 1983 - 84 as a midfield player, and made his league debut versus West Bromwich, at Highbury in December 1983. His career never materialised at Arsenal and he was granted a free transfer during the summer of 1984 when he joined Charlton. Later played for Reading, Los Angeles, USA, Crystal Palace, Birmingham and Maidstone United.

	Games	Goals
League	2	0
Friendly Matches	6	2
Combination League	25	3
Total	**33**	**5**

Honours:
Football Combination Champions   1983-84

MAGILL, Eddie — 1959-65

Birth Place: Carrickfergus, Northern Ireland
Date of Birth: 17th May 1939

Eddie Magill joined Arsenal from the Irish side Portadown in May 1959. Made his league debut versus Sheffield Wednesday in December 1959, and was considered at the time a possible replacement for Dennis Evans. He played in seventeen league games that season, but the following season, 1960 - 61, lost his place to both Len Wills and Dave Bacuzzi. In 1961 - 62 season he shared the right back position with Bacuzzi and won the first of his twenty six Irish caps. In the next two seasons (1962 - 63, 1963 - 64) he became a regular in Arsenal's defence, playing in seventy one of Arsenal's eighty four league matches. He lost his place however, when Don Howe was signed from West Bromwich in April 1964. Over the next eighteen months he was a regular member of the reserve team. He became unsettled and was transferred to Brighton for £10,000 in October 1965. He spent three seasons there, before returning to Northern Ireland in 1968. Later became coach to B1909 Odense (Denmark) and then manager of Frederikshavn (Denmark).

	Games	Goals
League	116	0
FA Cup	11	0
UEFA Cup	4	0
Friendly Matches	35	0
Tour Matches	9	0
Combination League	96	2
London Challenge Cup	7	0
Southern Floodlight Cup	1	0
Metropolitan League	1	0
Metropolitan Cup	2	0
Total	**282**	**2**

Eddie Magill

Honours:
26 Northern Ireland Caps
1 Under - 23 Cap
London FA Challenge Cup
   runners - up   1960-61
Metropolitan League Professional Cup
   winners   1960-61

MANCINI, Terry — 1974-76

Birth Place: Camden Town, London
Date of Birth: 4th October 1942

Terry Mancini began his football career with Watford, joining them as a professional in July 1961. In his five seasons at Vicarage Road he played in only sixty six league games. Released on a free transfer at the beginning of the 1965-66 season, he decided to try his luck in South Africa and for the next two years played for the Port Elizabeth side. Was tempted back to English football by Orient in November 1967. During the following four seasons he played in one hundred and sixty seven league matches, winning a Third Division Championship medal in 1969 - 70. QPR signed him in October 1971 for £20,000, and during his three years at the club became a firm favourite with the crowd. Played in ninety four league matches for Rangers, helping them win promotion to the First Division in 1972 - 73. After selling Frank McLintock at the end of the 1972 - 73 season, Arsenal lacked an experienced centre half, and surprisingly in October 1974, they signed Mancini for £20,000. Played for the Republic of Ireland side, winning the first of his five Eire caps versus Russia in 1973. In his two seasons at Highbury, Terry played in fifty two league games helping the club through two of its worst ever seasons. Released on a free transfer in September 1976 when he rejoined Orient. Later coached several teams and in 1983 - 84 became a coach with Fulham. Now running a car hire business in New Malden.

Terry Mancini

	Games	Goals
League	52	1
FA Cup	8	0
League Cup	2	0
Friendly Matches	7	0
Tour Matches	7	1
Combination League	12	0
Total	**88**	**2**

Honours:
5 Eire Caps
(WITH ORIENT)
Third Division Championship Medal 1969-70

MARDEN, Ben   190-55

Birth Place: Fulham, London
Date of Birth: 10th February 1927

☛ Ben Marden joined Arsenal from Chelmsford City after a two month trial in January 1950. He spent the first of his six seasons with the club playing in the reserve side. Was a regular member of the reserve side during 1950 - 51 before making his league debut versus Manchester United in March 1951. Played in the final eleven league matches of that season. Started the 1950 - 51 season as a regular winger of the league side but returned to the reserves and made only seven league appearances during that season. Played in eight league matches during the championship winning season of 1952 - 53, and a further nine league games in 1953-54, which included scoring a hat

trick versus Charlton in October 1953. Played in a further seven league games during 1954-55 before transferring to Watford in June 1955. In his six seasons at Highbury, Ben Marden never established a first team place. He played in a total of only forty two league matches; although for the reserve team he played in over one hundred matches, scoring sixty three goals. He later served Bedford Town and Romford.

Ben Marden

	Games	Goals
League	42	11
Friendly Matches	20	13
Tour Matches	8	1
Combination League	74	38
Combination Cup	45	25
London Challenge Cup	5	3
Eastern Counties League	11	10
Eastern Counties Cup	1	0
London Midweek League	14	9
Total	**220**	**110**

Honours:
Football Combination Champions   1950-51

MARINELLO, Peter   1970-73

Birth Place: Edinburgh, Scotland
Date of Birth: 20th February 1950

☛ Peter Marinello joined Arsenal from Hibernian for £100,000 in January 1970. It was the first time Arsenal had ever paid a six figure fee for a player, Marinello, with the film star image, the long hair and the fantastic ball control was regarded as the new George Best. He was highly sought after by the advertising medium, selling everything from records to toothpaste. Unfortunately, the pressures of all the publicity affected the twenty year old Marinello, and although scoring on his debut

versus Manchester United in January 1970, he played in only fourteen league matches that season, and was not even included in the club's Inter Cities Fairs Cup winning side. Even worse was to follow, during the great Double season of 1970-71, he played in only three league games. By this time the press and the media had come to the conclusion that Marinello was one of the most over rated and expensive flops in the history of British football. Played in only eight league matches in 1971 - 72 and thirteen in 1972 - 73. With George Armstrong as consistent as ever on Arsenal's right wing, his days at Highbury were numbered, and in July 1973 Peter was transferred to Portsmouth for £40,000. Later returned to Scotland to play for Motherwell in 1975. Played for Fulham 1978, Phoenix, USA, and back to Scotland with Hearts in 1981. The career which promised so much collapsed, due mainly to media pressure. After a spell running a pub in Edinburgh, Peter is now living in Bournemouth where he was officially declared bankrupt by the local County Council in March 1995.

Peter Marinello

	Games	Goals
League	38	3
FA Cup	1	0
League Cup	5	1
European Cup	2	1
UEFA Cup	5	0
Friendly Matches	12	1
Tour Matches	8	2
Combination League	75	22
Combination Cup	2	2
London Challenge Cup	3	1
Total	**151**	**33**

Honours:
(WITH ARSENAL)
2 Scottish Under - 23 Caps
Football Combination Cup Winners
 Medal   1969-70
(WITH HIBS)
Scottish League Cup Finalist Medal 1968-69

MARLOW, Fred   1947-50

Birth Place: Sheffield, Yorkshire
Date of Birth: 9th November 1928

☞ Fred Marlow joined Arsenal from the Sheffield side, Hillsborough Boys Club in September 1947. He did not turn professional until March 1949, after his release from HM Forces. Played regularly in Arsenal's third team during 1949 - 50. Was released on a free transfer in September 1950, when he joined Sheffield Wednesday. Later played for Buxton, Grimsby, Boston United and York City.

	Games	Goals
Combination League	2	1
Combination Cup	1	0
Eastern Counties League	9	1
Eastern Counties Cup	4	1
London Midweek League	5	1
Other Youth Matches	7	0
Total	**28**	**4**

MARSHALL, Tom   1957-58

Birth Place: Beadford, Yorkshire
Date of Birth: June 1938

☞ Tom Marshall joined Arsenal as a promising half back from a West Riding youth side in May 1957. During season 1957-58 played in only sixteen matches, predominantly for Arsenal's London Midweek side. Was released on a free transfer in March 1958.

	Games	Goals
Friendly Matches	6	1
Eastern Counties League	2	0
London Midweek League	11	0
Total	**19**	**1**

MATTHEWS, John   1971-78

Birth Place: Islington, London
Date of Birth: 1st November 1955

☞ John Matthews joined Arsenal as an apprentice in July 1971, turning professional in August 1973. In his first two seasons at Highbury he played consistently for the successful youth team, either in defence or midfield. Won a regular place in the reserve side during 1973-1974. Made his league debut on the opening day of the 1974-75 season versus Leicester City. Played in twenty league games that season, at full back, centre back, and in midfield. In 1975-76, John played in only one league match due to a series of injuries. In the following season he fought his way back to full fitness and played in seventeen league games. In 1977 - 78, because of the availability of players like David O'Leary and Willie Young, he played in only seven league games. With Steve

Walford and Steve Gatting also emerging, his first team chances were limited. In August 1978 he was transferred to Sheffield United for £80,000. He spent four seasons at Bramall Lane. Later played for Mansfield, Chesterfield, Plymouth Argyle and Torquay.

John Matthews

	Games	Goals
League	45	2
FA Cup	6	1
League Cup	6	2
Friendly Matches	44	5
Tour Matches	17	0
Combination League	123	6
London Challenge Cup	5	0
South East Counties League	57	6
Youth Cup	13	1
Other Youth Cups	15	0
Youth Tour Matches	15	6
Total	**346**	**29**

Honours:
South East Counties League
    Champions   1971-72
South East Counties League Cup
    runners - up   1971-72

MELDRUM, Colin   1958-60

Birth Place: Glasgow, Scotland
Date of Birth: 26th November 1941

☞ Colin Meldrum joined Arsenal's groundstaff in August 1958, turning professional in December 1958. Was a regular in Arsenal's Metropolitan League side during 1958 - 59. Played regularly for the reserve side either at full back or half back, in the 1959 - 60 season. Lost his place during the first half of the 1960 - 61 season and returned to the Metropolitan side. Was released on a free transfer in December 1960 and joined Watford. Later played for Reading (who he served well for seven seasons), Cambridge United and Workington Town.

	Games	Goals
Friendly Matches	10	2
Combination League	16	0
London Challenge Cup	1	0
Southern Floodlight Cup	1	0
Metropolitan League	39	3
Metropolitan Cup	6	0
South East Counties League	13	1
Youth Cup	12	6
Other Youth Cups	6	0
Youth Tour Matches	2	0
Total	**106**	**12**

Colin Meldrum

Honours:
Metropolitan League Championship
    Medals   1958-59, 1960-61
South East Counties League Cup Winners
    Medal   1959-60

MERCER, Joe OBE   1946-55

Birth Place: Ellesmere Port, Cheshire
Date of Birth: 9th August 1914

☞ Joe Mercer was one of the most influential players Arsenal have ever had. He started his long career with Everton as a sixteen year old in 1932. Made his debut for them during the 1933 - 34 season, winning a regular place during the 1935 - 36 season. Up to the beginning of the war he had made one hundred and fifty nine league appearances. Won five England caps and a League Championship medal in 1938 - 39. During wartime he added twenty two England international caps. In December 1946, at the age of thirty two, Joe was surprisingly transferred to Arsenal for £8,000. With Arsenal in trouble at the foot of the table he and Ronnie Rooke were instrumental in helping the side out of trouble. In 1947 - 48 he captained Arsenal to the League Championship and in 1949 - 50

METCHICK, Dave   1970-72

Birth Place: Derby
Date of Birth: 14th August 1943

Dave Metchick served his football apprenticeship with Fulham, under the influence of Johnny Haynes, Bobby Robson and Jimmy Hill, before turning professional in August 1961. Spent three years at Craven Cottage before joining Leyton Orient in December 1964. Transferred to Peterborough then QPR, before joining Arsenal for a small fee in December 1970. Served Arsenal's reserve side well for two seasons and was a great influence on all the young players during that period. Was given a free transfer in May 1972, going to the USA where he played for the Atlanta Chiefs. Returned to English football with Brentford in September 1973 where he finished his career. He supplemented his football income by working as a male model.

	Games	Goals
Friendly Matches	7	1
Combination League	60	1
London Challenge Cup	4	1
Total	**71**	**12**

Honours: (WITH FULHAM)
4 England Youth Caps

MILLEN, Billy   1966-67

Birth Place: Northern Ireland
Date of Birth: March 1948

Billy Millen joined Arsenal from the Irish side Distillery, in September 1966. During the 1966-67 season he was a prominent member of Arsenal's Metropolitan League side. Unluckily suffered many niggling injuries during his spell at the club and did not settle. Was granted a free transfer in November 1967 when he returned to play in Irish League football, where he won many honours.

	Games	Goals
Friendly Matches	5	2
Combination League	1	0
Combination Cup	2	0
Metropolitan League	15	9
Metropolitan Cup	4	3
South East Counties League	7	5
Other Youth Cups	2	0
Total	**36**	**19**

MILNE, Andrew   1965-67

Birth Place: Renfrew, Scotland
Date of Birth: 17th July 1948

Andrew Milne was yet another young Scotsman to travel South. Joined Arsenal in July 1965 as a professional on his seventeenth birthday, from the Scottish junior side Glasgow United. Was a regular in Arsenal's youth side during 1965 - 66 as a goalscoring inside forward. Played regularly in the Metropolitan League side during 1966 - 67. Released on a free transfer in March 1967.

	Games	Goals
Friendly Matches	5	6
Combination League	3	1
Combination Cup	1	1
London Challenge Cup	1	0
Metropolitan League	22	12
Metropolitan Cup	3	3
South East Counties League	19	11
Youth Cup	3	1
Other Youth Cups	9	9
Youth Tour Matches	7	0
Total	**73**	**44**

Honours:
FA Youth Cup Winners Medal   1965-66
Southern Junior Floodlight Cup
  Winners Medal   1965-66
South East Counties League Cup
  Finalists Medal   1965-66

MILNE, Dennis   1962-65

Birth Place: Kennelmouth, Scotland
Date of Birth: 1945

Dennis Milne was an apprentice joiner before joining Arsenal as an amateur in August 1962. Played regularly in Arsenal's successful youth side at centre half during the 1962-63 season. Turned professional in April 1963 and progressed to the Metropolitan League side during the following season. Retained his place during the first part of the season 1964-65, before sustaining a serious leg injury in October 1964 which kept him out of action for four months. Released on a free transfer in May 1965.

	Games	Goals
Friendly Matches	3	0
Combination League	3	0
Metropolitan League	30	0
Metropolitan Cup	5	0
South East Counties League	31	0
Youth Cup	6	0
Other Youth Cups	8	0
Total	**86**	**0**

he led them to a FA Cup victory over Liverpool and was voted Footballer of the Year. Led Arsenal back to Wembley for the 1952 FA Cup Final, when losing against Newcastle, and captained the championship winning team of 1952-53. Announced his retirement in May 1953, but his love for the game was too great and he was back at the opening of the next season. Unfortunately, during a match against Liverpool at Highbury in April 1954, he collided with his team mate Joe Wade and broke his leg, ending his playing career on a low note. Was appointed manager of Sheffield United in August 1955. Later managed Aston Villa, Manchester City and Coventry City. Led Manchester City to First and Second Division Championships as well as the FA Cup, the League Cup and the European Cup Winners Cup. Managed the England team for two months in the early 1970's. Joe Mercer was one of footballs' most dedicated men. Was a director of Coventry City 1972 - 81. Awarded the OBE for his excellent services to football in 1976. Died on his 76th birthday in 1990.

	Games	Goals
League	247	2
FA Cup	26	0
Charity Shield	2	0
Friendly Matches	17	1
Tour Matches	9	0
Combination Cup	2	0
Total	**303**	**3**

Honours:

(WITH ARSENAL AND EVERTON)
5 England Caps
22 England War-Time Caps
2 Football League Caps
Footballer of the Year   1949-50
2 League Championship Medals
    1938-39, 1947-48, 1952,53
FA Cup Winners Medal   1949-50
FA Cup Finalist Medal   1951-52
2 FA Charity Shield Winners Medals
    1949-49, 1953-54

Joe Mercer

Honours:

Metropolitan League Professional Cup
   Winners Medal   1962-63
S.E. Counties League Cup Winners Medal 1963-64

MILTON, Arthur   1945-55

Birth Place: Bristol, Avon
Date of Birth: 10th March 1928

☛ Arthur Milton will be remembered as the man who played both football and cricket for England. Joined Arsenal as an amateur in April 1945, turning professional in July 1946. Made his debut in Arsenal's reserve side in October 1946, just before he was called up for National Service. Returned to Highbury two years later and played regularly at outside right in the reserve side during seasons 1949-51, making his league debut versus Aston Villa in March 1951. Became the regular first team right winger at the beginning of the 1951-52 season, and such was his progress that after only twelve league appearances was chosen to play for England versus Austria in November 1951. Totalled twenty league appearances and in the following championship season of 1952 - 53, played twenty three times. During the next two seasons played in only a further twenty nine league matches before being transferred to Bristol City in February 1955. Retired at the end of that season to concentrate on his cricket career. During his twenty three year career with Gloucestershire he totalled over thirty two thousand runs and played in six test matches for England during 1958-59.

Arthur Milton

	Games	Goals
League	75	18
FA Cup	9	3
Friendly Matches	13	6
Combination League	44	15
Combination Cup	25	10
London Challenge Cup	1	0
Eastern Counties League	10	7
London Midweek League	4	0
Youth Tour Matches	15	5
Wartime	6	1
Total	**202**	**65**

Honours:

1 England Cap
League Championship Medal   1952-53
Football Combination Champions   1950-51
London FA Challenge Cup Winners 1953-54

MITCHELL, Geoff   1951-55

Birth Place: Bradford, Yorkshire
Date of Birth: July 1934

☛ Geoff Mitchell joined Arsenal as an amateur from the Bradford youth side Frasley Celtic in January 1951, turning professional in November 1951. In the 1951-52 and 1952-53 season, played regularly at wing half in Arsenal's Eastern Counties League side. During the next two seasons his appearances were restricted due to him being called up for National Service. On his return to Highbury was granted a free transfer in February 1955.

	Games	Goals
Friendly Matches	5	0
Combination League	1	0
Eastern Counties League	37	1
Eastern Counties Cup	5	0
London Midweek League	17	2
Total	**65**	**3**

Honours:

London Midweek League Championship
   Medal   1952-53
East Anglian Cup Finalist Medal   1951-52

MORGAN, Stan   1938-48

Birth Place: Abergwynfi, Wales
Date of Birth: 10th October 1920

☛ Stan Morgan joined Arsenal during 1938 as an amateur from the Welsh side Gwynfi Welfare. Turned professional during the war in December 1941. After the war he played regularly either on the wing or at inside forward in Arsenal's reserve side. In season 1946-47 he played in thirty five reserve games and scored fourteen goals, this form, in December 1946, winning him a place in the league side, playing two matches versus Grimsby Town and Portsmouth. During 1947-48 was again a regular member of the reserve side before being released on a free transfer in June 1948 when he joined Walsall. Later played for Millwall for five seasons, finishing his career with Leyton Orient in 1956.

	Games	Goals
League	2	0
Friendly Matches	5	5
Combination League	49	16
Combination Cup	27	13
London Challenge Cup	3	0
Wartime	9	5
Total	**95**	**39**

Stan Morgan

Honours:

Football Combination Champions   1946-47
Football Combination Cup
   Runners - up   1946-47

MORTON, Alan   1959-61

Birth Place: Peterborough, Cambridgeshire
Date of Birth: 6th March 1942

☛ Alan Morton was an amateur with Peterborough when joining Arsenal in April 1959. Played regularly for Arsenal's Metropolitan League side for two seasons, 1959-61, as a promising winger. However, never fulfilled his early potential and subsequently transferred back to Peterborough in October 1961. Later played for Lincoln City and Chesterfield.

	Games	Goals
Friendly Matches	7	4
Combination League	4	4
Metropolitan League	26	16
Metropolitan Cup	5	2
South East Counties League	8	4
Youth Cup	5	3
Other Youth Cups	5	2

Alan Morton

Youth Tour Matches	2	1
Total	**62**	**36**

Honours:

2 England Youth Caps

NEILL, Terry   1959-70

Birth Place: Belfast, Northern Ireland
Date of Birth: 8th May 1942

Terry Neill joined Arsenal from the Irish side Bangor, in December 1959. In his first season at Highbury he played regularly at either centre half or wing half in the Metropolitan League side as well as playing in youth cup competitions. In 1960-61 he made his league debut versus Sheffield Wednesday in December 1960, and at the age of eighteen, won the first of his fifty nine Irish caps versus Italy. In 1961-62 at the age of nineteen he became Arsenal's youngest ever captain. However, over the next three seasons 1961-63, although being a regular in the Northern Ireland side, could not claim a regular place in the Arsenal league side. In 1964-65 he recaptured his form and played in twenty nine league matches, and in 1965-66 missed only three league games. In 1966-67 he played in a further thirty four league games, and thirty seven league games and a place in Arsenal's League Cup Final team versus Leeds in 1967-68. Around this time Terry Neill was appointed captain of Northern Ireland as well as becoming the PFA secretary. In 1968-69 a series of injuries including contracting yellow jaundice restricted him to only twenty two league games as well as missing the League Cup Final versus Swindon. In 1969-70 he played in only seventeen league matches, although during that season he did win his forty third Irish cap to become (at the time) the most capped Arsenal player of all time. He later broke Danny Blanchflower's record of Irish caps (a record later broken by Pat Jennings). Was transferred to Hull City as player/manager for £40,000 in July 1970, and at the age of twenty eight years two months was one of the youngest ever football managers. Managed Hull (1974-76) and the Northern Ireland national team,before returning to Highbury in July 1976, at thirty four he became Arsenal's youngest ever manager. In his eight seasons as manager at Highbury, he guided Arsenal to three consecutive FA Cup Finals and a Cup Winners Cup Final in 1980. Arsenal never finished outside the top ten during his time as manager, thus vindicating his transfer dealings totalling over twelve million pounds. However, not long after a defeat by Walsall in a League Cup match, he was dismissed as Arsenal's manager. He now owns and runs Terry Neill's Sports Bar in Holborn, London. He is also a director of Hendon FC.

	Games	Goals
League	241	8
FA Cup	13	0
League Cup	16	2
UEFA Cup	5	0
Friendly Matches	50	1
Tour Matches	40	4

Combination League	71	4
Combination Cup	3	0
London Challenge Cup	6	1
Metropolitan League	32	3
Metropolitan Cup	3	1
Youth Cup	2	0
Other Youth Cups	1	0
Youth Tour Matches	5	1
Total	**488**	**25**

Honours:
59 Northern Ireland Caps
4 Under 23 Caps
League Cup Finalist Medal   1967-68
Football Combination Champions   1962-63
Metropolitan League Champions   1960-61

Terry Neill

Terry Neill

NEILSON, Gordon   1964-68

Birth Place: Glasgow, Scotland
Date of Birth: 28th May 1947

Gordon Neilson joined Arsenal from the Scottish junior side Glasgow United in July 1964. In 1964-65 he was a regular member of Arsenal's successful youth team of that season. The following season he played regularly in the reserve side and made his league debut versus Everton at Highbury in March 1966. He played in twelve league matches during 1966-67, when he vied for the right wing spot with George Armstrong, 1967-68 was a complete disaster for him as he played in only nine competitive matches due to a string of injuries. Regained full fitness at the beginning of the 1968 - 69 season when he again played regularly for the reserves, but in October 1968 was transferred to Brentford for £8,000.

	Games	Goals
League	14	2
FA Cup	3	1
Friendly Matches	20	4
Tour Matches	2	0
Combination League	39	14
Combination Cup	11	4
London Challenge Cup	4	1
Metropolitan League	31	10
Metropolitan Cup	6	0
South East Counties League	20	3
Youth Cup	4	0
Other Youth Cups	4	0
Youth Tour Matches	10	4
Total	**168**	**43**

Gordon Neilson

Honours:

London FA Challenge Cup	
Runners - up	1965-66
FA Youth Cup Runners - up	1964-65
South East Counties League	
Champions	1964-65
London Minor Challenge Cup	
Runners - up	1964-65

NELSON, Sammy   1966-81

Birth Place: Belfast, Northern Ireland
Date of Birth: 1st April 1949

Sammy Nelson joined Arsenal as a professional on his seventeenth birthday in April 1966. He began his career as a left winger in the Arsenal youth side, but was soon converted to a left back. He established himself as a regular in the reserve side in 1966-67. Over the next three seasons, 1967-69, he played in well over one hundred reserve team games. It was not until October 1969 that he made his league debut versus Ipswich, although during that season, 1969-70, he won the first of his fifty one Irish caps (forty seven won while at Arsenal). During the double season of 1970-71 he was Bob McNab's left back understudy, playing in six first team games. However, in 1971-72 owing to a series of injuries to McNab, he won a regular place in the league side playing in twenty four matches. Returned to the reserve side over the following two seasons, 1972-74, playing in only twenty five league matches during that period. Bob McNab was released during the summer of 1974 and Sammy Nelson (after eight seasons with the club) was at last Arsenal's first choice left back. In 1975-76 he missed only six league matches, and in 1976-77 he played in a further thirty games. In seasons 1978-80 he played in one hundred and nine of Arsenal's one hundred and twenty six league games as well as playing in all three FA Cup Finals (1978-80), and making a Cup Winners Cup Final appearance versus Valencia. With the arrival of Kenny Sansom in June 1980, he found himself back in the reserve side during the whole of that season. With apparently no future at Highbury, and after a testimonial match versus Celtic (which netted Nelson £30,000) he was transferred to Brighton for £10,000 in September 1981. Was a member of the Brighton squad which reached the FA Cup Final in 1983. In his fifteen years at Highbury, Sammy Nelson played seven hundred and sixty eight competitive matches for Arsenal, a number bettered by only six other players (Simpson, Armstrong, Storey, Rice, Radford and O'Leary). Was coach at Brighton 1983 - 84. Now works for Save & Prosper and lives in Brighton.

	Games	Goals
League	255	10
FA Cup	35	1
League Cup	27	1
European Cup	5	0
Cup Winners Cup	7	0
EUFA Cup	9	0
Charity Shield	1	0
Friendly Matches	83	7
Tour Matches	43	0
Combination League	197	14
Combination Cup	30	0
London Challenge Cup	12	0
Metropolitan League	17	5
Metropolitan Cup	5	1
South East Counties League	9	3
Youth Cup	6	1
Other Youth Caps	9	1
Youth Tour Matches	18	3
Total	**768**	**47**

Sammy Nelson

Honours:

51 Northern Ireland Caps	
2 Northern Ireland Under 23 Caps	
4 Northern Ireland Youth Caps	
FA Cup Winners Medal	1978-79
2 FA Cup Finalists	
Medals	1977-78, 1979-80
European Cup Winners Cup Finalist	
Medal	1979-80
FA Charity Shield Finalist	
Medal	1979-80
Football Combination	
Champions	1968-69, 1969-70
London FA Challenge Cup	
Winners	1969-70
FA Youth Cup Winners	1965-66
Southern Junior Floodlight Cup	
Winners	1965-66
London Youth Challenge Cup	
Winners	1966-67
South East Counties League Cup	
Runners - up	1965-66

Sammy Nelson gets to grips with Pat Rice

NEW, Martin
1975-78

Birth Place: Swindon, Wiltshire
Date of Birth: 11th May 1959

☛Martin New had played for Swindon and represented England schoolboys (eight caps) when he joined Arsenal as an apprentice in July 1975, turning professional in March 1977. In his first season at Highbury 1975-76 he played in seventeen youth matches followed in 1976-77, by winning a regular place in the reserve team. Went on tour with the Arsenal first team to Singapore in July 1977,and in the following season played regularly in goal for the reserve side. With Jennings, Barron and Wilmot all on the books, Arsenal decided to let New go, and in June 1978 was given a free transfer to Mansfield. Later played for Barnsley and a series of non league clubs including Nuneaton, Burton Albion, Worksop Town and Kings Lynn.

	Games	Goals
Friendly Matches	7	0
Tour Matches	3	0
Combination League	45	0
South East Counties League	37	0
Youth Cup	3	0
Other Youth Cups	6	0
Total	**101**	**0**

Honours:
England Schoolboy Int.

NEWMAN, Eric
1946-50

Birth Place: Romford, Essex
Date of Birth: 24th November 1924

☛Eric Newman joined Arsenal from Ipswich Town in October 1946. During his first season with the club was restricted in his appearances by a back injury. During the following two seasons he was sidelined by injuries including a cartilage operation in June 1949. Transferred back to Ipswich in September 1950.

	Games	Goals
Friendly Matches	1	0
Combination League	24	0
Combination Cup	5	0
London Challenge Cup	1	0
Eastern Counties League	5	0
London Midweek League	9	0
Other Youth Matches	14	0
Total	**59**	**0**

NEWTON, Charlie
1969-72

Birth Place: Tylortown, Rhondda, Wales
Date of Birth: 8th December 1953

☛Charlie Newton was a Welsh schoolboy international when he joined Arsenal as an apprentice in July 1969, turning professional in May 1971. In his first two seasons at Highbury was a regular member of the youth team, playing in the FA Youth Cup and South East

Counties League winning side of 1970 - 71. In 1971 - 72 he won a regular midfield place in the reserve side as well as winning three Welsh youth caps. Granted a free transfer in June 1972.

	Games	Goals
Friendly Matches	21	4
Combination League	32	1
London Challenge Cup	2	0
South East Counties League	55	10
Youth Cup	17	2
Other Youth Cups	15	0
Youth Tour Matches	13	2
Total	**155**	**19**

Honours:
3 Welsh Youth Caps
FA Youth Cup Winners Medal 1970-71
South East Counties League Championship
Medal 1971-72
South East Counties League Cup Winners
Medal 1970-71
South East Counties League Finalists
Medal 1971-72

NICHOLAS, Ken
1953-59

Birth Place: Northampton
Date of Birth: 3rd February 1938

☛Ken Nicholas joined Arsenal's groundstaff as an amateur in May 1953, turning professional in May 1955. As a fifteen year old schoolboy he represented Northampton and England schools. In season 1953-54 he won himself a regular place in Arsenal's Eastern Counties League side and in 1954-55, he captained Arsenal's first ever youth team in the South East Counties League. This season also saw him win the first of his three England youth caps, versus Wales. Played regular youth team football the following season before being called up for National Service in September 1956. During these two years he played in only twenty competitive matches. On his return to Highbury in September 1958 he could not recapture his previous form, and was released on a free transfer to Watford in May 1959, where he spent six seasons, playing in over two hundred first team games.

	Games	Goals
Friendly Matches	10	2
Combination League	15	0
London Challenge Cup	2	0
Eastern Counties League	12	0
Eastern Counties Cup	1	0
London Midweek League	35	0
Metropolitan League	17	1
Metropolitan Cup	2	0
South East Counties League	45	4
Youth Cup	3	0
Other Youth Cups	2	0
Youth Tour Matches	5	0
Total	**149**	**7**

Honours:
3 England Youth Caps
Metropolitan League Championship

Medal 1958-59
South East Counties League Championship
Medal 1955-56

NICHOLAS, Peter
1981-84

Birth Place: Newport, Wales
Date of Birth: 10th November 1959

☛Peter Nicholas started his football career with Crystal Palace, turning professional for them in December 1976. Spent five seasons at Selhurst Park, playing in over one hundred and fifty first team games. Won the first of his seventy three Welsh caps in 1978-79. Transferred to Arsenal for £400,000 in March 1981 and didn't finish on a losing Arsenal side during the remainder of the season. He played in thirty one league matches during 1981-82 and was also made captain of the Welsh National team. However in 1982 - 83 a series of injuries sidelined him for over half the season, allowing him to play in only twenty three league matches.After regaining full fitness for the beginning of the 1983-84 season, could only command a place in the reserve side. Was loaned to Crystal Palace in October 1983 for the rest of the 1983-84 season with the option of a £150,000 transfer at the end of the season and duly signed for Palace. Later played for Luton Town, Chelsea, Aberdeen and Watford and coached Chelsea Juniors. Peter is now youth team boss at Selhurst Park.

Peter Nicholas

	Games	Goals
League	60	1
FA Cup	8	0
League Cup	8	2
UEFA Cup	4	0
Friendly Matches	5	1
Tour Matches	7	0
Combination League	20	0
Total	**112**	**4**

Honours: (WITH ALL CLUBS)
73 Welsh Caps
3 Welsh Under - 21 Caps
(WITH CRYSTAL PALACE)
Division 2 Championship Medal 1978-79
(WITH CHELSEA)
Division 2 Championship Medal 1988-89
(WITH ABERDEEN)
Scottish League Cup Finalists Medal 1987-88

NUTT, Gordon   1955-60

Birth Place: Birmingham
Date of Birth: 8th November 1932

☛Gordon Nutt started his football career with Coventry City in 1949. He spent five years at Highfield Road before joining Cardiff City in December 1954. Transferred to Arsenal with Mike Tiddy for a joint fee of £30,000 in September 1955. Made his league debut on the 24th September versus Sunderland. Unfortunately he broke an ankle at Everton a fortnight later and was out of the game for two months. He played in only one league match in 1956 - 57, but the following season, 1957 - 58, he shared the first team left wing position with Joe Haverty. Over the next three seasons, 1958 - 60, although being a regular member of the reserve side, played only occasionally in the league team. Transferred to Southend in October 1960, later also played for PSV Eindhoven, Holland (1961), Hereford United (July 1962), Rugby Town (Dec 1963) and Bexley United (Feb 1964). Later went to Australia to play for Corinthians of Sydney.

Gordon Nutt

	Games	Goals
League	49	10
FA Cup	2	0
Friendly Matches	25	6
Tour Matches	1	0
Combination League	118	32
London Challenge Cup	12	1
Southern Floodlight Cup	4	1
Metropolitan League	7	9
Metropolitan Cup	1	2
Total	**219**	**61**

OAKES, Don   1945-55

Birth Place: Rhyl, Wales
Date of Birth: 8th October 1928

☛Don Oakes joined Arsenal as an amateur in 1945, turning professional in July 1946. During his ten seasons with the club he played in only eleven league matches, being content to spend the majority of his playing career in the reserve side. Played very little football in his first two seasons at Highbury due to National Service. On being demobbed in 1948, he played regularly for the Eastern Counties League side for two seasons (1948-49 and 1949-50) at either inside forward or wing half. For the next three seasons played regularly in reserve team football, and made his league debut versus Aston Villa on the opening day of the 1952-53, season scoring the winning goal. Spent the whole of the 1953 - 54 season in the reserve side but played in a further nine league matches during 1954 - 55 before a series of injuries forced him to retire. Died 1977 aged 48.

Don Oakes

	Games	Goals
League	11	1
Friendly Matches	25	13
Combination League	98	43
Combination Cup	59	25
London Challenge Cup	12	5
Eastern Counties League	31	9
London Midweek League	5	1
Other Youth Matches	9	2
Wartime	2	0
Total	**252**	**99**

Honours:

Football Combination Champions	1950-51
Football Combination Cup Winners	1952-53
Football Combination Runners-Up	1950-51
London FA Challenge Cup Winners	1953-54
	1954-55

O'BRIEN, Noel   1972-75

Birth Place: Islington, London
Date of Birth: 18th December 1956

☛Noel O'Brien joined Arsenal as an apprentice in June 1972, turning professional in January 1974. Had previously played for Camden, London and Middlesex schools. Settled down at either full back or in midfield for Arsenal's youth team during the 1972 - 73 season. Established a regular place at the age of seventeen in the reserve side in 1973 - 74. Played reserve team football during

0
1945-1985

1974 - 75 until being given a free transfer during the summer of 1975 when he joined Mansfield.

	Games	Goals
Friendly Matches	21	0
Combination League	71	2
London Challenge Cup	3	0
South East Counties League	39	1
Youth Cup	9	1
Other Youth Cups	11	0
Youth Tour Matches	14	1
Total	**168**	**5**

O'FLANAGAN, Dr Kevin   1946-47

Birth Place: Dublin
Date of Birth: 10th June 1919

☛Dr Kevin O'Flanagan was one of the most talented sportsmen of pre war years, not only was he excellent at athletics, but represented Ireland at both rugby and football. He was a qualified MD and when one of his colleagues was injured he would quickly be in attendance. O'Flanagan was playing for the Irish club Bohemians when Arsenal signed him as an amateur in May 1946. He spent one season at Highbury, playing in fourteen league matches, including his league debut versus Blackburn Rovers, 4th September 1946 and also won three Irish caps, to add to the seven he won pre war while with Bohemians. Later played for Barnet and Brentford.

	Games	Goals
League	14	3
FA Cup	2	0
Friendly Matches	1	0
Tour Matches	1	0
Combination Cup	2	1
Total	**20**	**4**

Honours:
10 Irish Caps
2 Victory Internationals.

O'NEILL, Frank   1959-61

Birth Place: Dublin
Date of Birth: 13th April 1940

☛Frank O'Neill was an amateur with the Home Farm club when joining Arsenal in April 1959. Played regularly in all forward positions for the reserve and third team. In 1960-61 he was a prolific scorer in the Metropolitan and reserve sides, scoring thirty five goals in fifty six matches. Played in two league matches during the season, his debut versus Nottingham Forest resulting in a 5 - 3 victory for Arsenal. Was released during the summer of 1961 when he returned to Ireland to play for Shamrock Rovers, playing for them for over ten seasons and winning twenty Republic of Ireland caps. Later played for Watford.

Frank O'Neill

	Games	Goals
League	2	0
Friendly Matches	17	11
Combination League	45	15
London Challenge Cup	5	3
Metropolitan League	36	28
Metropolitan Cup	8	5
Youth Tour Matches	3	0
Total	**116**	**62**

Honours:
20 Eire Caps
London FA Challenge Cup Finalist
  Medal 1960-61
Metropolitan League Championship
  Medal 1960-61
Metropolitan League Challenge Cup Winners
  Medal 1960-61
Metropolitan League Professional Cup
  Winners Medal 1960-61

O'ROURKE, Jim   1965-67

Birth Place: Glasgow
Date of Birth: 17th October 1948

➴ Jim O'Rourke joined Arsenal from the Scottish junior side Possilpark in October 1965. In his two seasons at Highbury, Jim O'Rourke played at either wing half or full back in both the South East Counties and Metropolitan league sides. However, with a strong nucleus of young full backs on the books at this time, ie Pat Rice and Sammy Nelson, Jim was granted a free transfer and joined Carlisle in October 1967.

	Games	Goals
Friendly Matches	7	1
Combination League	3	0
Metropolitan League	34	1
Metropolitan Cup	7	1
South East Counties League	14	2
Youth Cup	7	0

Other Youth Cups	7	0
Youth Tour Matches	4	3
Total	**83**	**9**

Jim O'Rourke

Honours:
London Youth Challenge Cup Winners
  Medal 1966-67

O'ROURKE, Ken   1967-68

Birth Place: Lambeth, London
Date of Birth: 8th December 1949

➴ Ken O'Rourke joined Arsenal in April 1967 after a trial period of two weeks. Had previously been an apprentice with Leyton Orient. Spent only one full season at the club, playing centre forward in Arsenal's junior side. Released on a free transfer in August 1968 when he joined Ipswich. Later played for Colchester.

	Games	Goals
Friendly Matches	5	1
Combination League	2	0
Combination Cup	4	0
Metropolitan League	9	4
Metropolitan Cup	4	1
South East Counties League	2	1
Youth Cup	4	2
Other Youth Cups	6	1
Youth Tour Matches	6	2
Total	**42**	**12**

Honours:
London Youth Challenge Cup Winners
  Medal 1966-67
Southern Junior Floodlight Cup Finalists
  Medal 1967-68

OLLERENSHAW, John   1945-50

Birth Place: Stockport, Lancashire
Date of Birth: 3rd April 1925

➴ John Ollerenshaw joined Arsenal as an amateur from an army team, turning

professional in September 1946. After being demobbed from the army in 1947, he played for the junior side at full back. During seasons 1948-49, 1949-50 he played regularly in Arsenal's Eastern Counties League side. Released on a free transfer in June 1950, when he joined Hartlepool. Later played for Oldham.

John Ollerenshaw

	Games	Goals
Combination League	4	0
Eastern Counties League	35	0
Eastern Counties Cup	2	0
London Midweek League	8	0
Other Youth Matches	19	0
Wartime	1	0
Total	**69**	**0**

O'SHEA, Danny   1979-84

Birth Place: Kennington, London
Date of Birth: 26th March 1963

➴ Danny O'Shea joined Arsenal as an apprentice in 1979, turning professional in December 1980. Played regularly in Arsenal's South East Counties League side, either at full back or centre half during seasons 1978-79 and 1979-80. He won a place in the reserve side in 1981-82. Made six league appearances during 1982-83 but returned to reserve team football during 1983-84, spending a period on loan to Charlton. Granted a free transfer in May 1984 when he joined Exeter City. Danny has since played for Southend United, Cambridge United and Northampton Town.

	Games	Goals
League	6	0
League Cup	3	0
Friendly Matches	50	3
Tour Matches	1	0
Combination League	108	4
South East Counties League	58	3
Youth Cup	6	2
Other Youth Cups	17	0
Youth Tour Matches	4	0
Total	**253**	**12**

PACK, ROY   1962-66

Birth Place: Islington, London
Date of Birth: 20th September 1946

➤Roy Pack joined Arsenal as an apprentice in June 1962 after impressing in England schools trial matches, turning professional in November 1963. In his first two seasons with Arsenal he played regularly at full back for the South East Counties league side. During the next season (1964-65) won a place in the Metropolitan League side, and the following season played regular reserve team football. Made his one and only first team appearance versus Leeds in May 1966. Was granted a free transfer the following month when he joined Portsmouth.

Roy Pack

	Games	Goals
League	1	0
Friendly Matches	23	1
Combination League	23	1
London Challenge Cup	5	0
Metropolitan League	48	0
Metropolitan Cup	7	0
South East Counties League	47	3
Youth Cup	12	0
Other Youth Cups	17	1
Youth Tour Matches	27	0
Total	**220**	**6**

Honours:
London FA Challenge Cup
  runners up   1965-66
FA Youth Cup runners up   1964-65
South East Counties League Cup
  winners   1963-64
Southern Junior Floodlight Cup
  winners   1962-63
London Minor Challenge Cup
  runners up   1964-65

PARKER, Brian   1975-77

Birth Place: Chorley, Cheshire
Date of Birth: 4th August 1955

➤Brian Parker began his football career with Crewe in 1972, and won a regular place in their league side during 1973-74. Around this time Arsenal required a reserve team goalkeeper and signed Parker for £30,000 as cover for Jimmy Rimmer. Spent two seasons at Highbury but, because of Rimmer's consistency, never played for the league side. Granted a free transfer during the summer of 1977. Later played for Yeovil.

	Games	Goals
Friendly Matches	9	0
Combination League	57	0
Total	**66**	**0**

PEARCE, Trevor   1970-71

Birth Place: Canterbury, Kent
Date of Birth: 30th May 1949

➤Trevor Pearce joined Arsenal for a small fee from the Southern League side Folkestone in February 1970. He spent only one season at Highbury (1970-71), playing regularly in the Combination side on either wing, finishing the season as the team's leading scorer with thirteen goals. However, his progress stopped there and he was subsequently granted a free transfer during the summer of 1971 when he joined Aldershot.

	Games	Goals
Friendly Matches	5	0
Combination League	36	13
Combination Cup	6	1
London Challenge Cup	3	0
Total	**50**	**14**

Honours:
Football Combination Cup Winners
  Medal   1969-70

PETTS, Johnny   1954-62

Birth Place: Edmonton, London
Date of Birth: 2nd October 1938

➤Johnny Petts joined Arsenal's groundstaff in April 1954 after playing for Edmonton, Middlesex and London schools. Turned professional in May 1956. Played regularly for Arsenal's first ever South East Counties youth side as wing half or inside forward during seasons 1954-55 and 1955-56. At this time he also won the first of his seven England Youth caps. Won a regular place in Arsenal's reserve side during 1956-57 before being called up for National Service in September 1957. Made his league debut versus Bolton in February 1958 and played in eight further league matches that season. Was back in the reserve team during 1958-59, playing in only three league games that season and seven and one respectively in the following two seasons. It was now obvious that the early promise was not to be fulfilled,

and although he played in a further twelve league matches in season 1961-62, John was transferred to Reading in October 1962. Later spent five seasons with Bristol Rovers and then became assistant manager of Northampton Town (1974-75). His son, Paul, played for Shrewsbury Town.

Johnny Petts

	Games	Goals
League	32	0
Friendly Matches	39	10
Tour Matches	7	0
Combination League	141	22
London Challenge Cup	11	1
Southern Floodlight Cup	2	0
London Midweek League	3	0
Metropolitan League	8	2
Metropolitan Cup	5	1
South East Counties League	31	1
Youth Cup	6	0
Other Youth Cups	7	0
Youth Tour Matches	9	0
Other Youth Matches	2	0
Total	**303**	**37**

Honours:
7 England Youth Caps
South East Counties League
  Champions   1955-56
South East Counties League Cup
  Winners   1955-56
London FA Challenge Cup
  Runners up   1960-61
Metropolitan League Challenge Cup
  Winners   1960-61
Metropolitan League Professional Cup
  Winners   1960-61

PETROVIC, Vladimir — 1982-83

Birth Place: Belgrade, Yugoslavia
Date of Birth: 1st July 1955

Vladimir Petrovic had been one of his country's leading players for well over ten years. He joined Red Star Belgrade at the age of thirteen in 1968. Scored two goals for them versus Real Madrid on his debut in 1971 at the age of sixteen. Served Red Star well for fourteen years, playing in over four hundred first team games and helping them to European honours as well as Yugoslav league and Cup wins. Was voted Yugoslav Footballer of the Year on three occasions. Captained his country many times, winning forty two caps and played in the 1974 and 1982 World Cup Finals. After much speculation and drawn-out transfer negotiations Petrovic joined Arsenal for £400,000 in December 1982, making his league debut versus Swansea. His stay at Highbury was one of only five months, during which time he helped Arsenal to both the FA Cup and Milk Cup semi finals. Unfortunately his deft skills and penetrating passes were lost to English football when he joined the Belgium club Lokeren during the summer of 1983.

Vladimir Petrovic

	Games	Goals
League	13	2
FA Cup	6	1
League Cup	3	0
Combination League	2	1
Total	**24**	**4**

Honours:
Yugoslav Footballer of the Year 3 times
42 Yugoslav Caps
5 Yugoslav Under-23 Caps
4 Yugoslav Championship Medals   1972-73,
      1976-77, 1979-80, 1980-81
Yugoslav Cup Winners Medal 1981-82. UEFA
Cup Finalist Medal   1978-79

PILKINGTON, Les — 1948-50

Birth Place: Darwen, Lancashire
Date of Birth: 23rd June 1925

Les Pilkington joined Arsenal from Darwen Corries as an inside forward in March 1948. He spent two seasons at Highbury, playing in the Eastern Counties and London Midweek League sides. Released on a free transfer in March 1950 when joining Watford.

Les Pilkington

	Games	Goals
Combination League	2	1
Combination Cup	3	1
Eastern Counties League	14	0
Eastern Counties Cup	2	0
London Midweek League	16	6
Other Youth Matches	6	2
Total	**43**	**10**

PITTAWAY, Mick — 1977-81

Birth Place: London
Date of Birth: 1962

Mick Pittaway joined Arsenal as an apprentice during the close season of 1977, turning professional in June 1979. Played regularly either at full back or centre back in the club's South East Counties League side during 1977-78 before winning a place in the reserve side during 1978-79. Played reserve team football for three seasons before being given a free transfer in May 1981 joining non league side Barnet. Later moved on to Maidstone United.

	Games	Goals
Friendly Matches	10	1
Combination League	72	4
South East Counties League	47	3
Youth Cup	7	0
Other Youth Cups	15	1
Youth Tour Matches	4	0
Total	**155**	**9**

Honours:
South East Counties League Cup Winners
  Medal   1979-80
Presidents Cup Winners Medal   1979-80

POPPLE, Ralph — 1953-56

Birth Place: Leeds, Yorkshire
Date of Birth: 1935

Ralph Popple joined Arsenal in February 1953 after representing West Riding youth. Turned professional in June 1953. Unfortunately, in July 1953, called up for two years National Service, this reducing his appearances to only nine over the following two seasons. Demobbed in September 1955 and spent the 1955-56 season as right half in the London Midweek League side. Was granted a free transfer during the summer of 1956.

	Games	Goals
Friendly Matches	2	0
Combination League	1	0
Eastern Counties League	6	0
Eastern Counties Cup	2	0
London Midweek League	14	1
Other Youth Matches	7	0
Total	**32**	**1**

POWLING, Ritchie — 1971-81

Birth Place: Barking, Essex
Date of Birth: 21st May 1956

Ritchie Powling

Ritchie Powling joined Arsenal as an apprentice in September 1971 after representing both London and Essex schools. Made his league debut at the age of sixteen versus QPR whilst still an apprentice. During the 1971-72 season, at the age of fifteen, played regular reserve team football. Turned professional in July 1973. Held his place in the reserve side over the following three seasons and played two league games in 1973-74 and eight in 1974-75. Won three England Youth caps during the 1973-74 season. In 1975-76 won a regular first team place, playing in all defensive positions. However, his injury problems began during the 1976-77 season when he played in only eleven league matches. On his return to full fitness played in the first five league matches before suffering a serious leg injury versus Nottingham Forest in September 1977. He spent virtually two seasons out of action, making a come back in the reserve side at the end of the 1979-80 season. Further injuries followed soon after and in the summer of 1981 he announced his retirement when still only twenty five years old. Played non league football for Barnet and Grays Athletic, later managing non league teams Tiptree United and Sudbury Town.

	Games	Goals
League	55	3
FA Cup	2	0
League Cup	2	0
Friendly Matches	50	5
Tour Matches	14	0
Combination League	148	3
London Challenge Cup	5	0
South East Counties League	29	2
Youth Cup	16	1
Other Youth Cups	12	0
Youth Tour Matches	20	1
Total	**353**	**15**

Honours:
3 England Youth Caps
South East Counties League
  Champions   1971-72
South East Counties League Cup
  runners-up   1971-72

PRICE, David   1970-81

Birth Place: Caterham, Surrey
Date of Birth: 23rd June 1955

David Price

David Price joined Arsenal (after stiff opposition from at least twelve other league clubs) as the England schoolboys captain in July 1970. In his first season at the club was a member of the youth team which won both the South East Counties League and the FA Youth Cup. Maintained his progress the following two seasons, establishing himself in the reserve side and making his league debut versus Leeds in May 1973, as well as winning six England youth caps. Played regular reserve team football for the next three seasons (spending part of the time on loan to Peterborough) although his appearances during 1975-76 were limited due to injury. He played in eight league matches during 1976-77 and became a regular member of the league side over the next three seasons (1977-80) helping Arsenal to three consecutive FA Cup Finals and playing in one hundred of Gunners' one hundred and twenty six league matches. However, lost his first team place to John Hollins in the 1980-81 season and was subsequently transferred to Crystal Palace for £140,000 in March 1981 in the deal which took Peter Nicholas to Highbury. Later played for Leyton Orient, but was forced to quit the game through injury at the age of 27. Now a mini-cab driver and plays for West Wickham in the Southern Amateur League.

	Games	Goals
League	126	16
FA Cup	26	1
League Cup	11	0
Cup Winners Cup	6	2
UEFA Cup	6	0
Charity Shield	1	0
Friendly Matches	60	5
Tour Matches	20	1
Combination League	211	29
London Challenge Cup	5	1
South East Counties League	31	0
Youth Cup	16	0
Other Youth Cups	17	1
Youth Tour Matches	33	2
Total	**569**	**58**

Honours:
FA Cup Winners Medal   1978-79
2 FA Cup Finalist Medals   1977-78,
                                1979-80
European Cup Winners Cup Finalists
  Medal   1979-80
FA Charity Shield Finalists Medal 1979-80
6 England Youth Caps
FA Youth Cup Winners Medal   1970-71

South East Counties League Cup Winners
                                1970-71
South East Counties League Cup Finalist
                                1971-72

PROSSER, Sidney — 1954-55

Birth Place: Shoreditch, London
Date of Birth: 1936

☛ Sid Prosser joined Arsenal as a professional in May 1954 after previously playing in three London Midweek League games (scoring three goals) as an amateur. However, he was called up for National Service during the summer of 1954 which resulted in him missing the whole of season 1954-55. Released on a free transfer during the summer of 1955.

	Games	Goals
London Midweek League	3	3
Total	**3**	**3**

PROUTON, Ralph — 1949-52

Birth Place: Southampton, Hampshire
Date of Birth: 1st March 1926

☛ Ralph Prouton signed for Arsenal as a professional in August 1949 on the recommendation of former Arsenal captain Tom Parker. During seasons 1949-50 and 1950-51 played regularly at wing half in the Eastern Counties League side. Unfortunately a series of injuries sidelined him for most of the 1951-52 season and Ralph was subsequently given a free transfer in August 1952, joining Swindon.

Ralph Prouton

	Games	Goals
Friendly Matches	4	0
Combination League	2	0
Combination Cup	3	0
Eastern Counties League	44	0
Eastern Counties Cup	1	0
London Midweek League	22	0
Total	**76**	**0**

QUINN, William — 1948-50

Birth Place: Northern Ireland
Date of Birth: 1930

☛ Bill Quinn joined Arsenal as a professional in September 1948. Served the Eastern Counties League and London Midweek League sides well for two seasons at either wing half or inside forward. Was released on a free transfer during the summer of 1950.

William Quinn

	Games	Goals
Friendly Matches	2	0
Combination League	1	0
Eastern Counties League	18	1
Eastern Counties Cup	3	0
Other Youth Matches	14	3
Total	**38**	**4**

John Radford

RADFORD, John — 1962-76

Birth Place: Hemsworth, Yorkshire
Date of Birth: 22nd February 1947

☛ John Radford spent fourteen years at Highbury during which time, in all competitive matches, he scored more goals (over three hundred) than any other player in Arsenal's history. Joined Arsenal as an apprentice in October 1962, turning professional soon after his seventeenth birthday in February 1964. In his first season he established a regular place in Arsenal's youth side and in all youth team matches that season scored forty two goals in thirty eight matches. John maintained his terrific striking rate the following season (a further forty nine goals in sixty nine matches) this resulted in him making his league debut versus West Ham in March 1964. In 1964-65 he played in thirteen league matches (seven goals) before winning a regular place over the next two seasons, either playing inside or centre forward. However, during the 1968-69 season switched with great success to the right wing position, scoring nineteen first team goals as well as winning four England Under-23 Caps and helping Arsenal to the League Cup Final versus Swindon. In 1969-70 he added a full England Cap (versus Rumania) and an Inter Cities Fairs Cup winners medal to his honours and also finished the season as the club's leading scorer with nineteen goals. In the Double season, Radford returned to centre forward where he enjoyed notable success alongside Ray Kennedy, their goal tally for that season being forty seven. He aided Arsenal's return to Wembley for the 1971-72 FA Cup Final versus Leeds, and again scored nineteen first team goals that season. Between 1972-75 played regularly, although his selection was not automatic. In 1975-76 a series of injuries resulted in Radford playing in only fifteen league matches. Played a further two league games in 1976-77 before losing his place to the up-and-coming Frank Stapleton. Was transferred to West Ham for £80,000 in December 1976. Later played for Blackburn and had further success with non league Bishops Stortford. In all John Radford scored nearly one hundred and fifty first team goals for Arsenal; only Cliff Bastin has scored more.

	Games	Goals
League	379	111
FA Cup	44	15
League Cup	34	12
European Cup	5	3
UEFA Cup	19	8
Friendly Matches	50	41
Tour Matches	38	14
Combination League	74	40
London Challenge Cup	5	4
Metropolitan League	20	16

Metropolitan Cup	7	4
South East Counties League	22	26
Youth Cup	16	10
Other Youth Cups	9	10
Youth Tour Matches	24	14
Total	**746**	**328**

Honours:
2 England Caps
4 England Under-23 Caps
2 Football League Caps

League Championship Medal	1970-71
FA Cup Winners Medal	1970-71
FA Cup Finalist Medal	1971-72
Inter Cities Fairs Cup Winners Medal	1969-70
Two League Cup Finalists Medals	1967-68, 1968-69
FA Youth Cup runners-up	1964-65
Metropolitan League Professional Cup runners-up	1962-63

John Radford

Q/R
1945-1985

Since he retired from playing, John has run two public houses in Essex and Hertfordshire. He is now General Manager of Bishops Stortford.

John Radford in action flanked by Everton's John Hurst (left) and Brian Labone.

READ, John 1957-61

Birth Place: London
Date of Birth: 1941

John Read joined Arsenal as an amateur in July 1957, turning professional in November 1959 after representing London at youth level. During season 1957-58, as a defender, played regularly in the South East Counties League side, later progressing to the Metropolitan team in 1959-60, playing a total of forty five matches. However, although a regular in the team during the first half of the 1960-61 season, was released on a free transfer in March 1961.

	Games	Goals
Friendly Matches	2	0
London Challenge Cup	1	1
Metropolitan League	34	4
Metropolitan Cup	6	0
South East Counties League	50	11
Youth Cup	13	3
Other Youth Cups	9	0
Youth Tour Matches	2	0
Total	**117**	**19**

Honours:
Metropolitan League Championship
  Medal 1960-61
Metropolitan League Cup Winners
  Medal 1960-61
South East Counties League Cup Winners
  Medal 1959-60
Southern Junior Floodlight Cup Finalists
  Medal 1957-58.

REES, Tony 1982-84

Birth Place: Swansea, Wales
Date of Birth: 13th September 1966

Tony Rees was offered apprenticeship terms with Arsenal, when only fifteen years old, during the season of 1982. He won a regular midfield place in the South East Counties League side during 1982-83 and added Welsh under seventeen honours to his schoolboy caps. Turned professional in February 1983 and it was hoped that in 1983-84 he would gain a regular place in the reserve team. However, a series of injuries sidelined him for nearly half the season. Granted a free transfer during the summer of 1984.

	Games	Goals
Friendly Matches	3	0
Combination League	3	0
South East Counties League	49	9
Youth Cup	8	2
Other Youth Cups	13	2
Total	**76**	**13**

Honours:
3 Welsh Youth Caps
Southern Junior Floodlight Cup Winners
  Medal 1983-84

RHODES, Trevor 1963-66

Birth Place: Southend, Essex
Date of Birth: 9th August 1948

Trevor Rhodes joined Arsenal as an apprentice in July 1963, turning professional in September 1965. During his three seasons at Highbury was a regular in both the Metropolitan and South East Counties sides, playing at either wing half or inside forward. Was released on a free transfer in September 1966 when he joined Millwall. Later played for Bristol Rovers.

Trevor Rhodes

	Games	Goals
Friendly Matches	8	1
Combination League	2	0
Metropolitan League	40	7
Metropolitan Cup	4	0
South East Counties League	47	5
Youth Cup	5	2
Other Youth Cups	18	1
Youth Tour Matches	13	0
Total	**137**	**16**

Honours:
FA Youth Cup Winners
  Medal 1965-66
Metropolitan League Challenge
  Cup Winners Medal 1965-66
South East Counties League
  Championship Medal 1964-65
Southern Junior Floodlight
  Cup Winners Medal 1965-66.

RICE, Pat 1964-80

Birth Place: Belfast, Northern Ireland
Date of Birth: 17th March 1949

Pat Rice joined Arsenal as an apprentice in December 1964, turning professional in March 1966. Pat Rice, through hard work and determination, only just survived the apprenticeship stage at Highbury to become one of the most loyal players the club has ever had. During his sixteen years at Highbury Pat Rice played in no fewer than five Wembley FA Cup Finals (a record he shares with Frank Stapleton, Joe Hulme and Johnny Giles). Won forty nine Northern Ireland Caps and played in over five hundred first team matches (only George Armstrong and David O`Leary have played in more) and in all competitive matches for the club he totalled over eight hundred and twenty games (only Simpson, Armstrong, Storey and O`Leary can better this total). Pat Rice's career had a very unimpressive start. During his first five seasons with the club he progressed from youth team football to reserve team football rapidly enough, but during this time played in only fifteen first team matches. However, when Peter Storey was switched from right back to a midfield position, Pat Rice was drafted in to the right back position for the beginning of the 1970-71 season, and in his first full season helped Arsenal to the incredible League and FA Cup Double. He had already won the first of his Irish caps two seasons previously (while still in Arsenal's reserve side) versus Israel. Over the next ten seasons Pat Rice was undoubtedly Arsenal's most consistent player, playing in every league match during 1971-72, 1975-76 and 1976-77 (becoming one of the few Arsenal players to be an ever-present in three different seasons). He missed only one league match in seasons 1970-71 and 1973-74. Was made club captain in 1977 and skippered them to three consecutive FA Cup Finals between 1978-80 and the European Cup Winners Cup Final of 1980. Transferred to Watford for £10,000 in November 1980. Pat Rice will be remembered for his dedication to the club he loved and supported. For him it was an honour to play for and captain Arsenal and for Arsenal it was an honour to have a player like Pat Rice. Returned to Highbury as youth team coach in 1984. In the following ten seasons, Pat has managed the Arsenal youth team to two FA Youth Cup Final wins in 1987-88 and 1993-94 as well as the South East Counties League and Southern Junior Floodlight Cup double success in 1990-1991. Included in his 'discoveries' have been Kevin Campbell, Andy Cole, Paul Merson, David Rocastle and Micheal Thomas to name but a few. Pat Rice is undoubtedly one of Arsenal's unsung heroes.

Pat Rice in action

	Games	Goals
League	397	12
FA Cup	67	1
League Cup	36	0
European Cup	6	0
Cup Winners Cup	6	0
UEFA Cup	14	0
Charity Shield	1	0
Friendly Matches	61	3
Tour Matches	50	2
Combination League	94	3
Combination Cup	33	0
London Challenge Cup	8	0
Metropolitan League	14	0
Metropolitan Cup	3	0
South East Counties League	19	0
Youth Cup	8	0
Other Youth Cups	12	0
Total	**829**	**21**

Pat Rice

Honours:

49 Northern Ireland Caps	
2 Northern Ireland Under-23 Caps	
League Championship Medal	1970-71
2 FA Cup Winners Medals 1970-71,	1978-79
3 FA Cup Finalists Medals 1971-72, 1977-78,	1979-80
European Cup Winners Cup Finalist Medal	1979-80
FA Charity Shield Finalist Medal	1979-80
Football Combination Champions	1968-69, 1969-70
Football Combination Cup Winners	1967-68
London FA Challenge Cup Winners	1969-70
FA Youth Cup Winners	1965-66
Southern Junior Floodlight Cup Winners	1965-66
South East Counties League Cup runners-up	1965-66

RIDLEY, David 1980-83

Birth Place: Essex
Date of Birth: 1965

David Ridley appeared for Arsenal during the 1980-81 season while still only on associated schoolboy terms. Became an apprentice in June 1981 and during the 1981-82 season served the South East Counties League and Combination sides well either in defence or midfield. This season also saw him win three England youth caps. However, during the following season his early promise was not fulfilled and he was not offered professional terms. Subsequently released early in 1983.

	Games	Goals
Friendly Matches	5	0
Combination League	17	0
South East Counties League	39	1
Youth Cup	5	0
Other Youth Cups	8	0
Total	**74**	**1**

Honours:
3 England Youth Caps

RIMMER, Jimmy 1974-77

Birth Place: Southport, Lancashire
Date of Birth: 10th February 1948

Jimmy Rimmer joined Manchester United straight from school as a fifteen year old in 1963, turning professional in May 1965. Made his league debut during the 1967-68 season and was substitute goalkeeper in the 1968 European Cup Final versus Benfica. Spent seven seasons at Old Trafford as understudy to Alex Stepney, playing in only thirty four league matches. Was loaned to Swansea City in October 1973, and under the guiding influence of Harry Gregg, turned in some magnificent performances for the Swans. At this time Arsenal were in need of a top class goalkeeper to fill the gap caused by the retirement of Bob Wilson, and in February 1974 Arsenal paid Manchester United £40,000 for him. Made his Arsenal league debut the following month versus Liverpool at Anfield. During his three seasons at Highbury he showed great consistency, missing only three league matches. In 1976-77 he won an England cap versus Italy on the American tour of 1976. However, when Pat Jennings joined Arsenal in August 1977 Rimmer realised his days at Highbury were over and during the same week was transferred to Aston Villa for £80,000. Served Aston Villa well for six seasons, helping them win both the League Championship and European Cup before losing his place to the up and coming Nigel Spink. Left Villa in the summer of 1983 when he joined Swansea City. Now Youth Team Coach at the Vetch Field.

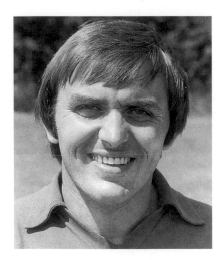
Jimmy Rimmer

	Games	Goals
League	124	0
FA Cup	12	0
League Cup	10	0
Friendly Matches	17	0
Tour Matches	18	0
Combination League	6	0
Total	**187**	**0**

Honours:
1 England Cap
(WITH ASTON VILLA)
League Championship Medal 1980-81
European Cup Winners Medal 1981-82
European Super Cup Winners
  Medal 1982-83

RITCHIE, Bob 1968-70

Birth Place: Kettering, Northamptonshire
Date of Birth: 1952

Bob Ritchie joined Arsenal as an apprentice in May 1968, turning professional in June 1969. During his two seasons at the club played regularly for the junior sides both in the Metropolitan and South East Counties League sides. However, he did not meet the standard required and was eventually released during the close season of 1970. Younger brother of John Ritchie who played for Stoke City and Sheffield Wednesday.

Bob Ritchie

	Games	Goals
Friendly Matches	16	7
Combination League	7	0
Combination Cup	1	0
London Challenge Cup	2	0
Metropolitan League	26	3
Metropolitan Cup	8	1
South East Counties League	11	2
Youth Cup	6	4
Other Youth Cups	3	0
Youth Tour Matches	4	0
Total	**84**	**17**

RITCHIE, John 1972-74

Birth Place: Paddington, London
Date of Birth: 28th February 1951

John Ritchie was an England amateur international with Slough Town when he and his team mate Pat Cruse joined Arsenal in April 1972. Spent two seasons at Highbury as the regular centre forward in the reserve side, and was leading scorer for them with twenty goals, in the 1972-73 season. Was never able to gain a place in the league side and subsequently transferred to Hereford United in March 1974.

	Games	Goals
Friendly Matches	10	8
Combination League	72	30
London Challenge Cup	5	3
Total	**87**	**41**

Honours:
1 England Amateur Cap

RIXON, Peter 1971-74

Birth Place: London
Date of Birth: 1955

Peter Rixon was already an associated schoolboy with Arsenal when he joined them as an apprentice in April 1971, turning professional in July 1973. In his first full season at Highbury he established himself in the South East Counties League side. During seasons 1972-73 and 1973-74 he was a regular in the Combination side, playing either at full back or centre half. Released on a free transfer during the summer of 1974.

	Games	Goals
Friendly Matches	26	0
Combination League	74	0
London Challenge Cup	6	0
South East Counties League	52	1
Youth Cup	11	0
Other Youth Cups	10	0
Youth Tour Matches	14	0
Total	**193**	**1**

Honours:
South East Counties League Championship
  Medal 1971-72
South East Counties League Cup Finalists
  Medal 1971-72

ROBERTS, John — 1969-72

Birth Place: Swansea, Wales
Date of Birth: 11th September 1946

☞John Roberts started his professional career with Swansea Town in July 1964. Spent four years at Vetch Field before joining Northampton Town in November 1967. Transferred to Arsenal for £30,000 in May 1969 and went straight on tour the same month with the first team squad to Malta. During his first full season at Highbury he played in eleven league games, followed in 1970-71 by winning a League Championship Medal, playing in eighteen league games during Arsenal's Double season. Also that season won the first of his twenty two Welsh caps, versus England. Played in twenty three league games during 1971-72 and seven in 1973-74. Was transferred to Birmingham for £140,000 in October 1972. Spent four seasons at St Andrews before joining Wrexham. Finished his career with Hull City in 1981. John is now a driving instructor in the Chester area.

John Roberts

	Games	Goals
League	59	4
League Cup	12	1
European Cup	5	0
UEFA Cup	5	0
Friendly Matches	14	2
Tour Matches	10	1
Combination League	50	1
Combination Cup	7	0
London Challenge Cup	4	0
Total	**166**	**9**

Honours:
League Championship Medal	1970-71
22 Welsh Caps	
5 Welsh Under-23 Caps	
1 Welsh Under-21 Cap	
Football Combination Champions	1969-70
London FA Challenge Cup Winners	1969-70

ROBERTSON, James — 1948-53

Birth Place: Falkirk, Scotland
Date of Birth: 20th February 1929

☞James Robertson joined Arsenal from the Scottish junior side Dunipace Thistle in June 1948. During his first season at the club was right winger in the Combination League side. Called up for two years National Service in July 1949, restricting his appearances to under thirty during seasons 1949-50 and 1950-51. In 1951-52 was again a regular in the Combination League side, and appeared in his one and only league match for Arsenal versus West Bromwich in April 1952. Was a first choice in the reserves again in 1952-53, but with no chance of regular first team football was transferred to Brentford in September 1953 which was part of the exchange deal which brought Tommy Lawton to Highbury. He later played for Gravesend.

	Games	Goals
League	1	0
Friendly Matches	10	1
Combination League	65	13
Combination Cup	40	10
London Challenge Cup	3	0
Eastern Counties League	19	4
London Midweek League	1	0
Total	**139**	**28**

ROBERTSON, Jimmy — 1968-70

Birth Place: Glasgow
Date of Birth: 17th December 1944

Jimmy Robertson

☞Jimmy Robertson began his footballing career with St Mirren in 1962. Joined Tottenham in March 1964 for £25,000 and in four seasons at White Hart Lane played in over one hundred and

fifty league matches. Won a Scottish cap versus Wales during the 1964-65 season (to add to his four under-23 caps) and scored the first goal for Tottenham in the 1967 FA Cup Final versus Chelsea. Joined Arsenal for £50,000 in October 1968 in a deal which took David Jenkins to Tottenham. In his first season at Highbury he played in nineteen league matches and in 1969-70 he played in twenty seven league games. Due mainly to the presence of George Armstrong, Jimmy Robertson never really settled at Highbury and it was no surprise when he joined Ipswich Town for £80,000 in March 1970. Later played for Stoke City, Walsall and Crewe Alexandra. Jimmy now lives at Stoke-on-Trent where he works as a Director of the Task Force Group.

	Games	Goals
League	46	7
FA Cup	4	1
League Cup	4	0
UEFA Cup	5	0
Friendly Matches	2	0
Tour Matches	5	2
Combination League	8	1
Combination Cup	4	4
Total	**78**	**15**

Honours:
(WITH TOTTENHAM)
1 Scottish Cap	
4 Scottish Under-23 Caps	
FA Cup Winners Medal	1966-67

ROOKE, Ronnie — 1946-49

Birth Place: Guildford, Surrey
Date of Birth: 7th December 1911

☞Ronnie Rooke began his career with Crystal Palace during the 1932-33 season. Was a prolific goalscorer in their reserve side, scoring over one hundred and fifty goals. Managed to play only eighteen league matches for Palace, scoring four goals. Joined Fulham in November 1936 and led their attack until the outbreak of the war. Was their leading scorer for three consecutive seasons (1936-39) scoring fifty seven goals in eighty seven league games. Served in the RAF during the war years, and won an England Victory International Cap versus Wales in 1945. In the first half of season 1946-47, Arsenal badly needed a goalscoring centre forward in the Ted Drake mould. Surprisingly, perhaps, they sought Rooke's services and paid Fulham £1,000 for him in December 1946 (David Nelson and Cyril Grant going to Craven Cottage in part exchange). Ronnie Rooke found himself, at the age of thirty five, playing top level football for the first time. Made his debut versus Charlton on the 14th December 1946, scoring the winning goal. Scored twenty one goals in twenty four league appearances that season and thirty three goals the following season. This is still a post-war Arsenal goalscoring record. Finished that season as the First Division's leading goalscorer, and helped Arsenal win the League Championship. He scored a further fourteen goals in twenty two league games during the 1948-49 season. Rejoined Crystal Palace as player/manager in June 1949. During his first class career Ronnie Rooke scored one hundred and sixty seven league goals in two hundred and fifty seven league games. Also during the war time years he played in 201 games for Fulham scoring 129 goals. Later he became manager of Bedford Town. Died July 1985 aged 73.

Ronnie Rooke

	Games	Goals
League	88	68
FA Cup	5	1
Charity Shield	1	1
Friendly Matches	10	13
Tour Matches	6	6
Combination League	2	3
Combination Cup	2	1
London Challenge Cup	3	3
Total	**117**	**96**

Honours:
1 England Victory International Cap
League Championship Medal   1947-48
FA Charity Shield Winners Medal   1947-48

ROPER, Don   1947-57

Birth Place: Botley, Hampshire
Date of Birth: 14th December 1922

*Don Roper began his career with Southampton during the war years. Was originally a centre forward, but switched to the right wing during 1943. Joined Arsenal in 1947 for £10,000 (with Tom Rudkin going to the Dell in part exchange). In his first season

played in forty league games (ten goals) and helped Arsenal win the League Championship. Played a further thirty one league games in 1948-49 (mainly on the right wing), but during the following season established himself on the left wing where he played in twenty seven league games, unfortunately losing his place in the FA Cup Final side versus Liverpool to Denis Compton. Kept his place during the 1950-51 season, playing in thirty four league games. In 1951-52 he played a further thirty league games and won an FA Cup Finalists Medal versus Newcastle (when he had to deputise at full back for the injured Walley Barnes). The 1952-53 season was probably Roper's finest, missing only one league match. Scored fourteen goals, (five in one match versus Hibernian during a floodlit match at Highbury in October 1952). Won an England B Cap versus Scotland and helped Arsenal to their seventh league title. Played regularly during seasons 1953-54 and 1954-55, but during season 1955-56 lost his place and played in only sixteen league matches. Played reserve team football during the first half of the season 1956-57 and subsequently joined Southampton in January 1957. During his time at Highbury, Don Roper played in all five forward positions and in total played in three hundred and twenty one first team games for the club, scoring ninety five goals. He later played for Weymouth and Dorchester and was also a county cricketer with Hampshire. Don is now retired having worked as an engineer, living at Southampton.

Don Roper

	Games	Goals
League	297	88
FA Cup	22	7
Charity Shield	2	0
Friendly Matches	48	41

Tour Matches	26	8
Combination League	25	21
Combination Cup	8	4
London Challenge Cup	4	0
Total	**432**	**169**

Honours:
1 England B Cap
1 Football League Cap
2 League Championship Medals   1947-48,
                                 1952-53
FA Cup Finalist Medal   1951-52

ROSS, Trevor   1972-77

Birth Place: Ashton-Under-Lyne,
               Lancashire
Date of Birth: 16th January 1957

Trevor Ross

*Trevor Ross joined Arsenal as an apprentice in May 1972, after winning schoolboy honours for Lancashire and England schools. Turned professional in June 1974. During season 1972-73 played regularly for the South East Counties League side, but unfortunately the following season he was sidelined due to injury, playing only nineteen competitive matches. He made great strides during the 1974-75 season, playing twenty six matches for the reserve team, in various positions including full back, wing half and inside forward. Made his league debut versus Liverpool at Highbury in February 1975. For the following two seasons he held a regular place in the league side, playing in seventeen matches in 1975-76 and twenty nine during 1976-77. During that season he also won a Scottish Under-21 cap versus Wales. He lost his place in the league side to David Price at the beginning of the 1977-78 season and subsequently moved to Everton in November 1977 for £180,000. He spent six seasons at Goodison Park, playing over one hundred and twenty league games. During this time he had spells on loan to Portsmouth and Sheffield United. Was surprisingly granted a free transfer during the summer of 1983 when he joined AEK Athens of Greece. However, returned to English football with Sheffield United in February 1984. Later played for Bury and Altrincham. His father William played for Bradford City.

	Games	Goals
League	58	5
FA Cup	4	1
League Cup	6	3
Friendly Matches	39	10
Tour Matches	2	1
Combination League	68	14
South East Counties League	26	7
Youth Cup	7	1
Other Youth Cups	7	1
Youth Tour Matches	10	4
Total	**227**	**47**

Honours:
1 Scottish Under-21 Cap

ROSSITER, Don   1950-54, 1955-56

Birth Place: Strood, Kent
Date of Birth: 8th June 1935

☞ Don Rossiter joined Arsenal as an amateur in August 1950 and joined the groundstaff during the same month. Had previously played for Kent schoolboys, and was an England schoolboy trialist. While an amateur at Highbury he played for Middlesex boys and for Walthamstow Avenue, winning an Amateur Cup Winners Medal in 1952. Turned professional in June 1952, just after his seventeenth birthday. During his first full season at Highbury played regular Eastern Counties League football and won two England youth caps. He could not command a place the following season and was released on a free transfer in March 1954 when he joined Hartlepool. Returned to Highbury in July 1955 and in the 1955-56 season was a regular in the reserve team. Was again released on a free transfer in March 1956 when he joined Leyton Orient. Later played for Gillingham.

	Games	Goals
Friendly Matches	10	3
Combination League	24	4
Combination Cup	9	1
Eastern Counties League	37	6
Eastern Counties Cup	6	3
London Midweek League	43	16
Total	**129**	**33**

Honours:
2 England Youth Caps
FA Amateur Cup Winners Medal   1951-52

ROSTRON, Wilf   1972-77

Birth Place: Sunderland
Date of Birth: 29th September 1956

☞ Wilf Rostron played for Arsenal's South East Counties League side as an amateur during the 1972-73 season when his studying would allow. Became an apprentice in May 1973, turning professional in September the same year. In seasons 1973-74 and 1974-75 he played regularly on the right wing in Arsenal's Combination League side. Made his league debut versus Newcastle at Highbury in March 1975. He played in six league matches in 1974-75, five in 1975-76 and a further six in 1976-77. During this time although being a regular in the reserve side, could never command a regular place in the league side and joined Sunderland for £30,000 in August 1977. He spent just over two seasons at Roker Park before joining Watford in October 1979, where he was instrumental in their rise to the First Division, helping them to the 1984 FA Cup Final. Moved to Sheffield Wednesday in January 1989 and later Sheffield United in the same year, before joining Brentford as a player and later becoming coach.

Wilf Rostron

	Games	Goals
League	17	2
FA Cup	1	0
League Cup	1	0
Friendly Matches	37	9
Tour Matches	5	0
Combination League	129	24
London Challenge Cup	2	0
South East Counties League	33	14
Youth Cup	14	4
Other Youth Cups	8	1
Youth Tour Matches	14	4
Total	**261**	**58**

RUDKIN, Tom   1947

Birth Place: Worksop, Notts.
Date of Birth: 17th June 1919

☞ Tom Rudkin began his football career with Lincoln City in 1938. During the war years was on the books of Grimsby Town and after the war he joined the then non league club Peterborough United, where he caught the eye of an Arsenal talent scout. Moved to Highbury in January 1947, making his league debut versus Aston Villa on 18th January 1947. Played in five consecutive league matches before being demoted to the reserves. Became unsettled and transferred to Southampton in August 1947 as part of the deal which took Don Roper to Highbury. Later played for Bristol City.

	Games	Goals
League	5	2
Combination League	8	0
Combination Cup	1	0
Friendly Matches	2	0
Total	**16**	**2**

Honours:
Football Combination Cup
    runners-up   1946-47

RYAN, John   1964-65

Birth Place: Lewisham, London
Date of Birth: 20th February 1947

☞ John Ryan joined Arsenal from Maidstone United in October 1964. In his only season at Highbury, played regularly at full back or on the wing in Arsenal's Metropolitan League side. With a surplus of excellent youngsters on the books at Highbury at the time he was released on a free transfer in July 1965, joining Fulham. Spent the following seventeen seasons playing in all four divisions of the football league for Fulham, Luton, Norwich City, Sheffield United, Manchester City, Stockport, Chester and Cambridge United, as well as a spell in the United States playing for Seattle Sounders. In all he played in nearly five hundred league games. Was appointed manager of Cambridge United in February 1984. Managed Sittingbourne, but left to take over at Dover Athletic in February 1995. Also runs a transport business in Maidstone.

	Games	Goals
Friendly Matches	5	2
Combination League	6	0
Metropolitan League	20	3
Metropolitan Cup	2	0
South East Counties League	6	0
Other Youth Cups	2	0
Total	**41**	**5**

RYAN, Mike   1948-52

Birth Place: Welwyn Garden City, Hertfordshire
Date of Birth: 14th October 1930

🎯 Mike Ryan joined Arsenal from Chase of Chertsey in June 1948. After winning a place at inside forward in the Eastern Counties League side, was called up for two years National Service in March 1949. He still managed to play a considerable amount of football during those two years and in 1950-51 was a regular member of Arsenal's reserve side, playing in nineteen league and cup matches. Interchanged between the Eastern Counties and reserve sides during the 1951-52 season, playing at inside forward. Released on a free transfer in June 1952 when he joined Lincoln City. Later played for York City.

Mike Ryan

	Games	Goals
Friendly Matches	5	1
Combination League	29	10
Combination Cup	10	4
Eastern Counties League	49	14
Eastern Counties Cup	6	4
London Midweek League	13	3
Other Youth Matches	8	1
Total	**120**	**37**

Honours:
Football Combination
  Championship Medal   1950-51

SAMMELS, Jon   1961-71

Birth Place: Ipswich, Suffolk
Date of Birth: 23rd July 1945

🎯 Jon Sammels joined Arsenal as an apprentice in January 1961, turning professional in July 1962. In his first two seasons at Arsenal he played regularly in the successful youth team and graduated to the Metropolitan League side. In 1962-63 he won a place in the England youth side, winning a total of seven caps, Was also a member of the Little World Cup youth winners team versus Northern Ireland. During that season he made his league debut versus Blackpool in April 1963. He was not called into the league side during 1963-64, when he spent the season in the reserve side. However, after the sale of Geoff Strong to Liverpool during the following season, Sammels was drafted in for seventeen league matches. He won a regular place in the league side during 1965-66, playing in thirty two league matches. In 1966-67 season, after the transfer of George Eastham to Stoke City, Jon became the controlling influence in midfield. Played regularly throughout the season, scoring ten goals and winning the first of his nine under-23 caps, versus Wales. In seasons 1967-68 and 1968-69 he played regularly, missing only thirteen of Arsenal's eighty four league games, playing in successive League Cup Finals versus Leeds and Swindon. The following season, 1969-70, he played thirty six league games, and was a valuable member of the Inter Cities Fairs Cup winning team against Anderlecht (scoring one of the goals in the final). Unfortunately during Arsenal's double season of 1970-71, Sammels, despite being a valuable member of the squad, could not claim a regular place and although he qualified for a league championship medal by playing in fifteen league matches, he missed Arsenal's FA Cup Final victory over Liverpool. Disillusioned by this, he was placed on the transfer list at his own request and subsequently was transferred to Leicester City for £100,000 in July 1971. Served Leicester well for seven seasons, before joining Vancouver Whitecaps of Canada. Now working as a driving instructor in Leicester where he resides.

	Games	Goals
League	215	39
FA Cup	21	3
League Cup	19	3
UEFA Cup	15	7
Friendly Matches	39	27
Tour Matches	29	9
Combination League	77	31
Combination Cup	1	0
London Challenge Cup	5	0
Metropolitan League	26	10
Metropolitan Cup	14	4
South East Counties League	21	10
Youth Cup	7	4
Other Youth Cups	8	5
Youth Tour Matches	15	3
Total	**512**	**155**

Honours:
9 England Under-23 Caps
1 Football League Cap
7 England Youth Caps
League Championship Medal   1970-71
Inter Cities Fairs Cup Winners
  Medal   1969-70
Two League Cup Finalists Medal   1968-69
Football Combination Champions   1962-63
Football Combination Cup Winners   1969-70
London FA Challenge Cup
  Runners-up   1965-66
Metropolitan League Professional Challenge
  Cup Winners   1961-62
Metropolitan League Challenge Cup
  Winners   1965-66
South East Counties League Cup
  Winners   1960-61, 1961-62
Southern Junior Floodlight Cup
  Winners   1962-63
London Minor Challenge Cup
  Runners-up   1961-62

Jon Sammels

Arsenal
S
1945-1985

Jon Sammels

SANCHES, John   1956-59

Birth Place: Paddington, London
Date of Birth: 21st October 1940

☛ John Sanches was already an English schoolboy international when he joined the groundstaff during the summer of 1956, turning professional in October 1957. Made great strides in his first season at the club, becoming the regular full back in Arsenal's youth team and winning an England Youth Cap versus Luxembourg. Held his place in the South East Counties League side during 1957-58, also playing four reserve team matches. However, although he graduated into the Metropolitan League side in 1958-59, his early promise was not fulfilled and he was granted a free transfer in June 1959 when he joined Watford. Later emigrated to Australia to play league football.

	Games	Goals
Friendly Matches	7	0
Combination League	9	0
Southern Floodlight Cup	1	0
London Midweek League	6	0
Metropolitan League	23	0
Metropolitan Cup	2	0
South East Counties League	27	1
Youth Cup	21	0
Other Youth Cups	14	1
Youth Tour Matches	4	0
Total	**114**	**2**

Honours:
1 England Youth Cap
Metropolitan League Championship
   Medal   1958-59
Southern Junior Floodlight Cup Finalist
   Medal   1957-58

SAXBY, Ron   1953-59

Birth Place: Rolvendon, Kent
Date of Birth: 1937

☛ Ron Saxby joined Arsenal as an amateur in May 1953 after representing Kent and England schoolboys. Turned professional in October 1954 making rapid progress in his first season at Highbury (1953-54) and his Combination League debut that season. In 1954-55 he was a regular in the South East Counties League side, scoring seventeen goals in thirty matches. He gained a permanent place in the reserve side during 1955-56, also winning the first of his England Youth Caps. Unfortunately, over the next two seasons, 1956-57 and 1957-58 he was called away for his National Service and during those seasons he played in only fourteen matches. On his return to Highbury he spent the 1958-59 season as the regular in the Metropolitan League side but was granted a free transfer in May 1959, when he joined Hastings United.

	Games	Goals
Friendly Matches	13	6
Combination League	32	9
Combination Cup	1	0
London Challenge Cup	1	0
Eastern Counties League	14	3
Eastern Counties Cup	1	0
London Midweek League	26	3
Metropolitan League	29	10
Metropolitan Cup	2	1
South East Counties League	38	22
Youth Cup	3	1
Other Youth Cups	2	0
Youth Tour Matches	4	1
Total	**166**	**56**

Honours:
4 England Youth Caps
Metropolitan League Championship
   Medal   1958-59
South East Counties League Championship
   Medal   1955-56

SCURR, John   1959-61

Birth Place: North Shields, Durham
Date of Birth: 30th September 1940

☛ John Scurr joined Arsenal as an amateur from a North Shields boys club in April 1959, turning professional in September 1959. He held a regular place in the club's Metropolitan League side as an inside forward for two seasons (1959-61) before being granted a free transfer in January 1961, when he joined Carlisle United.

	Games	Goals
Friendly Matches	6	4
Combination League	4	1
London Challenge Cup	2	0
Metropolitan League	41	13
Metropolitan Cup	3	4
Total	**56**	**22**

Honours:
London FA Challenge Cup Finalist
   Medal   1960-61
Metropolitan League Championship
   Medal   1960-61

SEXTON, Bernard   1948-49

☛ Bernard Sexton spent only one season at Highbury (1948-49), playing at inside forward for the Eastern Counties League side.

	Games	Goals
Combination League	3	0
Combination Cup	2	0
Eastern Counties League	17	5
Eastern Counties Cup	1	0
Other Youth Matches	3	0
Total	**26**	**5**

Bernard Sexton

SHAW, Arthur   1948-55

Birth Place: Limehouse, London
Date of Birth: 9th April 1924

☛ Arthur Shaw had considerable amateur experience during the latter war years playing for Hounslow, Hayes, Southall, and Queens Park Rangers. Joined Brentford as a professional in May 1946. He spent two seasons at Griffin Park as a reserve wing half, before surprisingly joining Arsenal for a small fee in April 1948. He made his league debut versus Chelsea in August 1949, after spending the 1948-49 season as a regular member of the reserve side. He made five league appearances in 1949-50 followed by sixteen during the 1950-51 season. After Ray Daniel suffered a fractured arm during a match at Blackpool over Easter in 1952, Shaw stepped in to deputise for the last eight league matches of that season. He played regular first team football the following season (1952-53), sharing the right half position with Alex Forbes. Played in twenty three matches and won a League Championship Medal. However, after the signing of Bill Dickson in October 1953, and the consistency of Forbes, Arthur Shaw played in only two further league games during the 1953-54 season and in 1954-55 played in only one league match. In his seven seasons at Highbury he played in only fifty seven league matches, although during that period he was a valuable and versatile reserve. Joined Watford in June 1955.

	Games	Goals
League	57	0
FA Cup	4	0
Friendly Matches	18	0
Tour Matches	6	0
Combination League	93	8
Combination Cup	31	2
London Challenge Cup	9	0
Eastern Counties League	2	0
Eastern Counties Cup	1	0
London Midweek League	4	0
Total	**225**	**10**

Arthur Shaw

Honours:

League Championship Medal	1952-53
Football Combination Cup	
runners-up	1950-51
London FA Challenge Cup winners	1954-55

SHERRATT, James   1946-48

Birth Place: Warrington, Lancashire
Date of Birth: 24th December 1921

James Sherratt joined Arsenal from Southampton in December 1946 after a trial period. He spent two seasons at Highbury as a goalscoring inside forward in the reserve side, scoring thirty goals in less than fifty matches. However, was never able to command a place in the league side and was granted a free transfer in December 1948 when he joined Hartlepool. Later played for Leyton Orient and Workington.

James Sherratt

	Games	Goals
Friendly Matches	2	1
Combination League	27	12
Combination Cup	19	18
Eastern Counties Cup	2	1
Other Youth Matches	18	6
Total	**68**	**38**

SHOVELAR, Micky   1969-72

Birth Place: Gravesend, Kent
Date of Birth: 6th October 1953

Micky Shovelar joined Arsenal as an apprentice in April 1969 after representing both Tonbridge and Kent schoolboys. Turned professional in May 1971. In his first two seasons at Highbury he was a regular in the South East Counties League side, playing defence or midfield, and he was a member of Arsenal's victorious FA Youth Cup and South East Counties League championship sides of 1970-71. He won a regular place in the reserve side during season 1971-72 but progressed no further and was granted a free transfer during the summer of 1972. Later played in non league football.

	Games	Goals
Friendly Matches	24	6
Combination League	41	1
London Challenge Cup	4	0
Metropolitan League	5	1
South East Counties League	46	5
Youth Cup	19	3
Other Youth Cups	14	1
Youth Tour Matches	21	0
Total	**174**	**17**

Honours:

FA Youth Cup Winners Medal	1970-71
South East Counties League Cup	
Winners Medal	1970-71
South East Counties League Cup	
Finalists Medal	1971-72

SIMMONS, Dave   1964-69

Birth Place: Gosport, Hampshire
Date of Birth: 24th October 1948

Dave Simmons joined Arsenal as an apprentice in April 1964, turning professional in October 1965. In his early years with the club was one of the most prolific youth team goalscorers the club has ever had. In seasons 1964-65 and 1965-66 he played regularly in all youth competitions and he scored seventy goals in ninety four matches. This form brought him the chance of reserve team football during 1966-67 and 1967-68. However, his goalscoring rate was not as high as in the youth team days, and during the next season, although he played in first team friendly matches, was allowed to leave Highbury on loan to Bournemouth in November 1968. On his return to the club was transferred to Aston Villa for £10,000 in February 1969. He later played for Colchester, Cambridge United and Brentford.

	Games	Goals
Friendly Matches	27	19
Tour Matches	4	2
Combination League	47	17
Combination Cup	22	5
London Challenge Cup	1	0
Metropolitan League	30	16
Metropolitan Cup	2	2
South East Counties League	45	38
Youth Cup	9	9
Other Youth Cups	18	15
Youth Tour Matches	20	5
Total	**225**	**128**

Dave Simmons

Honours:

Football Combination	
Championship Medal	1968-69
Football Combination Cup	
Winners Medal	1967-68
FA Youth Cup Winners	
Medal	1965-66
Metropolitan League Challenge	
Cup Winners Medal	1965-66
South East Counties League	
Championship Medal	1964-65
South East Counties League	
Finalists Medal	1965-66
Southern Junior Floodlight	
Cup Winners Medal	1965-66
Southern Junior Floodlight	
Cup Finalists Medal	1967-68

SIMPSON, Peter — 1960-78

Birth Place: Gorleston, Norfolk
Date of Birth: 13th January 1945

Peter Simpson joined Arsenal's groundstaff in May 1960, became an apprentice in October 1961, and turned professional in May 1962. In his first season at the club he played regularly in the South East Counties League side and for the next two seasons became a consistent member of the Metropolitan League side. Progressed to the reserve side during the 1963-64 season and made his league debut versus Chelsea in March 1964. He made six league appearances that season, but during seasons 1964-65 and 1965-66 he totalled only twelve league games and during that period it looked as though he would never gain a regular place in the league side. His fortunes changed during the 1966-67 season when he made thirty six league appearances, playing these matches in virtually every position except goalkeeper. He held his place during 1967-68 and 1968-69 (when settling down in the left half position) and he figured in both League Cup Finals of those seasons. In 1969-70 he missed only three league games and played his part in the winning of the Inter Cities Fairs Cup. During that season he was also called in to several England squads, although he never won a full international cap (along with George Swindin and George Armstrong must be considered as one of Arsenal's best club players never to win a full international cap). He played a leading role in the Arsenal team when the club performed the Double in 1970-71. He also appeared for the club in the 1972 FA Cup Final versus Leeds and from then until the 1974-75 season he held his place in the league side. However, during his final three seasons 1975-78 he played in only thirty seven league matches and he had to settle for reserve team football up to his retirement. Peter Simpson, during his eighteen years at Highbury, played in more competitive matches (eight hundred and eighty six) than any other player in Arsenal's history, a record later broken by David O`Leary. He finished his career playing for New England Teamen in USA and later for Hendon. Now working for a roofing materials firm in Hertfordshire.

Peter Simpson

	Games	Goals
League	370	10
FA Cup	53	1
League Cup	33	3
European Cup	5	1
UEFA Cup	16	0
Friendly Matches	65	2
Tour Matches	43	0
Combination League	125	16
Combination Cup	2	0
London Challenge Cup	9	1
Metropolitan League	71	8
Metropolitan Cup	21	2
South East Counties League	30	9
Youth Cup	15	2
Other Youth Cups	17	3
Youth Tour Matches	11	1
Total	**886**	**59**

Honours:

League Championship Medal	1970-71
FA Cup Winners Medal	1970-71
FA Cup Finalists Medal	1971-72
Inter Cities Fairs Cup Winners Medals	1969-70
League Cup Finalists Medals	1967-68, 1968-69
Football Combination Winners	1969-70
Metropolitan League Champions	1962-63
Metropolitan League Professional Cup Winners	1961-62
runners-up	1962-63
Metropolitan League Challenge Cup Winners	1965-66
South East Counties League Cup Winners	1960-61, 1961-62
Southern Junior Floodlight Cup Winners	1962-63
London Minor Challenge Cup Runners-up	1960-61

Peter Simpson

SINGFIELD, Ken — 1957-58

Birth Place:
Date of Birth:

☞ Ken Singfield spent only one season at Highbury as a wing half, playing mainly in the London Midweek League side. He also played in one game for the Combination League team. Was granted a free transfer at the end of the 1957-58 season.

	Games	Goals
Friendly Matches	5	1
Combination League	1	0
London Midweek League	9	1
Total	**15**	**2**

SKIRTON, Alan — 1959-66

Birth Place: Bath, Avon
Date of Birth: 23rd January 1939

☞ Alan Skirton joined Arsenal from Bath City in January 1959, while he was still completing his National Service. Unfortunately soon after joining the club he contracted pleurisy and pneumonia which kept him out of action for well over eighteen months. When regaining full fitness at the start of the 1960-61 season he made his league debut versus Burnley at Highbury in August 1960. He played in sixteen league games that season and shared the right wing position with Danny Clapton. During the following season he established a permanent place in the league side (missing only four matches) and finished that season as the club's leading goalscorer with nineteen goals. About this time he switched to the left wing position after the signing of right winger Johnny MacLeod. In 1962-63 he appeared in twenty eight league matches followed in 1963-64 by only fifteen, due mainly to the emergence of George Armstrong as a first team player. Over the next two seasons he played in roughly half of the club's league matches the other half being played by George Armstrong, due to the club operating in most matches with only one winger. He played in the first two games of the 1966-67 season before being transferred to Blackpool for £30,000 in September 1966, spending two seasons at Bloomfield Road. Was transferred to Bristol City in November 1968. Finished his league career with Torquay United in 1971-72. Later played for Durban City (South Africa) and Weymouth. On finishing playing (1975) he became assistant commercial manager at Weymouth and commercial manager at Bath City. Is currently commercial manager at Yeovil Town.

	Games	Goals
League	145	53
FA Cup	8	0
UEFA Cup	1	1
Friendly Matches	40	38
Tour Matches	19	10
Combination League	47	19
London Challenge Cup	14	5
Metropolitan League	7	5
Metropolitan Cup	2	1
Total	**283**	**132**

Alan Skirton

Honours:
London FA Challenge Cup Winners 1961-62
Metropolitan League Challenge Cup
Winners 1965-66

SLOAN, J W (Paddy) — 1946-48

Birth Place: Lurgan, Northern Ireland
Date of Birth: 30th April 1921

J. W. Sloan

☞ Paddy Sloan joined Arsenal from Tranmere Rovers in May 1946. He made his league debut as an inside forward versus Wolves on the opening day of the season 1946-47. Was soon switched to wing half and played in twenty seven league games that season. However, after the signings of Alex Forbes and Archie Macaulay he lost his place and played in only six league games. Was transferred to Sheffield United in February 1948. Later played for

Norwich City, after playing in Italy for nearly four years with Milan, Turin, Udinese and Brescia. He went on to coach in Turkey and Australia. Died January 1993, aged 71.

	Games	Goals
League	33	1
FA Cup	2	0
Friendly Matches	6	4
Tour Matches	2	0
Combination League	14	6
Combination Cup	4	3
London Challenge Cup	2	0
Total	**63**	**14**

Honours:
3 Irish Caps
2 Victory International Caps.

SMAILES, Jim — 1952-58

Birth Place: Tow Law, Durham
Date of Birth: 1934

☞ Jim Smailes joined Arsenal from Romford in June 1952 after winning two England youth caps during the 1950-51 season. Won a regular place in the reserve side as a wing half during the first part of the 1952-53 season. Was called up for National Service in November 1952. Returned to Highbury in November 1954 after missing the whole of the 1953-54 season. He established himself in the reserve side over the next four seasons, playing in nearly one hundred matches for them without ever winning a first team place. Released on a free transfer at the end of the 1957-58 season.

	Games	Goals
Friendly Matches	10	1
Tour Matches	3	0
Combination League	89	1
Combination Cup	3	0
London Challenge Cup	7	0
Eastern Counties League	11	0
Eastern Counties Cup	2	0
London Midweek League	13	0
Total	**138**	**2**

Honours:
2 England Youth Caps
London FA Challenge Cup Winners
Medal 1954-55

SMITH, Alan — 1946

Birth Place: Newcastle, Durham
Date of Birth: 15th October 1921

☞ Alan Smith joined Arsenal as a professional in May 1946. He spent only six months at Highbury, playing left wing for the reserve team. He made three league appearances, his debut being versus Sunderland at Highbury in September 1946. Transferred to Brentford in

December 1946. Later played for Leyton Orient.

	Games	Goals
League	3	0
Friendly Matches	2	1
Combination League	14	3
Combination Cup	12	2
Wartime	2	1
Total	**33**	**7**

Honours:
Football Combination Championship
Medal   1946-47

SMITH, Edward   1938-47

Birth Place: Stoke, Staffordshire
Date of Birth: 19th October 1920

☛Edward Smith joined Arsenal from their nursery side Margate before the outbreak of the war in May 1938. On the resumption of league football in 1946 he made five reserve team appearances, playing at inside forward. Released during the summer of 1947 when he joined Aldershot.

	Games	Goals
Friendly Matches	1	0
Combination League	5	0
Combination Cup	1	0
Wartime	3	0
Total	**10**	**0**

SMITH, John   1979-81

Birth Place: Hull, Humberside
Date of Birth: 1963

☛John Smith Joined Arsenal as an apprentice during the summer of 1979, having already been on the books as a schoolboy. Turned professional in June 1980. During his two seasons at Highbury played regularly as an inside forward in the South East Counties League side. Released on a free transfer during the summer of 1981.

	Games	Goals
Friendly Matches	5	0
Combination League	1	0
South East Counties League	53	7
Youth Cup	4	1
Other Youth Cups	8	1
Total	**71**	**9**

SMITH, Norman   1947-52

Birth Place: Darwen, Lancashire
Date of Birth: 2nd January 1925

☛Norman Smith joined Arsenal from Darwen in July 1947 after having previously been an amateur with Bolton Wanderers. Throughout the 1947-48 season played at wing half for the reserve side. Held his place during the 1948-49 season, but was sidelined

during the following two seasons when undergoing three leg operations. Returned to full fitness in the 1951-52 season, re-establishing himself in the reserve side. Transferred to Barnsley in October 1952, playing regularly for them for seven seasons. During his five years at Arsenal Norman Smith played in over one hundred reserve team games without ever playing first team football.

Norman Smith

	Games	Goals
Friendly Matches	7	0
Tour Matches	2	0
Combination League	87	3
Combination Cup	33	0
London Challenge Cup	7	0
Eastern Counties League	6	0
Eastern Counties Cup	2	0
London Midweek League	2	0
Other Youth Matches	14	0
Total	**160**	**3**

Honours:
Football Combination Championship
Medal   1950-51

SMITH, Ron   1954-55

Birth Place: Aberystwyth, Wales
Date of Birth: 9th April 1934

☛Ron Smith joined Arsenal after being demobbed from the army in July 1954. He spent only one season at Highbury, playing at right back in the Eastern Counties League side. Was released on a free transfer in August 1955 when he joined Watford. Died 1987 aged 53.

	Games	Goals
Friendly Matches	1	0
Eastern Counties League	18	0
Eastern Counties Cup	1	0
London Midweek League	3	0
South East Counties League	3	0
Total	**26**	**0**

Honours:
Eastern Counties League Championship
Medal   1954-55

SMITH, Terry   1952-56

Birth Place: London
Date of Birth: 1936

☛Terry Smith joined Arsenal as an amateur in August 1952 after representing Edmonton boys. Turned part time professional in March 1953 enabling him to train as a draughtsman. Was called up for two years' National Service in May 1953 and subsequently during seasons 1953-54 and 1954-55 played in only twelve matches. Released on a free transfer in January 1956.

	Games	Goals
Friendly Matches	8	0
Combination League	1	0
Eastern Counties League	31	0
Eastern Counties Cup	6	0
London Midweek League	17	0
Total	**63**	**0**

SMITHSON, Rodney   1959-64

Birth Place: Leicester
Date of Birth: 9th October 1943

☛Rodney Smithson was an England schoolboy international when joining Arsenal's groundstaff in June 1959. Became an apprentice in July 1960 and turned professional in October the same year. In his first two seasons at Highbury played either at half back or full back for the South East Counties League side. Won a place in the Metropolitan League side in 1961 -62 when he also won three England youth caps. Made his league debut versus Fulham at Craven Cottage in September 1962 after playing several reserve team games. Played in one further league match that season. He spent all of season 1963-64 in the reserve side. With little chance of maintaining a first team place, he was transferred to Oxford United for £5,000 in July 1964, playing ten seasons for them.

	Games	Goals
League	2	0
Friendly Matches	16	0
Combination League	62	2
London Challenge Cup	7	0
Metropolitan League	58	8
Metropolitan Cup	24	6
South East Counties League	33	0
Youth Cup	13	1
Other Youth Cups	12	4
Youth Tour Matches	19	4
Total	**246**	**25**

Honours:
Football Combination Champions   1962-63
London FA Challenge Cup Winners   1962-63
Metropolitan League Champions   1960-61,
                                       1962-63
Metropolitan League Challenge Cup
   Winners   1960-61
Metropolitan League Pro. Cup Winners   1960-61,
                                       1961-62
South East Counties League Cup
   Winners   1959-60,1961-62
3 England Youth Caps

SNEDDEN, John   1958-65

Birth Place: Bonnybridge, Scotland
Date of Birth: 3rd February 1942

John Snedden was a Scottish schoolboy international when he joined Arsenal as an amateur in October 1958. Turned professional in February 1959. He played regularly for the club's youth teams during 1958-59, and was promoted to the reserve side in 1959-60. Made his league debut the same season versus Tottenham at White Hart Lane in January 1960, when only seventeen years old. He won a regular place in the league side as a wing half during the 1960-61 season before, unfortunately , breaking an ankle versus Sheffield Wednesday in December 1960. In 1961-62 he shared the wing half position with Terry Neill and played in fifteen league matches that season. Played in twenty seven league games in 1962-63, and fourteen in 1963-64. Lost form and confidence altogether in the 1964-65 season and played in only three league games, his place being taken by both Terry Neill and Frank McLintock. Transferred to Charlton for £15,000 in March 1965. Later played for Leyton Orient. Finished playing at 25 and now living in Germany.

John Snedden

	Games	Goals
League	83	0
FA Cup	10	0
UEFA Cup	1	0
Friendly Matches	42	1
Tour Matches	9	0
Combination League	72	0
London Challenge Cup	5	0
Metropolitan League	19	0
Metropolitan Cup	3	0
South East Counties League	8	0
Youth Cup	10	0
Other Youth Cups	7	0
Youth Tour Matches	2	0
Total	**271**	**1**

Honours:
London FA Challenge Cup Winners 1961-62
South East Counties League Cup
Winners   1959-60

SPARROW, Brian   1978-84

Birth Place: Bethnal Green, London
Date of Birth: 24th June 1962

Brian Sparrow joined Arsenal as an apprentice during the summer of 1978 and turned professional in January 1980. Began his career as a left winger in the South East Counties League side during seasons 1977-78 and 1978-79. He played regularly for the reserve team between 1980-84, switching to a midfield position, (later moving to full back). Had played in nearly one hundred and fifty Combination matches for the club without a first team place. Was with Wimbledon and Gillingham during seasons 1982-83, and 1983-84 on loan periods.His brother John has also played league football for Chelsea and Exeter. Released on a free transfer to Crystal Palace in June 1984. Joined non league Enfield and later Crawley. Brian has been reserve team coach at Wimbledon since 1992.

Brian Sparrow

	Games	Goals
League	2	0
Friendly Matches	49	3
Tour Matches	2	0
Combination League	149	11
South East Counties League	59	26
Youth Cup	5	0
Other Youth Cups	13	5
Youth Tour Matches	4	0
Total	**283**	**45**

Honours:
Football Combination Champion   1983-84
South East Counties League Cup Winners
                                                          1979-80

STANDEN, Jim   1953-60

Birth Place: Edmonton, London
Date of Birth: 30th May 1935

Jim Standen joined Arsenal from Rickmansworth in April 1953. However, in October 1953 he was called up for National Service which limited his appearances to twenty during seasons 1953-54 and 1954-55. After being released in October 1955 he played in nine matches during the 1955-56 season. He won a place in goal for the reserve side during 1956-57, sharing the position with Con Sullivan. Made one league appearance in 1957-58 versus Burnley at Turf Moor in December 1957. He deputised for Jack Kelsey in thirteen league matches in 1958-59 and shared the first team spot with him in 1959-60 when he appeared in twenty league matches. Transferred to Luton Town in October 1960 after the arrival of Jack McClelland. Joined West Ham in November 1962 and served them well for six seasons, helping them win the FA Cup in 1964 and the European Cup Winners Cup in 1965. Later played for Detroit Cougars in the United States, Millwall and Portsmouth. He also played county cricket for Worcestershire for twelve years between 1959 and 1970, and topped the national bowling averages in 1964. Now lives in Clayton, California where he works for a Honda car leasing company.

Jim Standen

	Games	Goals
League	35	0
FA Cup	3	0
Friendly Matches	22	0
Tour Matches	5	0
Combination League	66	0
Combination Cup	1	0
London Challenge Cup	11	0
Southern Floodlight Cup	3	0
Eastern Counties League	16	0
London Midweek League	14	0
Metropolitan League	3	0
Total	**179**	**0**

Honours:
(WITH WEST HAM)
FA Cup Winners Medal	1963-64
European Cup Winners Medal	1964-65
League Cup Finalists Medal	1965-66
FA Charity Shield Winners Medal	1964-65
(WITH ARSENAL)
| London FA Challenge Cup Winners | 1957-58 |

STANLEY, Ernie   1948-51

Birth Place: London
Date of Birth: 1930

➤ Ernie Stanley joined Arsenal in July 1948 after playing for Eton Manor. Ernie spent three seasons at Highbury playing either on the wing or at inside forward for the club's Eastern Counties League side. Played in one reserve match in 1949-50. Released on a free transfer during the close season of 1951.

Ernest Stanley

	Games	Goals
Friendly Matches	5	1
Combination League	1	0
Combination Cup	3	0
London Challenge Cup	1	0
Eastern Counties League	63	15
Eastern Counties Cup	1	0
London Midweek League	19	10
Other Youth Matches	6	1
Total	**99**	**27**

STANTON, Tom   1966-67

Birth Place: Glasgow, Scotland
Date of Birth: 3rd May 1948

➤ Tom Stanton was a Scottish schoolboy international when he joined Liverpool as a professional in May 1965. Surprisingly joined Arsenal on a free transfer in September 1966. He spent one full season at Highbury in 1966-67, playing in both the Metropolitan and Combination League sides. Released on a free transfer in September 1967 when he joined Mansfield. He later spent eight seasons with Bristol Rovers.

	Games	Goals
Friendly Matches	5	0
Combination League	15	0
Combination Cup	4	0
London Challenge Cup	2	0
Metropolitan League	14	2
Metropolitan Cup	7	0
Total	**47**	**2**

STAPLETON, Frank   1972-81

Birth Place: Dublin
Date of Birth: 10th July 1956

➤ Frank Stapleton joined Arsenal as an apprentice in June 1972 and turned professional in October 1973. In his first season at Highbury we glimpsed the great promise he fulfilled becoming one of the most respected centre forwards in world football. He scored forty two goals in fifty two youth matches and won five Republic of Ireland youth caps. Progressed to the reserve team in season 1973-74 and maintained his place during 1974-75, making his league debut versus Stoke at Highbury in March 1975. He established himself in the league side in 1975-76, playing in twenty five matches, In 1976-77 he became an automatic choice and formed a great goalscoring partnership with Malcolm Macdonald (scoring forty six goals between them) and won the first of his seventy Eire caps versus Turkey. During the next three seasons, 1977-80, he missed only seven of the Club's one hundred and twenty six league matches and was leading goalscorer for the club from 1978-81. Helped Arsenal to three consecutive FA Cup Finals 1978-80, scoring one of the goals in the 1979 FA Cup Final versus Manchester United. By this time he had found a new goalscoring partner in Alan Sunderland and many of the goals he scored were set up by his Irish team mate Liam Brady. However, he like Liam Brady wanted to move after the expiry of his contract and joined Manchester United for £900,000 (the fee being set by a tribunal after Arsenal had asked for £1,500,000) in August 1981. During his time at Old Trafford he still remained one of the great centre forwards of this era and helped United to both FA Cup and League Cup Finals. He left Old Trafford in July 1987 when he joined Ajax (Holland). His stay was for only eight months before returning home to join Derby, March 1988, later joined Le Harve (France). Signed for Blackburn Rovers, July 1989 spending two seasons at Ewood Park. He played Non Contract with both Aldershot and Huddersfield. In December 1991 he became Player Manager of Bradford City where he spent three seasons before leaving. During the 1994-95 season he was invited back into league football by his old pal Liam Brady at Brighton. In his career which spanned over twenty seasons, he played in over six hundred league games. Frank Stapleton, in all competitive matches for Arsenal, scored nearly two hundred and fifty goals of which over one hundred were for the first team. After a brief spell as reserve team coach at QPR, Frank has returned to his home in the north of England seeking a coaching or managerial position.

	Games	Goals
League	225	75
FA Cup	32	15
League Cup	27	14
Cup Winners Cup	9	0
UEFA Cup	6	4
Charity Shield	1	0
Friendly Matches	59	36
Tour Matches	21	7
Combination League	72	31
London Challenge Cup	3	0
South East Counties League	41	39
Youth Cup	12	9
Other Youth Cups	12	10
Youth Tour Matches	15	5
Total	**535**	**245**

Frank Stapleton

Honours:
(WITH ARSENAL AND MANCHESTER UNITED)
70 Eire Caps
5 Eire Youth Caps
FA Cup Winners
    Medals   1978-79,1982-83, 1984-85
FA Cup Finalists
    Medals   1977-78,1979-80
League Cup Finalists
    Medal   1982-83
European Cup Winners Cup
    Finalists Medal   1979-80
FA Charity Shield Winners
    Medal   1982-83
FA Charity Shield Finalists
    Medals   1979-80, 1984-85
PFA Team Award
    Division One   1984

STEAD, Kevin 1977-79

Birth Place: West Ham, London
Date of Birth: 2nd October 1958

Kevin Stead joined Arsenal on a free transfer from Tottenham in July 1977. He spent the 1977-78 season in the Combination League side, playing in forty matches. Was again a regular in that side during the 1978-79 season when he appeared in thirty eight matches. Played in many positions for the reserves but usually at full back. That season also saw him play in two league games, including his debut versus Southampton at Highbury in October 1978. Was released on a free transfer in September 1979 when he joined Oxford City. His brother Mike Stead has also played league football for Tottenham and Southend.

	Games	Goals
League	2	0
Friendly Matches	7	0
Combination League	80	11
Total	**89**	**11**

STILL, Ron 1961-65

Birth Place: Aberdeen, Scotland
Date of Birth: 10th June 1943

Ron Still joined Arsenal from Woodside junior side in August 1961. In his first season at Highbury (1961-62) played regularly at left back in the Metropolitan League side. He never progressed as expected and spent the following three seasons (1962-65) playing in the Metropolitan League side, although he did appear in the odd reserve game. Was granted a free transfer during the summer of 1965 when he joined Notts County. Later played for Brentford.

	Games	Goals
Friendly Matches	8	0
Combination League	20	0
Metropolitan League	72	1
Metropolitan Cup	17	0
South East Counties League	1	0
Youth Tour Matches	4	0
Total	**122**	**1**

Honours:
Metropolitan League Championship
 Medal 1962-63
Metropolitan League Professional Cup
 Winners Medal 1961-62

STOREY, Peter 1961-77

Birth Place: Farnham, Surrey
Date of Birth: 7th September 1945

Peter Storey was an England schoolboy international when he joined Arsenal as an apprentice in May 1961, turning professional in September 1962. He started his career as a young right back in the South East Counties League side in 1961, progressing to the Metropolitan League side during the next two seasons. Became a regular in the reserve side in 1964-65, and made his league debut in October 1965 versus Leicester at Filbert Street. He won a regular place in the league side that season, replacing Billy McCullough, and played in twenty eight league games. Played in thirty four league games the following season and during seasons 1967-68 and 1968-69 he missed only three league games and appeared in both League Cup Finals versus Leeds and Swindon. In 1969-70 he appeared in thirty nine league games and was a member of the club's Inter Cities Fairs Cup winning team. During the double year of 1970-71 he equalled Bobby Smith's record of winning League Championship, FA Cup Winners Medal and England Caps in the same season. Established himself in the England side, taking over from Nobby Stiles during seasons 1971-72 and 1972-73. Also played for Arsenal in the 1971-72 FA Cup Final versus Leeds. During this time he had switched from his original full back position to a wing half, midfield defensive position, and became known as one of the hardest tacklers in the game. Unfortunately this occasionally brought him into conflict with referees. Remained a regular for three further seasons (1973-75) before losing his place during the 1975-76 season when he appeared in only eleven league games. Played in a further eleven league games in 1976-77 but was unhappy with reserve team football and subsequently transferred to Fulham for £10,000 in March 1977. During his sixteen seasons at Highbury Peter Storey played in five hundred first team matches, a total only surpassed by Pat Rice, George Armstrong and David O'Leary. Peter has led a colourful life since retiring from the game and ran a market stall in London's West End after managing public houses.

	Games	Goals
League	391	9
FA Cup	51	4
League Cup	37	2
European Cup	3	0
UEFA Cup	19	2
Friendly Matches	56	2
Tour Matches	40	0
Combination League	60	1
London Challenge Cup	4	0
Metropolitan League	80	2
Metropolitan Cup	17	0
South East Counties League	26	1
Youth Cup	8	0
Other Youth Cups	12	0
Youth Tour Matches	18	0
Total	**822**	**23**

Honours:
Nineteen England Caps
One Football League Cap
League Championship Medal 1970-71
FA Cup Winners Medal 1970-71
FA Cup Finalist Medal 1971-72
Two League Cup Finalist Medals 1967-68,
 1968-69
Inter Cities Fairs Cup Winners
 Medal 1969-70
Rothmans Team Award 1970-71
Metropolitan League Champions 1962-63
South East Counties League Cup
 Winners 1963-64
Southern Junior Floodlight Cup
 Winners 1962-63
London Minor Challenge Cup
 Runners-up 1961-62

Peter Storey

STRONG, Geoff   1957-64

Birth Place: Kirkheaton, Northumberland
Date of Birth: 19th September 1937

Geoff Strong joined Arsenal as an amateur from Stanley United in November 1957, turning professional in April 1958. He won a place in the Metropolitan League side in 1958-59, scoring seventeen goals in fourteen matches. This resulted in him being promoted to the Combination team for the rest of the season. Became a regular in that side during 1959-60 before being called up for National Service in April 1960. However this did not effect his footballing career and after he had scored seven goals in six reserve team matches he was drafted in to the league side, making his debut versus Newcastle in October 1960. Played in nineteen league games that season, scoring ten goals and in 1961-62 scored twelve goals in twenty league matches. Forming a deadly goalscoring partnership with Joe Baker, he became an automatic choice in the 1962-63 season, playing in thirty six league games and scoring eighteen goals. This partnership flourished in 1963-64, when between them they scored sixty two first team goals (each scoring thirty one times). However, after playing in a further eleven league games in the first half of the 1964-65 season he became frustrated at the club's lack of success and was transferred to Liverpool for £40,000 in November 1964. While at Anfield he became one of the great utility players of the period, playing in every position except goalkeeper. Served Liverpool well for six seasons, winning both FA Cup and League Championship Winners Medals. Later played for Coventry City. Geoff now lives in Birkdale and is a successful businessman on Merseyside where he owns a thriving hotel furnishing company. Also co-owns a pub with his former Liverpool team mate Ian Callaghan.

Geoff Strong

	Games	Goals
League	125	69
FA Cup	8	5
UEFA Cup	4	3
Friendly Matches	31	21
Tour Matches	10	7
Combination League	42	33
London Challenge Cup	1	2

Metropolitan League	42	50
Metropolitan Cup	4	5
Total	**267**	**195**

Honours:
(WITH ARSENAL)

Metropolitan League Champions	1958-59
(WITH LIVERPOOL)	
FA Cup Winners Medal	1964-65
League Championship Medal	1965-66
European Cup Winners Cup Finalist	
Medal	1965-66.

SULLIVAN, Con   1954-58

Birth Place: Bristol, Avon
Date of Birth: 22nd August 1928

Con Sullivan began his footballing career with Bristol City in 1949. He spent five seasons at Ashton Gate before joining Arsenal in February 1954. Made his league debut versus Newcastle at St James Park in April 1954. Became the regular reserve team goalkeeper and played in two first team games during 1954-55, and the following season deputised for Jack Kelsey in a further ten. Returned to the Combination League side during 1956-57 and 1957-58, only managing to play in fifteen league games during that period. Retired at the end of 1958-59 season with a back injury sustained during training.

Con Sullivan

	Games	Goals
League	28	0
FA Cup	4	0
Friendly Matches	19	0
Tour Matches	2	0
Combination League	94	0
Combination Cup	6	0
London Challenge Cup	10	0
Southern Floodlight Cup	4	0
London Midweek League	2	0
Total	**169**	**0**

Honours:
London FA Challenge Cup Winners 1954-55

SULLIVAN, Nick   1976-80

Birth Place: Forest Gate, London
Date of Birth: 4th January 1961

Nick Sullivan joined Arsenal as an apprentice during the summer of 1976, turning professional in January 1979. Established himself as the regular youth team goalkeeper in seasons 1976-77 and 1977-78. Unfortunately he missed a number of matches due to injury in 1978-79 when it appeared he could attain the reserve team goalkeeping position. These injuries reduced his appearances to only nine in 1979-80 and he was released on a free transfer during the close season of 1980. Nick then played Non league football with Tooting, Bromley, Dulwich, Sutton United and Welling.

Nick Sullivan

	Games	Goals
Friendly Matches	7	0
Combination League	27	0
South East Counties League	44	0
Youth Cup	6	0
Other Youth Cups	9	0
Total	**93**	**0**

SULLIVAN, Terry   1953-56

Birth Place: Merthyr Tydfil, Wales
Date of Birth: 1936

Terry Sullivan was a Welsh schoolboy international when he joined Arsenal in October 1953. However remained at Highbury for only five months (as a regular in the Eastern Counties League side) before being called up for National Service in February 1954. He only played in three matches during 1954-55 season and was granted a free transfer on his release in February 1956.

	Games	Goals
Friendly Matches	1	0
Combination League	1	0
Eastern Counties League	9	1
London Midweek League	9	1
Total	**20**	**2**

SUNDERLAND, Alan   1977-84

Birth Place: Mexborough, Yorkshire
Date of Birth: 1st July 1953

Alan Sunderland will be remembered by Arsenal fans as the man who scored the winning goal in the final minute of the 1979 FA Cup Final versus Manchester United. Alan began his career with Wolves, turning professional in June 1971. He spent seven seasons at Molineux and played in nearly two hundred first team games as well as playing in the League Cup winning side of 1973-74 and the Second Division Championship side of 1976-77. Joined Arsenal for £220,000 in November 1977, immediately establishing himself in the league side and playing in the Cup Final versus Ipswich the same season. Played in thirty seven league games in 1978-79, scoring six goals in Arsenal's victorious FA Cup campaign. Won an England under 21 cap to add to the under 23 cap he had won at Wolves.

Scored twenty eight first team goals in 1979-80 when he formed a goal scoring partnership with Frank Stapleton. Helped Arsenal to both the FA Cup and European Cup Winners Cup Finals of that season as well as winning an England cap versus Australia. During seasons 1980-81 and 1981-82 he played in thirty four and thirty eight league games respectively and was the club's leading scorer with eleven goals in 1981-82. A series of injuries plagued him during the 1982-83 season and he played in only twenty five league games. After the signing of Charlie Nicholas during the summer of 1983 he found himself in the reserve side, and when Paul Mariner joined the club in February 1984 he realised his first team chances were limited. Alan joined Ipswich on loan in February 1984, eventually signing for them on a full time basis on a free transfer in July 1984. He later played in Ireland for Derry City. Alan ran a property rental company and sold insurance, before becoming licensee of the 'Halberd Inn' near Ipswich.

	Games	Goals
League	206	55
FA Cup	34	16
League Cup	26	13
Cup Winners Cup	7	4
EUFA Cup	7	3
Charity Shield	1	1
Friendly Matches	21	9
Tour Matches	22	5
Combination League	6	3
Total	**330**	**109**

Honours:
(WITH ARSENAL AND WOLVES)
1 England Cap
7 England 'B' Caps
1 England Under 23 Cap
2 England Under 21 Caps

FA Cup Winners Medal	1978-79
League Cup Winners Medal	1973-74
Division Two Championship Medal	1976-77
FA Cup Finalist Medal	1977-78, 1979-80

Alan Sunderland

European Cup Winners Cup Finalist
Medal | 1979-80
FA Charity Shield Finalist Medal | 1979-80

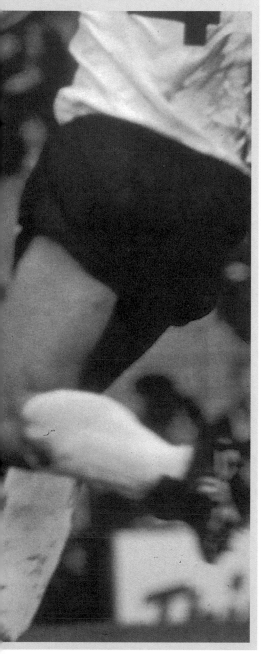

Alan Sunderland

SWALLOW, Ray   1952-58

Birth Place: Southwark, London
Date of Birth: 15th June 1935

Ray Swallow had represented Surrey youth when joining Arsenal's groundstaff in September 1952, turning professional in December 1952. Established himself either at wing half or inside forward in the Eastern Counties League side during 1952-53. Was called up for National Service in October 1953 but he still managed to play in twenty five matches that season. Played regularly in the Eastern Counties League side in 1954-55 resulting in him winning a place in the reserve side. Made his league debut versus Cardiff in April 1955. After his release from National Service in October 1955 he became a permanent member of the reserve team for three seasons and managed to play in a further twelve league games until being transferred to Derby County in September 1958. Ray also played county cricket for Derbyshire.

Ray Swallow

	Games	Goals
League	13	4
Friendly Matches	3	4
Combination League	98	67
London Challenge Cup	8	10
Southern Floodlight Cup	1	0
Eastern Counties League	52	18
Eastern Counties Cup	4	2
London Midweek League	13	6
Metropolitan League	1	0
Total	**193**	**111**

Honours:
London FA Challenge Cup
Winners | 1957-58
Eastern Counties League
Champions | 1954-55
London Midweek League
Championship Medal | 1952-53

1945-1985

TAPPING, Terry   1959-64

Birth Place: London
Date of Birth: 1943

Terry Tapping joined Arsenal's groundstaff in August 1959, became an apprentice in July 1960 and turned professional in January 1961. During his first two seasons at Highbury he played regularly for the South East Counties League side, graduating to the Metropolitan League team in 1961-62. Was a regular in that side during seasons 1962-63 and 1963-64, playing at either full back or wing half. Was granted a free transfer during the summer of 1964 when he joined Romford.

	Games	Goals
Friendly Matches	18	4
Combination League	4	0
Metropolitan League	91	15
Metropolitan Cup	19	4
South East Counties League	41	11
Youth Cup	10	3
Other Youth Cups	12	1
Youth Tour Matches	16	0
Total	**211**	**38**

Honours:
Metropolitan League Championship
Medal | 1962-63
Metropolitan League Cup Winners
Medal | 1960-61
Metropolitan Professional Cup Winners
Medals | 1961-62, 1962-63
South East Counties League Cup Winners
Medal | 1960-61, 1961-62

TAPSCOTT, Derek   1953-58

Birth Place: Barry, South Wales
Date of Birth: 30th June 1932

Derek Tapscott joined Arsenal from Barry Town in October 1953. Derek made his debut in the reserve team two days later and played in fifteen matches for that side scoring thirteen goals. He made his league debut versus Liverpool at Highbury in April 1954 scoring twice. He played in five league games (five goals) in 1953-54 and continued to progress when during the summer of 1954 he won the first of his fourteen Welsh caps versus Austria. Won a regular place in the league side in 1954-55, missing only five matches and scoring thirteen goals. Played in thirty six first team games in 1955-56 and was the club's leading scorer with twenty one goals. In 1956-57 he scored twenty five league goals (the most by an Arsenal player since Ronnie Rooke's thirty three in 1947-48). After representing Wales in the 1958 World Cup series he sustained several injuries to his ankle and knee, resulting in him playing in only eight league matches during season 1957-58. When regaining full fitness he could not reclaim his first team place and was subsequently transferred to Cardiff City for £15,000 in September 1958. He spent seven seasons with Cardiff before finishing his career with Newport County. Tapscott is currently self-employed,

Derek Tapscott

selling sports goods and is closely linked with multi-national sportswear company, Diadora, who recently signed Liverpool's Stan Collymore in a deal worth in excess of £2 million. A far cry from Derek's playing days when there were only two makes of boot to choose from!

	Games	Goals
League	119	62
FA Cup	13	6
Friendly Matches	17	28
Tour Matches	7	6
Combination League	32	30
Combination Cup	3	0
London Challenge Cup	7	5
Southern Floodlight Cup	2	2
Eastern Counties League	5	4
London Midweek League	1	1
Total	**206**	**144**

Honours:
14 Welsh Caps
London FA Challenge Cup Winners
Medals   1953-54,1957-58

TAWSE, Brian   1963-65

Birth Place: Ellon, Aberdeenshire, Scotland
Date of Birth: 30th July 1945

➤ Brian Tawse joined Arsenal as a professional in April 1963. In his first full season at Highbury (1963-64) he played on either wing in the Metropolitan League side. Progressed to the reserve side in 1964-65, also making the first of his five league appearances versus West Bromwich in November 1965. Was never able to maintain a regular place in the first team, and after spending the first half of the 1965-66 season

in the reserve side was transferred to Brighton for £5,000 in December 1965. Later

Brian Tawse

played for Brentford.

	Games	Goals
League	5	0
Friendly Matches	17	4
Tour Matches	2	1
Combination League	49	12
London Challenge Cup	7	2
Metropolitan League	43	14
Metropolitan Cup	9	2
South East Counties League	10	1
Youth Cup	4	0
Other Youth Cups	1	0
Youth Tour Matches	10	1
Total	**157**	**37**

Honours:
Southern Junior Floodlight Cup
Winners   1962-63

THEAR, Tony   1963-66

Birth Place: Edmonton, London
Date of Birth: 4th February 1948

➤ Tony Thear joined Arsenal as an apprentice in May 1963, turning professional in February 1965. During his three seasons at Highbury he played on either wing or inside forward in the South East Counties League side and the Metropolitan League team, and was also a prominent member of the club's successful youth team of that period. Was granted a free transfer in July 1966 when he joined Luton. Later played for Gillingham.

	Games	Goals
Friendly Matches	8	6
Combination League	4	1
Metropolitan League	57	22
Metropolitan Cup	4	0
South East Counties League	43	17
Youth Cup	6	0
Other Youth Cups	12	10
Youth Tour Matches	13	2
Total	**147**	**58**

Honours:
Metropolitan League Challenge Cup Winners
Medal   1965-66
South East Counties League Cup Winners
Medals   1963-64, 1964-65
London Minor Challenge Cup Finalist
Medal   1964-65

TIDDY, Mike   1955-58

Birth Place: Helston, Cornwall
Date of Birth: 4th April 1929

➤ Mike Tiddy began his career with Torquay United in November 1946. He spent four years at Plainmoor before joining Cardiff City in November 1950. He won a regular place in their league side, playing on either wing, and in five seasons at Ninian Park played in well over one hundred and fifty first team games. Transferred to Arsenal with Gordon Nutt for a joint fee of £30,000 in September 1955. He made his league debut versus Sunderland at Roker Park the same month. He played in twenty one league matches in the 1955-56 season, but unfortunately sustained several injuries the following season (including a cartilage operation) and played in only fifteen league games. When fully fit in 1957-58 he had to share the left wing position with Joe Haverty and Gordon Nutt, resulting in him having to return to reserve team football. Was subsequently transferred to Brighton for a small fee in October 1958.

Mike Tiddy

	Games	Goals
League	48	8
FA Cup	4	0
Friendly Matches	6	2
Tour Matches	5	0
Combination League	5	9
London Challenge Cup	7	2
Southern Floodlight Cup	2	1
Total	**123**	**22**

Honours:
London FA Challenge Cup Winners 1957-58

TILLEY, Don   1947-53

Birth Place: Ogmore Vale, Wales
Date of Birth: 1930

☛ Don Tilley was an amateur with the club before turning professional in February 1948. Unfortunately soon after joining Arsenal he was called up for National Service. Returned to Highbury in 1950 and spent the following three seasons (1950-53) at inside forward in the Eastern Counties League side. Granted a free transfer in the summer of 1953.

	Games	Goals
Friendly Matches	5	3
Combination League	11	4
Combination Cup	8	5
Eastern Counties League	53	21
Eastern Counties Cup	7	2
London Midweek League	20	16
Other Youth Matches	23	2
Total	**127**	**53**

Honours:
London Midweek League Championship
Medal   1952-53

TILLEY, Peter   1952-53

Birth Place: Lurgan, Northern Ireland
Date of Birth: 13th January 1930

☛ Peter Tilley joined Arsenal from Witton Albion in May 1952. In the 1952-53 season he played at inside forward in the Combination League side. He made his one and only league appearance versus Chelsea at Highbury in September 1953. Was transferred to Bury in November 1953. Later played for Halifax Town.

	Games	Goals
League	1	0
Friendly Matches	2	2
Combination League	29	8
Combination Cup	24	4
London Challenge Cup	6	2
Total	**62**	**16**

Honours:
Football Combination Cup Winners 1952-53

TILSED, Ron   1972-73

Birth Place: Weymouth, Dorset
Date of Birth: 6th August 1952

☛ Ron Tilsed began his career with Bournemouth in 1969-70, and the following season won four England youth caps. Joined Chesterfield in February 1972 and played in sixteen league matches for them that season. Joined Arsenal on a free transfer in September 1972 and during his six months at Highbury contested the reserve team

goalkeeper position with Geoff Barnett. Released on a free transfer in March 1973 when he joined Portsmouth. Later played for Hereford.

	Games	Goals
Friendly Matches	1	0
Combination League	13	0
Total	**14**	**0**

Honours:
4 England Youth Caps

TONES, John   1973-74

Birth Place: Silksworth, Durham
Date of Birth: 3rd December 1950

☛ John Tones spent five seasons with Sunderland and played in six league matches before joining Arsenal on a free transfer in July 1973. He spent one full season at Highbury, playing regularly as centre half in the Combination League side. Released on a free transfer during the summer of 1974. Later played for Swansea and Mansfield.

	Games	Goals
Friendly Matches	4	0
Combination League	33	1
London Challenge Cup	2	1
Total	**39**	**2**

TOWNSEND, Russell   1976-78

Birth Place: Reading, Berkshire
Date of Birth: 17th January 1960

☛ Russell Townsend played as a schoolboy with the club before joining them as an apprentice during the summer of 1976. He spent two seasons at Highbury, playing in defence or midfield in the South East Counties League side. Was never offered a professional contract and was released on a free transfer in January 1978 and joined Barnet. Later played for Northampton, then in non league football for Boreham Wood, Finchley, Harrow Borough and Leyton Wingate.

	Games	Goals
Friendly Matches	5	0
Combination League	23	2
South East Counties League	47	4
Youth Cup	7	1
Other Youth Cups	5	0
Total	**87**	**7**

TYRER, Alan   1965-67

Birth Place: Liverpool, Lancashire
Date of Birth: 8th December 1942

☛ Alan Tyrer began his career with Everton in December 1959. He spent four seasons at

1945-1985

Goodison Park before being transferred to Mansfield in July 1963 where he played in forty one league matches during his two year stay. He surprisingly joined Arsenal on a free transfer in August 1965. Was a regular in the reserve team that season, but was plagued by injuries during 1966-67, although he managed to play in two League Cup matches versus Gillingham. Granted a free transfer in August 1967 when he joined Bury. Later played for Workington where he stayed for eight seasons.

	Games	Goals
League Cup	2	0
Friendly Matches	9	1
Tour Matches	1	0
Combination League	44	13
Combination Cup	3	4
London Challenge Cup	6	2
Metropolitan League	2	0
Metropolitan Cup	2	2
Total	**69**	**22**

Honours:
London FA Challenge Cup
runners up   1965-66
Metropolitan League Challenge Cup
winners   1965-66

UPRICHARD, Norman   1948-49

Birth Place: Moyraverty, Northern Ireland
Date of Birth: 20th April 1928

Norman Uprichard

☛ Norman Uprichard joined Arsenal from the Irish side Distillery in June 1948. He spent the 1948-49 season as the regular Eastern Counties League goalkeeper. He never settled at Highbury and was transferred to Swindon Town in November 1949. He was their first team goalkeeper for three seasons before joining Portsmouth in November 1952. Spent seven seasons at Fratton Park in which time he played in nearly two hundred first team games and became Northern Ireland's regular goalkeeper (winning eighteen caps). Later played for Southend United. Returned to Ireland to run the bar at Queens University after his playing days, but came back to England after 12 years to retire in Hastings, East Sussex.

	Games	Goals
Combination League	8	0
Combination Cup	4	0
Eastern Counties League	23	0
London Midweek League	2	0
Other Youth Matches	6	0
Total	**43**	**0**

Honours:
18 Northern Ireland Caps

URE, Ian   1963-69

Birth Place: Ayr, Scotland
Date of Birth: 7th December 1939

☛Ian Ure began his professional career with Dundee in 1958. During his five years at the club he became one of the leading centre halves in Europe. Helped Dundee to their first and only Scottish League Championship in 1961-62 and the same season saw him win the first of his eleven Scottish caps. Played in the European Cup Semi-Finals the following season. Joined Arsenal in August 1963 for £62,500 then a world record fee for a centre half. Established himself in the league side in 1963-64, missing only one league game. However, during seasons 1964-65 and 1965-66 he played in only half the club's league matches matches due to poor form and a succession of injuries. Regained his place and fitness in 1966-67 when playing in thirty seven league games as well as winning back his Scottish international place. In 1967-68 he played in twenty one league games and the following season in twenty three. Appeared in both League Cup Finals of those seasons versus Leeds and Swindon Town. Played in the first three league matches of the 1969-70 season, when Arsenal, with a strong nucleus of half backs on the books, allowed him to leave. Was transferred to Manchester United for £80,000 in August 1969. He spent two seasons at Old Trafford before returning to play and manage in Scottish league football with St Mirren and East Stirling. Then coached in Iceland before returning to Scotland in 1977 to become a social worker based in Kilmarnock.

	Games	Goals
League	168	2
FA Cup	16	0
League Cup	14	0
EUFA Cup	4	0

Ian Ure

	Games	Goals
Friendly Matches	19	0
Tour Matches	24	0
Combination League	19	0
Combination Cup	11	2
London Challenge Cup	5	0
Total	**280**	**4**

Honours:
Eleven Scottish Caps
1 Scottish Under 23 Cap
3 Scottish League Caps
Scottish Championship Medal   1961-62
Two League Cup Finalists Medals   1967-68
                                                    1968-69

VAESSON, Paul   1977-83

Birth Place: Bermondsey, London
Date of Birth: 6th October 1961

Paul Vaesson

☛Paul Vaesson joined Arsenal as an apprentice during the summer of 1977, turning professional in July 1979. Paul Vaesson will be most remembered for scoring the only goal in the semi final of the European Cup Winners Cup versus Juventus in Turin in April 1980. In his first full season at Highbury Paul played at every level for the club (youth, reserve and league), making his league debut versus Chelsea

in May 1979. He appeared in fourteen league matches in 1979-80 and in only seven the following season, being plagued with injuries. Played in ten league games during 1981-82 but unfortunately his injury problems persisted, resulting in him missing virtually the whole of the 1982-83 season. On medical advice, he retired from the game in 1983. His father Leon played for Millwall and Gillingham. Paul went off the rails when injury ended his career and needed help with a drugs problem. Has worked on building sites and had a spell as a postman.

	Games	Goals
League	32	6
League Cup	2	2
European Cup Winners Cup	3	1
UEFA Cup	2	0
Friendly Matches	30	5
Tour Matches	3	0
Combination League	95	28
South East Counties League	20	5
Youth Cup	3	1
Other Youth Cups	10	5
Youth Tour Matches	4	3
Total	**204**	**56**

VALLENCE, Tom   1946-53

Birth Place: Stoke, Staffordshire
Date of Birth: 28th March 1924

☛Tom Vallence joined Arsenal as an amateur from Torquay United in November 1946, turning professional in July 1947. Was a left winger in the reserve side during 1947-48. Made his league debut versus Sheffield United in September 1948 and during that season shared the left wing position (fourteen games) with Ian McPherson. However the following season there was stiff competition for this position from McPherson, Denis Compton and Don Roper resulting in him playing only one league match, released on a free transfer in the summer of 1953. Died July 1980 aged 56. Brother-in-law of the legendary Sir Stanley Matthews.

	Games	Goals
League	15	2
Friendly Matches	4	2
Tour Matches	6	1
Combination League	44	18
Combination Cup	19	3
London Challenge Cup	2	0
Eastern Counties League	48	33
Eastern Counties Cup	8	4
London Midweek League	14	2
Other Youth Matches	29	16
Total	**189**	**81**

VASSALLO, Barrie
1971-74

Birth Place: Newport
Date of Birth: 3rd March 1956

☛Barrie Vassallo had played for Newport and Monmouth schoolboys when he joined Arsenal as an apprentice in July 1971, turning professional in May 1973. Played wing half in the South East Counties League side during seasons 1971-72 and 1972-73 and won the first of his eight Welsh youth caps during the summer of 1973. He won a place in the Combination League side in 1973-74, but unfortunately he progressed no further and was transferred to Plymouth for a small fee in November 1974. Later played for Aldershot and Torquay and in the non league fraternity with Bridgend, Kidderminster Harriers, Merthyr Tydfil and Gloucester City.

	Games	Goals
Friendly Matches	30	4
Combination League	36	3
London Challenge Cup	2	0
South East Counties League	68	9
Youth Cup	11	4
Other Youth Cups	9	1
Youth Tour Matches	6	4
Total	**162**	**25**

Honours:
8 Welsh Youth Caps
South East Counties League Championship
  Medal 1971-72

VERNON, Leslie
1955-57

Birth Place: London
Date of Birth: 1937

☛Leslie Vernon joined Arsenal from Enfield. He played in six friendly matches (six goals) at the end of the 1954-55 season, turning professional in August 1955. Unfortunately, during his two years at Highbury, his career was disrupted by National Service, although he did manage to play in eight reserve team games. Released on a free transfer in May 1957.

	Games	Goals
Friendly Matches	7	2
Combination League	8	3
London Challenge Cup	2	0
Eastern Counties League	3	3
Eastern Counties Cup	2	2
London Midweek League	18	6
Total	**40**	**16**

WADE, Joe
1944-56

Birth Place: Shoreditch, London
Date of Birth: 7th July 1921

☛Joe Wade joined Arsenal as an amateur in May 1944 and turned professional in August 1945. He will be remembered as one of the great stalwarts of the reserve side in the immediate post war years and during his twelve years stay at Highbury played in nearly three hundred reserve team games. Made his league debut versus Leeds at Highbury in November 1946, but over the following six seasons played in only fourteen league matches, being kept out of the side by the likes of Barnes, Scott and Smith. His first team chance came when Walley Barnes broke a leg in the 1952 FA Cup Final against Newcastle, and in 1952-53 he played in forty league games, helping Arsenal to the League Championship as well as winning a Football League cap against the League of Ireland. However, he played in only eighteen league games the following season due to a knee injury sustained versus Queens Park Rangers in a floodlit friendly match at Highbury. Played a further fourteen league games in 1954-55 but spent all of season 1955-56 in the Combination side helping the younger players through his knowledge of FA coaching. In the spring of 1956 he left Highbury to become player/manager of the then non league side Hereford United for six years. He then ran two sports shops in the area, a business which lasted 30 years. Now retired, Joe still lives in Hereford in a house named

Joe Wade

"Highbury". He recently went on the Ashes Tour to Australia, where he was reunited with his old team mate Denis Compton.

	Games	Goals
League	86	0
FA Cup	5	0
Friendly Matches	39	1
Tour Matches	13	0
Combination League	200	3
Combination Cup	74	0
London Challenge Cup	12	0
Eastern Counties League	2	0
London Midweek League	3	0
War Time	25	0
Total	**459**	**4**

Honours:
League Championship Medal 1952-53
1 Football League Cap
Football Combination Champions 1946-47,
  1950-51
London FA Challenge Cup Winners 1953-54
Football Combination Cup
  Runners up 1946-47,1950-51

WALFORD, Steve
1977-81

Birth Place: Highgate, London
Date of Birth: 5th January 1958

☛Steve Walford began his professional career with Spurs in April 1975, and although he won four England youth caps during his two year spell at White Hart Lane he managed to play in only four first team matches. Followed Terry Neill to Highbury in August 1977 for a fee of £20,000 and became a useful utility player at full back, centre half or midfield. He played in five league games in 1977-78 but won a regular place in the league side the following season when he played in thirty three matches and was the substitute in the FA Cup Final versus Manchester United. He played in nineteen league games in 1979-80 and twenty in 1980-81. Steve was transferred to Norwich City for £175,000 in March 1981. Spent two years at Carrow Road before joining West Ham for £140,000 in July 1983. Steve later played for Huddersfield, Gillingham, West Bromwich and Wycombe Wanderers, where he is now Youth Team boss.

Steve Walford

	Games	Goals
League	77	3
FA Cup	10	0
League Cup	5	1
European Cup Winners Cup	2	0
EUFA Cup	3	0
Charity Shield	1	0
Friendly Matches	12	0
Tour Matches	7	0
Combination League	59	11
Total	**176**	**15**

Honours:
4 England Youth Caps
FA Cup Winners Medal 1978-79
FA Charity Shield Finalist Medal 1979-80

WALLEY, Tom   1964-67

Birth Place: Caernarvon, North Wales
Date of Birth: 27th February 1945

☛ Tom Walley joined Arsenal from Caernarvon in December 1964, and during his first season at the club established himself at wing half in the reserve side. Played regularly for the same side in 1965-66, as well as playing in nine league games, his debut being versus Sheffield Wednesday in December 1965. He won the first of his four Welsh under 23 caps versus England in 1966-67, although playing in only a further four league games. Transferred to Watford for £5,000 in March 1967, staying with the club for four seasons and playing in over two hundred first team games. Won a full Welsh cap versus Czechoslovakia in 1970-71. Later played for Orient and Watford for a second spell. His brother John played league football for Spurs and Middlesbrough. Later Youth Team coach at Watford where he was responsible for the development of John Barnes. His team won the 1991 F.A. Youth Cup.

Tom Walley

	Games	Goals
League	14	1
FA Cup	1	0
League Cup	3	0
Friendly Matches	17	1
Tour Matches	1	0
Combination League	40	7
Combination Cup	2	0
London Challenge Cup	6	0
Metropolitan League	6	0
Metropolitan Cup	2	1
Total	**92**	**10**

Honours:
1 Welsh Cap
4 Welsh Under 23 Caps
London FA Challenge Cup
   Runners up   1965-66
Metropolitan League Challenge Cup
   Winners   1965-66

WALSH, Brian   1949-55

Birth Place: Aldershot, Hampshire
Date of Birth: 26th March 1932

☛ Brian Walsh was playing for Chase of Chertsey when he joined Arsenal as an amateur in March 1949, turning professional in August 1949. Appeared in youth team friendly matches for the club before being called up for National Service in 1950. On his return to Highbury in August 1952 he won a regular place in the reserve side. Brian made ten league appearances in 1953-54, his debut being versus Cardiff City in September 1953. Walsh was a regular in the reserves again in 1954-55, when he played a further six league games being followed by a single appearance in 1955-56, before joining Cardiff City in September 1955, staying with them for six seasons. Later played for Newport County.

Brian Walsh

	Games	Goals
League	17	0
Friendly Matches	19	6
Tour Matches	2	0
Combination League	60	15
Combination Cup	22	7
London Challenge Cup	5	1
Eastern Counties League	29	6
Eastern Counties Cup	4	1
London Midweek League	18	4
Other Youth Matches	3	1
Total	**179**	**41**

Honours:
Football Combination Cup
   Winners   1952-53
London FA Challenge Cup
   Winners   1954-55

WARD, Gerry   1952-63

Birth Place: Stepney, London
Date of Birth: 5th October 1936

☛ Gerry Ward had represented Leytonstone, London, Essex and England

Schoolboys when he joined Arsenal as an amateur in June 1952. Became a member of the groundstaff soon after and in his first season at the club won a place in the Eastern Counties League side and gained an England Amateur cap versus Northern Ireland. Made his league debut versus Huddersfield on 22nd August 1953 age 16 years 321 days and still holds the distinction of being the youngest player to play in a league match for Arsenal. Turned professional in October 1953 and appeared in three league games in 1953-54. Spent all of season 1954-55 in the Combination League side and was called up for National Service in February 1955. Managed to play in twelve reserve matches in 1955-56 and twenty two in 1956-57. Demobbed in February 1957. By this time he had switched from an orthodox left wing position to wing half and later occasionally to inside forward. Regained his league place in 1957-58 when he played in ten league games. Won a regular place in 1958-59, playing in thirty one league games and in fifteen the following season. During his final three seasons with Arsenal (1961-63) he played in only twenty two league matches, although he was a valuable member of the reserves. Granted a free transfer in July 1963 when he joined Leyton Orient. He later played for Cambridge City and managed Barnet. Died January 1994 aged 57.

Gerry Ward

	Games	Goals
League	81	10
FA Cup	3	0
Friendly Matches	29	7
Tour Matches	17	6
Combination League	158	40
Combination Cup	11	3
London Challenge Cup	22	7
Southern Floodlight Cup	3	0
Eastern Counties League	29	4
Eastern Counties Cup	7	4
London Midweek League	7	0
Metropolitan League	6	2

Metropolitan Cup	3	0
South East Counties League	15	10
FA Youth Cup	2	0
Total	**393**	**93**

Honours:
1 England Amateur Cap
6 England Youth Caps
Football Combination
  Champions   1962-63
Football Combination Cup
  Winners   1952-53
London FA Challenge Cup
  Winners   1953-54, 1961-62, 1962-63
  runners up   1960-61
Eastern Counties League
  Champions   1954-55

WATT, James   1980-82

Birth Place: Musselburgh, Scotland
Date of Birth: 2nd October 1963

☛ James Watt joined Arsenal as an apprentice in May 1980, turning professional in July 1981. Played regularly as a defender in the South East Counties League side in 1980-81, becoming a permanent member of the reserve side in 1981-82, when also winning three Scottish young caps. Was surprisingly granted a free transfer during the summer of 1982 and joined Hendon.

	Games	Goals
Friendly Matches	5	1
Combination League	32	0
South East Counties League	44	1
Youth Cup	5	0
Other Youth Cups	8	0
Youth Tour Matches	2	0
Total	**96**	**2**

Honours:
3 Scottish Youth Caps

WEBSTER, Malcolm   1966-69

Birth Place: Rossington, Yorkshire
Date of Birth: 12th November 1950

☛ Malcolm Webster represented Doncaster and England schoolboys before joining Arsenal as an apprentice in May 1966, turning professional in January 1968. Played regular Metropolitan League football as goalkeeper in seasons 1966-67 and 1967-68. Malcolm became the reserve team goalkeeper in season 1968-69 having won two England youth caps. Webster made three league appearances during the first half of the 1969-70 season, his debut being versus Tottenham at Highbury in September 1969. Soon after Geoff Barnett joined the club from Everton as reserve to Bob Wilson, subsequently he was

transferred to Fulham in December 1969. Later played for Southend and then Cambridge United. His career spanned over five hundred first class matches. Later became coach at Cambridge. Recently started up his own goalkeeping schools to add to his duties coaching aspiring keepers at various league clubs.

Malcolm Webster

	Games	Goals
League	3	0
League Cup	2	0
UEFA Cup	1	0
Friendly Matches	30	0
Tour Matches	1	0
Combination League	28	0
Combination Cup	6	0
London Challenge Cup	1	0
Metropolitan League	29	0
Metropolitan Cup	8	0
South East Counties League	19	0
Youth Cup	5	0
Other Youth Cups	7	0
Youth Tour Matches	17	0
Total	**157**	**0**

Honours:
2 England Youth Caps
Football Combination
  Champions   1968-69
London Youth Challenge Cup
  Winners   1966-67
Southern Junior Floodlight Cup
  Runners-up   1967-68

WHITTAKER, Ray   1960-64

Birth Place: Bow, London
Date of Birth: 15th January 1945

☛ Ray Whittaker joined Arsenal's groundstaff in May 1960, turning professional in May 1962. Already an England schoolboy international, he established himself in the South East Counties League side in 1960-61. In 1961-62

he and George Armstrong formed the most feared wing partnership in youth team football. Promoted in 1961-62 to the Metropolitan League side and won six England youth caps. During seasons 1962-63 and 1963-64 was a regular in the reserve side and at the time it seemed a promising future was assured. However he did not fulfil his early potential and was subsequently transferred to Luton Town in March 1964. Ray served them well for six seasons before finishing his career with Colchester United in 1970-71.

	Games	Goals
Friendly Matches	11	2
Combination League	35	7
London Challenge Cup	6	1
Metropolitan League	34	8
Metropolitan Cup	8	1
South East Counties League	25	8
Youth Cup	11	4
Other Youth Cups	17	4
Youth Tour Matches	2	0
Total	**149**	**35**

Honours:
6 England Youth Caps
Football Combination Championship
  Medal   1962-63
Metropolitan League Championship
  Medal   1962-63
London FA Challenge Cup Winners
  Medal   1962-63
South East Counties League Cup Winners
  Medal   1960-61
Southern Junior Floodlight Cup Winners
  Medal   1962-63
London Minor Challenge Cup Finalists
  Medals   1960-61, 1961-62

WHITSON, Richard   1960-61

Birth Place: Edinburgh, Scotland
Date of Birth: 1939

☛ Richard Whitson was an apprentice millwright engineer when joining Arsenal as a professional in July 1960. Richard had previously played in Scotland for the Royston Rosebery youth club and had represented Edinburgh at junior level. He spent only one season at Highbury as goalkeeper in the South East Counties League side. Released on a free transfer during the summer of 1961.

	Games	Goals
Friendly Matches	5	0
Metropolitan League	8	0
Metropolitan Cup	1	0
South East Counties League	21	0
Youth Cup	7	0
Other Youth Cups	5	0
Total	**47**	**0**

WILKINSON, Ernie — 1962-66

Birth Place: Chesterfield, Derbyshire
Date of Birth: 13th February 1947

Ernie Wilkinson joined Arsenal as an apprentice in June 1962 and turned professional in February 1964. Ernie spent four seasons at Highbury as a centre half in the South East Counties League side during 1962-64 and in the Metropolitan teams during 1964-66. Although progressing to the reserve side in 1965-66 (when playing in eighteen matches) was granted a free transfer in June 1966 when he joined Exeter City.

	Games	Goals
Friendly Matches	9	1
Combination League	18	0
London Challenge Cup	2	0
Metropolitan League	40	0
Metropolitan Cup	6	0
South East Counties League	59	3
Youth Cup	14	0
Other Youth Cups	17	0
Youth Tour Matches	39	3
Total	**204**	**7**

Honours:
FA Youth Cup Finalists Medal   1964-65
South East Counties League Cup Winners
   Medal   1963-64
Southern Junior Floodlight Cup Winners
   Medal   1962-63
London FA Challenge Cup Finalists
   Medal   1965-66
London Minor Challenge Cup Finalists
   Medal   1964-65

WILKINSON, John — 1953-56

Birth Place: Middlewich, Cheshire
Date of Birth: 17th September 1931

John Wilkinson joined Arsenal from Witton Albion in October 1953, immediately winning a regular place as the reserve team centre forward, (scored six goals in fifteen matches). Had a successful 1954-55 season when he was the reserve team's leading scorer with Cliff Holton, scoring seventeen goals in thirty matches and making his league debut versus Leicester City in February 1955. However, although a consistent goalscorer for the reserves again in 1955-56 was never given another chance in the league side. John was transferred to Sheffield United for a small fee in March 1956. Later played for Port Vale and Exeter City, returning to Witton Albion in 1963.

	Games	Goals
League	1	0
Friendly Matches	5	4
Combination League	61	33
Combination Cup	8	6
London Challenge Cup	8	8
Eastern Counties League	16	6

London Midweek League	4	1
Total	**103**	**58**

Honours:
London FA Challenge Cup Winners   1954-55

WILLS, Len — 1949-62

Birth Place: Hackney, London
Date of Birth: 8th November 1927

Len Wills joined Arsenal from the Eton Manor Boys Club in October 1949. During his first four seasons at Highbury (1949-53) was a consistent member of the reserve side playing in the wing half position. Len made his breakthrough into the league side when Joe Wade damaged his knee in a match against Queens Park Rangers in October 1953 and then deputised for him at right back on his league debut versus Spurs during the same month. Len performed so well that he kept his place for the rest of the season (playing in thirty league matches). Held his position in 1954-55, playing in twenty four league matches. However, played in only fourteen league games in 1955-56 due to the arrival of Stan Charlton in November 1955. During the next two seasons, (1956-57, 1957-58) he played in only thirty six league games, being kept out of the side by both Charlton and Denis Evans. Regained his place in the league side in 1958-59 after the sale of Stan Charlton to Leyton Orient. Wills played regular first team football for the next two seasons before losing his place to both Dave Bacuzzi and Eddie Magill in 1961-62, spending the whole of that season in the reserve side. Len Wills gave wonderful service during his thirteen seasons at Highbury, playing in well over two hundred first team games. He later played for Romford. Now retired from his job in the DIY Retail Trade and lives at Chigwell, Essex.

Len Wills

	Games	Goals
League	195	4
FA Cup	13	0
Charity Shield	1	0
Friendly Matches	64	4
Tour Matches	11	1
Combination League	185	6
Combination Cup	65	4
London Challenge Cup	12	0
Southern Floodlight Cup	8	1
Eastern Counties League	9	0
Eastern Counties Cup	1	0
Metropolitan League	1	0
London Midweek League	1	0
Total	**566**	**20**

Honours:
FA Charity Shield Winners Medal   1952-53
Football Combination Champions   1950-51
Football Combination Cup Winners   1952-53
   runners-up   1950-51
Southern Floodlit Challenge Cup
   Winners   1958-59

WILSON, Bob — 1963-74

Birth Place: Chesterfield, Derbyshire
Date of Birth: 30th October 1941

Bob Wilson was training to become a physical education teacher at Loughborough while playing as an amateur with Wolves. Joined Arsenal as an amateur during the summer of 1963 turning professional in March 1964, Arsenal having to pay Wolves £5,500. In 1963-64 he played regular reserve team football and also played in five league matches including his league debut versus Nottingham Forest in October 1963. After the signing of Jim Furnell in November 1963 he had to be content with reserve team football for the following three seasons, playing in only four league games. However, after Furnell made a costly mistake against Birmingham in the FA Cup fifth round in March 1968, Wilson took over and played the last thirteen league matches of the 1967-68 season. Bob played regularly in season 1968-69, being instrumental in Arsenal's seasonal defensive record at that time conceding only twenty seven goals in forty matches. In 1969-70, although suffering a broken arm, he played in twenty eight league matches and helped Arsenal to win the Inter Cities Fairs Cup. Figured prominently in Arsenal's league and FA Cup winning side of 1970-71, playing in the all of the clubs sixty four first team games. In 1971-72 he missed only five league games and won two Scottish Caps versus Holland and Portugal. Was plagued by injuries in 1972-73 playing in only twenty two league matches. Missed only one league game in 1973-74 before, surprisingly, announcing his retirement in May 1974 at the age of thirty two. Later became a leading sports broadcaster and returned to Highbury as goalkeeping coach. In 1994 Bob signed a lucrative contract with

WOOD, George 1980-83

Birth Place: Douglas, Lanarkshire, Scotl'd
Date of Birth: 26th September 1952

☞ George Wood began his career with the Scottish league side East Stirling in 1970. Transferred to Blackpool for £5,000 in Jan. 1972. George was their regular goalkeeper for four seasons, 1972-76, before being transferred to Everton for £180,000 in August 1977. Wood spent three seasons at Goodison Park, playing in over one hundred and twenty first team games, and winning three Scottish caps. Transferred to Arsenal for £140,000 in August 1980 as the possible successor to Pat Jennings. George played in eleven league games during 1980-81 and twenty six the following season. Also during season 1981-82 won his fourth Scottish cap, versus Northern Ireland and was selected for Scotland's World Cup squad. Shared the first team goalkeeper spot again in 1982-83 when playing in a

further twenty three league games. Was surprisingly granted a free transfer in May 1983 when he joined Crystal Palace. He spent five seasons at Selhurst Park before joining Cardiff City in January 1988. He had a loan period at Blackpool (March to May 1990). Was granted a free transfer by Cardiff City and signed for Hereford in August 1990. He later played for Merthyr Tydfil and Inter Cardiff. In a career spanning 20 years he played in over seven hundred first class games. George is now an ornithologist with Glamorgan Wildlife Trust and manager of Inter Cardiff F.C.

	Games	Goals
League	60	0
FA Cup	1	0
League Cup	7	0
EUFA Cup	2	0
Friendly Matches	4	0
Tour Matches	6	0
Combination League	53	0
Total	**133**	**0**

Honours:
4 Scottish Caps

George Wood

Carlton T.V. and switched channels after 20 plus years with the BBC.

	Games	Goals
League	234	0
FA Cup	32	0
League Cup	18	0
European Cup	6	0
UEFA Cup	18	0
Friendly Matches	44	0
Tour Matches	30	0
Combination League	90	0
Combination Cup	16	0
London Challenge Cup	9	0
Metropolitan League	28	0
Metropolitan Cup	6	0
Total	**531**	**0**

Honours:
2 Scottish Caps
League Championship Medal   1970-71
FA Cup Winners Medal   1970-71
Inter Cities Fairs Cup Winners
   Medal   1969-70
League Cup Finalists Medal   1968-69
Metropolitan League Challenge
   Cup Winners Medal   1965-66

Bob Wilson

WOODWARD, John   1966-71

Birth Place: Glasgow, Scotland
Date of Birth: 10th January 1949

☞ John Woodward joined Arsenal from the Scottish junior side Possilpark in Jan. 1966, on his 17th birthday. John made rapid progress from junior football, making his league debut versus Newcastle United in Oct. 1966 whilst still only seventeen. Played three league games during 1966-67 predominantly at centre half for the reserve side. Served the club well for four further seasons without ever getting another first team chance. Released on a free transfer during the summer of 1971 when he joined York City.

	Games	Goals
League	3	0
League Cup	1	0
Friendly Matches	34	1
Tour Matches 2		0
Combination League	121	9
Combination Cup	27	3
London Challenge Cup	10	0
Metropolitan League	13	1
Metropolitan Cup	4	0
South East Counties	6	0
Youth Cup 10		1
Other Youth Cups	11	1
Youth Tour Matches	17	0
Total	**259**	**16**

Honours:
Football Comb. Champions 1968-69,1969-70
Football Comb. Cup Winners
                1967-68, 1969-70
FA Youth Cup Winners   1965-66
Southern Jnr Floodlit Cup Winners   1965-66
South East Counties League Cup
   Runners up   1965-66
2 Scotland Youth Caps

YOULDEN, Tommy   1964-68

Birth Place: Islington, London
Date of Birth: 8th July 1949

☞ Tommy Youlden was an England Schoolboy International when joining Arsenal as an apprentice in July 1964, turning professional in July 1966. Progressed from the South East Counties side in 1964-65 to the Metropolitan League side in 1965-66. Tommy won a regular place in the reserve side at full back during 1966-67. Youlden was restricted through injury during season 1967-68 before being released on a free transfer in April 1968, joining Portsmouth. Later played for Reading and Aldershot.

	Games	Goals
Friendly Matches	23	0
Combination League	27	0
Combination Cup	7	0
Metropolitan League	55	6
Metropolitan Cup	6	1

South East Counties League	34	0
Youth Cup	16	0
Other Youth Cups	20	1
Youth Tour Matches	28	0
Total	**216**	**8**

Honours:
FA Youth Cup Winners Medal   1965-66
Metropolitan League Challenge Cup Winners
   Medal   1965-66
South East Counties League Championship
   Medal   1964-65
South East Counties Cup Finalists
   Medal   1965-66
Southern Junior Floodlight Cup Winners
   Medal   1965-66

YOUNG, Alan   1956-61

Birth Place: Hornsey, London
Date of Birth: 20th January 1941

☞ Alan Young joined Arsenal as an amateur in November 1956, turning professional in April 1959. Established himself in the South East Counties League side in 1957-58, progressing to the Metropolitan League side in 1958-59 and 1959-60. He won a regular place in the Combination League side 1960-61 also playing in four league matches, his debut being versus Sheffield Wednesday on Boxing Day 1960. Alan although playing regularly at centre half for the Combination League side during the first half of 1961-62, was transferred to Chelsea for £5,000 in November 1961. Stayed with Chelsea for eight seasons as understudy to Marvin Hinton before finishing his career with Torquay.

	Games	Goals
League	4	0
Friendly Matches	16	0
Combination League	34	0
Metropolitan League	60	2
Metropolitan Cup	6	0
South East Counties League	20	0
Youth Cup	13	0
Other Youth Cups	10	0
Youth Tour Matches	4	0
Total	**167**	**2**

Honours:
(WITH CHELSEA)
League Cup Winners Medal   1964-65
(WITH ARSENAL)
Metropolitan Lge Champs   1958-59, 1960-61
Sth. Jnr Floodlit Cup Runners up   1957-58

YOUNG, Willie   1977-81

Birth Place: Edinburgh, Scotland
Date of Birth: 25th November 1951

☞ Willie Young began his career with Aberdeen in 1970, taking over from Martin Buchan after he left to join Manchester United. Whilst at Pittodrie he played in over one hundred first team games and won five Scottish under 23 caps. Willie was transferred to Tottenham for £90,000 in September 1975, spending two seasons at White Hart Lane before joining Arsenal for £80,000 in March 1977. Willie made his Arsenal league debut versus Ipswich at Highbury during the same month, becoming a firm favourite at Highbury during the following four seasons. Played in thirty five league matches in 1977-78 and in the Cup Final versus Ipswich. The following season he played in thirty three league games and figured prominently in the cup winning side versus Manchester United. In 1979-80 he made thirty eight league appearances and was a member of the FA Cup and European Cup Finalists teams. In 1980-81 he played in forty league matches but after appearing in the first ten games in the league (1981-82) he lost his place to Chris Whyte and subsequently joined Nottingham Forest in November 1981 for £50,000. Young later played for Norwich, Brighton and Darlington. He now owns a picturesque country pub on the outskirts of Nottingham called the 'Bramcote Manor' in Bramcote.

	Games	Goals
League	170	11
FA Cup	28	3
League Cup	20	1
Cup Winners Cup	9	3
UEFA Cup	9	1
Charity Shield	1	0
Friendly Matches	13	1
Tour Matches	18	0
Combination League	10	2
Total	**278**	**22**

Honours:
5 Scottish Under 23 Caps
FA Cup Winners Medal   1978-79
FA Cup Finalists Medals   1977-78,1979-80
European Cup Winners Cup Finalists
   Medal   1979-80
FA Charity Shield Finalists Medal   1979-80

Willie Young

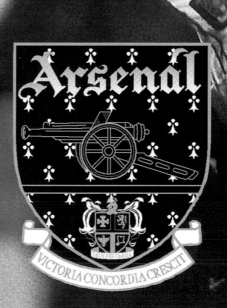

1985-1995

ADAMS, Tony   1983

Birth Place: Romford, Essex
Date of Birth: 10th October 1966

Tony was playing junior football in his home town, Romford, when signing for Arsenal as an associated schoolboy in November 1980 joining the apprentice ranks in April 1983, turning professional in the following January. Tony Adams has since gone on to become the most successful Arsenal captain in the club's history, and has now lifted more silverware than any of his predecessors which include Arsenal greats such as James, Hapgood, Mercer and McLintock. In his eight seasons as captain he has become the cornerstone of the meanest defence in Premier League football of the 1990's and it his commanding and dominating play which has been a key factor in all of Arsenal's recent successes.

Tony's ability was seen at a tender age, for he had played in the club's reserve side before ever appearing in any youth competitions for the club. In 1983-84, he became the England Youth team captain when winning the first of his eighteen youth caps and in November 1983, at seventeen years and twenty-six days, he became the second youngest player, in Arsenal's history to play in a league fixture against Sunderland. Adams finished that season appearing in three league games when deputising for the injured David O'Leary. During the next two seasons, he admirably covered for the likes of O'Leary and Tommy Caton although during this period he had the misfortune of receiving a stress fracture of his right foot which sidelined him for three months at the back end of 1985. However, in 1986-87, he was ever present when forming a formidable defensive partnership with David O'Leary. In that 1986-87 season, at the age of twenty years and four months, he made his England debut against Spain in February 1987, as well as helping the club in winning the League Cup versus Liverpool and on the same night as that final, Tony was voted P.F.A. Young Footballer of the Year, for that season. He was already being seen as the inspirational motivator and driving force behind the young team which George Graham had started to assemble and it came as no surprise in March 1988, when Tony was handed the Arsenal captaincy (taking over from Kenny Sansom) at the age of twenty-one years and five months, he was one of the youngest captains in the club's history. Also in that 1987-88 season, he was a key member of the side that reached the Littlewoods Cup Final against Luton Town and was involved with England in the European Nations Championships. In Arsenal's first League Championship winning campaign for eighteen years (1988-89), Tony led from the front when showing resilience, bravery and all the battling qualities of a born leader and it was at this stage when the Arsenal manager, George Graham, described Tony Adams as "My colossus". Adams, though, does have his flaws, he tends, at times, to rush in at tackles and because of his build it appears that he lacks the poise and grace of say, an Alan Hansen. Even so, the "donkey" taunts that greeted Tony nearly all over the country was not a testament to his ability, but in most cases, it grew out of jealously because of his success when

overcoming adversity. This was highlighted when he suffered the disappointment of being omitted from England's World Cup squad, followed, six months later, when he was given a three months prison sentence for a well publicised drink-drive offence. However, on his return to the side, he guided the club to their second League Championship in three seasons. The 1991-92 season, was possibly the most uneventful season in Tony's career, the only thing of note was that he had to undergo a hernia operation in November 1991, when missing six league games. However, in the 1992-93 season, he became the first captain to lift both the F.A. and League Cup trophies in the same season. After Tony had scored the most important goal of his Arsenal career when heading the only goal versus Tottenham in the F.A. Cup semi-final. Unfortunately, the Coca-Cola Cup victory was soured when Adams, who was in jubilant mood, had the misfortune of being involved in a freak accident which saw Steve Morrow crash to the ground in agony after accidentally slipping from Tony's grasp after he had been picked up and placed over his shoulder. In 1993-94 Tony had to put up with the comic strip newspapers hounding him every moment, when reporting on every trivial incident that Tony was involved in. The adversity had reared its ugly head again and it was with even more determination and passion, Adams instilled into his game when leading the club to the European Cup Winners Cup victory. He showed all these qualities again when guiding the side back to the following season's final and in 1994,

1985-1995

Arsenal Supporters Club voted him, for the third time as their Player of the Year. To put this honour in perspective, only Liam Brady had won this prize as many as three times, and this is proof of the popularity, respect and esteem in which Arsenal followers hold Tony Adams. To slightly change George Graham's quote, Tony Adams is "our colossus".

	Games	Goals
League	346	23
F.A. Cup	30	5
League Cup	49	3
Europe	20	2
Other First Team Matches	18	1
Friendly Matches	68	5
Tours	21	3
Football Combination	87	10
South East Counties League	17	3
Youth Cup	9	0
Other Youth Cups	15	2
Youth Tours	7	3
Total	**687**	**60**

Honours:
35 England Caps
4 England B Caps
5 England Under-twenty-one Caps
18 England Youth Caps
2 League Championship Medals
1988-89, 1990-91
F.A. Cup Winners Medal   1992-93
2 Football League Cup Winners Medals
1986-87, 1992-93
Football League Cup Finalists Medal
1987-88
European Cup Winners Cup Winners Medal
1993-94
European Cup Winners Cup Finalists Medal
1994-95
European Super Cup Finalists Medal   1995
F.A. Charity Shield Medal   1991
2 F.A. Charity Shield Finalists Medals
1989, 1993
P.F.A. Young Player of the Year   1986-87
P.F.A. Team Award - Division One   1987
Premier League   1994
Arsenal Player of the Year   1987, 1990, 1994
Fiat Young Player of the Year   1986-87
Mercantile Credit Centenary Trophy Winners
Medal   1988-89
Wembley International Tournament Winners
Medal   1988-89
2 Makita International Tournament Winners
Medals   1989, 1994
2 Makita International Tournament Finalists
Medals   1990, 1991
Football Combination League Championship
Medal   1983-84
Southern Junior Floodlight Cup Winners
Medal   1985-86

Tony Adams

ALLEN, Greg   1983-87

Birth Place: West Ham, London
Date of Birth: 18th October 1967

☛ Greg Allen had played for Newham, Essex and London Schoolboys before joining Arsenal as an apprentice in 1983. He was a regular in the club's midfield for two seasons in the South East Counties League side when helping the side in reaching two junior cup finals in 1985-86, after turning professional in July 1985. Greg played steadily for the combination team, 1985-87, before being released on a free transfer during the summer of 1987, when he linked up with Dagenham. Allen briefly returned to league action as a non contract player with Cambridge United.

	Games	Goals
Friendly Matches	10	4
Football Combination	68	13
South East Counties League	35	10
Youth Cup	9	0
Other Youth Cups	17	8
Youth Tours	19	3
Total	**158**	**38**

Honours:
Southern Junior Floodlight Cup Finalists
    Medal   1985-86
South East Counties League Cup Finalists
    Medal   1985-86

ALLINSON, Ian   1983-87

Birth Place: Stevenage, Hertfordshire
Date of Birth: 1st October 1957

☛ Ian joined Colchester United as a sixteen year old schoolboy in 1974, turning professional in October 1975 and had played for the Essex club in League football while still an apprentice. In eight seasons at Layer Road, he played in nearly three hundred League games when occupying virtually, every forward position. Ian was the clubs leading scorer in two of those seasons. However, in the summer of 1983 a secretarial blunder enabled Ian (at the age of 25) to be granted a free transfer, thus signing for Arsenal. Unfortunately, Allinson made his first team debut in the nightmarish League cup home defeat by Walsall on the 29th of November 1983, making his Arsenal League debut four days later (in the same game as Tommy Caton) against West Bromwich Albion at Highbury. An unassuming journeyman footballer, Ian, an Arsenal supporter as a boy, held no pretensions of grandeur. His strengths were his running ability and his fine crossing of the ball when at acute angles. In 1984-85 he surprised most people, finishing joint top League goal scorer on ten goals (with Talbot and Woodcock)

playing in twenty seven League games. In the following season, 1985-86, he was again a regular, when playing in thirty three League games. However, in 1986-87 Ian's feelings must have gone from euphoria to agony within a space of only a month, for although not being a first team regular during that season, he came on as a substitute in the League Cup semi final replay at White Hart Lane versus Tottenham and scored Arsenal's late equalising goal, with only minutes remaining which resulted in the Park Lane End of the ground erupting into sheer mayhem. In the history of the game, few players have scored such an important goal and then, within three months, have been handed a free transfer. Allinson joined Stoke City in June 1987, later playing for Luton Town and finished his League career back with Colchester United between 1988-90.

Ian Allinson

	Games	Goals
League	83	16
F.A.Cup	9	4
League Cup	13	3
Friendly Matches	29	15
Tours	2	1
Football Combination	69	40
Total	**205**	**79**

Honours:
(WITH ARSENAL)
Football Combination Championship Medal
                                            1983-84
(WITH LUTON)
Simod Cup Finalists Medal   1987-88

AMPADU, Kwame   1988-91

Birth Place: Bradford, Yorkshire
Date of Birth: 20th December 1970

☛ Kwame had played in Irish junior football with Sherrads United and Belvedere F.C. before joining Arsenal in July 1988. In his three seasons at Highbury, Kwame, a tricky winger, was mostly found playing for the Football Combination side although he did make two league appearances (both as substitute) of which his league debut was at the Baseball ground versus Derby County, 24th March 1990. He won Eire Youth honours as well as four under 21 caps. In 1990-91 he enjoyed loan spells with Plymouth Argyle and West Bromwich Albion and he was subsequently transferred to the latter for £50,000 in June1991. Ampadu was transferred to Swansea City for £15,000 in February 1994.

	Games	Goals
League	2	0
Friendly Matches	31	13
Football Combination	65	14
South East Counties League	26	23
Youth Cup	4	2
Other Youth Cups	2	1
Total	**130**	**53**

Honours:
4 Eire Under 21 Caps
3 Eire Youth Caps
Football Combination Championship Medal
                                            1989-90

Kwame Ampadu

Viv Anderson

ANDERSON, Viv   1984-87

Birth Place: Nottingham
Date of Birth: 29th August, 1956

Viv was an associated schoolboy with Nott'm Forest before becoming an apprentice in November 1972, turning professional in August 1974. In his time at the City Ground (ten seasons) he played in over four hundred first team games, won a League Championship Medal in 1977-78, he also won two European Cup Winners Medals, played in three League Cup Finals and was voted, three times in four seasons, 1979-82, the best right back in the First Division by his fellow professionals (P.F.A.). In November 1978 he made history by becoming the first black player to represent England in a full international. While at Forest he gained a further ten caps. In 1983-84, Colin Hill and Stewart Robson had filled in for Arsenal in the right back position, manager Don Howe, realising neither of them were playing in their rightful position, urgently required a top class right back and in July 1984 he paid £250,000 for Anderson's services. Although Viv was not at Highbury when the club reached its peak under George Graham in the late 1980's, he had a lot to do with the emergence of many of the younger players who were beginning their careers at this time, especially the encouragement he gave to the younger black players at the club, such as Davis, Rocastle and Thomas. Without doubt, at his peak, Viv Anderson was the most accomplished right back in the country. His build was his main asset for he was tall and willowy enabling him to be excellent in the air, but it was his long legs which seemed to be able to stretch to retrieve balls or to intercept tackles when it would have been a lost cause to many others. Allied to his great speed, his tactical sense and his hatred at being beaten, made him the ultimate competitor. In his first season at Highbury he settled into a back four which normally read Anderson, O'Leary, Caton and Sansom, between them they missed only seventeen league games. In 1985-86 he was just as consistent when missing only three league games and at this time was still considered England's premier right back. In his final season at the club, Viv was an inspirational member of the side who defeated Liverpool in the 1987 League Cup Final. However, with George Graham believing that he had a ready made right back in Michael Thomas, Anderson was allowed to leave Highbury when becoming Alex Ferguson's first major signing for Manchester United in July 1987. The fee, set by the tribunal, was £250,000. This angered Arsenal, Viv was at his peak, only thirty-one years old and was still England's number one choice right back. The club, had rightly believed that they had lost out through the tribunal just as they had six years previously on Frank Stapleton and this decision added insult to injury. In four seasons at Old Trafford he helped the club to win the F.A.Cup in 1989-90 and the European Cup Winners Cup the following year. In his thirty-fifth year he joined Sheffield Wednesday on a free transfer in January 1991 and was a member of their team in the losing finals of the F.A. and Coca Cola Cups in 1992-93, both against Arsenal. In July 1993, he was appointed player/coach of Barnsley with his former Wednesday team-mate, Danny Wilson and exactly a year later he joined Bryan Robson at Middlesbrough as player/assistant manager and Anderson played his part in helping the Teesiders to promotion to the Premier League.

	Games	Goals
League	120	9
F.A. Cup	12	3
League Cup	18	3
Friendly Matches	16	0
Tours	3	1
Football Combination	1	0
Total	**170**	**16**

Honours:
(WITH ARSENAL)
16 England Caps
League Cup Winners Medal   1986-87
P.F.A. Award - Division 1   1987
(WITH NOTT'M FOREST)
11 England Caps
7 England B caps
2 Football League Caps
1 Under-twenty-one cap
League Championship Medal   1977-78
2 European Cup Winners Medals
                1978-79, 1979-80
2 League Cup Winners Medal
                1977-78, 1978-79
League Cup Finalists Medal   1979-80
F.A Charity Shield Winners Medal   1978
European Super Cup Winners Medal   1980
European Super Cup Finalists Medal   1981
World Club Cup Finalists Medal   1980
Anglo-Scottish Cup Winners Medal   1976-77
3 P.F.A. Awards - Division 1 -
                1979, 1980, 1981
(WITH MANCHESTER UNITED)
3 England Caps
F.A. Cup Winners Medal   1989-90
European Cup Winners Cup Winners Medal
                1990-91
(WITH SHEFFIELD WEDNESDAY)
F.A. Cup Finalists Medal   1992-93
League Cup Finalists Medal   1992-93

BACON, John
1989-93

Birth Place: Dublin
Date of Birth: 23rd March 1973

☛ John Bacon was a young forward who joined Arsenal in July 1989. In his four seasons at Highbury John was an influential member of the club's Youth side, helping them win the South East Counties League Championship in 1990-91, he also won seven Republic of Ireland under 21 Caps as well as youth honours. In 1991-92, he went on loan to Shamrock Rovers for a three month period and by this time he had graduated to the club's reserve side. However, John was handed a free transfer at the end of the 1992-93 season.

	Games	Goals
Friendly Matches	34	16
Football Combination	29	10
South East Counties League	35	10
Youth Cup	4	1
Other Youth Cups	12	2
Youth Tours	10	2
Total	**124**	**41**

Honours:
7 Eire Under 21 Caps
Eire Youth Caps
South East Counties League Championship
   Medal   1990-91
Southern Junior Floodlight Cup Winners
   Medal   1990-91
Southern Junior Floodlight Cup Finalists
   Medal   1989-90

BALL, Jason
1984-87

Birth Place: Neath, Wales
Date of Birth: 7th December 1968

☛ Jason Ball joined Arsenal as an apprentice at the back end of the 1984-85 season, turning professional the following summer. Jason was a regular as a young versatile player in the Welsh under 18 side when appearing at centre back, centre midfield or at centre forward. In his two full seasons at Highbury he helped the Youth side to two cup finals. However, he was not retained and left the club in the close season of 1987.

	Games	Goals
Friendly Matches	7	0
Football Combination	31	0
South East Counties League	45	7
Youth Cup	6	0
Other Youth Cups	17	3
Youth Tours	7	1
Total	113	11

Honours:
Wales Youth Caps
South East Counties League Cup Finalists
   Medal   1985-86

Southern Junior Floodlight Cup Finalists
Medal   1985-86

BALL, Steve
1986-89

Birth Place: Colchester, Essex
Date of Birth: 2nd September 1969

☛ Steve had played for Essex Schoolboys and had England Schoolboy Trials and turned down the chance of going to the F.A. School of Excellence before joining Arsenal as a trainee, during the Summer of 1986, turning professional just after his eighteenth birthday in September 1987. In his time at Highbury he developed into a fine midfield player for the reserve side and was a member of the 1987-88 F.A. Youth Cup Winning Team (which included Miller, Hillier, Heaney and Campbell). Steve was granted a free transfer in the Summer of 1989 when he linked up, as a non contract player, with Colchester United before joining Norwich City in September 1990. He is currently playing with Colchester United.

	Games	Goals
Friendly Matches	16	6
Football Combination	55	12
South East Counties League	44	8
Youth Cup	7	3
Other Youth Cups	12	2
Youth Tours	10	2
Total	**144**	**33**

Honours:
F.A.Youth Cup Winners Medal   1987-88

BARTRAM, Vince
1994

Birth Place: Birmingham
Date of Birth: 7th August 1968

☛ Goalkeeper Vince had begun his footballing career as a trainee with Wolverhampton Wanderers before turning professional with them in August 1985. In his first full season at Molineux he was understudy to Tim Flowers and in six seasons with the club he played in only five League games, although he did gain experience while on loan to Kidderminster Harriers, Blackpool and West Bromwich Albion. Vince was transferred to Bournemouth for £65,000 in July 1991 and while at Dean Court he missed only six League games in three seasons. Bartram came to Highbury for a £400,000 transfer fee in August 1994 and he played in eleven League games when deputising for David Seaman. His Arsenal League debut was at Nottingham Forest 3rd December 1994. Vince sat on the bench for the European Cup Winners Cup Final versus Real Zaragosa.

	Games	Goals
League	11	0
Tours	3	0
Football Combination	10	0
Total	**24**	**0**

Honours:
European Cup Winners Cup Finalists Medal
                                     1994-1995
European Super Cup Finalists Medal   1995
Makita Trophy Winners Medal   1994

Vince Bartram

BERGKAMP, Dennis
1995

Birth Place: Amsterdam, Holland
Date of Birth: 10th May 1969

☛ Not for many years has an Arsenal signing caused as much media and general public attention as that of Dennis Bergkamp. Dennis is one of the leading lights of European football in the 1990's, where his glittering array of talents has taken him from Ajax to Arsenal via Inter Milan. His father was a Manchester United follower and he tried to name his son after the legendary Denis Law. However, the registrar would not accept Denis as a Dutch name because it was too close to the girls name Denise. Bergkamp joined Ajax when still a schoolboy and made his debut for them in December 1986, when only sixteen. In seven years with Ajax he scored just over one hundred goals in one hundred and eighty-five league appearances. He helped his side to the Championship in 1989-90 and the Cup in 1992-93. In European football he won a European Cup Winners Cup medal in 1986-87 and a losers medal the following season as well as a UEFA Cup Winners medal in 1991-92. In 1988 Dennis set a scoring record for the Netherlands when finding the net in ten consecutive league games, he was leading

goal scorer in Holland for three consecutive seasons (1991 - 93) which earned him the Dutch Footballer of the Year Award in both 1992 and 1993. On the international front Dennis won the first of his thirty-nine caps for Holland (twenty-three goals) against Italy in September 1990 and was an important member of his country's team in the 1994 World Cup. In the summer of 1993 he was involved with his team-mate Wim Jonk in a £12 million transfer to Inter Milan and in his first season in Italy, 1993-94 his eleven goals in eleven European ties helped Inter win the UEFA Cup that season. However, in 1994-95, a series of niggling injuries and a slight loss of form unsettled Bergkamp and in June 1995 Arsenal's new manager, Bruce Rioch, smashed the club's transfer record when paying £7.5 million for Dennis's services when he signed a four year contract.

Dennis had his first taste of a north London derby when he gave the Gunners the lead v. Spurs at White Hart Lane on November 18th, just before this book went to press. After a slow start, it was his 8th goal of the season.

Honours:
39 Caps for Holland
(WITH AJAX)
League Championship Medal   1989-90
Cup Winners Medal   1992-93
European Cup Winners Cup Winners Medal
     1986-87

European Cup Winners Cup Finalists Medal
     1987-88
Holland's Footballer of the Year   1992, 1993
U.E.F.A. Cup Winners Medal   1991-92
(WITH INTER MILAN)
U.E.F.A. Cup Winners Medal   1993-94

Dennis Bergkamp

BLACK, Michael   1993

Birth Place: Chigwell, Essex
Date of Birth: 6th October 1976

Michael is a tricky outside right and has a bright future in the game having played for Essex and England Schoolboys before joining Arsenal as a trainee during the summer of 1993. In 1993-94, he was a member of Arsenal's F.A. Youth Cup winning team against Millwall and in 1994-95 he appeared several times for the Football Combination side. He signed professional during the summer of 1995.

	Games	Goals
Football Combination	9	0
Friendly Matches	15	2
South East Counties	48	11
Youth Cup	10	3
Other Youth Cups	13	4
Youth Tours	6	1
Total	**101**	**21**

Honours:
England Under-fifteen international
F.A. Youth Cup Winners Medal   1993-94
Southern Junior Floodlight Cup Finalists
  Medal   1994-95

BOULD, Steve   1988

Birth Place: Stoke-on-Trent, Staffordshire
Date of Birth: 16th November, 1962

In Arsenal's history certain names have been linked together, Male and Hapgood, James and Bastin, Radford and Kennedy, spring to mind but in the latest generation of Arsenal players none have rolled off the tongue as easily as Bould and Adams. Of all of George Graham's signings, Steve, along with Lee Dixon and Nigel Winterburn were his greatest bargains. However, this may not have seemed the case when he first joined the club, for at six foot three inches he seemed gangly, crude and often rushed into tackles which led to free kicks being given away in dangerous positions. Added to this was the fact that he was signed to replace long term favourite, David O'Leary. Steve began his footballing career at the age of fifteen when signing associated schoolboy forms for Stoke City in September 1978. He became an apprentice in June 1979, turning professional in November 1980. In his first four seasons at the Victoria Ground he was usually found playing at right back and in October 1982, whilst still not being able to command a regular place at the club, was loaned out to Torquay United. Steve later converted to centre back, but in a league game at Blackburn Rovers in March 1987 he received a severe back injury which threatened his career. After a major

operation and seven months out of the game, Steve fully recovered. In June 1988, Steve followed his ex-team-mate at the Potters, Lee Dixon to Highbury when Arsenal paid £390,000 for his services. In Arsenal's League Championship winning campaign, Bould played in thirty league games, many as sweeper, making his Arsenal league debut in a 5-1 victory at Wimbledon on the opening day of the season. In 1989-90, he missed the first five months of the season through injury and many at Highbury were questioning Arsenal's form without Steve's availability. This question was answered in 1990-91 when he was ever present and Arsenal created a new club record when conceding only eighteen league goals with Steve undoubtedly instrumental in that achievement. The faithful at Highbury realised that the club had on their books a colossus of a defender. He was cool, efficient, reliable , virtually unbeatable in the air and the cornerstone of the meanest defence in European football. Many say that he developed these qualities when extra responsibility fell upon his shoulders with the absence of Tony Adams during the season of 1990-91, when he was honoured by being named as Arsenal Supporters Club Player of the Year. Coincidentally, in 1991-92 as in 1989-90, Bould missed the first four months of the season with an ankle injury and by the time he had returned to the side, Arsenal's season had virtually ended. In 1992-93, injuries, including a pulled thigh, resulted in Bould missing both the F.A. and Coca Cola Cup Finals. Again sidelined with further injuries at the beginning of the 1993-94 season , he returned when playing a gigantic

part in helping Arsenal lift the European Cup Winners Cup and deservedly, at the age of thirty-one, won his first England cap against Norway. In 1994-95, he again was a stalwart in the club's defence when playing in thirty-one league games, but after picking up a booking in the meaningless European Super Cup, Steve was sadly suspended for the 1995 European Cup Winners Cup Final.

	Games	Goals
League	192	5
F.A. Cup	17	0
League Cup	22	0
Europe	13	2
Other First Team Matches	9	1
Friendly Matches	27	0
Tours	18	0
Football Combination	26	3
Total	**324**	**11**

Honours:
2 England Caps
1 England B Caps
2 League Championship Medals
                          1988-89, 1990-91
European Cup Winners Cup Winners Medal
                                    1993-94
European Super Cup Finalists Medal   1995
Mercantile Credit Centenary Trophy Winners
  Medal   1988-89
Wembley International Tournament Winners
  Medal   1988-89
2 Makita International Tournament Winners
  Medals   1989, 1994
2 Makita International Tournament Finalists
  Medals   1990, 1991

Steve Bould

CAESAR, Gus   1982-91

Birth Place: Tottenham, London
Date of Birth: 5th March 1966

☛ Gus joined Arsenal as an apprentice in August 1982, turning professional in February 1984. His career started on a sorry note when he broke an ankle three times over a thirty month period. Caesar, who could play all along the back line, graduated from the Youth team to make his Arsenal League debut in a 1-0 victory at Old Trafford when replacing the suspended Viv Anderson on the 21st December 1985. In 1986-87, he became known as "The Five Minute Man", because is no less than ten first team games he came on as a substitute with less than five minutes to go. Although no way a regular at Highbury, he gained the first of his three England Under 21 Caps in June 1987. In 1987-88, Gus enjoyed a fine run in the League side, playing in twenty two League games, when deputising at centre half for the injured David O'Leary. However, a career which at one stage looked so promising came to a shattering end after the nervous looking Caesar made a catastrophic error when his fumbled clearance led to Luton Town's equaliser in the 1988 Littlewoods Cup Final. In normal circumstances the inexperienced Caesar would never have played, but because Arsenal at the time only had Gus as a centre half cover to Adams and O'Leary, George Graham had no other option and realising his error George then started collecting centre backs (i.e. Bould, Linighan, Keown,

Pates etc.). The Arsenal faithful crucified poor Gus and in his last three seasons at Highbury he played in only two other League games. He spent a loan period at Queens Park Rangers in 1990-91 and since leaving Arsenal on a free transfer in June 1991, Gus has been freed by Cambridge United in 1991, Bristol City in 1992 and Airdrie (where he won a Scottish F.A. Cup Finalists Medal versus Rangers), in 1994. He is currently playing for Colchester United. Has attained almost cult status in Arsenal's plethora of fanzines.

	Games	Goals
League	44	0
F.A.Cup	1	0
League Cup	5	0
Other First Team Games	4	0
Friendly Matches	45	1
Tours	18	0
Football Combination	142	12
South East Counties League	47	2
Youth Cup	6	1
Other Youth Cups	9	1
Total	**321**	**17**

Honours:
(WITH ARSENAL)
3 England Under 21 Caps
Football League Cup Finalists Medal 1987-88
F.A. Charity Shield Finalists Medal   1989
Makita Tournament Winners Medal   1989
Football Combination Championship Medal
                                    1989-90
(WITH AIRDRIE)
Scottish F.A. Cup Finalists Medal   1993-94

CAMPBELL, Gary   1981-85

Birth Place: Belfast
Date of Birth: 4th April 1966

☛ Gary joined Arsenal as an apprentice during the Summer of 1981, turning professional in January 1984. A midfield player, he won Northern Ireland Youth Caps as well as becoming a permanent fixture in Arsenal's Combination side. His potential was not fulfilled and at the end of 1984-85, and he was given a free transfer when he joined Leyton Wingate, he later enjoyed a long and distinguished career in non league football playing for Dagenham, Finchley, Barnet, Dartford, Finchley again and Bromley. Gary also returned to League action with Leyton Orient as a non contract player in January 1990. His brother Greg played League football for several clubs including West Ham United. The son of respected coach Bobby Campbell.

	Games	Goals
Friendly Matches	13	1
Football Combination	67	4
South East Counties League	66	12
Youth Cup	9	3
Other Youth Cups	18	6
Youth Tours	4	1
Total	**177**	**27**

Honours:
Northern Ireland Youth International
Football Combination Championship Medal
                                    1983-84
Southern Junior Floodlight Cup Winners
   Medal   1983-84

CAMPBELL, Kevin   1986-95

Birth Place: Lambeth, London
Date of Birth: 4th February, 1970

☛ Kevin signed associated schoolboy forms for Arsenal in October 1985 and became a trainee in the following July, turning professional in February 1988. Kevin was a product of South London Schools, who in the 1987-88 season, smashed all Arsenal goalscoring records' when finding the net fifty-nine times for the youth team and was a prominent member of the side that won the F.A. Youth Cup against Doncaster Rovers. This form earned him his league debut on the last day of the season at Goodison Park versus Everton. However, in the League Championship winning season of 1988-89, with Merson and Smith holding down the regular strikers positions, he was loaned out

Gus Caesar

to gain experience with Leyton Orient and although the Orient manager, Frank Clark, wanted to sign him permanently, he realised Arsenal would not sell a player with such potential. In 1989-90, after gaining further experience when on loan to Leicester City, he appeared for Arsenal in fifteen league games at the back end of that season and during this period Kevin won the first of his four England Under-Twenty-One Caps. No other player in Arsenal's League Championship winning season was more instrumental than Kevin Campbell, for up to February of that season he had appeared in only the odd game until bursting on to the scene scoring eight times in ten games, rejuvenating the side. At the age of twenty-one, Kevin had become a thoroughbred athlete whose sturdy build was more aligned to a middleweight boxer than to a footballer. His great attributes were his physical power, his pace over short distances and his ability to turn defenders when in close control with the ball. In 1991-92, he scored thirteen times in thirty-one league games and he found himself with a new striking partner in Ian Wright , at the end of that season. In 1992-93, Kevin's form wavered and he struggled when scoring only four league goals in the new Premiership. Ian Wright had put Kevin in the shade with his goal scoring exploits and "so called" Arsenal supporters spent most of their time reminding Kevin that George Graham should have kept Andy Cole and relieved Kevin of his services. He compensated his poor league form when scoring two late goals in League Cup ties against Millwall and Derby County. He was a member of the victorious double Cup winning team of that season. Kevin's goalscoring form returned, in 1993-94, when scoring fourteen times in thirty-seven appearances, these included two hat tricks against Ipswich and Swindon Town. Kevin was also a notable member of the European Cup Winners Cup winning team when scoring four times on route to the final. In his last season at Highbury, 1994-95, his form again suffered, due to a confidence crisis. This resulted in him not being in contention for selection for the European Cup Winners Cup Final against Real Zaragoza. In June 1995, the demoralised Campbell wanted away from his beloved Arsenal and in the following month, Frank Clark, now the Nott'm Forest manager, at last got his man when a tribunal set the transfer fee at £2.5 million.

	Games	Goals
League	166	46
F.A. Cup	19	2
League Cup	24	6
Europe	15	5
Other First Team Matches	9	1
Friendly Matches	43	30
Tours	17	9
Football Combination	89	94
South East Counties League	58	59
Youth Cup	10	12
Other Youth Cups	14	15
Youth Tours	4	1
Total	**468**	**280**

Honours:
1 England B Caps
4 England Under-twenty-one Caps
League Championship Medal 1990-91
F.A. Cup Winners Medal 1992-93
League Cup Winners Medal 1992-93
European Cup Winners Cup Winners Medal
1993-94
European Super Cup Finalists Medal 1995
F.A. Charity Shield Medal 1991
F.A. Charity Shield Finalists Medal 1993
2 Makita International Tournament Winners
Medals 1989, 1994
Makita International Tournament Finalists
Medal 1990
F.A. Youth Cup Winners Medal 1987-88
Football Combination League Championship
Medal 1989-90

Kevin Campbell

CAMPBELL, Stuart   1991-94

Birth Place: Bexley, Kent
Date of Birth: 2nd January 1975

Stuart had won England Under 15 and Under 16 Schoolboy Caps as a fine young left back. Joining Arsenal as a trainee from the F.A. School of Excellence during the Summer of 1991, turning professional two years later. In his three seasons at Highbury he was a mainstay in the club's Youth and reserve side. His chances of gaining first team recognition were slim due to the consistency of Nigel Winterburn and he was subsequently placed on the not retained list in the close season of 1993-94.

	Games	Goals
Friendly Matches	13	1
Football Combination	17	0
South East Counties League	49	3
Youth Cup	4	0
Other Youth Cups	22	2
Youth Tours	3	0
Total	108	6

Honours:
England Schoolboy International
2 Southern Junior Floodlight Cup Finalists
    Medals   1991-92, 1992-93

CARSTAIRS, Jim   1987-91

Birth Place: St Andrews, Fife, Scotland
Date of Birth: 29th January 1971

James was a young promising left back when joining Arsenal as a trainee in July 1987, turning professional in March 1989. In his four seasons at Highbury he helped Arsenal in winning the F.A.Youth Cup in 1988 and the Football Combination Championship in 1990. In February 1991 he had a loan period at Brentford before being given a free transfer in the following June when he joined Cambridge United. However, his stay with them was less than four months, being released from his contract when he linked up with Stockport County. James stayed there until the end of the season and was granted a free transfer for the third time in less than a year.

	Games	Goals
Friendly Matches	23	0
Football Combination	82	1
South East Counties League	57	1
Youth Cup	11	0
Other Youth Cups	7	0
Youth Tours	6	0
Total	**186**	**2**

Honours:
F.A.Youth Cup Winners Medal   1987-88
Football Combination Championship Medal
                                1989-90

CARTER, Jimmy   1991-95

Birth Place: Hammersmith, London
Date of Birth: 9th November 1965

Jimmy Carter had played for Islington Schoolboys when signing as an associated schoolboy with Crystal Palace in January 1980. He became an apprentice in July 1982 turning professional the following November. In nearly two seasons as a pro at Selhurst Park, he had not managed to play in any first class football for the club and at the age of nearly twenty, he was given a free transfer in September 1985, when he joined Queens Park Rangers. In eighteen months at Loftus Road he suffered the same fate and now in his twenty second year with still no League appearances behind him, he was transferred to Millwall in March 1987 for £15,000. Jimmy spent four successful years at the club, becoming a firm favourite with the crowd at the Den, helping the Lions to the Second Division Championship in 1987-88. However, even though he was not one of the first names written on the Millwall team sheet, Kenny Dalglish flabbergasted the average English football fan when signing him for Liverpool for £800,000 in January 1991. The question being asked at Anfield, was, "was Jimmy Carter signed to replace John Barnes?" If this was the case, it never materialised and after only five League games and under new management (Graeme Souness) Carter was just as surprisingly relieved of this awkward situation when George Graham paid £500,000 for his services in October 1991. Jimmy made his Arsenal League debut when coming on as a substitute at Nottingham Forest 8th December 1991 and although, on his day, he could produce a performance as good as most wingers, causing problems with his pace, his consistency, seemed lacking. In four seasons at Highbury he played in only twenty five League games and it must have come as a great disappointment when this life long Arsenal supporter was granted a free transfer in June 1995. In all of his performances for Arsenal Jimmy never gave less than one hundred percent and everyone must wish him well in his new career at Portsmouth.

	Games	Goals
League	25	2
F.A.Cup	3	0
League Cup	1	0
Friendly Matches	10	8
Tours	7	1
Football Combination	76	6
Total	**122**	**17**

Honours:
(WITH MILLWALL)
Division Two Champ'ship Medal   1987-88

Jimmy Carter

CATON, Tommy   1983-87

Birth Place: Kirkby, Liverpool, Lancs
Date of Birth: 6th October 1962

Tommy Caton was captain of England Schoolboys, at centre half, when joining Manchester City as an apprentice during the Summer of 1978, and in his first season at Maine Road, he helped the club to the F.A.Youth Cup Final versus Millwall. In 1979-80, Tommy made his City League debut as a sixteen year old apprentice, turning professional on his seventeenth birthday and during the season he became the youngest player in the history of the Football League to remain ever-present in a season. Caton also won five England Youth Caps and was still eligible to play in the 1980 F.A.Youth Cup Final against Aston Villa. Over the following two seasons he was the backbone of City's defence and was a member of their side against Tottenham Hotspur in the 1981 F.A.Cup Final, added to this he won the first of his nine Under 21 Caps. On 6th March 1982, in a League encounter at Maine Road against Arsenal he became the youngest player in the history of the Football League to reach the milestone of 100 First Division League games (at the age of nineteen years one hundred and fifty one days). However, when Manchester City were relegated to the Second Division in 1982-83, Caton became unsettled and requested a transfer. The day after Arsenal had suffered a humiliating League Cup home defeat against lowly Walsall, Tommy signed for the club in a £500,000 transfer, and made his Arsenal League debut three days later in a home fixture against West Bromwich Albion. For the rest of that season he remained virtually ever-present when linking up with David O'Leary at the heart of Arsenal's defence. Although tall and strong, Tommy seemed short of pace and sometimes struggled to regain position when out of his area. In 1984-85 he missed only seven League games. However, after being ever-present at the start of 1985-86, he was dropped after a League game at Southampton and was replaced by the young Martin Keown. With Tony Adams entering the fray, it was apparent that Tommy's future at Highbury was over and as a result, in January 1987 he joined Oxford United for £180,000 (too late to save the side from relegation to the Second Division). After less than eighteen months at the Manor ground he moved to Charlton Athletic in November 1988, but unfortunately endured another relegation from the top flight with them in 1989-90. In 1990-91 a long term injury resurrected itself after a League encounter against Blackburn Rovers on 1st January 1991. The injury was beyond repair and at the end of the 1991-92 season, after eighteen months of trying to regain full fitness, he was requested by doctors to retire from the game. In April 1993 the footballing public were shocked and stunned when hearing of the tragic and untimely death of Tommy Caton aged thirty.

	Games	Goals
League	81	2
F.A.Cup	4	0
League Cup	10	1
Friendly Matches	21	0
Tours	3	0
Football Combination	36	1
Total	**155**	**4**

Tommy Caton

Honours:
(WITH MANCHESTER CITY)
5 England Youth Caps
2 F.A.Youth Cup Finalists Medals
1978-79, 1979-80
F.A.Cup Finalists Medal   1980-81
(WITH MANCHESTER CITY & ARSENAL)
9 England Under 21 Caps.

CLARKE, Adrian   1991

Birth Place: Haverhill, Suffolk
Date of Birth: 28th September 1974

☛ Adrian had played for Suffolk County and England Under 15's before joining Arsenal as a trainee during the Summer of 1991, after making several appearances whilst still a schoolboy. A winger/midfield player, Adrian turned professional in July 1993 and became a permanent member of the reserve side as well as winning an England Youth Cap. His outstanding performances prompted George Graham to hand Adrian his full League debut on the last day of the year (1994) in a home fixture against Queens Park Rangers. This after he'd been a member of the club's F.A.Youth Cup Winning side against Millwall in 1993-94.

	Games	Goals
League	1	0
Friendly Matches	24	10
Tours	2	0
Football Combination	62	9
South East Counties League	51	12
Youth Cup	5	2
Other Youth Cups	23	7
Youth Tours	3	0
Total	**171**	**40**

Adrian Clarke

Honours:
England Schoolboy International
1 England Youth Cap
F.A.Youth Cup Winners Medal   1993-94
2 Southern Junior Floodlight Cup Finalists
Medals   1991-92 1992-93

CLEMENTS, Steve   1989-93

Birth Place: Slough, Berkshire
Date of Birth: 26th September 1972

☛ Steve joined Arsenal as a trainee from the F.A. School of Excellence at Lilleshall after he had represented Berkshire Schoolboys and England at under 16 level. However, after turning professional in 1990 a series of injuries including a hernia and a knee injury restricted his progress. Clements had begun his career as a full back later moving into the central midfield role. A promising career which looked so bright had not materialised and he was surprisingly given a free transfer at the end of the 1992-93 season when he joined Hereford United but unfortunately was released a year later.

	Games	Goals
Friendly Matches	20	0
Football Combination	49	1
South East Counties League	38	6
Youth Cup	6	3
Other Youth Cups	16	7
Youth Tours	9	0
Total	**138**	**17**

Honours:
England Under 16 International
South East Counties League Championship
Medal   1990-91
Southern Junior Floodlight Cup Winners
Medal   1990-91
Southern Junior Floodlight Cup Finalists
Medal   1989-90

COLE, Andrew   1986-92

Birth Place: Nottingham
Date of Birth: 15th October 1971

Alongside Herbert Chapman, George Graham was Arsenal's most successful manager of all time, if Herbert was alive today he would be the first to admit that he made mistakes within the transfer market. In George Graham's case, the biggest transfer blunder (in many Arsenal supporters eyes) was the transfer of Andy Cole for just £500,000 in July 1992. Andrew had joined Arsenal as a fourteen year old schoolboy in October 1985 before attending the F.A. School of Excellence at Lillishall and returning to Highbury to become a trainee in July 1988.

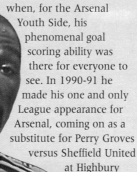

Already a schoolboy International, between 1987-1989, Cole was selected for the England Youth side on twenty occasions, when, for the Arsenal Youth Side, his phenomenal goal scoring ability was there for everyone to see. In 1990-91 he made his one and only League appearance for Arsenal, coming on as a substitute for Perry Groves versus Sheffield United at Highbury on 29th December, 1990.

eight months at Ashton Gate he joined Newcastle United for £1.75 million in March 1993. At the end of that season he had helped Newcastle to the First Division Championship. In 1993-94, Andrew became the talk of football when becoming United's record goal scorer in a season with forty one and was voted P.F.A Young Player of the year. However, in January 1995, the whole of Tyneside was aghast when Kevin Keegan accepted a £7 million offer, which was a new English transfer record, from Manchester United. Later on in that season Andrew won his first England Cap to complete a full set. In 1995-96, many eyes will be watching Andy Cole's progress.

	Games	Goals
League	1	0
Other First team games	3	0
Friendly Matches	34	15
Football Combination	60	30
South East Counties League	49	42
Youth Cup	9	10
Other Youth Cups	9	5
Youth Tours	9	1
Total	**174**	**103**

Honours:
(WITH ARSENAL)
England Schoolboy International
20 England Youth Caps
8 Under Twenty One Caps
F.A.Charity Shield Finalists Medal   1991
Makita Tournament Finalists Medal   1991
Southern Junior Floodlight Cup Finalists
   Medal   1989-90
(WITH NEWCASTLE)
2 England B Caps
Division One Championship Medal   1992-93
P.F.A. Young Player of the Year   1993-94
(WITH MANCHESTER UNITED)
1 England Cap

This was after he had turned professional in October 1989. In 1991-92, with the likes of Smith, Wright, Campbell and Merson ahead of him for selection he was given two loan spell opportunities at Fulham and Bristol City, George Graham seemed determined not to push Andrew into the forefront of attention, even though many at Highbury knew of the great all round talents that Cole possessed. This was even more pronounced when the England Under 21 selectors picked him eight times when still a reserve. Finally, in July 1992, Cole left Highbury to join Bristol City as a bemused and frustrated young man. His self confidence in his own ability, with his powerful running and his unbelievable awareness in front of goal, stood him in good stead and after less than

Andy Cole

CONNELLY, Dino   1986-90

Birth Place: Glasgow, Scotland
Date of Birth: 6th January 1970

☛ Dino joined Arsenal as trainee after being on the books of Celtic as a schoolboy, this after he had had trials with Dundee and Oldham. A Scottish Schoolboy International, this bright young star seemed to have everything going for him when from midfield he gained Scottish Youth International Caps and helped Arsenal win the Football Combination Championship in 1989-90. However, the brilliant career which was foreseen for him, after turning professional in February 1988, did not take shape. Connelly was released by the club in June 1990 when he joined Barnsley. He later played on loan for Wigan Athletic and Carlisle United. He was released by Barnsley in February 1993 when he was transferred to Wigan Athletic, but was released in June 1994. He linked up with Stockport County where his contract was cancelled during the 1994-95 season.

	Games	Goals
Friendly Matches	28	6
Football Combination	80	10
South East Counties League	37	5
Youth Cup	5	0
Other Youth Cups	7	3
Youth Tours	8	1
Total	**165**	**25**

Honours:
Scotland Schoolboy and Youth International
Football Combination Championship Medal
1989-90

CONNELLY, Tony   1991-93

Date of Birth: 17th June 1975

☛ A winger/forward, Tony joined Arsenal as a trainee during the Summer of 1991 having represented Eire at Under 15 and under 16 level. In his two seasons at Highbury he was unfortunately plagued by injuries which resulted in Connelly not being offered a new contract in June 1993.

	Games	Goals
Friendly Matches	11	7
Football Combination	5	1
South East Counties League	29	11
Youth Cup	1	0
Other Youth Cups	8	2
Youth Tours	2	0
Total	**56**	**21**

Honours:
Eire Under 15 and Under 16 Caps.
Southern Junior Floodlight Cup Finalists
Medal   1992-93

CORK, David   1978-85

Birth Place: Doncaster, Yorkshire
Date of Birth: 28th October 1962

☛ David was playing for Don Valley district and South Yorkshire Schoolboys before joining Arsenal in May 1978 (Schoolboy) May 1979 (apprentice) June 1980 (professional). David had been at Arsenal for the best part of five years, serving the Junior and reserve ranks with patience and no mean ability. During this time he had played in over one hundred and twenty reserve team games (in many positions) before making his League debut versus Watford at Highbury 17th December 1983. He finished that 1983-84 season playing in seven League games, mainly at right half and in 1984-85 his appearances were only for the reserve team. He was subsequently released and he joined Huddersfield Town in July 1985. David later played for West Bromwich Albion (loan), Scunthorpe United and Darlington.

	Games	Goals
League	7	1
F.A.Cup	1	0
Friendly Matches	66	16
Tours	2	0
Football Combination	163	15
South East Counties League	44	4
Youth Cup	6	1
Other Youth Cups	16	0
Youth Tours	6	0
Total	**311**	**35**

David Cork

DAVIS, Paul   1978-95

Birth Place: Dulwich, London
Date of Birth: 9th December, 1961

☛ Paul came to Highbury as an associated schoolboy in October 1977 whilst playing for South London Schoolboys and on leaving school he became an apprentice in June 1978, turning professional a year later. In his seventeen years at the club, Paul developed in to one of the most cultured midfield players in the country, so much so, if he had worn the yellow shirt of Brazil, he would not have looked out of place. However, although possessing a magical left foot when appearing to have so much time on the ball. he was never honoured by England at full international level and he must be considered, along with George Armstrong, John Lukic and Peter Simpson, as one of the finest Arsenal players never to have won an England cap. Paul rose through the ranks of the club and made his league debut in an experimental Arsenal side at White Hart Lane versus Tottenham Hotspur in April 1980. He became a regular in the side in 1981-82 season when missing only four league games as well as winning the first of his eleven England Under-Twenty-One Caps. In the following two seasons his place , on the right hand side of midfield, was virtually assured. However, in 1984-85, he spent two long periods out of the side through injury and this was to become a curse which would dog him for the rest of his career. In 1985-86 he had regained his place in the side when he suffered a groin strain which side lined him for three months. In the 1986-87 campaign, Paul missed only three league games and was a main influence in the Arsenal midfield when helping the club to lift the Littlewoods Cup when beating Liverpool and for a short while, at the end of that season, he was made team captain. Injuries plagued Paul yet again in 1987-88, when he was out for six weeks, this time with a ligament injury. However, Davis still managed to play in twenty-nine league games as well as playing in that season's Littlewoods Cup Final versus Luton Town. In the club's League Championship season, 1988-89, in the fourth league game of the season in a home fixture versus Southampton, Paul, uncharacteristically, lost his temper after a challenge by Glen Cockerill and video evidence was used to prove that Davis had elbowed Cockerill in the face which resulted in him having a broken jaw. Paul was handed a nine match suspension and fined a record £3,000. Although he returned to play in two short stints he was again beset by injuries and it was at this time that he lost out on his chance to play for England. There was no doubt that the incident with Cockerill had affected Paul and, in 1989-90, his future at the club looked on the bleak side when

playing in only eleven league games. As if to prove his critics wrong, Paul missed only one league game when being an integral part in Arsenal's 1990-91 League Championship winning season. After he had enjoyed a bumper testimonial against Celtic at the beginning of the 1991-92 season, Davis was dropped from the side, replaced by David Hillier after the club had crashed out of the European Cup against Benfica. In 1992-93, he was left out in the wilderness for nearly all of that campaign when manager George Graham, surprisingly selected him for both the F.A. and Coca Cola Cup Finals. Paul took up the challenge and in both games showed all of his old skills which had been lacking in the side. In his last two seasons at Highbury, although never an automatic choice, he was still a member of the European Cup Winners Cup winning team against Parma. The extremely talented Davis was left bemused and deeply hurt when the club he loved released him on a free transfer in June 1995. Paul linked up with Brentford three months later.

	Games	Goals
League	351	30
F.A. Cup	27	3
League Cup	51	4
Europe	16	0
Other First Team Matches	14	2
Friendly Matches	85	17
Tours	35	6
Football Combination	164	26
South East Counties League	31	4
Youth Cup	3	1
Other Youth Cups	9	2
Youth Tours	4	0
Total	**790**	**95**

Honours:

1 England B Cap
1 Football League Cap
11 England Under-twenty-one Caps2 League Championship Medals

1988-89, 1990-91
F.A. Cup Winners Medal   1992-93

2 League Cup Winners Medal
                    1986-87, 1992-93
League Cup Finalists Medal   1987-88
F.A. Charity Shield Medal   1991
F.A. Charity Shield Finalists Medal   1993
1 European Cup Winners Cup Winners
    Medal   1993/94
Mercantile Credit Centenary Trophy Winners
    Medal   1988-89
Wembley International Tournament Winners
    Medal   1988-89
Makita International Tournament Winners
    Medal   1994
2 Makita International Tournament Finalists
    Medals   1990, 1991
South East Counties League Cup Winners
    Medal   1979-80
Presidents Cup Winners Medal   1980-81

Paul Davis

DICKOV, Paul   1989

Birth Place: Livingston, Scotland
Date of Birth: 1st November 1972

☛ Paul Dickov joined Arsenal as a trainee in July 1989, after he had starred for the Scottish Youth Team when helping his Country to the final of the 1989 Mini World Cup. Paul was a consistent member of the clubs South East Counties Youth side, scoring regularly before turning professional in December 1990, and helped the Youth side to the double, South East Counties League and Southern Junior Floodlight Cup Winners. In 1991-92. He won the first of his five Scottish Under 21 Caps versus Yugoslavia, before making his premier League debut as a substitute versus Southampton at Highbury 20th March 1993. He played in a further two League games that season, scoring in each, against Crystal Palace and Tottenham, as well as helping Scotland to the semi finals of the Toulon Under 21 Tournament.

Paul Dickov

In 1993-94, this small, skilful striker, who is a real competitor and has the ability to mature into a top class goal scoring inside forward, spent loan periods at both Luton Town and with Liam Brady at Brighton, although having played in only one League game for Arsenal, he won a European Cup Winners Cup Winners Medal when being named in the sixteen man squad against Parma in 1994. In 1994-95, he appeared in nine League games without scoring, although he did hit three goals in two League Cup ties. With the departure of Kevin Campbell and the unfortunate retirement of Alan Smith, many will be hoping that the talents of Paul Dickov will not be handed away because of limited first team opportunities, like the case of Andrew Cole.

	Games	Goals
League	13	2
League Cup	4	3
Friendly Matches	34	14
Tours	7	1
Football Combination	117	44
South East Counties League	39	14
Youth Cup	4	1
Other Youth Cups	19	6
Youth Tours	5	1
Total	**242**	**86**

Honours:

5 Scottish Under 21 Caps
Scottish Youth and Scottish Schoolboy Caps
European Cup Winners Cup Winners Medal
1993-94
South East Counties League Championship
Medal   1990-91
Southern Junior Floodlight Cup Winners
Medal   1990-91
Southern Junior Floodlight Cup Finalists
Medal   1989-90

DIXON, Lee   1988

Birth Place: Manchester, Lancashire
Date of Birth: 17th March, 1964

☛ There are not many players currently playing in the Premier League who have been granted a free transfer by a lower league side. But Lee Dixon's has been freed twice by lower division clubs, which shows his great tenacity when fighting back against all the odds. Lee had served his apprenticeship with Burnley before turning professional in July 1982. However, in less than twenty months at Turf Moor he played in only four league games and was released by Burnley boss, John Bond, in February 1984. He joined Chester City and although he played in more than fifty league games for the club over a season and a half, he was again rejected and moved to Bury in July 1985. In that 1985-86 season Lee missed only one league game for the Shakers and drew the attention of Stoke City boss, Mick Mills, who paid £40,000 for him in July 1986. In his first season at the Potteries he was ever present. Arsenal manager George Graham had tried replacing Viv Anderson with the young Michael Thomas, but having realised his destiny lay in midfield, turned to Lee Dixon when paying Stoke City £400,000 in January 1988. Lee made his Arsenal league debut in a home fixture versus Luton Town on 13th February 1988. In 1988-89, Lee Dixon and Nigel Winterburn began their Arsenal footballing careers together and in Arsenal's long history, only Hapgood and Male have been a finer full back combination. In 1994-95 they played in over three hundred Arsenal first team games together. Lee Dixon is one of the coolest, calmest players that Arsenal have had on their books in recent years, whose fleetness of foot and intercepting abilities allied to his now masterful defensive qualities, have made him into one of the finest right backs the club has ever had. It was his cool, calm approach which led George Graham to handing Dixon the penalty takers job in the early 1990's. However, if Lee is to be remembered for just one thing , in his time at Highbury, it would be for his involvement in the build up to Arsenal's dramatic last minute goal in the title decider at Anfield and how many Arsenal followers, reading this book, have relived that moment? When Lukic threw out to Dixon, on from Dixon to Alan Smith who knocked it on for Michael Thomas to score. Now in his ninth season at the club, Lee has been at the heart of all the club's recent successes, he has figured in over two hundred and fifty league games, being ever present in 1989-90 and in the second of his League Championship winning campaigns in 1990-91. Dixon won the first of his twenty-one England caps when appearing for his country against Czechoslovakia in 1989-90 and the only blemish on his record was when he missed the 1992-93 League Cup Final after being sent off a few weeks earlier in the F.A. Cup semi-final against Tottenham. Lee later added to his Arsenal honours list when appearing in both the 1994 and 1995 European Cup Winners Cup Finals. Lee Dixon must go down with Steve Bould and Nigel Winterburn as George Graham's best ever dealings in the transfer market.

Lee Dixon

	Games	Goals
League	254	16
F.A. Cup	26	1
League Cup	32	0
Europe	21	0
Other First Team Matches	15	0
Friendly Matches	32	4
Tours	21	1
Football Combination	18	3
Total	**419**	**25**

Honours:

21 England Caps
5 England B Caps
1 Football League Cap
2 League Championship Medals
               1988-89, 1990-91
F.A. Cup Winners Medal   1992-93
European Cup Winners Cup Winners Medal
                     1993-94
European Cup Winners Cup Finalists
  Medal   1994-95
European Super Cup Finalists Medal 1995
F.A. Charity Shield Medal   1991
2 F.A. Charity Shield Finalists Medals
                   1989, 1993
Mercantile Credit Centenary Trophy
  Winners Medal   1988-89
Wembley International Tournament
  Winners Medal   1988-89
Makita International Tournament
  Winners Medal   1994
Makita International Tournament
  Finalists Medals   1990, 1991

Lee Dixon

DOLAN, Pat — 1984-86

Birth Place: Dagenham, Essex
Date of Birth: 20th September 1967

A centre half, Patrick had represented Essex Schoolboys when joining the club as an apprentice in the Summer of 1984. In two seasons with the club he represented the Youth side with distinction and gained Republic of Ireland Youth Honours. His twin brother Eamonn played for West Ham and Birmingham City. Patrick was given a free transfer in the Summer of 1986 when he joined Walsall.

	Games	Goals
Friendly Matches	3	0
Football Combination	3	0
South East Counties League	48	4
Youth Cup	8	0
Other Youth Cups	17	2
Youth Tours	9	0
Total	**88**	**6**

Honours:
Eire Youth Caps
2 South East Counties League Cup Finalists
  Medals   1984-85, 1985-86
Southern Junior Floodlight Cup Finalists
  Medal   1985-86

ESQULANT, Danny — 1986-89

Birth Place: Islington, London
Date of Birth: 28th September 1969

Every generation of schoolboy and youth team football has produced players who, it seemed, would reach the very top in the professional game One of these players was Danny Esqulant. Unfortunately for Danny, fate took an upper hand and the glittering career forecast was not forthcoming. A product of Islington/Camden schoolboys, Danny had won fifteen England Schoolboy Caps when he became one of the first boys to attend the first F.A. School of Excellence in 1985. He joined Arsenal in the Summer of 1986, turning professional the following October. In 1987-88, he gained England Youth Caps and was a regular member, as an attacking midfield player, for both the Youth team and the reserves. No one knows how or why his career never materialised and George Graham released him in the Summer of 1989. Esqulant later played for Fisher, Croydon and Sutton.

	Games	Goals
Friendly Matches	13	5
Football Combination	45	7
South East Counties League	47	14
Youth Cup	6	3
Other Youth Cups	10	3
Youth Tours	9	3
Total	**130**	**35**

Honours:

15 England Schoolboy Caps
3 England Youth Caps

FLATTS, Mark — 1989

Birth Place: Islington, London
Date of Birth: 14th October 1972

Mark was playing for Haringey/Middlesex Schoolboys when signing Associated Schoolboy Forms for Arsenal in January 1987. He became a trainee in July 1989, after he had enjoyed a term at the F.A. School of Excellence at Lillishall. In 1989-90 he won an England Youth Cap before turning professional in December 1990. During this time, although very slight, his skilful displays were seen week in week out in the club's Youth side. In 1991-92 Mark progressed into the Combination side, but injuries hampered his progress that season. In 1992-93, George Graham gave Mark ten League opportunities, of which his Arsenal League debut was at Sheffield United 19th September 1992. However, the following season he was restricted to only a few first team appearances and was loaned out to Cambridge United and Brighton. In 1994-95, Flatts was still unable to put a consistent run together and he was loaned out yet again, this time to Bristol City. Mark has undoubted talents, but at the age of nearly twenty three, 1995-96 could be the cross-roads of his career.

Mark Flatts

	Games	Goals
League	16	0
F.A.Cup	1	0
League Cup	1	0
Friendly Matches	30	5
Tours	5	0
Football Combination	85	13
South East Counties League	37	7
Youth Cup	6	1
Other Youth Cups	20	3
Youth Tours	10	2
Total	**211**	**31**

Honours:
1 England Youth Cap
South East Counties League Championship
  Medal   1990-91
Southern Junior Floodlight Cup Winners
  Medal   1990-91
Southern Junior Floodlight Cup Finalists
  Medal   1989-90

GRIGGS, Timmy — 1993

Birth Place: Bexley, Kent
Date of Birth: 9th November, 1976

Timmy was playing for Kent County Schoolboys when joining Arsenal as a trainee in the summer of 1993 and in his first season at Highbury he was the club's regular right back in the South East Counties League side and helped Arsenal in winning the F.A. Youth Cup versus Millwall. Griggs joined the professional ranks in the summer of 1995

	Games	Goals
Football Combination	3	0
Friendly Matches	9	0
South East Counties	48	2
Youth Cup	9	1
Other Youth Cups	13	0
Youth Tours	6	0
Total	88	3

Honours:
F.A. Youth Cup Winners Medal   1993-94
Southern Junior Floodlight Cup Finalists
  Medal   1994-95

FRANCIS, Lee — 1986-90

Birth Place: Walthamstow, London
Date of Birth: 24th October 1969

Lee was a young full back who had represented Waltham Forest and Essex Schoolboys, before joining Arsenal as a trainee in the Summer of 1986, turning professional in November 1987. Lee was a member of the victorious F.A. Youth Cup winning side versus Doncaster Rovers in 1987-88 and in March 1990, he spent a loan period at Chesterfield. However, in the Summer of 1991, Francis was granted a free transfer when again linking up with Chesterfield. In two seasons at the club (1990-92), although being a regular in the side, Lee's disciplinary record was not too favourable (20 bookings) and for partly this reason, his contract was terminated in June 1992.

	Games	Goals
Friendly Matches	17	1
Football Combination	90	3
South East Counties League	36	0
Youth Cup	8	0
Other Youth Cups	8	0
Youth Tours	6	0
Total	**165**	**4**

Honours:
F.A.Youth Cup Winners Medal   1987-88
Football Combination Championship Medal
1989-90

GAUNT, Craig   1989-93

Birth Place: Nottingham
Date of Birth: 31st March 1973

Craig had come to prominence when playing centre back for Nottinghamshire schools and he was yet another pupil of the F.A.School of Excellence at Lillishall, when joining Arsenal as a trainee in July 1989, turning professional the following year. A stalwart in the club's youth side of this period, injuries, however, hindered his career and Craig was subsequently released in June 1993.

	Games	Goals
Friendly Matches	26	0
Football Combination	44	0
South East Counties League	31	4
Youth Cup	3	0
Other Youth Cups	14	2
Youth Tours	3	1
Total	**121**	**7**

Honours:
South East Counties League Championship
Medal   1990-91
Southern Junior Floodlight Cup Winners
Medal   1990-91

GROVES, Perry   1986-92

Birth Place: Bow, London
Date of Birth: 19th April 1965

Perry, the nephew of Vic Groves who played for Arsenal between 1955-63, had played for Suffolk Schoolboys when becoming, in May 1980, an Associated Schoolboy with Wolverhampton Wanderers. He became an apprentice at Colchester United in September 1981 before turning professional in June 1982 and in four seasons at Layer Road played in over one hundred and fifty League games. Perry became George Graham's first ever signing for Arsenal when joining the club for £50,000 in September 1986. In 1986-87, Perry, played in all positions along the front line when appearing in twenty five League games and during this season he started his love hate relationship with the Arsenal faithful. Although he had more skill than many gave him credit for, his pace was undoubtedly his major asset. However, in his early days at the club he seemed to run with the ball in any direction with seemingly no idea of where he was going, or what he was going to do with it, having said that, one's mind must go back to a brilliant run he made past three Liverpool

defenders when laying the ball off for Charlie Nicholas to score the winning goal in the 1987 Littlewoods Cup Final. During the course of his career at Highbury he developed into possibly the best £50,000 the club has ever spent, serving the club he supported as a boy with great cause and enthusiasm. In 1987-88, he was instrumental in helping Arsenal reach the Littlewoods Cup Final versus Luton Town when he scored the only goal in the first leg Semi Final at Goodison Park versus Everton. In the championship winning season, 1988-89, Groves came on as substitute in no less than fifteen League games, including the title decider at Anfield. In 1989-90, his useful utility play was served well when filling in for the injured Brian Marwood. When Arsenal won the League Championship again, in 1990-91, Perry appeared in thirty two League games, but 'Tin Tin' remained on the field for the whole of the game in only seven of them. By this time competition in the forward line was getting stiffer and he found himself out in the cold in his last full season at the club and it came as no surprise when he was transferred to Southampton for £750,000, in August 1992. However, he had played in only fifteen League games for the Saints when suffering a serious leg injury at Middlesbrough in January 1993 and over the best part of the next two years he battled bravely to regain full fitness, but was

eventually advised to go into premature retirement. Perry, at the back end of the 1994-95 season, made a comeback with Dagenham and Redbridge.

	Games	Goals
League	155	21
F.A.Cup	17	1
League Cup	26	6
Europe	4	0
Other First Team Games	7	1
Friendly Matches	37	12
Tour	13	1
Football Combination	51	27
Total	**310**	**69**

Honours:
2 League Championship Medals
1988-89, 1990-91
Football League Cup Winners Medal 1986-87
Football League Cup Finalists Medal 1987-88
Mercantile Credit Centenary Trophy Winners
Medal   1988-89
Wembley International Tournament Winners
Medal   1988-89
Makita Tournament Winners Medal   1989
2 Makita Tournament Finalists Medals
1990, 1991

Perry Groves

HALL, Graeme 1992-95

Birth Place: Cleveland
Date of Birth: 22nd November 1975

☛ Graeme was a six foot two inch, seventeen year old, centre back who joined Arsenal as a trainee in the Summer of 1992, after he had played for Stockton in senior football and had won Cleveland County honours. Graeme was a member of the F.A.Youth Cup Winning side of 1993-94, having turned professional in November 1993. Hall was one of six players not retained at the end of the 1994-95 season.

	Games	Goals
Friendly Matches	20	2
Football Combination	22	1
South East Counties League	42	0
Youth Cup	11	0
Other Youth Cups	13	0
Youth Tours	3	0
Total	**111**	**3**

Honours:
F.A.Youth Cup winners Medal 1993-94
Southern Junior Floodlight Cup Finalists
Medal 1992-93

HANNIGAN, Al James 1987-90

Birth Place: Islington, London
Date of Birth: 26th January 1971

☛ Al James was yet another product of Islington/Camden Schools who had also represented London when joining Arsenal as a trainee in the Summer of 1987. In 1987-88 he settled down at centre back, being a member of the F.A.Youth Cup winning team as well as winning Northern Ireland Youth Caps. Hannigan turned professional in March 1989. However, with a surplus of centre backs on the club's books, he was released from his contract in June 1990, after he had spent a loan period with Torquay United. Al-James later played for Marlow, Harlow, Harwich, Barnet and Enfield.

	Games	Goals
Friendly Matches	18	1
Football Combination	21	0
South East Counties League	55	2
Youth Cup	11	1
Other Youth Cups	3	0
Youth Tours	8	1
Total	**116**	**5**

Honours:
Northern Ireland Youth Caps
F.A.Youth Cup Winners Medal 1987-88
Football Combination Championship Medal
1989-90

HAMMOND, Nicky 1983-86

Birth Place: Hornchurch, Essex
Date of Birth: 7th September 1967

☛ Nicky had played for Havering District side at Under 15 level and for Essex County before becoming the regular youth team goalkeeper at the end of the 1982-83 season. This after fellow youth team keeper, Kenny Veysey, was injured. He turned professional in July 1985 and gained experience whilst spending a loan period with Bristol Rovers in August 1986. With a surplus of fine goalkeepers on the books, Hammond was given a free transfer in July 1987 when he joined Swindon Town and served them well for eight seasons before joining Plymouth in the Summer of 1995.

	Games	Goals
Friendly Matches	4	0
Football Combination	10	0
South East Counties League	61	0
Youth Cup	13	0
Other Youth Cups	21	0
Youth Tours	15	0
Total	**124**	**0**

Honours:
Southern Junior Floodlight Cup Winners
Medal 1983-84
Southern Junior Floodlight Cup Finalists
Medal 1985-86
2 South East Counties League Cup Finalists
Medals 1984-85, 1985-86

HARPER, Lee 1994

Birth Place: Chelsea, London
Date of Birth: 30th October 1971

☛ Lee was playing for Eltham Town before joining Sittingbourne in August 1993. Lee signed for Arsenal in June 1994 for £150,000 and in his one season so far at Highbury he has been a regular fixture in the Combination side although he did sit on the bench in several League games.

	Games	Goals
Friendly Matches	6	0
Tours	1	0
Football Combination	26	0
Total	**33**	**0**

HARTFIELD, Charlie 1988-91

Birth Place: Lambeth, London
Date of Birth: 4th September 1971

☛ Charles had made his name in the South London side that won the England Schools Trophy in 1987, he also turned out for London Schools, before turning professional

in September 1989. Charlie had joined Arsenal as a trainee in July 1988, after he had gained England Under 17 Honours (four caps). In his time at the club he played either full back or midfield for the Youth and reserve sides and was granted a free transfer in August 1990 when Dave Bassett saw his potential and signed him for Sheffield United.

	Games	Goals
Friendly Matches	14	3
Football Combination	27	2
South East Counties League	41	10
Youth Cup	8	0
Other Youth Cups	6	0
Youth Tours	5	0
Total	**101**	**15**

Honours:
4 England Youth Caps.

HARTSON, John 1995

Birth Place: Swansea, Wales
Date of Birth: 5th April 1975

☛ John was a trainee at Luton Town, signing professional forms for them in December 1992. In two years at Kenilworth Road, John, still only nineteen, had figured in over fifty League games scoring eleven times as well as winning four Welsh Under 21 Caps. Although Hartson was on the wanted list of several premiership clubs, it surprised most people at Highbury when George Graham paid £2.5 million for his services in January 1995. What people were asking was, why had George Graham questioned paying large fees for established players, yet was prepared to pay this vast amount for a nineteen year old unknown? However, soon after John had made his Arsenal League debut versus Everton at Highbury, 14th January 1995, it soon became apparent that, in John Hartson, Arsenal had a throw back from a different era as far as the centre forward position goes and in many Arsenal supporters eyes, who were old enough to remember, he is a combination of John Radford and Ray Kennedy. Having Kennedy's power and strength, the great ability to shield and hold up the ball and his ability to make space for others, and Radford's heading ability and deft touches when laying the ball off. His striking ability makes John potentially, one of the big names of the future. It was John's goal in the Final of the European Cup Winners Cup which gave hope to every Arsenal supporter of Gunners retaining that trophy. A full Welsh international, John looks to have a fine future in the game if he can improve his suspect disciplinary record.

	Games	Goals
League	15	7
Europe	5	1
Other First Team Games	2	0
Tours	1	0
Total	**23**	**8**

Honours:
(WITH LUTON AND ARSENAL)
5 Welsh Under 21 Caps
(WITH ARSENAL)
3 Welsh Caps
European Cup Winners Cup Finalists Medal
1994-95
European Super Cup Finalists Medal   1995

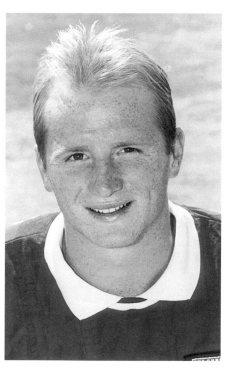

John Hartson

HAYES, Martin   1981-90

Birth Place: Walthamstow, London
Date of Birth: 21st March 1966

☞ Martin was playing for Waltham Forest and Essex Schoolboys when joining Arsenal as an apprentice in June 1982, after previously signing amateur forms in 1981. In 1982-83, when still only sixteen, he went through the ranks from youth team football to the reserves and was named as substitute in the last game of the season at Aston Villa. He was also invited to join the England Under-seventeen squad in training. In November 1983 he turned professional and in that season Martin developed into a first class striker when playing all along the front line. He continued his progress in 1984-85 for the reserve side before making his Arsenal league debut in a home fixture against Oxford United on 16th November 1985 and in that first season of first team

football he played in eleven games when initially deputising for Graham Rix. In 1986-87, Martin finished as the first team leading goal scorer with twenty-four goals, twelve of these being penalties (the most ever converted in one season by an Arsenal player). The youngster, who had nearly joined Huddersfield Town for £20,000, was now the talk of Highbury. He gained three England Under-Twenty-One Caps and played a significant role when Arsenal beat Liverpool in the 1987 Littlewoods Cup Final. In 1987-88, Martin's goalscoring ability took a dramatic turn for the worse when he scored just one league goal in twenty-seven appearances and although he scored the opening goal in the 1988 Littlewoods Cup Final against Luton Town, people could tell that his confidence was sapped when he contrived to hit a post from less than one foot out, in the same game, which would have undoubtedly settled the issue in Arsenal's favour. At this stage, Martin's self belief had reached an all time low and although he featured in seventeen league games (fourteen as substitute) in the 1988-89 League Championship winning season, he was now regarded as just a member of the first team squad. In 1989-90, with the forward line virtually picking itself, he played in only twelve league games before accepting that his Arsenal career was over and in May 1990, Hayes was transferred to Glasgow Celtic for £650,000. However, this move proved to be a disaster for both club and player when playing in only seven league games which cost the club nearly £100,000 for each appearance. Martin spent a loan period with Wimbledon in February 1992 before joining Swansea City on a free transfer in January 1993. Hayes spent two and a half years at Vetch Field before, at the age of twenty-nine, he was given a free transfer in June 1995, and joined Dover Athletic.

1985-1995

	Games	Goals
League	102	26
F.A. Cup	9	3
League Cup	21	5
Other First Team Matches	6	0
Friendly Matches	71	31
Tours	9	2
Football Combination	165	69
South East Counties League	59	28
Youth Cup	9	5
Other Youth Cups	17	7
Youth Tours	4	2
Total	**472**	**178**

Honours:
(WITH ARSENAL)
3 England Under-Twenty-One Caps
League Championship Medals   1988-89
Football League Cup Winners Medal 1986-87
Football League Cup Finalists Medal 1987-88
Wembley International Tournament Winners
Medal   1988
Makita Tournament Winners Medals   1989
2 Football Combination Championship
Medals   1983-84, 1989-90
Southern Junior Floodlight Cup Winners
Medal   1983-84
(WITH SWANSEA CITY)
Autoglass Trophy Winners Medal   1993-94

Martin Hayes

HOWELL, Jamie — 1993

Birth Place: Worthing, Sussex
Date of Birth: 19th February 1977

☛ Jamie was England's Under Fifteen and Under Sixteen captain when joining Arsenal as a trainee from the F.A. School of Excellence in the summer of 1993. A dynamo of a midfield player who broke into the Football Combination side at the back end of 1994-95, after being an important member of the F.A. Youth Cup winning side in 1993-94. Howell turned professional in the summer of 1995

	Games	Goals
Friendly Matches	13	0
Football Combination	5	0
South East Counties League	46	9
Youth Cup	10	1
Other Youth Cups	14	3
Youth Tours	6	1
Total	**94**	**14**

Honours:
England Under-Fifteen and Under-Sixteen
   International Honours
F.A. Youth Cup Winners Medal   1993-94
Southern Junior Floodlight Cup Finalists
   Medal   1994-95
2 England Youth Caps

HOYLE, Colin — 1988-90

Birth Place: Derby
Date of Birth: 15th January 1972

☛ Colin was spotted by Arsenal scouts when playing for the Derbyshire County Schools side and became a trainee during the Summer of 1988, turning professional in January 1990. He spent only two seasons at Highbury winning an England Youth Cap before being granted a free transfer in June 1990 when he joined Barnsley, after he had been on loan to Chesterfield.

	Games	Goals
Friendly Matches	10	6
Football Combination	2	1
South East Counties League	45	15
Youth Cup	6	4
Other Youth Cups	5	3
Youth Tours	3	0
Total	**71**	**29**

Honours:
1 England Youth Cap.

HEANEY, Neil — 1988-94

Birth Place: Middlesbrough, Cleveland
Date of Birth: 3rd November 1971

☛ Neil, a winger who can play on either flank, was playing for Teesside Schoolboys when signing associated schoolboy forms for Arsenal in January 1987 and achieved the remarkable record of being in the club's F.A. Youth Cup Winning side in 1987-88 versus Doncaster Rovers, when still only a schoolboy. two months later in July 1988 he signed as a trainee. In 1988-89 Neil was a regular in the South East Counties League side when gaining three England Youth Caps. Neil turned professional in November 1989, before, in 1990-91, he spent a loan period with Hartlepool United. During the 1991-92 season he enjoyed a further loan experience with Cambridge United, returning to Highbury, he made his Arsenal League debut as substitute at Bramall Lane versus Sheffield United, 18th April 1992. Neil's potential was so vast that after that one League appearance he was capped four times by England Under 21. The 1992-93 season saw Heaney playing in five League games and his future at the club looked quite bright when showing considerable pace, subtle skills and brilliance at crossing the ball. However, in 1993-94, after playing in just one further League game, George Graham accepted a cheque for £300.000 from Southampton for his signature in March 1994. Many thought, at the time, that this was shrewd business, but many Arsenal supporters, having since seen Heaney in action for Saints will now have their doubts.

	Games	Goals
League	7	0
League Cup	1	0
Friendly Matches	27	5
Tours	1	0
Football Combination	115	27
South East Counties League	46	16
Youth Cup	10	1
Other Youth Cups	14	4
Youth Tours	9	0
Total	**230**	**53**

Honours:
4 England Under 21 Caps
3 England Youth Caps
F.A. Youth Cup Winners Medal   1987-88
Football Combination Championship Medal
                                 1989-90
Southern Junior Floodlight Cup Finalists
   Medal   1989-90

HELDER, Glenn — 1995

Birth Place: Leiden, Holland
Date of Birth: 28th October, 1968

☛ Glenn Helder will always be remembered as George Graham's last signing for the club, when joining Arsenal for £2.3 million in February 1995. Glenn, a natural left winger, possesses pace which he uses to great effect when bamboozling opposing full backs with his glittering array of subtle skills and movements which can only be compared to the very top class of international footballers. A product of the Ajax youth system, because of the great amount of talent on the club's books, he was forced to join Sparta Rotterdam to get any chance of first team football in 1989. Glenn spent four seasons in a very ordinary Rotterdam side before joining Vitesse in a £250,000 transfer in 1993 and helped the club to fourth position in the Dutch League in 1993-94. In 1994-95 he was drew the attention of the Dutch international management, winning his first cap against France. In only thirteen league appearances for the club, of which his Arsenal league debut was against Nott'm Forest at Highbury on 21st February 1995, he became a firm favourite with the massed Arsenal legions and much is expected of him in the future.

	Games	Goals
League	13	0
Tours	2	0
Total	**15**	**0**

Honours:
1 Holland International Cap

Glenn Helder

HILL, Colin — 1980-86

Birth Place: Uxbridge, Middlesex
Date of Birth: 12th November 1963

☛ Colin had played for Middlesex Schoolboys and was a prolific goal scorer in Junior Football with Hillingdon when signing Associated Schoolboy forms for Arsenal in December 1977. A champion sprinter and javelin thrower as a schoolboy, he signed amateur forms in 1979, becoming an apprentice in June 1980 before finally turning professional in July 1981. From striker, he turned defender and became a more than capable full or centre back. Colin graduated from the Junior and reserve ranks to make his Arsenal League debut at Carrow Road versus Norwich City, 20th April 1983, playing in the last seven League games of that season. By far Colin's best season at Highbury was in 1983-84, when he played in thirty seven League games (mostly at right back). However, after the signing of Viv Anderson, Colin's last two seasons at the club were spent permanently playing combination football and he was given a free transfer in the close season of 1986 when he joined CS Maritimo of Madeira who play in the Portuguese League. Colin spent fifteen months there before returning to England to play for Colchester United in October 1987. His fine form for the Essex club over two seasons earned him considerable recognition and Dave Bassett, the Sheffield United manager, paid £85,000 for his signature in August 1989. In his first season at Bramall Lane he helped the club to promotion to Division One and won the first of his eight Northern Ireland Caps when playing against Norway in March 1990. Colin was transferred to Leicester City (after being on loan) in July 1992 for £200,000 and has since assisted them to three Second Division play offs. Like David Platt, Colin Hill is a fine example of how you can resurrect your career even when having the misfortune of being discarded as a youngster.

Colin Hill

	Games	Goals
League	46	1
F.A.Cup	1	0
League Cup	4	0
Friendly Matches	57	4
Tours	6	0
Football Combination	147	12
South East Counties League	33	12
Youth Cup	7	1
Other Youth Cups	6	1
Youth Tours	2	0
Total	**309**	**31**

Honours:
(WITH LEICESTER & SHEFFIELD UNITED)
8 Northern Ireland Caps

HILLIER, David   1986

Birth Place: Blackheath, Greater London
Date of Birth: 18th December 1969

David signed Associated Schoolboy forms for Arsenal in January 1984 after he had attended two England Schoolboy Trials and played for South East England. In July 1986 he became a trainee, turning professional in February 1988. In 1987-88, David was captain of the Arsenal Youth Team which won the F.A.Youth Cup versus Doncaster Rovers. In 1989-90 he was a member of the Football Combination Championship winning side although during this period and the season before, he was plagued with injuries. Hillier, a strong tackler with plenty of stamina and a whole hearted approach to the game, made his first team debut in a League Cup tie at Chester in September 1990, making his League debut a few days later when coming on as a substitute versus Leeds United at Elland Road, 29th September, 1990. In his first season of League Football, 1990-91, David helped the club to the League Championship when appearing in sixteen League fixtures as well as gaining an England Under 21 Cap. In the following season, 1991-92, he was out injured for the first three months before returning and playing in twenty six League games when helping Arsenal in their magnificent run at the end of the season. David had played in thirty League games in 1992-93 but was extremely unfortunate when receiving a serious leg injury at Middlesbrough in April 1993, which resulted in him missing both the Coca Cola and F.A.Cup Finals. In 1993-94, David was again ill fated when, although being a steady member of the side, injury again dealt David another tragic blow, causing him to miss the 1994 European Cup Winners Cup Final versus Parma. However, fortune was on his side in 1994-95, when although having played in only nine League Fixtures, he was chosen by Stuart Houston to feature in the 1995 Cup Winners Cup Final versus Real

Zaragoza. With new manager Bruce Rioch at the helm David is one of several players whose careers are in question. Off field activities have given further cause for concern.

	Games	Goals
League	97	2
F.A.Cup	15	0
League Cup	13	0
Europe	7	0
Other First Team Games	3	0
Friendly Matches	49	10
Tours	9	2
Football Combination	111	4
South East Counties League	42	7
Youth Cup	9	2
Other Youth Cups	5	0
Youth Tours	6	1
Total	**366**	**28**

Honours:
1 England Under Twenty One Cap
League Championship Medal   1990-91
European Cup Winners Cup Finalists Medal
                                                        1994-95
European Super Cup Finalists Medal   1995
F.A.Charity Shield Winners Medal   1991
Makita Tournament Trophy Winners Medal
                                                        1994
Makita Tournament Trophy Finalists Medal
                                                        1991
F.A. Youth Cup winners Medal   1987-88
Football Combination Championship Medal
                                                        1989-90

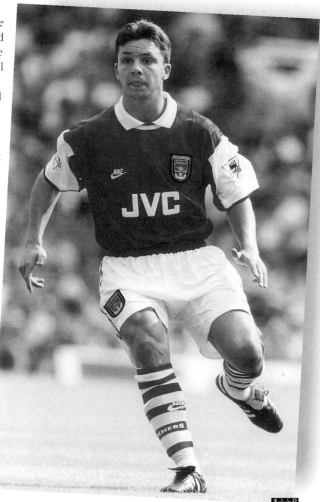

HUGHES, Stephen 1993

Birth Place: Wokingham, Berkshire
Date of Birth: 18th September 1976

☞ Stephen had represented Berkshire and England Under 15 before joining Arsenal as a trainee in the Summer of 1993. In the previous season, 1992-93, he had played in the Youth side while still a schoolboy. In 1993-94 he was a member of the club's F.A.Youth Cup winning team versus Millwall. At the beginning of the 1994-95 season his promising displays from midfield prompted George Graham in handing Stephen his League debut versus Aston Villa at Highbury on Boxing Day 1994.

	Games	Goals
League	1	0
Friendly Matches	14	0
Tours	3	0
Football Combination	17	1
South East Counties League	45	10
Youth Cup	11	3
Other Youth Cups	13	1
Youth Tours	2	0
Total	**106**	**15**

Honours:
6 England Youth Caps
England Schoolboy International
F.A.Youth Cup Winners Medal 1993-94
Southern Junior Floodlight Cup Finalist
  Medal 1994-95

Steve Hughes

IMBER, Noel 1993

Birth Place: Harrow, Middlesex
Date of Birth: 4th December 1976

☞ Noel, a young goalkeeper, was playing for Harrow District side when he became an Arsenal trainee during the summer of 1993. Imber produced many vital saves when helping Arsenal's youth side win the F.A. Youth Cup in 1993-94 against Millwall, resulting in him signing professional with the club in the close season of 1995.

	Games	Goals
Friendly Matches	6	0
Football Combination	5	0
South East Counties League	54	0
Youth Cup	12	0
Other Youth Cups	13	0
Youth Tours	5	0
Total	**95**	**0**

Honours:
F.A. Youth Cup Winners Medal 1993-94
Southern Junior Floodlight Cup Finalists
  Medal 1994-95

ISAACS, Tony 1983-85

Birth Place: Brixton, London

☞ Tony Isaacs joined Arsenal on a Youth Opportunities Scheme at the end of the 1982-83 season, making steady progress during 1983-84 when becoming a regular in the South East Counties League side. Unfortunately, he cracked a fibula which kept him out of action for more than two months. He turned professional during the Summer of 1984. Tony had previously played for Wandsworth and London Schoolboys. However, during his term at Highbury he was very unlucky with injuries and was released on a free transfer during the Summer of 1985. He later played for Dartford.

	Games	Goals
Friendly Matches	3	0
Football Combination	22	0
South East Counties	38	3
Youth Cup	3	1
Other Youth Cups	11	1
Total	**77**	**5**

Honours:
Southern Junior Floodlight Cup
  Winners Medal 1983-84

JENNINGS, Pat MBE, OBE 1977-85

Birth Place: Newry, Northern Ireland
Date of Birth: 12th June 1945

☞ Pat Jennings' career spanned twenty-three seasons of which twenty-one had been played in the First Division. The young lad who left Irish shores in May 1963, won virtually every honour as well as breaking many records during his fabulous career. He joined Watford in May 1963 and spent thirteen months at Vicarage Road, winning several youth caps as well as the first of his 119 Irish caps. He was transferred to Tottenham for £27,500 in June 1964 as a replacement for the ageing Bill Brown. His career with Spurs spanned thirteen years, during which time he won F.A. Cup, League Cup and UEFA Cup Winners Medals. He broke Tottenham's league appearance record (four hundred and seventy-two), (later to be bettered by Steve Perryman) and became Spurs' most capped international (sixty-eight caps). Pat was the first player to win both the Football Writers' and PFA Footballer of the Year awards. He was surprisingly transferred to Arsenal for £40,000 in August 1977 and remained first choice keeper for eight seasons (1977-84). He played a major role in enabling Arsenal to appear in three consecutive F.A. Cup Finals in the years 1978-80. When Jennings won his one hundredth Northern Ireland cap against Austria in September 1983, he also broke several other records which included:
1) The first Northern Ireland player to win one hundred international caps.
2) The first British and only the third goalkeeper in world football history to win one hundred international caps.
3) Only the fourth British player ever, behind Wright, Charlton and Moore, to win one hundred international caps.
4) Became only the fourteenth player in the history of international football to win one hundred caps.
5) His twenty-one year international career has only been bettered by Stanley Matthews and Billy Meredith.
Further notable achievements include:
1) First player in Football League history to have played in one thousand first-class competitive matches (versus West Bromwich Albion in February 1983).
2) First goalkeeper and only the twelfth player in league history to play in as many as seven hundred league matches.
3) Helped Northern Ireland to the World Cup Finals in 1982.
4) Was awarded the MBE in 1981 and OBE in 1987.
5) His one hundred and nineteen caps was a world record until beaten by Peter Shilton. Pat Jennings is a football legend.

1985-1995

Pat now divides his time between coaching the goalkeepers at White Hart Lane and making personal appearances.

	Games	Goals
League	237	0
F.A. Cup	38	0
League Cup	32	0
UEFA Cup	10	0
European Cup Winners Cup	9	0
Charity Shield	1	0
Friendly Matches	26	0
Tours	27	0
Football Combination	35	0
Total	**415**	**0**

Honours:
(WITH ARSENAL & TOTTENHAM)
119 Irish Caps
1 Irish Under-Twenty-three cap
8 Irish Youth Caps
(WITH TOTTENHAM)
F.A. Cup Winners Medal   1966-67
2 Football League Cup Winners Medal
                    1970-71, 1972-73
U.E.F.A. Cup Winners Medal   1971-72
U.E.F.A. Cup Finalists Medal   1973-74
Footballer of the Year   1972-73
P.F.A. Footballer of the Year   1975-76
F.A. Charity Shield Winners Medal 1967-68
2 Rothmans Golden Boot Awards
                    1973-74, 1974-75
2 First Division P.F.A. Awards
                    1973-74, 1974-75
(WITH ARSENAL)
F.A. Cup Winners Medal   1978-79
2 F.A. Cup Finalists Medals
                    1977-78, 1979-80
European Cup Winners Cup Finalists
  Medal   1979-80
F.A. Charity Shield Finalists Medal
                                1979-80

Pat Jennings

JENSEN, John   1992

Birth Place: Copenhagen, Denmark
Date of Birth: 3rd May 1965

John began his footballing career with Bronby in the early 1980's and during this period with the club he won the first of his seventy two Danish Caps as well as helping them to the League Championship in 1986-87 and to the Cup Final in the same season. Jensen then joined the German club Hamburg S.V. soon after the European Championships of 1988. He spent two seasons in the Bundesliga before returning to Bronby in 1990. Although John was known in European Footballing circles, he rose to world wide fame when scoring a stunning goal in the 1992 European Championship Final for Denmark versus Germany. This performance attracted Arsenal's attention and manager George Graham paid £1.1 million for his services in August 1992. However, poor John has had a shadow cast over him as it was his transfer which caused 'The George Graham allegations' to be probed. In his first season at Highbury after making his Arsenal League debut on the opening day of the season versus Norwich City at Highbury, he struggled at first to make any sort of impact within the English game and, although a great tackler with a work rate second to none, he found the pace of the Premier League too frenzied. John missed the Coca Cola Cup Final 1993 v. Sheffield Wednesday but bounced back to put in two sterling performances in the F.A.Cup Final against the same opposition two months later. In 1993-94, he was of paramount importance to the side when he received a ghastly tackle in an international match versus Hungary, which resulted in him missing this European Cup Winners Cup Final v. Parma (although along with Ian Wright he was later granted a medal). In 1994-95, although playing in twenty four League games he had to endure the pain of missing yet another European Final when not selected by caretaker boss Stewart Houston. At this time anyone who knew anything about football knew that John had an extremely potent shot, but had inexplicably failed to score in nearly 100 matches. This brought about many mickey-taking actions, such as, supporters high in the executive boxes at the clock end of the ground ducking every time John shot. However, the magical moment arrived when on the last day of 1994, in his ninety eighth first team game for the club, he eventually scored a magnificent curling shot past the startled Roberts, in the Queens Park Rangers goal. The euphoria that greeted this had not been heard or seen at Highbury for an average League game for many years (if at all). Without doubt, in his short period at Highbury, John Jensen has become a cult figure for reasons good and bad. However, as

this is being written, John's career with Arsenal could be in jeopardy with the appointment of new manager Bruce Rioch.

	Games	Goals
League	83	1
F.A.Cup	7	0
League Cup	10	0
Europe	13	0
Other First Team Games	4	0
Friendly Matches	10	0
Tours	10	0
Football Combination	6	0
Total	**143**	**1**

John Jenson

Honours:
(WITH DENMARK)
European Nations Championship Medal 1992
(WITH BRONBY AND ARSENAL)
72 Danish Caps
(WITH BRONBY)
Danish League Championship Medal 1986-87
Danish Cup Finalists Medal   1986-87
(WITH ARSENAL)
F.A.Cup Winners Medal   1992-93
European Cup Winners cup Winners Medal
                                     1993-94
F.A.Charity Shield Finalists Medal   1993
European Super Cup Finalists Medal   1995
Makita Tournament Trophy Winners Medal
                                     1994

JONSSON, Siggi   1989-92

Birth Place: Akranes, Iceland
Date of Birth: 27th September 1966

'Siggi' had started his playing career with his home town club I.A.Akranes before moving to Sheffield Wednesday in February 1985. He spent over four years at Hillsborough which included a loan spell at Barnsley. Jonsson, an Icelandic International, joined Arsenal in July 1989 after a tribunal had set his value at £475,000. 'Siggi' made

his Arsenal League debut at Highbury versus Manchester City 14th October 1989. However, in twenty seven months at Highbury, due to injury and the fierce competition in midfield, he played in only seven League games for the club before a serious back injury forced him to retire from football in January 1992.

	Games	Goals
League	7	1
F.A.Cup	1	0
League Cup	1	0
Friendly Matches	21	2
Football Combination	31	4
Total	**61**	**7**

Honours:
21 Iceland International Caps

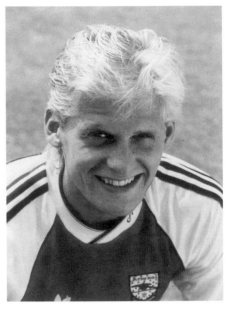

Siggi Jonsson

JOSEPH, Matthew   1989-92

Birth Place: Bethnal Green, London
Date of Birth: 30th September 1972

Matthew Joseph had played for Islington/Camden Schoolboys as well as for Inner London when joining the F.A.School of Excellence at Lillishall, joining Arsenal as a trainee in July 1989, turning professional two summers later. A fine utility player, he appeared for the club in midfield, on the right wing and at right back. This ability gaining him three England Youth Caps and although he was a successful member of the Youth Team in 1990-91, with stiff competition for the reserve full back place (Dixon and Winterburn), Matthew was surprisingly given a free transfer in June 1992 when he joined Gillingham. His career was seemingly going nowhere when Cambridge United signed him at the start of the 1993-94 season but over the last two seasons he has become one of the most sought after full backs in the lower Leagues.

	Games	Goals
Friendly Matches	20	2
Football Combination	22	3
South East Counties League	45	3
Youth Cup	7	0
Other Youth Cups	21	1
Youth Tours	8	1
Total	**123**	**10**

Honours:
England Schoolboy International
3 England Youth Caps
South East Counties League Championship
   Medal   1990-91
Southern Junior Floodlight Cup Winners
   Medal   1990-91
Southern Junior Floodlight Cup Finalists
   Medal   1989-90

KEOWN, Martin   1982-86 and 1993

Birth Place: Oxford
Date of Birth: 24th July 1966

☛ Martin had played for Oxford and Oxfordshire schoolboys when joining Arsenal as an associated schoolboy in October 1980, becoming an apprentice in June 1982 and turning professional in February 1984. In seasons 1982-83 and 1983-84 Martin progressed from the junior ranks, and won four England Youth Caps, stepping up to the reserve side in the latter season. In 1984-85, he gained experience while on loan to Brighton and returned to Highbury to make his Arsenal league debut at the Hawthorns versus West Bromwich Albion on 23rd November, 1985. Martin kept his place (when taking over from Tommy Caton) for the remainder of that season, appearing twenty-two times in the league side. However, after a dispute concerning a new contract, he was transferred to Aston Villa for £125,000 in July 1986. Keown spent just over three years at Villa Park, playing in nearly one hundred and fifty first team games and winning eight England Under-21 Caps. In August 1989, he was transferred to Everton for £750,000 and whilst at Goodison Park won the first of his eleven England caps against France in 1991-92. Surprisingly, in February 1993, Martin became the first player in nearly seventy years to "rejoin Arsenal," George Graham paying £2 million to reclaim his services. Martin played in sixteen of the club's last seventeen league games but missed out in playing in both the 1993 Coca Cola and F.A. Cup Finals when being cup-tied. He also added two more England caps to his collection. In 1993-94, Keown played in thirty-three league games but was ruled out with injury when missing the European Cup Winners Cup Final against Parma. He was again an important member

of the squad in 1994-95, when helping Arsenal to reach their successive European Cup Winners Cup Final and without doubt played his finest for the club in the semi-final victory against Sampdoria. Keown has now developed into a first class experienced centre back. He is excellent in the air, distributes the ball with economic ease and has fine pace, although at times he puts in unnecessary tackles, risking injury. Martin's enthusiasm and love of Arsenal Football Club is still obviously evident.

	Games	Goals
League	102	1
F.A. Cup	10	0
League Cup	8	0
Europe	12	0
Other First Team Matches	2	0
Friendly Matches	36	1
Tours	3	0
Football Combination	74	2
South East Counties League	46	6
Youth Cup	11	0
Other Youth Cups	7	0
Youth Tours	2	0
Total	**313**	**10**

Honours:
(WITH ARSENAL)
   2 England Caps
      4 England Youth Caps
         European Cup Winners Cup
         Finalists Medal   1994-95
         F.A. Charity Shield Finalists Medal
                              1993
         European Super Cup Finalists Medal
                              1995
         Football Combination Championship
         Medal   1983-84
         Southern Junior Floodlight Cup
         Winners Medal   1983-84
  (WITH ASTON VILLA)
  8 England Under-21 caps
  (WITH EVERTON)
  9 England Caps
  1 England 'B' Cap

Martin Keown

KIRBY, Ryan   1991-94

Birth Place: Redbridge, London
Date of Birth: 6th September 1974

☛ Ryan was originally a mid-fielder when joining Arsenal as a trainee during the Summer of 1991. Kirby, who represented Essex Schoolboys, then moved to the right back position where he produced many fine displays for the Youth Team before turning professional in July 1993. Like so many other young full backs who had been on the club's books during the last eight years Ryan's chances of first team football were slim and in June 1994 he was granted a free transfer when he joined Doncaster Rovers. In 1994-95 Ryan was one of many Rover's players who came under scrutiny from the Premier League Clubs. A fine future may still lie ahead.

	Games	Goals
Friendly Matches	16	1
Football Combination	31	0
South East Counties League	50	2
Youth Cup	5	1
Other Youth Cups	22	0
Youth Tours	3	0
Total	**127**	**4**

Honours:
2 Southern Junior Floodlight Cup Finalists
  Medals   1991-92, 1992-93

KIWOMYA, Chris   1995

Birth Place: Huddersfield, Yorkshire
Date of Birth: 2nd December 1969

☛ Chris joined Ipswich Town as a trainee in July 1986, turning professional in March 1987. In his seven seasons at Portman Road, he fluctuated from being as good as any striker/winger in the country to mediocrity. He had played in over two hundred and fifty first team games for Ipswich, scoring nearly sixty goals and helping them win the Second Division Championship in 1991-92, and although he was the club's leading League goal scorer for three consecutive seasons 1990-93, his all round confidence and ability in front of goal seemed to have nose dived when George Graham surprisingly paid £1.25 million (tribunal) to resurrect his career in January 1995. On the same day, Graham had also acquired John Hartson. This meant that he would have to permutate two strikers from Campbell, Dickov, Hartson, Kiwomya, Smith and Wright. He made his Arsenal League debut in the same game as Hartson at Highbury versus Everton, 14th January, 1995 and by the end of the season he had done reasonably well when scoring three times in fourteen League appearances. Kiwomya's brother, Andrew also played League Football.

	Games	Goals
League	14	3
Europe	3	0
Tours	3	2
Football Combination	5	1
Total	**25**	**6**

Honours:
(WITH IPSWICH)
Second Division Championship Medal
               1991-92
(WITH ARSENAL)
European Cup Winners Cup Finalists Medal
               1994-95

Chris Kiwomya

LEE, Justin   1990-93

Birth Place: Abingdon, Oxfordshire
Date of Birth: 19th September 1973

☛ Justin had played for Oxfordshire Schoolboys and England Under 15's as well as being a guest player on the 1990 F.A.School of Excellence Tour to Italy. He had already played for the club when signing as a trainee in 1990. Justin, who could play either left back or in a midfield role, skippered Arsenal's Youth Team in 1991-92, becoming a regular in the combination side in 1992-93. Lee was released by the club in the Summer of 1993.

	Games	Goals
Friendly Matches	19	0
Football Combination	27	0
South East Counties League	41	1
Youth Cup	3	1
Other Youth Cups	16	2
Youth Tours	5	0
Total	111	4

Honours:
England Under 15 International
South East Counties League Championship
  Medal   1990-91
Southern Junior Floodlight Cup Winners
  Medal   1990-91
Southern Junior Floodlight Cup Finalists
  Medal   1991-92

LEE, Ray   1987-90

Birth Place: Bristol, Avon
Date of Birth: 19th September 1970

☛ Ray was a product of the Avon County Schools side when joining Arsenal as a trainee during the Summer of 1987 (he had already appeared for the club as a school-boy). A right winger/midfield player, Lee was a member of the 1987-88 F.A.Youth Cup Winning side, later graduating into the combination team after he had turned professional in October 1988. However, his promising career never blossomed and his contract was cancelled when joining Scarborough.

	Games	Goals
Friendly Matches	18	1
Football Combination	37	4
South East Counties League	51	10
Youth Cup	8	1
Other Youth Cups	5	0
Youth Tours	9	1
Total	**128**	**17**

Honours:
F.A.Youth Cup Winners Medal   1987-88
Football Combination Championship Medal
               1989-90

LEE, Terry   1981-85

Birth Place: London
Date of Birth: 15 July 1965

☛ Terry Lee had already played in twelve Youth team games at the end of the 1980-81 season before joining Arsenal as an apprentice in July 1981. He became a regular in Arsenal's reserve side during his first full season (1981-82) keeping his place the following season after turning professional in September 1982. Terry toured Indonesia with the first team squad at the end of the 1982-83 season. In 1983-84 Terry won three

England Youth Caps and was a regular in Arsenal's reserve side between 1983-85, before being released in that summer. He later had spells in Finland with Sepsi 78 and HJK Helsinki as well as playing for Dartford, Gravesend and Tooting and Mitcham. His brother, Trevor Lee, played for several League clubs including Millwall and Colchester.

	Games	Goals
Friendly Matches	20	8
Tours	3	1
Football Combination	127	32
South East Counties League	37	9
Youth Cup	4	1
Other Youth Cups	10	2
Youth Tours	2	1
Total	**203**	**54**

Honours:
3 England Youth Caps
Football Combination Championship Medal
1983-84

LIMPAR, Anders   1990-94

Birth Place: Solna, Sweden
Date of Birth: 24th September 1965

➤Anders began his career playing in Sweden for Brommapojk and Orgryte before joining Young Boys of Switzerland in 1988-89. Anders tried his luck in Italian football with Cremonese in 1989-90, joining Arsenal for £1 million in July 1990. Although many Arsenal supporters had heard of the name Anders Limpar, many would never have guessed the delights that he would conjure up during that following Championship campaign. The buzz of excitement and anticipation when Anders received the ball had not been seen or heard at Highbury since the days of Liam Brady. Arsenal, with their unruffled professionalism and their machine like efficiency, were now a team with a new dimension, for in Limpar they had a totally unknown quantity tearing defences apart with his exhilarating runs and sparkling array of skills. Add his speed of thought, his ability to create openings and deadly shooting capabilities and you had, on his day, the almost perfect wing forward. On the debit side, at times he seemed to drift in and out of matches and sometimes his fans would wonder if he was actually on the field of play. Also in that initial season at the club (although he was heavily tackled on many occasions) Anders did tend to overreact and some of his dramatic falls in the penalty area when looking for a decision in his favour made Klinnsman's appeals look justified by comparison. Looking back at that 1990-91 season Anders scored eleven times in thirty four League appearances, many of which were spectacular. Cast your mind back to the

two strikes at Elland Road versus Leeds, two goals in the last minute at Coventry City, the cheeky effort which was the decider in the infamous game at Old Trafford versus Manchester United and the never to be forgotten hat-trick he scored in the 6-1 home defeat of Coventry City, in the last game of the season. In 1991-92 Limpar seemed to be waging a running battle with manager George Graham (over his get out clause to play for his country Sweden). He did, however, play in twenty nine League games scoring four goals one of which is described by many as the greatest goal ever seen at Highbury when, from literally the half way line, he chipped a fifty yard shot over the bemused Mike Hooper in the Liverpool goal. In 1992-93 Limpar figured in only twenty three League games when injuries forced him to miss both the F.A. and Coca Cola Cup Finals. However, with George Graham not seemingly over enthusiastic with any player who possessed an abundance of skill (remember Marwood, Rocastle, Nicholas etc.) George decided to sell Anders to Everton for £1.6 million in March 1994. The sales of the aforementioned plus Michael Thomas, were hard enough to take, but the sale of Limpar (and at that price) caused considerable heartache at Highbury. The question being asked was, "would you rather go to Highbury and watch a stereotype outfit dig out a 1-0 win or would you rather see an open ended 3-3 draw where you could appreciate the

scintillating delights of such players as Anders and Rocky?" Most, I think, would prefer the latter. In his one full season at Goodison Park, the Swedish International with fifty two caps was inspirational in their 1995 F.A.Cup Final victory over Manchester United.

	Games	Goals
League	96	17
F.A.Cup	7	2
League Cup	9	0
Europe	3	1
Other First Team Games	5	1
Friendly Matches	10	3
Tours	9	3
Football Combination	17	4
Total	**156**	**31**

Honours:
52 Swedish Caps
1 Football League Cap
League Championship Medal   1990-91
F.A.Charity Shield Finalists Medal   1993
2 Makita Tournament Finalists Medal
1990, 1991
(WITH EVERTON)
F.A.Cup Winners Medal   1994-95

Anders Limpar

LINIGHAN, Andy — 1990

Birth Place: Hartlepool, Cleveland
Date of Birth: 18th June 1962

☛ Andy comes from a footballing family, his father, Brian played for Lincoln and Darlington in the 1950's, his twin brothers, Brian and John have been on the books of Sheffield Wednesday and his older brother, David, has appeared for Hartlepool, Shrewsbury and Ipswich Town. Andy was playing Junior football with Smiths Dock before joining Hartlepool United in September 1980, spending the best part of four years at the club before Leeds United secured his services for £200,000 in May 1984. In his twenty months at Elland Road he was virtually everpresent before surprisingly being transferred to Oldham Athletic in January 1986 for £65,000. It was during this part of his career that his six foot three inch frame seemed to dominate the penalty area, with his thoughtful reading of the game and his powerful heading ability. Norwich City, looking for a replacement for Steve Bruce, snapped Andy up for £350,000 in March 1988 and in his two seasons at Carrow Road, his consistent displays earned him International recognition when winning four England B Caps. However, (with Adams, Bould, O'Leary and Pates already on Arsenal's books) it did come as a surprise when George Graham paid £1.25 million for his services in July 1990. Andy made his Arsenal League debut, as a substitute, in a home encounter versus Chelsea, 15th September, 1990. Little did Andy know that he would have to wait until December 1990 before making his full League debut. In that Championship season, Linighan replaced Tony Adams whilst Tony was being unavoidably detained at Her Majesties Pleasure, when playing in seven League games (ten in total). In 1991-92, he filled in admirably for the injured Steve Bould, when playing in fifteen League fixtures. However, this quiet, no nonsense centre half, won a place in the Arsenal history books for all time when scoring the last minute goal, with a thunderous header in the 1993 F.A.Cup Final replay versus Sheffield Wednesday. Andy had previously been a member of the victorious Coca Cola Cup side, also against the Owls. In 1993-94, he again was a more than adequate deputy for Adams and Bould when playing in twenty one League games. Possibly Andy's greatest game for the club was in the European Cup Winners Cup Final versus Real Zaragoza, when he replaced the suspended Steve Bould. If Linighan had been with virtually any other League club, he would have been an automatic choice, but even so, in five seasons at Highbury, Andy has done a fantastic job. when deputising for either Steve Bould or Tony Adams.

Andy Linighan

	Games	Goals
League	89	4
F.A.Cup	13	1
League Cup	12	1
Europe	7	1
Other First Team Games	1	0
Friendly Matches	34	2
Tours	14	2
Football Combination	75	3
Total	**245**	**14**

Honours:
(WITH NORWICH)
4 England B Caps
(WITH ARSENAL)
F.A.Cup Winners Medal — 1992-93
League Cup Winners Medal — 1992-93
European Cup Winners Cup Winners Medal — 1993-94
European Cup Winners Cup Finalists Medal — 1994-95
F.A.Charity Shield Finalists Medal — 1993
European Super Cup Finalists Medal — 1995
Makita Tournament Trophy Winners Medal — 1994
2 Makita Tournament Trophy Finalists Medal — 1990, 1991

LUKIC, John — 1983-90

Birth Place: Chesterfield, Derbyshire
Date of Birth: 11th December 1960

☛ Without doubt, along with George Swindin, John Lukic is the finest goalkeeper to have played for Arsenal without ever gaining full international honours. John, the son of Yugoslavian parents, had played for Chesterfield and Derbyshire schoolboys when signing associated schoolboy forms for Leeds United in October 1975. John became an apprentice in May 1977 and under the watchful guidance of his schoolboy goalkeeping hero, David Harvey, he turned professional in December 1978. Lukic made his league debut for the Elland Road club in October 1979 and went on to play in a club record one hundred and forty-six successive league games. During this period he held off the challenge of two reserve team goalkeepers, who were both later given free transfers and who both later became full internationals, Henry Smith, who later played for Hearts and Scotland and David Seaman. However, in March 1983 he requested a transfer and was dropped for the last thirteen games of that season when his mentor David Harvey replaced him. Whilst at Elland Road, he gained England Youth and Under-Twenty-one honours. Four months after putting in his transfer request, Lukic was transferred to Arsenal for £75,000 in July 1983, as goalkeeping cover for the legendary Pat Jennings. John had to wait nine months for his Arsenal league debut, in a home fixture versus Stoke City on the 7th April 1984 and finished that season playing in just four league games. In 1984-85, he took over from the master when establishing himself in the side in December of that season. In 1985-86, he missed only two league games when becoming a permanent fixture in the Arsenal league side. It was in the 1986-87 season that John showed the English footballing public that he was now one of the leading goalkeepers in the country. At this time he was the best shot stopper and penalty saver in the game and his confidence grew when dealing with corners or crosses and he had a presence which all great goalkeepers have. In that 1986-87 season, he missed only six league games, playing an influential part in the club's Littlewoods Cup Final victory against Liverpool. In 1987-88, John was ever present and was a mainstay when helping the club back to Wembley for the following seasons Littlewoods Cup Final against Luton Town. In Arsenal's League Championship campaign of 1988-89, John was again ever present and had by this time, become one of the firm favourites of the North Bank faithful. Again ever present in 1989-90, John was put in an awkward position, when in March 1990, George Graham went public in announcing the fact he was keen to sign the Q.P.R. goalkeeper, David Seaman. This brought about certain demonstrations outside the ground in protest at the lack of loyalty being shown to John. However, when it became clear that he was no longer wanted at the club, Lukic re-joined Leeds United in a £1 million transfer in May 1990. John later had the last laugh when being a member of the Leeds United League Championship team in 1991-92, so becoming one of the elite to have won League Championships with two different clubs. In 1994-95, John joined only a handful of players who have remained ever present in as many as eight seasons. As this book went to press in late November 1995, he was still between the posts as Leeds mounted an F.A. Carling Premiership title challenge.

	Games	Goals
League	223	0
F.A. Cup	21	0
League Cup	32	0
Other First Team Matches	8	0
Friendly Matches	46	0
Tours	11	0
Football Combination	40	0
Total	**381**	**0**

Honours:
(WITH ARSENAL)

1 England 'B' Cap	1988-89
League Championship Medal	1988-89
League Cup Winners Medal	1986-87
League Cup Finalists Medal	1987-88
F.A. Charity Shield Finalists Medal	1989
Mercantile Credit Centenary Trophy Winners Medal	1988-89
Wembley International Tournament Winners Medal	1988
Makita Tournament Winners Medals	1989
Football Combination Championship Medals	1983-84

(WITH LEEDS UNITED)
7 England Under-21 caps
10 England Youth Caps

League Championship Medal	1991-92
F.A. Charity Shield Winners Medal	1992

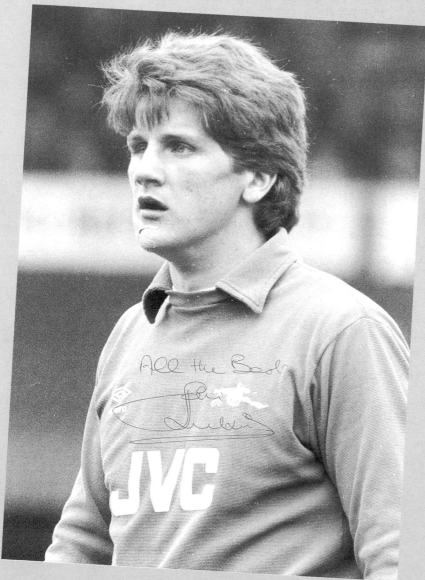

John Lukic

LYDERSEN, Pal   1991-95

Birth Place: Norway
Date of Birth: 10th September 1965

☛ Pal Lydersen was a Norwegian International defender who George Graham paid Ik Start £500,000 for in November 1991. He was signed as cover to Dixon and Winterburn and in that 1991-92 season he played in seven League games of which his League debut was at Selhurst Park versus Wimbledon, 28th March, 1992. In 1992-93, Pal made a further eight League appearances when deputising for all and sundry in the club's F.A.Cup Final run in. However, although a Norwegian International with seventeen caps, and named in their squad for the 1994 World Cup, in his last two seasons at Highbury, 1993-95, he did not get another League opportunity,. Pal was unfortunate in his Highbury career, he was deputy to two of the most consistent full backs in the Premiership, and suffered a continuous stream of injuries. At the end of 1994-95 he was released from his contract and granted a free transfer when he returned home to Norway.

	Games	Goals
League	15	0
League Cup	1	0
Friendly Matches	8	1
Tours	2	0
Football Combination	61	2
Total	**87**	**3**

Honours:
17 Norwegian Caps

Pal Lydersen

McDONALD, Chris   1992-95

Birth Place: Edinburgh, Scotland
Date of Birth: 14th October 1975

☛ Chris was a Scottish Schoolboy International who joined Arsenal midway through the 1991-92 season as a trainee. However, soon after he required a cartilage operation. A midfielder, he turned centre back when helping the club win the F.A.Youth Cup in 1993-94, this after turning professional in December 1993. McDonald was released on a free transfer in June 1995, and any hopes of another 'Super Mac' at Highbury went with him.

	Games	Goals
Friendly Matches	23	0
Football Combination	24	0
South East Counties League	52	10
Youth Cup	8	0
Other Youth Cups	12	2
Youth Tours	3	0
Total	**122**	**12**

Honours:
Scotland Schoolboy International
F.A.Youth Cup Winners Medal   1993-94
Southern Junior Floodlight Cup Finalists
    Medal   1992-93

McGOLDRICK, Eddie   1993

Birth Place: Islington, London
Date of Birth: 30th April 1965

☛ Eddie originally signed Schoolboy forms with Peterborough United in December 1979, he was not offered an apprenticeship with the London Road club and drifted into the Gola League with Kettering Town and later Nuneaton Borough. His old boss at Nuneaton remembered his talents and signed him for Northampton Town for £10,000 in August 1986. In his first season with the club, with Richard Hill and Trevor Morley, he helped the Cobblers to the Fourth Division Championship in 1986-87. In January 1989, Steve Coppell, the Crystal Palace manager, secured his services for £200,000 and in the remainder of that season he helped the Eagles to promotion to Division One (via the play offs). In 1989-90, he was a regular in the side until receiving a long term injury which resulted in him missing the 1990 F.A.Cup Final against Manchester United. Whilst at Palace, Eddie played in nearly two hundred first team games for the club and won the first of his fifteen Eire Caps versus Switzerland in March 1992. The versatile McGoldrick, who can play full back, sweeper, midfield or on either wing, joined Arsenal for £1 million in June 1993 and in 1993-94, he played in twenty-six League games of which his Arsenal League debut was as a substitute against Coventry City at Highbury, 14th

August, 1993. Eddie also added further Republic of Ireland Honours and crowned his finest moment when coming on for the last thirteen minutes of the European Cup Winners Cup Winning triumph against Parma. However, in 1994-95, he managed to play in only eleven League games and at this present moment in time his career at the club seems to be in question. An obviously talented player, whose confidence has been dented by so called Arsenal supporters who feel it their duty to barrack poor Eddie at every opportunity.

Eddie McGoldrick

	Games	Goals
League	37	0
F.A.Cup	2	0
League Cup	9	0
Europe	7	1
Other First Team Games	3	0
Friendly Matches	9	0
Football Combination	13	0
Total	**80**	**1**

Honours:
(WITH NORTHAMPTON TOWN)
Division Four Championship Medal 1986-87
(WITH CRYSTAL PALACE)
8 Eire Caps
(WITH ARSENAL)
7 Eire Caps and 1 B Cap
European Cup Winners Cup Winners Medal
    1993-94
European Cup Winners Cup Finalists Medal
    1994-95
F.A.Charity Shield Finalists Medal   1993
Makita Tournament Winners Medal   1994

McGOWAN, Gavin   1992

Birth Place: Blackheath, Kent
Date of Birth: 16th January 1976

☛ When Gavin McGowan made his Arsenal League debut versus Sheffield Wednesday at

Hillsborough, 6th May, 1993 aged seventeen years one hundred and ten days, only five players in Arsenal's history had made their debut at a younger age. Gavin had joined Arsenal as a trainee during the summer of 1992, this after he had captained the Inner London Schoolboys side as well as winning England Schoolboy Caps. A versatile young player he either plays full back, centre back or midfield and was still a trainee when he played in two League games in 1992-93. In 1993-94, he helped Arsenal win the F.A. Youth Cup versus Millwall as well as winning two England Youth Caps. He followed this in 1994-95, after turning professional in July, by being a regular member of the Football Combination side and played in Arsenal's last League game of the season at Stamford Bridge versus Chelsea.

	Games	Goals
League	3	0
Friendly Matches	22	0
Tours	3	0
Football Combination	40	0
South East Counties League	50	4
Youth Cup	9	3
Other Youth Cups	17	1
Youth Tours	3	1
Total	**147**	**9**

Honours:
England Schoolboy International
2 England Youth Caps
F.A.Youth Cup Winners Medal   1993-94
Southern Junior Floodlight Cup Finalists
    Medal   1992-93

McKEOWN, Gary   1987-92

Birth Place: Oxford
Date of Birth: 19th October 1970

☛ Gary was yet another Arsenal youngster who attended the F.A.School of Excellence, and before joining Arsenal as a trainee in the Summer of 1987, he had represented Oxfordshire County and England Under 16's. In his five seasons at Highbury, he won three England Youth Caps and a F.A.Youth Cup Winners Medal in 1987-88. In 1990-91 and 1991-92 he was the penalty taker while being a mainstay in the reserves. Before leaving Highbury, Gary spent a time on loan at Shrewsbury Town. He was released on a free transfer in June 1992 when he linked up with Scottish Premiership 'new boys' Dundee.

	Games	Goals
Friendly Matches	29	2
Football Combination	91	23
South East Counties League	42	8
Youth Cup	10	3
Other Youth Cups	4	0
Youth Tours	5	0
Total	**181**	**36**

Honours:
3 England Youth Caps
England Under 16 International
F.A.Youth Cup Winners Medal   1987-88
Football Combination Championship Medal
                                    1989-90

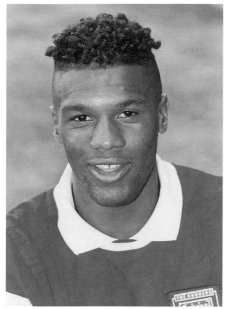

Gary McKeown

McKERNON, Craig   1989-92

Birth Place: Gloucester
Date of Birth: 23rd February 1968

☛ Craig was an excellent up and coming full back, who had played in over one hundred first team games for Mansfield Town, when he joined Arsenal as 21 year old for £200,000 in December 1989. (as cover for Lee Dixon). However, he suffered a succession of serious knee injuries (and after three months of a comeback) he was finally advised to retire from the game in 1992. McKernon, later overturned that decision and made a comeback with the G.M. Vauxhall side Kettering Town.

	Games	Goals
Friendly Matches	2	0
Football Combination	24	1
Total	**26**	**1**

MARINER, Paul   1984-86

Birth Place: Bolton, Lancashire
Date of Birth: 22nd May 1953

☛ Paul Mariner began his footballing career with non-league Chorley, being transferred to Plymouth Argyle for a small fee in July 1973. During his three seasons at Home Park he developed into a fine centre forward, scoring fifty-six league goals in one hundred and thirty-five appearances and played a large part in helping the

Pilgrims to the semi-final of the League Cup in 1974. Bobby Robson, the Ipswich Town manager, noted his talents and produced a £200,000 cheque to secure his signature in October 1976. During his eight seasons at Portman Road he became one of the elite centre forwards of this era. Paul was capped thirty-three times by England (fourteen goals) which included representing England in the 1982 World Cup. At club level, he helped Ipswich in becoming one of the most consistent sides in the country, being a member of their side that won the F.A. Cup against Arsenal in 1977-78 as well as inspiring the club to First Division runners-up in 1981 and 1982. Paul was also a member of their U.E.F.A. Cup winning team of 1980-81 against AZ 67 Alkmaar. In total, Mariner played in three hundred and thirty-five first team games for Ipswich, scoring one hundred and twenty-four goals. Paul was transferred to Arsenal in February 1984 for £150,000, this signing in many Arsenal supporters eyes was three years too late, for although Arsenal required a target man to feed the likes of Woodcock and Nicholas, someone like Mariner should have been brought after the sale of Frank Stapleton in 1981. For Paul, although hardly in the veteran stage, had seen his best years, even though at the age of thirty, his touch play was as good as any and he remained a brave, unselfish leader, still majestic in the air. In his first season at Highbury he played in the last fifteen games of the season scoring seven times. His Arsenal league debut was on the 18th February 1984 in a home fixture against Aston Villa. In 1984-85, he made thirty-four

league appearances scoring seven goals, but his form was still good enough to gain a further two England caps, However, in 1985-86, he played in only nine league games one of which was at centre half when playing against Leicester City. With the emergence of the young Niall Quinn one of the new Arsenal manager George Graham's first tasks was to release Paul on a free transfer in August 1986. Paul joined Portsmouth and in his first season at Pompey helped the club gain First Division recognition for the first time in nearly thirty years. Mariner was granted a free transfer by Portsmouth in 1988 and later played in Malta for Naxxar Lions and back in England, in non-league circles, at Chorley and Bury Town. Had a brief spell as Commercial Manager at Colchester United and now coaches in the USA, but when home, commentates for radio and cable television as well as helping to train youngsters at a private school in Lancashire.

	Games	Goals
League	60	14
F.A. Cup	6	2
League Cup	4	1
Friendly Matches	9	4
Tours	3	1
Football Combination	10	6
Total	**92**	**28**

Honours:
(WITH IPSWICH)
33 England Caps
7 England 'B' Caps
F.A. Cup Winners Medal
                        1977-78
U.E.F.A. Cup Winners
    Medal   1980-81
F.A. Charity Shield Finalists
    Medal   1978
Division One P.F.A. Team
    Award   1980-81
(WITH ARSENAL)
2 England Caps

Paul Mariner

MARRIOTT, Andrew 1987-89

Birth Place: Sutton-in-Ashfield, Notts
Date of Birth: 11th October 1970

Andrew had played for Nottingham County and England Schoolboys before joining Arsenal as a trainee goalkeeper from the F.A.School of Excellence, during the Summer of 1987, turning professional in October 1988. Andrew was unfortunate to be at the club at the same time as Alan Miller. Andrew won two England Youth Caps in 1988-89 before George Graham decided to sell him to Nottingham Forest for £50,000 in June 1989. He spent over four seasons at the City Ground as reserve custodian to Steve Crossley and was loaned out at different periods to West Bromwich Albion, Blackburn Rovers, Colchester United and Burnley (helping Burnley win the Fourth Division Championship in 1991-92). Andrew was transferred to Wrexham in October 1993 for £200,000, after he had gained an England Under 21 Cap and helped Forest win the Full Members Cup in 1991-92.

	Games	Goals
Friendly Matches	4	0
Football Combination	2	0
South East Counties League	36	0
Youth Cup	4	0
Other Youth Cups	1	0
Youth Tours	3	0
Total	**50**	**0**

Honours:
(WITH ARSENAL)
England Schoolboy International
2 England Youth Caps
(WITH NOTTINGHAM FOREST)
England Under 21 Cap
Full Members Cup Winners Medal 1991-92
(WITH BURNLEY)
Fourth Division Championship Medal
1991-92

MARSHALL, Scott 1989

Birth Place: Edinburgh, Scotland
Date of Birth: 1st May 1973

Scott Marshall comes from a distinguished footballing family. His father, Gordon, was a goalkeeper who played for Hearts, Newcastle United and England Under 23's. His brother, Gordon Jnr., is presently the Celtic and Scottish goalkeeper. At any other club Scott would have been a regular fixture in their side by now. For in six seasons at Highbury he has managed to play in only two League games, of which his debut was at Hillsborough versus Sheffield Wednesday 6th May 1993. Marshall joined Arsenal as a trainee in July 1989 after having helped Scotland reach the Mini World

Cup Final. A Scotland Under 16 International, later adding Youth and Under 21 Caps, he signed professional in March 1991. Scott has enjoyed loan periods at Rotherham United, 1993-94, and Sheffield United, 1994-95.

	Games	Goals
League	2	0
Friendly Matches	50	3
Football Combination	109	5
South East Counties League	45	4
Youth Cup	6	0
Other Youth Cups	20	1
Youth Tours	11	0
Total	**243**	**13**

Honours:
2 Scottish Under 21 Caps
3 Scottish Youth Caps
Scottish Schoolboy Caps
South East Counties League Championship
Medal 1990-91
Southern Junior Floodlight Cup Winners
Medal 1990-91
Southern Junior Floodlight Cup Finalists
Medal 1989-90

Scott Marshall

MARWOOD, Brian 1988-90

Birth Place: Seaham Harbour, Durham
Date of Birth: 5th February 1960

Brian Marwood was on Associated Schoolboy Forms with Hull City when

signing as an apprentice in June 1976, turning professional in February 1978 and in six seasons at the club he averaged a goal in every third League game when making over one hundred and fifty appearances and was inspirational in their 1982-83 Division Four promotion campaign. Sheffield Wednesday snapped him up for £115,000 in August 1984. A small but clever winger, Brian could have carved out a career as a cricketer, for as a youngster he was offered the chance to play for Northants Second Eleven. Whilst at Hillsborough, he developed into one of the most consistent wingers in the First Division his trademark being electrifying pace and his ability to control the ball at high speed and centre all in one devastating action. In March 1988 Arsenal paid Wednesday £600,000 for his services. Brian made his Arsenal League debut on 30th March 1988 versus Oxford United. In Arsenal's 1988-89 Championship season he was an influential member and he became a firm favourite with the North Bank crowd. The amount of goals that he set up for Alan Smith alone were decisive that season, this vein of form gaining Marwood his only England Cap against Saudi Arabia in November 1988. Although Brian missed the last five League games of that historic season, he chipped in with nine goals in thirty one appearances. However, in 1989-90, there was no less than seven periods when Marwood was out with various injuries and he managed to play in only seventeen League games. In September 1990, with the newly signed Anders Limpar occupying the club's left wing position, Brian was transferred to Sheffield United for £350,000. He finished his career with Swindon Town, 1993, and Barnet, 1993-94, after he had had a short loan spell at Middlesbrough in October 1991. Brian is now the respected P.F.A. Chairman. In the post war era only Ronnie Rooke and Joe Mercer can be considered as better short term buys for the club.

	Games	Goals
League	52	16
F.A.Cup	2	0
League Cup	6	1
Other First Team Games	6	4
Friendly Matches	20	8
Tours	9	0
Football Combination	14	7
Total	**109**	**36**

Honours:
(WITH ARSENAL)
1 England Cap
League Championship Medal 1988-89
F.A.Charity Shield Finalists Medal 1989
Mercantile Credit Centenary Trophy Winners
Medal 1988-89
Wembley International Tournament Winners
Medal 1988-89

MEADE, Raphael 1978-85

Birth Place: Islington, London
Date of Birth: 22nd November 1962

Raphael was playing for Islington Schoolboys when joining Arsenal on Schoolboy Forms in 1977, becoming an apprentice in June 1979, turning professional a year later. In his first two seasons at Highbury he played in many games for the Youth Team before breaking through to the reserve side in 1980-81. Raphael was the Combination League side's leading goal scorer in both 1980-81 and 1981-82, this form earning him his League debut at centre forward when scoring the only goal of the game versus Manchester City at Highbury, 17th October, 1981. All told, he played in sixteen League games that season. A cartilage operation kept him out for most of the 1982-83 season but on his return, in February 1983, he scored twice versus Brighton. In December 1983, he hit a rich vein of form when scoring a hat-trick versus Watford and nine days later, two in a 4-2 victory at Tottenham. In 1984-85 with Mariner, Woodcock and Nicholas operating in the striking positions his first team chances were limited and in the summer of 1985 he was transferred to Sporting Club Lisbon for £60,000. Over the following eight years, Meade Interloped from country to country at will. He played in Scotland, for Dundee United, in England for Luton Town and Ipswich, he had two spells in Denmark with OB Odense and then came back to England to play for Plymouth Argyle, Brighton and Dover as well as playing in Singapore. Raphael Meade had all the potential and ability to go to the very top in his profession, he was quick, fleet footed, powerful, had an eye for goal and was a clone of a young Kevin Campbell. Someone, somewhere must know why it never materialised.

	Games	Goals
League	41	14
F.A.Cup	3	0
League Cup	4	1
Europe	3	1
Friendly Matches	46	40
Tours	6	2
Football Combination	133	90
South East Counties League	43	18
Youth Cup	9	7
Other Youth Cups	18	7
Youth Tours	4	2
Total	**310**	**182**

Honours:
Football Combination Championship Medal
    1983-84
South East Counties League Cup Winners
  Medal   1979-80
Presidents Cup Winners Medal   1980-81

Raphael Meade

MERSON, Paul   1984

Birth Place: Harlesden , London
Date of Birth: 20th March 1968

🔫 When, in November 1994, Paul Merson announced to the outside world that he was going to seek professional help for his, off field problems, everyone in football must have admired his bravery and courage for openly admitting this in public. For here was a footballer, at the peak of his career, who was finding his fame too hard to cope with. Happily, all of this is behind him, and all Arsenal supporters must relish Paul linking up with Platt and Bergkamp. Merson had played for Brent, Ealing District and Middlesex Schoolboys, when after trials, he had been turned down by Chelsea, Queens Park Rangers and Watford. In April 1982, when only fourteen, he joined Arsenal as an associated schoolboy, he became an apprentice in July 1984, turning professional in December 1985. Merson worked his way through the Arsenal ranks before being loaned out to Brentford in January 1987. This was to help him gain valuable league experience, after he had made his Arsenal league debut when coming on for Niall Quinn in a 3-0 home victory against Manchester City in November 1986. In 1986-87, Paul consolidated his position at the club when appearing in fifteen league fixtures usually replacing or substituting for Perry Groves. In the championship winning season of 1988-89, he scored ten vital goals in thirty seven league appearances, but of those thirty seven he remained on the field for the ninety minutes in only thirteen. However, it proved to be a marvellous season, he won the first of his four England under twenty one caps and was voted P.F.A. Young Player of the Year. It was at this stage that Paul started to have "run ins" with boss, George Graham, and from an outside point of view it seemed that the gutter press were hell bent on destroying his career after it had only just began. Several incidents were reported, many of them trivial, and each time Graham accepted Paul's version of the story. This led the "Merse" to be nick named "The son of George". However, Paul bounced back in the 1990-91 championship campaign when netting thirteen times in thirty seven league appearances. Merson came into his own, in 1991-92, when in a roaming forward role he was one of the few players in the top flight, who was capable of the unexpected. His main forte being having the ability to be able to run down the left flank and cut in at any angle to unleash a ferocious right footed shot. In this term he was ever-present, scored his only ever

Paul Merson

league hat trick against Crystal Palace in April 1992 and won the first of his fourteen England caps when playing against Germany. In the cup double winning season, 1992-93, Paul was a key member of both winning sides and scored the first goal in the Coca Cola Cup Final, when being named man of the match against Sheffield Wednesday. Paul later played a vital role for the club, when helping Arsenal reach two successive European Cup Winners Cup Finals in 1994 and 1995. Paul was given a rapturous welcome when returning to the side in the first leg of the European Super Cup Final against A.C. Milan. Merse is undoubtedly one of the finest talents in English football today and everyone at Highbury wishes him well for the future.

	Games	Goals
League	257	67
F.A. Cup	28	4
League Cup	30	9
Europe	20	5
Other First Team Matches	16	1
Friendly Matches	56	25
Tours	20	15
Football Combination	82	44
South East Counties League	32	13
Youth Cup	9	6
Other Youth Cups	17	9
Youth Tours	13	1
Total	**580**	**199**

Honours:
14 England Caps
3 England B Caps
4 England Under-twenty-one Caps
3 England Youth Caps
2 League Championship Medals
1988-89, 1990-91
F.A. Cup Winners Medal 1992-93
League Cup Winners Medal 1992-93
European Cup Winners Cup Winners Medal
1993-94
European Cup Winners Cup Finalists Medal
1994-95
F.A. Charity Shield Medal 1991
2 F.A. Charity Shield Finalists Medal
1989, 1993
P.F.A. Young Player of the Year 1988-89
Mercantile Credit Centenary Trophy Winners
Medal 1988-89
European Super Cup Finalists Medal 1995
Wembley International Tournament Winners
Medal 1988
2 Makita International Tournament Winners
Medals 1989, 1994
2 Makita International Tournament Finalists
Medals 1990, 1991
2 South East Counties League Cup Finalists
Medals 1984-85, 1985-86
Southern Junior Floodlight Cup Finalists
Medal 1985-86

MILLER, Alan 1986-94

Birth Place: Epping, Essex
Date of Birth: 29th March 1970

☛ Alan joined Arsenal as an Associated Schoolboy in July 1984 and later played for Essex County and England Schoolboys before being invited to the F.A. School of Excellence. He learned his goal keeping trade at this time before becoming a trainee in July 1986. In 1987-88, he was a member of the victorious F.A.Youth Cup Winning side versus Doncaster Rovers, turning professional in May 1988. Unbelievably, he made his England Under 21 debut just after signing Pro before ever having played in a full League game. Over the following four seasons Alan, would have been automatic choice at most clubs, unfortunately, with Lukic and Seaman around he never got a look in. Although, during this time he had loan spells at Plymouth Argyle, West Bromwich Albion and Birmingham City, in 1991-92, he helped Birmingham to promotion from Division Three. Alan was highly regarded at Highbury and although he had seen off Schoolboy and Youth Inter-nationals such as Marriott, Rust and Will, he seemed destined to be unable to achieve his ultimate ambition of being Arsenal's regular goalkeeper. However, in 1992-93, at the age of twenty two, he made history when becoming the club's first ever goal keeping substitute when making his Arsenal League debut at Elland Road versus Leeds United 21st November 1992. In 1993-94, he deputised in the League on four occasions for David Seaman and although he had won many honours whilst at the club (sitting on the bench) he wanted away and joined Middlesbrough for £500,000 in the summer of 1994 and in his first season at Ayrsome Park he helped the club to the First Division Championship.

	Games	Goals
League	8	0
Friendly Matches	49	0
Tours	4	0
Football Combination	131	0
South East Counties League	48	0
Youth Cup	10	0
Other Youth Cups	13	0
Youth Tours	8	0
Total	**271**	**0**

Honours:
(WITH ARSENAL)
England Schoolboy International
4 England Under 21 Caps
F.A. Cup Winners Medal 1992-93
League Cup Winners Medal 1992-93
European Cup Winners Cup Winners Medal
1993-94
F.A.Charity Shield Finalists Medal 1993
2 Makita Tournament Winners Medals
1989, 1994
2 Makita Tournament Finalists Medals
1990, 1991
F.A. Youth Cup Winners Medal 1987-88
Football Combination Championship Medal
1989-90
(WITH MIDDLESBROUGH)
Division One Championship Medal 1994-95

Alan Miller

MILTON, Russell 1988-89

Birth Place: Folkestone, Kent
Date of Birth: 12th January 1969

☛ Russell had represented Kent as a Schoolboy at both football and cricket before joining Arsenal as a trainee during the Summer of 1985 from Folkestone. Originally a left back, he moved in to midfield before turning professional in June 1987. Like many other young midfield players of this period, he failed to bridge the gap between reserve and League football and was subsequently released in June 1989. Russell later tried his luck playing in Hong Kong, returning home to play for Dover Athletic.

	Games	Goals
Friendly Matches	20	4
Football Combination	110	10
South East Counties League	25	2
Youth Cup	4	1
Other Youth Cups	7	2
Youth Tours	12	1
Total	**178**	**20**

Honours:
Southern Junior Floodlight Cup Finalists
Medal 1985-86
South East Counties League Cup Finalists
Medal 1985-86

MOCKLER, Andrew — 1987-90

Birth Place: Middlesbrough, Cleveland
Date of Birth: 18th November 1970

➤ Andrew was a midfield player who had represented Cleveland when joining Arsenal as a trainee in July 1987, turning professional in November 1988. In his three seasons at the club, Andrew was unfortunate with injuries, this partly contributing to him being granted a free transfer in July 1990 when he teamed up with Scarborough.

	Games	Goals
Friendly Matches	8	2
Football Combination	5	0
South East Counties League	32	7
Youth Cup	2	2
Other Youth Cups	4	1
Youth Tours	3	1
Total	**54**	**13**

MORROW, Steve — 1987

Birth Place: Belfast, Northern Ireland
Date of Birth: 2nd July 1970

➤ Steve had played for Northern Ireland Schoolboys when signing for his local side, Bangor, as a fifteen year old schoolboy. He played twenty six matches for them when still under seventeen, as well as winning Northern Ireland Youth honours, captaining the side. Steve joined Arsenal as an apprentice in July 1987, turning professional in May 1988. In his first four seasons at Highbury he was a permanent fixture in the reserves as understudy to both Dixon and Winterburn and although he had still to play a League game for the club, he won the first of his seventeen Northern Ireland caps versus Uruguay in May 1990. He continued to play for his country even though still a reserve. In 1990-91, he had a loan period at Reading and in 1991-92 he had further loan periods at Watford, Reading again and Barnet. Steve returned to Highbury at the end of that season and made his Arsenal League debut as a substitute at Carrow Road versus Norwich City, 8th April, 1992. He had been a member of the F.A. Youth Cup winning team in 1987-88, and had suffered with more than his fair share of injuries, which included, a hernia and a groin strain. In 1992-93 he stepped in, originally to replace the injured Nigel Winterburn, but found himself playing in a new midfield role, when making sixteen League appearances. However, after he had scored the winning goal in the Coca Cola Cup Final versus Sheffield Wednesday a freak injury in the post match celebrations, which has since been well documented, kept him out for the rest of the season, which included the F.A. Cup Final, against the same opposition two months later. In 1993-94,

although playing in only eleven League games, he came into the side at the last minute to play in the Cup Winners Cup Final versus Parma and in 1994-95 he played in the losing final versus Real Zaragosa. In the last twenty years there have been few finer servants to the club than Steve Morrow.

	Games	Goals
League	44	1
F.A.Cup	5	0
League Cup	8	2
Europe	5	0
Other First Team Games	1	0
Friendly Matches	37	0
Tours	2	0
Football Combination	134	1
South East Counties League	14	0
Youth Cup	8	0
Other Youth Cups	3	2
Youth Tours	3	0
Total	**264**	**6**

Honours:
17 Northern Ireland Caps
Northern Ireland Schoolboy International
3 Northern Ireland Youth Caps
3 Northern Ireland Under Twenty One Caps
1 Northern Ireland B Cap
League Cup Winners Medal   1992-93
European Cup Winners Cup Winners Medal
1993-94
European Cup Winners Cup Finalists Medal
1994-95
European Super Cup Finalists Medal   1995
Makita Tournament Trophy Winners Medal
1994
F.A. Youth Cup Winners Medal   1987-88
Football Combination Championship Medal
1989-90

Steve Morrow

NICHOLAS, Charlie — 1983-88

Birth Place: Glasgow, Scotland
Date of Birth: 30th December 1961

➤ Charlie Nicholas joined Celtic as a seventeen year old in 1979 making his league debut for the club in 1980-81. Still not yet twenty, he finished that season scoring twenty-five goals in forty-two games when helping Celtic to the Scottish League Championship. In the following season, 1981-82, a series of injuries, including a broken leg, sidelined him for most of the season, although he did manage to play in enough games to help Celtic retain the League Championship. However, it was in 1982-83 when Charlie started hitting the headlines. He scored over fifty competitive goals for Celtic as well as scoring a tremendous goal for Scotland in his international debut versus Switzerland. Charlie finished as Scotland's leading scorer, was voted Scottish footballer of the Year, won six Scottish caps and gained a Rothmans special award. Arsenal beat off the challenge of both Liverpool and Manchester United when securing his signature for £800,000 in June 1983. It was the most publicised transfer for many years and many likened it to Peter Marinello's transfer some fourteen years earlier. Charlie became the instant idol of the North Bank legions and only Charlie George and possibly Liam Brady had ever received the hero worshipping welcome that Nicholas had bestowed upon him. For here was a working class boy made good, with his boyish grin and his long flowing dark locks, he was able to charm the public with his film star qualities off the field and on the field with his cheeky carefree attitude. On his day in the mid 1980's there was no more skilful footballer than Charlie. He was a wizard in the dribble, had speed of thought and instinctive passing ability, performing feats with the ball which most players would not even dream of. His razor sharp shooting ability completed the package. In this transitional period in the club's history, Charlie was looked upon as a "Messiah" like figure. But he was only human and he did have his weaknesses. Charlie was not strong in the air, lacked genuine pace, flitted in and out of games when not seemingly interested in the proceedings and his work rate could never be described as industrious. The beginning of Nicholas's career at Highbury did not exactly go to plan, for although he missed just one league game, he scored only eleven goals in the 1983-84 season. Although he did net two spectacular efforts (one of these was an exquisite lob) against Tottenham at White Hart Lane on Boxing Day 1983. In 1984-85, his goal scoring performance did not improve when scoring only nine league goals in thirty eight appearances. By this time, though, he had

moved back into a deeper midfield position. In 1985-86, he missed only one league game and scored a memorable hat trick in an F.A. Cup third round tie at Grimsby Town. With new manager, George Graham in charge, Charlie spent no less than five periods, during the 1986-87 season, out of the side, with a definite rift between the two Scotsmen apparent. Charlie was determined to have the last laugh and appeared to have done so when scoring both goals in the 1987 Littlewoods Cup Final against Liverpool. NIcholas played in the first three league games in 1987-88 and with only one goal scored in these matches, he was dropped from the side when Perry Groves replaced him. In January 1988, the "King" of the north bank was transferred to Aberdeen for

£400,000. Charlie spent three seasons at Pittodrie before returning to Celtic for the 1990-91 season, and in 1994-95 he was still an important member of their squad despite being briefly discarded by boss Lou Macari in May 1994 and then reinstated by new manager Tommy Burns. Joined Clyde in the summer of 1995.

	Games	Goals
League	151	34
F.A. Cup	13	10
League Cup	20	10
Friendly Matches	34	14
Tours	7	2
Football Combination	23	20
Total	**248**	**90**

Honours:
(WITH ARSENAL)
13 Scottish Caps

1 Scottish Under-twenty-one Caps
League Cup Winners Medal 1992-93
(WITH CELTIC)
6 Scottish Caps
5 Scottish Under-twenty-one Caps
Scottish Footballer of the Year   1982-83
2 Scottish League Championship Medals
                                    1980-81, 1981-82
Scottish League Cup Winners Medals
                                    1982-83
(WITH ABERDEEN)
1 Scottish Cap
Scottish Cup Winners Medal   1989-90
Scottish League Cup Winners Medal 1989-90
Scottish League Cup Finalists Medal 1988-89

Charlie Nicholas

O'LEARY, David 1973-93

Birth Place: Stoke Newington, London
Date of Birth: 2nd May 1958

David O'Leary joined Arsenal as an apprentice in June 1973, turning professional in July 1975, and became one of Arsenal's great discoveries. At fifteen years of age he held a regular place in Arsenal's South East Counties League side, and at seventeen, after playing reserve team football regularly (1974-75), made his league debut versus Burnley in August 1975. During the 1975-76 season he played in thirty first team matches and, still seventeen, was one of the youngest ever players to win a regular place in the Arsenal first team. He held a regular place in the heart of the Arsenal defence for seventeen seasons. Won the first of his sixty seven Eire caps in October 1976 versus England when only eighteen years old. He played in thirty three and forty one league matches respectively in 1976-77 and 1977-78 and helped Arsenal to the F.A. Cup Final of 1978

versus Ipswich. He played in thirty seven league matches in 1978-79 and won an F.A. Cup winners medal versus Manchester United. He appeared again at Wembley in the 1979-80 final versus West Ham and played in a further thirty four league matches. A succession of injuries reduced his league appearances to only twenty four in 1980-81 but in 1981-82 he missed only two league matches and was made club captain. After a further thirty six league matches in 1982-83, he relinquished the captaincy to Graham Rix at the beginning of the 1983-84 season and surprisingly lost his place in the Eire international team. David O'Leary made his four hundredth first team appearance for the club in April 1984 a month before his twenty sixth birthday. He already held the record of the youngest Arsenal player to play one hundred and two hundred first team games. At the time, in the late 1970's, and early 80's, David was considered not only the best centre back in England, but also in Europe and throughout his career it was his ability to

read the game so well that made his job look so easy. He was unruffled, calm and used the ball as well as any in his position. Allied to these attributes was his speed of thought as well as a great positional sense and it was not often that David was dragged out of position. David, who had also played for the Republic of Ireland at schoolboy and youth level, served Arsenal for twenty years, Leslie Compton being the only player in the club's history to have served Arsenal longer. David smashed George Armstrong's league appearance record for the club in November 1989 and by the time he had finished his career at Highbury, he had played in five hundred and fifty eight league games, held the record for the most F.A. Cup and League Cup appearances for the club as well as the record for overall first team appearances (seven hundred and twenty two). In his final season at Highbury, David appeared in his fourth F.A. Cup Final for Arsenal and became the first player in the club's long history to play one

David O'Leary in action against Spurs

thousand competitive games for the Gunners. This Arsenal legend bowed out after a bumper testimonial against Manchester United and he finished his playing days with Leeds United. His brother, Pierce, played for Celtic and the Republic of Ireland. He officially retired due to injury in October, 1995.

	Games	Goals
League	558	11
F.A. Cup	70	1
League Cup	70	2
Europe	21	0
Other First Team Matches	8	0
Friendly Matches	91	4
Tours	51	2
Football Combination	89	2
South East Counties League	28	0
Youth Cup	5	0
Other Youth Cups	6	0
Youth Tours	8	0
Total	**1005**	**22**

Honours:
67 Eire Caps
Eire Youth and Schoolboy Caps
2 League Championship Medals
1988-89, 1990-91
2 F.A. Cup Winners Medals
1978-79, 1992-93
2 F.A. Cup Finalists Medals
1977-78, 1979-80
2 League Cup Winners Medals
1986-87, 1992-93
European Cup Winners Cup Finalists Medal
1979-80
F.A. Charity Shield Medal 1991
2 F.A. Charity Shield Finalists Medal
1979, 1989
3 Division One P.F.A. Awards
1978, 1979, 1981
Makita International Tournament Winners
  Medals 1989
2 Makita International Tournament Finalists
  Medals 1990, 1991

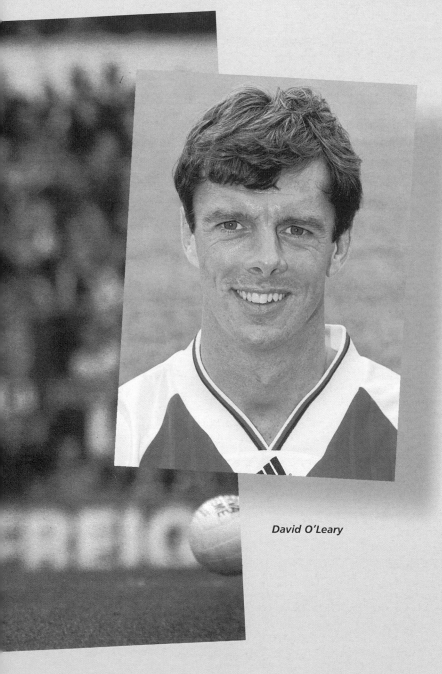

David O'Leary

O'BRIEN, Roy   1991-95

Birth Place: Cork, Eire
Date of Birth: 27th November 1974

Roy O'Brien is a young centre back who arrived at Highbury from Cork during the summer of 1991, after he had won Schoolboy honours for the Republic of Ireland's under 15 and under 16 sides. He was the Youth Team captain in 1992-93 when winning youth honours and for the last two seasons 1993-95, has become a regular in the Combination Team. Only time will tell if he can follow his fellow country, David O'Leary, into the first team!

	Games	Goals
Friendly Matches	18	0
Football Combination	47	1
South East counties League	42	3
Youth Cup	4	0
Other Youth Cup	20	1
Total	**131**	**5**

Honours:
Eire Under 15 and under 16 Caps
2 Southern Junior Floodlight Cup Finalists
  Medal 1991-92, 1992-93

OSBORNE, Lawrie   1983-87

Birth Place: West Ham, London
Date of Birth: 20th October 1967

Lawrence had played for Newham, Essex and London Schoolboys before establishing himself in Arsenal's South East Counties League side in 1983-84, when still a school-boy. Osborne became an apprentice during the summer of 1984, later turning professional in July 1985. After leaving Arsenal he played for Wycombe Wanderers, Huddersfield Town, Newport County, Dagenham, Maidstone United and Gillingham.

	Games	Goals
Friendlies	13	8
Football Combination	36	5
South East Counties League	50	20
Youth Cup	9	6
Other Youth Cups	21	10
Youth Tours	14	7
Total	**143**	**56**

Honours:
South East Counties League Cup Finalist
  Medal 1984-85 1985-86
Southern Junior Floodlight Cup Finalist
  Medal 1985-86

OWEN, Dafydd   1993

Birth Place: Bangor, Wales
Date of Birth: 3rd June, 1977

➤ Dafydd suffered with a terrible cruciate ligament injury during his first season at Highbury after joining the club as a Welsh schoolboy international left back as a trainee in the close season of 1993. During the 1994-95 season he had to contest the youth team left back position with Ross Taylor, However, in the summer of 1995 he was good enough to sign professional forms for the club after playing in less than thirty games.

	Games	Goals
Friendly Matches	10	0
South East Counties	12	0
Youth Tours	5	0
Total	**27**	**0**

Honours:
Wales Under-fifteen and Under-sixteen
    International

PARLOUR, Ray   1989

Birth Place: Romford, Essex
Date of Birth: 7th March 1973

➤ Ray Parlour is no different to any other young man of his generation. He has a carefree attitude, a wicked sense of humour and enjoys a night out. However, the biased tabloid press seem to pick up on every trivial misdemeanour he is allegedly involved in. Stories concerning young women, skirmishes with cab drivers and the letting off of a fire extinguisher are of minor significance. Ray has undoubtedly suffered from the reports of these incidents and should now be left alone to continue his promising football career and let him respect the name of Arsenal Football Club, who have backed him through all these troubled episodes. Ray joined Arsenal as a trainee in July 1989 having been associated with the club as a schoolboy since January 1988. Parlour, with his blond shaggy locks, is a clever midfield performer with an impressive range of passing skills, as well as an "engine" which makes it seem that he can run forever. Ray became a full professional in March 1991 and within a year had made his Arsenal League debut at Anfield versus Liverpool, 29th January, 1992 when he unfortunately onceded a penalty in a 0-2 defeat. He finished that season making six league appearances as well as winning the first of his twelve England under twenty one caps. In 1992-93 Ray, a former Essex schoolboy star had an outstanding season when helping Arsenal win both the F.A and Coca Cola Cups. In 1993-94, although not appearing in any of the European fixtures, he won a winners medal when being one of the non playing reserves (sitting on the bench) and at the end of that season he was voted man of the match when England won the Toulon under Twenty One International Tournament. In 1994-95, he figured in twenty nine league fixtures and appeared in the European Cup Winners Cup Final. With all his ability, the only thing lacking in Ray's game is that for all his skills, he does not score as many goals as he should, if he could rectify this he would be the almost complete midfield player.

Ray Parlour

	Games	Goals
League	83	4
F.A.Cup	9	1
League Cup	11	0
Europe	8	0
Other First Team Games	1	0
Friendly Matches	43	8
Tours	8	0
Football Combination	62	11
South East Counties League	51	5
Youth Cup	7	0
Other Youth Cups	19	1
Youth Tours	7	0
Total	**309**	**30**

Honours:
12 England Under Twenty One Caps.

F.A.Cup Winners Medal	1992-93
League Cup Winners Medal	1992-93
European Cup Winners Cup Winners Medal	
	1993-94
European Cup Winners Cup Finalists Medal	
	1994-95
European Super Cup Finalists Medal	1994-95
South East Counties League Championship Medal	1990-91
Southern Junior Floodlight Cup Winners Medal	1990-91
Southern Junior Floodlight Cup Finalist Medal	1989-90

PATES, Colin   1990-93

Birth Place: Carshalton, Surrey
Date of Birth: 10 August 1961

➤ Colin joined Chelsea as an apprentice in Aug. 1977, turning professional in July 1979. A polished defender, he played eleven times for England Youth, helping his country to win the 1980 U.E.F.A Youth competition. In the best part of ten years at Stamford Bridge Colin made nearly three hundred and fifty first team games for the club and was ever-present when helping Chelsea to the Second Division Championship in 1983-84. In Oct. 1988, Charlton Athletic paid £430,000 for his services, however, his duration at the club was one of only fifteen months before being transferred to Arsenal for £500,000 in Jan. 1990. Arsenal, already having Bould, Adams, O'Leary and Linighan seemed hell bent on collecting centre halves. With the aforementioned dominating the centre back positions Colin was reduced to playing in only twelve full League games in his stay at Highbury of over two and a half years. His Arsenal debut being at Hillsborough versus Sheffield Wednesday, 17th February, 1990. Colin was loaned out to Brighton for two months at the back end of the 1990-91 season before joining them on a full time basis after Arsenal had granted Pates a free transfer in August 1993. Brighton severed his contract midway through the 1994-95 season when he was forced to quit due to a knee injury. Colin joined Crawley and was appointed their manager in May 1995. Also helped out at the Arsenal school of excellence.

Colin Pates

	Games	Goals
League	21	0
League Cup	2	0
Europe	2	1
Friendly Matches	18	0
Tours	4	0
Football Combination	48	4
Total	**95**	**5**

Honours:
(WITH CHELSEA)
11 England Youth Caps

Division Two Championship Medal	1983-84
Full Members Cup Winners Medal	1985-86

PLATT, David   1995

Birth Place: Chadderton, Lancashire
Date of Birth: 10th June, 1966

☛ David Platt's footballing story sounds as if it should come out of a boy's fantasy comic strip, for no player in the history of the world of football has gone from a rags to riches situation quite like David has done, and it is a great testament to his will power and determination, that he succeeded against the odds. It's a tale any young footballer who has been discarded should take note of. Platt was playing for his local side, Chadderton, when he was offered a professional contract with Manchester United in July 1984. However, with the likes of Moses, Muhren, Strachan, Robson, Wilkins and Whiteside to compete with, his chances of breaking into the team were hopeless and after only six months at Old Trafford he was released on a free transfer and signed with Dario Gradi at Crewe Alexandra. He was still determined to break back into the big time and he underlined his ambition by scoring fifty five times in one hundred and thirty four league games. His scoring exploits once again drew the attention of the big clubs and in February 1988, Crewe accepted a £200,000 offer from Aston Villa for his services. In two and a half seasons at Villa Park, David developed into one of the most accomplished all round midfield players in the country, scoring twenty first team goals or more in seasons 1989-90 and 1990-91 when helping the club to promotion to the First Division and to runners up spot the following season. David had already won England under twenty one honours when he gained the first of fifty five England caps against Italy in 1989-90. If there was one moment which changed David Platt's life forever it was when he scored a brilliant goal against Belgium in the final phase of the 1990 World Cup series. This strike alerted the attention of club's all round Europe. In July 1991, Italian side Bari paid Aston Villa £5.5 million for his services and in his one season there he finished top goal scorer with eleven goals. In the summer of 1992 he moved to Juventus in a £6.5 million transfer. Unfortunately, with the three foreign players allocation over subscribed, he was often left in the shadows when battling for a place in the side with the likes of Cesar, Möeller and Köhler, and although he won a U.E.F.A. Cup Winners medal, as a non playing reserve, he

managed to play in only sixteen league games. David was on his travels again when he joined Sampdoria for £5.2 million in the summer of 1993, where over the course of the following two seasons he scored seventeen goals in fifty five league outings. In 1994-95, David took his England goal tally up to twenty six, which meant only seven players have scored more times for England. In June 1995, Bruce Rioch sent shockwaves through the F.A. Carling Premiership when persuading David to return to English football with Arsenal. The England captain cost the club £4.75 million. This means that in the last five years Platt has been involved in five transfers which have totalled a staggering total £22 million. David is renown for his great stamina, which enables him to help defenders and support attackers alike. He also has the ability to time late runs beyond the main strikers when finding space to score many of his goals. Added to his drive and great enthusiasm for the game, on his day he is virtually the complete midfield player. After scoring two goals in his first four games an untimely cartlidge operation halted his progress at the strat of 1995-96, but he came back to play against Man. Utd. after missing seven matches.

Honours:
45 England Caps
2 England B Caps
4 England Under-twenty-one Caps
U.E.F.A. Cup Winners Medal   1992-93
PFA Player of the Year   1990

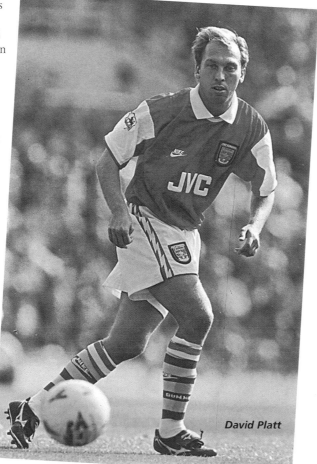

David Platt

PURDIE, Jon   1982-85

Birth Place: Corby, Northamptonshire
Date of Birth: 22nd February 1967

☛ Jon was playing for England schoolboys when he impressed Gunners Scouts in 1981-82 (and had played for the club as a schoolboy) before joining Arsenal as an apprentice during the summer of 1983, turning professional in January 1985. However, his early promise was not fulfilled and he was given a free transfer when joining Wolves in July 1985. He played in nearly one hundred first team games for them, and later played for Cambridge United, Oxford United, Brentford and Shrewsbury and for non League clubs Worcester City, Cheltenham Town as well as being a member of the Kidderminster side which had a great F.A.Cup run in 1993-94

	Games	Goals
Friendly Matches	4	3
Football Combination	11	2
South East Counties League	58	16
Youth Cup	7	1
Other Youth Cups	16	5
Youth Tours	4	0
Total	**100**	**27**

Honours:
England Schoolboy International
Southern Junior Floodlight Cup Winners
   Medal   1983-84
South East Counties League Cup Finalist
   Medal   1984-85

QUINN, Niall   1983-90

Birth Place: Dublin
Date of Birth: 6th October, 1966

☛ Niall was playing junior football in his native Ireland for Manortown United when joining Arsenal in November 1983 and before starting his footballing career he excelled at both Gaelic football and hurling. In his first two seasons at the club he was a consistent member of the youth side when playing either centre half or centre forward and he gained Republic of Ireland youth honours. Niall progressed through the reserve ranks to make his Arsenal league debut (when scoring) against Liverpool in December 1985, replacing the out-of-touch Tony Woodcock. In his first season of league football he failed to convince when playing in twelve league games. For at that time, Niall looked completely bemused when having the ball at his feet and seemed to jump for any ball in the penalty area within a proximity of ten yards. When he did have the ball, it seemed that he had no idea what to do with it. The saying, only time will tell, definitely applies to Niall Quinn, for over the years he has blossomed into one of the most respected strikers in Europe. Like a good bottle of wine, he has matured and improved with age. No one in the modern game causes more havoc in the air in opponents penalty areas, more than Niall Quinn. His once awkward looking frame has added weight which gives him a less gainly style. Added to his fantastic work rate, his neat distribution and the brilliant way he holds up the ball, he was now the finished article. In 1986-87, Niall's persistence gained him a regular place in the league side when missing only seven league games and scoring his all-important goal when equalising against Tottenham in the second leg, cup semi final of the league cup, which helped Arsenal to the final that year. In the following three seasons (after the arrival of Alan Smith) Niall became a fringe member of the first team squad when playing in only twenty league games, and in March 1990 Arsenal accepted an £800,000 bid from Manchester City for his services. Since joining the Maine Road club, he has averaged a goal every third game and at international level represented the Republic of Ireland in two World Cups taking his caps total to the half century mark. When Arsenal accepted that £800,000 fee for Niall in 1990, it seemed as if they'd got the better part of the deal. However, in 1995, as this book is being written, following the retirement of Alan Smith, the transfer didn't look such good business. In the summer of 1995 a speculative transfer to Porto involving Quinn broke down and he stayed at Maine Road. At the end of

November 1995, the Mancunians were shoring up the F.A. Carling Premiership and looked relegation favourites.

	Games	Goals
League	67	14
F.A. Cup	10	2
League Cup	16	4
Other First Team Matches	2	1
Friendly Matches	44	19
Tours	8	1
Football Combination	101	59
South East Counties League	44	17
Youth Cup	4	0
Other Youth Cups	8	6
Youth Tours	9	1
Total	**313**	**124**

Honours:
(WITH ARSENAL)
13 Eire Caps
6 Eire Under-twenty-one Caps
Eire Youth Caps
League Cup Winners Medal   1986-87
F.A. Charity Shield Finalists Medal   1989
Southern Junior Floodlight Cup Winners
    Medal   1983-84
South East Counties League Cup Finalists
    Medal   1984-85
(WITH MANCHESTER CITY)
37 Eire Caps
2 Eire B Caps

RAWLINS, Matthew   1992-95

Birth Place: Bristol, Avon
Date of Birth: 12th September 1975

☛ Matthew was playing for Avon County and had played for the club whilst still a schoolboy before joining Arsenal as a trainee in the summer of 1992, turning professional two years later. Matthew was the youth team's top goal scorer in 1992-93 (twenty goals) and in 1993-94 (twenty eight goals) when gaining an F.A Youth Cup Winners Medal versus Millwall. In 1994-95, he failed to consolidate his position in the combination side and he was granted a free transfer in June 1995.

	Games	Goals
Friendlies	23	12
Football Combination	11	2
South East Counties League	54	35
Youth Cup	11	5
Other Youth Cups	13	8
Youth Tours	2	0
Total	**114**	**62**

Honours:
F.A Youth Cup Winners Medal   1993-94
Southern Junior Floodlight Cup Finalist
    Medal   1992-93

READ, Paul   1990

Birth Place: Harlow, Essex
Date of Birth: 25th September 1973

☛ Paul had played for Essex and England schoolboys when joining Arsenal as a trainee during the summer of 1990 (turning professional in October 1991). In 1990-91 and 1991-92 the "Two Pauls" Read and Shaw wreaked havoc with defences when scoring over one hundred goals between them. Read alone netting forty eight times in all matches in 1991-92. Paul was sidelined for most of the following two seasons when he received ruptured knee ligaments, this after winning an England Youth Cap. At the back end of the 1994-95 season Paul gained valuable experience when playing in eleven league games whilst on loan to Leyton Orient.

	Games	Goals
Friendly Matches	33	30
Football Combination	61	28
South East Counties League	39	48
Youth Cup	5	6
Other Youth Cups	12	10
Youth Tours	11	9
Total	**161**	**131**

Honours:
1 England Youth Cap
England Schoolboy International
South East Counties League Championship
    Medal   1990-91
Southern Junior Floodlight Cup Winners
    Medal   1990-91
Southern Junior Floodlight Cup Finalist
    Medal   1991-92

REID, Wesley   1985-87

Birth Place: Lewisham, London
Date of Birth: 10th September 1968

☛ Wesley had played for South London and had won Inner London County Honours when joining Arsenal as an apprentice in July 1985, turning professional in July 1986. A tough tackling midfield player, he could also play full back. He was not retained by the club in June 1987 when he joined Millwall. Wesley later played for Bradford City, and in Scotland with Airdrie whom he helped to the Scottish Cup Final Versus Glasgow Rangers in 1991-92.

	Games	Goals
Friendlies	8	0
Football Combination	34	3
South East Counties League	21	1
Youth Cup	5	0
Other Youth Cups	8	0
Youth Tours	8	0
Total	**84**	**4**

Honours:
(WITH AIRDRIE)
Scottish Cup Finalists Medal   1991-92

Niall Quinn

RICHARDSON, Kevin   1987-90

Birth Place: Newcastle, Durham
Date of Birth: 4th December 1962

🦅 Kevin joined Everton as an associated schoolboy in July 1978, becoming an apprentice in May 1979, turning professional in December 1980. Whilst at Goodison Park, the slightly built Richardson was never an automatic choice having to dispute the midfield places with Bracewell, Reid and Sheedy. However, he appeared for Everton in both the League Cup and F.A. Cup Finals of 1983-84. As well as playing in fourteen league games in their League Championship season of 1984-85. In September 1986 he was transferred to Watford for £225,000. His stay at Vicarage Road was just under a year before he joined Arsenal for £200,000 in August 1987. Kevin's attributes were his never say die attitude, a great competitive spirit and for a player with slight build, a very strong tackle. In his first season at Highbury he staked a claim for a first team place when taking over from Graham Rix on the left hand side of midfield. He played in twenty nine league games of which his Arsenal league debut was as substitute in a 6-0 home victory versus Portsmouth, Kevin was also a member of the Littlewoods Cup Final side against Luton Town in 1988. In the championship winning campaign on 1988-89, he moved to the right hand side of midfield when predominately replacing the injured Paul Davis. Richardson was the unsung hero of that side, doing the spade work of denying opponents space and stifling the opposition's play makers. He played in thirty two league games that season and it was his injury which enabled injury time to be played, allowing Michael Thomas the time to score in that never to be forgotten title decider at Anfield. Although Kevin was still an integral part of the 1989-90 league side (thirty three appearances) there seemed to be a difference of opinion between himself and George Graham and in May 1990 he joined Real Sociedad for £750,000 when linking up with John Aldridge and Dalian Atkinson. Both parties must have finished up pleased with the situation, Arsenal had made a profit of over half a million pounds on the player and Richardson, whilst at Highbury, had become one of the very few players to have won League Championship medals with two different clubs. He returned to England when signing for Aston Villa for £450,000 in August 1991 and in his first season he was ever present in all of Villa's fifty one first team games, achieving a remarkable record of playing in every minute of those fixtures (not once

substituted). In the best part of four seasons at Villa Park he played in nearly one hundred and fifty league games, was made club captain, helped the club to victory over Manchester United in 1994 Coca Cola Cup Final and in 1993-94, Kevin deservedly won an England cap versus Greece. In February 1995, Kevin followed his old boss Ron Atkinson to Coventry City signing for them in a £300,000 transfer.

	Games	Goals
League	96	5
F.A. Cup	9	1
League Cup	16	
2Other First Team Matches	8	0
Friendly Matches	11	2
Tours	7	2
Football Combination	10	0
Total	**157**	**12**

Honours:
(WITH EVERTON)
League Championship Medal   1984-85
F.A. Cup Winners Medal   1983-84
League Cup Finalists Medal   1983-84
F.A. Charity Shield Winners Medal   1986
F.A. Charity Shield Finalists Medal 1984
(WITH ARSENAL)
League Championship Medal   1988-89
League Cup Finalists Medal   1987-88
F.A. Charity Shield Finalists Medal 1990
Wembley International Tournament Winners Medal   1988
Makita International Tournament Winners Medals   1989
(WITH ASTON VILLA)
1 England Cap
League Cup Winners Medal   1993-94

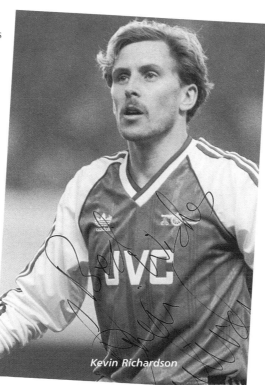
Kevin Richardson

RIVERO, Francis   1984-87

Birth Place: Santa Cruz, Tenerife
Date of Birth: 29th December 1968

🦅 Francis was a full back whose father was a Venezuelan, and had represented the district of Wandsworth when joining Arsenal as an apprentice in the summer of 1985 (turning professional one year later). Originally a midfield player, he was converted to full back when helping Arsenal to three Junior Finals in the mid 1980's. He was released on a free transfer at the end of the 1986-87 season. Francis later played for Farnborough, Wealdstone and Staines.

	Games	Goals
Friendly Matches	5	0
Football Combination	9	0
South East Counties League	55	8
Youth Cup	5	0
Other Youth Cups	20	1
Youth Tours	12	0
Total	**106**	**9**

Honours:
2 South East Counties League Cup Finalist Medals   1984-85, 1985-86
Southern Junior Floodlight Cup Finalist Medal   1985-86

RIX, Graham   1974-88

Birth Place: Askern, Doncaster, Yorkshire
Date of Birth: 23rd October 1957

🦅 Graham Rix joined Arsenal as an apprentice in June 1974, turning professional in January 1975. This was after he had represented Doncaster and Yorkshire schools. Graham worked his way through the club's ranks and eventually made his league debut at Highbury against Leicester City on the 2nd April 1977 (Graham scoring the first goal) in a 3-0 victory. And he finished that season playing in seven of the club's last ten league games. In 1977-78, he took over the left sided midfield position from George Armstrong, playing in thirty nine league games and came on as a substitute in that seasons F.A. Cup Final versus Ipswich Town. In 1978-79, Graham missed the first three league games of the season but for the rest of that campaign he was ever present, when with Liam Brady, he was the main influence in Arsenal's midfield and it was Graham's excellent cross which was turned in by Alan Sunderland for Arsenal's winning goal in the final minute of the 1979 F.A. Cup Final versus Manchester

United. Rix followed this, in 1979-80, by playing in his third consecutive F.A. Cup Final against West Ham and was the unfortunate Arsenal player who missed the final spot kick in the penalty shoot out against Valencia in that season's European Cup Winners Cup Final. In the following season, 1980-81, he made Arsenal history when he became the club's first player to win caps at four different levels when he won the first of his seventeen full England caps versus Norway, (to add to the youth, under twenty one, and B caps that he had won previously). With the departure of Liam Brady to Italy, the added responsibility seemed to rejuvenate Rix and he thrived on this. Graham was a member of the England World Cup squad in the 1982 World Cup and in 1982-83 he was a leading figure when Arsenal reached both major cup semi finals. In the next term, Graham was appointed club captain when playing in thirty-four league games, although being out of action for six weeks with an Achilles tendon injury. Graham's game was based on his natural footballing ability, whose rather slender frame was deceptive in the fact that on occasions, his shot was as ferocious as any. But it was his play making ability and ball control which were Graham's hallmark. In 1984-85, a re-occurrence of the Achilles injury reduced his league appearances to only eighteen, but in 1985-86, when fully recovered, he missed only four league games that term. In 1986-87, he lost his automatic left sided midfield position to Martin Hayes and in the December of that season he went on a month's loan to Brentford. With George Graham now having a fine nucleus of midfield players at his disposal, he freed Graham in June 1988, who moved to the French club, Caen. He later joined Le Havre before returning home to play for Dundee and later became player/youth coach with Glenn Hoddle at Chelsea. Graham's career

was a long and distinguished one, however, it might have been even more notable if he had not suffered from the media's obsession of comparing him to his master and mentor, Liam Brady.

	Games	Goals
League	351	41
F.A. Cup	44	7
League Cup	47	2
Europe	21	1
Other First Team Matches	1	0
Friendly Matches	79	7
Tours	32	2
Football Combination	124	10
South East Counties League	17	2
Youth Cup	7	4
Other Youth Cups	9	0
Youth Tours	12	1
Total	**744**	**77**

Honours:
17 England Caps
3 England B Caps
7 England Under-twenty-one Caps
2 England Youth Caps
F.A. Cup Winners Medal 1978-79
2 F.A. Cup Finalists Medals 1977-78, 1979-80
European Cup Winners Cup Finalists
    Medal 1979-80
F.A. Charity Shield Finalists Medal 1979

Graham Rix

Stewart Robson

ROBSON, Stewart   1980-87

Birth Place: Billericay
Date of Birth: 6th November 1964

Stewart Robson was an associated schoolboy in December 1978 with Arsenal before joining them as an apprentice in April 1981, (becoming one of the few footballers to have had a public schoolboy education). In the 1980-81 season he was a regular in the South East Counties side. He turned professional in November 1981, and made his league debut during the same month versus West Ham at Upton Park. He played in twenty league matches in 1981-82 and won the first of his eighteen England youth caps. In 1982-83 he was again a regular in the league side, playing in thirty-one matches, although he was unfortunately injured in the F.A. Cup semi-final versus Manchester United. However, after regaining full fitness he played in the club's first sixteen league matches of 1983-84 before sustaining a serious leg injury versus West Brom in December 1983, resulting in him being out of action for three months. He finished that season playing in twenty-eight league games and he won the first of his six Under-twenty-one caps. Stewart, who was an excellent cricketer with Essex Second Eleven, was good enough to have forged out a cricketing career. At this time in his career, other than Norman Whiteside, he was possibly the most talented young footballer in the country. The problem with Stewart, though, was that he was too versatile for his own good, being able to play at full back, centre back or midfield. Stewart's strengths were his formidable power, his great competitiveness and his powerful tackling which was his hallmark. However, on many occasions he went into tackles which hardly any other player would have dared to attempt and it was his fearless approach in these situations, which he would regret later in his career. In 1984-85, he missed only two league games, was drafted into the England squad and was voted Arsenal supporters' player of the year. However, in 1985-86 he again received another serious injury which put him out of action for nearly three months, although he did manage to play in twenty-six league games. With new Arsenal manager, George Graham, at the helm, Robson played in the first five league games of the 1986-87 season before losing his place to Steve Williams and many Arsenal supporters were shocked and saddened when he was transferred for £700,000 to West Ham United in January 1987. Except for the 1987-88 season (when he was voted Hammer of the Year), Stewart's career at Upton Park was one long sorry tale of persistent injuries and in the seasons 1988-91, he played in only fourteen league games. After a loan spell at Coventry City, he joined them on a full time basis when given a free transfer by West Ham in May 1991 and in his first season at

Highfield Road he was back to full fitness when missing only five league games. However, with everyone thinking that his terrible injury problems were behind him, he was unfortunate again when firstly being struck down by an eye infection and then when returning to the side, in February 1993, a recurrence of the hamstring injury brought his season to a close. Stewart returned to the City side in the opening day of the season versus Arsenal at Highbury, but received a horrific knee injury. Stewart battled bravely to save his career for the best part of two years before doctors advised him to retire from the game in June 1995. He was just thirty years of age. Stewart Robson should have been part of Arsenal's glory years of the late eighties and early nineties, but fate ruled otherwise. He received the ultimate accolade from the fans by being voted Player of the Year at every club he played for. A great testament to his whole hearted endeavour and surely a record in itself.

	Games	Goals
League	151	16
F.A. Cup	13	1
League Cup	20	3
Europe	2	1
Friendly Matches	41	4
Tours	12	1
Football Combination	32	4
South East Counties League	18	6
Youth Cup	5	2
Other Youth Cups	6	0
Total	**300**	**38**

Honours:
(WITH ARSENAL)
6 England Under-21 Caps
18 England Youth Caps
Division One P.F.A. Award 1986
(WITH WEST HAM)
7 England Under-21 Caps

ROCASTLE, David   1983-92

Birth Place: Lewisham, London
Date of Birth: 2nd May 1967

☛ Without doubt, David "Rocky" Rocastle was one of the most popular players that Arsenal have had on their books over the last twenty years. The way in which he played his football was a throw back to a bygone age. However, although when things were going right he seemed to play with a smile on his face but after encountering the wisdom of both Viv Anderson and Steve Williams, he became known throughout the length and breadth of the country as someone with great footballing skills which were being spoilt by his, sometimes, temperamental behaviour. But, this did not distract from the fact that during the late 1980's and early 90's he was one of the most talented players in English football. On his day, David was the complete footballer, being able to dazzle

defences with his Brazilian like movements with the ball, which at times seemed magnetised to his feet. He was beautifully balanced, had the instinct of knowing when to release the ball when delivering delightful cross field passes or driving in hard low crosses for his fellow forwards to move in on. Having said all this, George Graham never seemed totally happy with Rocky's performances and the result was that in virtually one quarter of all the league games Rocastle played for Arsenal, George substituted him. David was playing for South London Schoolboys when signing Associated Schoolboys forms for Arsenal in May 1982 and he appeared for the club as a schoolboy before becoming an apprentice in August 1983, turning professional on the last day of 1984. Rocastle had been a regular in both the youth and reserve teams before making his league debut against Newcastle United at Highbury in September 1985, and in the rest of that season he filled in for the injured Stewart Robson in sixteen league games. In 1986-87, he enjoyed a rapid rise to fame when missing only six league games, he won the first of fourteen England under twenty-one caps versus Sweden and was honoured with the 1986 Arsenal Player of the Year Award as well as being voted by his fellow professionals in the Division One P.F.A. side. However, his greatest moment was when scoring the last minute extra time goal against Tottenham which helped Arsenal to the Little-woods Cup Final against Liverpool in 1987. In 1987-88, he was ever present when helping the club back to Wembley for the following season's Littlewoods Cup Final versus Luton. In Arsenal's championship winning campaign of 1988-89, he was again ever present and his form gained him the first of his fourteen England caps when making his debut against Denmark. Rocastle was again voted into the Division One P.F.A side and was elected as Barclays Young Eagle of the Year. However, in 1989-90, although he played in thirty three league games, he suffered a loss of form and had to undergo a knee operation. Worse was to follow in the club's League Championship season of 1990-91, when he played in only sixteen league games due to more injuries amongst which was a broken toe. However, in 1991-92, he took up a new role when playing in a central midfield position and missed only three league games, scoring one of the goals of the season against Manchester United at Old Trafford. He was disappointed at missing out on selection for the 1990 World Cup series but must have been more shattered, when not being included for the 1992 European Championships. All Arsenal followers were stunned when David left his beloved Gunners in August 1992, when George Graham sold him to Leeds United for £2 million. Has since moved on to Manchester City in a further £2 million transaction and in December 1993 he returned to London to join Chelsea. In late November 1995 he was finding it difficult

to get into Glenn Hoddle's side on a regular basis.

	Games	Goals
League	217	24
F.A. Cup	20	4
League Cup	33	6
Europe	4	0
Other First Team Matches	13	3
Friendly Matches	63	7
Tours	13	4
Football Combination	71	11
South East Counties League	48	13
Youth Cup	8	2
Other Youth Cups	18	5
Youth Tours	13	2
Total	**521**	**81**

Honours:
14 England Caps
2 England B Caps
14 England Under-twenty-one Caps
2 League Championship Medals
                    1988-89, 1990-91
League Cup Winners Medal   1986-87
League Cup Finalists Medal   1987-88
F.A. Charity Shield Winners Medal   1991
F.A. Charity Shield Finalists Medal 1989
2 Division One P.F.A. Awards   1987, 1989
Mercantile Credit Centenary Trophy Winners
   Medal   1988-89
Wembley International Tournament Winners
   Medal   1988
Makita International Tournament Winners
   Medal   1989
2 Makita International Tournament Finalists
   Medals   1990, 1991
South East Counties League Cup Finalists
   Medals   1984-85
Southern Junior Floodlight Cup Winners
   Medal   1983-84
Barclays Young Eagle of the Year 1988-89

David Rocastle

ROSE, Matthew   1992

Birth Place: Dartford, Kent
Date of Birth: 24th September 1975

☞ Matthew had played for Kent County at Under 15 and 16 level and played for the club in the 1991-92 season whilst still a schoolboy, becoming a trainee in the summer of 1992. Matthew began as a midfield player but moved to centre back or sweeper in 1993-94 when he skippered Arsenal's F.A Youth Cup Winning team. In 1994-95 he was a regular in the Combination side after turning professional in July 1994.

	Games	Goals
Friendly Matches	18	3
Football Combination	41	3
South East Counties League	50	1
Youth Cup	11	2
Other Youth Cups	13	1
Youth Tours	3	0
Total	**136**	**10**

Honours:

F.A Youth Cup Winners Medal   1993-94
Southern Jnr Floodlight Cup Finalist 1992-93

RUSSO, Donato   1984-86

Birth Place: Bedford
Date of Birth: 28th November 1967

☞ Donato was playing for Bedford Boys and Bedfordshire County under 18's when joining Arsenal as a schoolboy halfway through the 1983-84 season. During the summer of 1984 he became an apprentice, turning professional a year later. Although being a regular in the club's youth side, he was released on a free transfer in June 1986.

	Games	Goals
Friendly Matches	1	0
Football Combination	6	0
South East Counties League	54	0
Youth Cup	5	0
Other Youth Cups	15	0
Youth Tours	4	0
Total	**85**	**0**

Honours:

Southern Junior Floodlight Cup Winners
    Medal   1983-84
Southern Junior Floodlight Cup Finalist
    Medal   1985-85
South East Counties League Cup Finalist
    Metal   1985-86

SANSOM, Kenny   1980-88

Birth Place: Camberwell, London
Date of Birth: 26th September, 1958

☞ Kenny had played for South London, Surrey and England Schoolboys when joining Crystal Palace as an apprentice in 1974, after, like his future team mate, Graham Rix, he had failed a trial at Leeds United. Kenny signed professional forms for The Eagles in December 1975 and over the course of the following five seasons he played in nearly two hundred first team games for the club, won England youth and under twenty one international honours, helped the club to the Second Division Championship in 1978-79 and won the first of his eighty six England caps when playing against Wales. In 1979-80, he started a remarkable record, when he was voted for the first of his eight consecutive left back Division One P.F.A. awards of which no other outfield player has got remotely close to in the near twenty five year history of the awards. By this time, the twenty one year old Sansom, with over two hundred first team games to his credit and already an English International was being regarded as the best left back in the country. In August 1980, Arsenal paid Palace £1.25 million pounds (a world record fee for a full back) in a deal which took Clive Allen and Paul Barrow to Selhurst Park. In his eight seasons at Highbury, Kenny was voted Arsenal Player of the Year in 1981, became the most capped Arsenal player in history (seventy seven) and captained Arsenal in a League Cup Final versus Liverpool in 1986-87. What made Sansom into the great player he was was his remarkable consistency, being ever present in his first two seasons at Highbury. Kenny only missed two league games in 1982-83 and only three in 1984-85. By this time Kenny was easily recognised by many pundits as the finest left back in the country. However, in George Graham's second season at the club, he like many other star names at Highbury were facing fresh challenges from George's "new boys" and at the start of Arsenal's League Championship campaign in 1988-89, Sansom found himself wasting away in the combination side having been replaced by Nigel Winterburn. In December 1988 Newcastle United ended his nightmare when paying Arsenal £300,000 for his talents. However, his stay on Tyneside was only six months and he became homesick, and returned to London in June 1989 when joining Queens Park Rangers. Kenny later played for Coventry City, where in 1991-92, he played in his six hundredth league game. In 1994-95, he was player youth coach at Watford, after a short spell at Brentford and Everton. Eddie Hapgood was regarded as Arsenal greatest ever left back, but if one was to choose a second choice then only Lionel Smith, Bob McNab and Nigel Winterburn would challenge Kenny to that position. Now lives at Bromley, Kent and was promoted to Asssitant Manager of Watford after assisting Chertsey Town.

	Games	Goals
League	314	6
F.A. Cup	26	0
League Cup	48	0
Europe	6	0
Friendly Matches	40	1
Tours	18	1
Football Combination	16	0
Total	**468**	**8**

Honours:
(WITH CRYSTAL PALACE)
9 England Caps
2 England B Caps
8 England Under-twenty-one Caps
7 England Youth Caps
England Schoolboy International
Second Division League Championship
    Medal   1978-79
Division One P.F.A. Award   1979-80
(WITH ARSENAL)
77 England Caps
League Cup Winners Medal   1986-87
League Cup Finalists Medal   1987-88
7 Division One P.F.A. Awards (inc.) 1981-87

Kenny Samson

SCULLY, Pat   1986-91

Birth Place: Dublin, Eire
Date of Birth: 23rd June 1970

☞ Pat had captained the Republic of Ireland Schoolboys Team before joining Arsenal as a trainee in the summer of 1986, turning professional in September 1987. In his four seasons at Highbury, Scully, a centre half, never once had the chance to break into the League side, owing to the presence of Adams O'Leary, Bould, Linighan and Pates. However, Pat's career at Highbury was not all doom and gloom for he helped the club win the F.A Youth Cup in 1987-88 and he also won one Eire Under-23 Cap, nine Under-21 Caps, two B Caps and played in a full

International against Tunisia in 1988-89. Pat also had loan spells at Preston North End and Northampton Town before being transferred to Southend United for £100,000 in January 1991. He joined Huddersfield Town in March 1994 and helped them to promotion to Division One in 1994-95.

	Games	Goals
Friendly Matches	29	0
Football Combination	95	3
South East Counties League	33	4
Youth Cup	8	1
Other Youth Cup's	12	0
Youth Tours	6	0
Total	**183**	**8**

Honours:
Eire Schoolboy International
1 Eire Under 23 Cap
9 Eire Under 21 Caps
2 Eire B Caps
1 Eire Cap
F.A Youth Cup Winners Medal   1987-88
Football Combination Championship Medal
1989-90

SCHWARZ, Stefan   1994-95

Birth Place: Malmo, Sweden
Date of Birth: 18th April 1969

☛ Stefan, the son of a German, began his career in Sweden with his local side Kulldal. His talents were soon being admired and it was not long before he was on the move to Malmo, where in 1988-89, he helped the club to that season's Swedish League Championship. Schwarz was transferred to Bayer 40 Leverkusen of Germany in the 1989-90 season, before Benfica paid a seven figure sum to acquire his services in the close season of 1990-91. By this time Stefan had won the first of his thirty six Swedish caps. In his four seasons at the "Stadium of Light" he was instrumental in the defeat of Arsenal when playing for Benfica in the 1991 European Cup, and he won Portuguese League Championship medals in 1990-91 and 1993-94 as well as a Cup Winners Medal in 1992-93. He was one of Sweden's stars, who finished third in the 1994 World Cup series and joined Arsenal soon after for £1.8 million. His first displays were seen at Highbury in the Makita Tournament when Gunners fans witnessed his great enthusiasm for the game, fantastic stamina, a biting tackle and ferocious shooting power. His League debut was on the opening day of the season versus Manchester City 20th August 1994 and went on to play 43 league games last season. Stefan was also an influential member of the side which helped Arsenal through to the 1995 European Cup Winners Cup Final, his goal sending the game into extra time. However, his Portuguese wife wanted to live in a warmer climate than England, so unsettled Stefan accepted a £3 million move to Fiorentina of Italy in July 1995.

	Games	Goals
League	34	2
F.A Cup	1	0
League Cup	5	0
Europe	8	2
Other First Team Games	4	0
Friendlies	2	0
Tours	4	0
Total	**58**	**4**

Honours:
36 Swedish Caps
(WITH ARSENAL)
European Cup Winners Cup Finalists Medal
1994-95
European Super Cup Finalists Medal   1995
Makita Tournament Trophy Winners Medal
1994
(WITH BENFICA)
2 Portuguese League Championship Medals
1990-91, 1993-94
Portuguese Cup Winners Medal   1992-93
(WITH MALMO)
Swedish League Championship Medal
1988-89

SEAMAN, David   1990

Birth Place: Rotherham, Yorkshire
Date of Birth: 19th September 1963

☛ All great goalkeepers have a certain presence about them, Jennings, Shilton, Zoff and Yashin had this aura and without doubt, David Seaman has too. The greatness of his goalkeeping is emphasised by his commanding and calm approach, which is one of the main features of his game. But above all it is his magnificent reflexes allied to his fantastic positional sense which earmarks him as a goalkeeper out of the top draw. David began his career with Leeds United after he had represented Rotherham schoolboys. He had become an apprentice at Elland Road in March 1980, turning professional in September 1981 and in his eleven months as a professional at the club he never made a league appearance, due to the consistency of former Gunner, John Lukic. Seaman was transferred to Peterborough United for £4,000 in August 1982 and his brilliant form for "The Posh" was noted by Birmingham City manager,

Jim Smith, who paid £100,000 for his services in October 1984, as a replacement for Tony Coton who had been transferred to Watford. In his first season, at St. Andrews, he helped the club to promotion to Division One. However, in 1985-86, although being ever present and winning England Under-twenty-one honours he could not save City from relegation and in order to remain playing in the First Division he joined Q.P.R. for £225,000 in August 1986. In four seasons at Loftus Road, David was a first team fixture in the side and in 1988-89 he won the first of his seventeen England caps when appearing against Scotland. Although John Lukic had performed magnificently for Arsenal, George Graham went public when declaring his interest in Seaman and in May 1990, Arsenal paid out a British record fee for a goalkeeper of £1.3 million when obtaining Seaman's services. No Arsenal follower could have realised the impact David would have on the side and in that League Championship winning season, when being ever present, he broke two club records when conceding only eighteen league goals, and keeping twenty-four clean sheets. Again, ever present in 1991-92, he followed this in the next season

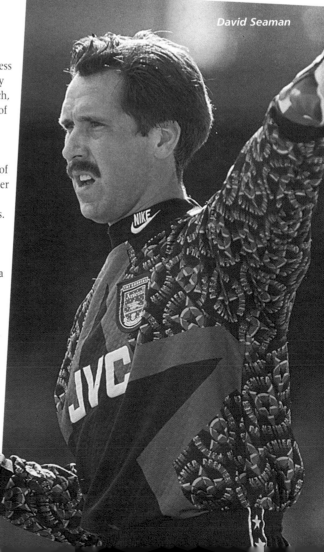

David Seaman

when helping the club to the F.A. and Coca-Cola Cup Double and it was David alone who had kept Arsenal in the Coca-Cola Cup when saving three penalties in a penalty shoot-out against Millwall at the Den. In 1993-94, he was a key member of the side which won the European Cup Winners Cup against Parma, this after he had bravely battled on with a painful rib injury which resulted in him having to have six pain-killing injections before the final. No Arsenal follower will ever forget his performance against Sampdoria in the European Cup Winners Cup semi-final in the penalty shoot-out, his goalkeeping was nothing less than miraculous and one particular save from Lombardo will live on in the memory of many. However, in the final, Nayim, scored arguably one of the all-time great goals, for which the press inexplicably blamed David, stating that he was too far off his line. The question to be asked though is how many goalkeepers would have been on their line, with the ball in that position at that time. Unfortunately, for David, things got even worse when he suffered a serious leg injury in Arsenal's close season tour of China. But he was an ever-present up to and including the North London derby clash with Spurs at White Hart Lane on November 18th, 1995.

	Games	Goals
League	189	0
F.A. Cup	22	0
League Cup	27	0
Europe	22	0
Other First Team Matches	10	0
Friendly Matches	16	0
Tours	15	0
Total	**301**	**0**

Honours:
(WITH ARSENAL)
17 England Caps
6 England B Caps
10 Under-twenty-one Caps
1 Football League Cap
League Championship Medals 1990-91
F.A. Cup Winners Medal 1992-93
League Cup Winners Medal 1992-93
European Cup Winners Cup Winners Medal
1993-94
European Cup Winners Cup Finalists Medal
1994-95
F.A. Charity Shield Medal 1991
F.A. Charity Shield Finalists Medal 1993
Division One P.F.A. Award 1991
European Super Cup Finalists Medal 1995
Wembley International Tournament Winners
Medal 1988
Makita International Tournament Winners
Medals 1994
2 Makita International Tournament Finalists
Medal 1990, 1991

SELLEY, Ian 1990

Birth Place: Chertsey, Surrey
Date of Birth: 14th June 1974

☛ Ian was playing for Surrey County Schoolboys when joining Arsenal as an associated schoolboy in October 1988, before becoming a trainee in July 1990, after he had been a guest player on the F.A School of Excellence tour of Italy. In 1990-91, he showed his great versatility when playing for the Youth Team playing in midfield, on the wing and on one occasion, as a stand in goalkeeper. In 1991-92 he became a regular member of the reserves, turning professional during the close season of 1992. In his first term as a professional, 1992-93, he appeared on the substitutes bench in both the Coca Cola and F.A Cup Finals (without coming on), and Ian won two England Youth Caps and made nine League appearances of which his League debut was at Highbury versus Blackburn Rovers in September 1992. In 1993-94 he figured in eighteen League games, won three England Under-21 caps and was the youngest player on the pitch when Arsenal beat Parma in the European Cup Winners Cup Final in Copenhagen. However, in 1994-95, a serious leg injury ruined Ian's progress. The undoubted brilliant skills of Selley will hopefully be back in action for the New Year. In May 1994, Ian was a 1990's version of Cliff Bastin in the sense that he had won F.A, Coca Cola and European Cup Winners Cup Winners medals and played for England-21, all before his twentieth birthday.

	Games	Goals
League	40	0
F.A Cup	3	0
League Cup	6	0
Europe	8	2
Other First Team Games	2	0
Friendly Matches	43	7
Tours	4	0
Football Combination	47	2
South East Counties League	42	5
Youth Cup	3	0
Other Youth Cups	13	2
Youth Tours	4	0
Total	**215**	**18**

Honours:
3 England Under Twenty One Caps
2 England Youth Caps
F.A Cup Winners Medal 1992-93
League Cup Winners Medal 1992-93
European Cup Winners Cup Winners Medal
1993-94
European Super Cup Finalists Medal 1995
Makita Tourn. Trophy Winners Medal 1994
South East Counties League Championship
Medal 1990-91
Southern Junior Floodlight Cup Winners
Medal 1990-91
Southern Junior Floodlight Cup Finalists
Medal 1991-92

SHAW, Paul 1990

Birth Place: Maidenhead, Berkshire
Date of Birth: 4th September 1973

☛ Paul's partnership with Paul Read was quite phenomenal for Arsenal's Youth Team in the early 1990's, after he had joined the club as a trainee in the summer of 1990, having previously played for the club as a schoolboy. Paul had played for Berkshire County and for their Under 19 team when only fifteen. Shaw turned professional in September 1991 when breaking into the football Combination side. Paul has been a regular for the reserves over the last three seasons, eventually receiving his League opportunity when making his Arsenal debut versus Nottingham Forest at the City Ground 3rd December 1994. An England Youth International with one Cap, he gained experience when scoring four times in ten League games for Burnley at the back end of the 1994-95 season whilst on loan.

	Games	Goals
League	1	0
Friendly Matches	37	21
Tours	1	0
Football Combination	103	37
South East Counties League	48	31
Youth Cup	4	0
Other Youth Cups	17	11
Youth Tours	7	1
Total	**218**	**101**

Honours:
1 England Youth Cap
South East Counties League Championship
Medal 1990-91
Southern Junior Floodlight Cup Winners
Medal 1990-91
Southern Junior Floodlight Cup Finalists
Medal 1991-92

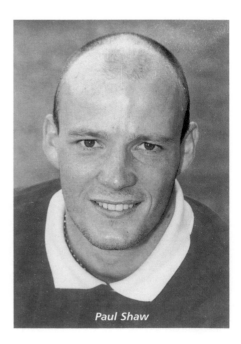
Paul Shaw

SMITH, Alan 1987-95

Birth Place: Birmingham
Date of Birth: 21st November, 1962

☛ Everyone connected with Arsenal football club must have been saddened by the news of Alan's premature retirement from the game in July 1995, when just thirty two years of age. Alan Smith was a centre forward who was a throw back to the days when players would take a barrage of physical abuse, pick themselves up and get on with the game. In the best part of six hundred first class games, Alan was booked on just one occasion, this being for the most petty of things in the F.A. Cup Final replay of 1992-93 against Sheffield Wednesday and it would have been understandable if Alan had turned round and said to the referee "Do you know who I am?" During the course of his career at Highbury he scored two of the most crucial goals in the club's history. The first being the opening goal at Anfield versus Liverpool in the 1989 title decider and the other being when his crisp volley beat the Parma goalkeeper to win the European Cup Winners Cup in 1993-94. Alan had played for Birmingham and West Midlands and was playing junior football for West Hills Athletic when joining non-league Alvechurch. While at the non-league club he represented the English Semi-professional international side. His form soon drew the attention of Leicester City and he joined them for £22,000 in June 1982. In his first season at Leicester his thirteen goals, when partnering the up and coming Gary Lineker, helped the Filberts to promotion to the First Division. Whilst at Leicester he scored over eighty first team goals in less than two hundred and twenty games. His transfer to Arsenal was a strange affair, for he signed after the transfer deadline in March 1987. This resulted in him being loaned back to Leicester for the rest of that season. The first installment on the £800,000 which was paid out for Smith was soon to be paid back, when he scored a hat trick in the 6-0 demolition of Portsmouth at Highbury in the fourth league game of the season, after making his Arsenal league debut in front of a near fifty five thousand crowd at Highbury v. Liverpool. He did not reach expectations in that initial season at the club when he seemed to lack confidence, although Alan did score the second goal in the 2-3 defeat in the League Cup Final against Luton Town in 1988. However, in Arsenal's championship winning campaign of 1988-89 his form took a turn for the better, in fact, he was a revelation. He became a master of being able to control long passes out of defence when retaining possession on either flank or in his orthodox centre forward position and the way he could control the ball when holding up proceedings for the others to join the attack, was bettered by none. He scored twenty three league goals as the First Division's top goal scorer in thirty six appearances which included a hat trick in

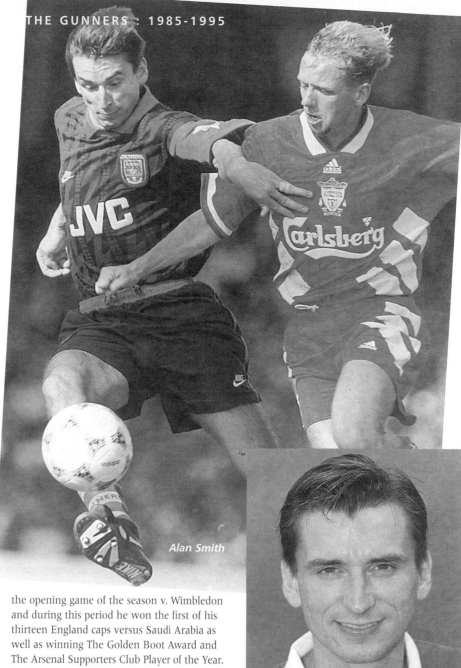

Alan Smith

the opening game of the season v. Wimbledon and during this period he won the first of his thirteen England caps versus Saudi Arabia as well as winning The Golden Boot Award and The Arsenal Supporters Club Player of the Year. In 1989-90, Alan scored only ten league goals in thirty eight league appearances, but in 1990-91 Smith answered the critics when scoring twenty two times in thirty seven games, helping The Gunners to their second League Championship in three seasons. In 1991-92, up until his premature retirement, he became more a provider than goal scorer, although by this time he had become one of only thirteen Arsenal players to have reached the milestone of scoring one hundred first team goals for the club. Alan reaped a bumper benefit when old adversaries Sampdoria appeared at Highbury on November 9, 1995 for his testimonial match watched by a crowd of over 17,000. The match raised £250,000.

	Games	Goals
League	264	86
F.A. Cup	27	5
League Cup	38	16
Europe	17	7
Other First Team	15	3
Friendly Matches	36	21
Tours	19	9
Football Combination	18	9
Total	**434**	**156**

Honours:
(WITH ARSENAL)
13 England Caps
5 England B Caps
2 League Championship Medals
1988-89, 1990-91
F.A. Cup Winners Medal 1992-93
League Cup Finalists Medal 1987-88
European Cup Winners Cup Winners Medal 1993-94
F.A. Charity Shield Medal 1991
F.A. Charity Shield Finalists Medal 1989
Mercantile Credit Centenary Trophy Winners Medal 1988-89
Division One P.F.A. Award 1989
2 Golden Boot Awards 1989, 1991
Wembley International Tournament Winners Medal 1988
2 Makita International Tournament Winners Medals 1989, 1994
Makita International Tournament Finalists Medal 1990

SMITH, Paul   1984-87

Birth Place: Wembley, Middlesex
Date of Birth: 5th October 1967

☛ Paul, a right winger, was a product of Brent, whom in the mid 1970's had developed the likes of Luther Blissett, Ricky Hill and Cyrille Regis. Paul represented Middlesex and having played for Arsenal as a schoolboy he joined them as an apprentice in the Summer of 1984. A regular on the club's right wing in the Youth side, Paul turned professional in Oct. 1985 and was understudy to Martin Hayes in the reserve side. Soon after he was released by the club in July 1987, later played for Brentford, Bristol Rovers and Torquay.

	Games	Goals
Friendly Matches	11	0
Football Combination	23	1
South East Counties League	39	5
Youth Cup	8	1
Other Youth Cups	13	2
Youth Tours	19	1
Total	**113**	**10**

Honours:
2 South East Counties League Cup Finalists
   Medals   1984-85, 1985-86
Southern Junior Floodlight Cup Finalists
   Medal   1985-86

STANISLAUS, Roger   1984-87

Birth Place: Hammersmith, London
Date of Birth: 2nd November 1968

☛ Roger had played for Inner County London Boys, appearing as a schoolboy for the South East Counties League side in 1984, becoming an apprentice in 1985. At this point of his career he was playing a midfield role, turning professional in July 1986, when converting to full back. With a surplus of full backs on the club's books at this time, Stanislaus was given a free transfer in Sept. 1987 when joining Brentford. He later moved to Bury for £90,000 in July 1990 and in the last eight seasons he has played in over 300 league games and has developed into one of the most respected full backs in the lower Leagues. Roger moved to Leyton Orient in the summer of 1995.

	Games	Goals
Friendly Matches	8	2
Football Combination	33	2
South East Counties League	32	2
Youth Cup	8	0
Other Youth Cups	21	2
Youth Tours	16	1
Total	**118**	**9**

Honours:
Southern Junior Floodlight Cup Finalists
   Medal   1985-86
South East Counties League Cup Finalists
   Medal   1985-86

TALBOT, Brian   1979-85

Birth Place: Ipswich, Suffolk
Date of Birth: 21st July 1953

☛ Brian Talbot began his career as an apprentice with Ipswich Town in July 1968, and before turning professional in August 1972, he had a two year loan spell with Toronto Metros. He spent seven seasons at Portman Road, playing in well over two hundred first team matches and won five England caps. He was also a member of the F.A. Cup winning team versus Arsenal in 1978. Brian was transferred to Gunners for a then club record fee of £450,000 in January, 1979 and made his league debut in a home fixture versus Nott'm Forest on 13th January 1979. He was a member of Arsenal's F.A.Cup winning team (scoring the first goal) against Manchester United in the 1979 F.A. Cup Final and thus became, and still is, the only player ever to play for different cup winning teams in successive seasons. Talbot created an Arsenal club record, in 1979-80, when he appeared in all of the club's seventy first team games, (the most first team games played by an Arsenal player in one season) also in that campaign he played in both losing major finals, in the F.A. Cup versus West Ham and in the European Cup Winners Cup versus Valencia. His commitment to the club, in the game against the Hammers, was so great that when the final whistle blew he collapsed with exhaustion. However, he recovered to play in England's Australia tour during the summer of 1980 when he won his sixth and final England cap. Brian's play was built around his great stamina. He literally spent the whole of the ninety minutes running his heart out for Arsenal. Talbot was the workhorse, the dynamo and the driving force behind Arsenal's midfield, when toiling for his more skilled team-mates such as Brady and Rix. To call him an unsung hero would be an understatement. In just over six seasons at Highbury, he played in a staggering three hundred and eighty games for the club. This averages out at sixty-three games per year. He missed only two league games in 1980-81 and one league game in 1984-85 and was ever-present in 1981-82 and 1982-83. Talbot, is one of only five Arsenal players in the club's history (Lukic, Parker, Rice and Sansom being the others) to have been ever-present for the club in as many as three different seasons. However, after the signing of Steve Williams, Brian realised his Highbury days were over and he joined Watford for £150,000 in June 1985. Talbot later played for Stoke City, West Bromwich Albion and Fulham. After serving as chairman of the P.F.A., he went into management with West Bromwich and player-manager of Aldershot. He is now managing Hibernians of Malta.

	Games	Goals
League	254	40
F.A. Cup	30	7
League Cup	27	1
Europe	15	1
Other First Team Matches	1	0
Friendly Matches	22	9
Tours	26	3
Football Combination	5	2
Total	**380**	**63**

Honours:
(WITH ARSENAL AND IPSWICH)
6 England Caps
8 England B Caps
1 England Under-21 Cap
1 Football League Cap
2 F.A. Cup Winners Medals 1977-78, 1978-79
1 F.A. Cup Finalists Medal   1979-80
European Cup Winners Cup Finalists Medal
                                    1979-80
2 F.A. Charity Shield Finalists Medals
                          1977-78, 1978-79
Division One P.F.A. Award   1976-77

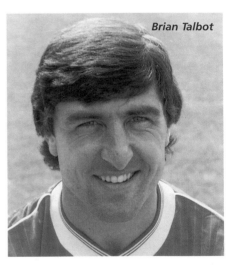
Brian Talbot

TAYLOR, Ross   1993

Birth Place: Southend, Essex
Date of Birth: 14th January, 1977

☛ Ross had appeared for Essex Schoolboys and had won England representative honours at under fifteen and under sixteen level, when joining Arsenal as a trainee in the summer of 1993. This young left back had played for the youth team while still a schoolboy. In 1994-95, he became a member of the combination league side whilst winning England youth honours. The previous season he had been a part of the F.A. youth cup winning side against Millwall. A fine future is predicted. Ross signed professional forms in the summer 1995.

	Games	Goals
Football Combination	16	0
Friendlies	13	0
South East Counties	43	1
F.A. Youth Cup	11	0
Other Youth Cup	12	0
Total	**95**	**1**

Honours:
England Under-fifteen and Under-sixteen
  International
3 England Youth Caps
F.A. Youth Cup Winners Medal   1993-94
Southern Junior Football Cup Finalists Medal
                                      1994-95

THOMAS, Michael   1983-91

Birth Place: Lambeth, London
Date of Birth: 24th August 1967

☛ On the 26th May 1989, Michael Thomas wrote himself into the Arsenal record books for all time, for without any doubt, of all the near 6,000 league goals Arsenal have scored in their long history, not one has been more important or precious than Michael's injury time goal, in the last game of the season, when deciding the League Championship against Liverpool at Anfield. This goal has been described as comic strip fiction and an epic of theatrical drama. Certainly the amount of times, Arsenal supporters had hit stop-rewind-play on their video recorders, must have made it the most recorded goal in Football League history. One even now can see Michael bursting through the Liverpool defence with Brian Moore stating "It's up for grabs now", when in this magnificent counter attack, he evaded Nichol's challenge and delicately clipped the ball pass the advancing Grobbelaar. In the dying seconds Michael nonchalantly laid the ball back to Lukic in his own penalty area, surrounded by Liverpool forwards. Michael had played for South London and England schoolboys, as captain, when he signed associated schoolboy forms with Arsenal in September 1982. Thomas progressed through the ranks as an apprentice when signing in August 1983, turning professional on the last day of 1984. In 1984-85, he won the first of his twenty-two England Youth Caps as captain. In 1986-87, he enjoyed a loan period at Portsmouth in January 1987 and although being a deputy at full back for both Anderson and Sansom he made his first team debut in the Littlewoods Cup semi-final in the home leg versus Tottenham. In 1987-88, Michael missed only five league games when appearing mainly in the right back position and he won the first of his twelve England Under-twenty-one Caps versus Yugoslavia. In 1988-89, in that League Championship winning season, he was drafted into midfield when becoming Arsenal's player of the year and winning his first England Cap versus Saudi Arabia, thus becoming the first player in Arsenal's history to play at five different levels for his country. This thoroughbred, versatile, athletic, midfield player had played for England at schoolboy, youth, Under-twenty-one, 'B' and full level. In 1989-90, Thomas missed only six league games,

followed by, in 1990-91, thirty-one league games when being an important part of the League Championship winning side. However, after playing in only ten league games in 1991-92, he lost his place to David Hillier and was subsequently transferred to Liverpool for £1.5 million in December 1991. This elegant midfield player, who has wonderful stamina and ability to make runs on and off the ball, joined Liverpool to strengthen their midfield. During his four seasons at Anfield, Michael has been plagued with injuries, but paid back some of his transfer fee when scoring a stunning first goal in the 1991-92 F.A. Cup Final versus Sunderland. It came to light that Michael never wanted to leave Highbury and that his main qualm had been that he had had certain disagreements with Arsenal manager George Graham. In February 1992, Michael had his story published in a national newspaper criticising George Graham. The F.A. took stern action when fining Michael £3,000. Whatever happens to Michael in the rest of his playing career nothing will remotely compare to that unbelievable evening of 26th May 1989.

	Games	Goals
League	163	24
F.A. Cup	17	1
League Cup	24	5
Europe	2	0
Other First Team Matches	14	1
Friendly Matches	54	4
Tours	14	0
Football Combination	105	11
South East Counties League	44	3
Youth Cup	16	1
Other Youth Cups	19	1
Youth Tours	17	2
Total	**489**	**53**

Honours:
(WITH ARSENAL)
2 England Caps

Michael Thomas

5 England B Caps
1 Football League Cap
12 England Under-twenty-one Caps
22 England Youth Caps
England Schoolboy International
2 League Championship Medals
                          1988-89, 1990-91
League Cup Winners Medal   1986-87
League Cup Finalists Medal   1987-88
F.A. Charity Shield Medal   1991
F.A. Charity Shield Finalists Medal   1989
Mercantile Credit Centenary Trophy Winners
  Medal   1988-89
Wembley International Tournament Winners
Medal   1988
Makita International Tournament Winners
  Medal   1989
2 Makita International Tournament Finalists
  Medals   1990, 1991
Football Combination League Championship
  Medal   1983-84
South East Counties League Cup Finalists
  Medal   1984-85
Southern Junior Floodlight Cup Winners
  Medal   1983-84
Southern Junior Floodlight Cup Finalists
  Medal   1985-86
(WITH LIVERPOOL)
F.A. Cup Winners Medal   1991-92
League Cup Winners Medal   1994-95

TURNER, Paul   1984-87

Birth Place: Cheshunt, Hertfordshire
Date of Birth: 13th November 1968

☛ Paul had won Hertfordshire Schoolboy honours and was on Associated Schoolboy Forms with Tottenham before joining Arsenal as an apprentice in the Summer of 1985. A young midfielder, he turned professional in July 1986, but spent just over a year at Highbury before being released and joining Cambridge United in September 1987. He later played for Farnborough and Enfield.

	Games	Goals
Friendly Matches	9	1
Football Combination	27	2
South East Counties League	30	1
Youth Cup	5	0
Other Youth Cups	10	0
Youth Tours	6	0
Total	**87**	**4**

Honours:
Southern Junior Floodlight Cup Finalists
  Medal   1985-86
South East Counties League Cup Finalists
  Medal   1985-86

WARD, Stephen   1986-88

☛ Stephen Ward was an England School-boy International winger who joined Arsenal as a trainee during the Summer of 1986 and before officially joining the club he suffered a broken leg in a practice match. Stephen was offered a professional contract in June 1987 but persistent leg injuries meant that he spent much of this time at the F.A.'s Lilleshall Rehabilitation Unit to speed his recovery. The injuries by this time had taken their toll and Stephen was forced into retirement.

	Games	Goals
Friendly Matches	1	0
South East Counties League	1	0
Total	**2**	**0**

Honours:
England Schoolboy International

WEBSTER, Kenny   1989-94

Birth Place: Shepherds Bush, London
Date of Birth: 2nd March 1973

☛ Kenny had played for Inner London and England Under 15's before joining Arsenal as a trainee in July 1989, after he had appeared for the club as a schoolboy in 1988-89. He was a regular member of Arsenal's Youth Team, playing either full back or centre back as well as winning an England Youth Cap. Webster turned professional in the Summer of 1991. He was a consistent performer at full back in the Combination side in his last three seasons with Arsenal. Like so many mentioned before, he was yet another young full back who was discarded when given a free transfer in June 1994. Kenny moved on to Peterborough United.

	Games	Goals
Friendly Matches	36	4
Football Combination	81	2
South East Counties League	42	1
Youth Cup	6	0
Other Youth Cups	20	2
Youth Tours	14	1
Total	**199**	**10**

Honours:
England Under 15 International
England Youth Cap
Southern Junior Floodlight Cup Winners
    Medal   1990-91
Southern Junior Floodlight Cup Finalists
    Medal   1989-90

WHYTE, Chris   1977-86

Birth Place: Islington, London
Date of Birth: 2nd September 1961

☛ Chris was playing for Islington and Inner London Schoolboys when signing Associated Schoolboy Forms for Arsenal in May 1977 (apprentice) turning professional three weeks after his seventeenth birthday in September 1978. In his first four seasons at Highbury he rose through the ranks when playing at either full back or centre half and after the sale of Willie Young to Nottingham Forest, Chris was given his League debut versus Manchester City at Highbury, 17th October, 1981 and from then until the end of the season, he missed only one League game. To anyone who had seen Chris at that time most would have backed him to have gone on to win Full International Honours. Still not twenty one years of age, his partnership with David O'Leary, in the centre of defence was outstanding and at this stage his coolness and his confidence in his own ability was there for all to see. Unlike most centre halves, he seemed to be comfortable with the ball at his feet and his distribution was immaculate. These performances gaining "Huggy" (after the character in Starsky and Hutch) four England Under Twenty One Caps. In 1982-83, he missed only six League games when helping the club to both the F.A. Cup and League Cup Semi Finals. However, in 1983-84, although starting the season in a back line of three centre backs, (Hill and O'Leary being the others) he was dropped after a disastrous League Cup home defeat against Walsall and other than four League games, he was replaced for the rest of that season by newly signed Tommy Caton. This experience shattered Chris's self belief and he was now just a shadow of his former self. In 1984-85, his position was made even worse with the emergence of the young Tony Adams. However, in 1985-86, he became an emergency striker for the reserve side and he scored six goals in a game against Charlton Athletic. This resulted in Don Howe giving him a short run in the League side as a striker. In June 1986, at the age of twenty four, Chris was granted a free transfer, amazingly no English club offered him a contract and so, disillusioned and disgruntled, Whyte packed his bags and headed off to the United States where he spent two years playing in the USA Indoor Soccer League for New York Express and for Los Angeles Lazers. In the Summer of 1988 he was offered a trial by West Bromwich Albion's manager, Ron Atkinson, and he returned to England to play for the 'Baggies' for two seasons. In June 1990, Chris

Whyte returned to the big stage when Howard Wilkinson, the Leeds United manager, paid £400,000 for his services. He was everpresent in 1990-91 and in 1991-92, this one time footballing outcast, helped Leeds United to the ultimate prize, The Football League Championship. In August 1993, approaching his thirty second birthday, Chris was transferred for £250,000 to Birmingham City and in 1994-95 he was a mainstay in the club's defence when winning the Second Division Championship.

	Games	Goals
League	90	8
F.A.Cup	5	0
League Cup	14	0
Europe	4	0
Friendly Matches	58	2
Tours	13	0
Football Combination	163	15
South East Counties League	58	3
Youth Cup	3	0
Other Youth Cups	13	0
Youth Tours	4	0
Total	**425**	**28**

Honours:
(WITH ARSENAL)
4 England Under 21 Caps
Football Combination Championship Medal
                                   1983-84
South East Counties League Cup Winners
    Medal   1979-80
Presidents Cup Winners Medal   1980-81
(WITH LEEDS UNITED)
League Championship Medal   1991-92
(WITH BIRMINGHAM CITY)
Division Two Championship Medal   1994-95

Chris Whyte

WILL, Jim   1989-94

Birth Place: Aberdeen, Scotland
Date of Birth: 7th October 1972

➤ James Will was a brilliant young goalkeeper who joined Arsenal as a trainee in July 1989 after playing for Scotland Under 15's and helping his country to the final of the Mini World Cup in 1989, when he was voted player of the Tournament. He was a regular with the Juniors for two seasons before turning professional during the Summer of 1991. However, although becoming Scotland's Under 21 goalkeeper, he had to share the reserve team goalkeeping position with Alan Miller, 1991-94. Jim was granted a free transfer in June 1994 when he joined Dunfermline Athletic.

	Games	Goals
Friendly Matches	32	0
Tours	2	0
Football Combination	68	0
South East Counties League	42	0
Youth Cup	4	0
Other Youth Cups	21	0
Youth Tours	1	0
Total	**179**	**0**

Honours:
Scottish Schoolboy International
Scottish Youth International
3 Scottish Under 21 Caps
South East Counties League Championship
    Medal   1990-91
Southern Junior Floodlight Cup Winners
    Medal   1990-91
Southern Junior Floodlight Cup Finalists
    Medal   1989-90

WILLIAMS, Steve   1984-88

Birth Place: Hammersmith, London
Date of Birth: 12th July 1958

➤ In the 1970's there were many naturally gifted footballers who should have won more International Caps than they did. Eight names immediately spring to mind (remembering they won just over fifty caps between them) Bowles, Currie, George, Hudson, Marsh, Osgood and Worthington, the eighth name is Steve Williams. To think that he only won six England caps is an insult to his footballing ability for no one, other than the aforementioned, plus Glenn Hoddle have made football look so easy. On his day he could control a game like no other over the past twenty five years. Steve seemed to have so much time on the ball it was untrue and, with his upright posture and his seemingly arrogant way, he was like a thoroughbred amongst plain horses. Steve was full of grace and composure, but it was his distribution from almost a sweeper position, which was his forte and his ability with tantalising passes which were floated with almost effortless ease just beyond the opposition's defence for forwards to run on to. Unfortunately for Williams (like so many other great talents) it was his temperament that let him down and on many occasions instead of getting on with his wonderful footballing talents, he would spend the game having a running battle with an opposition player or spending time throwing abuse at the referee, for not giving a certain decision. Steve began his career as an apprentice with Southampton before turning professional in September 1975 and over the course of the following nine seasons he played in nearly three hundred and fifty League games helping them to the League Cup Final of 1979 and to the First Division Runners up position in 1983-84. He also won six England Caps, four B Caps and fourteen Under twenty one Caps before signing for Arsenal (the club he had supported as a boy) for £550,000 in December 1984. In his initial season at the club he played in fourteen League games which included his Arsenal League debut as a substitute in a home fixture against Tottenham on New Years Day 1985. However, in 1985-86 he suffered with injuries which included a broken toe and a hamstring injury which reduced his League appearances to only seventeen. In 1986-87, under the new management of George Graham (and after taking over from the unfortunate Stewart Robson) he formed with Viv Anderson, Paul Davis and the young David Rocastle a formidable right sided triangle and Steve, without doubt, played the best football of his career when he featured in thirty four League games and helped the Gunners to the Littlewoods Cup victory against Liverpool. However, after playing in the first twenty six League games in 1987-88, Steve was dropped after a 1-2 home defeat by Manchester United and in the following game, George Graham performed a master stroke which was to be significant in the winning of the Championship the following season. He switched Michael Thomas from his right back position to play midfield for the first time and Michael's place was taken by Lee Dixon, who was making his Arsenal League debut. Consequently Williams missed the 1988 Littlewoods Cup Final against Luton Town and the rift between himself and Graham became untenable. In July 1988 Williams was transferred to Luton Town for £300,000. Williams spent two seasons at Kenilworth Road before finishing his career with his ex-Southampton team mate Alan Ball at Exeter City. Steve now works for a football publishing company in Exeter, Devon.

	Games	Goals
League	95	4
F.A.Cup	11	0
League Cup	15	1
Friendly Matches	21	0
Tours	1	0
Football Combination	24	2
Total	**167**	**7**

1985-1995

Honours:
(WITH SOUTHAMPTON)
6 England Caps
4 England B Caps
14 England Under 21 Caps
League Cup Finalists Medal   1978-79
(WITH ARSENAL)
League Cup Winners Medal   1986-87

WILMOT, Rhys   1978-89

Birth Place: Newport, Gwent
Date of Birth: 21st February 1962

➤ In the best part of ten seasons at Highbury as a professional, Rhys Wilmot showed his loyalty and dedication to Arsenal. For his commitment to the club overshadowed financial rewards and acclaim for stardom as possibly a first team regular at another top club. During this time he played in only eight League games for Arsenal whilst understudy to Pat Jennings, John Lukic and George Wood. Rhys had played junior football for Rogiet Juniors and was a Welsh Schoolboy International when joining Arsenal as a schoolboy in 1977. In July 1978 he signed apprenticeship forms turning professional in January 1980. Whilst at Highbury he had four loan periods, to Hereford United in 1983, Swansea City in 1988, Plymouth Argyle in 1989 as well as in 1984-85 when he created a record when being everpresent whilst on loan to Leyton Orient. Wilmot added three Youth and six Under Twenty One Caps to his Schoolboy Caps whilst at Highbury before eventually making his Arsenal League debut in a 4-1 away victory at Villa Park, versus Aston Villa, 28th March, 1986. In 1986-87 he deputised six times in the League for John Lukic and after his final loan spell at Home Park, he was snapped up by Plymouth Argyle for £100,000 in July 1989. Rhys later played for Grimsby Town and in 1994-95 found himself back in the top flight as deputy to Nigel Martyn at Crystal Palace.

	Games	Goals
League	8	0
League Cup	1	0
Friendly Matches	76	0
Tours	6	0
Football Combination	179	0
South East Counties League	49	0
Youth Cup	5	0
Other Youth Cups	12	0
Youth Tours	4	0
Total	**340**	**0**

Honours:
Welsh Schoolboy International
3 Welsh Youth Caps
6 Under 21 Welsh Caps
Football Combination Championship Medal
1983-84
South East Counties League Cup Winners
Medal   1979-80
Presidents Cup Winners Medal   1980-81

Rhys Wilmot

WINTERBURN, Nigel   1987

Birth Place: Nuneaton, Warwickshire
Date of Birth: 11th December 1963

🏹 Nigel became an apprentice at Birmingham City in May 1980 before turning professional in 1981, after he had played for Nuneaton schoolboys. Whilst at St. Andrews, he won an England Youth cap but failed to make the first team and after an unsuccessful trial at Oxford United he joined Wimbledon in August 1983. In four seasons with The Dons, Nigel missed only seven out of one hundred and seventy-two league games for the club whilst being ever present in 1986-87. Nigel helped them to promotion from Division Three to Division Two in 1983-84 and Division Two to Division One in 1985-86. Nigel was voted player of the year for the club in four consecutive seasons. In May 1987 he was transferred to Arsenal for £400,000 becoming one of George Graham's most shrewd signings although, at the time, he had been signed as reserve cover to Kenny Sansom. Nigel made his Arsenal league debut as a substitute in a home fixture versus Southampton on the 21st November 1987 and in the remainder of that season he played in seventeen league games, playing in the League Cup Final when missing a penalty in the 3-2 defeat by Luton Town. Since his debut for the club, Nigel Winterburn has been one of the most consistent left backs the club has ever had when between the 1988-89 League Championship season and the end of 1994-95, he missed only twenty-seven of the club's two hundred and eighty-two league games. His

main attributes being his brilliant distribution of the ball, stamina and commitment as well as having the most potent of shots within the club, although this has not been evident in recent seasons. In 1988-89, he was ever present when helping the club to the League Championship. Nigel won his first England cap the following season versus Italy and again in 1990-91 he was ever present in Arsenal's last League Championship winning campaign. In 1992-93 he won a second England cap versus Germany and was a proud member of the club's double winning Cup season when winning F.A. Cup and Coca-Cola Cup winners medals, in two Wembley meetings with Sheffield Wednesday. In the following two seasons Nigel was again a stalwart in the defence when helping the club to two European Cup Winners Cup Finals. Without doubt, Nigel is one of the finest left backs to have played for the club. He was an ever-present up to and including the 2-1 North London derby defeat at Spurs on November 18th 1995.

	Games	Goals
League	272	5
F.A. Cup	30	0
League Cup	35	3
Europe	22	0
Other First Team Matches	17	0
Friendly Matches	35	2
Tours	24	1
Football Combination	19	0
Total	**454**	**11**

Honours:
(WITH ARSENAL)
2 England Caps
3 England B Cap
1 Football League Cap
2 League Championship Medals
1988-89, 1990-91
F.A. Cup Winners Medal   1992-93
League Cup Winners Medal   1992-93
League Cup Finalists Medal   1987-88
European Cup Winners Cup Winners Medal
1993-94
European Cup Winners Cup Finalists Medal
1994-95
European Super Cup Finalists Medal   1995
F.A. Charity Shield Medal   1991
2 F.A. Charity Shield Finalists Medal
1989, 1993
Mercantile Credit Centenary Trophy Winners
Medal   1988-89
Wembley International Tournament Winners
Medal   1988
2 Makita International Tournament Winners
Medals   1989, 1994
2 Makita International Tournament Finalists
Medals   1990, 1991
(WITH BIRMINGHAM)
1 England Youth Cap
(WITH WIMBLEDON)
1 England Under-twenty-one Cap

Nigel Winterburn

WOODCOCK, Tony   1982-86

Birth Place: Nottingham
Date of Birth: 6th December, 1955

Tony began his career as an apprentice with Nottingham Forest in August 1972, signing professional forms in January 1974. Unbelievably, at the beginning of Brian Clough's reign at Nottingham Forest, it appeared that Woodcock had no future with the club when he was loaned out twice in 1976, to Lincoln City and Doncaster Rovers. However, Tony established himself in the Forest team which won promotion from the Second Division in 1976-77. In the following three seasons, Tony helped the club to the League Championship in 1978-79, to two League Cup Final victories and to The European Cup in 1978-79. Tony also won six England caps in the summer of 1979, he was transferred to Cologne, The West German side, where he spent three successful seasons before returning home to join Arsenal after the World Cup Finals in July 1982 for a fee of £500,000. Without doubt, on his day, Tony Woodcock was as lethal as any other striker in the country and although he possessed all the qualities of a top flight striker, the Highbury followers, at the back of their minds, felt that Tony had much more to offer, for although he scored his fair share of goals, a lot less skilful players have scored more. Even so, Woodcock was the club's leading league goal scorer in each of his four seasons at Highbury. In 1982-83, he netted fourteen times in thirty-four appearances, which included a hat trick against Luton Town at Highbury in March 1983, and he played in every cup tie when helping the club to both the F.A. Cup and League Cup semi-finals. In the following campaign, 1983-84, he improved his goal tally to twenty-one and in a game at Aston Villa on the 29th October 1983 it seemed as if he was on course to equal Ted Drake's record of seven goals, when scoring five times. In 1984-85, Tony had scored ten times in twenty-seven league appearances before receiving a serious injury (again at Villa Park) in March 1985, which ruled him out for the rest of the season. In his final season at Highbury, he found the net on eleven occasions when playing in thirty-three league games. In May 1986, after the appointment of George Graham, Tony's career at the club came to close and in July of the same year Arsenal received £140,000 when he returned to West Germany to play for Cologne. He later spent one season with Fortuna Dusseldorf. If Tony had been four years younger and he had had the chance of playing in the late 1980's Arsenal side, with his scorching pace and splendid ability to hold the ball up for others to come into play, then everyone at Highbury might have seen a different Tony Woodcock. For in a nutshell, he was a star within a side of stars which never shone. Tony has now made Germany his adopted home and lives in Cologne. A qualified coach, his most recent post was manager of VFB Leipzig until mid 1995.

	Games	Goals
League	131	56
F.A. Cup	14	7
League Cup	22	5
Europe	2	0
Other First Team Matches	17	0
Friendly Matches	17	5
Tours	8	1
Football Combination	8	9
Total	**202**	**83**

Honours:
(WITH ARSENAL)
18 England Caps
1 England B Caps
(WITH NOTT'M FOREST)
6 England Caps
2 England Under-twenty-one Caps
League Championship Medals   1977-78
2 League Cup Winners Medals
                              1977-78, 1978-79
European Cup Winners Medal   1978-79
F.A. Charity Shield Winners Medal   1978
(WITH COLOGNE)
18 England caps

Tony Woodcock

WRIGHT, Ian   1991

Birth Place: Woolwich, London
Date of Birth: 3rd November 1963

➤ Over the last twenty-five years only three Arsenal players, Charlie George, Liam Brady and Charlie Nicholas have been held with as much as admiration, esteem and awe as Ian Wright. He can turn a game with one dazzling moment of brilliance. His hallmarks being his speed, aggression, two quick feet, strength whilst running at defenders and his natural goalscoring instincts. In recent seasons Ian has scored some of the most remarkable goals ever witnessed by Arsenal followers, these include two devastating strikes against Nott'm Forest in 1992-93, an unbelievable effort v. Everton at Highbury in the same season and a truly marvellous chipped goal at Swindon Town in 1993-94. Ian Wright grew up on the same housing estate as former Arsenal star, David Rocastle. When leaving school he became a labourer and plasterer whilst playing Sunday League football for local side, Ten-em-bee. Wright was playing for Greenwich Borough when spotted by Crystal Palace manager Steve Coppell and joined The Eagles in August 1985. In six seasons at Selhurst Park he forged a wonderful goalscoring partnership with Mark Bright, scoring over one hundred goals between them. Ian was Palace's leading league goalscorer, in three of those campaigns. In 1989-90, Ian suffered a broken leg twice during the season but was selected, as substitute, for the 1990 F.A. Cup Final against Manchester United and when coming on, scored two stunning goals which took the game into a replay. In 1990-91, Ian won the first of his twenty England Caps when coming on as a substitute against Cameroon. Although many Arsenal followers had heard of Ian Wright many of them must have been stunned when in September 1991 George Graham paid out a new club record transfer fee of £2.5 million to secure Wright's services and little did they know what was to follow! Ian wasted no time in proving his worth when scoring on his first team debut in a League Cup tie at Leicester City and three days later he helped himself to a hat trick on his league debut at the Dell versus Southampton. Ian finished his first term with Arsenal by scoring twenty-four league goals in only thirty appearances, which included two other hat tricks (four versus Everton and another against Southampton) and was the First Division and Europe's leading league goalscorer (Ian winning the Golden Boot). In 1992-93, Wright was instrumental in helping Arsenal secure the F.A. and Coca-Cola Cups. He scored in both the F.A. Cup Final games against Sheffield Wednesday and he finished the season having scored on thirty occasions. This was after his temperament got the better of him and he was suspended for three matches after throwing a punch at Tottenham's David Howells. In the

following term Ian was again the club's leading goalscorer but unfortunately was suspended for the European Cup Winners Cup Final against Parma. This after, in November 1993, he had scored four times for England against San Marino. He was also fined £5,000 by the F.A. after he had supposedly made an improper gesture to a linesman in the previous season's F.A. Cup Final replay. In 1994-95, Ian broke all European club cup goalscoring records when he scored in each tie of every round up to the final of the European Cup Winners Cup which was tragically lost to Real Zaragoza in Paris. Again, for the fourth consecutive season, Ian was the club's leading league goalscorer when netting eighteen times in thirty-one appearances and he also reached the milestone of his one hundredth first team goal for Arsenal (only the fourth player in the club's history to do so). In his near four years at Highbury, Ian has missed nearly thirty league games and although some of these were through injury many were for suspension (thirty-three bookings). If he could control that part of his game he would be looked upon as the complete striker. However, many have their doubts, for they believe this is part of Ian Wright's make up and if you took that away from him, he would not be the same Ian Wright, Wright, Wright!

	Games	Goals
League	131	80
F.A. Cup	12	11
League Cup	18	16
Europe	15	13
Other First Team Matches	5	1
Friendly Matches	7	6
Tours	1	8
Football Combination	3	5
Total	**201**	**140**

Honours:
(WITH CRYSTAL PALACE)
4 England Caps
F.A. Cup Finalists Medal   1989-90
P.F.A. Team Award - Division Two   1989
(WITH ARSENAL)
16 England Caps
3 England B Caps
F.A. Cup Winners Medal   1992-93
League Cup Winners Medal   1992-93
European Cup Winners Cup Winners Medal
                                                      1993-94
European Cup Winners Cup Finalists Medal
                                                      1994-95
European Super Cup Finalists Medal   1995
F.A. Charity Shield Finalists Medal   1993
Golden Boot Award   1991-92
P.F.A. Team Award - Premier   1993
Arsenal Player of the Year   1992, 1993
Makita International Tournament Winners
   Medal   1994
League Championship Medal   1988-89

Ian Wright

ZUMRUTEL, Soner   1991-95

Birth Place: Islington, London
Date of Birth: 6th October 1974

☛ Soner had played for Islington/Camden Schoolboys when joining Arsenal as a trainee in June 1991. He was a Youth Team regular when playing on the right wing. Zumrutel turned professional in July 1993 and broke into the Combination side in 1993-94. However, although being small and tricky scoring his fair share of goals, he was released on a free transfer in June 1995, when he joined Cambridge United.

	Games	Goals
Friendly Matches	21	7
Football Combination	31	2
South East Counties League	45	18
Youth Cup	5	4
Other Youth Cups	23	2
Youth Tours	2	1
Total	**127**	**34**

Honours:
2 Southern Junior Floodlight Cup Finalists
  Medals   1991-92, 1992-93

WHO'S WHO
SUBSCRIBERS

PRESENTATION COPIES

DAVID DEIN
KEN FRIAR
PHIL CARLING
JOHN HAZELL
LES GOLD
RICHARD LERMAN
ANDREW MILLER
GERALD TOON

SUBSCRIBERS

DANIEL AND PAUL GODFREY
DAVID JEWELL
TONY GREEN
JOE REDKNAPP
JASON TEGG
COLIN DAVID CLARKE
STUART JOHN JARMAN
SHAUN C. COLBY
STEVE MANN
ANTHONY STANGER
P.W.AVIS
TOMMY GOSTIC
DOMINIC DUCELLIER
JOHN EDWARD GILKS
MITCHELL CARTER
ROBERT SALISBURY
MARK AUGHTERLONY
MARK JERVIS
GARETH WEEKLY
ANDREW HOOKWAY
MIKE CANTWELL
JOE STUDMAN
PAUL SWEENEY
LEE DAWSON
TERENCE PETTITT
JOE WATERS
JONATHAN WITHERS
RICHARD JOHN HAWKINS
HOWARD PANAS
RICHARD GRIFFITH
NORMAN ALFRED FLEMING
MARK SHEARS
IAN LAWRENCE
MR L. FISHER
MR S. FISHER
MR M. FISHER
ANDREW BELL
NEIL DAVID CAMPBELL
LLOYD TOWN
MR R.J. UPTON

JOHN AND BEV. KERNS
TONY JUDD
DANIEL BENJAMIN GREEN
JON STEPHENSON
D.C. WHELLER
TERRY HONE
PADRAIG McCORMACK
DAVID BRADSHAW
BARRY JACKSON
IAN LOWE
PHIL DURSTON
ANDREW SPROAT
LEE MURCUTT
IAN PORTER
STEPHEN MALCOLM BEDDOES
JAMES ELKIN
THOMAS PATRICK COLLINS
ROBERT PAUL O'DONNELL
MICHAEL JOHN WILDERS
GRAHAM PARKIN
GARETH DAVIES
OWEN LUDER
FRANKIE SPENCER
J. DENIS. FOSTER
SIMON HARVEY
KELLY CHRISTOPHER BRYAN
STEPHEN MEARS
SHARON COOKE
PAT AND DANIEL BROWN
PETER STRAKER
ALEX REEVE
ALAN LIGHT
STEPHEN SKITT
JULIAN WILLIAMS
JOHN WELLING
SID WELLING
RICHARD GIST
RICHARD MORGAN
ROBERT BUTLER
LYNNE HEAD
ROBERT DENHAM
ALEX MASON
NEIL MUNN
WILLIAM J. AMOS
DAVID JAMES
JUNE JAMES
KEITH "DEL" SHANNON
DAVID SMITH
CAROL SMITH
GRAHAM SMITH
CHLOE SMITH
KENNETH E. HARPER
VIC HUGHES
TERRENCE WILLIAM DEAN
SANDRA PLOWMAN

RICKY GOLDBOURNE
ODHRAN O'KEEFFE
CLIVE NEEDHAM
JONATHAN LINFOOT
STEPHEN WEEKS
GLEN LAWRENCE WARNER
ANDREW T. MEALE
MARTIN UNIACKE
ADRIAN DUKE-COHAN
ALAN D. GUNNER
FRANK BROWN
PETER BLOYCE
CLIFFORD
GRANT WICKS
MICHAEL ADAMS
MISS MICHELLE BURTON
PHILLIP BAKER
GARY BERRY
LESLEY ANN KEELING
ANDY COXALL
RAYMOND GRIFFITHS
STEVE JONES
CHRIS WILKS
JAMES CHRISTOPHER EVANS
BERNADETTE KELLY
KEITH SIMPSON
BERNADETTE RASMUSSEN
KEITH P. WINMILL
C. TIMBRELL
SEAN CLARKE
ALAN MACBETH
ANTHONY BALSEIRO
CLINT BUTCHER
MARK HESP
KEVIN BLAKE
PETER REID
CHRIS HINDSON
IAN HINDSON